# THE BLUE GUIDES

Austria
Belgium and Luxembourg
China
Cyprus
Czechoslovakia
Denmark
Egypt

FRANCE
France
Paris and Versailles
Burgundy
Normandy
Corsica

GREECE
Greece
Athens and environs
Crete

HOLLAND
Holland
Amsterdam

Hungary

ITALY
Northern Italy
Southern Italy
Florence
Rome and environs
Venice
Tuscany
Umbria
Sicily

Jerusalem
Malta and Gozo

Moscow and Leningrad
Morocco
Portugal

SPAIN
Spain
Barcelona

Switzerland

TURKEY
Turkey: the Aegean
    and Mediterranean Coasts
Istanbul

UK
England
Ireland
Scotland
Wales
London
Museums and Galleries
    of London
Oxford and Cambridge
Gardens of England
Literary Britain and Ireland
Victorian Architecture in Britain
Churches and Chapels
    of Northern Engalnd
Churches and Chapels
    of Southern England
Channel Islands

USA
New York
Boston and Cambridge

Yugoslavia

*Portrait of Isablella Brant, Rubens' first wife, by P.P. Rubens. The Mauritshuis, The Hague*

*BLUE GUIDE*

# Holland

## Charles Ford

**A & C Black**
London

**WW Norton**
New York

First edition 1933
Second edition 1961
Third edition 1982 by John Tomes
Fourth edition 1987 by John Tomes

Fifth edition 1993

Published by A & C Black (Publishers) Limited
35 Bedford Row, London WC1R 4JH

©A & C Black (Publishers) Limited 1992

ISBN  0-7136-3653-8

Maps and plans by Doug London and Andras Bereznay revised for this edition by John
Flower and Thames Cartographic Services Ltd.

A CIP catalogue record for this book
is available from the British Library

Published in the United States of America by
W W Norton & Company, Inc
500 Fifth Avenue, New York, NY 10110

Published simultaneously in Canada by
Penguin Books Canada Limited,
2801 John Street, Markham, Ontario L3R 1B4

ISBN  0-393-30968-1

The publishers and the author have done their best to ensure the accuracy of all the
information in Blue Guide Holland; however, they can accept no responsibility for any
loss, injury or inconvenience sustained by any traveller as a result of information or
advice contained in the guide.

Please write in with your comments, suggestions and corrections. Writers of the best
letters will be awarded a free Blue Guide of their choice.

**Charles Ford** lectures in the History of Art at University College London. He has
published many articles, reviews and translations on matters relating to the history of
Dutch painting and art theory. He is presently preparing a book on Dutch writings on
art during the seventeenth century.

Printed in Great Britain by The Bath Press, Avon

# PREFACE

What the Dutch have they have wrested from the most difficult of natural circumstances. Their story begins with the first communities of Celtic and Germanic peoples who raised islands above the bogs and whose earliest governmental organisations were structured around the daily necessities of land drainage; these were farmers and fishing folk. The story begins also with cities, some, like Maastricht, dating back to Roman times; cities which thrived on the land and river traffic between southern and northern Europe. The story continues through the glories of the cities of medieval Flanders, now Belgium but culturally the ancestors of the Dutch towns, whence so many craftsmen and merchants fled northwards during the religious wars of the sixteenth century taking with them the mysteries of the production of and trade in luxury goods. The remarkable human wealth was augmented by the riches of colonial adventures made possible by a huge navy. As a consequence the Netherlands derived an influence far out of proportion to its size. A land without forests the Netherlands built Europe's ships; a land without significant mineral resources it manufactured and controlled Europe's armament production—both these achievements in the 'Golden Age', the seventeenth century, when the Dutch commanded trade in raw materials from the Baltic and through the Rhine. A nation which eschewed art in its churches, whose outraged citizenry perpetrated the iconoclasm against sacred art, the Netherlands nevertheless trained and employed several generations of artists during that 'Golden Age' and the country remains rich in art. Since the Second World War the Netherlands has been a showpiece of European reconstruction. It would be hard for anyone who saw the country stripped of every movable thing in 1945—stripped of its art, stripped of its machine-tools, even stripped of its railway lines—to imagine that the bustling, civilised, prosperous cities and the ordered, opulently productive countryside could have come about within a generation.

Each town has a core of flamboyantly gabled canal houses and public buildings, many dating back to medieval times. The churches are as diverse as the many sects which have thrived here since the (relatively) tolerant Dutch Reformation—one finds handsome synagogues a step away from medieval churches stripped for Calvinist worship; up some backstairs in the next street a 'secret' Catholic chapel, sumptuously furnished. In the town by town guide these treasures are catalogued and for the visitor who makes the time available the wealth of the past is simply stunning. Each town has its own museum and its independent perspective upon national and international history, each industry and trade and human pastime is catalogued—all human life, as they say, is there.

The Netherlands remain a favourite choice for travellers on all budgets. For the motorist there is arguably Europe's most efficient road network— certainly one of Europe's most well-mannered nations of road users. For the traveller on public transport there is the astonishing prospect of a bus, tram and rail network where the staff are polite and multilingual, where fares are integrated and tickets transferable and where timetables are more than bewildering sheets of numbers to be read as one waits. For the cyclist and pedestrian the cities and the countryside are safe and relatively healthy places to wander, while a boating enthusiast could devote a whole holiday switching from one cruise to another, either salt water or exploring the maze of rivers and canals. And when you arrive, or before you set out, there are in every town VVV offices (Vereniging voor Vremedelingenverkeer, the Association for Foreigners' Travel) where information about hotel, guest-house and campsite accommodation is readily accessible, where the staff are helpful and will supply you with information on travel, opening times and cultural events.

This fifth edition of *Blue Guide Holland* continues the tradition of embracing not only the well-known and obvious features but also less generally familiar aspects and corners of the country, some of the latter rarely visited by the average tourist yet often of real charm and character. Two of the most important galleries have been renovated, the Mauritshuis at the Hague and the Rijksmuseum in Amsterdam, and the entries for these have had a major re-writing.

**Comments and Suggestions.** First published in 1933 as *Holland and the Rhine*, a continually evolving guide such as this can profit immensely from the contributions of its users. Comments and suggestions—whether on fact, on the general layout and style of the book, or the result of personal discovery—will always be most welcome.

**Acknowledgements** must go first to all those who over more than half a century have played their part in the story of *Blue Guide Holland*. The most recent author and editor, John Tomes, has made my task a very easy one. The surest acknowledgement of that must be the degree to which this edition depends upon his own revised edition. John Tomes is a fine historian and an unerringly competent guide. This book is alive with his knowledge and enthusiasm and my hope is that in re-drafting and re-presenting it for a new generation of what he called 'discerning travellers' I have lost none of those essential qualities. When I took it up this was the best small book on the Netherlands, on its history, culture and topography; my hope is that it continues to be so.

**Background sources.** In addition to some specialist works mentioned elsewhere, the following have been particularly valuable for reference and background and are offered as a selective bibliography: Svetlana Alpers, *The Art of Describing*, Chicago, 1983; Pierre Brachin, *The Dutch Language: A survey*, (English tr. by Paul Vincent), Cheltenham, 1985; *The Encyclopaedia Britannica*; Van Dale's dictionaries; Giovanni Fanelli, *Moderne architectuur in Nederland, 1900–1940*, The Hague, 1978; Pieter Geyl, *The Revolt of the Netherlands*, London, 1958; Paul Groenendijk, et al., *Gids voor Moderne Architectuur in Nederland*, Rotterdam, 1987; *Grote Winkler Prins Encyclopedie*; Bob Haak, *The Golden Age, Dutch painters of the seventeenth century*, London/New York, 1984; Adam Hopkins, *Holland*, London, 1988; J.A. van Houtte, et al., *Algemene Geschiedenis der Nederlanden*, Utrecht/Antwerp, 1949–58; J. Huizinga, *The Waning of the Middle Ages*, Harmondsworth, 1953; L. de Jong, *Het Koninkrijk der Nederlanden in de Tweede Wereldoorloog*, The Hague, 1969–1990; Tim Killian, *Amsterdam Canal Guide*, Utrecht/Antwerp, 1978; E.H. Kossmann, *The Low Countries, 1780–1940*, Oxford, 1978; R. de Leeuw, et al. *The Hague School: Dutch Masters of the 19th century* London, 1983; R.P. Meijer, *The Literature of the Low Countries*, Assen, 1971; P.C. Molhuysen, et al. *Nieuw Nederlandsch Biliographisch Woordenboek*, Leiden, 1911—37; Gerald Newton, *The Netherlands: an historical and cultural survery 1795–1977*, London, 1978; Geoffrey Parker, *The Dutch Revolt*, Harmondsworth, 1985; The relevant Pelican Histories of Art; J.L. Price, *Culture and Society in the Dutch Republic during the 17th century*, London, 1974; Simon Schama, *The*

*Embarrassment of Riches*, London, 1987; Simon Schama, *Patriots and Liberators: Revolution in the Netherlands*, London, 1977; Sir William Temple, *Observations upon the United Provinces of the Netherlands*, London, 1673; W. Uitterhoeve, et al., *De Staat van Nederland*, Utrecht/Nijmegen, 1990; Christopher White, *Paintings in Dutch Museums*, Oxford, 1985; Paul Zumthor, *Daily Life in Rembrandt's Holland*, London, 1952.

Considerations of space does not allow mention to be made of the many museum guides and catalogues, exhibition catalogues, articles in periodicals and the like which have also been useful.

For permission to reproduce illustrations the publishers would like to thank: A.F. Kersting, the Rijksmuseum-Stichting, the Frans Halsmuseum, the Maurithuis, the Rijksmuseum Kröller-Müller, the Museum Boymans van Beuningen, the Rijksmuseum Huis Lambert van Meerten, Fries Museum, Aerocamera Hofmeester, Rijksvoorlichtingsdienst, the Netherlands National Tourist Office.

# NOTES ON USING THIS GUIDE

*Blue Guide Holland* is in two parts. The first provides Background and Practical Information, the main subjects covered being listed in the Contents. Intending visitors with no firm plans as to where to tour may be helped by the Introduction which briefly outlines the main features of the country. The second part of the book comprises descriptions of the historic Provinces out of which the Netherlands grew, and introduces 39 Routes covering virtually the whole country. These Routes are designed for motorists and I have myself followed them by car in preparing this new edition. I am, however, principally a cyclist and have also done many of the routes by a judicious mixing of train and cycle-path travelling which has been a little slower, often damper, but very much more rewarding both intellectually and physiologically. Cycle-paths (fietspad) are as thoroughly signposted as the motorways and extend from the outskirts of the towns as a distinct and separate network. *Blue Guide Holland* will serve the motorist, the cyclist or the traveller on the Netherlands' public transport system equally well both as a series of itineraries and as a handbook. For the most part these Routes are grouped by provinces, but this is not always the case and where it has seemed more appropriate some Routes cover more than one province. The overall scheme of the Routes can be seen at a glance by referring to the map of Routes at the end of the book. The description of each town starts from the main square, usually near the VVV office; from there you are given a basic orientation and a series of walks that will take you past the significant monuments, curiosities and cultural and historical sites.

**Distances.** The preamble to each Route gives its total distance. In both the preambles and texts italicised distances are those between points along the basic Route, i.e. each italicised distance is the distance from the previous one. Other distances (e.g. along diversions) are in roman print. For a number of reasons distances can only be approximate.

**Maps.** An overall map of the Netherlands showing all places of principal interest appears at the end of the book. Since Routes not infrequently run close to one another it is advisable to look up in the General Index places lying either side of the road being travelled and thus ensure that places within easy reach but described under other Routes are not missed.

Three great rivers—the Rhine, the Maas and the Scheldt—are, with their tributaries, offshoots and linking channels, the key to much of the country. The courses and even the names of these rivers can be confusing. They are therefore the subject of a special map on pp 18–19.

**Indexes.** There are two indexes, a *General Index* and an *Index of Artists* (painters, engravers, sculptors, metalworkers, glassworkers), this especially convenient when visiting museums, galleries and historical sites. Names appearing in the latter index, which gives dates and other information, are not repeated in the General Index.

**Asterisks** draw attention to places (and objects) of special attraction or interest.

**Opening Times** are indicated for most sites. Although these are believed to have been substantially correct at the time of compilation, the warning must be given that few sites are willing to commit themselves for even a year ahead and that times can change without notice. Easter and public holidays can add to the uncertainty, and it should be noted that even when a Holiday opening time is given this does not necessarily apply to all public holidays and virtually never to Christmas and New Year. Often, of course, sites will be visited simply on an opportunist basis. However, where a site is a positive objective, to avoid possible disappointment intending visitors are urged first to check with the VVV.

Particulars given are normally inclusive, e.g. April–September means 1 April to 30 September. In most cases the closing time shown is the actual closing time and, particularly in the case of larger sites, the sale of tickets may end well before this. For admission charges, see Practical Information, Museum Card.

*Churches* pose their own problem. Whereas a few years ago it would have been normal to expect most churches to be open at reasonable times, today's vandalism has closed most doors other than those of the more famous edifices which in effect rank as museums. Visitors keen to get into a particular church should consult VVV or chase the sacristan or other key holder whose name is sometimes posted on the door. Persistence may then bring success.

The interior of the *Stadhuis* (Town Hall) of many towns is often worth a visit for its pictures, rich furnishings and other features. In some cases there are formal entry arrangements; in others, provided civic activities allow, it is often possible on request to look around during working hours.

# A Note on Blue Guides

The Blue Guide series began in 1915 when Muirhead Guide-Books Limited published 'Blue Guide London and its Environs'. Finlay and James Muirhead already had extensive experience of guidebook publishing: before the First World War they had been the editors of the English editions of the German Baedekers, and by 1915 they had acquired the copyright of most of the famous 'Red' Handbooks from John Murray.

An agreement made with the French publishing house Hachette et Cie in 1917 led to the translation of Muirhead's London guide, which became the first 'Guide Bleu'—Hachette had previously published the blue-covered 'Guides Joannes'. Subsequently, Hachette's 'Guide Bleu Paris et ses Environs' was adapted and published in London by Muirhead. The collaboration between the two publishing houses continued until 1933.

In 1933 Ernest Benn Limited took over the Blue Guides, appointing Russell Muirhead, Finlay Muirhead's son, editor in 1934. The Muirhead's connection with the Blue Guides ended in 1963 when Stuart Rossiter, who had been working on the Guides since 1954, became house editor, revising and compiling several of the books himself.

The Blue Guides are now published by A & C Black, who acquired Ernest Benn in 1984, so continuing the tradition of guidebook publishing which began in 1826 with "Black's Economical Tourist of Scotland'. The Blue Guide series continues to grow: there are now 50 titles in print with revised editions appearing regularly and many new Blue Guides in preparation.

'Blue Guides' is a registered trade mark.

# CONTENTS

# PROVINCES AND ROUTES

## PROVINCES OF NOORD AND ZUID HOLLAND AND ZEELAND

## PROVINCE OF UTRECHT

## PROVINCE OF GRONINGEN

## PROVINCE OF FRIESLAND

# MAPS AND PLANS

## TOWN PLANS

## GROUND PLANS

# INTRODUCTION

## Landscape and people

*Blue Guide Holland* has carried its misnomer for many years; it should be *Blue Guide Netherlands* but it is not, and with good enough reason. English-speaking people have always called the Netherlands Holland and probably always will. Perhaps the essential inelegance of a noun which appears to be both plural and singular is the problem. The ancestry of 'Netherlands' as a word is impressive enough, it derives from the medieval Latin 'inferior terra' which has English (Low Countries) and French (Pays-Bas) equivalents which have usually been applied to the region as a whole. I have not sought to alter the time-honoured title of this book but throughout the new edition I have uniformly used the term Netherlands when referring to the country as a whole. Holland has been more properly used as the name of two of the provinces of the present day Netherlands. Every Welshman or Scotswoman who has been called 'English' will understand how important clarity is in such matters. In fact the Netherlands is made up of 12 provinces in all—each quite distinct. Eleven of them—Noord Holland, Zuid Holland, Zeeland, Utrecht, Noord Brabant, Limburg, Gelderland, Overijssel, Drenthe, Groningen and Friesland—are very old established. The twelfth, Flevoland, comprises entirely reclaimed land and achieved provincial status only in 1986.

The conventional picture of the Dutch countryside is of flat polder, canals, bulb-fields and windmills (see separate sections on Horticulture and Windmills). This is a picture which is not unjustified since over half of the country with some 60 per cent of the total population of 14 million is reclaimed or dike-protected land lying below sea level. Waterland scenery will be found over much of the western part of the country, notably around the IJsselmeer (the former Zuider Zee) and is discussed at some length in this introduction. The conventional picture of a Dutch town is the water-town: compact, neat and characterised by row upon row of ornately gabled canal houses. The reality which visitors first confront is in some contrast to both of these—the so-called Randstad (literally, rim-town), the great crescent of cities and towns formed by Amsterdam and Utrecht to the N, then curving S and SE to include Haarlem, Leiden, The Hague, Delft, Rotterdam and Dordrecht. The Randstad is thoroughly modern, its distinguishing features are the factory, the vast municipal housing project, the motorway and the airport. The Randstad itself has two of Europe's largest seaports, one west of Amsterdam and one at Rotterdam. Yet the Randstad is no continuous conurbation but rather a chain of highly individual places separated by green and in some cases wooded countryside. The individual towns are all that one would expect when one gets to them, but they lie far from the motorway exit and often a stiff walk away from the railway station, cocooned within their mantles of brightly coloured business parks and 19C suburbs.

It is virtually impossible to consider the physical geography of the Netherlands as if it were independent from the human geography. All of Europe has been shaped by man but the Netherlands have for a large part been made by man. The Netherlands sit upon clays, stones and sands dumped by the retreating icesheet at the close of the last Ice Age; in the following centuries the myriad temporary lakes and confused meanderings of rivers rich in silt shaped, graded and added to this amalgam. All along the coast the sea, loosed by the same warming process, began sweeping the coastline and piercing the low dunelands to form lagoons and brackish inlets. In the south the Rhine and the Maas, which in pre-glacial times had flowed far away to the north when the British Isles were still a peninsula, brought thousands of tonnes of rich soils to make Europe's largest delta. As the landscape emerged so it was colonised—by forests and heathland, by peat, by fresh and salt water life and by millions of wildfowl. The wildlife adapted to the conditions. The most recent coloniser, man, demanded the adaptation of the conditions themselves. This was a slow and uncertain adventure initiated at first piecemeal by local communities and now carried out by government with EC grants. Great storms have swept away towns and villages, reshaping the coastline and re-routing the rivers within recorded history, but the painstaking process of reclamation has gone on. Other than the story of little Hans Brinker of Spaarndam who put his finger into a hole in the dike the reclamation has not provided a theatre for heroic narratives, but in a gale force wind, with huge waves visible for miles along the shore, there is a certain heroism in the mundane cosiness of a small Dutch town living its daily life yards from the maelstrom.

*Fishermen on the bank of the Amstel, Arent Arentsz (called Cabel) (1585/6–c 1635)*

The curve of the West Frisian islands, from Texel in the S to Rottumeroog in the N, defines the original coast. It is known that in Roman times there was a large freshwater lake (Flevo Lacus) to the NE of the present site of Amsterdam, and that between this lake and the sea stretched a waste of peat bog. During the 11–13C a combination of sinking land and rising sea level led to flooding and general encroachment by the sea, the lake increasing in size until by c 1300 (and now known as the Almare—literally 'all sea', the large lake), it had effectively become a southward bay of the ocean reaching into the heart of the country. Shallow and tidal, part salt and part brackish, the bay had an inner and an outer part, the two separated by a strait some 20km broad (S of today's Afsluitdijk); the inner would become known as the Zuider Zee (south sea), the outer as the Wadden Zee (mud sea). Among the islands of the Zuider Zee were Urk, Schokland and Marken, all now mainland and all having interest for tourists.

From prehistoric times primitive attempts at land reclamation were undertaken, communities perched huts on artificial mounds (terps), traces of which survive throughout the north of the country and can be recognised in the ground plans of 'ring-towns'. The next step, dictated by the demands of both communication and protection, was the construction of linking dikes, the first of these perhaps dating back to c 800 or earlier, and the land thus enclosed eventually coming to be known as polder (the word derives from the old word 'pol', meaning a stake, such stakes, supporting seaweed or grass, being a main feature of early dikes). However, while these dikes gave protection against flooding from outside, there arose the new problem of the ground and rain water now confined within the dikes. Sluices, probably introduced before 1000, provided some relief (the first true polder is officially dated to 1150), but the real breakthrough came with the introduction of the windmill, and particularly (16C) of the rotating turret windmill which could operate regardless of wind direction. Water could now be pumped out and kept out and the first recorded successful use of this system is dated 1528. Between 1612 and 1626 Jan Leeghwater, using a 'gang' of 26 windmills each raising the drainage by a few feet, created the Beemster, Wormer, and Purmer polders, all to the N of Amsterdam, although these had been diked off from the sea as early as the 14C.

Towns such as Harderwijk, Kampen, and Staveren, all on the mainland S and E shores, were already flourishing when in the 14C and 15C Amsterdam and other W shore towns, protected by their lake and river dikes, also began to grow in importance. Typically the shore town sits at the mouth of a dammed river which has been diverted into two or more encircling canals.

In 1667 the engineer Hendrik Stevin drew up the first plan for enclosing and partially draining the Zuider Zee. With the development of the steam engine the idea was advanced again in the mid 19C, after the successful draining of the Haarlemmer Meer which had lain between Amsterdam, Haarlem and Leiden (itself substantially a man-made lake caused by centuries of peat excavation). It was, however, the work of Dr C. Lely at the end of the century that led to the Zuider Zee Reclamation Act of 1918 and the start of work the following year.

The first stage, during the 1920s, was the construction on the lake's western side of a dike between Den Oever and Medemblik, this being followed by the draining in 1930 of the Wieringermeer and the creation of the polder (20,000 ha.) of the same name. The key to the Zuider Zee project, the sealing of the lake from the sea, was achieved by the completion of the Afsluitdijk (barrier dike) in 1932. The Zuider Zee then became the IJsselmeer.

The Noord-Oost Polder (48,000 ha.) was drained in 1942; Oostelijk Flevoland (54,000 ha.) in 1957; and Zuidelijk Flevoland (44,000 ha.) in 1968. The dike road (32km long) across the IJsselmeer from Enkhuizen to Lelystad was completed in 1976 as the first step in the reclamation of the Markerwaard (60,000 ha.) lying along the E side of Noord Holland between Amsterdam and Enkhuizen. Reclamation is projected for the 1990s.

The *Informatiecentrum Nieuw Land* (Rte 29) at Lelystad is the best starting point for anyone interested in studying the Zuider Zee (IJsselmeer) project. This covers the historical, technical, agricultural and social aspects. For those more interested in the past history of the region there is the *Zuider Zee Museum* (Rte 3) at Enkhuizen. At *Ketelhaven* (Rte 29), on Oostelijk Flevoland, there is a marine archaeological museum with ship remains and other marine material discovered after draining, while at

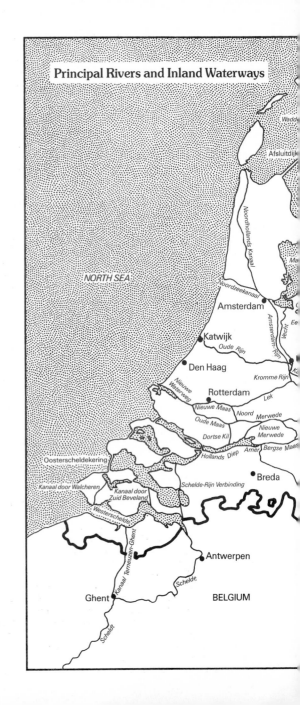

# Principal Rivers and Inland Waterways

Wadd

Afsluitdijk

*Noordhollands Kanaal*

Ma

*NORTH SEA*

*Noordzeekanaal*

Amsterdam

Ee

*Amsterdam Rijn*

*IJchel*

Katwijk

*Oude Rijn*

Den Haag

*Kromme Rijn*

K

*Nieuwe Waterweg*

Rotterdam

*Lek*

*Nieuwe Maas*

*Noord*

*Merwede*

*Oude Maas*

*Nieuwe Merwede*

*Dortse Kil*

*Amer*

*Bergse Maas*

*Hollands Diep*

Oosterscheldekering

Breda

*Kanaal door Walcheren*

*Kanaal door Zuid Beveland*

*Schelde-Rijn Verbinding*

*Westerschelde*

*Kanaal Terneuzen-Ghent*

Antwerpen

*Schelde*

Ghent

*Schelдt*

BELGIUM

*Aerial view of the Haringvlietdam (Delta Plan)*

*Schokland* (Rte 32A) on the Noord-Oost Polder a small museum exhibits general and local material similarly revealed.

Waterlands and water-towns are certainly the most characteristic Dutch environments, but the Netherlands has an even greater diversity of landscapes. Much of the length of the coastline, for instance, provides magnificent beaches, backed by dunes and resorts of a variety to suit all tastes and standards. The dunes between Haarlem and the sea have been a resort for Dutch townsfolk for centuries, the springs providing the pure water necessary for Haarlem's principle industries of early times: brewing and linen-bleaching. The great delta of Zeeland is a province of fertile island-peninsulas separated by broad channels (their waters tamed now by the ambitious Delta Plan) across which the motorist travels by massive dikes, long and graceful bridges, or by ferry. By contrast, Limburg, at the southeast corner of the country, is in part made up of steep, wooded hills known for their caves. These have been humorously called the Dutch Alps. Until recently there was an active coal-mining industry in this region. From south to north along much of the centre of the Netherlands and crossing the Maas, Waal and Rhine, there is heath and woodland, a part of this near Arnhem forming the Hoge Veluwe National Park, near and within which are the famous Openlucht (Open Air) and Kröller-Müller (Van Gogh and other modern artists) museums. The Achterhoek (back corner) is the quiet, pastoral, and little visited south-eastern corner of Gelderland, to its north being the largely industrial towns of the district of Twente. Further north again the province of Drenthe is crossed from south to north by the ridge of the Hondsrug along which prehistoric man built his massive communal burial chambers (the hunebeds). Both Drenthe and Groningen to its north are known for the curious former peat-colonies (veenkolonien), dense networks of ditches and canals with villages several kilometres long lining the larger waterways. These villages were founded by shrewd speculators from the cities of Holland who stripped the peat and shipped it back to the cities for fuel, returning boats full of nightsoil to manure the land they then profitably rented to landless peasants. In both Groningen and Friesland many villages indicate from their circular shape that they originated as 'terps', hillocks first made by people of some 2000 years ago so that they could settle above the ubiquitous marsh. The Frisian islands are popular holiday resorts—remote, windblown and in the sunshine exhilaratingly beautiful. Finally, occupying southern Friesland and north-western Overijssel, there is an expanse of broads and waterways as popular with boat users as it can be attractive and colourful to those on land.

Virtually all of the towns of The Netherlands are historic and there can be few which do not repay a visit. The Randstad towns are all places of exceptional interest and character, and it is here that will be found the best of the great museums and art galleries, places which for themselves alone merit a visit to the Netherlands. Among several may be listed the Rijksmuseum and the Van Gogh Museum in Amsterdam; the Centraal Museum art gallery and the St Catherijns Museum of religion and religious arts at Utrecht; Haarlem's Frans Hals Museum; the National Museum of Antiquities at Leiden; the Mauritshuis Royal Picture Gallery in The Hague; and at Rotterdam the Boymans-Van Beuningen Museum. Of the larger towns outside the Randstad perhaps special mention may be made of Breda, with the fine Orange-Nassau monuments in its Grote Kerk; 's Hertogenbosch for its magnificent Gothic cathedral; historic, part still fortified Maastricht; Arnhem, a name poignantly recalling the tragedy and gallantry of 1944 and today a place much visited for the variety of attractions in its environs; Nijmegen, standing high above the Waal and with both Roman and Frankish associations, a favourite retirement spot for gentlefolk a few generations ago; and Leeuwarden, a town with an attractive old centre and home of the Netherlands' most important provincial museum. Additionally the Netherlands is rich in smaller towns (most of them mentioned in the province descriptions in the second part of this Guide), ancient, historic, picturesque and—despite a certain sameness with their canals, 17C and 18C façades, and encircling boulevards, moats, or ramparts—nevertheless somehow all managing to be individual.

Centuries of struggle against nature, centuries of struggle against foreign domination, and, ever since the towns began to grow on the few spots that were dry, crowded and confined urban living have made the Dutch as a people and as individuals. Out of this background have emerged broad characteristics: individualism, a sense of community, respect for order, pragmatism. On the one hand the Dutch are individualists who have maintained the tradition of liberal toleration asserted in the Union of Utrecht and who perhaps more than any other European nation are quick in their defence of human rights. At the same time the population density in the urban areas, while perhaps enhancing the need for toleration, demands order and neatness and has been the continuing seed-bed for an emphasis on community welfare which reaches back to the many charitable institutions of the 17C or earlier. Pragmatism, especially in the conduct of foreign affairs, is the hallmark of a small, wise nation determined to survive; it is apparent, despite the profound conservatism of Dutch society, in the toleration of drugs, pornography and prostitution which invariably shocks visitors from the English-speaking world.

The Dutch, however, are as diverse as their landscapes and although the previous paragraph might accurately characterise the multi-racial, cosmopolitan populations of the Randstad it does not accommodate the variety of the nation as a whole. Friesland, for example, has its own independent history and its own language spoken daily by 350,000 people. It is said that the Frisian fishermen who from medieval times roamed the British coast following the herring shoals could converse readily with Yorkshire folk. The Dutch from the eastern provinces have regional dialects which are as much German as Dutch and their culture (and more obviously architecture) can reflect this mixed heritage. In the northern parts of The Netherlands one comes across communities such as Staphorst-Rouveen, near Meppel, which have, like the Amish of Pennsylvania, preserved the customs and costumes of their Puritan forebears (if only on Sundays). South of the great rivers the population is almost uniformly Catholic. The Dutch nation was created when towns and communities keen to preserve their own privileges and rights revolted against the centralising ambitions of the Habsburg monarchy, the Dutch Constitution (see below) still attempts to balance the national against the local.

The present Dutch Royal Family have ruled as monarchs since 1815. For the early story of the houses of Orange and Nassau, their first associations with the Netherlands and their fusion, see under National History. The Dutch royal family does not have the glamour of the House of Windsor, nor the film-star glossiness of the House of Monaco. It is one of northern Europe's 'bicycle monarchies', paradoxically middle class. Queen Juliana (consort Prince Bernhard von Lippe-Biesterfeld) abdicated on 30 April 1980, reverting to the title of Princess and being succeeded by her eldest daughter Beatrix (born 1938). Queen Beatrix is married to Prince Claus von Amsberg, who now holds the title of Prince of the Netherlands; she has three sons: Willem-Alexander, Johan, and Constantijn (born 1967–69).

The Dutch State is headed by the Crown, a term which includes the sovereign and his or her ministers. As in the United Kingdom the monarch is above politics but the ministers are responsible to the States General (Parliament). This last comprises a First (upper) Chamber of 75 members elected indirectly by the Provincial Councils (see below) and a Second (lower) Chamber with 150 directly elected members. All nationals over 18 may vote. Both chambers have the right of inquiry but only the Second Chamber may introduce and amend legislation. Thus the States General is the legislature, while the Council of Ministers (Cabinet) led by the Prime Minister co-ordinates policy and functions as the executive. Ministers may be helped by State Secretaries.

There are two other important bodies. The Council of State is the highest advisory body and has to express its views on all legislation. Presided over by the sovereign, the Council has a maximum of 24 members, people of proven public service merit appointed for life. The General Chamber of Audit has the responsibility of supervising the public accounts; the members are appointed for life.

At the provincial level administration is through an appointed Sovereign's Commissioner and a directly elected Provincial Council. It is the members of these councils who elect the members of the First Chamber of the States General. At municipal level there are directly elected municipal councils who appoint their aldermen. Burgomasters are normally appointed by the Crown and serve for six years.

The Netherlands has an independent Judiciary functioning through a

Supreme Court and three lower levels of courts (appeal, district, local). There is no jury system.

**Horticulture** is very much a feature of life and landscape in the Netherlands. It is in itself one of the country's most important industries as well as attracting hundreds of thousands of tourists each year—hence this special section. Flowers fill the windows of private houses and public buildings, they line many streets and brighten shopping precincts; in the cities flower shops are as ubiquitous as betting shops in England. No town is without flower-filled gardens or parks, and flowers provide the excuse for pageants, shows, and parades with decorated floats. One does not arrive for supper at a Dutch home without a bunch of flowers for one's hosts. Some detail is given below, but visitors with a special interest are advised to obtain the Netherland Board of Tourism's (NBT) annual leaflet which lists and gives dates of the year's floral highlights. Technical and statistical detail may be found in 'Bulb Growing in the Netherlands', a booklet issued by the Netherlands Ministry of Agriculture and Fisheries at The Hague.

Tulip bulbs were introduced into the Netherlands from the Near East around the turn of the 16C/17C, causing a speculation that came to be known as 'Tulipomania', after the height of the boom the market crashed during the mid 1630s ruining many fortunes (including that of the landscape painter Jan van Goyen). Local cultivation started in the sandy soil near Haarlem, at once spreading southwards towards Leiden to form what are today the world's most famous bulb-fields (*De Bloembollenstreek*). At about the same time there was northward expansion into Kennemerland (main centre, Limmen); later the industry spread further north and northeast in Noord Holland (main centres, Breezand and Andijk); and modern times have seen development on the Noord-Oost Polder, in Friesland, and on the delta island-peninsulas of Zuid Holland and Zeeland, these last to a great extent concerned with gladioli.

The principal bulbs (including tuberous plants) now cultivated are crocus, daffodils and narcissus, tulips, gladioli and hyacinths, and if these are to be seen at their best the fields should be visited in April and May at which time 'bulb routes' are signposted through De Bloembollenstreek and many establishments are open. For more detail, including the Keukenhof, see Rte 6. During these months there are also coach excursions from Amsterdam and other centres. De Bloembollenstreek can become extremely crowded, with queues of cars, and some people may prefer to visit the less obviously spectacular but still beautiful and certainly much quieter other fields mentioned above; if the weather is mild a short train journey and a rented bicycle can make the experience far more memorable—simply ask how at the nearest station.

Fruit blossoms are another April and May attraction in several districts of The Netherlands, some principal ones being the Betuwe (Rte 25) and elsewhere along the large rivers, the Noord-Oost Polder near Kraggenburg and Marknesse (Rte 32A), around Bergen op Zoom (Rte 18B), and in Zuid Beveland (Rte 13). Vast expanses of brilliant yellow rape seed splash the landscapes of Groningen, Friesland, the Noord-Oost Polder and Flevoland during mid to late May, while the heathers of the eastern Netherlands are at their glorious best in August and September.

Flower auctions and markets are a feature of many towns. The most famous flower auction is that at *Aalsmeer* (Rte 9), a scene of efficiency and colour that has become one of the country's leading tourist attractions. There are other auctions, also open to visitors, at Bleiswijk (north of

*Tulips by Jac. Marrel (1614–81)*

Rotterdam), at Honselersdijk in Westland (Rte 11), and at Rijnsburg (Rte 6) near Leiden. Among the country's many flower markets the best known is that in Amsterdam (weekdays) on the Singel, behind the Muntplein. Others are at Amersfoort (Friday), Delft (Thursday), Groningen (Tuesday, Friday, Saturday), Utrecht (Saturday).

**Windmills** have served two basic purposes, powering heavy industrial tasks and removing water in drainage schemes. Industrial mills came first and may well have been in use by the 11C although the first record is one of the 13C; the first polder mill was recorded in 1414. The early industrial mills were of the Trestle Post type, the shaft and machinery being contained in a wooden body (the buck), the whole resting and turning on a massive wooden post to face the wind. This design would not work for drainage purposes where the scoop-wheel had to remain in a fixed position regardless of wind direction. The solution was found in the Hollow Post mill which enabled the shaft to be carried down within the post. The disadvantage of both these types was that to get the sails to face the wind the entire buck had to be turned on its post. Change came in the early 16C with the invention of the rotating cap set on a fixed buck, easy to 'wind' being much lighter. The wooden Post mills were in turn superseded by brick Tower mills, which, especially in towns, grew taller and taller in order to catch the wind; some had several levels, often incorporating a 'smok' construction of thatch which provided sheltered storage and accommodation space. Windmills powered many industries: seed grinding for oil or other products; grinding wheat; wood sawing; mulching rags for paper; grinding tobacco for snuff; fulling cloth—indeed a whole range of activities which contributed to Dutch industrial and mercantile ascendancy during the early modern period.

Drainage windmills at first operated under the disadvantage that a scoop-wheel could not raise water more than about two metres, but improvement came with the invention of the screw-pump carrying water some three times higher. But even with this the differences in level were too great and a system evolved by which mills were used in rows and in series. A ring-dike enclosing a ring-canal was first built around the marsh or lake to be drained, a row of windmills then raising water into the canal which carried it away to a river or the sea; when the water in the lake fell below reach, a second and lower row of mills was installed, these raising the water to a catchment at the first row and so to the canal. This process was repeated at as many levels as might be necessary, as many as 60 mills sometimes being required for a large reclamation.

For centuries the setting of the sails of windmills has been a method of conveying messages (birth, mourning, etc.), and it is also the custom on special occasions to hang the sails with traditional ornaments. One often comes across windmills in Dutch landscape paintings. It is generally agreed by modern art historians that as well as being part of the plausible scenery of a picture, the windmill can be understood to serve a symbolic function within landscapes. This can happen both directly on account of its cruciform shape, and subliminally by allusion to emblematic writings which stated that man was like the windmill, immobile unless motivated by the breath of God. The windmill was also a symbol of God's generosity and remains the emblem of one printing house, a symbol of the labour of learning turning rude experience into palatable knowledge.

Windmills continued in use until the turn of the 19C/20C when oil and steam began to take over. At that time there were some 10,000 windmills in the Netherlands. Of these, thanks to conservation measures, around 1000 survive, some 200 of which still function. Windmills are now used as private houses, museums, tourist attractions, and some even for industrial pur-

*Portrait of a girl in traditional costume by J.H. Maris (1837–1917)*

poses. Windmills are be seen throughout the Netherlands, especially in the west and the north. Four places at which there are good groups are Kinderdijk (Rte 12A), Zaanse Schans (Rte 2), Schermerhorn (Rte 3), and the town of Schiedam (Rte 11). There are also several mills in the Openlucht Museum at Arnhem, and there are windmill museums at Koog a.d. Zaan (Rte 2), Leiden (Rte 6) and Assumburg (Rte 18B). For further information see 'Windmills' by Suzanne Beedell (David & Charles), a general work with a chapter on Dutch Windmills.

**Traditional Dutch Costumes** are still worn throughout the Netherlands on certain occasions, in certain places. Although there are variations in detail, regional costumes have certain main features in common. For women, long, loose, and often pleated skirts, usually dark in colour; tight-fitting jackets; striped or coloured aprons; shawls or wide yokes; white peaked or winged caps, normally worn only on Sundays over a weekday's black inner cap; and the curious ear-irons, thought to date from the 16C as a means of fixing the cap to the hair and now developed with intricate extensions. For men long baggy trousers with silver buckles and buttons. Not only are there variations of detail between regions, there are also variations within regions, also between weekday and Sunday wear, and between children and adults.

Volendam and Marken are the most celebrated living museums of traditional costume, both places are popular with tourists. There are other places where costume is worn more naturally. One such is Urk (Rte 32A), once an island but now a village on the shore of the Noord-Oost Polder, where the light blue plastrons of the women are distinctive, as are also the men's trousers which, although baggy as elsewhere, are shorter and reveal intricately knitted stockings. At Bunschoten-Spakenburg (Rte 16A), to the N of Amersfoort, the women still wear costume, this distinguished by curved yokes of brightly coloured cotton. The long village of Staphorst-Rouveen (Rte 30B) near Meppel has long preserved an identity as a strict, enclosed community and here the costume worn on Sundays is certainly not for the benefit of tourists who are in fact discouraged from taking photographs; here the women's costume is generally dark blue while a local feature is the way in which gold spirals hang from the ear-irons. Within the Randstad costume is quite frequently worn by the women of old Scheveningen (Rte 7), particularly around the harbour, local characteristics being coloured shawls and ear-irons which extend up the head and are backed by pearl-ended pins. Costume may also be found in Zeeland, usually only on Sundays or market days at, for example, Goes or in Zeeland Flanders; here the women's caps are known for their Flanders lace.

Clogs (Dutch, Klompen), normally of poplar or willow, are still quite frequently worn, particularly in polder districts. Clogmakers' workshops are often a feature of folk museums, probably the best known being at Arnhem's Openlucht Museum. Most local museums exhibit examples of costume or accessories. The best national display is at the Openlucht Museum at Arnhem.

For further information on costume see 'National Costumes in Holland' by Riet Hijlkema (J.M. Meulenhoff, Amsterdam) and 'Dutch Costumes' by Elsa M. Valeton (De Driehoek, Amsterdam), both works being available in English.

# National History

The physical appearance of the Netherlands has changed dramatically over the centuries, as was explained in the Introduction. Until the 17C only primitive flood protection and reclamation had been attempted, the land area was much less than it was even in the 19C, let alone today. This is especially true of the provinces of Noord and Zuid Holland and Zeeland (see history of these provinces) and the lands around the IJsselmeer. Much of the rest of the country was marsh or barren heath, notably large tracts of Friesland, Groningen, Overijssel, and Drenthe.

## Roman and Frankish Period (BC–c 1000)

Few traces were left by the prehistoric inhabitants of this region of Europe. Apart from the 'hunebedden' (literally—giants' graves), the long dolmens of people of perhaps 3000–2000 BC scattered along the Hondsrug (Dog's back) in the province of Drenthe, and the 'terps' (low, man-made hills found in Friesland and Groningen) raised by settlers of some 2000 years ago in their search for safety above semi-tidal marsh there are no notable monumental remains. We know that the hunebedden were made by the 'Funnel Beaker folk', so called from their style of pottery, who had drifted in from the north-east following the line of sandy ridges such as the Hondsrug. Pliny wrote in AD 47 of the terp-dwellers as living like sailors at high tide, and like castaways at low tide. They warm themselves, he added, by cutting, drying and then burning mud—he cannot have understood the use of peat. Insignificant though the terps may seem it is perhaps worth noting that 1260 of them have been counted and that it has been estimated that together they make up a volume some thirty times greater than the largest of Egypt's pyramids. Julius Caesar, who conquered Egypt and its Queen, did not manage to extend his Empire very far into this watery desert. He encountered a mixture of Gallo-Celtic and Germanic tribes, the former (Belgae) being to the south by the great rivers, and the latter (Batavi) living among the islands and meres of the rivers; the coastal strip from the Scheldt estuary northwards was the home of the Germanic Frisians. Caesar subdued the Belgae, their lands in 15 BC becoming the imperial province of Gallia Belgica, and in AD 13 Drusus brought the Batavi under Roman influence, not as part of Gallia Belgica but as allies who soon became valuable recruits for the legions. The Batavi spoke a Frankish dialect, which over the centuries would provide one of the elements of modern Dutch.

The Batavian-Roman alliance was broken in AD 69–70 when the Batavian Claudius (or Julius) Civilis (the Roman and only recorded name of this native leader) rebelled. Supported by the Frisians, who had in part been conquered in AD 47, he drove out or massacred Roman garrisons along the northern Rhine and before long much of northern Gaul was in revolt. The Emperor Vespasian then sent Petilius Cerialis who quickly suppressed the uprising. Claudius Civilis was defeated at Trier and Nijmegen but nevertheless succeeded in negotiating favourable conditions for his people. The Claudius Civilis story became a key episode in the patriotic historiography of Dutch writers during the Revolt against Spain. It was the subject of a painting (now in Stockholm) commissioned from Rembrandt to decorate the great hall of the new Town Hall (now Royal Palace) in Amsterdam, the building of which was begun in 1648, the year of the peace treaty which acknowledged the Netherlands' independence from Spain.

The principal Roman remains in the Netherlands are at Coriovallum (modern Heerlen, in Limburg), a civilian settlement, later fortified, on the road from Cologne to the coast.

By the 3C things were changing as Rome's hold weakened and Frankish penetration began (Franks being the name for a loose federation of several Germanic tribes). This penetration was at first more successful in the southern Netherlands where Clovis (466–511) imposed his authority over the various Frankish tribes and became converted to Christianity. Along the coast though, from the Scheldt to the Ems, the pagan Frisians retained their independence, while the Saxons—a Germanic people from the Schleswig peninsula who since the late 3C had been raiding westward along the coast and who had settled around today's Cuxhaven (Germany)— now penetrated into much of what are today Gelderland, Overijssel, and Drenthe. Christianity, although established by Clovis in the south, was slower to take root elsewhere and an early church built at Utrecht in c 500 was destroyed in c 630 by the Frisians. But in 689 the Frankish King Pepin of Herstal defeated the Frisian Radbod at Wijk bij Duurstede, and the next year St Willibrord (c 657–c 738), a Northumbrian missionary of Saxon origin, landed with a few companions near the mouth of the Scheldt. Befriended by Pepin, who sent him to Rome, Willibrord was later appointed Bishop of Utrecht, rebuilding the church there and from this base spreading Christianity throughout the north. He was much helped by St Boniface, martyred by the Frisians in 754.

In 768 Charlemagne ascended the Frankish throne, by 800, in which year the Pope declared him Emperor of the West, he ruled an empire which extended from Denmark to southern Italy and from northern Spain to the river Oder. By this date, too, the Frisians and the Saxons had been fully Christianised. But this period of stability ended with Charlemagne's death in 814, his vast domain being split up and the Netherlands experiencing a sequence of changes of overlordship. After much fighting between Charlemagne's descendants the Treaty of Verdun of 843 gave to his grandson Lothair the so-called Middle Kingdom along the Rhine and the Rhône. West Francia (roughly today's France) was separated from East Francia and that hodge-podge of states and dominions, including most of the Netherlands, which would eventually become the Holy Roman Empire, was given its first primitive form. But this Middle Kingdom was short-lived and on Lothair's death his son Lothair II received only the northern part, this being described as Lotharii Regnum (later corrupted in turn to Lotharingia and Lorraine) and including the Netherlands. Lothair II had no heir, so for nearly a century after his death in 869 his lands were in dispute; in 870 they were partitioned between East and West Francia (Treaty of Meerssen), in 879 they went to East Francia, from 912 to 924 they belonged to West Francia, and finally in 924 they returned to East Francia. In 953 Otto I (King of East Francia, crowned Emperor in 962) handed Lorraine as a fief to his brother Bruno, Archbishop of Cologne, he in turn dividing it into the two duchies of Upper and Lower Lorraine, the Netherlands being a part of the latter, although in practical terms Friesland and Groningen were independent.

It may here be noted that the 9C and 10C were centuries of raiding and limited settlement by Vikings. The need for defence against this constant menace, and the difficulties in exercising imperial authority in the distant and inaccessible Netherlands, led to increasing reliance on local authority and the parallel (and in many ways analagous) development of the feudal system and the independent town.

## The Burgundian Period (c 1000–1482)

During the 11C to the 15C there were two important trends throughout the Netherlands. One was the growth of the towns; the other the gradual consolidation of Burgundian power.

From the 11C and 12C onwards the towns of the Netherlands were growing in size, importance and independence. This was formalised through charters, the earliest ones dating from the 12C. Town charters were contracts between local lords and towns or other communities setting down agreed rules on such questions as taxation, the administration of justice, inheritance, access to natural resources and obligations for labour and military service. The Town Charter Movement started in the south with the great cloth centres of Ghent, Bruges and Ypres, soon spreading northwards. The 13C saw the chartering of, amongst others, Amsterdam, Rotterdam, Dordrecht, Leiden, Haarlem, Delft, Utrecht, Groningen and Leeuwarden. During the following century many towns with maritime trade further strengthened their position by joining the Hanseatic League, a federation (originating in Germany and led by Lübeck) some of the aims of which included common legal and commercial customs, protection against piracy and the establishment of 'factories', agencies which might secure uniform justice and acquire trading rights. These links were important for the subsequent Dutch domination of the Baltic trade in corn and lumber during the 'Golden Age'.

During the 11C to the 14C the feudal lords, with an often tenuous allegiance to the German emperor or the French king, occupied themselves with petty warfare and the crusades, but by the middle of the 14C five lords had emerged as the principal powers in the Netherlands. These were the Count of Flanders, the Duke of Brabant and Limburg, the Duke of Gelder, the Count of Holland (with also Zeeland and Hainaut) and the Bishop of Utrecht, whose lands included Overijssel, Drenthe and the town of Groningen. Frisia (by now without the territory to the south of the Zuider Zee, this having been absorbed into the county of Holland) and the Ommelanden or country districts of Groningen stood apart and were ruled as many small fiefs. In 1419 Duke Philip the Good of Burgundy succeeded to the countship of Flanders. He ruled until 1467, widely and thoroughly consolidating Burgundian power both territorially and administratively. He bought Namur in 1421; in 1430 he inherited Brabant, Limburg, and Antwerp; in 1433 he caused Countess Jacqueline (of Bavaria) to be deposed and took over Hainaut, Holland, and Zeeland; in 1443 he bought Luxembourg; in 1456 he had his nephew Louis de Bourbon elected Bishop of Liège and he also made his bastard son Bishop of Utrecht. It was during Philip's time that there occurred the disastrous St Elisabeth Flood (18 November 1421) when an inundation of the sea caused immense damage and loss of life, carving out the Hollands Diep and flooding what are now the Biesbos and Alblasserwaard.

Given the diversity of histories and traditions within his small empire, Philip knew that he had to assert his own centralised authority and to this end he determined to curtail or abolish the chartered privileges of the towns. Bruges (1438) and Ghent (1453) were to be the principal victims. More constructively, he summoned representatives from the various 'states' (estates, or assemblies) to a central States General in Brussels (1465), and he appointed a Grand Council with supreme judicial and financial authority over the whole of the Netherlands.

Philip was succeeded by his son Charles the Bold. Although he acquired

*St. Elisabeth's Day Flood 18–19 November 1421 by the Master of the St. Elisabeth Panels*

Gelder by reversion purchase in 1473 Charles was less concerned with the Netherlands than with his quarrels with the French, the Austrians, and the Swiss, these ending with his death in battle at Nancy in 1477. Turmoil followed, with the French taking Burgundy and Artois while in the Netherlands representatives of Flanders, Brabant, Hainaut, and Holland seized Charles's daughter and heir, Mary of Burgundy. She was forced to sign the Great Privilege, a charter conferring far-reaching local rights, this to be repaid with support against France. In the same year Mary married Archduke Maximilian of Austria. The Burgundian federation created by Philip the Good thus passed to the Habsburgs (but for temporary local independence, see provincial histories of Gelderland, Friesland, Groningen, Drenthe, and Utrecht).

During the Burgundian period, despite the tensions engendered between nominal overlord and local privilege, the geographical and political identity of the Netherlands took form. This was the larger Netherlands of the sixteenth century—the 13 provinces straddling the great rivers which were eventually to divide north and south into the independent United Provinces and the Spanish Netherlands. To some extent there was unity—Dutch was by far the most important language. Certainly there was a unity of civilisation—at all levels this most urbanised corner of Europe had a distinctive character evidenced in its material culture, its literary and religious life and its fine and decorative arts.

## The Habsburgs (1482–1555)

In 1482 Mary was killed in a riding accident. Maximilian became regent during the infancy of their son, later known as Philip the Handsome. Maximilian brought order to the Netherlands and on his election as Holy Roman Emperor in 1494 he handed the territory over to Philip, now aged 15. Philip married Joanna of Aragon, on his early death in 1506 his Burgundian lands passed to his son Charles (aged six). His aunt, Margaret of Austria, acted as governor during Charles' minority establishing a lavish court at her capital, Mechelen. In 1515 the States General declared Charles of age. In 1516 Charles became King of Spain and in 1519 Holy Roman Emperor—thus succeeding to all the Habsburg possessions. In 1524 he bought Central Frisia (modern Friesland); in 1527 he bought the temporal rights of the bishops of Utrecht; in 1536–38 he subjugated Groningen, Drenthe, and Gelder. Despite this territorial consolidation the Netherlands were to Charles V but a small part of a scattered empire, their wealth ensured that they were a rich source of revenue for his wars. Busy elsewhere, he continued to leave much of the administration to Margaret and, after her death in 1530, to his sister Mary of Hungary. Charles V abdicated in 1555 to be succeeded by his son, Philip II.

Territorial changes apart, the most significant feature of this period was the growth of Protestantism throughout the region. Protestantism spread rapidly through the highly literate urban populations where the Devotia Moderna had thrived in the previous century. Criticism of the medieval Catholic church, its corruption and its decadent dogma, had been led early in the century by humanist scholars like Erasmus of Rotterdam. Among common people and upper classes alike the most distinctively Netherlandish form of popular heresy was Anabaptism, though Lutheranism was also strong; Calvinism was later to become the dominant movement. All this was accompanied by persecution. The Edict of Blood of 1550 decreed death for all convicted of heresy and, even allowing for a tolerant attitude on the part of Catholic magistrates, 2000 in this region alone died for their beliefs before the end of Charles V's reign.

## The Revolt against the Habsburgs (1555–79)

Philip II's adamant Catholicism is the stuff of legend. He ruthlessly persecuted heretics, introducing the shock troops of Catholic reform, the newly formed Jesuit Order and garrisons of Spanish troops into the Netherlands. This did not inhibit increasing opposition, unrest, and further spread of Protestantism. Allied to the popular opposition, springing from religious and social grievances, there was the resistance of the nobles (mostly Catholic, and some of them stadholders, or provincial governors) who were resentful of the increasing centralisation of power into Spanish hands and the loss of powers of patronage under Philip's plans for the reorganisation of the Church. Unlike his father who was a Burgundian by birth, Philip was raised as a Spaniard and ruled through his agents, never seeking to understand the inhabitants of his richest province. Soon Prince William of Orange-Nassau (1533–84, known as the Silent), Stadholder of Holland, Zeeland and Utrecht, emerged as leader.

*Orange*, today a town and district of the Rhône in southern France, was an independent principality at the time of Charlemagne. From 1174 the princely line was that of the De Baux family but in 1393 when John of Châlons married Marie de Baux the inheritance passed to the Châlons line. Philibert (1502–30), the fifth in this Orange-Châlons line, gave loyal service to the Emperor Charles V for which he was rewarded in 1522 with lands in the Netherlands, these soon regarded as of more importance than those of Orange.

The countship of *Nassau* seems to have stemmed from one Drutwin (died 1076), builder of a fortress on the river Lahn, a tributary of the Rhine between Bonn and Wiesbaden. In 1255 two brothers, Walram and Otto, divided the now extensive inheritance, Walram taking the left bank of the Lahn and Otto the right bank (his seat was Siegen). In 1404 Otto's descendant Count Engelbert I of Nassau married Johanna van Polanen who had inherited the lands of Breda, thus starting the line of Breda-Nassau (he also made Breda his principal residence).

The two houses of Orange and Nassau merged with the marriage between Hendrik III of Breda-Nassau (1483–1538), great-grandson of Count Engelbert I, and Claudia de Châlons, sister of Philibert and, since her brother died childless, Princess of Orange. Their son Réné de Châlons became the first Prince of Orange-Nassau. He died childless in 1544, the titles then passing to his cousin William van Nassau-Dillingen (William the Silent). Although the eldest of five brothers, William's succession had not been automatic since his parents were staunch Protestants and Charles V only approved his assuming the titles on condition that he was separated from his parents, educated and given a household in the Netherlands and brought up a Catholic. Despite this William became the leader of the revolt, and from that time until the present day the family has provided Holland and the other provinces with stadholders, kings, and queens.

Having been seized by Louis XIV in 1672, the principality of Orange was officially transferred to France by the Treaty of Rijswijk in 1697, thereafter only the princely title surviving. The combined title of Orange-Nassau became extinct in 1702 when William III, prince of Orange-Nassau and king of England, died childless, the Nassau title then passing to Jan Willem Friso, a descendant of John, brother of William the Silent.

Forced to accede to a demand by the States General that all Spanish troops be withdrawn, Philip II retired to Spain, leaving Margaret of Parma (natural daughter of Charles V) in Brussels as governor, with as chief counsellors Cardinal Granvelle, a French adviser to Philip, and Berlaymont, a Walloon (i.e. French-speaking, from the southern part of present-day Belgium) nobleman. Opposition hardened, the Inquisition was defied, Protestantism (in particular Calvinism) spread to the nobility, and in 1564 Granvelle was recalled. The following year saw the formation of the League of the Nobility, a religious and political opposition group. William the Silent's brother Louis of Nassau and Hendrik van Brederode were among the League's northern members. The League, many of whose members were still Catholic, petitioned for moderation of the anti-Protestant edicts. It was dismissed by Berlaymont who contemptuously referred to its members as *'ces gueux'* (those beggars), a taunt which was soon adopted as an honorific title. Calvinism now spread rapidly, the year 1566 being marked by rioting and the destruction of Church property, especially in Antwerp.

Known as the Iconoclastic Fury (in Dutch, *De Beeldenstorm*) this development did the Protestant cause great harm, frightening and alienating many
people, splitting the opposition to Spain and enabling Margaret to play off
the popular party against the aristocratic and to regain the support of many
of the nobles. William and Count Egmont, the Stadholder of Flanders,
attempted to steer a middle course but failed in the face of a Calvinist
uprising in Flanders supported by Van Brederode, and William retired to
his Nassau estates.

Determined on the absolute suppression of heresy Philip now sent the
Duke of Alva with an army of 10,000 to the Netherlands, the Duke without
delay setting up the so-called Council of Blood to deal ruthlessly with
heretics and rebels, outlawing William and executing Egmont and many
other nobles. From Nassau William attempted to raise an army but, although his brother Louis won a battle at Heiligerlee near Groningen, lack
of money and lack of support from the towns, all now garrisoned by Spanish
troops, made continued resistance impossible.

It was on 1 April 1572 that the tide began to turn when the Sea Beggars
(*Gueux de Mer*, or, in Dutch, *Watergeuzen*), privateers commissioned by
William and hitherto operating out of England, captured Brielle at the
mouth of the Maas and, soon afterwards, Vlissingen (Flushing) and, in the
Zuider Zee, Enkhuizen. By June 1572 the entire county of Holland except
for Amsterdam was in the hands of the rebels, the States of Holland
assumed responsibility for administration and William, now a declared
Protestant, settled in Delft. Alva, however, far from defeated, beat Louis of
Nassau at Mons and then marched north, brutally sacking Mechelen and
subduing the whole of Gelder and Overijssel, while his son Don Frederick
of Toledo sacked Zutphen and Naarden and, in July 1573 after a siege of
seven months, took Haarlem, slaughtering over half the garrison and all
the Calvinist ministers. But these successes were not enough to defeat the
resistance of the townspeople of Holland and Zeeland; the dikes were cut,
Don Frederick had to withdraw, and Alva, his fleet defeated in the Zuider
Zee and his army now mutinous and unpaid, left for Spain. The northern
rebels, their strongest element now Calvinist, controlled all Holland (except
for Amsterdam and Haarlem) and Zeeland (except for Middelburg and
Zierikzee).

Alva was replaced by Luis Requesens and the fighting continued, with
the North determined on religious freedom but the South ready for compromise. The year 1574 saw the defeat and death of Louis of Nassau near
Nijmegen, but also the relief of the Spanish siege of Leiden and the taking
of Middelburg and Zierikzee. Then in 1576 Requesens died, William
seizing this opportunity, advancing into Flanders and taking Ghent, and
starting the negotiations with the Brussels States General which led to the
signing (8 November 1576) of the Pacification of Ghent. Under this agreement freedom of religious belief was accepted in principle and all edicts
against heresy were lifted, although the supremacy of Catholicism was
established in all provinces other than Holland and Zeeland in which
William was officially recognised as Stadholder. The unity of the whole of
the Netherlands (the 13 provinces) was also accepted in principle and the
chances of its continuation seemed reasonable.

Requesens' successor was Philip II's bastard brother Don John of Austria
who at the time of the signing of the Pacification was waiting in Luxembourg with a fresh Spanish army. William persuaded the States General to
withhold recognition until Don John accepted the terms of the Pacification;
this resulted in deadlock until William's hand was strengthened in 1577 by

the signing of the Union of Brussels under which all the provinces represented in the States General (many, of course, staunchly Catholic) demanded the departure of all foreign troops and the implementation of the Pacification, and in return formally accepted Philip's sovereignty. At this Don John yielded, coming to Brussels and signing the Perpetual Edict accepting virtually all the demands of the States General.

But the unity apparently now achieved was short-lived, largely because the spread of Calvinism was awakening widespread fears in the Catholic provinces of Brabant, Groningen and Limburg, and also in the Walloon country in the south. The mistrust was especially strong among the Catholic nobility. Don John withdrew to Namur, Haarlem was reoccupied by the North in 1577, and the year 1578 saw a series of significant events—a secret conspiracy by southern Catholic nobles resulting in the proclamation as governor of the Archduke Mathias, later Emperor; the expulsion of the Spanish garrisons from Kampen and Deventer by, respectively, William's rigidly Calvinist brother John, appointed Stadholder of Gelderland, and Count Renneberg, Stadholder of Overijssel; the overthrow of the pro-Catholic authority in Amsterdam; and, finally, Philip II's determined attempt to settle the Netherlands problem by despatching there Alexander Farnese, Duke of Parma, at the head of yet another army. By the end of the year Spanish authority was again established over most of the South.

The last hope of unity between North and South disappeared on 5 January 1579 when Hainaut, Artois, and Douai signed the Union of Arras, declaring faith in Catholicism and allegiance to Philip. The North replied with the Union of Utrecht.

The Union of Arras and the Union of Utrecht may be regarded as the starting points of the two separate countries of Belgium and the Netherlands. The former (see *Blue Guide Belgium and Luxembourg*) would progress through being the Spanish Netherlands (until 1713); the Austrian Netherlands (1713–94); a part of revolutionary France (1794–1814); reunion with the North as a part of the United Kingdom of the Netherlands (1815–31); and finally the Kingdom of Belgium.

The history of the North from the republic of the United Provinces to today's Kingdom of the Netherlands (or, to English speakers, Holland) continues below.

## The United Provinces (1579–1795)

Apart from a truce between 1609 and 1621, the years 1579 to 1648 were years of continuing and ultimately victorious warfare against Spain. These were also the years in which the new republic established itself. It seems therefore appropriate to summarise the religious and constitutional situations which would change little over the following 200 years. A note is also included on Public Order and the role of the shooting guilds in its enforcement.

*Religion*. Prior to the Union of Utrecht there had been Calvinist outbreaks of iconoclasm (notably in 1566), and in 1572, as the Sea Beggars increasingly took over the towns, churches and monasteries were plundered or handed over to civic authorities and some Catholics were murdered. The Union of Utrecht, however, stipulated freedom of conscience for all, and there was compelling reason for this. The struggle against Spain was by no means simply a religious one; many Catholics in the United Provinces were as set on independence and as much opposed to Spain as were the Calvinists, and the leaders of the revolt had no wish to alienate support.

Nevertheless, while freedom of conscience was allowed, this did not extend to automatic freedom for Catholics, or for members of some other sects, to hold public office (this varied from place to place and from time to time), nor, especially in Holland and Zeeland, did it fully permit open Catholic worship. In fact a compromise soon emerged—more a matter of connivance than anything official—by which the Catholics could worship provided that they were not seen to do so. This led to a proliferation of clandestine or hidden churches, virtually always enjoying immunity from interference even if sometimes the Catholics found it wise to pay protection money to the civic authorities.

Full and open freedom of worship for everybody came only with the arrival of the French Revolutionary armies in 1795.

*Constitution.* The situation on the signing of the Union of Utrecht was that the northern provinces had merely formalised themselves as a loose and essentially military federation (the United Provinces), comprising Holland (by far the most populous and richest and thus the most influential), Zeeland, Utrecht, Friesland, Overijssel, Gelderland (less the Roermond quarter which being largely Catholic remained in Spanish hands), and Groningen. Sparsely inhabited Drenthe enjoyed no provincial status, nor, later, did the 'generality' lands captured from the south along the borders in Zeeland Flanders and Brabant. These United Provinces were far from being a state even of a federal kind—in fact after the formal deposing of Philip II in 1581 there was no head of state—and indeed at the start the leaders were not clear what kind of state they wanted, or for that matter whether they wanted one at all. While historically the Union of Utrecht is now hailed as the birth of the modern state of the Netherlands, to William and many other leaders of the time, whose aim had always been the unity of the Netherlands and who now had to accept that this could probably never be achieved, the Union in some measure represented defeat.

In its main essentials the above constitutional looseness, born of an absolute insistence on provincial independence, was to be the pattern throughout the 200 years of the United Provinces; there would be no *de jure* head of state, no central taxation, no central or even uniform legal system and courts. The only central institution was the States General, the assembly of the delegations of the provinces which met in the Binnenhof at The Hague, but, without authority to enact domestic legislation, the assembly could concern itself only with foreign affairs and war and even in these fields its decisions had to be unanimous. Answerable to the States General were the Union's only two federal servants, the Captain General and the Admiral General, both appointments usually held by the Stadholder of Holland. Such indeed was the insistence on local autonomy that the States General had to exercise marine administration through no fewer than five district admiralties.

Each province had its Stadholder, although more often than not the same man held the post for two or more provinces. Formerly the stadholders had been provincial governors, and now, in the United Provinces, they were still powerful men and usually members of the House of Orange-Nassau, a man such as Maurice, William the Silent's son, Prince of Orange, a brilliant commander, and Stadholder of Holland, Zeeland, Utrecht, Gelderland and Overijssel, being virtually a national ruler.

The provinces were administered by their States (assemblies of the various 'estates' or interest groups—nobility, merchants, towns, country parishes, etc), but the means of choosing delegates for these varied widely. Each State had a permanent official, the Council Pensionary (Raadspensionaris; earlier, Advocate), these being men of high local repute who, in modern terms, acted as chief executive. The Pensionary of the States of Holland was a particularly powerful figure, always accompanying his delegation to the meeting of the States General and often achieving the status of something akin to a national statesman.

The delegates to the provincial States were sent by the towns and the country parishes, the former ruled by councils made up, largely on a hereditary basis, of members of an oligarchy of leading families, the parishes generally controlled by a local lord. A city such as Amsterdam had immense national influence, but smaller places had little and could only be heard through the provincial States.

In the absence of any formal apportionment of power either as between the stadholders and their provincial States, or as between the stadholders, the States, and the States General, lay the seeds of much future trouble. Nevertheless, despite their decentralised, slow, and by any normal standards inefficient system, the United Provinces achieved internationally recognised independence, celebrated a Golden Age (see below), and survived until the arrival of a new order with the French Revolutionary armies.

*Public Order (the Shooting Guilds).* The 13C saw the start of the negotiating of town charters, the independence thus achieved brought with it the need to do something about public order. For long this was largely a matter of self-help with bands of marksmen forming vigilante guilds (or companies, or corporations) under such names as St George, St Sebastian, or St Adrian, armed at first with bows and arrows but soon with firearms (arquebuses) and exercising in the Doelen (target) yards. The social aspect soon became important and even pre-eminent, banquets in particular being a popular feature of guild activities; these could be protracted and sumptuous and indeed an order of 1633 complains that such festivities often lasted a whole week. In course of time the original defensive purpose of the guilds lapsed while the number of such companies proliferated and little more than the festivities and the outward show remained. One popular form of display was the commissioning of group portraits to hang in the Doelen hall (the high period for such portraits was roughly 1550 to 1650) and each guild kept a museum of armaments and militaria—pieces from the collection of the Kloveniersdoelen enhance the richness and sense of living history in Rembrandt's *Nightwatch* (Rijksmuseum, Amsterdam).

With Parma at the head of a fresh army, his rear secured by the conclusion of peace by the southern provinces, militarily the situation could hardly have been less favourable for the new federation, and to make things worse the town of Groningen soon withdrew from the Union. Delfzijl and Steenwijk were lost to Parma in 1580 and Philip II, encouraged by these successes, declared William to be an outlaw and promised a large reward to any man who killed him. William, convinced now that only foreign help could save the United Provinces, offered sovereignty to the Duke of Anjou, brother of Henry III of France. Anjou accepted, but discredited by several defeats returned to France in 1583. The following year (July 1584) the outlawed William was assassinated in Delft by a French Catholic.

The leadership of the United Provinces now passed nominally to William's 17-year-old second son Maurice of Nassau (his eldest son was in the hands of the Spanish) but practically to Jan van Oldenbarneveld (1547–1619) who in 1586 became Advocate of the province of Holland. With defeats continuing (Nijmegen, Doesburg, and Antwerp all fell), and with sovereignty refused by Henry III of France, Oldenbarneveld turned for help to Protestant England, offering sovereignty to Elizabeth. This she refused, instead sending troops under her favourite the Earl of Leicester but at the same time demanding and holding the towns of Vlissingen and Brielle as surety against her expenses. Leicester, however, was an even more disastrous failure than Anjou, making himself unpopular in many ways, not least by failing to halt Parma. Grave, Venlo, Deventer, and Sluys all fell and finally, after an attempted coup-d'état, Leicester returned to England at the end of 1587.

Oldenbarneveld, Maurice of Nassau and William Louis (son of John of Nassau and Stadholder of Friesland) next formed a triumvirate, with Maurice, already Stadholder of Holland and Zeeland, now given the same title for Utrecht, Gelderland, and Overijssel. The two cousins Maurice and William Louis soon showed themselves to be soldiers of genius, quick to profit from the change of fortune as Philip II's resources were weakened by the disastrous Armada and as Parma was diverted southward to campaigns against the French. The decade 1589–99 became one of virtually continuous victory. Breda and Steenbergen were the first towns to be taken (1590), the following year it was the turn of Zutphen, Deventer, Delfzijl, Hulst and Nijmegen; in 1592, the year in which Parma died, Steenwijk and Coevorden were taken, and in 1593–94 Geertruidenberg and Groningen. William Louis became Stadholder of the Groningen. With the signing in 1596 of the Triple Alliance with the French and English it could be said that the United Provinces had achieved internationally recognised statehood, and by the following year, with a victory at Turnhout and the taking of Grol, Enschede, Ootmarsum and Oldenzaal, for all practical purposes there were no Spanish garrisons within the Provinces' borders.

Nor was it only at home that the United Provinces were active. Already by 1595 their first ship had sailed for the East Indies, and by 1602, the date of the founding of the East Indies Company, the Provinces' ships were trading in competition with Spain and Portugal in both the East and the West Indies. This contributed to the refusal of Albert and Isabella (the 'Archdukes'), now joint sovereigns in the Spanish Netherlands, to consider tentative proposals for union based on religious toleration. Fighting continued, with Albert laying siege to Ostend, an isolated United Provinces' port which they could supply only by sea and which fell in 1604 to Spinola, the Spanish commander, as did also one or two other places (Grol and Oldenzaal), largely because the position of the United Provinces had been weakened by James I's decision to make peace with Spain. But these losses were amply offset by the taking by Maurice of Cadzand and Sluys and by the destruction by Admiral Heemskerk of the Spanish silver fleet off Gibraltar (1607). This last perhaps more than anything else convinced the Spanish that they had had enough and in April 1609 a 12-year truce was arranged.

The truce recognised the United Provinces as independent free states, their frontiers to be as existing on signing, this last provision gave the United Provinces what is now Noord Brabant, a territory then termed 'generality land' which, without provincial status, was directly administered by the States General. A later secret agreement recognised the United Provinces' trading rights in the Indies and trade continued to expand both there and in Europe where between 1609 and 1612 trading factories (agencies) were established at Venice, Gothenburg and Istanbul. In 1613 Vlissingen and Brielle, since 1585 held as surety by England, were returned.

The main feature of the period of the truce was a domestic quarrel, part political and part religious, which ended in tragedy. The quarrel had its roots in the very strained relations that now existed between Maurice and Oldenbarneveld. The enmity arose out of disagreement over the truce, the chief architects of which had been Oldenbarneveld and the States of Holland. Maurice, supported by his cousin William Louis together with the military leaders and the Calvinist clergy, took the view that the truce was a Spanish ruse to gain a breathing space. Into this already strained atmosphere there erupted in 1612 an abstruse religious dispute arising out of the assertion by the Leiden theologian Jacobus Arminius that predestination, a firm Calvinist tenet, was conditional and not absolute. Opposed by the rival theologian Franz Gomarus, the followers of Arminius addressed a remonstrance (they were henceforth known as the Remonstrants) to the States of Holland, which, with the support of Oldenbarneveld, upheld the Remonstrants' rights to their opinions. However, Maurice and four provinces out of the seven supported the orthodox view and the States General suggested a synod (the Synod of Dort, 1618) to resolve the argument. This the States of Holland arrogantly refused to attend, passing a resolution which asserted the principle of provincial independence, demanding oaths of allegiance, raising a provincial militia, and even advising the 'generality' troops for which they were financially responsible that they owed no allegiance to the States General. Thus what had started as a theological debate escalated into a constitutional dispute on the respective powers of the provincial States and the States General, a dispute which Maurice and his supporters saw as a grave threat to the Union. Backed by his army Maurice quickly overcame all opposition and arrested Oldenbarneveld, the jurist Hugo Grotius and others. Oldenbarneveld was hauled before a special court, allowed no facilities for defence, and executed in May 1619, while Grotius was sentenced to life imprisonment (he was dramatically rescued by his wife 20 months later)

As Prince of Orange (since the death of his elder brother in 1618, who had been a life-long prisoner/hostage in Spain), as Stadholder of Holland, Zeeland, Utrecht, Overijssel, and Gelderland, and as Captain General and Admiral General, Maurice was now undisputed leader of the United Provinces.

The *Thirty Years' War* (of complex, mainly religious origins) had broken out in 1618 and the hostilities between Spain and the United Provinces, automatically renewed in 1621, now became a part of a general European conflict.

Initially things went badly for the United Provinces, with Spinola taking Breda in 1625 and the death that same year of Maurice; but Frederick Henry, Maurice's younger half-brother who succeeded to all the titles, soon proved himself as good a commander as his brother and far more of a statesman. His twenty years as national leader saw not only the triumphant end of the long struggle with Spain but also the start of what came to be known as the Golden Age (see below).

Militarily there now followed a series of victories on land and at sea against a Spain increasingly weakened by her fight with France. Oldenzaal and Grol were retaken in 1624 and 1627; in 1628 Admiral Piet Heyn, sponsored by the West Indies Company, captured the Mexican silver fleet; in 1629 Frederick Henry took first 's-Hertogenbosch, then gained control of the lower Rhine by seizing Wesel; Maastricht, Roermond, Venlo and Breda all fell between 1632 and 1637, while 1639 saw Admiral Tromp destroy the Spanish fleet in the Downs. Further land victories came in 1644 and 1645 with the taking of Sas van Gent and Hulst, actions which assured the United Provinces' control of the south shore of the Scheldt (Zeeland Flanders). Politically also Frederick Henry scored a signal success through the marriage in 1641 of his son William with Mary, daughter of Charles I of England, a match which marked the first step of the House of Orange-Nassau towards royal status.

Frederick Henry died in 1647, and the following year Philip IV of Spain, hard pressed by France, signed the Treaty of Münster, this being a part of the more general Peace of Westphalia which ended the Thirty Years' War. The independence of the United Provinces was recognised, their claim to the 'generality' lands confirmed, and, perhaps the most important provision, the Scheldt was officially closed to trade, a move which ruined Antwerp and transferred commercial prosperity from the Spanish Netherlands to the United Provinces.

*The Golden Age.* The years of Frederick Henry roughly covered the first half of what has come to be called the Golden Age, an era which extended into the early 18C. These were the years of the United Provinces' brilliance, success and prestige not only militarily and politically as outlined above but also in many other spheres, notably art, learning and overseas trade. The artists active during this period are not outshone in brilliance by those of any other age or place (see article on Dutch Art). Applied art was represented by such craftsmen as Jan Lutma and the Van Vianen family. Architects such as Jacob van Campen and sculptors such as Artus Quellin and Rombout Verhulst were quick to seize the opportunities offered by the fast expanding towns, and the universities flourished, among the many learned men of the time being Christiaan Huygens, astronomer, mathematician and inventor of the pendulum clock; Hugo Grotius, the jurist; the classicists Daniel and Nicolaas Heinsius; and the great philosopher Baruch Spinoza.

Another feature of the Golden Age was the extent of religious toleration, though it fell short of today's standards it was incomparably greater than that in other countries. The connivance at clandestine Catholic worship has already been noted and this continued increasingly throughout the 17C, especially after the annexation of Noord Brabant which brought the Catholic population up to about one-third of the United Provinces' total. Additionally, within the Protestant Church, sects of many kinds were tolerated and also, in contrast to most of Europe, Jews were accepted, being allowed to worship freely and, despite certain restrictions, becoming commercial leaders in many cities.

The wide and rapid expansion in overseas trade was concentrated in the activities of the East and West Indies companies.

The *East Indies Company* was formed through a States General charter of 1602, its terms of reference being first the regulation and protection of trade (many companies had been fighting one another since 1595 when, after failing to find a north-east passage, the first United Provinces' ship sailed round the Cape of Good Hope to Java), and secondly to contribute to the war of independence. In Europe the company was run by a central board at The Hague controlling several local boards; it enjoyed trading monopoly and freedom from import duties and was allowed to raise its own armed forces and to establish colonies. One of the company's early acts was (1609) to send Henry Hudson to find a north-west passage, a voyage which led the navigator to what is now New York. In the Indies the company was in effect the government, and, with its capital established at Batavia, it in turn drove the English out of Malaya and the Moluccas and the Portuguese out of Ceylon and Malacca. In 1652 a colony was established on the Cape of Good Hope and by about 1670 the company was at its most prosperous, with a network of trading depots, 150 merchantmen, about 40 warships, and able to call on some 10,000 troops. Due largely to its rigidly monopolistic attitude and the consequent conflict with other powers, notably England and France, the company was in decline by the end of the 17C, although, then bankrupt, it was not until 1798 that it was finally wound up by the French.

The *West Indies Company* arose out of a States General charter of 1621, its role being to regulate and protect the contraband trade with the Spanish and Portuguese possessions in Africa and the Americas and also to establish colonies. Organised similarly to the East Indies Company it was more tightly controlled by the States General. Nevertheless it enjoyed a trade monopoly over a huge area, ran its own armed forces, and had the right to sign treaties and wage war. From 1609, when Hudson had anchored in New York bay, there were moves (though not all by the West Indies Company) towards the establishment of trade and colonists in this area, and the colony of New Netherland was formally constituted in 1623. Already by this same year the company was active in what is now Brazil, although it pulled out in 1661. Posts were established in St Eustatius, Curaçao, and Aruba in 1634–35, at Saba in 1640, and on St Martin in 1648. Later the emphasis was on the development of Surinam. Never as commercially successful as the East Indies Company, the company was dissolved in 1674, reconstituted in 1675, and finally wound up by the French in 1798.

**Prince William II (1648–1650)**, another able soldier, succeeded his father Frederick Henry, his brief period of power (he died of smallpox in 1650) being marked by a constitutional dispute the basis of which was on the one hand the Orangist urge for personal authority and centralisation and, on the other, the desire of the urban oligarchies (especially Amsterdam's) and the provinces (especially Holland) to run the country in their own way. The States General, still wary of former enemies and influenced by William who had military ambitions, wished to keep in service at least key elements of the regiments rendered redundant by the Treaty of Münster, but the States of Holland would have none of this and unilaterally cashiered their own troops. William then acted as effectively as had Maurice against Oldenbarneveld, locking up the Holland leaders at Loevestein while his kinsman William Frederick, Stadholder of Friesland, moved against Amsterdam which put up no fight. Generous and diplomatic in success, William then released his prisoners. Three months later he died.

A week after William's death the son was born who in 1689 would become King William III of England. But now the leaders of the States of Holland were quick to seize the opportunity offered by an infant Prince of Orange, calling together a special Great Assembly of the provinces which decided that there should be no stadholders (except in Friesland and Groningen which remained loyal to William Frederick), that the powers of the States General should be drastically reduced, and that all effective authority should be decentralised to individual provinces. One natural result of this was that the province of Holland became even more powerful than before, in foreign eyes being regarded as representing the whole nation. In 1651 Jacob Cats was appointed Council Pensionary (Raadspensionaris; what had formerly been Advocate) to the States of Holland, and in 1653 he was followed by Johan de Witt, the great statesman and dominant political figure of the next 20 years; they were to be 20 years of war.

The First English War (1652–54), the perhaps inevitable result of years of commercial and colonial competition, was an entirely naval affair, the United Provinces' admirals being Maerten Tromp (died 1653) and Michiel de Ruyter. On the whole the English were the winners, and under the Treaty of Westminster the United Provinces paid East Indies trade compensation while, on Cromwell's insistence and with the anti-Orange De Witt readily agreeing, the States of Holland secretly undertook (Act of Seclusion) that the Prince of Orange would never become Stadholder (this was confirmed in 1657 when by the Perpetual Edict the States General abolished the stadholderate). This is the period 'of Dutch history so scrupulously and acutely observed by Sir William Temple (see Background Sources in the Preface). The Cavalier knight was full of respect for Dutch bourgeoise values and for the republican gravitas of men such as Johan de Witt who was incorruptible, overpoweringly modest and terrifyingly efficient. Like so many travellers in the Netherlands during this period he was also intrigued by the technological advances made by Dutch manufacturers and scientists, by the independence of Dutch women and by the frequency and prosperity of Dutch towns. The United Provinces seemed to be in competition with every one of their European neighbours in every aspect of political and commercial life.

The years 1657–61 saw war with Portugal over Brazil which led to the United Provinces dropping their claims. In 1658–59 a successful naval war was fought against Sweden to safeguard the Provinces' trading interests in Danish waters (De Ruyter expelled the Swedes from the island of Fyn).

Colonial rivalry continued with England, the English seizing New Netherland and its capital New Amsterdam in 1664 and renaming it New York. The resulting Second English War (1664–67) was again fought largely at sea, the best known action being the daring raid which burnt the English fleet in the Medway. Again the war was inconclusive and the main provision of the Treaty of Breda was that the English kept New Netherland in exchange for Surinam. A year later a triple alliance aimed at curbing the ambitions of France's Louis XIV was signed between the United Provinces, Sweden and England. England's Charles II was a half-hearted partner (the Medway raid rankled more than was commonly supposed), making a secret treaty with Louis XIV of France in 1670 and openly siding with him when in 1672 he marched against the Spanish Netherlands and the United Provinces. Most of the Provinces' military effort had gone into the navy, while the army, little used and the cause of constant bickering between the States General and the provincial States, had been neglected. Now, without allies and apparently helpless before a powerful threat on land, the United Provinces turned once again to the House of Orange, in February 1672 appointing William III Captain General and Admiral General and in July repealing the Perpetual Edict and declaring him Stadholder of Holland and Zeeland, the title to be hereditary.

William's rise inevitably meant the fall of Johan de Witt who was blamed, however unjustly, for present troubles. He had signed the Act of Seclusion and had opposed both the repeal of the Perpetual Edict and the offer of titles to William. In June de Witt was wounded in an attempt on his life, and in July a rumour spread that his brother Cornelis had conspired to poison William. The brothers were held and put to torture in the Gevangenpoort at The Hague and in August were murdered by a pro-Orange mob. The savagery of the assassination was appalling and is recorded in a small painting in the historical section at the Rijksmuseum in Amsterdam.

William has never been associated with this crime, but he did later reward its instigators.

**Prince William III (1672–1702)**. Louis XIV quickly overran almost the whole of the southern and eastern United Provinces, but William saved the west by opening the dikes while at the same time De Ruyter held the combined French and English fleets. By 1674 William had retaken all the lost fortresses except Maastricht, England making peace with the Treaty of Westminster and relations between the two countries so improving that three years later William married Mary, daughter of the Duke of York (later James II). In 1678 Maastricht was recovered and under the Treaty of Nijmegen Louis XIV gave up all claims in the United Provinces.

In 1688 the scene shifted to England where with the revolution against James II the crown was offered jointly to William and his wife Mary. In the same year Anthonie Heinsius became Council Pensionary of Holland.

William, now dividing his time between England and the United Provinces, soon (1690) again found himself at war with France, this time as the leader of the Augsburg League (or Grand Alliance) comprising England, the United Provinces, Spain, Sweden, and several German states. In 1692 the combined fleets of England and the United Provinces defeated the French at La Hogue; in 1695, as part of a series of land victories, William took Namur in the Spanish Netherlands; and in 1697 Louis XIV had little choice but to sign the Treaty of Rijswijk recognising William as King of England and giving the United Provinces commercial advantages. But the respite from war was brief for in 1700 Charles II, the last of the Spanish Habsburgs, died childless, willing the crown of Spain and of the Spanish Netherlands to Philip of Anjou, grandson of Louis XIV. At once seizing this opportunity, Louis forced his grandson to hand the Spanish Netherlands over to France, upon which William set up the Triple Alliance of England, the United Provinces and Austria. William died in March 1702. In May the three powers declared war (War of the Spanish Succession).

William III died childless, his heir in the United Provinces being Jan Willem Friso who although Stadholder of Friesland and Groningen was unacceptable to the province of Holland. So once again all the other provinces embarked on a period without any stadholder. That despite this the War of the Spanish Succession was successfully prosecuted was in large measure due to the co-operation between Anthonie Heinsius the Council Pensionary, the Duke of Marlborough who commanded the armies of England and the United Provinces, and Prince Eugène of Savoy, a Frenchman who had fallen foul of Louis XIV and entered the service of Austria.

### War of the Spanish Succession (1702–13)

1702: Marlborough advanced S from the United Provinces taking the Maas fortresses (Venlo, Liège, Huy).

1703: A comparatively inactive year. Marlborough wished to invade France, but the States General persuaded him to divert to Bonn, which he took. Marlborough took Limburg.

1704: Louis XIV marched against Austria, but Marlborough's and Eugène's campaigns on the Danube ended in victory at Blenheim. At sea the United Provinces' Admiral Callenberg defeated the French off Malaga.

1705: Little action. The French took Huy, but Marlborough broke through their lines at Tienen.

1706: Marlborough's defeat of the French at Ramillies led to their withdrawal from virtually the whole of the Spanish Netherlands.

1707: A year of lull during which the French recovered.
1708: The French overran much of Flanders, taking Ghent and Bruges, but Marlborough then defeated them at Oudenarde and went on to take Lille.
1709: Marlborough and Eugène took Tournai and fought an indecisive battle at Malplaquet.
1710–13: The war dragged on. Marlborough, the victim of jealous intrigue in England, was dismissed by Queen Anne on 31 December 1711.
1713: Treaty of Utrecht.

Under the Treaty of Utrecht France abandoned all claim to the Spanish Netherlands which now, under the Emperor Charles VI, became the Austrian Netherlands, while the United Provinces gained parts of Gelderland and Limburg, small reward for years of war which had exhausted the country's finances at a time when economic decline was already setting in. The national policy now became one of avoiding entanglement, an aim soon thwarted when the Emperor Charles VI established an East Indies Company at Ostend, a move which threatened the huge trade advantage which the United Provinces still enjoyed through the continuing closure of the Scheldt. In return for the suppression of this company the United Provinces had to agree to become guarantors of the Pragmatic Sanction which sought to assure that Charles VI was succeeded by his daughter Maria Theresa. Thus when Charles died in 1740 the United Provinces could not avoid becoming involved in the War of the Austrian Succession (1743–48). At first this involvement was indirect, even when in 1744 the French under Marshal Saxe occupied the whole of the Austrian Netherlands, but when in 1747 they also took over Zeeland Flanders the United Provinces turned again to the House of Orange. William Friso of Friesland, now by inheritance Prince William IV of Orange, was elected Stadholder of all seven provinces (the United Provinces thus for the first time in their history having a head of state) and also Captain General and Admiral General. Soon afterwards all these titles were made hereditary.

Under the Treaty of Aix-la-Chapelle of 1748 France evacuated and gave up all claim to United Provinces' and Austrian Netherlands' territories.

The United Provinces now entered its final 50 years, a period of decline the causes of which were many and complex, domestic and international. The country was crippled by debt, its fleet practically non-existent; the commercial drive of the past was giving way to complacency and a love of consumption, financial markets proving more attractive than overseas risk and the cautious rentier taking the place of the adventurous investor; neither Prince William IV nor his son William V were men of sufficient character to persuade the conservative oligarchies still ruling the towns and provinces to carry out the many reforms which were becoming increasingly urgent for the recovery and survival of a modern state; above all, with the removal of the French threat the initial enthusiasm for the stadholders waned, and the familiar conflict between them (the Orangists, between 1751 and 1768 represented by unpopular foreign regents) and the ruling families (now increasingly liberal in outlook, pro-French, and calling themselves the Patriots) sharpened until by 1787 it resulted in civil war and foreign invasion.

In 1751 William IV died, his successor being his infant son William V for whom his mother Anne of Hanover, daughter of George II of England, acted as regent. She was pro-English at a time when the majority of the people were not, and she had little feeling for the United Provinces' attitudes or problems. Anne died in 1759 to be succeeded as regent by the Duke of

Brunswick, a distinguished soldier whom William IV had made commander of the army and who had since achieved great influence and wealth. As regent he was disliked by the Patriots who saw him as a soldier committed to centralised authority and war whereas they wanted decentralisation and peace.

When William V entered his majority in 1766 the Duke of Brunswick, knowing William's weakness of character, drew up a secret Act of Consultation under which William would continue to be advised by him. In 1767 William married the strong-willed Princess Wilhelmina of Prussia. The outbreak of the American War of Independence saw William favouring England while most of his people sympathised with the colonials. Despite his resistance diplomatic relations were established between the American Congress and the United Provinces in 1779. In the following year the United Provinces joined the League of Armed Neutrality, a defensive measure against English interference with neutral shipping, and England declared war. The only United Provinces' success was a naval action (1781) off the Dogger Bank. This apart, the Provinces suffered continual defeats, losing most of their colonies and finishing the war economically ruined.

Under the Treaty of Paris of 1784 the United Provinces had to cede the last of their Indian possessions (Negapatam), allowing the English full freedom of East Indies trade. With William receiving the blame for the disasters of the war the Patriots grew in strength and when now they learnt about the Act of Consultation the Duke of Brunswick left the country. Civil war loomed. In 1785 the Patriots organised an armed Free Corps which soon gained control of several towns. By the summer of 1786 William had retaken the small towns of Hattem and Elburg. In Utrecht, however, there was open Patriot revolt and in September the States of Holland suspended the stadholderate. In a skirmish near Utrecht in the following year the Free Corps killed 80 Orangists. William was now established at Nijmegen, from where in June his wife Wilhelmina offered to mediate. Although the Patriots granted her a safe-conduct to The Hague, she was intercepted and held for several hours near Gouda. The King of Prussia determined to avenge this insult to his sister and in September his army invaded the United Provinces at Wesel and William returned to The Hague. The Act of Guarantee (1788) settled the dispute, the provinces agreeing to respect the stadholderate and William agreeing to limitations to his powers, but many Patriots were banished or chose to leave.

The French Revolution erupted onto the European scene in 1789. At war with Austria from 1792–95 the French invaded the Austrian Netherlands, occupying the whole territory by mid 1794 and opening the Scheldt to commerce. War was declared on England and the United Provinces in 1793, and in 1794, led by General Charles Pichegru and actively helped by the Patriot faction (both those in the country and the many who had been refugees in France) the French swept into the United Provinces, occupying Amsterdam in January 1795 and soon afterwards seizing the fleet. William fled to England.

## French Rule (1795–1806)

The Batavian Republic was set up on the French model by the French and the Patriots, the outstanding personality among the latter being Rutger Jan Schimmelpenninck. The stadholderate was abolished, the antiquated constitutional machinery of the United Provinces was swept away, and a National Assembly met in March 1796, its most obvious achievements being the disestablishment of the Church, the introduction of religious freedom, and a move towards direct political representation. But whatever the domestic advances, militarily the republic, now of course at war with England, faced disaster and by 1801 Admiral Rodney had driven the Dutch out of Ceylon, the Cape of Good Hope, the West Indies, and Java while nearer home Admiral Duncan destroyed the fleet at Camperduin (1797). There was though some compensation in the defeat at Castricum in 1799 of an English invasion (which included a Russian element) under the Duke of York.

Hostilities were briefly suspended under the Peace of Amiens of 1802, the republic receiving back all the lost colonial territories except Ceylon; it was also a part of the agreement that the exiled William V formally handed over to the republic all the Orange lands within its borders, in return receiving certain estates in Germany where he died in 1806. But the Peace of Amiens lasted only a little over a year, fighting breaking out again in 1803 and continuing until 1815. Very quickly the republic again lost its colonies and, facing economic disaster, began to show such antipathy towards the war that Napoleon reversed the new constitution so as to permit government through a Council Pensionary, appointing Schimmelpenninck to this post. But a year later, determined to make effective his Continental System by which there was to be no trade between the Continent and Britain, he installed his brother Louis Bonaparte as king.

Matters did not work out as Napoleon had planned, Louis following an independent course and generally putting his new country's interests before those of his brother and France. Specifically, he refused to introduce conscription, he reduced the financial contribution, and, from Napoleon's point of view the worst failing of all, he made no attempt to curb the smuggling trade with Britain, thus disregarding the principal reason for his having received his crown. In 1810, after the British had bombarded Antwerp and briefly occupied Walcheren during the previous year, Napoleon told Louis to abdicate and the Netherlands became part of the French Empire.

The years as a part of the French Napoleonic empire saw the end of the trade with Britain, conscription, press censorship, secret police and heavy financial contributions to the ever growing costs of Napoleon's campaigns. The turning point came with the loosening of French control after the retreat from Moscow in 1812 and the French defeat at Leipzig in 1813. The Orangist faction (led by Leopold van Limburg-Stirum and Karel van Hogendorp), underground since 1795 but now quick to profit from the general discontent, invited (Frederick) William, son of William V, to return from exile. He landed at Scheveningen in November 1813.

Prince William VI of Orange was a stronger, more distinguished, but also more obstinate character than his father had been. Even before having to leave his country in 1795 he had fought against the French in the Austrian Netherlands, and later, in 1799, he had taken part in the Duke of York's unsuccessful invasion. He fought at Jena, and was wounded at Wagram.

## The Kingdom of the Netherlands

On landing, William, who had expected to become Stadholder, was proclaimed Prince Sovereign of the Netherlands, and only eight months later he was crowned King William I. Like his ancestor William the Silent his dream was of a united Netherlands—which well suited the Allies who

sought to establish a deterrent to any future French northward ambitions—
and when at the Congress of Vienna Austria gave up all claim to the
Netherlands the way seemed clear for the amalgamation of the North and
South into a United Kingdom of the Netherlands with William as sovereign.
The 'Hundred Days' intervened briefly, but soon after Waterloo William
was crowned in Brussels.

But the union thus achieved was to be brief, the two Netherlands no
longer had much in common and their new sovereign was unwilling to
adapt to this. Obstinately a northerner, he refused equality of representation in the States General, despite the South having nearly double the
population of the North; he insisted on Dutch (Flemish) as the official
language; he insisted too on the principle of total religious liberty, something which the Catholic Church in the South was not yet ready to accept;
finally he turned down all proposals for administrative autonomy within
the South. By 1828 the South was approaching revolution and William's
continuing obstinacy and his suppression of the press ensured that it broke
out in 1830. Starting in Brussels the revolt spread quickly through the
southern provinces and, despite an invasion and a northern success at
Hasselt, was so successful that the London Conference of January 1831
recognised an independent Kingdom of Belgium with Leopold of Saxe-
Coburg as its sovereign. Refusing to accept this, William again invaded but
had to retreat, although he held on to Maastricht and Antwerp (the latter
only until December 1832). Not until 1839 did William admit defeat, though
one of the agreements then reached gave him what, with minor changes,
makes up the present Dutch province of Limburg.

**King William I (1814–40)** found himself unpopular partly because of the
cost of the years 1831–39 and partly because he was out of sympathy with
the popular demand for constitutional change. On arrival he had inherited
the centralised system of the latter years of the French occupation, a system
which suited his autocratic character (to a large extent he governed by royal
decrees) and which equally suited his conservative chief minister Cornelis
van Maanen. Nevertheless in 1839 William was forced to adjust the number
of seats in the States General because the pretence that there were Belgian
delegates no longer held water, and a further measure (1840) transferred
the control of colonial finance (after 1816 most of the colonies had been
returned), one of the main sources of the national revenue, from the Crown
to the States General. Profoundly disliking what was going on, and also
wishing to marry a Belgian Catholic, William abdicated in 1840 in favour
of his son.

**King William II (1840–49)**, was a distinguished military man, he had been
wounded at Waterloo. During his reign he came under increasing pressure
for liberal constitutional change and after riots in 1845 he set up a constitutional commission under J.R. Thorbecke, the leading liberal. A new
constitution came into force in October 1848, the Year of Revolutions in
Europe. Among the main provisions were freedom of association, direct
elections, public elementary education, ministerial responsibility, and control by the States General of public finance.

**King William III (1849–90)**, son of William II, was despite personal
autocratic inclinations the Netherlands' first genuinely constitutional
sovereign. British readers will recognise some of the main trends and events
of his long reign as thoroughly Victorian. Firstly there was the development
of Cabinet government and the continuing growth of 'liberalism'. There

were many cabinets, J.R. Thorbecke heading three of these (1849–53, 1862–66, 1872) and establishing himself as the outstanding political figure of the century. The Franchise Bill passed by Thorbecke's first cabinet set up constituencies, each represented by two delegates one of whom would have to stand again every second year. The bill also provided that the powers of the First (upper) Chamber of the States General should be limited to approving or disapproving bills, and that the right to initiate legislation should be confined to the Second Chamber. The growth and proliferation of political parties was witnessed by the election of the first Socialist member in 1887. The abolition in 1870 of the Cultivation System (Cultuur-stelsel), the government monopoly of colonial trade was a liberalisation of a peculiarly Dutch innovation in colonial administration. The administration of the colonies in the East Indies through royal agents and local princes had come under fierce criticism, indeed, had been exposed as a public scandal in Multatuli's novel of 1860, *Max Havelaar.*

At home there were many developments in public administration, notably public health and postal laws. Throughout the second half of the 19C the contesting interests of the Calvinist, Catholic and other churches were resolved by the policy known as the 'Verzuiling' (pillaring), a kind of cultural apartheid within the nation which allowed the different religions and the secular state to co-exist as separate but equally supportive elements of the fabric of the society. Meanwhile, as elsewhere, there was the development of a national railway network and a general growth in industry, especially textiles and shipbuilding. The internal economy of the Netherlands, which had barely progressed in terms of technology from the 17C and 18C, whose luxury industries and colonial goods trades were sapped by the advances of Britain, the new Germany and the United States, was brought into the Industrial Age. This was accompanied by the growth of Rotterdam as a major port, linked to the sea in 1872 by the Nieuwe Waterweg. Amsterdam's revival was encouraged by the opening in 1876 of the Noordzee Kanaal.

In the world of art, the achievements of the Hague School in the 1860s and 70s recalled, sometimes even by specific reference, the achievements of the Dutch Golden Age. This was in part a nationalistic school, the references to the glorious past therefore playing a part in defining and asserting 'Dutch national character'; it was also a naturalistic school, the daily-life scenes, town views and landscapes exploring daily experience in the modern world in the manner of the French Impressionists.

William III died in 1890, and since his two unmarried sons had predeceased him he was succeeded by his daughter Wilhelmina (born 1880) whose reign lasted 57 years until her abdication in 1948. The longevity of the Orange-Nassau family is impressive. The main events prior to the First World War were a new franchise act of 1896; the enlightened social legislation passed between 1887 and 1891 by the cabinet of Goeman Borgesius; and, in 1899 at The Hague, the international conference for the suppression of war which set up, also at The Hague, a Permanent Court of Arbitration. Even though the hopes of the last years of the 19C were never fulfilled, and were betrayed by the appalling violence of the succeeding hundred years, such pacific ambitions remain a major feature of Dutch national consciousness.

Although the Netherlands remained neutral throughout the First World War they were gravely affected economically, partly because of the Allied blockade which refused to allow into the Netherlands anything that might pass on to Germany and partly because of the German policy of unrestricted

*Queen Wilhelmina and General Snijders (right) reviewing an army exercise, 1914*

submarine warfare. Nevertheless the cabinet of Cort van den Linden succeeded in 1917 in bringing about the changes in the constitution necessary to solve two long outstanding domestic problems; from now on the Netherlands enjoyed universal suffrage and proportional representation, and from now on there was no state financial discrimination between public and private education.

Among the events of the years between the wars were the first KLM air service between Amsterdam and London (1920); the 9th Olympic Games held at Amsterdam in 1928; and the sealing off in 1932 of the Zuider Zee as the start of major reclamation schemes around what became the IJssel-meer. The spirit of social welfare established by progressively enlightened social policies found expression in the suburbs of the cities of the Randstad in public housing projects which, unlike so many elsewhere, seem to work. Of particular interest to a visitor might be the work of the Amsterdam School of architects, based ultimately upon a modernistic interpretation of tradi-tional styles, and especially well represented in the area around the Olympic Stadium in southern Amsterdam.

In the Second World War Nazi Germany refused to respect Dutch neutral-ity, crossing the border on 10 May 1940 and on 14 May destroying much of Rotterdam by aerial bombing—after playing a curious trick by flying first out to sea as if to attack England, and then doubling back to catch the civilian population unawares. Under the threat of a similar bombardment of Utrecht the Dutch had little choice but to capitulate, Queen Wilhelmina and her family crossed to England where a government in exile was formed. There followed five years during which the full horrors of Nazi occupation were experienced, but during which also a gallant Resistance did much to sabotage the enemy war effort and also helped large numbers of Allied airmen. Overseas, all the East Indies colonies were lost to the Japanese. As elsewhere in occupied Europe the Nazis operated through local fascists under a Reichskommissar, the Netherlands were to be the 'Westland' of the New Europe. Liberation came in 1944–45 (see immediately following article), but a heavy price in lives and material was paid as the result of flooding, bombing and land fighting. The darkest hour was indeed before the dawn, in the winter of 1944–45. By September 1944 the Royal Family were poised to return, Allied troops liberated Vlissingen (Flushing) in November and all looked set. However, the German forces broke through in the Ardennes offensive and the focus of the war was turned away from liberating the Netherlands. The Allies would not drop food or supplies for fear of helping the occupying forces, the occupying forces stripped the Netherlands of all that they had and the Dutch population suffered the terrible famine of the Hunger Winter. Pneumonia, influenza and diptheria raged in a country where medical supplies were non-existent and malnutri-tion was widespread. Gas and electricity were cut off, fuel was virtually unobtainable. Conditions, already bad, were unimaginably appalling. When the Queen and the government returned to The Hague in May 1945 she discovered that George VI had already flown in ahead of her to meet Montgomery at Eindhoven. The slow and sometimes ugly business of normalisation began and the question was asked of every citizen whether they had been 'goed' or 'fout'. Dutch Nazis were tried and executed and known collaborators 'disappeared'. The capitulation of Japan in September of the same year brought to an end the occupation of the colonies.

The principal concerns of the immediate post-war years were, at home, reconstruction and economic revival, and overseas, the demands of the colonies for independence, this being achieved first by Indonesia between 1946 and 1949. In 1948 Queen Wilhelmina abdicated, being succeeded by her daughter Juliana whose reign saw Dutch membership of Benelux (the agreement was actually signed in London in 1944), the European Economic Community, and the North Atlantic Treaty Organisation; the further development of the great port of Rotterdam, notably by the construction of the Europoort; continuing major reclamation work around the IJsselmeer (Flevoland); after tragic flooding in 1953, the start of work on the Delta Plan for Zuid Holland and Zeeland; and overseas, the conclusion of colonial liberation.

As discussed in the Introduction, the character of modern Dutch life is marked by a distinctly different approach to many social problems from those followed in the English-speaking world. This is as much a result of pressures from below as it is of direction from above. During the 1960s the post-war Baby Boom generation of the Netherlands found a voice in the radical politics of the provos, so called from the description of a group of politicised young intellectuals as 'provocateurs' in a government report. Initially the provos focussed their attacks on pollution (particularly cigarette smoking in the early days), property developers and (most famously) in protesting against the marriage of Princess Beatrix to the German Claus von Amsberg. No long-lasting conventional political party has emerged from this, but the generally liberal tenor of Dutch society with regard to sex, drugs and non-violent protest—in the Randstad cities at least—can be traced back to this influence. In part it was pragmatic, the weight of numbers of young people who flooded into Amsterdam during the late 1960s and early 1970s made the policing of the drug laws impracticable— though the subculture did frame its own laws, the sign 'Dope yes, Heroin no' hung on the doors of rock music venues. The authorities therefore, and often with strong denials, allowed the sale and use of cannabis; it can be bought nowadays in many cafés.This trade is centred upon the bohemian quarters of Amsterdam, especially in the red-light district. The sale and use of hard drugs has not been so readily tolerated. It is true that registered addicts are supplied with clean needles (since AIDS) and drugs, but the international criminal traffic in all illegal substances is as ruthlessly pursued in the Netherlands as elsewhere in the world.

On 30 April 1980 Queen Juliana abdicated in favour of her daughter Beatrix. In 1986 the reclaimed polders of Flevoland, together with the Noord-Oost Polder, became the Netherlands twelfth province and, later in the year, the Delta Plan was realised by the completion of the OosterscheldeKering.

# Liberation 1944–45

By *Major I.M. Tomes, M.C., MBE*

**The Opening Situation**. By early September 1944 the Allies had defeated the German forces in northern France and followed this with a rapid advance through Belgium. Antwerp was entered on 4 September and further E a bridgehead established over the Escaut canal just short of the Dutch frontier near Neerpelt. This advance saw the first part of the Netherlands liberated when troops of 1st American Army (Gen. Hodges) entered Maastricht on 14 September, and by the end of the month they had cleared northward from there to just beyond Sittard. However, this fast advance meant that the Allies were now facing increasing logistic difficulties; the Germans still controlled the mouth of the Scheldt, and all supplies were having to be brought up from Normandy along communication routes badly disrupted by the fighting and earlier bombing. In addition, German resistance was stiffening.

This enforced slow-down of the Allied advance was to result in a long campaign to liberate the Netherlands lasting through the autumn of 1944 to the early months of 1945. The campaign may conveniently be divided into four main phases: first the Arnhem operation of September 1944; second, the clearance of the Scheldt and operations N to the Maas in September and October; third, the advance to the Rhine during the winter; and, finally, the liberation of the North and West in April and May 1945.

**The Arnhem Operation**. The Arnhem operation ('Market Garden'; see also Rte 26) was intended to outflank the German West Wall, thus cutting off the escape route of the Germans still in western Netherlands, Allied forces then planning to swing eastwards and drive into the Ruhr. The operation commenced on Sunday 17 September when the 1st British Airborne Division parachuted into the Oosterbeek area some 10km W of Arnhem. Three battalions headed for the town and its bridge, but in the face of strong and rapid German reaction only one was able to reach the N end of the bridge and was unable to take the S end. On the same date 101st and 82nd American Airborne divisions dropped to secure bridges in the Son-Veghel area (SE of 's-Hertogenbosch) and over the Maas near Grave and the Waal at Nijmegen. On the ground British 30th Corps advanced N out of the Neerpelt bridgehead to link up with the three airborne divisions and reached Valkenswaard (S of Eindhoven) that evening.

Events were, however, not to turn out as planned. During the week following the landings the Allies fought to drive a link through to Arnhem in the face of continual German counter-attacks, and at first all went reasonably well. 30th Corps linked up with 101st Division on the 18th, with 82nd Division the next day, and after a brave flanking attack across the Waal the Nijmegen bridges were captured on the 20th. Thereafter, though, continued German pressure which threatened, and at times even split, the narrow corridor, coupled with the difficulties in moving N from Nijmegen, resulted in the planned capture of Arnhem turning into a relief operation. 1st Airborne Division had fought gallantly, but in spite of further air landings was unable to reinforce the now isolated troops at the N end of the Arnhem bridge. The battalion there fought on until the 21st, but the remainder of the Division was forced back into a tightening perimeter at Oosterbeek and withdrawal across the river took place during the night of the 25th.

Although the Arnhem operation failed in its main objective, it nevertheless resulted in a solid wedge or corridor being driven through Eindhoven to N of Nijmegen, a wedge which would be expanded E and W during the following month.

**Clearance of the Scheldt and Advance to the Maas**. Although Antwerp had been captured, it could not be used as a port while the Germans still controlled the Scheldt estuary. The clearance was to be achieved by 1st Canadian Army (Gen. Crerar) in three parts; sealing off and clearing Zuid Beveland, clearing the S bank, and finally the capture of Walcheren, then an island. Before these main operations took place though, part of the S bank had already been freed. On 16 September 1st Polish Division (Maj. Gen. Maczek) had entered the Netherlands S of Hulst, and after an initial repulse successfully crossed the Axel-Hulst canal near Kijkuit on the 18th. On the 19th 4th Canadian Division (Maj. Gen. Foster) crossed the frontier to take Sas van Ghent that day and Philippine on the 20th. The Poles had meanwhile also captured Hulst on the 17th and after the canal crossing they fanned out to take Terneuzen on the 20th. By the 22nd the Netherlands S of the Scheldt and E of the (then bigger) Braakman inlet was clear.

The main operations began in early October with a move to secure the

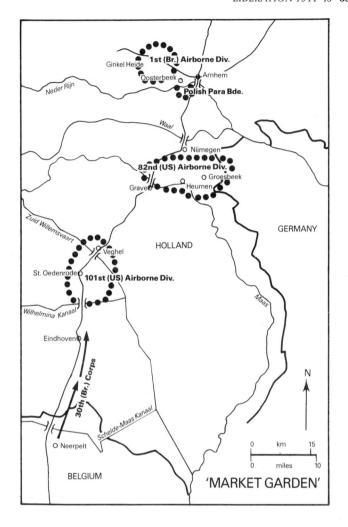

1st (Br.) Airborne Div.
Ginkel Heide
Oosterbeek
Arnhem
Neder Rijn
Polish Para Bde.
Waal
Nijmegen
82nd (US) Airborne Div.
Groesbeek
Grave
Heumen
Zuid Willemsvaart
GERMANY
HOLLAND
Veghel
St. Oedenrode
101st (US) Airborne Div.
Wilhelmina Kanaal
Maas
Eindhoven
30th (Br.) Corps
N
Schelde-Maas Kanaal
O Neerpelt
0        km        15
0        miles      10
BELGIUM
'MARKET GARDEN'

right flank. On 3 October Baarle was taken, and Alphen, just N, on the 5th. Further W 2nd Canadian Division (Maj. Gen. Foulkes) crossed the frontier N of Antwerp at Putte on the 5th and captured Ossendrecht on the 6th. Thereafter German resistance in the area stiffened, and although Hooger-heide was taken on the 7th it was not until the 16th that the Canadians were able to seal off the Zuid Beveland peninsula W of Woensdrecht.

South of the Scheldt operations started on the 7th to clear the Breskens pocket, with 3rd Canadian Division (Maj.Gen. Spry) forcing crossings of the Leopold canal SE of Aardenburg on that date. It was not until the 16th though that nearby Eede was taken and Aardenburg itself only on the 19th. On the 9th elements of the Division launched a water-borne assault just E of Hoofdplaat. Serious fighting followed with the Germans bringing over reinforcements from Walcheren, but Hoofdplaat was taken on the 10th and Biervliet on the 11th. The strain proved too much for the enemy by around the 18th, and Breskens was taken on the 21st, Schoondijke on the 24th, Oostburg on the 26th, and Zuidzande and Cadzand on the 29th. By 2 November (with the capture of Knokke in Belgium) all resistance in the Netherlands S of the Scheldt had ceased.

Zuid Beveland was also cleared during the latter half of the month. 2nd Canadian Division launched an attack on the isthmus on the 24th and were in Rilland and Krabbendijke the next day, as well as taking Kortevan to the north-east. On the 26th 52nd (Lowland) Division (Maj.Gen. Hakewell-Smith) crossed the estuary from Terneuzen to land between Ellewoutsdijk and Hoedekenskerke, and, having fought across the Beveland canal on the 27th and 28th, the Canadians took Goes and linked up with this Division at 's-Gravenpolder on the 29th. By the end of the month Zuid Beveland was clear, and a small operation took Noord Beveland on 1 and 2 November.

The clearance of Walcheren was to prove more difficult, and again involved amphibious assault. Since early October Bomber Command had successfully breached the sea dikes in several places, resulting in much of the island being flooded and the Germans becoming separated and isolated. It was not though until 3 November, and after a flanking move by boats and across the mud, that the very narrow (in 1944) causeway from Zuid Beveland could be forced. On 1 November amphibious landings were made at Vlissingen by No. 4 Commando and No. 155 Infantry Brigade, and at Westkapelle by 4th Special Service Brigade. There were considerable casualties in the Westkapelle landings but Zouteland was captured on the 2nd, while the troops that had now crossed the causeway took Veere on the 6th, and on the same day met up with the forces from Vlissingen at Middelburg. Vlissingen was not completely cleared until the 4th, and the final strongpoint on the island surrendered on the 8th. With the taking of Walcheren both shores of the Scheldt were now in Allied hands and the port of Antwerp could be used.

Whilst the Scheldt was still being cleared the advance continued northwards to the Maas. 12th Corps advanced on 22 October from the line established after 'Market Garden', and, after meeting stiff opposition in Middelrode, 53rd (Welsh) Division (Maj. Gen. Ross) gained a foothold in 's-Hertogenbosch on the 24th and cleared the town on the 27th. To their immediate S 51st (Highland) Division (Maj. Gen. Rennie) took Schijndel and Boxtel while 7th US Division cleared Udenhout a short way to the west. Converging attacks were then launched on Tilburg which was finally cleared on the 28th.

Subsequently the Afwaterings canal was crossed on 4 November and the Maas reached on the 5th. Concurrently with 12th Corp's advance, 1st British Corps (to the west) fought north. Zundert was captured by 104th US Division (Maj. Gen. Allen) on 27 October, Breda by 1st Polish Division on the 29th, and Roosendaal by 49th (West Riding) Division (Maj. Gen. Barker). By 5 November the line along the Mark canal had been breached, and by the 8th the Maas and Hollands Diep were reached although the Germans managed to blow the Moerdijk bridges as they withdrew.

**Winter Operations**. With the Scheldt cleared and the line of the Maas secured W from near Oss (between 's Hertogenbosch and Nijmegen), major

Allied redeployments took place. 1st Canadian Army became responsible for the front from the sea to E of Nijmegen and 2nd British Army (Gen. Dempsey) from there S to Maastricht. The four American divisions (82nd and 101st Airborne, 7th Armoured, 104th Infantry) which had taken part in the Arnhem and subsequent operations returned to their own Armies. Allied efforts were now to be directed to defeating the enemy W of the Rhine, the first step being 2nd Army's clearance of the remaining enemy W of the Maas. This operation started on 14 November when 12th Corps (Gen. Ritchie) crossed the Wessem canal near Weert and by the 16th had cleared nearly up to the Zig canal (now the Uitwaterings canal). Beringe was captured on the 18th, although wet ground and tank obstacles then slowed the advance. Further N 8th Corps (Gen. O'Connor), after an initial hold up on the Deurne canal, fought east. By the 19th the enemy started to withdraw and 2nd Army were up to the Maas by the 25th, with a well organised attack clearing Blerick opposite Venlo on 3 December.

There was little activity in the Netherlands during December and early January, largely due to the Ardennes offensive by the Germans in Belgium and the Allies' need to devote their efforts to defeating this. However, several attacks were beaten off in the Nijmegen area, and after extremely stiff fighting a German outpost at Kapelsche Veer, S of the Maas near Tilburg, was finally crushed on 30 January.

With the Ardennes attack defeated the Allies could advance again, and it was during three subsequent operations that the strip of the Netherlands E of the Maas was liberated. The first of these was Operation 'Blackcock', launched on 16 January to clear a German salient W of the little Roer river. It involved 12th Corps advancing NE from Sittard; Echt and Susteren were cleared on the 17th, St Joost on the 21st, and the Corps was along the line of the Roer by the 26th. The subsequent two operations cleared to the Rhine. Operation 'Veritable' commenced on 8 February with 2nd Canadian Corps and 30th British Corps fighting SE from the Nijmegen area. Gennep was cleared on the 11th, Afferden on the 18th, and Well on 3 March. South of 'Veritable', Operation 'Grenade' was launched on 23 February with 9th US Army moving NE from the Roer river. By 4 March the two operations had linked up E of the Maas.

**The Final Advance**. On 23 March the Allies assaulted across the Rhine near Wesel in Germany, and while 2nd British Army launched itself towards the north of Germany, 1st Canadian Army turned to clear northern Nether-lands. The advance against a disintegrating enemy was rapid. Enschede was cleared by 30th British Corps on 1 April as it drove towards Bremen, while to their W 2nd Canadian Corps reached the Twente canal on 2 April and broke N from it on the 4th. Parties of Special Air Service troops were dropped ahead of the advance on 7 April both to confuse the enemy and to save bridges and airfields for the following Canadians. The drops were in the Zwolle and Groningen areas and were soon linked up by 2nd Canadian Division who reached Ommen on the 11th, Assen on the 12th and, after four days hard fighting, took Groningen on the 16th. On the right 4th Canadian Division reached Almelo on the 4th and then swung E, whilst 1st Polish Division cleared the general line of the border taking Coevorden on the 9th, Emmen on the 10th and reaching the Dollard estuary on the 15th. To the W 3rd Canadian Division reached Zwolle on the 14th and, after a seventy mile dash, Leeuwarden and the coast to the N on the 18th. By the 19th the whole of northern Netherlands was free with the exception of an enclave around Delfzijl, which was not to fall until after a bitter fight that ended on 2 May.

While 2nd Corps moved N, 1st Canadian Corps attacked west. After concentrating near Zutphen, 1st Canadian Division crossed the IJssel on 11 April and in the early hours of the 17th occupied Apeldoorn. To their S 49th Division crossed the IJssel on the 12th and by the 14th had cleared Arnhem. 5th Canadian Division was then passed through, but it was not until the 18th that they were able to reach the IJsselmeer as the Germans had striven to retain a corridor on its S side along which to get as many of their troops as possible into western Netherlands.

This last part of the Netherlands was not to be liberated until the final German surrender. It had been necessary to bypass it in order to concentrate on the main drive into Germany, and additionally it was considered that to defeat the estimated 200,000 enemy in the area would result in unnecessary civilian and military casualties. Conditions though in the area had become increasingly serious with severe food shortages, and it was largely for these reasons that a local truce existed for the last two weeks or so of the war, with rations being sent in by land and air from 29 April onwards. On 5 April the German commander, General Blaskowitz, surrendered all German troops in western Netherlands to General Foulkes, commanding 1st Canadian Corps, at Wageningen. The 1st Corps drove into western Netherlands on the 7th and the liberation was complete.

It is fitting to record here the brave activities of the Dutch Resistance. Although geographically the Netherlands was not well placed greatly to help the Allied strategic aims, the Resistance fought an extremely fierce and brutal war. Over 23,000 members lost their lives.

The Dutch experience of the war is explored in literature and film. English-speakers might know of the Diaries of Anne Frank, and a visit to the Anne Frank Museum in Amsterdam is a moving experience even for those who have not read the book. Two powerful novels tell of the moral confusions of occupation. Willem Frederik Herman's 'The Dark Room of Damocles', 1958, explores the experience as one of actual schizophrenia. Harry Mulisch's novel 'The Assault', 1983, is a compelling thriller which shows how the murder of a pro-Nazi policeman, the moral choices of Resistance fighters and the elimination of a harmless family still reach down to the present day. The film after this book won an Oscar.

# INTRODUCTION TO DUTCH ART AND ARCHITECTURE

'(Flemish painting) will please the devout better than any painting in Italy. It will appeal to women, especially to the very old and the very young, and also to monks and nuns and to certain noblemen who have no sense of true harmony. In Flanders they paint with a view to external exactness, or such things as may cheer you and of which you cannot speak ill, as for example saints and prophets. They paint stuffs and masonry, the green grass of the fields, the shadow of trees, and rivers and bridges...And all this, though it pleases some persons, is done without reason or art, without symmetry or proportion, without skilful choice or boldness and finally, without substance or vigour.' Words attributed to Michelangelo in 'Four dialogues on Painting' (c 1550), by Francisco de Hollanda.

'Cattle and shepherd, by Albert Cuyp, the best I ever saw of him; and the figure is likewise better than usual: but the employment which he has given the shepherd is not very poetical: it must, however, be allowed truth and nature; he is catching fleas or something worse.' Sir Joshua Reynolds, in 'A Journey to Flanders and Holland', 1781.

'Dutch painting was not and could not be anything but the portrait of Holland, its external image, faithful, exact, complete, life-like, without any adornment.' Eugene Fromentin, 'Les Maitres d'autrefois', 1876.

## Before 1600

Zeeland, Utrecht and Holland, being the most economically advanced provinces, and those most intimately connected with the more sophisticated regions further south in Europe, provide the most important centres for the production of art and architecture during the later Middle Ages. Many factors encouraged the development of painting, not least the proximity of the French, German and Flemish schools. The presence of the influential bishopric at Utrecht favoured Utrecht painters with a constant influx of major artists, and much patronage. Institutional developments might favour particular places—in Haarlem, for example, painters had their own guild from early on. Early records show that the St Luke's Guild, although comprised of many trades (dyers, engravers, architects, chairmakers and others), was controlled by the painters. Within the town, only guild members might practise and take pupils; they controlled and directed much patronage, and organised sales of work. This guild survived, in name at least, until the end of the 18C, and played a significant role in the artistic life of the 'Golden Age'

*Geertgen tot Sint Jans* (c 1455/1465–c 1485/95), a native of Leiden, was attracted to Haarlem not, it seems, by the advantages of a local guild, but to paint for the religious community from whom he took his unusual surname, the Knights of the Order of Saint John. Painting just one huge altarpiece for them (6 x 1.5 metres) must have taken up a large part of his short working life, for he died at the tragically early age of twenty-eight. The altarpiece can stand as an emblem of what we know, or do not know, about late medieval Dutch religious painting. Firstly because, following the Reformation and the suppression of the Orders, little has survived intact and that which remains is dispersed. Secondly, that which survives is more tantalising than satisfying. We should like to know more. The picture surface is precise and brilliant. Doll-like figures people the naturalistic landscape settings. The idealised and rather stereotypical Bible characters are supported by strikingly portrait-like and individualised extras; these are the members of the Order of Saint John. Geertgen condensed the spiritually charged naturalism of the Flemish school (Van Eyck and Rogier van der Weyden) into a highly decorative narrative style which is as pictorially sophisticated as the International Gothic miniature illumination it seems to echo. He has been described as 'charming', but the technical mastery of jewel-like paint, the careful organisation of space and telling symbolic resonances, should caution us that he and his Dutch fellows were by no means naive or ingenuous primitives.

*St. Mary Magdalen by Jan van Scorel, Rijksmuseum, Amsterdam*

Geertgen's fairy-tale world, a consummation of early Dutch painting, was supplanted over the next few generations by successive waves of outside influence. Many Dutch painters travelled as far as Italy and experienced the Renaissance at first hand—included among them were *Jan van Scorel* (1495–1562) and *Maerten van Heemskerk* (1498–1574). But all painters did not become Italianisers. In the 1450s *Hugo van der Goes* (fl. 1467–1482) had visited Italy, become known to some of the quintessentially Renaissance artists like Piero della Francesca and remained profoundly un-influenced. In the 1550s *Pieter Bruegel* (fl. 1551–after 1569) had travelled the length of Italy, and although not unmoved by what he saw, he has never been described as Italianate. Many saw the Italian Renaissance through eyes informed by that great German communicator of new ideas, Albrecht Dürer—the effect of the print, German, Italian, and Flemish, on the development of Dutch painting cannot be over-estimated. It is with some caution that anyone treats of external influence on Dutch art—an important influence, however, was to ensure the elevation of the painter from out of the ranks of craftsmen. The celebration of the artist finds its most comprehensive utterance at the end of the period, in the 'Schilderboeck' (1604) of *Karel van Mander* (1548–1606). The shift away from descriptive attributions such as 'the Master of the x Madonna' to conventional names makes the change quite apparent to the average museum goer. An informed eye might detect precise quotations from Roman or Florentine works, but all will note the proliferation of monumentalised human figures, more often than not 'heroically' nude or part-nude, setting forth narratives within a far more lively set of compositional formulae.

One of the more successful painters in the Italian idiom was Jan van Scorel. Widely celebrated in his own time and much travelled, he was fortunate enough to be in Rome during the pontificate of the Dutch Pope, Hadrian VI, and hold the office of leading painter to the papal see (in which office he was successor to Raphael). His style, dignified and monumental, is often more reminiscent of Venetian than any other Italian school of painting. A native of Utrecht, he settled in several Dutch towns successively, and was influential over a whole generation of painters.

Other travellers included *Jan Mostaert* (c 1472/3–1555/6) who became the court painter to Margaret, Regent of the Netherlands from 1506 to 1529, and *Anthonis Mor* (c 1517/21–76/7), portraitist to Philip II of Spain. Both managed a scrupulous attention to detail in their work, Mor, or Antonio Moro as he was known, doing so with a distinctly Titianesque flair. Maerten van Heemskerk returned to his native Haarlem and dominated the town's artistic life throughout a long career after making the southward journey. *Cornelis Cornelisz.* (1562–1638) travelled no further than France in the more turbulent 1560s, but met the northward-moving Mannerist style head-on while there. Karel van Mander, a Fleming, had travelled Italy and worked briefly at the sumptuous court of Vienna in Austria before settling finally in Haarlem. Stay-at-home painters were as open to European trends as their more mobile peers, though some, like *Pieter Aertsen* (1507/8–75) of Amsterdam, developed distinctive styles and kinds of subject matter in relative isolation. Aertsen's complex combinations of still life, everyday scene and Biblical story herald many qualities of 17C painting. *Lucas van Leyden* (?1494–1533), apart from a tour of the Low Countries, stayed in his native town. He kept in touch with, and influenced, other artists through his masterly command of the engraver's burin. Other artists, like *Hendrik Goltzius* (1558–1617), also an engraver and painter, found that their talent brought the world to their doorsteps. Profound though the effect must have been of his journey through Italy to Naples, Goltzius, by the nature of his training and the opportunities offered by the exchange of prints and drawings, was never working in isolation in his adopted home of Haarlem.

The wealth of Gothic architecture in the older parts of the Dutch towns betrays contact with the Europe-wide movements in medieval building, and well into the later periods churches continued to be built in traditional styles. Italian influence, the Renaissance concern with 'correct' proportion and the use of the orders, was not to find pure expression before the 17C.

What we find towards the end of this period is an often weird and wonderful combination of late Gothic decoration and 'copy-book' Renaissance detail, which adds a proud (if eccentric) splendour to many town squares.

We must assume that sculpture, especially polychrome wood sculpture, was a prominent part of the decoration of churches before the Reformation. The *beeldenstorm*, the iconoclastic outrages of the 1560s, saw to the removal of much, and the protestant settlement, a more bureaucratic and thorough purge, dispersed the rest. The Dutch were late and in some ways pragmatic converts to the Reformation, and a surprisingly large proportion remained Catholic—it was in the area of present-day Belgium, in industrial towns like Ghent and Antwerp, where the real battles of the Reformation were fought. No doubt the general Protestant disapproval of 'graven images' contributed to the fact that sculpture did not become an important art-form in the Netherlands until modern times. The wars brought one unlooked for blessing with them, a massive influx of refugees from the southern Netherlands and the neighbouring German states. Although largely made up of the poverty-stricken victims of a generation's fighting who were doomed to be the cheap labour to fuel the Dutch economic miracle, a significant number were well to do, merchants and craftsmen, artists and intellectuals.

## The 'Golden Age'

The 17C has justly been described as a Golden Age of Dutch history. Not, of course, because it was a time when the poor were fed, the sick were healed, and all the evils of the world were kept at bay. For the majority of the people conditions were as hard as could be imagined, though the constant visitations of plague, influenza, typhoid and the rest made sure that the nasty and brutal battle of life was at least mercifully short. But in a world ever more devastated by wars and revolutions, the Netherlands were relatively peaceful, and in the general famine of the age, the Dutch were relatively well fed. National wealth grew phenomenally, and the arts and the study of the more abstract sciences benefitted from the patronage and involvement of a sophisticated ruling class.

One can analyse Dutch 17C painting in various kinds of category—by town, by 'school', and by genre (that is, by subject type). Each method has its advantages. Amsterdam was the home of the group portrait, the earliest militia group portraits date from the 1530s and the Amsterdam Historical Museum has a magnificent display of them. Utrecht, a Catholic stronghold whose painters kept in close contact with Roman fashions, was the home of the 'Utrecht Caravaggisti'—here, as is often the case, a town designation is also a school designation. The painters of Leiden during the middle decades of the century were famed for their painstaking technique, best exampled by *Gerrit Dou* (1613–75), a former pupil of Rembrandt, and have been nicknamed the 'fijnschilders'. The quiet pastel shades of the 'Delft school' are immediately recognisable. Each town—Middelburg in Zeeland, Franeker in Friesland—had its group of painters. Successful painters and teachers drew like-minded painters around them, there are distinct Rembrandt and Hals schools. 'Schools' formed where sympathetic painters tackled similar subjects (presumably in response to buoyant markets), thus the 'Italianate landscapists' who included not only painters who had travelled to Italy, like *Claes Berchem* (1620–83), but stay-at-home painters like *Aelbert Cuyp* (1620–91). 17C painting has usually been analysed by genre. It was a distinct feature of painting during the period that individual masters tended to specialise in certain subject types. This has always been understood to evidence the rational economics of Dutch art, through specialisation painters could practise alongside each other without spoiling each others' chance of a good living. The genres—history (that is, narrative paintings on religious and classical themes), portrait, 'genre' (i.e. everyday life scenes), landscape, animal painting and still life, in decending order of prestige—will shape this account of the painters of the Golden Age.

Although history painting has generally been played down in accounts of Dutch 17C art, excepting, that is, the career of Rembrandt, one should bear in mind that most painters capable of drawing a figure made some attempt at it. *Rembrandt van Rijn* (1606–69), *Jan Vermeer* (1632–75), *Jan Steen* (1625/6–79), and many more worked with varying degrees of success, although a contemporary might never have thought to mention these minor masters, preferring to point out the achievements of *Govert Flinck* (1615–60) at the Amsterdam Town Hall (now the Royal Palace), or *Caesar van Everdingen* (c 1616/17?–78), *Pieter de Grebber* (c 1600–c 1652/3), *Gerrit van Honthorst* (1590–1656) and *Jan Lievens* (1607–74) in the Huis ten Bosch near the Hague.

History painting in the Netherlands was dramatically affected by a series of Italian influences. At the turn of the century the italianate Mannerism of the Haarlem painters, and a similar group in Utrecht around *Abraham Bloemaert* (1564–1651), and *Joachim Wttewael* (c 1566–1638), lent what has often been considered an untypical glamour to Dutch painting. Although out of step with most peoples' expectations of seventeenth century Dutch painting these artists clearly attracted clients, as they continued to produce in their Cinquecento style well into the third decade. It was the influence of two other painters in Rome at the turn of the century, however, who were to have the most lasting impact upon Dutch history painting--- *Michelangelo Merisi Caravaggio* (1571–1609/10), and the German *Adam Elsheimer* (1578–1610). Both painters are strikingly 'realist'. Caravaggio, whose moody *chiaroscuro* turns the eye away from the setting and focuses it instead upon the human action, was immediately influential—Rubens brought a variant of the style home to Antwerp in 1608. The Utrecht painters most usually associated with the style include Gerrit van Honthorst, *Hendrik Terbrugghen* (?1588–1629), and *Dirk van Baburen* (fl. 1611–24). Vermeer and Rembrandt received the influence at second hand, and in their own ways made far more of it. Elsheimer gathered a group of young Dutch painters about him which included *Jan Pynas* (1583/4--1631), *Jacob Pynas* (c 1585–after 1650), *Moses van Uyttenbroeck* (c 1595/1600--1647) and most importantly, for he was to become one of Rembrandt's teachers, *Pieter Lastman* (1583–1633). All worked, at least for a time, in the characteristic Elsheimer manner—small exquisitely modelled figures in elaborate costumes, set solidly and logically into airy landscape settings. This is the influence most evidently at work in the earlier paintings of Rembrandt. That group of Dutch followers in Rome has been given the resonant if absurd title of 'pre-Rembrandtists'. Elsheimer's paintings were engraved by *Count Hendrik Goudt* (1585–1630), reaching a large Dutch audience, and having a lasting influence on landscape painting. During the century successive fashions in painting never lost the monumental illusionism of these two influential styles.

Small scale 'histories', such as the many Bible scenes of Rembrandt, evidence a widespread taste for 'serious' painting to decorate the bourgeois home—they competed on the market with 'genre' pictures. After the Reformation the Church was no longer the major source of patronage for large scale 'public' pictures. The court of the Stadholder at the Hague (only rarely a major patron during this period—the Stadholdership of Frederick Henry (1625–48) was a minor golden age of its own) tended to favour foreigners, or those with foreign success behind them like Honthorst and Lievens. In the towns, though, the real rulers of the Republic——the 'regents' of the charitable institutions, the municipal authorities, the wealthier guilds, militia companies and so forth—found a place for this kind of picture, and paid native masters very well for it.

Portraiture was a serious business. The commonplace defence for this (to theorists) depressingly imitative activity, was that one was recording the likenesses of great men to serve as images of virtue to future generations. The Dutch had supplied successful portraitists to the rest of Europe for many years. Anthonis Mor, *Cornelis Ketel* (1548–1616), *Michiel van Miereveld* (1567–1641), and others had fed the home market and found patrons abroad. Miereveld was reputed to have painted 10,000 portraits in his lifetime. A pupil of his, *Daniel Mytens* (c 1590–before 1648) took the precise Dutch style to England, and until the arrival of Van Dyck was London's leading painter. Throughout the period there were 'precise' masters, capable of making an expensive looking image, elaborating it a little with a *memento mori* or a *vanitas*, and perhaps venturing across the divide into history painting with the suggestion of an appropriate story. A handful of painters stand out—Rembrandt, Frans Hals, and *Bartholomeus van der Helst* (?1613–70).

Although a painter in many genres, it is in his portraiture that Rembrandt seems most truly to excel, for he brought to it a personal style which impresses the spectator as a personal vision, and makes of every sitter a 'Rembrandt'. Many myths surround this extraordinary man, but a few facts locate him. Born in Leiden, the son of a prosperous miller, he trained with a local master *Jacob van Swanenburgh* (c 1571–1638), who specialised in Hell scenes. At an early age he went to Amsterdam to train under Pieter Lastman; he went with his fellow townsman Jan Lievens, with whom he returned to Leiden to set up a studio. His first painting dates from 1627, his first etching from a year later. A distinguished courtier, Constantijn Huygens, saw them both at their Leiden workshop at this time, and prophesied great things for them. At this point Lievens was apparently the more precocious talent. By 1631 Rembrandt had moved to Amsterdam, and a year later produced the astonishing group portrait *The Anatomy lesson of Dr Tulp* (in the Mauritshuis, The Hague), effectively making his mark. From then on his career as a portraitist bloomed, he produced a painting a month for several years, each one notable for its detailed glossy finish. He married a burgomaster's daughter from Leeuwaarden in Friesland, Saskia van Ulenborch, and fell in with her uncle, a successful Amsterdam art dealer. He took on numerous pupils, and made enough money from painting portraits and teaching to cut a figure in the art salerooms and buy a substantial house on the Jodenbreestraat. This golden career lost direction in the early 1640s. After securing an enviable commission to paint a militia company, *The Night Watch* (in the Rijksmuseum, Amsterdam), Rembrandt seems to have gone into a semi-retirement from portrait painting. It has been generally supposed that this innovative picture, which shows guardsmen in action rather than ranked in rows, was not well received, and that Rembrandt retired, rather like Achilles to his tent, to nurse his misunderstood genius. There is no evidence for this, and it is unlikely anyway. Saskia's death in 1642 may have contributed to his retirement, but again, that is mere conjecture. What is certain is that Rembrandt threw himself into a new career, painting histories (something he had always found time for) and etching. That this second career was a financial disaster is evidenced by his bankruptcy in 1656, but that bankruptcy was a long time coming. The foggy *chiaroscuro* of this second period, heralded in smaller works long before the *Night Watch*, lends a captivating imprecision to his painted work, nowhere more than in his self-portraits. A poetic majesty is admired in his late paintings, in works such as *The Jewish Bride*, and *The Syndics of the Cloth Guild* (both in the Rijksmuseum, Amsterdam). *The Syndics* proves that Rembrandt was quite capable of gaining prestigious commissions even after his bankruptcy.

*The Jewish bride. Portrait of a couple from the Old Testament by Rembrandt, after 1665, Rijksmuseum, Amsterdam*

In comparison Frans Hals seems a prosaic painter. This is a pity, for as a technician he is second to none. In capturing the characteristic 'it' of a face he stands alone. His brilliant, 'unfinished' brushwork can convey a sense of rapidly seized likeness; in late works it can seem to hang in front of the canvas and trick the eye. Apart from a few excursions into everyday life scenes (his brother, *Dirk Hals* (1591–1656) was a leading 'genre' painter), Frans Hals was a pure portraitist. So little is known of him (the drunken Frans Hals who beat his wife was another man) that we must suppose that he lived a blameless life. We know that he was respectable enough to serve as an officer in the Haarlem painters' guild. His most impressive suite of paintings, the militia group portraits in Haarlem's Frans Halsmuseum, show that he could work on a scale, and to a degree of complexity, which was the equal of Van Dyck or Rubens. The group portrait is very much a Dutch speciality, an emphatic assertion of community and fellowship. Hals was one of the first to take it out of the boring 'row of heads' tradition. He enlivened it with the sweeping diagonals of Baroque art, giving each of a dozen or more figures their own distinct personality within the group. In individual portraits Hals experimented with a number of formulae, some casual, some formal.

The finest portrait of the Golden Age, judged by its sumptuousness, elegance and sheer mesmeric panache is surely Bartholomeus van der Helst's *Banquet of the Civic Guard* in the Rijksmuseum, Amsterdam. Van der Helst managed to combine brilliance of touch with a much more highly finished technique than any contemporary so far discussed. His portraits never fail to impress in their rendering of rich fabrics and the varieties of human flesh. He was to succeed Rembrandt as Amsterdam's most fashionable portraitist before himself falling upon hard times, and dying in poverty.

In all the genres of painting there were vast variations in quality—not artistic quality, but in that readily measurable quantity, the amount of work that appears to have been done. *Gerrit Dou* (1613–75) could ask his own price, his scrupulously finished panels bear the weight of many weeks of skilful labour. Many painters worked in a freer technique—Hals in portraiture, *Quiringh Brekelenkam* (fl. 1648–67/8) in 'genre' painting, *Jan van Goyen* (1596–1656) in landscape. We know little about the prices of paintings on the open market, but it would seem that a sketchy technique could mean one of two things—either that the painting was a cheap one, and this must usually have been the case with Brekelenkam's works, or that the painter was respected enough as a manipulator of paint to be admired by the *cognoscenti* and be paid for his skill rather than for his labour. This may have sustained the prices of Hals during part of his career.

This variety in quality is nowhere more apparent than in 'genre' works— clearly, one must assume, this type of painting was consumed by a wide variety of economic classes. The 'genre' painters took scenes of everyday life and 'commented'—using anecdote, witty juxtapositions of caricatures, and the popular symbolism of Emblem Books. The pictures are rarely large in scale, neither their subject matter nor intended location (the parlour) merited that.

The origins of Dutch 'genre' painting lie in a variety of 16C and early 17C painting fashions. Pieter Bruegel's grotesque 'pastorals' of peasants (known widely through prints), inspired followers like *Adriaen van de Venne* (1589–1662), *David Vinckboons* (1576–1632), *Adriaen Brouwer* (1605/6–38), and *Adriaen van Ostade* (1610–85). The rural poor, especially before 1650, were scrutinised with a fascinated loathing—examples and symbols of idle, drunken and violent degradation of humanity. The outdoor settings of peasant kermises (fairs) make many of these paintings almost landscapes. Similar compositions giving a kind of 'all human life is there' view of the world (by *Hendrik Avercamp*, 1585–1634, for example) often have a jollier feel. Marketplaces had furnished Pieter Aertsen with a richly symbolic setting for his Biblical parables. 17C painters (Jan Steen, *Jan Miense Molenaer*, ?1609/10–68, and others) used images of material abundance to powerful ironic effect. Common themes included man's ready disintegration into brutish violence, the bad example given by adults to children, and the vicious effect of riotous living on misguided youth. This last subject derived from a long tradition of representing the 'Prodigal son' story in contemporary dress.

The elegance of earlier italianate painting was echoed in the work of the Haarlem painters Dirk Hals, *Esaias van de Velde* (c 1590?–1630), and *Willem Buytewech* (1591/2–1624) in 'merry company' scenes. Well dressed groups of young people display and indulge themselves—the presence of a *vanitas*, or a *memento mori* hinting at the more important things from which their attention has been diverted. Later variations of the high-life 'genre' scene, paintings by people like *Gerard Terborch* (1617–81), *Gabriel Metsu* (1629–67), *Pieter de Hooch* (1629–after 1683) and Jan Vermeer, have so much captured the imagination of our own times that it can be difficult to observe them in context, with their original meaning intact. It is important to realise that some of the most memorable images of Dutch everyday life are much more complicated than they initially appear. Vermeer's *A woman weighing pearls* is a minor thesis on the final judgement of mankind. Vermeer's young women at their music are believed to represent prostitutes, or at least highly compromised innocence. So little is known about Jan Vermeer and his work is so rare (in both senses of the word), that one is constantly at a loss to explain or analyse his achievement. Vermeer was a Catholic, he kept an inn in Delft (his native town), his mother-in-law was a picture dealer who is known to have owned some of the paintings which appear in the backgrounds of his interiors. If the aim of painting was, in John Calvin's words, simply to represent 'that seen by one's own eyes', then he was the most successful painter of all time. It has been suggested, with good supporting evidence, that he used a camera obscura to achieve the precise spatial accuracy in his work. Certainly he worked in a studied and highly finished style, one which is strikingly independent of his *fijnschilder* contemporaries in Leiden—for rather than emphasising the solidity of objects with mere dark and light, he span an illusionistic web of colour in tiny blobs and puddles of paint. If we consider how these works simultaneously undermine the 'realities' they so compellingly reproduce, with their symbolic references to religious and moral 'truths', then we must wonder at their inventor. At a much profounder level than that suggested by Fromentin's remark at the beginning of this essay, we look in upon not only 17C life, but into 17C mentality—the journey into the past becomes doubly exciting.

As with the other genres, landscape had a history in northern painting going back to medieval art—Michelangelo sneered at the Netherlander's preoccupation with this (to him) lamentably imitative tradition. The landscape painters of the first decade (*Gillis van Coninxloo*, 1544–1607, for example, though the landscape settings of the mannerist history painters could make the point as easily) used expressive, if formulaic, images. It was a manifestation of a long-lasting fashion for the fantastic. It was continued during the 17C, with a degree more emphasis upon the plausibility of the scene, in the works of *Hercules Seghers* (1589/90–after 1635), and the highly dramatic landscape paintings of Rembrandt.

It is with 'realistic' landscape painting that 17C painters are most readily associated. Spacious views of the Dutch countryside, with the minor incident of daily life going on quietly all around, are for us the most typical scenes of Golden Age painting. Several important formal and stylistic innovations mark the development of this characteristically Dutch phenomenon: the gradual lowering of the horizon in the picture, so that as much as four-fifths of the scene became sky, giving the strong sensation of 'being there', occurred during the 1630s. The various planes in depth of the land itself, rather than being linked by forceful perspectival 'corridors', were more naturalistically rendered with interconnecting diagonals (one of the key innovators here was *Pieter de Molijn* (1595–1661). The great emphasis upon 'local colour', so much a part of the earlier, more decorative schools, was generally played down in the interests of atmospheric unity. Indeed, during the 1630s and 1640s many painters worked in a near monochrome

*(Jan van Goyen* (1596–1656), and *Salomon van Ruysdael* (c 1600/1603?–70)). Some of these innovations can be found in other European schools—in Rome, the work of Adam Elsheimer, and later *Claude Lorraine* (1600–82) and *Nicolas Poussin* (1594–1665), was invariably naturalistic, though intentionally more 'poetic', and attracted the attention and emulation of many Dutchmen. Painters who used the Italian style with Italian subject matter (views in the Romagna, nostalgic images of Antique ruins populated by Italian peasants) included *Jan Both* (c 1618?–52) and Claes Berchem. This stylistic choice becomes most interesting when, as in the work of Aelbert Cuyp, it depicted of the Dutch countryside. Cuyp's extraordinary cows and milkmaids, illuminated as they are by a golden, Claudian light, create an obvious fiction about the day to day realities of the landscape around his native Dordrecht. These paintings are strongly reminiscent of the far more zoologically informed animal 'portraits' of specialist animal painters like *Paulus Potter* (1625–54), whose huge painting of livestock in the Mauritshuis never fails to hold a crowd of admirers.

The great figure in landscape painting was *Jacob van Ruisdael* (?1628/9–82). Ruisdael was born in Haarlem, many of the 'realistic' painters were associated with Haarlem—Esaias van de Velde, Pieter de Molijn, and *Cornelis Vroom* (c 1590/1–1661). He is believed to have studied under his father, *Isaak van Ruisdael* (1599–1677). It was to Ruisdael, and his follower *Meindert Hobbema* (1638–1709), that English landscapists like Gainsborough and Constable looked for inspiration. His mature compositions can have a moody and disturbing quality which never loses its naturalistic grip. Later in life he moved to Amsterdam where he turned his hand to urban and suburban scenes such as views of the Dam, and the *Jewish Cemetery* (in Dresden). This last, like the *Mill at Wijk bij Duurstede* (in the Rijksmuseum, Amsterdam), conveys a meditated and rather melancholic atmosphere which has encouraged research into the symbolic meanings of his landscapes.

The town and its buildings were popular subjects for painters. Again, the genre had late medieval and 16C antecedents. *Pieter Saenredam* (1597–1665) developed his luminous church interiors out of elaborately finished drawings, and *Emmanuel de Witte* (c 1615/17–91/2) and *Jan van der Heyden* (1637–1712) continued to produce architectural paintings late into the century. The townscapes of *Job Berckheyde* (1630–93) and *Gerrit Berckheyde* (1638–98) are no less than photographic. Many landscapists and townscape painters did not paint the figures in their own compositions—van der Heyden, *Jan Wynants* (fl. 1643–84), and even Jacob van Ruisdael collaborated to varying degrees. Some painters never collaborated, Salomon van Ruysdael, and the nightscene specialist *Aert van der Neer* (1603/4–77), for example.

Still life paintings, another northern speciality, range in subject matter from the simplest fish breakfast (a kind of 'banquet piece') to the richest displays of worldly goods *(pronkstilleven)*. Once again, this is a genre in which there is usually more in the painting than meets the eye. A *memento mori*, such as a skull, or a *vanitas* symbol such as a dying candle, an hour glass, or a bubble, turn the riches of the world into metaphorical ashes before our eyes. It would be foolish, however, not to see these pictures as also celebrating material things. There are various categories of still life, and each of the categories had its specialist masters. The game-piece is associated with *Willem van Aelst* (c 1625/6?–c 1683) and *Jan Baptist Weenix* (?1642--1719), though Rembrandt was one of many who tried his hand at the same subject. Close to these game-pieces were the pictures of wild and domesticated fowl, the outstanding master in these was *Melchior d'Hondecoeter* (1636–95).

The most admired sub-genres of still life were the flower- pieces and the banquet pieces. The flower-piece, an eloquent memorial to the Dutch passion for horticulture, was one of the oldest 'pure' still life subjects. Van Mander tells us that many of his contemporaries in the last quarter of the 16C painted flower-pieces. This is no surprise when we learn that such pictures were highly prized—Ambrosius Bosschaert the Elder (1573–1621), as well as founding a dynasty of painters in his adopted home of Middelburg, could command 1000 guilders for a single painting. Bosschaert and his followers arranged their subjects in elegant vases stood in niches. A kind of 'hyper-realism', the result of minute and uniform detail, is the most characteristic quality of these paintings. He was followed by his three sons, and his brother-in-law *Balthasar van der Ast* (1593/4–1657), all of whom reproduced his style, with little real variation, into the second half of the century. This school blends easily into the work of such 18C century painters as *Rachel Ruysch* (1664–1750), gaining only in elaboration as it goes.

The banquet-piece, like many still life subjects, was popular throughout Europe. *Floris van Dyck* (1575–1651), *Floris van Schoten* (fl. 1610–55) and *Nicolaes Gillis* (fl. 1601–32), three Haarlem painters, produced carefully laid-out tables, the objects rarely overlapping, all viewed from a slight elevation. This was painting to 'show off', and enjoyed as such. It was the next generation which, while still seeking to thrill the eye, took still life painting into a different dimension. *Pieter Claesz.* (1597/8–1661), the father of Claes Berchem, and *Willem Claesz. Heda* (1594–1680), both started in Haarlem and both show the early influence of their teachers. However, during the 1630s both painters turned to depicting the breakfast-piece, a simple meal of herring, beer and bread, set on the corner of a table. The viewpoint was lowered and local colour reduced, much as in contemporary landscape painting. Light and atmosphere, combined with the more casual arrangement, gives these pictures a powerful immediacy, as if the diner had just stepped out on an errand. Heda later turned to specialising in rather richer subjects, lobsters and wine glasses and golden vessels, but he never abandoned the casual arrangement with its consequent sense of immediacy.

*Jan de Heem* (1606–83/4), who learned much during his brief spell in Leiden in the mid 1620s, had started his career under Balthasar van der Ast. After his move to Antwerp in 1636 he became one of the most celebrated painters in Europe. His work displays a scale, and a magnificence, quite beyond most Dutch painters. *Willem Kalf* (1619–93) painted some of the most stunning still lifes. He developed a manner of combining *chiaroscuro* and Vermeer-like colour which enabled him to make pictures of astonishing illusionistic power.

The architecture of the Golden Age is dealt with monument by monument elsewhere, this small account is merely to sketch in the general points. The florid 'gable' style of 16C mannerist architecture had its last, rich flowering during the early 17C. *Lieven de Key* (c 1560–1627) the municipal architect of Haarlem, sums up this style in his ornate façades for the Haarlem Meat Hall (1602–03) and Leiden Town Hall (1597). Both have the attention to detail one might expect from an architect originally trained as a stonemason. *Hendrik de Keyser* (1565–1621), a sculptor of importance, designed the Amsterdam Zuiderkerk (1606–14) in a basically Gothic manner, applying Renaissance details, such as columns, as decoration. His later Westerkerk (begun 1620), a rectangular basilica, was much more 'classical' in inspiration and marks a key point in Dutch building. The 1620s saw a great change. French example, and the ready availablity of illustrated Italian books such as Andrea Palladio's 'Quattro Libri', brought in the international style of the day, though the lack of a large court and the traditional tastes of the urban regents made its acceptance piecemeal. The most striking of the 'modern' buildings was the Mauritshuis (designed c 1633) in The Hague, designed by *Jacob van Campen* (1595–1657). Van Campen went on to design the Amsterdam Town Hall (begun 1648), a building which is still capable of impressing the visitor's eye, lulled by mile upon mile of gabled conformity. Much of the rest of the century's building was dominated by the work of Van Campen's pupils and followers—*Pieter Post* (1608–69), the architect of the Huis ten Bosch, in The Hague, *Arent van 's Gravesande* (?–1662) who designed the Leiden Cloth Hall (now the Lakenhal Museum), and *Philips Vingboons* (1614–78) architect of the Trippenhuis in Amsterdam. The last decades of the century were dominated by a massive rather featureless classical style.

## The Eighteenth Century

Many accounts of Dutch art begin the 18C as early as 1672. Frans Hals and Rembrandt were dead, Vermeer soon to follow. The important event, however, was the Dutch defeat and French invasion of 1672 (see National History). Just as the defeated and reconquered nations of Europe steeped themselves in American style and culture after 1945, the Dutch became fascinated with France. This fascination was to be more or less loyally maintained until the very different French invasion of 1795. Some flirtation with German and English culture occurred, but the important point was that the Dutch now looked abroad for their inspiration. The period has been called the *pruikentijd*, the age of wigs, and condemnation of its artificiality and decadence has been almost universal.

The 100 or so years between 1672 and 1795 were marked by a very different economic environment from the Klondike days of the 17C. Polarisation occurred—the rich got richer, and the poor got poorer. Amsterdam was still the banker to Europe, the Dutch merchant marine was still enormous, the colonies continued to return their annual tribute of valuable raw materials. The profits from all this were channelled into the coffers of the urban patriciate who abandoned their pretentions to inconspicuous citizenship and followed the fashions of Europe's aristocracy. This involved buying foreign art and importing foreign artists. The patrons of Dutch art turned away from styles of a defeated culture, and aped their victors and the strongest market for native art was the antiquarian market for 17C old masters. The art theorists of the 18C remarked upon this collapse and argument raged over whether the decline was one of the artists making, or the result of the perfidy of dealers and the stupidity of patrons. The lower middle-classes were progressively forced out of the art/craft painting business by the rise of academies for gentlemen, and the guilds declined. As rents rose and investment fell the Dutch peasantry, aspiring to leather shoes during the Golden Age, adopted the cheaper wooden clog.

An example of the new sensibility can be found in the person of *Gerard de Lairesse* (1641–1711), called the 'Dutch Raphael' by his contemporaries. A Walloon, de Lairesse arrived in Amsterdam in 1665. There he had Rembrandt paint his portrait, at a later date he wrote of of this event 'I do not want to deny that I once had a special preference for his manner; but at that time I had hardly begun to understand the rules of art ..(Rembrandt's art).. was based upon nothing but light and fantastic conceits, without models, and which had no firm foundation upon which to stand'. Until he went blind in 1690 de Lairesse was the most fashionable painter in the country, laying down the law and example of French academic art. He specialised in cloud-borne allegory, and established the decorative tradition followed by *Jacob de Wit* (1695–1754), who combined the Flemish baroque of Rubens and Van Dyck into this repertoire. The undeniable grandeur of such painters fell out of favour during the 1750s, and a return to a more 'domestic' painting ensued.

*Regents of the Aalmoezeniersweeshuis by Cornelis Troost, 1729, Rijksmuseum, Amsterdam*

The genres of 17C painting did not die out during the 18C. There were however certain general changes, all of which have been treated as changes for the worse by critics. As a whole, the work became glossier. Not simply glossier in finish but in other ways too. Sentiment rules in the depiction of the poor by *Jacob Ochterveld* (1634–'82), as it does in the increasingly popular genre of patrician interiors, which followed the example of *Gerard Terborch* (1617–81) and *Frans van Mieris* (1635–81). *Godfried Schalcken* (1643–1706) took Dou's precision to new heights with his tiny, *chiaroscuro* collector's pieces. Names such as *Adriaen van der Werff* (1659–1722), now only known to enthusiasts, were of European renown. Such painters were believed to have 'improved' Dutch painting for the new age in ways de Lairesse would have approved of. Van der Werff was one of several millionaire painters, he worked for the Elector Palatine. Many Dutch painters turned to the German courts for patronage. *Cornelis*

*Troost* (1697–1750) painted group portraits in life size, and many 'conversation' (rather than 'genre') works in a manner which has earned him the title of 'the Dutch Hogarth'. Troost's work in pastels places him firmly in the European 18C mainstream—as does his delight in theatrically presented picture series (for example the *NELRI* pictures in the Mauritshuis). Like Hogarth, too, he was capable of portraiture in the grand manner.

There was a taste for foreign portraitists. *Jean Etienne Liotard* (1702–89) and *Jean Baptiste Perronneau* (1715–83) both catered for Dutch patrons. *Charles Howard Hodges* (1764–1837) settled in Amsterdam and brought with him the London fashions. The court at the Hague preferred the German *Johann Friedrich August Tischbein* (1750–1812).

Some essential features of the 17C tradition never died out. The portrait and 'genre' works of painters such as *Wijbrand Hendriks* (1744–1831) and *Jan Ekels* (1759–93) evidence a continuing and growing interest in the Dutch tradition towards the end of the century. In still life the work of the Middelburg master *Adriaen Coorte* (fl. 1685–1723) is outstanding. Tiny in scale, it is the antithesis of the flamboyant contemporary fashion exhibited by Rachel Ruysch and *Jan van Huysum* (1682–1749).

In architecture, the classicism of the later 17C was superseded by a variant of French Baroque, brought north by the Huguenot refugee *Daniel Marot*. He was employed by William III as an interior architect both in the Netherlands and in England. The interior and the park at Het Loo were designed by him. In the Hague the Royal Library (formerly the Hotel Huguetan) shows him at his ornamental best. Marot's style, out of fashion by 1715 in France, continued to be influential into the middle of the century. More up to date French influence can be observed in the buildings of *Pieter de Swart* (?1709–73). A number of foreign architects contributed individual buildings, but the late 17C classicism was never properly displaced in public and large-scale private buildings.

## The Nineteenth and Twentieth Centuries

After the Battle of Waterloo and the creation of the Kingdom of the Netherlands, which for a while included present-day Belgium, the development of Dutch art and architecture conformed very much to that of the arts in the rest of Europe. A keen interest in the Dutch Golden Age was fostered by patriotic sentiment typical of European Romanticism. In the work of the three most notable painters, *J.B. Jongkind* (1819–91), *Jozef Israels* (1824–1911), and *Vincent van Gogh* (1853–90), there is a 'Dutch-ness' which enhances their European reputation. Israels's work, very well represented at the Rijksmuseum, brings a grandeur, Rembrandt-like in many ways, to representations of everyday life. His images of the Jewish community, and fishermen, are infused with a thoughtfulness and compassion which repays close study. Jongkind's seascapes, dissolving the view into light and vapour as Turner had done in England, made a major contribution to the development of Impressionism. His prints demonstrate just how luminous mere ink and paper can be. Van Gogh can hardly be understood without an awareness of his Dutch origins. He has been remembered as the painter of brightly coloured canvasses, but for the greater part of his life he worked in a number of employments, as a picture dealer, a teacher, and a missionary, turning to full-time painting only in his thirties. His early work is dominated by his vigorous drawings of Dutch peasants, and caricature-like monochrome paintings such as *The potato eaters* (in the Van Gogh Museum, Amsterdam). When he arrived in Paris Impressionism, though ten years old, was scarcely known outside a small circle, and came as a complete surprise to him. The last years of his life are now the stuff of legend. However, one can detect associations with his Dutch roots—the generous brushstrokes, a preoccupation with the problems of representation, a concentration upon rural landscape and (of course) those stunning sunflower still lifes.

The 'Victorian' Dutch painters will not surprise anyone familiar with the work of their English and American contemporaries. The painters of the 'Hague School' all explored landscape with a new earnestness. *J.H. Weissenbruch* (1824–1903), and the three Maris brothers *Jacob Maris* (1837), *Matthijs Maris* (1839–1917) and *Willem Maris* (1844–1910) show the diversity from common roots which the school achieved. Weissenbruch worked very much within the idioms of the Golden Age masters, though with a Romantic tendency to rusticity. Jacob Maris echoes the Barbizon painters. Matthijs Maris, who worked for much of his career in London, was more preoccupied with the mystic than the natural vision. Willem Maris studied the life of the countryside and introduced a generation of Dutch painters to open-air study. *Anton Mauve* (1838–88) made of landscape painting something akin to photography, so capable was he of exact representation and capturing the effects of light. Together the group indicate the contexts for Van Gogh's passionate commitment to telling the 'truth' about nature—another kind of truth from that of contemporary scientists. This quiet, traditional painting was continued into the 20C by painters such as *G.H. Breitner* (1857–1923). There remain many riches to be enjoyed by the visitor to provincial museums throughout the Netherlands.

Sculpture began to come to the fore in the late 19C with the work of such sculptors *L. Zijl* (1866–1947) and *J. Mendes da Costa* (1883–1939), followed by *J. Bronner* (born 1888), *J. Raedecker* (1885–1956) and *H. Krop* (born 1884). In the Graphic arts notable artists of this century include *Jessurin de Mesquita* (1868–1944) and the members of the De Ploeg group (see below), *H. Werkman* strikingly developing this group's experiments. Other names in this field are *Paul Citroen* (born 1896) and *Maurits Escher* (1898–1972).

The more startling trends of Parisian painting were easily absorbed by the conservative institutions of Dutch art, but the steady war of attrition waged by the modernists began to make real advances during the first decade of the 20C. Guerrilla incursions by *Jan Sluyters* (1881–1957) brought Fauvism in 1908, soon to be followed by Cubism and Expressionism. The Great War inhibited development, but was immediately followed by the rise of several important 'schools'. Expressionism informed the 'Bergen School' and the 'Ploeg School'—the latter, based in Groningen, was close to German Expressionism. However, it was the De Stijl group which put Dutch painting on the map. Taking their name from Doesburg's magazine (founded in 1917), the painters and architects associated with De Stijl—*Piet Mondriaan* (1872–1944), *Theo van Doesburg* (1883–1935), *J.P. Oud* (1890–1963) (who only built in Rotterdam) and *G. Rietveld* (1888–1964), with others—sought to exclude decoration and subjectivity from art and architecture. They were the main influence upon Gropius and the Bauhaus. Rigorous discipline in design saw to the eradication of all but horizontal and vertical lines, only primary colour was to be used. The universal truth which this style against style sought to achieve was explained in manifestos of remarkable opacity. The influence of De Stijl upon 20C art has been profound, notably in the applied arts. Modern architecture is generally informed from this group—not only in the Netherlands, but throughout the world. There can be few areas in the world better than the

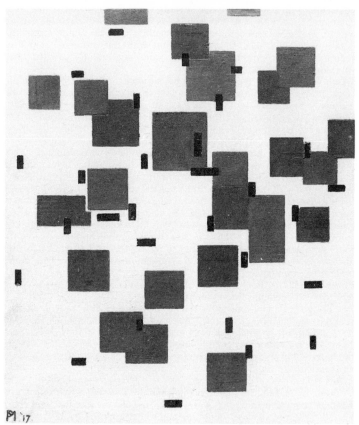

*Composition in blue by Piet Mondriaan, 1917, Rijksmuseum Kröller-Müller, near Arnhem*

the Randstad for exploring all the varieties of European modernism. Visitors especially to Amsterdam will also be impressed by a parallel architectural style in unassuming brick rooted in the imaginative innovations of *H.P. Berlage* (1856–1934). Berlage's Exchange on the Damrak, Amsterdam provided a break with Victorian historicism (e.g. *P.J.H. Cuyper's* (1827–1921) Central Station nearby). The many delightful buildings of the Amsterdam School combine modernist functionalism with an expressionist flair and fine attention to detail. Housing estates and suburbs throughout the Netherlands built between the wars provide ubiquitous examples of this handsome building tradition.

One disciple of De Stijl, *Willem de Kooning*, left for the United States in 1926, and has since made an international reputation in action painting. Echoes of contemporary currents in figurative painting are apparent in the work of *Carel Willink* (1900– ) and *Pyke Koch* (1901– ). Their works have the treacherous appeal of Neue Sachlichkeit and Surrealism combined. Using a hyper-realistic technique, they explored decadent and fetishistic images with an untiring eye.

The optimism which followed the liberation of the Netherlands after the Second World War manifested itself in a remarkably generous government policy to the arts. This has ensured a vital artistic life (for example, specially commissioned sculptures are now a feature of many towns) but has not created international 'stars'. The COBRA group, an international axis between Copenhagen, Brussels and Amsterdam included *Karel Appel* (born 1921) who is well represented in collections outside the Netherlands. A visitor conversant with the latest styles of New York and Berlin will discover that the commercial galleries of the Netherlands are a home from home. The more adventurous artistic tourist will discover that there is a large semi-official and underground art scene in the major cities where experimental rock music, jazz and the visual arts thrive in a culture of constant change. Local information sheets, such as the 'Uitkrant' in Amsterdam, as well as posters and word of mouth are the ways to connect with all of this.

# PRACTICAL INFORMATION

This section sets out the basic information you will need to know to get by in the Netherlands. The first part covers accommodation and travel, the second is a quick reference list of topics organised alphabetically.

# Tourist Organisations

The **Netherlands Board of Tourism** (National Bureau voor Toerisme. NBT), a central organisation charged with the encouragement of tourism, will be mainly of interest to intending visitors planning their tour and requiring information before leaving their own countries. To meet this need the Board publishes several maps and brochures, among the subjects of the latter being watersports, cycling, facilities for young people, museums, castles and architecture, annual events, facilities for the handicapped, fishing, bird sanctuaries and golf and tennis (prices and postal charges from the addresses below).

NBT offices also market the *Holland Leisure Card*, a wallet which includes a map, a calendar listing major events, a booklet setting out useful hints, a 'Good Time Guide' and a Holland Leisure Credit Card. Valid for the calendar year of purchase, the card entitles the holder to a wide range of discounts.

**NBT Addresses.** *The Netherlands*: Vlietweg 15, 2266 KA Leidschendam. *United Kingdom*: 25–28 Buckingham Gate, London SW1E 6LD. Tel: 071-630 0451. *USA (East)*: 355 Lexington Avenue (21st Floor), New York NY 10017. Tel: 212-370-7367. *USA (Midwest)*: 225 N Michigan Avenue, Suite 326, Chicago IL 60601. Tel: 312-819-0300. *USA (West)*: Suite 305, 90 New Montgomery Street, San Francisco, CA 94105. Tel: 415-543-6772. *Canada*: 25 Adelaide Street East, Suite 710, Toronto. Ont. M5C 1Y2. Tel: 416-363-1577. *Australia*: Suite 302, 5 Elizabeth Street, Sydney, NSW 2000. Tel: 02-276-921.

**VVV (Vereniging voor Vreemdelingenverkeer)** offices for tourist information abound throughout the Netherlands at province, district and town levels. Clearly signed (blue VVV triangle), these offices, invariably English-speaking, provide full local information and will also help with local accommodation, bookings for entertainment and such-like. In the larger centres the VVV offices bear the additional sign 'i-Nederland', such offices providing information and reservation and other facilities for any part of the country. VVV offices are generally open Monday–Friday 09.00 to 17.00, Saturday 10.00 to 12.00, but in summer many are open for longer hours as well as on Sunday afternoons.

Information regarding any particular town can be requested simply by addressing a letter to VVV, followed by the name of the town concerned. For province information the addresses are VVV *Noord Holland*, Florapark 6, 2012 HK Haarlem. *Zuid Holland*, Markt 85, 2611GS Delft. *Zeeland*, Postbus 123 4330 AC Middelburg. *Utrecht*, Maliesingel 38, 3581 BK Utrecht. *Noord Brabant* Postbus 90, 5260 AB Vught. *Limburg*. Postbus 811, 6300 AV Valkenburg. *Gelderland* Postbus 988, 6900 AZ Arnhem. *Overijssel*, Postbus 500, 7600 CA Almelo. *Drenthe* Postbus 95, 9400 AB Assen. *Groningen*, Naberpassage 3, 9712 JV Groningen. *Friesland*, Stationsplein

1, 8911 AC Leeuwarden. *Flevoland*, Postbus 548, 8200 AM Lelystad.

The **National Reservations Centre** (NRC) is a joint booking organisation of the Netherlands' hotel trade. Reservations may be requested in writing, by telephone or by telex. It is important that requests should reach NRC in good time and that requirements be clearly and fully stated (e.g. place; arrival and departure dates; price range; number of people and number of rooms; whether private bath or shower required). National Reservations Centre, Postbus 404, 2260 FK Leidschendam. Tel: (070) 3202500. Telex: 33755. Fax: 01031 70 202611. Monday–Saturday, 08.00 to 20.00.

For **ANWB**, the national motoring club, see below.

# Getting to the Netherlands

**By Sea.** The following principal services, all carrying cars, cross between England and the Netherlands. Addresses and telephone numbers of operators are given, but annual brochures with up-to-date information on timetables and fares are obtainable through motoring clubs and travel agents. Budget travel by rail or coach remains popular and travellers from the United Kingdom should consult their local railway and coach stations, or travel agents, for information on the best deals. It is worth considering the extra expense which a journey of this kind will necessitate; you may spend up to 24 hours on such a journey and the meals and incidental costs of travel should be set against the savings you make on the price of a 45 minute flight.

Harwich to Hoek van Holland. Crossing 6¾ hours (day) to 8¾ hours (night). Sealink Stena Lines, Charter House, Park Street, Ashford TN24 8EX. Tel: 0233-47047 or 0255-240980. Also at London's Victoria Station.

Sheerness to Vlissingen. Crossing 7 hours (day) to 8½ hours (night). Olau Line Terminal, Sheerness, Kent ME12 1SN. Tel: 0795-660776.

Hull to Rotterdam. Crossing 13 hours (night). North Sea Ferries, King George Dock, Hedon Road, Hull HU9 5QA. Tel: 0482-795141.

Shorter crossings may be made from Dover to the Belgian ports of Ostend (4 hours) or Zeebrugge (4½ hours). This approach can be recommended to visitors aiming for Zeeland Flanders (Rte 14) or wishing to enter the Netherlands from the SW across the delta region (Rte 13). P and O European Ferries, Channel House, Dover CT17 9TJ. Tel: 0304-203388.

**By Air.** There is a choice of air services, the principal airlines being British Airways, KLM, NLM and British Midland, all operating between London (Heathrow and Gatwick) and Amsterdam (Schiphol). Other services link Scotland, Wales, Ireland and English provincial centres with Amsterdam, Rotterdam, Eindhoven and Maastricht.

*Schiphol* is the Netherlands' principal international airport and serves all the Randstad towns. With its own railway station and flanking the A4 motorway (which, in fact, tunnels below one of the runways), the airport is some 10km from central Amsterdam, 40km from The Hague and 50km from Rotterdam, all rapidly reached by rail or road, as indeed are all the Randstad cities. Schiphol is also the home of the Netherlands' national airline, KLM. The initials stand for Koninklijke Luchtvaart Maatschappij, literally Royal Aviation Company but normally known as Royal Dutch Airlines. Founded in October 1919, KLM on 17 May 1920 inaugurated between Amsterdam and London the world's first scheduled air service.

# Getting around the Netherlands

**By Car.** The Netherlands has an excellent network of motorways and other roads, the traffic laws and signs generally following western European continental practice, though there is perhaps more emphasis on road-surface signs (arrows, route numbers and pictograms of bicycles) than in many other countries. Motorways linking the Netherlands with neighbouring countries are signed green with the letter "E' (though this system is under review); internal motorways (Autosnelweg) are indicated by an 'A' symbol in red; other main roads bear yellow signs and the letter 'N'.

It is advisable to be member of a home motoring organisation (e.g. British Automobile Association or Royal Automobile Club; or American Automobile Association), such membership conferring use of the facilities of the Dutch motoring club (ANWB), while home clubs' specialised publications contain detailed information on local Dutch facilities, regulations and much else. The Dutch motoring club is the *Koninklijke Nederlandse Toeristenbond (ANWB)*, founded in 1883 as a bicycling association, ANWB standing for Algemene Nederlandse Wielrijdersbond or General Netherlands Bicyclists' Association. The club's headquarters are at 220 Wassenaarseweg, The Hague, and there are many local offices throughout the country. Offices are normally open Monday–Friday, 08.45 to 16.45 and Saturday, 08.45 to 12.00. Traffic information (24-hour service) can be obtained by telephoning (070) 3313131. Most of ANWB's facilities are available to visiting motorists on proof of membership of an affiliated club. In addition to the wide range of activities normally covered by motoring clubs, ANWB has organised signed Tourist Routes through particularly picturesque or interesting districts. These routes are marked by hexagonal signs bearing the appropriate name, and detailed maps and descriptions (some only in Dutch) can be obtained from ANWB or VVV offices.

As noted above, details regarding motoring facilities and regulations on the Continent generally, as also in individual countries, are set out in clubs' annual specialised publications. Selected aspects for the Netherlands are mentioned in alphabetical order below; while the information is believed to have been correct at the time of going to press, it should be borne in mind that regulations can change, sometimes at short notice.

*Accidents and Breakdowns.* In the event of an accident of any significance, and invariably if there is any question of personal injury, the police must be called before any vehicle involved is moved. Warning triangles, which must be carried in all cars, should also be placed as quickly as possible. For Police and Ambulance in Amsterdam or The Hague, Tel: 222222; in Rotterdam, Tel: 141414. Elsewhere, emergency numbers will be found in the front of local telephone directories. Alternatively contact the State Police Emergency Centre, Tel: 03438 14321.

In the event of a breakdown the motorist should first try to manoeuvre their car to the edge of or off the road and then place the warning triangle to the rear of the vehicle to warn following traffic. ANWB "Wegenwacht' road patrols operate along main roads throughout most of the country between 07.00 to midnight and, if one does not soon turn up, may be contacted by telephoning (070) 3147714. Before receiving free breakdown service, foreign motorists will usually be asked to provide evidence of affiliated club membership or of the breakdown cover provided by, for example, the AA's Five Star or the RAC's Travellers Bond schemes.

*Bicycles,* from a motorists point of view, can be a hazard. Bicycle tracks, indicated by signs and painted lines, frequently run along one or both sides of the road and even, at intersections, into the middle of the road. Be aware also when you are turning that cyclists continuing ahead normally have priority. Parking is never allowed on bicycle tracks. If you are cycling in the Netherlands see the section below.

*Documents.* For most foreign motorists the only documents required are passport, driving licence and vehicle registration. Additionally, all vehicles must display an approved national disc (e.g. GB) identifying the country of registration.

*Ferries.* There are a number of ferries throughout the Netherlands, ranging from sizeable ships down to small craft crossing rivers and canals. Most, though not all, carry cars. The more important car ferries are listed below (from S to N). Motorists should enquire locally regarding times of first and last sailings.

1. Breskens-Vlissingen (Rtes 14 and 13A). Crossing 20 minutes. Half-hourly. This can be a particularly interesting crossing, often offering good views of Scheldt shipping.

2. Kruiningen-Perkpolder (Rtes 13A and 14). Crossing 20 minutes. Half-hourly, but hourly on Saturday and Sunday.

3. Rozenburg-Maassluis (Rtes 10E and 11). Crossing 15 minutes. Frequent.

4. Hembrug-Zaanstad (Rte 2). Crossing 5 minutes. Frequent.

5. Den Helder-Texel. See Rte 2.

6. Harlingen-Vlieland and Terschelling. See Rte 39A.

7. Holwerd-Ameland. See Rte 38.

*Insurance.* Most British motor policies should provide sufficient Third Party cover to meet the Dutch minimum legal requirement, but this does not necessarily mean that full home cover is automatically extended abroad. Motorists should consult their insurance broker or company, and will in any case be wise to arrange for a Green Card extending the home policy to use abroad for a contracted period. If a caravan or other trailer is towed, the Green Card must be endorsed to this effect. Motorists are also strongly advised to travel under the protection of one of the special breakdown, get-you-home or other insurance packages offered by motoring clubs and some other organisations (e.g. AA, Five Star; RAC, Travellers Bond).

*Lights.* Dipped (low beam) headlights must be used between dusk and dawn and whenever visibility is poor. It is forbidden to drive showing only parking or side lights. Headlights must be adjusted (e.g. by fitting converters or deflectors) so that the dipped beam does not light the incorrect side of the road and thus possibly dazzle oncoming drivers.

*Seat belts* must be worn by the driver and front passenger. Children under the age of 12 may only occupy the front seat if over the age of four and wearing a hip-type safety belt; if under four, then in an approved safety seat.

*Speed limits.* In built-up areas, 50kph (31mph), such areas normally extending between place name signs; walking pace in residential areas indicated by a white house on a blue background. Motorways, maximum 100kph (62mph). Other roads, 80kph (49mph). The limit with a trailer or caravan is 80kph (49mph). The above are the general rules, but frequently there are special speeds signed for particular places or circumstances.

*Tolls.* There are no motorway tolls. However, there are some bridge and tunnel tolls: Zeelandbrug (Rte 13A); Kiltunnel from Dordrecht (Rte 12B) to the Hoekse Waard (Rte 13A); Prins Willem Alexanderbrug across the Waal near Tiel (Rte 25).

*Traffic Sign words.* Following are some of the wordings likely to be seen on traffic signs.

Alle Richtingen = All Directions (i.e. to all destinations)
Bromfietsen = Mopeds
Bushalte = Bus Stop
Doorgaand Verkeer = Through Traffic
Fietsen = Bicycles
Fietsers Oversteken = Cycle Crossing
Fietspad = Cycle Track
Filevorming = Get into Lane
Geen = No
Gestremd = Forbidden, Obstructed
Gevaar = Danger
Inhaalverbod = No overtaking
Langzaam Rijden = Drive slowly
Pas Op! = Attention!
Rijwielpad = Cycle Track
Tegenliggers = Two-way Traffic
Tussen = Between (usually with parking times)
Uit = Exit
Voetpad = Footpath
Weg Omlegging = Diversion
Werk in Uitvoering = Road Works
Woonerven = Ramps, 'Sleeping policeman'

*Warning Triangles* must be carried by all cars and, in the event of a breakdown or accident, be placed behind a stopped vehicle at such a distance and in such a position as to give adequate warning to traffic approaching from the rear.

**By Bicycle.** In the Netherlands—a flat country with a network of special cycle tracks which to a large extent traverse country inaccessible to motorists—bicycling (including moped) is not only a national means of transport and a national recreation but also increasingly popular with visitors as a relaxed means of touring (cycle track maps available from ANWB, Netherlands Railways and VVV offices). Tours may be an independent venture, or alternatively use may be made of one of the several package arrangements available. Details are set out in an NBT annual publication.

Bicycles can readily be hired throughout the country, including from a large number of railway stations.

Intending cyclists should take great care that their lights are as visible for right-hand drive conditions as they are for British roads. A very secure lock is recommended; and when securing your bicycle in one of the large cities you are recommended to remove all removable parts (lights, saddles and wheels with quick-release mechanisms) as there is a lively trade in exotic machinery (most British machines qualify as such) and for spare parts. Every town has a bicycle shop, it seems, so a puncture or a dented wheel need not be more than a temporary disaster.

**By Coach.** The Netherlands enjoys an extensive network of inter-urban coach services, town terminals normally being close to railway stations. The starting point for any journey should be the VVV office (usually near the station). Coach, bus, tram and rail travel all share an integrated ticket system which makes for very easy (and easily rectifiable!) travelling.

**By Rail**. The first train in the Netherlands ran between Haarlem and

Amsterdam in 1839, and there was great expansion during the reign of William III, a Railways Act being passed in 1860. The present national railway company is *Nederlandse Spoorwegen (NS)*, founded in 1917 and with its headquarters at Utrecht.

NS operates a dense network commonly regarded as one of the most modern and most efficient in the world, the trains being clean, well maintained, frequent and, despite numerous stops, remarkably fast. So good is the service that NS boasts that few people find it necessary to study a timetable since an early departure for any destination in the country can be relied upon. Travel is made easy by means of the timetable (Spoorboekje), published annually in May or June and containing a series of maps; excellent yellow departure boards at stations, showing destination, time of departure and platform, and giving route diagrams; automatic indicators over platforms; and destinations marked on coaches. However, passengers should be careful to board the correct portion of trains since some consist of two or more parts going to different places.

Among the many special facilities offered are Rover tickets of various types and periods; season tickets; reduced fare concessions for senior citizens and for young people; family tickets; bicycle hire; and a particularly good range of reduced-fare combined rail, bus and boat excursions. If you are basing yourself in one or another city you are recommended to go to the station, or the VVV, and collect the booklet of excursions; such excursions will often be cheaper than travelling by car, and the experience of the train journey itself might well be one of the highlights of your stay.

For further information apply Netherlands Railways, 25–28 Buckingham Gate, London SW1E 6LD. Tel: 071-630 1735, or at NBT offices.

**By Air.** Air travel in the Netherlands Internal air services are provided by NLM Cityhopper (Nederlandse Luchtvaart Maatschappij = Netherlands Aviation Company), a subsidiary of KLM founded in 1966. Amsterdam, Eindhoven, Enschede, Groningen, Maastricht and Rotterdam are all served by frequent flights.

# Accommodation

The Netherlands offers the complete range of *Hotels* that the visitor would expect of a western European country, NBT's annual 'Hotel Guide' listing most of these under place names. Hotels are given both a national classification (stars) and also a category-numbered Benelux classification; prices (which include VAT and service) are indicated, while further information is provided by symbols. The guide also advises on how to make reservations; but see also under Tourist Organisations above.

Rather fuller local lists are obtainable from VVV offices, these lists also including *Guest Houses* and *Private Homes* with rooms to let; such accommodation, usually with something of a family atmosphere, offers an opportunity to meet local people.

*Self-catering Bungalows* are a popular choice for accommodation in holiday regions, but reservations must be made many months in advance. For such accommodation there are regional central booking addresses, these being updated annually in NBT's general publication 'Holland'.

*Youth Hostels*. There are over 50 Youth Hostels throughout the country.

Information from visitors' home organisations or from Stichting Nederlandse Jeugdherberg Centrale, Prof. Tulpplein 4, 1018GX Amsterdam. Tel:
020- 264433.

*Camp and Caravan Sites.* NBT publishes annually a list detailing a large
number of selected sites. This, however, represents only a fraction of the
sites available, lists of local sites normally being obtainable from VVV
offices.

# Food and Drink

Traditional Dutch food tends to be substantial and straightforward, the
result, it is said, of climate, of centuries of battle against watery and muddy
nature, and even of propelling a bicycle. Among popular traditional
dishes—each with infinite variations—may be mentioned thick soups,
notably pea soup (Erwtensoep), and mashed vegetable dishes (stamppot-
ten), frequently reinforced with bacon fat. Straightforward though these
and similar dishes may be (and no one eating a meal in the Netherlands is
in danger of leaving the table still hungry), they are, nevertheless, almost
invariably well prepared and tasty.

But tradition—at any rate in its older and extremer forms—is on the wane
as more and more Dutch become calorie conscious. And also the expansion
of international air travel means that the fare in the larger hotels and
restaurants, though always generous, is tilted more towards international
rather than local taste.

The Netherlands is probably best known for its cheese of which some 26
varieties are produced, the most famous being Edam and Gouda. Then
there are Dutch herrings, swallowed raw or salted with chopped onions,
especially popular in May and June, the time of the '*nieuwe haring*', the
first of the season. Eels, too, are popular, while from the bakers come small
pancakes called '*poffertjes*' and quite a variety of biscuits, such as the
ubiquitous gingery '*speculaas*'; local specialities include the sweet 'siroopwafels' of Gouda. 'Drops' (liquorice) are sold widely—sometimes you will
come across a market stall devoted to them; there are many shapes and
sizes and two distinct flavours: salty and sweet. Do taste before you buy as
even the sweetest can be too harsh for the foreigner's palate and on the
whole they can not be recommended as presents for children.

Restaurants (usually open in the evening rather earlier than in England)
are of the standards and variety to be found elsewhere in western Europe.
However, thanks to the many settlers native to the former colonies, the
country enjoys a particularly good choice of oriental restaurants, the best
known being the Indonesian serving 'Rijstafel', a base of rice with a
daunting variety of often highly spiced meat, fish and vegetable dishes.
Visitors in search of a genuine 'rijstafel' should take local advice as not only
do standards vary but the distinction also tends to become blurred between
Chinese, Indo-Chinese and genuine Indonesian restaurants. A traditional
Dutch 'short order' meal is a 'pannekoek' (pancake), these are available
with many fillings—particularly recommended is the bacon and syrup. If
you wish to remain on your feet and walk around while eating 'frites' (chips)
are a cheap and filling option; they are usually eaten with mayonnaise and
salt.

A Tourist Menu scheme operates throughout the country, the menu comprising three courses at a reasonable price fixed annually. Over 500 restaurants provide this menu, these being listed in a NBT brochure and also being identified by a special blue sign, bearing a fork between the words Tourist Menu. Another sign—a red, white and blue soup tureen—identifies the 500 or so 'Neerlands Dis' restaurants, establishments offering distinctively Dutch dishes (leaflets from NBT or VVV offices).

As to drink, the Netherlands is famous for its many excellent beers. Also for 'Jenever' (= juniper) or 'Hollands' gin, a potent spirit produced either as old (oude) or young (jonge); and 'Advocaat', a type of egg-nog liqueur. Dutch beer is on the whole of the bland international lager type, fortunately served too cold to be tasted, but the Dutch are great connoisseurs of exotic beers, especially Belgian, German and British and these are all widely available.

*Cafés* are very much a feature of the Netherlands, they often have a period character or theme and can seem far removed from the conventional picture conveyed by the word. With comfortable chairs, and tables covered by thick carpet-like cloths (just like the Vermeer interiors), the ambience can often be more like that of a large and welcoming dark-panelled living room. This is especially the case with the 'brown cafés'; there are also 'white cafés', modernist in design (for example 'Het Land van Walem', Keizersgracht 449 in Amsterdam, originally designed by Gerrit Rietveld in 1920). Cafés and bars generally open at around lunchtime and remain open until one in the morning (later at weekends). Here Dutch beer, or, perhaps, jenever guarantees an experience uniquely Dutch; bar snacks include such delights as 'bitter ballen'—try them.

# General Information

**Banking and Currency.** The Dutch monetary unit is the Guilder (Gulden), confusingly sometimes also called a Florin, prices usually being marked as such with a f or fl. The guilder divides into 100 cents. There are six notes, values (in guilders) 1000, 100, 50, 25, 10 and 5. There are five coins, all being nickel except for the 5 which is bronze; the coin values are f5, f2.50 (rijksdaalder), f1 (guilder), 25 cents (kwartje), 10 cents (dubbeltje) and 5 cents (stuiver).

There are no foreign exchange restrictions. Visitors may either carry Travellers' Cheques or use the Eurocheque system. The latter, which has the merit of avoiding the outlay involved in buying Travellers' Cheques, involves obtaining a Eurocheque Card (valid only for the year printed on it) and as many special Eurocheques as may be needed from your bank. You make out a cheque in the normal way (max. £100, but many countries, the Netherlands included, set a lower limit) and present it at any bank or other exchange displaying (as most do) the Eurocheque sign. Eurocheques have the further advantage of being widely used by the Dutch themselves and are accepted at all shops, restaurants and (even) bars. For purchases greater than the limit two or more cheques can be made out. Cheques and currency can often be exchanged other than at banks; for instance, some VVV offices, several railway stations, hotels, frontier crossings, etc. (look for the sign GWK = Grenswissel Kantoren = Border Exchange Offices. Open daily from early morning to late evening. Tel: 020-3221324).

All the main credit cards (some with cash facilities) are widely accepted.

**Casinos.** There are casinos (roulette, black jack and baccarat) at Rotterdam, Scheveningen, Valkenburg and Zandvoort. They are open all year, daily, 14.00 to 02.00 but Baccarat does not normally start until 21.00. The minimum age is 18, and all visitors must produce official identification (e.g. passport or driving licence). Correct dress (for gentlemen, jacket and tie) is required.

**For the Children.** In addition to magnificent beaches and an exciting choice of both town and country boat excursions, many attractions are likely to be of especial appeal to children. These include, to name only a few, the miniature towns of Madurodam and Walcheren at respectively The Hague and Middelburg; the fairy-tale park of De Efteling near Tilburg (allow a full day for this); dolphins at Haderwijk, Zandvoort and Rhenen; excellent zoos at Amsterdam, Rotterdam, Emmen and Arnhem; the windmills of Kinderdijk; the leisure park of Linneaushof near Haarlem, claiming to be the world's largest and with over 300 play attractions for children; and the fun and safari park of Beekse Bergen. In addition there are numerous local attractions, some ephemeral, and if you want to entertain your children you are recommended to ask at the local VVV to find out what is going on. If you are fortunate enough to be in the Netherlands when the ice is good then be sure to get some cheap lash-on skates (most toyshops) and join the locals in one of the most delightful experiences known to mankind—unrestricted access to miles upon miles of good skating. The traditional Dutch long skates take some half an hour to learn to manage and, apart from the skates, the only essential equipment is a stout pair of gloves (you will fall over several times).

**Commonwealth War Graves.** Over 19,000 men from the countries of the Commonwealth, in particular from the United Kingdom (12,400) and Canada (5700), died in the Netherlands during the Second World War and are buried or commemorated here. The greater number of the graves are in war cemeteries in the eastern part of the country, the largest being Oosterbeek near Arnhem; Groesbeek near Nijmegen (Canadian); Holten (Canadian); and Jonkerbos near Nijmegen. There are also cemeteries in the west, notably two near Bergen op Zoom, while several aircrew rest in graves in the Frisian islands, principally Terschelling, Ameland and Schiermonnikoog. Additionally the Groesbeek Memorial records the names of those who have no known grave.

The great majority of the war graves are directly maintained by the Commonwealth War Graves Commission, 2 Marlow Road, Maidenhead, Berkshire SL6 7DX (Tel: 0628-34221), while others are maintained on the Commission's behalf by the Nederlandse Oorlogsgravenstichting (Netherlands War Graves Authority).

Anyone wishing to visit a particular grave will find a printed register near the cemetery entrance. Those who are uncertain about the location of a grave or memorial are advised to refer to the Commission's head office (see above). The Commission also publishes material of interest to relatives and the general public and can at a small charge obtain photographs of graves. The Royal British Legion (49 Pall Mall, London SW1Y 5TG) can arrange for poppy wreaths to be laid for a reasonable charge.

**Consulates.** *British: Amsterdam Koningslaan 44. Tel: 020-6764343. USA*: Amsterdam, Museumplein 19. Tel: 020-6790321. *Canada*: The Hague, Sophialaan 7. Tel: 070-3614111. *Australia*: The Hague, Koninginnegracht 23. Tel: 070-3630983.

**Contact with local people.** There are a number of VVV offices able to help foreign visitors wishing to meet Dutch people. Amsterdam, in particular, has a special programme.

**Disabled.** The Netherlands prides itself on the high standard of the facilities it provides for the disabled. A special NBT brochure aims to help the handicapped plan a holiday making the best use of the facilities.

**Events.** As might be expected, the emphasis in the Netherlands tends to be on floral events, with, for example, the Hillegom 'Kerstflora' show of hothouse plants (around Christmas), the flower parade between Haarlem and Noordwijk towards the end of April, and the Giethoorn waterborne flower procession on the last Saturday in August. Other annual events occur in such fields as folklore, sport, the arts, cycling, ice-skating, motor racing, and religion, with Carnival celebrated in February mainly in the Catholic southern provinces and the performance, at Naarden in the week before Easter, of Bach's 'St Matthew Passion'. An annual list of Events is published by NBT.

**Medical.** Foreign tourists are entitled to medical help when they originate from a country with which the Netherlands has signed a health treaty, when treatment cannot be delayed, or if covered by internationally valid insurance. A health treaty has been concluded with all EC countries, and eligible United Kingdom travellers should obtain leaflet SA30 from their Department of Health and Social Security office, or from the leaflets office at PO Box 21, Stanmore, Middlesex HA7 1AY; this explains eligiblity and contains an application for Form E111 certifying entitlement to medical treatment throughout the EC. Visitors may well judge that the cover provided is not sufficient—it does not, for instance, cover repatriation—and the importance of good travel insurance cannot be over-emphasised.

**Museums and Art Galleries** are very much a feature of the Dutch scene, the former (not infrequently including a room or rooms devoted to art) being ubiquitous and ranging from the world-famed Rijksmuseum in Amsterdam or The Hague's Gemeente Museum down to modest village efforts, while themes range from large and distinguished collections down to, for instance, curiosities such as money-boxes, footwear, clay pipes and even taxation. The Dutch have enthusiastically and skilfully seized their opportunity and the majority of museums—certainly the larger ones—are models of modern and in many cases inspired presentation.

Many museums, and most art galleries, own more than they can display at one time, a situation aggravated by a laudable antagonism to anything suggestive of clutter. It is therefore increasingly the policy to rotate pictures (although famed masterpieces of course remain permanently on show), this not only enabling pictures to be enjoyed which might otherwise languish in storerooms but also attracting more visitors who can now reasonably expect to see at least some works different from those enjoyed on a previous visit. Museums and galleries are also well aware of the attraction of well-publicised temporary exhibitions; but, admirable as these often are, they can sometimes oust significant parts of the permanent collection which may well have been the touring visitor's objective.

Stedelijk (Municipal) museums abound—whether large and distinguished such as those in Amsterdam, The Hague and Rotterdam, or the simple Oudheidkamer (Antiquities room) of many small towns and villages—their purpose being to preserve and display material telling the local story. Foreign visitors sometimes shun these on the reasonable enough ground of lack of interest in the past of some relatively obscure Dutch town. Yet it is worth bearing in mind that there are discoveries to be made here—such as, to mention but two, an extraordinary school learning-to-read wheel in Amersfoort's Museum Fléhite or an ingenious window-cleaning spray in the museum at Zwolle.

Most of the larger museums and galleries provide guides and descriptions in English, and many of the smaller ones will produce a modest typed explanatory sheet or even a helpful ground plan. It is always worth asking.

**Museum Card.** Most Dutch museums charge for entry, and the fee can often be surprisingly high. Any tourist proposing to visit several museums should consider buying a Museum Card. The cost is most reasonable (there are three age-related bands; under 26, between 26 and 64, and 65 or over) and, once bought, the card, which is valid for the calendar year, allows entry without further payment to some 300 museums. A booklet listing those organisations recognising the card can be obtained when you purchase the card itself. Cards are available at NBT offices, principal VVV offices and also at most of the museums and galleries. See also Pensioners, below.

**Passports.** Citizens of most European countries, of USA, Canada, Australia and New Zealand, and of many other countries, require no visa. A passport or, in many cases, a national identity card will suffice. For documents required if entering with a car, see under Motoring above.

**Pensioners.** There is quite a range of reductions for visitors over 65 years of age, including the entrance fees for many museums and art galleries and also the cost of rail travel, for which in fact the qualifying age is 60. Visitors may be asked to produce evidence of eligiblity.

**Post and Telephone (PTT).** Post Offices are normally open Monday–Friday 08.30 to 17.00. The more important offices may remain open until 19.00 and also open Saturday, 08.30 to 12.00.

The Dutch telephone system is fully automatic, and most public telephone boxes display instructions in English. It should be noted that long distance and international calls cannot be made from all boxes.

**Public Holidays.** The following are to a greater or lesser extent public holidays:
New Year's Day.
Good Friday. Many shops remain open, especially in the north.
Easter Sunday and Monday.
Queen's Day (30 April).
Liberation Day (5 May). Most shops open.
Ascension Day.
Whit Sunday and Monday.
Christmas Day and Boxing Day.

**Shopping** hours are flexible and can vary from place to place. Some shops close for lunch and, during each week, virtually all close for a half or whole day. Many places enjoy late shopping on Thursday or Friday, while in holiday centres many shops stay open late or throughout the weekend. The following opening hours are given as a basic guide. Monday, 13.00 to 17.30 or 18.00, though food shops may well be open during the morning; Tuesday–Friday, 08.30 or 09.00 to 17.30 or 18.00; Saturday, 08.30 or 09.00 to 16.00 or 17.00.

Clogs, model windmills, costumed dolls and pottery (notably Delft and Makkum) are among the more popular choices of souvenir hunters. Many visitors also buy flower bulbs, while more specialised tastes may seek out the glass and crystal of Leerdam, the silver of Schoonhoven or even diamonds from Amsterdam.

**Time.** The Netherlands is in the Central European Time Zone, but during the summer months (roughly end March to end September) the clocks are advanced one hour. Put you watch forward one hour—what you lose on your departure you will regain on your return.

**Tipping.** Custom is as vague, personal and flexible as in most other countries. Hotel and restaurant bills will virtually always be inclusive of service and VAT. So also are taxi meters, though here it is customary to tip as well.

**Voltage** in the Netherlands is 220; plugs are different and if you wish to use electrical equipment a universal adaptor is essential.

**On the Water.** *Beaches.* Along its mainland and around its islands the Netherlands boasts over 300km of really magnificent beaches, the many resorts along these ranging from sophisticated Scheveningen through smaller family resorts down to mere villages. NBT booklet 'The Dutch Seaside' provides general descriptions by regions and resorts and also gives information regarding accommodation, naturists' beaches, water sports, events and suchlike.

*Boat Excursion* possiblities—within towns, along rivers and canals, on the sea—are almost unlimited and in summer can be made from any place of significance which is close to water. Of outstanding interest are the canals of Amsterdam; the port of Rotterdam; the Oosterscheldedam; the Biesbos; the strange village of Giethoorn; the broads of Overijssel and Friesland; and IJsselmeer cruises, these even including sailing trips on traditional local craft.

**Young People.** Many special facilities are available for young people, including reduced entry prices for museums, reduced travel costs, and accommodation choices which include youth hostels, student hotels, camping houses and camping farms. For details ask for the special NBT booklet.

# The Dutch Language

The Dutch language is of Germanic ancestry, its lineage then being through the Frankish dialects spoken first by the Batavi and then by the Franks who moved in as the Romans withdrew. The language was early influenced by the dialects of the raiding Frisians and Saxons. Various dialects developed, notably in the southern Netherlands and each city has its street patois, a phenomenon further enriched with the arrival of immigrant communities from former colonies since the last war. The best introduction for anyone seriously interested in finding out about, or even learning, Dutch is 'The Dutch Language, A Survey' by Pierre Brachin, tr. Paul Vincent, Stanley Thornes (Publishers) Ltd, Cheltenham, 1985 (which also has information on Frisian).

**Pronunciation**. The Dutch are simply not used to foreigners attempting to speak their language—whereas an English-speaker can cope with bad pronunciation and grammar, the Dutch can seem impatient and will usually reply in English. They will, however, respect persistence and the following rough guide may be useful when dealing with placenames and menus.

CONSONANTS are pronounced roughly as in English, but with the following exceptions:
*ch* as in the Scottish loch
*g* as ch
*j* as in yellow
*ng* as in bring (not in linger)
*nj* as in onion
*'s* preceding a place name is a shortening of *des* (of the) and is pronounced run straight into the word following
*sch* (now increasingly written *s*) as in kiss
*v* almost as English f
*w* almost as English v
*y* is normally only used in words of foreign origin. See *ij* below

VOWELS. When a vowel sound is to be drawn out, this is achieved either by doubling or by adding a consonant followed by *e* (e.g. there is no pronounciation difference between *groot* and *grote*, both being pronounced as groat, with the g rolled on the soft palette with the back of the tongue).
*a* as in hat
*aa* as in cart
*e* almost as in bet, but with a touch of bear
*ee* as in late
*i* as in bit
*o* as in cop
*oo* as in cope
*u* as in wood
*uu* a thin sound unknown in English but like the French u or the German ü

DIPTHONGS are pronounced thus:
*au* as in cow
*ei*—nearly as in fly
*eij* as in lay
*eu* something like English firm
*ie* as in peer
*ij* is virtually y and is regarded as a single letter (hence when initial and capitalised it must be written IJ). Pronounced somewhere between English pile and pale. But note that mijnheer (Mr) is pronounced short (m'nair).
*oe* as in boor
*ou, au, ouw, auw* as in out
*ui* as in French oeil

STRESS. There are many exceptions but the general rule is that the stress falls on the last syllable but one or but two.

# GLOSSARY

*Aan Zee*, On sea
*Aarde*, Earth
*Accijns,*Excise duty
*Achter*, Behind. At the rear of
*Afslag*, Dutch auction. Discount
*Afsluitdijk*, Closing dike
*Aken*, Aachen. Aix-la-Chapelle
*Ambacht*, Trade. Craft
*Apenheul*, Monkey refuge
*Arm*, Poor. Needy

*Baan*, Path. Way. Track
*Bad*, Bath. Seaside resort
*Bakker*, Baker
*Barrevoets*, Barefoot
*Basiliek*, Basilica
*Bedd (ancient)*, Stone. Ancient
  tomb
*Beek*, Brook. Stream
*Beeld*, Image. Picture. Sculpture
*Beer*, A bear
*Beest*, Animal
*Begijn*, Beguine (member of a
  lay sisterhood
*Beirer (eij-)*, Bavarian
*Beneden*, Below. Lower
*Benoordenhoutseweg*, North of
  the Wood Road
*Berg*, Hill
*Beurs*, Exchange. Bourse
*Bevrijding*, Liberation
*Bezem*, Broom
*Bezoeker*, Visitor
*Bezuidenhoutseweg*, South of
  the Wood Road
*Bibliotheek*, Library
*Bier*, Beer
*Bij*, By. Near
*Binnen*, Interior. Inner
*Bisschop*, Bishop
*Blauw*, Blue
*Blik*, Tin
*Bloem*, Flower
*Boer*, Peasant. Farmer
*Bolwerken*, Fortifications
*Boog*, Bow (weapon)
*Boom*, Tree
*Boos (bose)*, Angry
*Bo(e)rderij*, Farmhouse

*Bos*, A wood
*Botanische Tuin*, Botanic garden
*Boter*, Butter
*Bourgonje*, Burgundy
*Boven*, Above. Upper
*Brandweer*, Fire service
*Breed (bredde-, bree-)*, Road
*Brink*, Village green
*Broeder*, Brother
*Broederschap*, Brotherhood
*Broekland*, Marshy land
*Brug*, Bridge
*Buiten*, Outside. Outer
*Buitenland*, Abroad
*Burcht*, Castle
*Burg*, Castle
*Burgemeester*, Burgomaster.
  Mayor
*Buur*, Neighbour
*Buurt*, Neighbourhood

*Catharijn*, Catherine
*Centraal*, Central. Principal
*Centrum*, Centre
*Chirurg*, Surgeon
*Choor*, Choir
*Clok (klok)*, Clock. Bell (on a
  tower)
*Clovenier*, Arquebusier
*Crom (krom)*, Crooked

*Dal*, Valley
*Dam*, Dam. Dike
*De*, The
*Deel*, A part of
*Diep*, Deep. Canal. Waterway
*Dierenpark*, Animal park. Zoo
*Dijk*, Dike
*Dis*, Dish
*Doel*, Target. Butt
*Dok*, Dock
*Donker*, Dark. Gloomy
*Door*, Through
*Dorp*, Village
*Drager*, Porter. Carrier
*Dreef*, Avenue
*Droom*, Dream
*Duif (duiv-, duyv-)*, Pigeon. Dove
*Duin*, Dune

*Duivel*, Devil
*Dun*, Thin

*Eendracht*, Union
*Effecten*, Stocks. Securities
*Egelantier*, Eglantine
*Eier*, Egg
*Eiland*, Island
*Eind*, End
*En*, And
*Engel*, Angel
*Erf*, Premises
*Ezel*, Donkey

*Fantoon*, Ghost
*Feilzuster*, Fallible sister (of a religious order)
*Fluw(e)el*, Velvet
*Fries*, Frisian

*Galg*, Gallows
*Gans*, Goose
*Gasthuis*, Hospice. Hospital
*Gat*, Gap. Opening (of a water inlet)
*Gebouw*, Building
*Gedemte*, Filled-in
*Geel (gele-)*, Yellow
*Geertruide (a)*, Gertrude
*Geest*, Spirit
*Geit*, Goat
*Gemeente*, Municipal. Of the community
*Gemeentehuis*, Town Hall (usually of a small place)
*Gerechtsgebouw*, Law Courts
*Geschiedenis*, History
*Geschiedkundig*, Historical
*Gevangen*, Captive. Prisoner
*Gevel*, Façade
*Gier*, Manure
*Gild(e)*, Guild. Corporation
*Gist*, Yeast
*Glad*, Smooth
*Goor*, Dark. Dingy
*Goud*, Gold
*Goudsmid*, Goldsmith
*Graaf (grave-)*, Count (title)
*Gracht*, Moat. Canal
*Gratie*, Grace
*Grauw*, The rabble
*Gravensteen*, Literally the Count's Stone (castle, prison)

*Griet*, Meg
*Groen*, Green
*Groot (grote)*, Large
*Grot*, Cave. Grotto

*Hal*, Hall. Entrance hall
*Hals*, Neck
*Haring*, Herring
*Haven*, Harbour. Port
*Haver*, Oats
*Heden*, Today
*Hedendaags*, Modern
*Heer*, Army
*Heide*, Heath
*Heil*, Welfare
*Heilig*, Holy
*Hek*, Fence. Hedge
*Helm*, Helmet. Type of grass
*Hendrik*, Henry
*Here-*, of the gentry
*Herinnering*, Memory
*Hert*, Stag
*Hervormd (herv)*, Reformed
*Het*, The
*Heul*, Refuge
*Heuvel*, Hill
*Hoek*, Corner
*Hof*, Court. Yard. House
*Hofje*, Almshouse
*Hondsrug*, Dog's Back
*Hoofd*, Main. Principal
*Hoofdwacht*, The Watch (guard patrol)
*Hoog (hoge-)*, High
*Hooi*, Hay
*Hout*, Wood
*Huis (huys)*, House

IJzer, Iron

*Jaarbeurs*, Industrial Fair
*Jan* (abbr. of Johan), John
*-je*, (diminutive suffix)
*Jenever*, Gin
*Johan*, John
*Jong*, Young
*Jood*, Jew
*Joris*, George
*Juffer*, Young woman
*Justitie*, Justice

*Kaars*, Candle
*Kaas*, Cheese
*Kade*, Quay

*Kalf (kalv-)*, Calf
*Kamer*, Room. Chamber
*Kamp*, Camp. Field. Battle
*Kansel*, Pulpit
*Kanselarij*, Chancellery
*Kant*, Side
*Kantoor*, Office
*Karel*, Charles
*Kasteel*, Castle. Château
*Kathedraal*, Cathedral
*Kazemaaten*, Casemates
*Kazerne*, Barracks
*Keizer*, Emperor
*Kering*, Dam. Storm-surge barrier
*Kerk*, Church
*Kerkhof*, Churchyard. Close
*Keuken*, Kitchen
*Kijk*, View
*Kind*, Child
*Kleermaker*, Tailor
*Klein*, Small
*Klompen*, Clogs
*Klooster*, Cloister. Religious
  House
*Klovenier*, Arquebusier
*Koe*, Cow
*Koek*, Cake. Cookie
*Kolk*, Pool (now usually a small
  street)
*Koning*, King
*Koningin*, Queen
*Koninklijk*, Royal
*Kooi*, Cage
*Koopman*, Merchant
*Koor*, Choir
*Kop*, Head
*Koper*, Buyer. Copper
*Koppel*, Cupola
*Koren (Koorn)*, Corn. Grain
*Korenmeter*, Corn weigher
*Korf*, Basket
*Kort*, Short
*Kraan*, Crane. Derrick
*Krom*, Crooked
*Kruidenier*, Grocer
*Kruis*, Cross
*Kuiper*, Cooper
*Kunst*, Art
*Kwartier*, Quarter
*Kweek*, Nursery
*Kweekschool*, Training school

*Laan*, Avenue
*Laatste*, Last
*Lakenhal*, Cloth Hall
*Lang*, Long
*Laurens*, Lawrence
*Ledig*, Empty. Vacant
*Leger*, Army
*Lening*, Lending
*Lieve*, Dear. Beloved
*Lijnbaan*, Rope walk
*Linde*, Lime. Linden
*Lodewijk*, Ludwig. Louis
*Looier*, Tanner
*Lucht*, Air
*Luisteren*, Listen

*Maaltijd*, Meal (meal time)
*Maas*, Meuse (river)
*Markt*, Market
*Maurits*, Maurice
*Meer*, Lake. Mere
*Melk*, Milk
*Midderste*, Central
*Mijl op Zeven*, Roundabout way
*Minderbroeder*, Franciscan (Friar
  Minor)
*Moer*, Mother
*Molen*, Mill. Windmill
*Mond*, Mouth
*Munt*, Coin. Mint

*Neder Rijn*, Lower Rhine
*Neer*, Down. Lower
*Nering*, Trade
*Nieuw*, New
*Noord*, North
*Noteboom*, Walnut tree

*Oever*, River bank
*Onderwijs*, Education
*Outspanning*, Relaxation
*Onze Lieve Vrouw*, Our Dear
  Lady
*Oog*, Eye
*Oord*, Place. Region
*Oorlog*, War
*Oost*, East
*Op*, On. Upon
*Oranje*, Orange
*Os*, Ox
*Oud*, Old
*Oudheiden (heden)*, Antiquities
*Over*, Over. Beyond

*Paard*, Horse
*Paleis*, Palace
*Parochie*, Parish
*Passiebloem*, Passion Flower
*Paus*, Pope
*Pauw*, Peacock
*Peel*, Marshy land
*Pels*, Fur
*Penning*, Medal
*Peper*, Pepper
*Pest*, Plague
*Pierement*, Barrel organ
*Pijl*, Arrow
*Plantage, Plantsoen*, Public
  garden
*Plas*, Pool
*Plein*, Square (in a town)
*Pluim*, Feather
*Polder*, Reclaimed land
*Poort*, Gate
*Pop*, Doll. Puppet
*Provenier*, Inmate of an
  almshouse
*Punt*, Point. Summit
*Put*, Well

*Raad*, Council
*Raadhuis*, Council House. Town
  Hall
*Raam*, Window
*Rak*, Stretch of water
*Ramp*, Disaster
*Raspen*, To grate
*Recht*, Right. Straight
*Rechtshuis*, Law Court
*Reveraat*, Reserve (e.g. nature
  reserve)
*Ridder*, Knight
*Rij*, Row. Line
*Rijk (Rijks-)*, The State (National-)
*Rijn*, Rhine
*Rogge*, Rye
*Rood (rode)*, Red
*Rozelaar*, Rosebush
*Rozen*, Rose
*Rug*, Back
*Ruim*, Space

*'s = des*, Of the
*Saai*, Serge
*Saal (zaal)*, Hall
*Schaap*, Sheep

*Schans*, Entrenchment
*Schatkamer*, Treasure room
*Scheepvaart*, Shipping activity.
  Navigation. Maritime
*Schepenzaal*, Aldermen's hall
*Schilder*, Painter. Artist
*Schilderij*, Picture
*Schippersbeurs*, Shipping
  exchange
*Schoon*, Beautiful
*Schot*, A Scot
*Schouwburg*, Theatre
*Schreien*, Weep
*Schutter*, Marksman
*Schuur*, Barn
*Singel*, Girdle. Ring
*Sint*, Saint
*Slachten*, Kill
*Sloot*, Ditch
*Slot*, Castle
*Sluis (pl. sluizen)*, Lock (on a
  waterway). Sluice
*Smeden*, To forge or weld
*Spaans*, Spanish
*Speel*, Toy. Game
*Speeldoos*, Musical box
*Spelen*, To play
*Spelonk*, Cave. Grotto
*Spoor*, Track
*Sprookje*, Fairy tale
*Spui*, Sluice
*Staal*, Sample
*Staalmeesters*, Syndics
*Staat*, Authority. Rank
*Stad*, Town
*Stadhuis*, Town Hall
*Stedelijk*, Municipal
*Steeg*, Alley
*Steen*, Stone (here normally
  stone building, i.e., castle
  prison)
*Stelsel*, System
*Stempel*, Stamp (of quality,
  authentication, etc)
*Stichting*, Foundation.
  Organisation
*Stijlkamer*, Period Room
*Straat*, Street
*Streek*, District
*Strooi*, Straw
*Stuiver*, Penny (5 cent coin)

*'t = het*, The
*Tamboer*, Drummer
*Te. Ter*, At. In
*Tijd*, Time
*Timmer*, Carpenter
*Toren*, Tower
*Trouwzaal*, Marriage room
*Tuchthuis*, House of correction
*Tuig*, Harness
*Tuin*, Garden
*Turf*, Peat
*Tussen*, Between
*Tweekbak*, Biscuit. Pastry

*Uit*, Out
*Uiteste*, Outermost

*Vaart*, Navigation. Canal
*Valk*, Falcon
*Van*, Of
*Varken*, Pig
*Vee*, Cattle
*Veen*, Moor. Marsh (usually peat). Fen
*Veer*, Ferry
*Veiling*, Auction
*Verbinding*, Connection. Link
*Verdronken*, Submerged
*Vereniging*, Union. Association
*Vergulden*, Gilded
*Vergunning*, Permission
*Verzet*, Resistance
*Vesting*, Fortification
*Vierschaar*, Tribunal
*Vijver*, Pond. Lake
*Vijzel*, Mortar
*Vis*, Fish
*Vlaams*, Flemish
*Vlaanderen*, Flanders
*Vlag*, Flag
*Vlakte*, Plain. Flat ground
*Vlaming*, A Fleming
*Vlas*, Flax
*Vlees*, Flesh. Meat
*Vleeshal*, Meat market
*Vleeshouwer*, Butcher
*Vleugel*, Wing
*Vloedlijn*, High water mark
*Voet*, Foot
*Voetboog*, Foot bow
*Vogel*, A fuller
*Volkskunde*, Folklore. Ethnology

*Voor*, Before. For
*Voorlichting*, Information
*Vos*, Fox
*Vrijheid*, Freedom
*Vrouw*, Woman. Lady

*Waag*, Weigh house
*Waard*, Foreshore
*Wacht*, Guard
*Wad*, Mud flat
*Wal*, Rampart. Embankment
*Walvis*, Whale
*Wandel*, Walk
*Warmoe-*, Market garden
*Waterleiding*, Water authority. Waterworks
*Weeshuis*, Orphanage
*Weg*, Way. Road. Track
*Werf*, Shipyard. Wharf
*Wering*, Protection
*West*, West
*Wetenschap*, Science
*Wielrijder*, Cyclist
*Wier*, Seaweed
*Wijd*, Wide
*Wijde*, A broad or mere
*Wijn*, Wine
*Wild*, Game animals
*Willem*, William
*Winkel*, Shop
*Wit*, White
*Wol*, Wool
*Wolde*, Wold
*Woud*, Forest. Wood

*Zaad*, Seed
*Zaal*, Hall
*Zadel*, Saddle
*Zak*, Bag. Sack
*Zand*, Sand
*Zee*, Sea. Large lake
*Zeeuws*, Zeeland
*Zeevaart*, Navigation. Maritime
*Zeewering*, Sea protection
*Ziekenhuis*, Hospital
*Zijd*, Side. Flank
*Zijl*, Watercourse. Lock
*Zonne*, Sun
*Zout*, Salt
*Zuid*, South
*Zuster*, Sister
*Zwan*, Swan

*Zwart*, Black
*Zweefvliegen*, Gliding

**Numbers**

| | |
|---|---|
| 1 | Een |
| 2 | Twee |
| 3 | Drie |
| 4 | Vier |
| 5 | Vijf |
| 6 | Zes |
| 7 | Zeven |
| 8 | Acht |
| 9 | Negen |
| 10 | Tien |
| 11 | Elf |
| 12 | Twaalf |
| 13 | Dertien |
| 14 | Veertien |
| 15 | Vijftien |
| 16 | Zestien |
| 17 | Zeventien |
| 18 | Achttien |
| 19 | Negentien |
| 20 | Twintig |
| 21 | Eenentwintig |
| 22 | Tweenentwintig |
| 30 | Dertig |
| 40 | Veertig |
| 50 | Vijftig |
| 60 | Zestig |
| 70 | Zeventig |
| 80 | Tachtig |
| 90 | Negentig |
| 100 | Honderd |
| 1000 | Duizend |

1st = eerst
2nd = tweede
3rd = derde

4th = vierde
5th = vijfde
6th = zesde
7th = zevende
8th = achtste
9th = negende
10th = tiende
11th = elfde
12th = twaalfde
13th = derdiende
20th = twintigste

**Days**

| | |
|---|---|
| Monday | Maandag |
| Tuesday | Dinsdag |
| Wednesday | Woensdag |
| Thursday | Donderdag |
| Friday | Vrijdag |
| Saturday | Zaterdag |
| Sunday | Zindag |
| Ascension | Hemelvaart |
| Christmas | Kerstmis |
| Easter | Paas |
| New Year | Nieuwjaar |
| Whitsun | Pinksteren |

**Months**

| | |
|---|---|
| January | Januari |
| February | Februari |
| March | Maart |
| April | April |
| May | Mei |
| June | Juni |
| July | Juli |
| August | Augustus |
| September | September |
| October | Oktober |
| November | November |
| December | December |

# PROVINCES OF NOORD AND ZUID
# HOLLAND AND ZEELAND

**Capitals.** *Noord Holland*: Haarlem. *Zuid Holland*: The Hague. *Zeeland* Middelburg.

**History.** Historically, as the former county of Holland, the provinces of Noord and Zuid Holland can be treated as one, and Zeeland can be included since it was annexed by Holland as early as 1323, prior to this it was disputed territory fought over by the counts of Flanders and Holland. The joint history of the three, up to 1436 when the county of Holland became merely a part of the wide lands of Duke Philip of Burgundy, covers some 500 years, during which there were only three lines of counts. During most of the early period only primitive flood protection and land reclamation had been attempted and for this reason the land area was very much smaller than it was even in the 19C, let alone today. To the N of Amsterdam, the extensive polder area of Beemster, Purmer, and Wormer, and, further N, Wieringermeer, were all tracts of water or marsh with islands; to the SW of Amsterdam there was (until the mid 19C) a huge shallow lake system, the Haarlemmer Meer, the waters of which at times reached the gates of Amsterdam or in the S flooded parts of Leiden. Because of this the main N to S route through the county ran between the coastal dunes and the lake; Zeeland was largely a waste of marshy islands, with Sluis, in Zeeland Flanders, an important port on a wide estuary.

The name Holland derives from a Frankish word meaning marshy scrub, this describing the district around Dordrecht which from 1015 onwards became the power centre of the county. The county's origins, though, are more associated with Egmond near the coast N of IJmuiden, land here being given in 922 by Charles the Simple to a Frisian who has come to be known as Count Dirk I. His son, Dirk II, founded an abbey here and, with land grants from the Emperor Otto III, vastly extended his territory. Dirk II died in 988, being succeeded by his son Arnulf who was killed fighting the West Frisians in 993, he in turn being succeeded by his son Dirk III, the first of the line to assume the title of Count of Holland. As such, he both consolidated and extended his lands, particularly at the expense of the bishopric of Utrecht, and in 1015 built a castle (around which would grow the town of Dordrecht) from which he levied tolls on river shipping. This so much reduced the prosperity of the up-river towns, even as far as Cologne, that in 1018 Count Godfrey of Lorraine invaded, though without success. The security of the southern part of his county thus established, Dirk III went on to subject Friesland in the north.

Dirk III was followed in 1039 by his son Dirk IV, during whose countship began the long dispute with the counts of Flanders over the ownership of Zeeland. In 1047 he defeated an imperial army in Zeeland, but two years later he was killed (it is believed at Dordrecht) fighting Bishop William of Utrecht. His successor, his brother Floris I, defeated Bishop William and his allies (Cologne, Liège, and others) in 1058 and again in 1061, when he was killed. The title then passed to his child son Dirk V, who lost virtually everything to Bishop William but regained it all on the latter's death in 1076. Dirk V died in 1091; he was followed by Floris II (died 1122), Dirk VI (died 1137), and Floris III (died on the Third Crusade in 1190). Dirk VII, son of Floris III, defeated his brother William when the latter stirred up revolts in

Zeeland and West Friesland, later, though, pardoning him and creating him Count of East Friesland.

On Dirk VII's death in 1204, William defeated the former's daughter and in 1206 declared himself Count of Holland. A born fighter, he took part in several campaigns, including the Fourth Crusade, but his countship is best known for the early town charters which he granted (Geertruidenberg in 1213, Dordrecht in 1220). His son Floris IV, who succeeded in 1222, was murdered in 1235.

There now followed two notable counts. William II, son of Floris IV, was elected King of the Romans (in place of the deposed and excommunicated Frederick II) in 1247 and was crowned in Aachen the following year. In 1256 he was about to leave for Rome to be crowned Emperor when, on an expedition against the West Frisians, he was killed when his horse fell through the ice. His son Floris V succeeded at the age of two and reigned for 40 years. A man of outstanding ability he did much for his county, granting many charters, including one to which Amsterdam traces its formal origin, and also, through his friendship with England's Edward I, negotiating many commercial advantages. Later the nobles became disaffected, disliking charters and other measures which reduced their status, and Floris was murdered at Muiden in 1296. With the death of his childless son John I in 1299 there ended a long line of remarkable rulers who over a little less than 400 years had established a county that was strong both militarily and commercially, in which the towns increasingly flourished, and in which much of the original marsh and scrub had become rich agricultural and pastoral land.

The new line was that of Avesnes, John I's successor being John II, son of William II's sister who had married John of Avesnes. Successful in his campaigns he defeated and killed the Bishop of Utrecht in 1301 and in 1304 expelled the Flemings from Zeeland. William III (the Good) followed, his countship being notable for the settlement of the Zeeland Flanders question under which its ownership was accepted in return for his dropping any claim to imperial Flanders. Continuing the traditions of the first line of counts, William III did much to foster the towns and to develop his county both agriculturally and commercially.

In 1337 William III was followed by his son William IV, whose death, childless, in battle against the Frisians in 1345 brought the civil war which marked the beginning of the end for the county. William IV's sister Margaret, wife of the Emperor, having been accepted as Countess of Holland, Zeeland, and Hainaut, appointed her son William of Bavaria as Stadholder, but when she abdicated in 1349 the Stadholder became Count William V. It was now that internal dissentions sharpened into civil war, the Hollanders grouping as Kabbeljauws (Cods), the party of the citizens and merchants and supporters of William V, and as Hoeks (Hooks), the party of the nobles who resented the growing power of the towns. (The name Cods symbolised the fat and prosperous merchants, Hooks the means by which they were to be caught and killed.) The Hoeks, helped by England's Edward III, won a sea engagement off Veere in 1351, but soon afterwards were decisively defeated at Vlaardingen. When in 1357 William V started to go insane, his younger brother Albert of Bavaria became regent, ruling with real wisdom for 46 years, becoming Count in 1388, and on his death in 1404 being followed by his son William VI, a firm supporter of the Hoeks who now enjoyed supremacy.

William VI was succeeded in 1417 by his daughter Jacqueline (also sometimes called Jacoba), and there now began 20 years of intrigue and strife, and, for Jacqueline, of treachery and tragedy. In 1416 both the Kabbeljauws and the Hoeks had sworn support for Jacqueline, but as soon as her uncle John of Bavaria claimed her lands she was deserted by the Kabbeljauws, while at about the same time (1418) she was tricked into marrying Duke John IV of Brabant. In 1420 she fled to England, declared her marriage to have been illegal, married (1422) Duke Humphrey of Gloucester and, in 1424, accompanied by Duke Humphrey, invaded Holland where, John of Bavaria having been poisoned, her enemy now was her 'husband' John of Brabant. Duke Humphrey soon deserted Jacqueline, who now fled to her cousin Philip the Good of Burgundy, Count of Flanders, who promptly imprisoned her at Ghent, thus in effect presenting her lands to John of Brabant, who now mortgaged to Philip the counties of Holland and Zeeland. Jacqueline soon escaped, but, despite a gallant struggle, stood no chance against the combined forces of John of Brabant (died 1427) and Philip. In 1428 a treaty recognised Jacqueline as nominal Countess but also ensured that Philip both exercised the power and was named heir should Jacqueline have no children. Soon afterwards Philip mortgaged Holland and Zeeland to Franck van Borssele, head of a leading Zeeland family, whom in 1432 Jacqueline married. Philip reacted quickly, invading Holland, imprisoning Van Borssele, and making his release conditional on Jacqueline's abdicating her titles. She could only submit, and when in 1436 she died childless she was succeeded by Philip. Holland now lost its independent identity and its history became merged with that of the Burgundian Netherlands. Not until the latter half of the next century, with the development of the Revolt of the Netherlands, would Holland regain that independence as the most Calvinist, populous, prosperous and influential of the northern provinces.

The border between Noord and Zuid Holland runs roughly E to W about halfway between Amsterdam and The Hague. Features common to both provinces are that they include the so-called Randstad, the great loop of towns made up of Amsterdam, Haarlem, Leiden, The Hague, Delft, and Rotterdam, and also that both have a coastline of magnificent beaches, dunes and resorts.

**Noord Holland**, most of which is below sea level, divides into two unequal parts, S and N of the Noordzee Kanaal. To the S are Amsterdam, the country's largest city and the national capital, the international airport of Schiphol, and the historic and interesting town of Haarlem, associated with the painter Frans Hals.

The *Noordzee Kanaal*, 22km in length, 140m in average width, and following the early course of the IJ, links Amsterdam with the sea at IJmuiden; the surface level is maintained at 50 centimetres below the 'Amsterdam zero'. The canal, dug in 1865–76 when the Noordhollands Kanaal (see below) was proved to have failed in recovering for Amsterdam its role as a deep-water port, can be well seen from the car ferry at Hembrug, and further W it is crossed by the triple-tube Velsertunnel. The great locks at IJmuiden are also of interest.

The northern part of the province, bounded on the W by open sea and on the E by the IJsselmeer (including the Markerwaard which may be reclaimed during the 1990s), contains nearly all that is considered typical of Holland: canals; polders, with the striking local large farms with their pyramid roofs; bulbs, though not the main fields which are in Zuid Holland; windmills, old towns, small wooden houses and costumes. Historically the area includes what was known as the Noorderkwartier-West Friesland, the seven principal towns here (Hoorn, Alkmaar, Enkhuizen, Medemblik, Edam, Monnickendam, and Purmerend) boasting their own regional council which met in the fine Staten-College (now the Westfries Museum) in Hoorn. Of these towns, Hoorn, Edam and Alkmaar, with its cheese market, are among the most attractive in Holland. West Friesland, the name recalling one of the Frisian districts recognised by Charlemagne (see Province of Friesland), is today the district enclosed by Schagen, Hoorn and Enkhuizen, and is not a part of Friesland.

Among other features of this northern part of Noord Holland are the Beemster, Wormer, and Purmer polders (just N of Amsterdam), now quiet agricultural and pastoral corners but once the home of whaling ports; the over-visited 'tourist triangle' of Monnickendam-Marken-Volendam; the Zuider Zee Museum at Enkhuizen; the two remarkable dike roads across the water, one across the IJsselmeer linking Enkhuizen to Lelystad, the other (the Afsluitdijk) sealing off the lake and providing the road link to Friesland; and the island of Texel. The *Noordhollands Kanaal*, 80km long and running from Amsterdam to Den Helder, was cut in 1819–25 with the purpose of regaining for Amsterdam the transit trade that had been lost by the silting up of the approach from what was then the Zuider Zee. Though a remarkable achievement at the time, the canal, too narrow and too shallow, was soon found inadequate and was superseded by the Noordzee Kanaal.

**Zuid Holland**. The province's principal cities—all historic places of great interest and character, and with fine museums and art galleries—are The Hague, Leiden, Delft, Rotterdam and its huge port area, Gouda, and Dordrecht. Except in the industrial areas surrounding the large towns the province is concerned with agriculture and horticulture, the most famed and visited district being that of the bulbfields stretching northward between Leiden and Haarlem. Other districts of interest are Westland (to the S of The Hague) with a vast expanse of glasshouses, the tree nurseries around Boskoop (N of Gouda), and, to the N of Dordrecht, the Alblasserwaard with the Kinderdijk windmills. To the S of Rotterdam are the two agricultural 'islands' of Voorn-en-Putten and Goeree-Overflakkee, both with beaches and many facilities for water sports. Either side of the Haringvliet, they are linked at the E end by the Haringvlietbrug and at the W end by Haringvlietdam.

**Zeeland**, with, true to its name, nearly as much water as land and with much of the land below sea level, embraces the southern mainland district known as Zeeland Flanders, connected to the remainder of the province only by ferries, and also two peninsulas either side of the Oosterschelde and linked in the W by the Oosterscheldedam and, further E, by the long and graceful Zeelandbrug. The northern peninsula comprises Schouwen, Duiveland and, to the E across the Philipsdam, St Philipsland and Tholen; the southern peninsula is made up of Noord and Zuid Beveland and Walcheren. To the visitor Zeeland offers ever-changing water vistas; beaches, marinas, and many facilities for water sports; quiet agricultural polder areas, with remote corners awaiting discovery; the giant Oosterscheldedam, with its storm-surge sluices and exhibition; and a number of historic and attractive old towns, some of them flourishing ports until the silting up of their approaches. Towns especially worth visiting are Brouwershaven, Zierikzee, Middelburg, and in Zeeland Flanders, Hulst and Sluis.

# Amsterdam

**AMSTERDAM** (700,000 inhab.), the Netherlands' largest city and the national capital (though not the seat of the government, which is at The Hague), stands on the S side of the IJ, a chain of lagoons, now almost entirely docks, forming a long inlet at the SW corner of the IJsselmeer, here the Markerwaard. Connected with the North Sea by the Noordzee Kanaal, constructed for ocean-going vessels in 1865–76, Amsterdam has the largest freshwater harbour in Europe. Much of the city rests on huge piles driven some 20m through the marshy surface soil to reach firmer ground below.

The city is visited principally for its many picturesque canals, crossed by around 1000 bridges and in large part lined by attractive old houses, many built by prosperous merchants, and also for its wealth of museums, notably the Rijksmuseum with its magnificent collection of Dutch paintings. Amsterdam can also be a convenient base from which to sample much of the essence of the Netherlands, whether famed nearby cities or such typically Dutch features as bulb-fields and windmills. See City Tours and Other Excursions, below.

In plan the main city is a crescent (this shape dating from the planned expansion of the early 17C), with concentric rings of canals, intersected by radiating streets and, on the SE, by the main stream of the Amstel, the original dam at the mouth of which gave the city its name. The canals are flushed into the Amstel roughly every two days, thus ensuring that there is no stagnant water. The outermost ring-canal is the Singelgracht, marking the limit of the city until the mid 19C; further in, Prinsengracht, Keizersgracht, and Herengracht mark the successive stages of the 17C expansion. Further in again, although some waterways have been filled in, Singel, Kloveniersburgwal, and Geldersekade form the line of the 16C moat, while the boundary of mid 14C Amsterdam was Voorburgwal (Oude Zijds and Nieuwe Zijds—old and new sides—respectively E and W of the Amstel, the course of which, until in recent times largely filled in, was along the line of Rokin and Damrak, the latter forming the inner harbour).

**Centre**. Dam.

**VVV**. There are three VVV offices, the principal one being in Stationsplein in front of the Centraal Station (Easter–June, Sept: Mon–Sat, 09.00 to 23.00; Sun, 09.00 to 21.00; July and Aug: daily 09.00 to 23.00; Oct–Easter: Mon–Sat 09.00 to 17.00; Sun 10.00 to 13.00. 14.00 to 17.00.) There is another office at Leidsestraat 106 (Leidseplein), possibly easier for motorists and conveniently close to the Rijksmuseum (Easter–Sept: daily, 09.00 to 22.30; Oct–Easter: Mon–Fri, 10.30 to 19.00; Sat, 10.30 to 21.00; Sun, 10.30 to 18.00). A third office is located at the A2 entrance to the S of the city just S of the bridge over the Amstel (the Utrechtsebrug) (Easter–Sept: Mon–Sat, 10.30 to 14.00. 14.30 to 18.30).

For postal or telephone enquiries: PO Box 3901, 1001 AS Amsterdam. Tel: (020) 6266444; after 17.00 and on Sundays, Tel: (020) 6221016.

**Station**. Centraal (800m NE of the Dam). Information office open Mon–Fri, 08.00 to 22.00; Sat, Sun, Holidays, 09.00 to 18.00. Tel: (020) 6238383).

**Post Office**. The principal post office is at Singel 250 (open Mon-Fri 08.30 to 21.00; Sat 09.00 to 12.00. Tel. (020) 555 8911).

**Airport**. Schiphol, off motorway A4 10km SW. Train link.

**Public Transport**. Metro, tram and bus services until midnight, then night buses. GVB (Municipal Transport Board) information and ticket offices in Stationsplein and at Leidseplein 15 (Mon–Fri, 07.00 to 22.30; Sat, Sun, 08.00 to 22.30. Tel: (020) 6272727). Amsterdam Day Tickets, valid on every metro, tram and bus line, can be bought from tram and bus drivers and at metro stations. Tickets valid for longer periods are obtainable only from the GVB offices in Stationsplein or Leidseplein.

**City Tours and Other Excursions**. Booking through VVV for a choice of Amsterdam tours (generally half a day). Also for a wide variety of excursions further afield (e.g. The Hague, Rotterdam, Delft, Alkmaar Cheese Market, Zuider Zee, Afsluitsdijk, Marken, bulb-fields and Keukenhof, windmills).

**City Canal Tours**. These are the traditional, most popular and most pleasant way to gain an impression of Amsterdam. Frequent departures, duration about one hour, multilingual commentaries. Several embarkation points, notably Prins Hendrikkade and Damrak, both near the station; Oude Turfmarkt (by Rokin); and points along the Singelgracht not far from the Rijksmuseum. For the independent, pedalos can be rented.

**Diamonds**. The art of diamond cutting and polishing was introduced to Amsterdam in 1576 or 1586 by Louis de Berguem of Bruges, a refugee from the Spanish Netherlands, and for long remained a Jewish monopoly. The trade received a boost early in the 18C when the United Provinces was granted a monopoly for handling the newly discovered Brazilian diamonds, and again after 1867 as the result of the opening of the South African fields. Such famed stones as the Cullinan and the Koh-i-Nohr were cut here. Until the Second World War diamond workshops were concentrated in the district around Waterlooplein, but firms are now in various parts of the city. Arrangements may be made through VVV, but listed below are some firms offering guided tours. All are normally open Monday–Saturday, but there are seasonal variations to Sunday opening.

Amsterdam Diamond Centre, Rokin 1–5. Tel: (020) 6245787.
AS Bonebakker, Rokin 86. Tel: (020) 6235972.
Coster Diamonds, Paulus Potterstraat 2–4. Tel: (020) 6762222.
Samuel Gasson, Nieuwe Achtergracht 17–23. Tel: (020) 6225333.
Holshuysen-Stoeltie, Wagenstraat 13–17. Tel: (020) 6237601.
Van Moppes, Albert Cuypstraat 2–6. Tel (020) 6761242.

**History**. Until the 13C the site of Amsterdam was occupied by a small fishing settlement held as a fief of the bishops of Utrecht by the lords of Amstel, whose seat was at Ouderkerk, 8km S of today's city centre. In 1204 Gysbert II of Amstel built a castle here, and some time during 1264–75 a dam was thrown across the mouth of the Amstel river, the site being that occupied today by the Dam, the city centre. By 1275 the township which had developed was of sufficient importance to be offered exemption from county taxes by Count Floris V of Holland, this gesture being part of the continual effort by the counts to annex the lands of the bishops, an effort which was soon successful in the case of Amsterdam; the document conferring the exemption is the earliest in which the name Amsterdam appears. In 1300 the town received municipal rights.

From the late 14C on Amsterdam became increasingly prosperous in the Baltic trade, particularly in grain, and by the 16C the town was an important commodities market, this prosperity being much helped by the persecutions in Flanders and elsewhere which drove many enterprising merchants, Jews and others, into the tolerant northern Netherlands. In 1578 Amsterdam sided formally with the enemies of Spain, this change from Roman Catholic to Calvinist becoming known as the 'Alteratie'.

Prosperity and immigration led to a rapidly increasing population which had to find space in a town which had grown little in area since the early 15C. By c 1600 it was obvious that major expansion was urgent and the following decades saw the growth of today's crescent shape with its concentric canals. For the most part this expansion was for the benefit of the wealthy—witness the patrician houses lining the canals—but the expansion also included the district known as the Jordaan, built to a more modest pattern by Hendrik Staets for artisans. This whole expansion stands as an example of early town planning, with land divided into plots, minimum distances between the backs of houses and restrictions on commercial and industrial use.

The Treaty of Münster (1648), which by closing the Scheldt ruined Antwerp, assured Amsterdam's prosperity for many years to come.

Amsterdam at first held out against the stadholders, in 1650 even opening the dikes to prevent the entry of William II, but by 1672 it was a staunch supporter of William III against Louis XIV. A century later, though, in 1795, the city was occupied by French revolutionary troops, becoming first a part of the Batavian Republic and then in 1806 capital of the Kingdom of the Netherlands, with Louis Bonaparte as King.

During the 17C and 18C Amsterdam was the banking centre of the world, this in large measure resulting from the asylum afforded to Jews, elsewhere much persecuted. Commercially, though, Amsterdam's trade was progressively threatened throughout the 18C by the silting of the Zuider Zee channels. The digging of the Noordhollands Kanaal (opened 1825) did not bring the expected relief, and in fact the valuable commodities transit trade did not really return until after the opening of the Noordzee Kanaal in 1876. With this return of prosperity came further increases in population, accompanied by a new social conscience in the field of housing and an increased awareness of the requirements of public health, the consequent building programme transforming much of the inner city as canals were filled in and streets widened; at the same time the city embarked on its continuing outward expansion.

Notable dates after the First World War were 1926 when the city took over what was then the small airport of Schiphol; 1928 when Amsterdam was the site of the Olympic Games; and 1936 when, to relieve unemployment, the recreation area of the Amsterdamse Bos was laid out. During the Second World War Amsterdam suffered little from direct military action, but the important Jewish colony virtually disappeared under German persecution.

**Natives and Others**. Amsterdam was the birthplace of Baruch Spinoza (1632–77), the philosopher, born of Portuguese Jewish parents; also of several painters, among these Thomas de Keyser (1596–1667), Salomon and Philips Koninck (1609–56, 1619–88), Jan Baptist and Jan Weenix (1621–before 1664, ?1642–1719), Karel Dujardin (?1621/2–78), Eglon van der Neer (?1634–1703), Werner van Valckert (c 1585–c 1627/8), Jan Verkolje (1650–93), Adriaen van der Velde (1636–72), Esaias van de Velde (c 1590–1630), Meindert Hobbema (1638–1709), Rachel Ruysch (1664–1750), and Cornelis Troost (1697–1750).

Kiliaen van Rensselaer (1595–1643), founder of the colony of Rensselaerwijk (now Albany, Rensselaer, and Columbia counties, New York), though born at Hasselt in Belgium, spent much of his life in Amsterdam, and is buried in the Oude Kerk. Wouter van Twiller, governor of New Amsterdam (New York), died here in 1646. John Locke (1632–1704), the English philosopher, lived in Amsterdam during his exile (1684–88), using the name Dr Van der Linden; later he moved to Rotterdam, then returned to England on the same ship that carried Mary, wife of Stadholder William III.

**Routes from Amsterdam**. To Alkmaar, Den Helder, and the Afsluitdijk, see Rte 2; to Hoorn, Enkhuizen, and Medemblik, see Rte 3; to Hilversum, see Rte 4; to Gouda and Rotterdam, see Rte 9; to Utrecht, see Rte 17A.

## Summary of Museums and Art Galleries

To help visitors make their choice the list below summarises Amsterdam's museums and art galleries. The list is in order of mention in the text. For opening times, see under individual entries.

**Koninklijk Paleis**: sculpture and paintings within a historic former town hall and royal palace.

**Museum Amstelkring**: clandestine 17C Catholic church (Our Lord in the Attic).

*****Amsterdams Historisch Museum**: the story of the growth of Amsterdam, displayed in former orphanage buildings.

**Madame Tussaud**: waxworks.

**University Library and Script Museum**: handwriting from prehistoric to modern days.

**Allard Pierson Museum**: Egyptian, Near Eastern, Greek and Roman antiquities.

*****Rembrandthuis**: Rembrandt's home, with his etchings.

**Joods Historisch Museum**: the story of the Jews in the Netherlands and Amsterdam.

**Nederlands Historisch Scheepvaartsmuseum**: national maritime history.

**'t Kromhout**: old marine engines at a 19C dock.

**Zoologisch Museum**: of the University.

**Tropenmuseum**: the peoples of the tropics and sub-tropics.

**Bijbelsmuseum:** the Bible; in two 18C canal houses.

**Informatie-Centrum Dienst Ruimtelijke Ordening**: Amsterdam town planning.

**Fodor Museum**: temporary exhibitions (Amsterdam artists).

**Museum van Loon**: a 17–18C patrician house showing contemporary family portraits.

**Museum Willet Holthuysen**: glass, ceramics, silver and goldware. Period rooms in a 17C house.

*****Six Collection**: works by Rembrandt and others shown in a house of c 1700.

**NINT**: industry and technology.

**Verzets**: the Dutch 1940–45 Resistance.

******Rijksmuseum**: the country's star national museum. Dutch and other paintings; sculpture, applied art, historical and oriental collections.

******Rijksmuseum Vincent van Gogh**: many works by Van Gogh and his contemporaries.

**Stedelijk Museum**: modern art. Frequent temporary exhibitions.

**Nederlands Film Museum**: film exhibits. Documentation.

**Electric Tram Museum**: vintage tram rides.

**Bosmuseum**: information on the Amsterdamse Bos.

**Aviodome**: air and space travel.

**Spaarpottenmuseum**: money-boxes.

*****Anne Frank Huis**: home and refuge of the Jewish family Frank (1942–44), the diary of whose daughter Anne became world-famous.

**Theatre Museum**: theatre material in a fine 17C house.

# A. Inner Amsterdam

Inner Amsterdam is described in four sections: around the Dam, and North-East, East, and South of the Dam. For the district West of the Dam, see D. Western Amsterdam.

## Around the Dam

The DAM, today a busy spacious square, has been the heart of Amsterdam ever since the first dam was thrown across the Amstel at this spot in c 1270. This is thus a fitting site for the *Nationaal Monument*, commemorating all who died in 1940–45; the urns contain soil from each province and from Indonesia.

The whole of the W side of the Dam is taken up by the **Koninklijk Paleis** (1648–55), designed by Jacob van Campen, completed by Daniel Stalpaert, and originally serving as the town hall, successor to a Gothic predecessor near this same site, burnt down in 1652. In 1808 the building was converted to a royal palace by Louis Bonaparte, but it was handed back to the city by King William I, so that the reigning monarch when in residence became the guest of the city. In 1935 the city sold the palace to the state. Resting on foundations of no fewer than 13,659 piles, the large square building is classical in style; the noticeable absence of any formal central doorway was deliberate, the object being to prevent sudden entrance being forced by a mob. It should be borne in mind that as well as being the administrative headquarters of city government and the principal place for receiving honoured guests, the Town Hall was also the seat of magistracy and the city bank. Untold wealth lay in its vaults. The external sculptural ornament is by Artus Quellin the Elder, the pediments representing Amsterdam as a port surrounded by marine deities on the front, and by river gods at the back. Above are figures of Peace, between Prudence and Justice; and Atlas, between Temperance and Vigilance. The cupola bears a weathervane in the form of a galleon ('t Koggeschip, the 'Dutch cog' of 15–16C English literature).

Inside the palace (June–mid Sept: daily, 12.30 to last entry at 15.40) the first room is the Vierschaar, or Tribunal, with SCULPTURES by Quellin, the main piece comprising reliefs of Justice, Wisdom, and Mercy, separated by caryatids. The magnificent Burgerzaal above (the citizens' hall; for Louis, his throne room) has a lower part entirely of marble. The sculptures here are of the school of Quellin, while the ceiling paintings date from the early 18C. Richly decorated galleries surround the Burgerzaal, a feature of the sculptures being that the subjects above the doors relate to the function of the room beyond. Two adjacent reliefs, symbolising Fidelity (a dog watching over his dead master) and Secrecy (a figure of Silence), are ascribed to Rombout Verhulst. The large paintings of early Dutch history are by Jan Lievens, Jacob Jordaens, Govert Flinck, and Juriaan Ovens. The painting by Ovens of the Conspiracy of Claudius Civilis was preferred by the municipal authorities to a rendering of the same subject by Rembrandt (the cut-down remainder is now in Stockholm)—the reason for this rejection probably being that Rembrandt did not follow the iconographical programme of the series from its source in an earlier 17C book by Otto van Veen. The Schepenzaal, the large room in the centre of the west wing, contains a picture of Moses the Lawgiver by Ferdinand Bol, above a rich chimneypiece. There are also fine chimneypieces in the rooms opening off the E wing, and paintings from Roman history by Flinck, Bol, and Lievens. Whereas the sculpture describes the functions of the various parts of the building, the paintings celebrate the values of the ruling group of patricians who saw themselves very much in the character of Roman senators. The balcony gallery, offering a view from above of the Quellin reliefs, was used for the reading of proclamations, while it was to the small room next door that the condemned were brought before stepping out to execution. The northern room beyond has scenes from the Old Testament by Flinck and J.G. van Bronkhorst, the Blessing of Moses (1736–38) by Jacob de Wit, and *trompe-l'oeil* paintings above the doors, also by De Wit.

*Façade of the Koninklijk Paleis (1648–55) with the Nieuwe Kerk (begun c 1408) in the background*

To the N of the palace stands the **Nieuwe Kerk**, which, despite its name, was begun in about 1408 (though twice burnt down and rebuilt during the ensuing century) largely through the benefactions of Willem Eggert, lord of Purmerend, who dedicated it to St Catherine. The north transept was completed in 1538–44, but the whole church was again badly damaged by fire in 1645, one result being that little of the interior furnishing is earlier than that date. It is here that the nation's royal investitures are solemnised. The church is in principle open Mon–Sat, 11.00 to 16.00; Sun, 12.00 to 15.00; closed Jan and Feb, but it is much used for exhibitions, concerts and suchlike, which may not only hide features of church interest, but may also confront the visitor with a stiff entry charge.

The interior contains a number of monuments to admirals: to the left of the west door, Van Kinsbergen (1735–1819) by P.J. Gabriel; in the north transept the tomb by Rombout Verhulst of Jan van Galen, who died in 1653 after a battle at Leghorn; in the choir a monument by Verhulst to De Ruyter (1607–76), who died at Syracuse of wounds received in battle against the French Admiral Duquesne; on a nearby pillar a bust-medallion of Admiral Bentinck (1745–1831). Also noteworthy are the panels of the organ case by J.G. van Bronkhorst; the pulpit of 1648 carved by Aelbert Vinckenbrink on the model of one lost in the fire; a window in the north transept containing all that is left of the stained glass of c 1650 by Bronkhorst (Count William IV granting arms to the city); in the S choir aisle a small painted memorial to Willem Eggert, the church's early benefactor; on a pillar in the south transept the urn of the poet Joost van den Vondel (1586–1679); and the brass and marble choir screen (c 1650) by Johan and Jacob Lutma.

Just N of the church a small street called Blaeuerf (Blaeu's premises) was where the famous atlases and globes of Johannes Blaeu were produced during the 17C. The main *Post Office* (1908) is immediately W of the palace and church.

## North-East of the Dam

Four parallel streets lead NE from the Dam towards the station, the most northerly being Nieuwe Zijds Voorburgwal, a broad street, once a canal, with some good façades. South of this runs Nieuwendijk, a narrow pedestrian shopping street, after Warmoesstraat (see below) the second of the city's early business streets. In Nieuwe Zijds Kolk, a small street linking the northern end of Nieuwendijk with Nieuwe Zijds Voorburgwal, is the attractive *Korenmetershuisje*, a small guildhouse of 1620. Next comes the broad and busy Damrak, once the inner harbour, today lined by hotels, cafés, and department stores (for an idea of the Damrak in the 17C, see picture by Jacob van Ruisdael in the Boymans-Van Beuningen Museum in Rotterdam). Damrak skirts BEURSPLEIN with the *Effectenbeurs* (Stock Exchange) and, to the N, the *Koopmansbeurs* (Commercial Exchange), a building of 1898–1903 by H.P. Berlage standing on 5000 piles; the decorative sculptures are by Mendes da Costa and L. Zijl. The water beside the N end of Damrak is all that is left of the former inner harbour. To the NE spreads the **Centraal Station**, a huge building of 1885 by P.J.H. Cuijpers which during its construction proved too heavy for its pile-foundations (9000) and partially subsided. The southernmost of the four streets is the narrow Warmoesstraat, the original main street of the city.

The **Oude Kerk** (Mon–Sat, 10.00 to 16.00), the oldest parish church in Amsterdam, is just E of Warmoesstraat about half-way along the street. The church was founded at the end of the 13C (there are Romanesque traces from this period), but the present Gothic building, dedicated to St Nicolaas in 1306, dates from the 14C, thereafter being gradually enlarged, principally during the two following centuries. The spire (1566) is by Joost

ALK

## Central Amsterdam

0 ——— 300m
0 ——— 300 yds

Claes Anslo

Noorderkerk
Noorder Plein

Brouwers Gracht

HEREN MARKT

Oude Ambachten

Nieuwe Luthersekerk

EGELANTIERS
EGELANTIERS GRACHT

BLOEM GRACHT
BLOEM STRAAT

Anne Frank Huis

Westerkerk

WESTER MARKT

Toneelmuseum

Spaarpotten Museum

Koninklijk Paleis

P.O.

Museum Amstelkring

Koopmansbeurs

Beurs Plein

Nieuwe Kerk

Effecten beurs

Oude Kerk

Dam

National Monument

ROZEN STRAAT

REE STR

DAMSTRAAT

ST. LUCIEN STEEG

Stadhuis

LAURIER GRACHT

BEREN STR

WOLVEN STRAAT

Historisch Museum

Begijnhof

Agnietenkapel

GEBED ZONDER END

ELANDS GRACHT

HUIDENSTRAAT

Bijbels Museum

University Library

Rasphuis

Allard Pierson Museum

Englis Churc

STAALSTRA

Munttoren

FLOWER MARKET

Amste

Raam Plein

Leidse

Munt Plein

Rembrandts Plein

AMSTEL

Stads Schouwburg

VVV

Thorbecke Plein

Museum Willet Holthuyse

Leidse Plein

Fodor Museum

STAD HOUDERS

WETERING

Museum Van Loon

SCHANS

NOORDER STRAAT

Rijksmuseum

Wetering plantsoen

WETERING SCHANS

JAN LUU KENN STRAAT

POTTER STRAAT

Van Gogh Museum

HOBBEMA KADE

Singel Gracht

Stedelijk Museum

Museum Plein

STAD HOUDERS

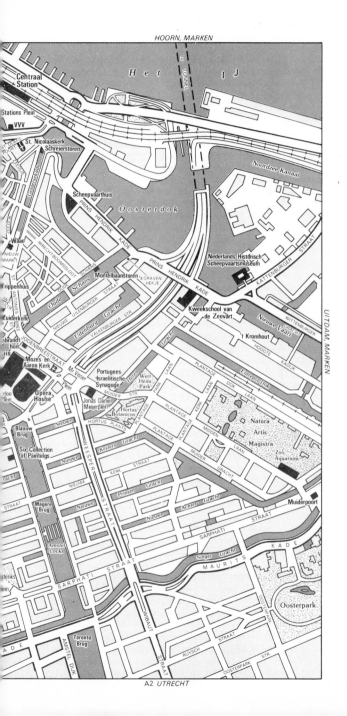

Bilhamer and contains a carillon of 1658 by François Hemony.

Features of the interior include 15C paintings on the vaults, revealed during restoration in 1955; the pulpit of 1642; in the choir ambulatory a memorial window to the Treaty of Münster, designed in 1655 and installed in 1911; the choir screen of 1681; and the two organs, the smaller in the north aisle dating from 1658 and the large one from 1724. In the north choir aisle (the Mariakapel) there are three fine windows (1555). Two of these, illustrating the Annunciation and the Adoration of the Shepherds, were carried out by Digman Meynaertsz. to designs by Lambert van Noort; the third, Death of Mary, is ascribed to Dirk Crabeth. A view of the interior as it was in the 17C can be seen in a picture by Emmanuel de Witte in the Mauritshuis in The Hague. Around the interior are memorials to admirals, all killed in action. These include, in the north choir aisle, Jacob van Heemskerk (1567–1607), who fell at the victorious battle of Gibraltar against the Spanish; at the crossing, Cornelis de Haan, killed in 1633 fighting Dunkirk privateers; at the west end of the north aisle, Willem van der Zaan, killed in 1669, this memorial being by Rombout Verhulst; and, in the south-west chapel, Abraham van der Hulst (1619–66), Gillis Schey (1644–1703), and Isaac Sweers, killed off Kijkduin in 1673, this monument also by Verhulst. A plaque on a pillar by the pulpit commemorates Kiliaen van Rensselaer, buried in this church in 1643.

Oude Zijds Voorburgwal road and canal, with many attractive old houses, run along the E side of the Oude Kerk. A short way N is the **Museum Amstelkring** (Mon–Sat, 10.00 to 17.00; Sun and Holidays, 13.00 to 17.00), occupying a merchant's house built in 1661–63 by one Jan Hartman; this was the time when Roman Catholic worship, although officially banned, was tolerated if practised inconspicuously, and Hartman, a Catholic, incorporated a church (St Nicolaas) in his attic, this extending over his canal-side house and the two smaller ones he built behind. This original attic was of three storeys, the church altar being on the lowest and the others having openings to enable worshippers to participate in the services. Later the church was enlarged and, as seen today, church and furnishings date from c 1735. The church served as parish church until the opening in 1887 of the large St Nicolaaskerk to the N on Prins Hendrikkade; after this it was taken over by a foundation and turned into a museum. Services, notably weddings, are still held in the church, now known as Our Lord in the Attic. The most notable furnishings are the altar picture The Baptism of Christ (1736) by Jacob de Wit and a curious revolving pulpit (late 18C). The church apart, the museum is worth visiting for its 17C and 18C rooms with contemporary furnishing. Among the many pictures are the Four Evangelists by Jacob de Wit (in the 17C backroom), a Virgin and a St John by Thomas de Keyser, Italian Landscape by Jan Wynants, and portraits by Jan van Bijlert and Abraham de Vries.

At its northern end Warmoesstraat reaches St Olafspoort, off which the rather sleazy Zeedijk runs SE; near the corner No. 2 is an old house with its original wooden façade. Follow Prins Hendrikkade eastwards, passing the *St Nicolaaskerk* (1887, see above) to reach the **Schreierstoren**, a rampart tower of c 1487, with a relief of 1560 and a weathervane recalling the departure of Henry Hudson from Amsterdam in 1609 on the voyage, on behalf of the Dutch East Indies Company, to find the North West Passage which led to the discovery of the Hudson River; the association between the tower's name (Weepers' Tower) and Hudson's departure seems to be more legend than fact. The tower bears plaques from the Greenwich

Village Historical Society (1927) and from the Port of New York Authority (1959).

For the district E of Oude Zijds Voorburgwal, see below (East of the Dam).

## East of the Dam

Much of the district E of the Dam—within the bounds of Warmoesstraat on the NW; Damstraat, Oude Doelenstraat, and Oude Hoogstraat on the S; and Nieuwmarkt and Geldersekade on the E—is sleazy and in part red-light. Nevertheless, with its three parallel canals and many façades parts of the district are picturesque and there are also buildings of interest.

From the Dam, Damstraat leads E to Oude Zijds Voorburgwal. On the corner the old house (No. 232) known as *Parijs* is named after its builder. In Pijlsteeg, the parallel street to the N of Damstraat, the tavern *Wynand Fockink* dates from 1609. Across the canal Damstraat is continued by Oude Doelenstraat to cross another canal, Oude Zijds Achterburgwal. (For the streets to the S, see South of the Dam.) You can follow Achterburgwal N to the short Koestraat, the second turning to the right. Here there are carvings of Faith, Hope, and Charity on Nos 7–11, while No. 10 was the guild-house of the wine merchants. From the E end of Koestraat, to the right across Kloveniersburgwal, can be seen the *Trippenhuis*, built in 1660–62 by Philips Vingboons for the brothers Louis and Hendrik Trip, two wealthy gun-makers, and between 1815 and 1885 the home of the Rijksmuseum; note the mortar chimneys and the gun-barrel motif on the pediment.

Kloveniersburgwal, followed N, ends at the NIEUWMARKT, with the pinnacled gateway originally known as *St Anthoniespoort*. There was a gate here at the end of the 14C, but the present building dates from 1488. By the end of the 16C, with the city expanding, there was no longer a requirement for a gate and in 1617 the ground floor was converted to a *Waag*, a weigh-house for the cannon and anchors being built nearby, while the rest of the building was taken over by the militia and by the various guilds (smiths, painters, surgeons, and masons; the mason's room is still preserved here). In the early 19C the weigh-house ceased to function, the guilds moved out, and the building served as furniture store, fencing academy, fire station, and (1891) archives. From 1926 until 1975 this was the home of the city's historical museum (now in Kalverstraat), and until 1986 the building housed the Joods Historisch Museum (now on Jonas Daniel Meijerplein). Plans are presently afoot to convert it into a TV studio.

From the NE corner of the Nieuwmarkt, Rechtboomssloot leads SE along a canal to reach the broad Oude Schans waterway. To the left, overlooking Oude Schans, stands the *Montelbaanstoren*, a rampart tower of 1512.

## South of the Dam

Two roads lead S out of the Dam; the broad Rokin, following the original course of the Amstel, all the northern part of which has been filled in, and, of more interest to the visitor, the narrow and lively Kalverstraat (pedestrians only), once serving as a cattle market but today with shops, cafés, and some pleasant façades.

At No. 92 Kalverstraat is **\*Het Amsterdams Historisch Museum** (daily, 11.00 to 17.00), where the story of the city is told in a series of rooms occupying a site with a history reaching back to the early 15C. The museum opened here in 1975 (on 27 October, precisely 700 years after the first mention of Amsterdam in an official document), moving from the cramped quarters it had occupied in the Waag since 1926. The Kalverstraat entrance is the main one, but there are others from the Begijnhof on the S and St Luciensteeg on the N; the latter gateway dates from the 16C (rebuilt 1634) and alongside there is a collection of façade stones from demolished houses.

At the beginning of the 15C this area was a triangular island enclosed by the Spui on the S, Nieuwe Zijds Voorburgwal on the W, and a large ditch, the Begijnensloot, on the E (running parallel to and immediately W of Kalverstraat). The S end of the island was occupied by the Begijnhof, and in 1414 a convent (of St Lucy) was built on the N end. In 1578, when Amsterdam sided with the Protestants, the convent was converted to Burgerweeshuis (municipal orphanage), with a new wing, by Hendrik de Keyser, built on the E side of the courtyard. Later, in c 1630, the orphanage took over an old men's home situated on the E side of the Begijnensloot, using this for orphan boys, and two years later a new gallery, attributed to Pieter de Keyser (son of Hendrik), was built to run E to W along the N side of what was now the boys' courtyard.

The orphanage now comprised two courtyards, for the boys on the E and for the girls (the old convent) on the west. In 1634 the convent buildings were demolished, giving way to new wings, designed by Jacob van Campen, on the N and W sides; the south wing, built rather later than the others, cut the old convent courtyard into two, the smaller part, alongside the Begijnhof, being used as a playground. As a part of this reconstruction the girls' orphanage was given its own entrance in St Luciensteeg. The next major change came in 1745 when Hendrik de Keyser's E wing was given external and internal renovation to bring it into harmony with the other wings. At about the same time a start was made with covering the Begijnensloot, which was entirely filled in by 1865. The orphanage moved out in 1960. Recent (1960s and 1970s) restoration and conversion to a museum (by B. van Kasteel and J. Schipper) has as far as possible retained the exterior façades, and has also produced one imaginative change, namely the Civic Guard Gallery, running along the former course of the Begijnensloot.

The gateway off Kalverstraat (Joost Bilhamer, 1581) carries figures of a boy and a girl orphan; the verse carved below (asking for contributions) is by the poet Joost van den Vondel. Beyond the gateway is Pieter de Keyser's gallery of 1632, with the restaurant to the right, on the site of the convent cowshed and later of the orphanage carpentry workshop; the restaurant takes its name from carved figures of David and Goliath (c 1650) which until 1862 stood in a maze in Jordaan (see D. Western Amsterdam). Opposite is the boys' courtyard, formerly that of the old men, the west wing of which is used for temporary exhibitions. The adjacent Civic Guard Gallery, with free entrance and detached from the museum proper, runs as a covered 'museum street' through to the Begijnhof. This Civic Guard Gallery displays a number of group portraits of militias.

At the end of the 14C, for the purpose of imposing law and order, groups of marksmen began to band together as guilds, e.g. of St George and St Sebastian. These guilds merged in 1580, and in 1672 a formal Civic Guard was formed. The practice of commissioning group portraits dates from c 1530 and lasted well over a century. The oldest groups here are of the first half of the 16C. A gallery within the museum offers a good alternative view of the pictures.

Leaving the Civic Guard Gallery on the left you approach the museum proper which surrounds the original convent courtyard, later that of the girls of the orphanage. The story of Amsterdam is illustrated—part chrono-

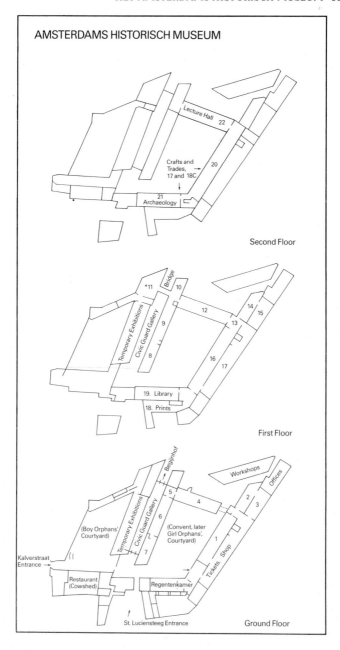

AMSTERDAMS HISTORISCH MUSEUM

Lecture Hall 22

Crafts and Trades, 17 and 18C 20

21 Archaeology

Second Floor

Bridge

*11 10

Temporary Exhibitions

Civic Guard Gallery 9 12 14 15

8 13

16 17

19. Library

18. Prints

First Floor

Begijnhof

Workshops Offices

5 2

Temporary Exhibitions

Civic Guard Gallery 6 4 3

(Boy Orphans' Courtyard)

(Convent, later Girl Orphans', Courtyard) 1

Tickets Shop

Kalverstraat Entrance

Restaurant (Cowshed) 7 Regentenkamer

St. Luciensteeg Entrance

Ground Floor

logically, part by themes—on three floors. Immediately right of the entrance is the Regentenkamer, the Regents' Chamber (not normally open), restored as nearly as possible to its 17C state.

On the GROUND FLOOR, **Room 1** is introductory, with a floor plan and an illuminated map together illustrating the growth of the city, while a large, striking painting of the IJ in 1686 by Willem van de Velde the Younger provides appropriate background. **Room 2** (Early History) is, understandably perhaps, somewhat short on material, and it is really only in **Room 3**, devoted to the growth of commerce and industry in the 14C and 15C, that the displays become interesting. Notable here are a huge metal cauldron, possibly used in shipbuilding (it was discovered during the excavation of the metro), as well as vitrines displaying shoes, tools, tailoring equipment, etc., all well presented with accompanying reproductions of old pictures showing the articles in use.

A short underground passage leads to **Room 4** and the 16C, with armour, some massive silver drinking horns, pictures by Dirk Barendsz. of The Longbowmen and by Hendrik Vroom of the IJ in c 1610, and portraits, all by unknown artists, of Charles V, Philip II, the Duke of Alva and William of Orange. But undoubtedly the most rewarding exhibit here is a bird's-eye view of Amsterdam (1538) by Cornelis Anthonisz. This is the oldest known plan of Amsterdam (N is at the bottom); the Amstel clearly divides the town, and the Dam and the adjacent old Stadhuis are clearly visible. **Room 5** illustrates marine development during the 17C and 18C, with maps and globes by Johannes Blaeu (c 1650), a portrait of Blaeu (1603) by Jan van Rossum, and several flamboyant sea scenes. The theme of **Room 6** is the growth of the city and of municipal organisations during the same two centuries. There are varied exhibits but the stars here are two picures. One, of 1656 by Johannes Lingelbach, shows the Dam with the new Stadhuis under construction and, in the centre, the old Waag (built 1565, demolished 1808), a building of key importance in the days of Amsterdam's supremacy in the commodities trade. The other picture is Adriaan van Nieulandt's * *Procession of Lepers on Copper Monday, absorbing for all its characters and other detail all admirably explained by a video film alongside. The ground floor ends with **Room 7**, concerned mainly with commerce, exemplified by portaits of the Bicker family, leaders within the Amsterdam oligarchy.

On the FIRST FLOOR, **Room 8** continues the theme of 17C and 18C commerce and finance, the latter emphasised by Job Berckheyde's picture of the courtyard of the Beurs in c 1660. (Rooms 8 and 9 both have windows offering good views of the Civic Guard Gallery.) **Room 9** describes the development of the city and daily life during the same period, with another bird's-eye view, this one by Jan Christiaan Micker, c 1620, and again with N at the foot of the picture. Church life in the 17C and 18C is the theme of **Room 10**, of particular interest being pictures of the interiors of the Oude Kerk and the Nieuwe Kerk.

A bridge across the Civic Guard Gallery leads to *°**Room 11**, a room which many visitors may well judge to be the museum's most rewarding. The theme here—Social Welfare in the 17C and 18C, or, more popularly and simply, Rich and Poor—is vividly brought home by several large portrait-groups of citizens concerned with charitable activities. Each group tells its story, and each reveals facets of contemporary life, particularly moving being two pictures of about 1650 by Jan Victors portraying the clothing and feeding of orphan girls, while a contrast is provided by Adriaen Backer's more stuffily formal group of the redoubtable Regentesses of the Burgerweeshuis (Orphanage).

Rooms 12 to 15, reached by returning across the bridge, cover further 17C and 18C themes. Elegance is the emphasis of **Room 12**, though a case of lances and muskets seems out of place; **Rooms 13** and **14** are devoted to both fine and applied art, with, among the pictures, works by Jan van Huysum and Rachel Ruysch; and **Room 15** looks at Instruction (Learned Institutions) and Amusements, notable here being the Anatomy Lesson of Professor Roëll by Cornelis Troost. **Rooms 16** and **17** bring you to the 19C and 20C; **Room 18** doubles as Print Room and home for temporary exhibitions, and **Room 19** is the Library.

On the SECOND FLOOR there is some archaeological material, but for many visitors the main interest will be provided by **Rooms 20** and **21**, Crafts and Trades of the 17C and 18C, imaginatively presented as a series of displays devoted to, for example, the baker, the distiller (with some fine old bottles), the silversmith, the brickmaker and the potter.

*The Munttoren, 1490, which formerly housed the mint. The steeple was added in 1620 by De Keyser*

You can reach the **Begijnhof**, founded in 1346, a peaceful courtyard of small old houses (16–18C), either by way of the Civic Guard Gallery, or from Spui, a street leading W off Kalverstraat, this latter entrance bearing a figure of a begijn. In the Begijnhof, the *Houten Huis* (No. 34), the wooden house, dates from c 1470 (restored 1957) and retains its wooden gables. No. 35 is a café and information centre. The church in the centre was granted to the Scottish Presbyterians in 1607 and rebuilt in 1727, while the inconspicuous little Roman Catholic chapel facing it dates from 1671 and functioned as a hidden church until 1795.

The waxworks museum, *Madame Tussaud*, formerly at Kalverstraat 156, is now on the Dam at the Peek & Cloppenberg building (open every day 10.00 to 17.30). Here, from both past and present but always changing, stand the famous and the infamous, and here too you can see models being fashioned in the workshop. Other attractions include a room devoted to Rembrandt and another to the grotesque world of Hieronymus Bosch.

Opposite the Begijnhof, Voetboogstraat leads S off Spui to reach Heiligeweg. Opposite the road junction is the doorway of the *Rasphuis*, with sculptures in the style of De Keyser (1603) and later (1663); this was once a small prison where petty criminals had to rasp brazilwood for use in dyeing. At its W end Spui reaches the Singel canal, the moat of 16C Amsterdam. To the left is the *University Library* (Mon–Fri, 10.00 to 13.00. 14.00 to 16.30), housing the Joost van den Vondel Collection and also a Script Museum tracing the story of writing from prehistoric to modern days. Across the bridge the S side of the canal may be followed eastward, passing the *Flower Market*, in operation since at least the 18C, and *D'Eendragt*, a picturesque warehouse with six storeys of numbered doors, to reach MUNT-PLEIN, at the S end of Rokin and in medieval times the sheep market. Here stands the **Munttoren**, a tower of 1490 with a steeple of 1620 by De Keyser, which formerly housed the mint.

*Houses in the Oude Turfmarkt*

For the district E of Muntplein, see B. Eastern Amsterdam.

The bridge leading NE from Muntplein crosses what is the end of the Amstel, where it becomes the Rokin, Oude Turfmarkt then running northwards beside the water and soon reaching the **Allard Pierson Museum** (Tues–Fri, 10.00 to 17.00; Sat, Sun, Holidays, 13.00 to 17.00), founded in 1934 in honour of the scholar and humanist Allard Pierson and housing the University of Amsterdam's archaeological collections, the emphasis on Egypt, the Near East and the Mediterranean.

In the HALL there is a shaft-grave of c 2000 BC. On the FIRST FLOOR, the first four rooms display Egyptian material, including a papyrus Book of the Dead, a model boat complete with oarsmen, and many everyday articles—bronze statuettes, jewellery, combs, etc.—the majority of these intended for the owner's use in the Nether World. The next three rooms are devoted in turn to the Near East (tablets with cuneiform writing, cylinder seals, and some notable Iranian pottery); Crete, Mycenaean Greece and Cyprus, notable here being a Mycenaean bowl of 1300 BC; and finally, in **Room 7** across a passage, Coptic material including some interesting clothing with a child's shoes and jerkin, the latter still retaining well its colour of the 5–9C.

On the SECOND FLOOR the progression (roughly anticlockwise) is through Greece and southern Italy (**Rooms 8–14**), through Etruria (**Room 15**) to the Romans (**Rooms 16–18**). Vases are the main theme of the Grecian rooms, these ranging from the 7C BC in **Room 8**; to (in **Room 9**) black-figured pottery of the Archaic period; on to red-figured vases of the 5C BC in **Room 11**; and finally, in **Room 12**, small black Attic pottery contrasting with some large vases from the Greek colonies in southern Italy. Beyond, the Etruscans are represented by votive offerings and bronzes; the Romans by a huge sarcophagus, jewellery (displayed on a special platform), small bronze gods, oil lamps and a variety of other homely articles.

Now follow Lange Brugsteeg and Grimburgwal east. A passage leading N off the latter, with the curious name Gebed Zonder End (Prayer without end), was in the 15C the route between several religious houses. Passing the S ends of Oude Zijds Voorburgwal and Oude Zijds Achterburgwal, Grimburgwal ends roughly opposite the entrance to a passageway called Oudemanhuispoort (the old men's house gate), once the gateway to a hospice, the buildings of which, rebuilt in 1754, now house a part of the university. The passageway is known for its second-hand bookstalls. There are many good façades along the Achterburgwal, and here too, on the W side at the S end, is the gateway of the *Agnietenkapel*, adapted in 1631–32 to house the Athenaeum Illustre, the forerunner of the university. Notable buildings on the Voorburgwal are the *Oude Vleeshuis* (No. 274), with cattle heads on the gable; alongside, a shop claiming to be the oldest butcher in Amsterdam; and the *Bank van Lening* (No. 300), the municipal pawnbroker, a picturesque group of which the oldest part dates from 1584. The *Stadhuis* (but see Waterlooplein below), between Voorburgwal and Achterburgwal, has since 1808 occupied a building erected in 1578 as a residence for the stadholders and almost completely rebuilt in 1927.

# B.  Eastern Amsterdam

From the Dam, Damstraat, Oude Doelenstraat, Oude Hoogstraat and Nieuwe Hoogstraat lead E to reach St Antonies Breestraat, coming from

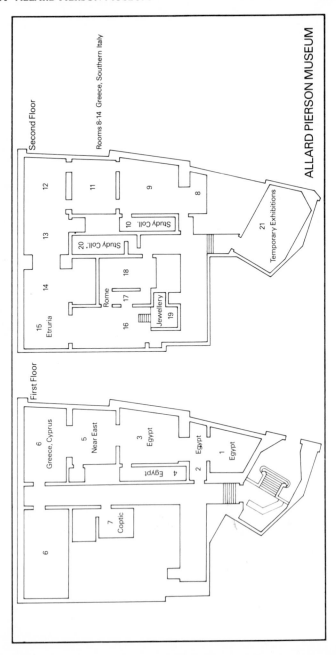

ALLARD PIERSON MUSEUM

Second Floor

Rooms 8-14 Greece, Southern Italy

12
11
9
8

13
10  Study Coll.

20  Study Coll.

14
18

Rome
17
16

15
Etruria

Jewellery
19

21
Temporary Exhibitions

First Floor

6
Greece, Cyprus

5
Near East

3
Egypt

4  Egypt

2

1
Egypt

Egypt

7
Coptic

6

the Nieuwmarkt. For the district N of this line of streets, see above (East of the Dam); for the district to the S, see above (South of the Dam).

The former *Zuiderkerk*, just S of Nieuwe Hoogstraat, was the first church founded in Amsterdam after the Reformation. Built in 1603–11 to a design by Hendrik de Keyser, the church is now used for concerts. Further S there are two quiet canals, the Raamgracht and, running S from it, the Groen Burgwal. On the bank of the latter is the *English Church*, and in the Staalstraat, which crosses Groen Burgwal, is the *Saaihal* (Cloth Hall) of 1641.

St Antonies Breestraat (with at No. 69 the *De Pinto Huis* of 1605, re-modelled after 1651; the building is now a library and information centre for European heritage projects), followed S, crosses a canal and becomes Jodenbreestraat, which until the German persecution of the Second World War was the chief thoroughfare of the Jewish quarter. After the murder or deportation of the inhabitants their deserted and gutted houses were pulled down for the sake of the timber during the wartime fuel famine, and much of the area was cleared by the construction of the approach to the IJ tunnel.

The \***REMBRANDTHUIS** (Mon–Sat, 10.00 to 17.00; Sun and Hol, 13.00 to 17.00; closed 1 January), at the W end of Jodenbreestraat, was built in 1606 and was Rembrandt's home from 1639–60, the lower floor being the domestic quarters, the upper floor the studio, and the attic (there was no third storey at this time) a studio for the pupils, who during these years included Govert Flinck, Jacob Backer and Ferdinand Bol. Rembrandt's son Titus was born here in 1641, and the following year his wife Saskia died here. The years here were, though, those of Rembrandt's decline into bankruptcy (1656), partly caused by the purchase and running of a house such as this. In 1658 he was forced to sell, although he was allowed to stay on in the house until 1660. Soon after he left, the house was given a third storey, the earlier step gable being replaced by a classical pediment. Purchased by the city in 1906, the house was restored and opened as a museum in 1911. Its general interest apart, the house is visited for its \*\*Collection of Rembrandt's etchings of which 250 out of a possible total of 280 are held here.

The etchings in the Sydelcaemer, to the left of the entrance, include Christ presented to the people (1655); Death of the Virgin (1639); The Three Crosses (1653–60). There are also portraits of the patrician patron Jan Six (1647), the physician Ephraim Bueno (1647), and the landscape artist Jan Asselyn (1647). Beyond there is a room in which the technique of etching is explained. In the Achterkamer, at the rear of the house, are a self-portrait with Saskia (1636); a self-portrait (1648); and portraits of the artist's parents, the receiver-general Jan Uytenbogaert (1639), the publisher Clement de Jonghe (1651) and the goldsmith Johannes Lutma.

The Tussenkamer, on the entresol, contains many notable works, of special interest being the *Series of Beggars and Vagabonds (c 1630) and also a depiction of Rembrandt himself as a beggar. Here too are the Ratcatcher (1632); Beggars at the door (1648); prints on mythological themes; and several self-portraits, and portraits of the artist's parents.

On the upper floor, the Schilderkamer exhibits two themes, landscapes and biblical. Among the former the View of Amsterdam (c 1640), with its line of windmills, is of particular interest. The many biblical subjects include Presentation in the Temple (c 1639); Triumph of Mordecai (c 1641); and Christ preaching (c 1652). The De Kunst Kamer is used for temporary exhibitions illustrating various aspects of Rembrandt's work.

WATERLOOPLEIN, just SW of the Rembrandthuis and now virtually taken over by the giant Stadhuis and Opera House (1987), was the birthplace in 1632 of the philosopher Spinoza. The Mozes en Aaron Kerk, marking the E corner, is a neo-classical work of 1837–41 by T. Suys the Elder. The Waterlooplein market (Mon–Sat 10.00–16.00) is well worth a visit.

Jodenbreestraat runs into the large MR VISSERPLEIN on the far side of which stands the **Portugees-Israelitische Synagoge**, built by Elias Bouman in 1671–75 and restored in 1953–69. The synagogue has an impressive, rich interior, and within the entrance passage are set several 17C gable-stones. The **Joods Historisch Museum** (daily, 11.00 to 17.00; closed Yom Kippur), on nearby Jonas Daniel Meijerplein, is a museum of (mainly Netherlands) Jewish history.

The Jews played an important part in the life of Amsterdam from the time when the Union of Utrecht opposed persecution, then at its height throughout much of Europe and especially in Spanish territory. The Sephardic, or Spanish, Jews many of whom had been leading a precarious existence as Maranos, or crypto-Jews, flocked to the North and soon took a leading part in the banking and exchange activities of a country rapidly growing wealthier. The Ashkenazic, or German, Jews tended to occupy an inferior position.

Amsterdam, known for its toleration, sheltered the largest Jewish community in the Netherlands. Although classified as foreigners and strictly controlled as commercial competitors, the Jews were allowed a generous measure of self-government, until in 1796 they were granted full civic status.

Jewish life and culture are illustrated through temporary exhibitions and a permanent collection, the latter covering both life at home and ceremony in the synagogue, and showing also works by Jewish artists and an important collection of Second World War documents.

From Mr Visserplein, Muiderstraat leads SE across the Nieuwe Herengracht to reach the PLANTAGE, a quarter laid out in the mid 19C as a garden city. The *Hortus Botanicus* (Mon–Fri, 09.00 to 16.00; Sat, Sun, Holidays, 11.00 to 16.00), the botanic garden of the university, is immediately to the right. Founded in 1682 for the cultivation of medicinal herbs, the garden today boasts over 6000 plant species of worldwide provenance.

At this point there is a choice between going NE to the Maritime Museum or SE to the zoo and the Tropical Museum.

NORTH EAST from the botanic garden Nieuwe Herengracht leads to Prins Hendrikkade, reached at the S end of the IJ tunnel and close to the *Kweekschool van de Zeevaart*, the school of navigation, founded in 1755 but now in a building of 1880.

To the W along Prins Hendrikkade there are buildings of interest. No. 176 was the East Indies Company building of the early 17C, while, on the corner of 's Gravenhekje, the warehouses (1642) were those of the West Indies Company. Further W No. 131 is the *Huis De Ruyter*, with a relief portrait of the admiral and, beyond, decorated with figures, is the conspicuous *Scheepvaarthuis* (J.M. van der Mey, 1912). Originally the office premises of six shipping companies, this building is generally recognised to be the earliest example of Amsterdam School architecture.

A short way E Prins Hendrikkade crosses water between Oosterdok and Nieuwe Vaart, with, just beyond, the **Nederlands Historisch Scheepvaarts-museum** (Tues–Sat, 10.00 to 17.00; Sun, Holidays, 13.00 to 17.00), the national maritime museum opened in 1979 in a building which was a marine warehouse of 1657 built to a design by Daniel Stalpaert. To the front and rear there are carved pediments, that on the E depicting the Maid of Amsterdam, a crown of ships, sea gods, etc., and that on the W Neptune and Amphitrite.

The museum, which will be under expansion for several years, is arranged chronologically by themes and provides a thorough survey of the Dutch maritime story. The themes are many and often overlapping—Fishing, Navigation and Cartography, War, Trade, East India Company, Clipper Ships, Polar Expeditions, Towards Steam, to mention but a sample—and are in virtually every case effectively illustrated by superb ship models, charts, instruments and suchlike, while throughout the museum and supporting many of the themes there is a wealth of fine paintings. Among the many artists are A. Willaerts (Dutch Anchorage, 1627. Anchorage in Batavia, 1649); Hendrik Vroom (Skirmish with the English, 1614. Warship, 1628); C. van Wieringen (Battle off Gibraltar, 1622); Karel Dujardin (Admiral de Ruyter, 1669); R. Nooms (View of the IJ); Willem van de Velde the Younger (Royal Charles, 1666. Battle at Kijkduin, 1673); Willem Schellinks (Expedition to Chatham, 1667). Among actual ships inside the museum are the Royal Barge and two towing barges, while moored outside can be seen a sailing lugger, a steam ice-breaker and a lifeboat. The major attraction, however, is the full-size replica of the VOC ship the *Amsterdam*.

Visitors wishing for more on the maritime theme may visit *'t Kromhout* (Mon–Sat, 10.00 to 16.00. Sun, 13.00 to 16.00) about 1km away to the SE on the S side of Nieuwe Vaart (entrance Hoogte Kadijk 187). Here, in a 19C dock and boat-building yard, are exhibited old marine engines and other machinery while various small old vessels are moored alongside.

SOUTH EAST from the botanic garden Plantage Middenlaan skirts *Natura Artis Magistra* (usually simply *Artis*, zoo), the somewhat curious official name (Nature, Mistress of the Arts) for the **Zoological Gardens** (daily, 09.00 to 17.00), founded in 1838 by G.F. Westerman (1807–90) in one small part of the present site it has since grown and today boasts some 6000 animals, including 2000 fish which swim in the Netherlands' first and still largest aquarium. Alongside is the *Zoologisch Museum* of the University of Amsterdam (daily, except Mon and Sat, 09.00 to 17.00; closed Holidays).

Just beyond the zoo and museum Plantage Middenlaan reaches the *Muiderpoort*, a gate rebuilt in 1770, beyond again, across the bridge over the Singelgracht, being the large Royal Tropical Institute which includes the **Tropenmuseum** (Mon–Fri, 10.00 to 17.00; Sat, Sun and some Holidays, 12.00 to 17.00) in which comprehensive aspects of the lives and problems of tropical and sub-tropical peoples are imaginatively presented.

# C.  Southern Amsterdam

## Within the Singelgracht

In many ways the inner part of southern Amsterdam, the 17C–18C quarter between the Singel and the Singelgracht, is the most charming and characteristic part of the city. It is intersected by three parallel concentric canals—Herengracht, Keizersgracht, and Prinsengracht—each lined with the houses, mostly tall and narrow and often with carved façade-stones, which were occupied by the more well-to-do citizens in the heyday of the city's prosperity. The quays, though now cluttered by parked cars, are tree-lined and still comparatively peaceful. Many of the most attractive houses are within easy reach of the three main streets (Leidse, Vijzel, and Utrechtse) radiating from the southern part of the inner city. Further out is a more modern quarter (after mid 19C), with broad avenues, some pleasant open spaces, and the three great museums (Rijks, Stedelijk, and Van Gogh).

REMBRANDTSPLEIN, between Vijzelstraat and Utrechtsestraat just S of the Amstel and just E of Muntplein, is, with Thorbeckeplein adjoining on the S, the cheerful centre of Amsterdam's café and night life. In the former there is a bronze statue of Rembrandt (1852) by Louis Royer, and in the latter a statue by F.C. Leenhoff commemorating J.R. Thorbecke (1795–1872), the liberal leader and outstanding political figure during the 19C.

LEIDSESTRAAT, the northernmost of the three radiating streets referred to above, soon crosses Herengracht, along which are perhaps the best of the canal houses. An impression of this part of Herengracht as it was during the 18C can be gained from a painting by Gerrit Berckheyde in the Six Collection. To the N Nos 410–412, 388, and 362–370 date from 1662–65. Among these Nos 362–368, the *Cromhout Huizen*, were built in 1662 by Philips Vingboons and are named from the crooked piece of wood (note stone tablet) that was the trademark of a builder, Jacob Cromhout, who lived at No. 366. This is now the *Bijbelsmuseum* (Tues–Sat, 10.00 to 17.00; Sun and Holidays, 13.00 to 17.00), a non-denominational museum devoted to the Bible—its origins and its contents—and also housing an important Netherlands religious documentation centre. At the corner of Leidsegracht, by the Boogbrug of 1722, No. 394 dates from 1672 and is notable for its curved gable on a high wooden façade. To the S the houses are slightly later. Nos 436, 446, 450, 458, 460, 468, and 476 are all of 1668–70.

The houses along Keizersgracht are also attractive, Nos 319 and 401 dating from the mid 16C, No. 324 from c 1778, and No. 446 from c 1725. Here, too, at No. 440, is the *Informatie-Centrum Dienst Ruimtelijke Ordening* (Tues–Fri, 12.30 to 16.30; also on Thurs, 18.00 to 21.00), where the many aspects of the town-planning policy for Amsterdam are set out. Along Prinsengracht the houses are more modest. Leidsestraat ends at the busy Leidseplein with the *Stads Schouwburg*, the municipal theatre built in 1894.

VIJZELSTRAAT runs due S from Muntplein and first crosses Herengracht. To the E Nos 524–526 are of 1666 and No. 539 of 1720. Along the next canal, Keizersgracht, No. 604 to the W dates from 1670–71. To the E No. 609 houses the *Fodor Museum* (Tel: (020) 249919), used for temporary exhibitions mainly by Amsterdam artists. Also to the E is the **Museum Van Loon** (Mon, 10.00 to 12.00; 13.00 to 17.00) at Nos 672–674, a fine 17–18C patrician house where the Van Loon Foundation exhibits family portraits which provide a unique record of one of the leading families of the period. The house, by Adriaan Dortsman, was built in 1671–72; and the first tenant (until 1680) was the painter Ferdinand Bol. There followed a series of owners, the most important of whom were Abraham van Hagen and his wife Catharina Trip (1752) who undertook major restoration. In 1884 the house was bought by Hendrik van Loon. Restoration to a late 18C–early 19C state was carried out by the Van Loon Foundation between 1964 and 1973. Among the portrait painters represented here are J.M. Molenaer, Dirk Santvoort, Cornelis van der Voort, and Adriaen Hanneman.

Beyond Prinsengracht, Vijzelstraat becomes Vijzelgracht (a drained canal).

*Reguliersgracht*, running S from Rembrandtsplein between Vijzelstraat and Utrechtsestraat, is a canal known for its series of similar bridges though it takes its name from the religious order.

UTRECHTSESTRAAT runs out of the SE of Rembrandtsplein to cross Herengracht, with, at No. 605 (E), the **Museum Willet Holthuysen** (Tues–Sat, 10.00 to 17.00; Sun and Holidays, 13.00 to 17.00), in a patrician house of 1689, renovated 1748–58. In 1855 the owner was Pieter Holthuysen, whose daughter and only child Sandrina in 1861 married Abraham Willet. It was these two who built up the collections of glass, ceramic, silver and goldsmiths' work, paintings, and objets d'art, which they bequeathed to the city which opened the museum in 1896. The museum's scope has since been extended, and it now contains several period rooms, including an 18C kitchen, while the garden has been laid out in 18C style. Notable among the paintings are a magnificent ceiling (1748, from another house) by Jacob de Wit, and decoration in painted imitation of stucco by the same artist; also portraits by Arnold Boonen, Frans and Jan van Mieris, Johann Tischbein, and M. van Musscher.

On the Amstel, between Herengracht and Keizersgracht, a house dating from 1680 contains the *SIX COLLECTION OF PAINTINGS**, the property of the descendants of Jan Six (1618–1700), Rembrandt's friend and patron, who was also burgomaster of Amsterdam in 1691 (see etching portrait in the Rembrandthuis). Visitors are **only** admitted by card of introduction from the Rijksmuseum, obtainable, at the Rijksmuseum Information Desk on production of your passport.

The paintings are exhibited in five rooms: in the first are family portraits by Caspar Netscher, Dirk Santvoort, Thomas de Keyser, and others, including one of Cretienne Six by Cornelis Ketel (1615); some works by Pieter Saenredam, and two small portraits by Lucas van Leyden. The large Drawing Room at the end of the corridor contains Rembrandt's **Portrait of Jan Six, painted in 1654 and by many considered to be the artist's finest portrait. Here too are Rembrandt's *Portrait of Anna Wymer, mother of Jan Six (1641); a portrait of Jan Six by Gerard Terborch (1640); a portrait of Dr Nicolaes Tulp (of the Anatomy Lesson) by Frans Hals; and portraits of Dr van der Hoeve and his wife by Michiel van Miereveld. In the remaining three rooms you can see *Moonlight landscape by Aelbert Cuyp; Interior of the Grote Kerk at Rotterdam by Antonie de Lorme; Portraits of a father and son by Nicolaes Maes; Prince Frederick Henry visiting the fair at Rijswijk with the King and Queen of Bohemia (1625) by Esaias van de Velde; Portrait of the wife of Jan Six by Govert Flinck; Landscape by Jacob van Ruisdael; and a portrait of Diederick Tulp by Paulus Potter. The furniture, porcelain and silverware are also noteworthy.

From the Six Collection, a walk southwards along the Amstel passes the *Magere Brug* (the Thin Bridge), a wooden bridge some 300 years old, and the Amstel locks to reach the bridge crossed by Sarphatistraat, offering a pleasant view. The next bridge is Torontobrug, beyond which Amsteldijk accompanies the river southward, in 800m reaching Tolstraat, with, at No. 129, *NINT*, the museum of the Netherlands Institute for Industry and Technology (Mon–Fri, 10.00 to 16.00; Sat, Sun, Holidays, 13.00 to 17.00). Housed in a former diamond-cutting factory, the museum's permanent collections cover such fields as Physics, Metal, Transport, Construction, Chemistry, Energy, Telecommunications and Computers, many of the models and displays being operated by the visitor. Those with an interest in the

Second World War can make their way another 800m S for the *Verzets-museum* (Tues–Fri, 10.00 to 17.00; Sat, Sun, 13.00 to 17.00) at Lekstraat 63, the museum of the Dutch Resistance.

# Outside the Singelgracht

The famous **Rijksmuseum** (see Section E) overlooks Singelgracht from the S between Leidseplein and Weteringplantsoen at the S end of Vijzelgracht. From behind the Rijksmuseum Paulus Potterstraat leads SW, with the Rijksmuseum Vincent van Gogh and the Stedelijk Museum at the end of the street.

The **\*\*Rijksmuseum Vincent van Gogh** (Tues–Sat, 10.00 to 17.00. Sun and Holidays, 13.00 to 17.00), designed by Gerrit Rietveld and built 1963–73, houses some 200 paintings, 500 drawings, and 700 letters.

On the death in 1891 of Vincent's devoted art dealer brother Theo, the latter's widow, Jo van Gogh-Bonger (1862–1925), was left with her husband's collection, comprising many of Vincent's works, his letters, and several works by contemporary artists. She spent the remainder of her life promoting Vincent's work by exhibitions, publishing his letters, and other means. Her son, Vincent Willem van Gogh (1890–1978; there is a bust of him on the second floor), continued his mother's work. In 1962 the collection was taken over by the Vincent van Gogh Foundation and in 1972 this museum was opened.

You enter from the street up broad steps at a right angle to the glass doors of the entrance (where you might find it necessary to queue for tickets, queues are rarely long here). Then you pass into a low dark foyer with a cloakroom to the right. From here a second set of glass doors leads into the central hall which runs the whole height of the building to the glazed roof; after the cramped entrance the effect is of light and air and is most impressive. From the centre of the hall you can see all four levels with people passing up and down the staircase. The museum shop is to your right, lifts to all floors ahead and to the right (behind the stall supplying audio guides in various languages), the entrance to the café (with a glazed open-air section during fine weather, mind the step if you go outside with a loaded tray) is directly in front of you and the exhibition starts to your left.

On the GROUND FLOOR there is a display of later 19C paintings, mostly Dutch and French. These are on the whole dark and serious-looking works, they are chosen to represent the various kinds of contemporary art that were known to Vincent from his early days in the art dealer's shop and in which he continued to show an interest throughout his life. The paintings are now and then changed around but among the collection you might see The Reading by *Honoré Daumier* and a number of works by *Thomas Couture*, notable among them The Realist, a mildly satirical piece showing a young artist painting a pig's head, surrounded by everyday articles and seated upon the head of a classical statue. Works by *Jan Toorop* and *Josef Israëls* are usually on display; Toorop's Self Portrait in a Studio is a very striking image which stands comparison with the self portraits by Vincent upstairs. *Fantin Latour* is often well-represented. One of the most striking images presently on show is a fruit Still Life by *Puvis de Chavannes*. Puvis, like Couture and Daumier, was an artist who was influential upon many of the young painters who themselves later became influential in the art movements of the last years of the 19C. Young artists such as *Maurice Denis* whose Japanese-style Two Sisters of 1891 is also presently on display.

The first floor currently displays a representative selection of Vincent's works in chronological order. The exhibition starts at the N end with brooding images from his time at his parents' house in Nuenen. Peasant heads, landscapes and topographical views (for example the Old Church Tower at Nuenen) frame his celebrated *Potato Eaters of April 1885. He was 32 years old and had turned to painting. Many of the pictures are given such precise dates; as one walks around one gets the impression that the time is being measured out in hours and days—we know that he did not have long to live and this is the essence of the power of Vincent's myth.

In striking contrast to Vincent's images of a dour Dutch countryside the Haymakers by *Leon Augustin Lhermitte* (1844–1925) is big and bright, celebrating a more lyrical ideal of rural work and community. Brighter colour is the first impression you get when you enter the section of paintings from Vincent's French years. Initially the colour is simply brighter, as in the *Hill of Montmatre with a Quarry of the autumn of 1866. But by the spring of 1887, with the View from Vincent's Room, Rue Lepic and the *Japonaiserie: The Flowering Plum Tree (after Hiroshige), (the pictures often have such laborious titles) one can observe a disintegration of the heavy brushstrokes which gave the earlier works much of their intensity. The influence here is from Impressionism, especially from the stylised developments such as Neo-Impressionism. But bright though the pictures are they do not lose any of the power of his earlier work. The *Self Portrait in a Grey Felt Hat, for example, is haloed by an orange-yellow radiance. In the Red Cabbages and Onions we see him using coloured lines to carve a structure onto the canvas, and in the *Still Life with Lemons, Pears, Apples, Grapes and an Orange he paints over the frame as well, the colour bursting out into our own space.

If he found his characteristic technique in Paris, he found his characteristic subject matter upon his return to the countryside. He left for Arles in the south of France. His dream was to set up a community of artists, the reality was a period of corrosive isolation although he managed to convince Gauguin to join him for a short while (the Sunflowers were for Gauguin's room). He produced an extraordinary number of paintings. He used so much paint and canvas that he had to write begging letters to his brother to send more. Rapidly produced pictures piled up—one often comes across marks left by one canvas pressed into the still wet paint of another. The fascination with places and personalities continued, evidenced by works such as *The Yellow House, Vincent's Room, Gauguin's Armchair and *The Zouave.

The surrounding countryside was painted with vivid (and now masterfully handled) colours. We can trace the seasons of 1888: Orchards in blossom, *The Harvest. The landscapes push higher and higher up the picture plane, crowding out the sky with a terrestial clutter reminiscent of Brueghel. Gauguin's departure and Vincent's despair led, as everyone knows, to a breakdown and the celebrated mutilation of his ear but despite that there are still lyrical episodes recorded, for example, the *Boats on the the beach at Saintes-Maries-de-la-Mer. Committed to an asylum at St Rémy Vincent ceased painting for a while, but in the summer of 1889 he began again and his continuing interest in older art is displayed in his free copies after *Delacroix (the Pieta), *Rembrandt (The Raising of Lazarus) and *Millet (a series after the Labours of the Field). It is difficult to tell whether

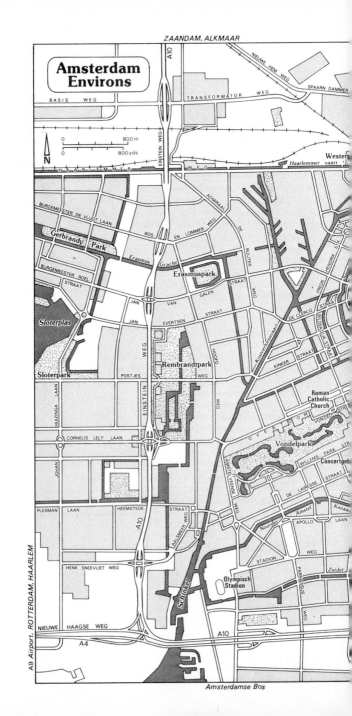

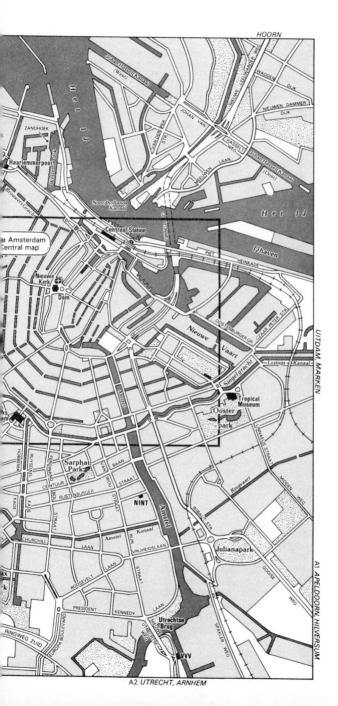

the contorted forms of the ivy and tree trunks in *Undergrowth should be considered a manifestation of his paranoia or of his tireless pursuit of nature. If the former it is hard to view them together with the simple pleasantness of the contemporary Vase with Irises. And the abstract frieze of *Roots and Tree trunks, painted at Auvers, is counterbalanced by the plain realism of Daubigny's Garden. On the last occasion that I visited this gallery a man whispered to his wife 'Was hij gek?' (was he mad?) by the painting of the Zoauve, 'Not yet' she replied. When they arrived at Undergrowth she announced 'Nu was hij gek' (now he's mad).

The paintings form a convoluted circuit of the first floor. Leaving the Van Gogh display one passes works by contemporaries inscribed with dedications. *Gauguin's* Self Portrait 'Les Misérables' and a Self Portrait by *Charles Laval*, both of 1888, Vincent's year of hopefulness.

The SECOND FLOOR is occupied by galleries specially darkened for the display of drawings and watercolours. Works by Gauguin, Redon, Pissarro and Toulouse-Lautrec might be on display with a host of pictures by lesser known but by no means less interesting artists. Here also is the Study Collection, scores of paintings, mostly by Van Gogh but including works by others, hung floor to ceiling behind a glass wall. The rest of the level is an exhibition gallery. The present policy of the Rijksmuseum Vincent Van Gogh is to keep the exhibition spaces in constant transformation. Recent shows have included displays of Japanese prints (there are many Japanese prints in the Collection once owned by Vincent), 19C paintings from The Hague and Post-Impressionist works. Both the exhibition space on the second and the third floors are given over to one or more exhibitions during the season.

The **Stedelijk Museum** (daily, 11.00 to 17.00) is Amsterdam's museum for modern art—roughly 1850 to the present day. The collection includes paintings, sculpture, graphic art, applied art, industrial design, posters, pop art, etc. Although some of the permanent collection is always on view, the main exhibition is between May and September (material being changed at intervals), while the remainder of the year is given over to special exhibitions.

The museum owes its existence to the bequest to the city in 1890 of the collections of Sophia de Bruyn-Suasso. Her house, which she had also bequeathed, was far too small, and it was therefore decided to build a new museum to house both the De Bruyn-Suasso collections and also the works of contemporary artists for which there was no space in the Rijksmuseum. This building, by A.W. Weissmann, was opened as a museum in 1895. A new S wing was added in 1954, and further extension and alteration continues.

The *Concertgebouw*, home of Amsterdam's renowned orchestra, is on Van Baerlestraat, just S of the Stedelijk Museum, while the VONDELPARK, the principal public garden of this part of Amsterdam, lies a short way NW. With its grass and ponds the park stretches almost 2km in a south-westerly direction. In the centre there is a statue of Joost van den Vondel (1587–1679), the poet, who was born in Cologne where his parents, refugees from Antwerp, found asylum before finally settling in the Netherlands. At No. 3 (a pavilion of 1880) is the *Nederlands Filmmuseum* (Mon–Fri, 09.00 to 17.00) which exhibits cameras and equipment and has a theatre, library, and documentation centre. The Roman Catholic church, at the NE corner, was designed by P.J.H. Cuijpers.

From the W end of Vondelpark, the Amstelveenseweg leads S, soon passing the former Haarlemmermeer Station, home now of an *Electric Tram*

*Museum* (April–late Oct: Sun and Holidays, 10.00 to 18.00; also Sat in early July to early Sept). Here are some 60 trams, with an average age of over 50 years, and of these, on summer weekends, 15 ply the 6km to the Amsterdamse Bos and beyond. Not far beyond, Amstelveenseweg passes the *Olympisch Stadion*, built for the games of 1928, and in another 2km, beyond the A10 motorway, reaches the NE corner of the **Amsterdamse Bos**, a large semi-wild recreation area of woodland and water, over 4km in length and some 2km wide, laid out during the 1930s as a means of relieving unemployment (*Bosmuseum* on Koenenkade at N corner off Amstelveense-weg: daily, 10.00 to 17.00, but closed Mon in Nov–March).

**Schiphol**, Amsterdam's international airport, lies to the W of the Amsterdamse Bos. Here the *Aviodome* (daily, 10.00 to 17.00; closed Mon in Nov–March) houses an air and space travel exhibition.

# D.  Western Amsterdam

The principal street of inner western Amsterdam is Raadhuisstraat, which starts from behind the Royal Palace on the Dam and crosses the four concentric canals, Singel, Herengracht, Keizersgracht, and Prinsengracht (see below, and for the district at the N end of these canals). Dating from the late 19C, Raadhuisstraat owes its name to the fact that the Palace was originally built as the Raadhuis (town hall). No. 20 houses the *Spaarpotten-museum* (Mon–Fri, 13.00 to 16.00), a museum devoted to money-boxes; some 12,000 of them of worldwide provenance, some of real artistry, and ranging from ancient boxes from Indonesia to modern piggy-banks. On the S side, Nos 23–55, put up in 1896–99 by A.L. van Gendt and Sons, form a pleasing gallery of shops in a style akin to Art Nouveau; the balcony rails and animal sculptures are noteworthy. Between Keizersgracht and Prinsengracht the road becomes WESTERMARKT, with the **Westerkerk** (May–mid Sept: Mon–Sat, 10.00 to 16.00), built in 1620–38 from designs by Hendrik de Keyser (died 1621). The fine tower (1638), the highest in Amsterdam (ascent in June–mid Sept: Tues, Wed, Fri, Sat, 14.00 to 17.00), is topped by a decorated coloured small cupola and has good chimes. Inside the church there is an organ of 1687, with allegorical decoration by Gerard de Lairesse; and Rembrandt and Claes Berchem are both buried here. No. 6 Wester-markt was the Amsterdam home of the philosopher Descartes (c 1630–c 1634).

Beside the S side of the church stands a small statue of Anne Frank (by Mari Andriessen), and just NW at No. 263 Prinsengracht is the *****ANNE FRANK HUIS** of 1635 (Mon–Sat, 09.00 to 17.00. Sun and Holidays, 10.00 to 17.00; open until 19.00 in June–Aug; closed Yom Kippur), home of the Jewish Frank family, refugees of 1933 from Germany, and between 1942 and 1944 their hiding-place, as also that of the Van Daan family and of a dentist called Dussel. The house extends well back, and it was this back-house (a rebuilding of 1740) that was prepared as a hiding-place into which the families moved in 1942, and it was here that Anne, the younger daughter, kept the diary that was to become world-famous. Betrayed in August 1944, all the occupants of the house were deported (the father being the sole survivor), and the diary was later found on the floor. Visitors see the whole of the back-house, including the concealed bookcase-door and such touching items as a small map with the Allied advance hopefully indicated, pencil marks recording the growth of the children, and magazine pictures pasted by Anne on the walls. The house is maintained by the Anne Frank Foundation, whose aim is to fight against prejudice and discrimination, and documentation is displayed recording German persecution and warning against today's trends.

Rozengracht, which beyond Westermarkt continues the line of Raadhuisstraat, is a filled-in canal. No. 184 was Rembrandt's modest home, from after he had had to leave the Rembrandthuis in 1660 until his death in 1669; here also died (1663) Hendrickje Stoffels (his model, mistress, and possibly second wife), and his son Titus (1668).

Rozengracht runs through the district known as JORDAAN (a corruption of the French 'jardin', garden), so called because the streets were, as they still are, named after trees and flowers. Much of the quarter, at one time the home of Huguenot and Walloon refugees, was designed in c 1612 by Hendrik Staets, his plan being to realise a self-contained artisan community. The district remains the home of many small businesses, and, with over 800 buildings listed as of architectural and other interest, is the object of continuing conservation plans. A short walk around the streets immediately N of Rozengracht enables many old houses to be seen, as attractive as, if more modest than, those further in along the main canals. Rembrandt's first Amsterdam home (from 1631) was in Bloemgracht, the second street parallel with Rozengracht and still with its canal, while Jan van Riebeek, founder of Cape Town, lived on Egelantiersgracht, the next canal to the N, in 1649–51. At Nos 34–54 on this latter street there are two rows of almshouses, mostly built in 1760 but belonging to a trust founded in 1626 by a Baptist cloth merchant, Claes Anslo. Restored in 1965 the almshouses are now used by students.

NORTH FROM RAADHUISSTRAAT. There are several good façades, principally to the N, along the main canals close to where they are crossed by Raadhuisstraat. Along Herengracht No. 168 (the Nederlands Theater-Instituut, with *Theatre Museum*; Tues–Sun, 11.00 to 17.00) was built by Philips Vingboons in 1638 and bears a sandstone gable, the first of this kind in Amsterdam; after modernisation in c 1730 the house was given rich interior decoration and, later, ceiling and wall paintings by Isaac de Moucheron and Jacob de Wit. No. 170–172 dates from 1618 and was designed by Hendrik de Keyser, but the right half of the house is largely rebuilding of c 1735. Along Keizersgracht No. 123 dates from 1622, and No. 177, by Jacob van Campen, from 1624. Further N, on Prinsengracht, the *Noorderkerk* was built in 1620–23 by Hendrik de Keyser and/or Hendrik Staets and has a ground plan in the shape of a Greek cross. On Monday mornings (07.30–13.30) the open space in front of the church is given over to the Noordermarkt—old clothes, junk and many treasures for the early-riser.

At their N end, all four concentric canals and their streets reach Brouwersgracht, lined by some old warehouses. The *Nieuwe Luthersekerk*, towards the N end of Singel, with a baroque dome, was built by Adriaan Dortsman in 1668–71, restored in 1823–26 after a fire, and closed as a church in 1935; beautifully restored in 1975 it now serves as a banquet hall for one of Amsterdam's leading hotels. Nearby, Nos 4 and 6 Kattengat are small houses of 1614 (restored 1930), while a short way N at 16 Nieuwendijk *Oude Ambachten* (daily, 10.00 to 17.00; closed Wed in Feb and March, and Mon in Nov and Dec; entrance charge) is a Dutch arts and crafts centre with demonstrations (products may be bought). Haarlemmerstraat (E) and

Haarlemmerdijk (W) run parallel to and N of Brouwersgracht. No. 75 Haarlemmerstraat (corner of Herenmarkt) was built as a meat hall in 1617, later becoming the House of the West Indies Company; the building was restored in 1979. Haarlemmerdijk, running W and becoming increasingly industrial, ends at the *Haarlemmerpoort*, a gate erected in 1840 to replace one by Hendrik de Keyser that had been pulled down three years earlier (see picture by Jan van Goyen in the Frans Hals Museum, Haarlem).

From near the junction of Haarlemmerstraat and Haarlemmerdijk, WESTER-DOK runs N, on its W side being a small area cut by many canals. Here, on Zandhoek, the small road along the NW of Westerdok, there is an attractive row of restored small houses.

# E.   The Rijksmuseum

The * *Rijksmuseum** (Tues–Sat, 10.00 to 17.00. Sun and Holidays, 13.00 to 17.00). The Netherlands' national museum contains the largest and finest collection of Dutch paintings in existence, almost every one of the great Dutch artists being represented. In addition, there is a small selection of Flemish, Italian, and Spanish paintings. The sculpture, applied arts (especially ceramics), Asiatic, and historical collections are in themselves worth a visit—as are the dolls' houses. The museum includes a print room, study collections, and library; and there are audio-visual shows with commentaries in English (David Roëll Room, First Floor).

The collection dates from 1808 when Louis Bonaparte decreed the establishment of a Royal Museum. Being housed in the palace (formerly the Town Hall) on the Dam, it at once received a fine collection of paintings 'on loan' from the city, including Rembrandt's Night Watch (none of which, of course, needed to be moved). With the departure of the French and the accession of William I the museum was re-established at the Trippenhuis (Kloveniersburgwal 29). This accommodation was always too cramped and *P.J.H. Cuijpers*, after much dispute and discussion (not a little of which was centred upon his Catholicism), was commissioned to design today's building, to which the museum moved in 1885. Cuijpers has been called the grandfather of Dutch modernism and this is due to his rationalistic approach to the design of buildings—his motto, borrowed from Viollet-le-Duc, was: all form not indicated by structure must be suppressed. For him, trained for 25 years as a church architect, it was natural to think a building all the way through from the basic ground plan (for the Rijksmuseum he adapted the plan of Van Campen's Town Hall) to the minutiae of decoration. If it were stripped of all its objects Cuijpers' building would still tell the history it was built to display. Cuijpers also designed the Centraal Station and the buildings stand at either entrance to Victorian Amsterdam (the museum looked out over fields) asserting his vision of a national style. Approached from the S the visitor is first impressed by the variety of the Gothic silhouette, as one comes closer you are presented with a cross-vaulted porch adorned with figures representing the crafts (the building as a whole straddles the road like a triumphal arch). The four façades of the building are all decorated with reliefs, designed by G. *Sturm*, not only depicting incidents in and aspects of the history of art and craft in the Netherlands but also celebrating the constitution of the nation. From the city side it is difficult to get any distant view, but as you approach up the Reguliersgracht the various masses and towers shift pleasingly in relation to each other. There has been much subsequent extension and alteration, notably in 1898 and 1909.

There are two entrances to the museum, both facing north onto the Stadhouderskade, one on either side of the road which passes under the building. The one usually employed is that on the right-hand side. Access is cramped and when one or another is closed, say for the installation of a large exhibition, you may have a short wait in the cold and the rain—dress up warm. From the main entrance (cloakrooms just inside, the café is on your immediate right as you enter) visitors ascend stairs to the large hall (**Room 237**), where there are information and sales desks. Application may be made at the information desk for introductory cards to the Six Collection of Paintings (see C. Southern Amsterdam), for this a passport is required. The hall has recently been whitewashed, the stained glass windows now appear more as works of art in their own right rather than mere fenestration. They are by *W.F. Dixon* of London and carry the date 1884. Together the windows in the hall form a massive triptych synthesising the literary, artistic, constitutional and economic histories of the nation, continuing, therefore, the themes of the decoration of the exterior.

Many visitors come primarily, or even only, to see Rembrandt's Night Watch and the museum's four Vermeers. The former (in Room 224, with explanatory material in 223) can be seen and approached direct from the information desk by way of the broad Gallery of Honour (Rooms 236–229, now hung with Golden Age masterpieces, see below); as you face the Night Watch the Vermeers are in Room 221a, to your left. If you have a longer stay in mind glance through the six sections below and then choose which part or parts of the museum to visit. To attempt to visit the whole of the museum in any worthwhile detail could easily absorb several days.

## Dutch Paintings, 15C–17C (First Floor. Rooms 201–224, 229–235)

The principal attraction, the Dutch paintings, are presently being re-hung following the huge 1991–92 Rembrandt exhibition. It is possible that there will be some variation from the listing provided below but the tour of the rooms includes all the pictures you are likely to come across—the most important works, if not out on loan, are always on display. Rooms are in places described in order of convenience of visiting and not necessarily in strict numerical sequence.

In the early years, in a Catholic Netherlands, much art was commissioned by the Church; functionally and iconographically this gives the dominant character to the art of the earlier period. The local, precious, Gothic style came under pressure for change in the early 16C when Dutch artists—most importantly Jan van Scorel—began to visit Italy and absorb Renaissance ideas.

**Room 201**. *Geertgen tot Sint Jans*: Tree of Jesse. Adoration of the Magi. *Master of the Virgo inter Virgines*: Mary and the Infant Jesus with saintly women (c 1490). Resurrection. *Dutch School (15C)*: An interesting series of 18 pictures on the Life of Christ. **Room 202**. *Master of Alkmaar*: The Seven Works of Charity, with a background of a late medieval town (1504). *Jan Mostaert*: Adoration of the Magi. Portrait of a Lady (c 1535–40). *South Holland Master*: Allegory of the Vanity of Human Life. *Anon*. St Catherine. **Room 203**. *J.C. van Oostsanen*: Portrait of Jan van Egmond (died 1523).

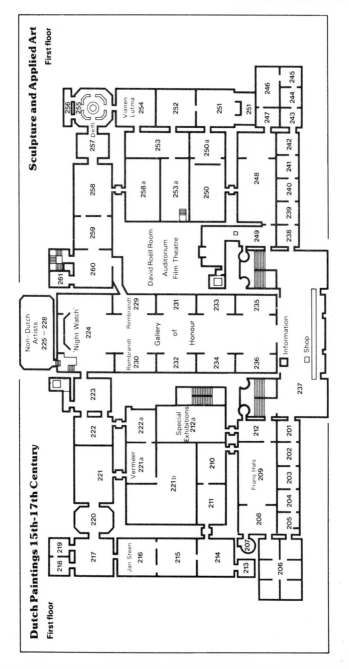

**Sculpture and Applied Art**
First floor

**Dutch Paintings 15th-17th Century**
First floor

Calvary. **Room 204**. *Cornelis Engebrechtsz*: Two scenes from the life of Christ. *Lucas van Leyden* (a pupil of Engebrechtsz): *Worship of the Golden Calf. **Room 205**. *Jan van Scorel*: Portrait of a man. Mary Magdalene, a Mona Lisa-like image set against a landscape. *Maerten van Heemskerck* (a pupil of Van Scorel): Portrait of Pieter Bicker Gerritsz. (c 1529, before the artist's visit to Italy). The Erythaean Sibyl (after the visit to Italy).

**Room 206**. This is a complicated room divided into several subsections. *Anthonis Mor van Dashorst (Antonio Moro)*: Portraits of Sir Thomas Gresham and his wife. *Jan van Scorel*: Bathseba. Later 16C painting from the Netherlands south and north is represented by *Joos de Momper* in landscape and *Adriaen Key* in portraiture, amongst others. *Pieter Aertsen* (The Egg Dance) from Amsterdam and *Joachim Bueckelaer* (The well-stocked kitchen), his follower from Antwerp where both had thriving careers, are recognised as having been important in combining daily life imagery with symbolic or narrative religious material. Here also are examples from the two principal Dutch Mannerist schools, Haarlem and Utrecht: from Haarlem the Flemish immigrant *Karel van Mander* (The Magnanimity of Scipio), who was also a distinguished poet and historian and *Cornelis Cornelisz* (Bathseba, The Fall of Man); from Utrecht came *Abraham Bloemaert* a man as important for his role as a teacher as for his painting. Note also the full-length militia portrait by *Cornelis Ketel*: The Company of Captain Rosecrans and Lieutenant Pauw; Amsterdam militia companies preferred full-length portraits from the late 16C onward (there is a very good display at the Amsterdam Historical Museum).

What came to be known as the Golden Age began properly during the stadholdership of Prince Frederick Henry (1625–47). Political and religious dissension eased, while trade and the arts flourished. Those elements of painting heralded in the previous room—individualised portraiture, daily life imagery, an exhibitionist approach to refined technique—came to the fore and Dutch painting can be said to have developed a national character. Artists also tended to specialise (as landscape, portrait, genre or still life painters) in the highly competitive market. The highest genre remained 'history' painting, the depiction of narratives taken from Biblical, Classical and historical sources.

**Rooms 207, 208, 209 and 210** are hung with a variety of works—a wide range of subject matters and scales are represented. Smaller paintings such as the minute pair of landscapes by *Jan Breughel* are in the tiny, circular Room 207.

**Room 208** is usually dominated by *Frans Hals*: *The Company of Captain Reynier Reael (the 'Lean Company', 1637), the figures on the right were finished by *Pieter Codde*—Hals did not feel inclined to travel all the way to Amsterdam (19 kms) to finish this most prestigious commission and an acrimonious correspondence over the matter remains. (Other Hals paintings in this and the following rooms include The Merry Toper and *The Marriage Portrait of Isaac Massa and Beatrix van der Laen.) An important group portrait of the Regents and Regentesses of the Leper Asylum, by *Werner van den Valckert* shows this peculiarly Dutch emphasis on group identity in another context. Superficially it is not so different from the Seven Works of Charity in Room 202 except, it may be noticed, those doing good in the Valckert painting are doing it for the good of the recipients rather than for the good of their own souls, a subtle distinction which indicates the Protestant nature of the commission. There are also examples of still life painting, the portraiture of things, notably by *Pieter Claesz* and *Willem Heda*; although the principal subject would seem to be the surfaces of

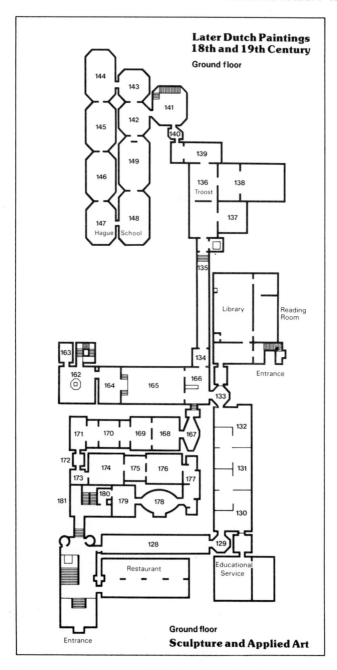

**Later Dutch Paintings 18th and 19th Century**

Ground floor

144

143

141

145

142

140

149

139

146

136
Troost

138

148

137

147
Hague School

135

Library

Reading Room

163

162

164

165

166

134

Entrance

133

132

171 170 169 168

167

172

131

174 175 176

177

173

181 180 179 178

130

128

129

Restaurant

Educational Service

Ground floor
**Sculpture and Applied Art**

Entrance

things, still life painters invariably represent the material world to comment upon human vanity, the transience of life and the deception of appearance. Vigorous figure paintings from this earlier period include works by *Jan Lievens* (Samson and Delilah) and *Gerrit van Honthorst* (The Merry Fiddler). Honthorst, a Utrecht artist, experienced at first hand the revolutionary painting of Caravaggio in Rome. The landscapes of *Hendrick Averkamp* (Winter landscape with ice-skaters) and the earlier works of *Isaias van de Velde* are crammed with incident like those of their 16C forebears, but already show that consideration for an overall and realistic atmosphere which characterised Dutch landscape painting. This could also be said for *Adriaen van de Venne* whose work combines portrait, landscape and genre—*Fishing for Souls is a satire on the Reformation (from a Calvinist point of view, he was painter to the Princes of Orange and a native of the extremely Calvinist city of Middelburg where his family ran a printing works).

Off Room 209, straight ahead of you as you enter from 208, is Room 212, not part of the gallery space; off this is Room 212A which is used for special exhibitions.

**Room 210**. Also by Van de Venne are The Harbour at Middelburg and Princes Maurits and Frederick Hendrick at the Valkenburg Horse Fair, vivid images which combine truthful renderings of particular places (the polder to the right of the Harbour, the town in the background of the Horse Fair) and personalities (the eponymous Princes and the painter and his family who bow to them). *Hendrick Averkamp's* Winterscene shows a similar 'all human life is there' image of the town of Kampen. The painting of social life, usually with a moral message, succeeded 16C representations of Biblical and moral tales in contemporary costume: examples from *Pieter Codde*, *Jan Miense Molenaer* (the husband of *Judith Leyster* whose Serenade hangs two rooms further on) and ** *Duyster* which introduce the kinds of bourgoise interior we more readily associate with later masters such as Vermeer and De Hooch. More typical of the 1620s are the *Buitenpartijen*, outdoor parties, by *Willem van Buytewech* and *Dirck Hals*— exquisite and self-evidently fanciful scenes.

**Room 211** is devoted to early Rembrandt—mainly influences: those upon him and his own upon others. *Pieter Lastman's* Dispute between Orestes and Pylades demonstrates the kind of archaelogically accurate narrative painting that held sway in Amsterdam during the 1620s and demonstrates why the young Rembrandt sought him out as a teacher. Lastman's precise use of gesture and emotional confrontation were very important for Rembrandt's own development. Jan Lievens (Portrait of Constantijn Huygens, Portrait of Rembrandt, An old woman reading) was Rembrandt's fellow student at Lastman's, they set up a workshop together in Leiden. From Rembrandt's Leiden period: The Musical Company and Tobias accusing Anna of stealing the kid; these two works show Rembrandt's variety as a painter even when still a young man. The brilliant colour of the Musical Company is reminiscent of some of the works by the Utrecht Caravaggisti, the scrupulous finish of the Tobias picture reminds us that Rembrandt was the teacher of *Gerrit Dou*, the principal Leiden *fijnschilder* (lit. precise painter) who is represented in this room by his own version of Rembrandt's mother. The earliest *Self Portrait securely attributed to Rembrandt is worth close attention—the young man engages us directly, his face half-shadowed; notice how the hair is rendered by scratching through dark paint to the lighter underlayers. Soon after his arrival in Amsterdam Rembrandt added to the moody chiaroscuro manner a looser application of paint apparent in *Jeremiah lamenting the Destruction of Jerusalem. Paint is rolled off the brush, opaque and translucent paints interlock to make the visionary substantial. A virtuoso treatment of paint is also apparent in the *grisaille* of Joseph telling his dreams.

**Rooms 213 and 214**. Both of these rooms show a similar range of landscape, townscape and still life painting; paintings are hung in one or another room according to size. The whole range of landscape painting is displayed, highly finished mythological and Biblical scenes by *Cornelis van Poelenburgh, Caesar van Everdingen* and *Moyses van Uytenbroeck* were prized by contemporaries and fetched hundreds of guilders. The new school of 'realist' landscapes employing local scenery by artists such as *Esaias van de Velde* (especially *The Ferry), *Jan van Goyen* (see especially his early roundels of Summer and Winter and the huge *Landscape with Two Oaks), *Salomon van Ruisdael* (among others a typical *River Scene) and *Aert van de Neer* (who specialised in moonlit scenes) could be bought for a few guilders. *Pieter Saenredam*, the son of a celebrated engraver and an official in the Painters' Guild at Haarlem, made scrupulous church interiors which are well represented here. His painting of Amsterdam's town hall (which burned down in 1652) is inscribed with a message on the neighbouring shop front stating that it was painted in 1657 after a drawing made in 1641. Unusual paintings include an early *Aelbert Cuyp* of a Mountainous Landscape and a view of a *River Valley by *Hercules Seghers*, an artist whose works in paint and print were avidly collected by Rembrandt. Still lifes by *Pieter Claesz* and others, notably Claesz's simple *ontbijtje*, breakfast piece, showing wine and fish set casually on the corner of a table and his more elaborate *Vanitas on human learning which includes a striking statuette of a small boy removing a thorn from his foot. Note also the Still Life (Allegory of Temperance) by Torrentius, a Haarlem artist prosecuted for witchcraft and obscenity.

**Room 215**. Here a variety of portraits, some of important 17C characters— for example, Andries Bicker (the Amsterdam burgomaster and merchant of whom it was said that with his brothers he ran the whole world's trade) by *Bartholomeus van der Helst* who also painted the fat boy by his side, Andries' son Gerard, and the *almost* informal full-length image of Maria Henrietta Stuart, widow of Stadholder William II, holding an orange. *Jan Verspronck*: Portraits of an old and a young man. *Michiel van Miereveld* was supposed to have painted 20,000 portraits. Of course, he did not, but his industrious studio certainly documented the faces of an entire generation of the ruling classes of The Hague and London—here two in his more relaxed late style. With the Bicker pictures and the brother and sister pastoral portraits of Martinus and Clara Alewijn by *Dirck Santvoort* (there is a later pair of portraits of Martinus and his wife Agatha Geelvinck, also by Santvoort), family portraits seem to be a minor theme in this room. *Jacob van Loo*'s Family Group with a Horse and Carriage (note the handsome contemporary frame) completes the suite.

Family is surely a principal theme of **Room 216**, devoted pre-eminently to *Jan Steen*. Many of the pictures feature the artist and his family—we can imagine it as an extended family which includes the bogus doctors (out of the *Commedia dell' Arte*) and mocking *pickelharings* from Dutch rhetoricians' dramas. Works here include *The Dancing Lesson (children teasing a cat); *The Sick Lady (we see pregnancy tests taking place); The Feast of St Nicholas (Steen did for the Dutch feast what Dickens later did for the English Christmas); *The Parrot's Cage; *The Merry Family (The moral is written on the cartellino at the top right-hand corner—As the old sing, so

do the young pipe); and a Self-portrait. Steen is the master of the comic/in-
structive commentary on daily life—English-speaking visitors should 'read'
his works in the same way that they read the comedies of British play-
wrights of the period. His Adoration of the Shepherds reminds us that Steen
had ambitions as a narrative painter, producing many scenes from the Bible
and classical literature. Three small pictures by *Paulus Potter*: Orpheus
charming the Animals, Landscape with Cattle and Herdsmen with Cattle—
all of which seem to share similar settings. The animal theme continues
with *Willem van Aelst's* Dead Birds.

Landscape is the dominant theme of **Room 217**. *Jacob van Ruisdael*:
*Landscape with a waterfall (c 1670). Rocky landscape. *The mill at Wijk
bij Duurstede (c 1665) is a magnificent landscape which although a picture
of a real place has been dramatised by Ruisdael onto an heroic scale.
Ruisdaels' interest in the dramatic is also evidenced in the Landscape with
a waterfall; Scandinavian subject matter was introduced into the Netherlands by Allart van Everdingen who had visited Sweden (see his picture of
the cannon foundry at Julitabroeck in Södermanland in the Historical
section in the north basement). Ruisdael's pupil *Meindert Hobbema* is well
represented with the Landscape with Fishermen and The Watermill—
thanks to the history of English taste both Ruisdael and Hobbema are better
represented in English collections. Landscape is the setting for *Adriaen van
der Velde's* Hunting Party (departing from the gateway of a country house),
a more intriguing picture is his Family in a Landscape where they promenade, the nurse too, while a shepherd pipes away like a hired extra to the
right. One of the most popular postcards in the shop is of *Jan Verspronck's*
*Girl Dressed in Blue, his portraits of Edward Wallis and Maria Strijp are
also worth some attention.

**Rooms 218 and 219** show small paintings in various genres. In the first a
group of genre scenes by the Haarlem artist *Adriaen van Ostade* including
Company of peasants, The Fish Woman, Travellers Resting, Interior with
Skaters (their skates lie on the floor) and an intriguing view of a Painter's
Studio, in the background you see the apprentice grinding colours on the
stone. More landscapes by *Jacob van Ruisdael*: a View of Haarlem with the
bleaching fields in the foreground; this view is taken from the dunes near
Bloemendaal, there is also a view of these dunes. Ruisdael's visit as a young
man to the German border is recorded in a romanticised view of Bentheim
Castle and a Forest Scene. The Winter Scene is astonishing for the leaden
sky characterising with a pitiless accuracy the bitter cold. *Thomas de
Keyser's* small-scale Equestrian Portrait of Pieter Schout, together with
Rembrandt's equestrian portrait in London, is a rare example of an aristocratic genre in Holland. Note the precise townscape by *Gerrit Berckheyde*
of the Spaarne at Haarlem. A fascinating exhibit in this room is the painter's
box decorated with landscapes, hunting scenes and battle scenes attributed
to *Anthonie van Croos* and *Jan Martszens II*.

Room 219 continues with town views by Berckheyde (The Herengracht)
and the master of the genre *Jan van der Heyden* (who also invented a
system of street lighting and a fire engine supplied by water from the
canals): German Town View, Nijenrode Castle and the Martelaarsgracht in
Amsterdam. The detail is such that visitors are frequently to be seen
counting the bricks and the paving stones. All the paintings in this room
demand scrupulous attention. More paintings by *Jan Steen*, including The
Quack, The Princes Birthday (a satire of ultra-Orangists?), The Village
Wedding and After the Drinking Bout. In the last a print of an owl above
the exhausted couple seems to ask: what use are a candle or spectacles if

you will not see? The Toilet is a rare venture into soft porn and The Baker Oostwaard into portraiture. Do not miss *Adriaen Coorte*'s *trompe l'oeil* of asparagus and *Melchior d'Hondecoeter*'s Plants and Animals.

**Room 220**. There was a widespread interest in and fashion for Italianate landscapes during the 17C—this room has examples from second generation practitioners (the first generation were displayed in Room 213)—painters like *Jan Asselijn, Adam Pijnacker, Nicolaes Berchem, Karel Dujardin* and *Jan Both* produced seemingly artless views crowded with motifs drawn from the Roman Campagna, peopled by peasants, shepherds and their beasts; the evening sun is invariably gilding the western sky, creating interesting shadows and gorgeous colours across the entire scene, the distance is hazy. The pure escapism of this art, rooted as it is in the poetry of Horace and Virgil, can be compared to the equally idyllic (though closer to home) elements in such paintings as *Jacob Esselens*'s The Shore, where townspeople buy fish from the fishermen, or *Lieve Vierschuier*'s Rippling Water (where we see a ship being tarred—not, admittedly, the stuff of elegiac verse). The sea is the main subject of most of the painting of *Jan van de Capelle* and *Willem van de Velde II* both of whom can range from the dramatic (Van de Velde's The Squall) to the lyrical (Van de Capelle's State Barge saluted by the Home Fleet). The continuing popularity of maritime subjects throughout the 17C and later is evidence of a strong patriotic sentiment.

**Room 221** includes some more Italianate landscapes but here they are set in the different context of the continuing 'classical' or 'academic' traditions within Dutch art represented by *Michiel Sweerts*, a painter who until recently has been hardly taken notice of (Portrait of Jeronimus Deutz, *The Painter's Studio, The Card Players, Visiting the Sick, Clothing the Naked). Here, too, is *Frans Post*'s remarkable View of Olinda. Post visited Brazil in the 1640s with the Dutch expedition led by Prince Maurits of Nassau; on his return he made his living almost exclusively by producing landscapes of Brazilian subjects often, as here, crowding the foreground with detailed representations of the flora and fauna including an anteater. The Threatened Swan by *Jan Asselijn* is a beast allegory in which the swan (*De raadpensionaris*, ie, Jan de Wit) is shown defending its eggs (Holland) from the attacking hound. (The room to the right, 221a, is dealt with below.)

**Room 222** is presently occupied with paintings by Rembrandt's pupils—these change from time to time as at present (1992) when several are abroad at the Rembrandt exhibition. Rembrandt had many pupils who became important masters in their own right—such as *Gerrit Dou* (see Room 222a), *Nicolaes Maes, Ferdinand Bol, Jacob Backer, Govaert Flinck* and *Aert de Gelder*. Their works are displayed here and in the Gallery of Honour (Rooms 229–236). Presently in this room is an example of Maes at his most Rembrandesque in Girl at a window and *Jan Victor*'s strange The Pork Butcher.

Backtrack a little and enter **Room 221a** and the difference could not be more striking. After the bombast, rhetoric and chiaroscuro of the Rembrandtists the works of the Delft School of the 1650s and '60s are so understated as to seem bland. Here are the four *Jan Vermeer* paintings: *The Milkmaid, *Woman reading a Letter, *The Love Letter and *The Little Street, all of them startlingly small. It is easy to understand how it was that Vermeer was 'rediscovered' by the generation that invented photography, the pictures seem so immediate and 'real'. A comparison with *Pieter de Hooch*, who was so influential upon Vermeer's style and subject matter, immediately highlight's Vermeer's extraordinary accomplishment. Even in one of De Hooch's most successful images, *The Linen Closet, there is a stiff, doll-like quality to the figures which gives the work a look of contrivance. There are three other paintings by De Hooch: an Interior where the child holds a whip (a motif which alludes to a contemporary emblem—the top will only spin for as long as it is whipped!), a Kitchen Interior with a mother and child, and The Country Cottage. *Gerard ter Borch* (also in Room 222a where you can see *Lady in front of a Mirror) was a painter who came close to Vermeer's artless realism, for example in the so-called *Parental Admonition (apparently, it seems, a whore and her client); powerful little portraits by Ter Borch are of François de Vicq and Aletta Pancras. *Emmanuel de Witte* specialised in church interiors which, unlike those of Saenredam, included telling incidents—thus his *Interior of Gothic Church, through the agency of the gravedigger who looks up from his work to speak to a burgher, might invite a meditation upon human mortality. The mixture of attention and inattention in the Interior of the Oudekerk, Amsterdam, invites speculation on the various spiritual destinies of the people we see.

**Room 222a**. After Rembrandt left Leiden his pupil *Gerrit Dou* emerged as the most important artist in the city, influencing several generations of younger artists with his painstaking and precise technique and creating the *finjnschilder*, fine painter, style. His works frequently employ distancing devices, such as curtains or a stone sill in the foreground, which cut us off from the dim and magically lit interiors beyond. The *Self Portrait is a rare example of his artistry turned toward portraiture, more familiar are The Hermit, The Fisherman's wife (virtuously seated by the window) and *The Night School. If one pays very great attention one can determine individual brushmarks, but Dou's appeal lies in his submergence of all technique behind a transparent, glossy wall—the end result being a surface like a coloured photograph. *Gabriel Metsu*, a follower, laid his paint on more freely but was more innovative in his treatment of the inner lives of his human subjects, one of the most sentimentally appealing images in the whole museum is his *Sick Child, equally compelling is the *Old Woman Meditating which derives ultimately from his master's versions, after Rembrandt, of Rembrandt's Mother. Note, too, his Old Drinker, Girl Feeding a Cat and The Huntsman's Gift, a sly and dirty joke. At a further remove still is the exquisite and classically informed manner of *Adriaen van der Werff* (A Painter, Two Lovers). Presently in this room are more works by Rembrandt pupils, notably *Samuel van Hoogstraaten* (Sick Woman); Hoogstraaten went on to write an important treatise on art.

**Rooms 223 and 224**, reached via 222 described above, are devoted to Rembrandt's *THE NIGHT WATCH, Room 223 contains background material and 224 the picture itself, handsomely restored after its slashing by a vandal (understandably, perhaps, an art student) in 1975. This is Rembrandt's largest and one of his greatest works.

The familiar name the 'Night Watch' is an 18C misnomer probably arising from the fact that the picture was long obscured by soot and the natural darkening tendency of oil paint. The correct name is 'The Company of Captain Frans Banning Cocq and Lieutenant Willem van Ruytenburch'. Painted in 1642, one of a suite of new pictures for the militia guild hall of the Kloveniers (arquebusiers), the picture shows the company emerging, in broad daylight, from the shadows beneath a triumphal arch upon which, in a large oval cartouche, the names of the officers are listed. The light falls strongly from the left, throwing the darkness of the deep archway into contrast, and there is again contrast between the tall Captain Cocq in his sombre garb and the shorter Lieutenant van Ruytenburch in his bright yellow buckskin (which, if you look closely, you will see is covered in embroidered detail). The small girl, whose figure catches the sunlight, has a cockerel hanging from her belt, perhaps a play on the captain's name—the prominent claws of the bird are probably a play in the name of the company (Kloveniers); an astute eye will notice that a number of the characters in the picture, although doubtless portraits, are also symbolically dressed. No doubt the two children (there is a boy 16C armour in the middle ground) are part of an allegorical scheme, but the exact plot of this allegory is now lost. It also seems likely the historical costumes celebrate the history of the militia guild and are probably drawn from its own collection—we know that they had a small museum in the building, as well as a series of group portraits of members going back a century.

Attention may be drawn to the difference between the treatment of the subject in this picture and in other group portraits and corporation pieces. In others the likeness of the sitters seems to have been the artists' principal aim, they are usually individuals posed in readily decipherable space. Rembrandt, though, asserts the dynamic of a whole picture over the demands of portraiture. It seems likely that this work was admired as a grand finishing touch to the militia hall and there is no reason to suppose that any of the sitters was dissatisfied with the picture when it was painted, this is part of the mythology around the 'Romantic' and misunderstood Rembrandt.

A 17C copy of the picture by *Gerrit Lundens* (in Room 223) shows that the original has been cut down by some 60cm on the left and by some 30cm at the top. This is thought to have occurred in the 18C, but the reason remains uncertain, it may have been to enable the picture to be hung between two doors in the War Council Room in the Town Hall on the Dam.

Also in **Room 224** are, to the left of the Night Watch, *Bartholomeus van der Helst*'s The Company of Captain Roelof Bicker (1639; in front of the tavern De Haen on the Geldersekade), and to the right his *Platoon of Cornelis Jansz Witsen and Lieutenant Johan Oetgens van Waveren celebrating the signing of the Treaty of Münster in 1648; opposite the Night Watch *Govert Flinck*'s The Company of Captain Albert Bas and Joachim von Sandrart's Corporalship of Captain Cornelis Bicker and Lieutenant Frederick van Banchem waiting to welcome Marie de Medici into Amsterdam in September 1638. These works, three of which originally hung in the same hall as the Night Watch, and two of which are by former pupils, provide an excellent context for Rembrandt's masterpiece emphasising its uniqueness and yet retaining a sense of real historical place and time.

Behind the Night Watch, approached by a staircase on the left, are **Rooms 225–228** into which are crowded the rather small and undistinguished collection of Italian, Spanish and Flemish works. These include: *Lorenzo Monaco*, a Madonna and Child, a St Jerome in his Study and a St Francis receiving the Stigmata; *School of Ferrara (15C)*, The Flood; *Piero di Cosimo*, Portraits of Giuliano da Sangallo the architect and Francesco Giamberti; *Filippino Lippi*: Portrait of a young man; *Fra Angelico*, a Madonna; *Tintoretto*, an Annunciation (in two halves) and Christ and the woman taken in adultery; *Ludovico Carracci*, Vision of St Francis; *Tiepolo*, Telemachus and Mentor; *Alessandro Magnasco*, Landscape with St Bruno; *Canaletto* two Venetian views; *El Greco*, a Crucifixion; *Murillo*, an Annunciation and a Madonna; *Goya*, Portrait of Don Ramon Satue; *Rubens (and studio)*, Portraits of Helena Fourment, the artist's wife, and of Anne of Austria (a replica of the portrait in the Louvre), Christ bearing the Cross (a study for the painting now in the Musée d'Art Ancien in Brussels) and a Caritas Romana (Cimon and Pero); *Van Dyck*, Portraits and a Penitent Magdalene; *Jordaens*, The Road to Calvary.

The wide parade of rooms leading directly from the Night Watch towards the shop and Information Desk is known as the Gallery of Honour (**Rooms 229–236**). The first rooms on either side (229–230) are usually dominated by Rembrandt's Jewish Bride and Syndics. The *Jewish Bride (usually in 229) was painted very late in Rembrandt's life, in about 1666. The picture is technically interesting for the way in which the colour is laid on freely with brush and palette knife and then qualified with transparent glazes of paint. These glazes seem to have been poured onto a high-relief latticework of paint; from a distance there is the powerful illusion of fabrics and figures in real space, close too there is the pleasure of the apparently arbitrary run of paint and the abstract allure of the colours. It is also a riddle. On the one hand it looks like a history painting and has been likened to representations of Jacob and Rachel, on the other hand it is understood to be a portrait. The bride's costume has led to the traditional name being adopted. 'Character' portraits are by no means rare, Hals' portrait of Isaac Massa and Beatrix van der Laen is an example of another marriage portrait of this kind.

The extraordinarily powerful St Paul Denying Christ, of the same date, is usually hung next to this picture. The *Syndics (*De Staalmeesters*), painted in 1661–62, represents the sampling masters of the cloth hall; they are frozen forever addressing a meeting. An arresting feature of the picture is that all the sitters seem to be interested in what we are doing or thinking, as if we were in the room with them, rather than performing their actions in that more or less unselfconscious manner typical of such corporation portraits. This is one of the rare pictures for which Rembrandt made sketches and each of the officials is highly individualised. This work proves that, although his reputation may have been in decline toward the end of his career, Rembrandt could still obtain important commissions—even after the bankruptcy of 1656.

Other important works by Rembrandt that you might see here (or in earlier rooms) include the Portrait of Maria Trip, *The Anatomical Lesson of Doctor Deyman (badly damaged by fire; if you have seen Rembrandt's Anatomy of Dr Tulp in the Mauritshuis at The Hague you would do well to see this for comparison), An Oriental Potentate, Portrait of Titus as a monk and the compelling *Self-portrait as the Apostle Paul.

The rooms are at the moment (1992) hung with paintings of the Rembrandt School. In 229: *Ferdinand Bol*, Six Regents of the Board of the Nieuwzijds Institute for Outdoor Relief of the Poor; *Govaert Flinck*, Rembrandt as a Shepherd; *Roelant Roghman*, Mountainous Landscape with Fishermen; *Philips Koninck*, Distant view, with Cottages lining a Road; *Aert de Gelder* (Rembrandt's last and most faithful follower), Hermanus Boerhaave, Professor of Medicine at Leiden, with his Family. In 230: Koninck, Entrance to a Wood; Bol, Peace negotiations between Claudius Civilis and Cerealis, a work associated with his commissions for the Town Hall decorations which has a spectacular *pentimento* where the ghostly figure of the protagonist, originally painted over, looms through the increasingly translucent oilpaint in the middle of the picture, and a *Portrait of a Man in a splendid contemporary gilt frame, the man dressed in some kind of historical costume; *Nicolaes Maes*, Woman Saying Grace, and a very grand portrait of Vice Admiral Cornelis Evertsen; *Carel Fabritius* (an artist who died young in an explosion at Delft and whose works are consequently rare), The Beheading of John the Baptist.

**Room 231** is presently dominated by *Karel Dujardin*'s Regents of the Spinhuis and New Workhouse of 1669 (the date is on the letter held by the man in the front centre). This is flanked by two handsome seascapes by *Allaert Bakhuysen. Ferdinand Bol*: a Self Portrait, Aenius at the Court of Latinus (with a delightful mixture of Roman armour and 17C ships' rigging), Consul Titus Manlius Torquatus Beheading his Son (an emblem of disinterested Justice), Venus and Adonis, and a pendant pair of portraits of Roelof Meulenaer and his wife Maria Rey.

**Room 233** shows examples of one of the more unusual sub-genres of 17C art, *penschilderij*, pen-painting. These are drawings in ink on a panel prepared for paint. All here are by *Willem van de Velde I*, two in their original frames, and they depict various sea-battles—off Dunkirk in 1639, Terheide in 1654, Livorno in 1653 and on the Downs in 1639.

**Rooms 234 and 235** have examples of Italianising and Classicising paint-ing. The first room has three *landscapes by *Aelbert Cuyp*. Cuyp is one of the few examples we can point to of a 'hard-line' Calvinist practising painting; we know that he married into the family of Gomarus, the leader of the Counter-Remonstrants (see History) and that he was a deacon in his local church in Dordrecht. Steen was a Catholic, like Vermeer; Rembrandt was nominally a member of the Reformed church as was Ruisdael; many painters were Mennonites (for example Flinck) and some seem to have had very little religion at all. It is not easy to relate a painter's religion and the style of painting—the idyllic, nostalgic and pseudo-classical world of many of Cuyp's pastorals seem as pagan as those of Claude (who was a devout Catholic, of course). Also *Cesar van Everdingen*, Young Woman Warming her Hands, possibly an allegory of Winter; *Jan de Bray*, The Haarlem Printer Abraham Casteleyn and his Wife (she is shown pulling him away from his books and into the garden, he is shown conceding with a play of reluc-tance); *Jan Steen*, *The Sacrifice of Iphigena, another example of Steen as a history painter, in which guise he received qualified praise from Joshua Reynolds. The second room has works by *Gerard de Lairesse*, now better known for his writings on art: Mars, Venus and Cupid, Ulysses urged on by Mercury to leave Calypso, and Diana and Endymion; *Adriaen van den Tempel*, Group Portrait of the Family of David Leeuw; *Jan Weenix*, Dead Game; *Melchior d'Hondercoeter* The Floating Feather, a display of exotic birds.

**Room 236** presently (1992) contains *Frans Hals'* Company of Captain Reinier Reael and Lieutenant Cornelis Michielsz Blaeuw and the Marriage Portrait of Isaac Massa and Beatrix van der Laen as well as still lifes by *Floris van Dijck*, *Willem Claesz Heda* and *Pieter Claesz* (discussed above, see Room 208). As well as works by these Haarlem artists there are portraits by *Michiel van Miereveld* and *Paulus Moreelse*.

## Later Dutch Painting (18C–19C) (Ground Floor. Rooms 135–137 and 141–149)

Having followed the patriotic trail from medieval art to the glories of the Baroque, visitors have to find their way to the back of the museum in order to pick up the scent and continue with the story of painting in the Nether-lands. The best route is to leave through the door out of Room 224 in the wall to the right of the Night Watch and follow the signs whih lead to **Room 135** (a corridor). Here you will find paintings by artists of c 1700, some of whose names will be familiar from the upper galleries: *Godfried Schalcken*, The Smoker; *Frans van Mieris the Elder*, The lute player; *Adriaen van der Werff*, *Self-portrait; *Gerard de Lairesse*, Antony and Cleopatra.

**Rooms 136 and 137** are dominated by *Cornelis Troost*, a painter of portraits and genre scenes reminiscent of Hogarth's work. Most prominent is his large group of the Regents of the Almoners' Orphanage in Amsterdam, painted in 1729. To the right **Rooms 137 and 138** are laid out in period style. There are some excellent portraits too by *George van der Mijn*. **Room 139** is the 'Pastels Room' with very fine examples, especially by the 18C Swiss artist *Jean-Etienne Liotard*, and amongst other by the French anarchist painter (though it is hardly apparent in the works on show) *Proud'hon*. Later Dutch Painting resumes beyond the small **Room 140** in which are displayed the collection of miniatures, some of which may be of particular interest to English visitors. This small room takes you into the Drucker Wing of the Museum devoted to Dutch 19C painting (the Druckers donated the bulk of this collection) and Islamic art (in the basement reached via the stairs in Room 141).

**Room 141** is a landing above an 18C staircase with stucco ceiling decoration. The group portrait of the Hasselaer family (1763) is by *George van der Mijn*. Here too are cases of 18C Chinese porcelain and, at the foot of the stairs, two magnificent Kang-hi vases. You, however, should remian on the same level and carry straight on.

**Rooms 142** and **143** contain late-18C and early-19C works, portraits by *Johann Tischbein* and *Wijbrand Hendriks*, including Hendriks' Woman sewing, and Man writing at his desk by *Jan Ekels the Younger*—both strikingly 'Golden Age' images. By *Adriaen de Lelie*, Jan Gildemeester's Gallery, and the Sculpture Gallery of the Felix Meritus Institute; *Pieter Kleyn*, Park at St Cloud; *Wouter van Troostwijk*, Snow scene on the ramparts of Amsterdam; *Pieter van Os*, In the Graveland; *J.L. Augustini*, Regents of the Leper House; *J. Jelgerhuis*, The Bookshop. It is clear from all of these that many characteristics of earlier art survived and indeed developed.

**Rooms 144 and 145** exhibit examples of Dutch Romantic painting in which painters not only come under the influence of other European Schools, but also explore varieties of earlier Dutch art now admired abroad. *Wijnand Nuyen*, Shipwreck on a rocky coast; *Barend Koekkoek*, Winter scene; *Jan* Kruseman, Regents and Regentesses of the Leper House; *Jan Weissenbruch*, Church of St Denis at Liège; *C. Springer*, View at Enkhuizen; *Andreas Schelfhout*, The Maas, frozen; *D.J. Blès*, Conversation; *A. Allebé*, Young girl, and Young Woman; *Charles Hodges* (a native of Portsmouth, England, who lived in the Netherlands, 1788–1837), a number of Portraits, notably of Johan Fraser and his family.

Rooms 146 to 149 display paintings of the Hague School and the Amsterdam Impressionists, both belonging to the latter part of the 19C and the early 20C.

**Room 146** provides an introduction, with a number of watercolours. **Rooms 147** and **148** are mainly Hague School works by the Maris brothers: *Willem Maris* whose speciality was animals, *Jacob Maris*, beaches and town views, and *Matthijs Maris* whose work was more various and included mystical themes, more like scenes from fairy tales. The Hague School painters sold well in England, they were the first painters for more than a hundred years to earn the Netherlands a reputation abroad. Together with *Anton Mauve* (see his Marshland, and the luminous *Morning Ride along the Beach) they have been seen as the first highpoint in the re-ascent of the Dutch national school and were tremendously influential on Van Gogh, Piet Mondriaan and many others. This room and **Room 149** include works by contemporary Amsterdam painters, the so-called Amsterdam Impressionists, who include *George Breitner*, who has stylistic and personal links with the Hague painters and *Jozef Israëls* who, like Rembrandt (with whom he was often compared) and like Van Gogh (who admired him), used paint dramatically and expressively—the expression is sombre and the drama often ironic: Portrait of Louis Jacques Veltman, Maternal bliss. Note also the Landscape by *Willem Roelofs*.

## Sculpture and Applied Art

The Sculpture and Applied Art Collections are in three sections. The 1st Floor, Rooms 238–261, includes the Middle Ages, Italy, the Renaissance, glass and silver, Colonial art, Delftware, and sculpture by Artus Quellin and Rombout Verhulst. On the Ground Floor, Rooms 162–181, are dolls' houses, lace, porcelain (German), and silver. In the Basement, Rooms 24–34 include glass, textiles, European and Dutch porcelain and work representative of the Empire and Art Nouveau periods.

FIRST FLOOR. **Rooms 238–248** are devoted to the Middle Ages and the 16C, a fine and varied collection of decorative art, mainly of ecclesiastical provenance. In **Room 238** a Tympanum from the abbey church of Egmond (c 1125–35), representing St Peter with Count Dirk VI and his mother Petronella; also Statues of Apostles from the abbey of St Odilienberg (1250–75). *Enamels and bronzes (13C); ivory hunting horn (South Italy, 11C); a small Scandinavian reliquary (11C); a Catalonian crucifixion (13C). **Room 239** *bronze statuettes from the tomb at Antwerp of Isabelle de Bourbon (died 1465), a macabre silver *head-reliquary of a bishop (1362) by *Elyas Scerpswert* of Utrecht, a French 14C Madonna. **Room 240**. Late 15C Dutch silver, including guild chains. **Rooms 241 and 242**, Dutch sculpture of the late 15C and early 16C, including fragments of altars, notably Death of the Virgin and St Joseph and an Angel choir by *Adriaen van Wesel* (c 1475), and a Meeting of Joachim and Anna by an unknown master. Also in this room a Flemish tapestry (Orange Harvest) of c 1500. Rooms 243–247 generally cover the 16C, a period during which the art of religious sculpture declined in the face of the iconoclasm of the Reformation. Noteworthy in **Room 243** are *a most original small carving showing riders (the Three Kings) descending through a rocky defile (Brussels, c 1500); three panels of knightly figures bearing shields, the panels being Rhenish workmanship from Naarden (1590) and part of an organ case; organ cases were one of the few forms of decoration allowed in post-Reformation churches and are often well worth close attention (look at the later examples at either end of the Entrance Hall (Room 237) as you leave. **Room 245** (principally German works) contains figures by the famous *Tilman Riemanschneider*; also a remarkably grouped Last Supper. **Room 246** (principally Netherlandish works) displays an Antwerp altar with scenes of the Passion, and also a balustrade with carved animals. In **Room 247** are ecclesiastical robes, silver, and a tapestry (Brussels, c 1520) representing the Washing of the Feet, perhaps from a work by *Bernard van Orley*. **Room 248**. Contains objects in copper and bronze, notably a bronze candelabrum by *Verrocchio*; also a Gothic rood screen from Helvoirt, as well as a tapestry (Brussels, c 1510) depicting the Triumph of Fame. **Room 249** is the Acquisitions Room.

**Room 250** illustrates the transition from Gothic to Renaissance, the emphasis being on tapestry, notably, in **Room 250A**, the Scenes from the Life of Diana woven in Delft and remarkable for their colouring, there are also examples of glass, sculpture and furniture. In **Room 251** the furniture and majolica represent the solid but stylish comforts of the 17C in that mix of showcase and room-setting display so loved by museum curators. **Room 251A** (the Treasure Room) displays jewellery, crystal, gold and silver, including guild silver, all part of the rich culture of the 16C and the Golden Age. **Room 252** is a panelled room from a house in Dordrecht, while **Room 253** shows Flemish Baroque and **Room 253A** presents colonial life. **Room 254**. *Dutch silver of the 17C, the principal artists being *Paulus van Vianen*

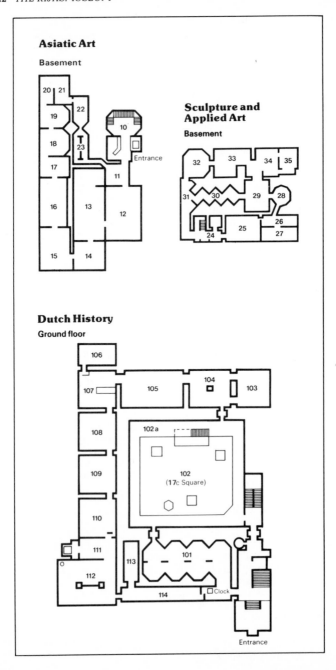

## Asiatic Art

Basement

## Sculpture and Applied Art

Basement

## Dutch History

Ground floor

(died c 1618), *Adam van Vianen the Elder* (died c 1625), *Christiaan van Vianen* (son of Adam), all from Utrecht, and *Johannes Lutma* of Amsterdam, the friend of Rembrandt. Especially noteworthy, by Lutma, are the *basin and ewer, with tritons and nereids, presented to Admiral Tromp in 1647. There is a portrait of Lutma by *Jacob Backer*.

**Rooms 255–257** contain the *Delftware Collection, both blue and polychrome; there are some remarkably unlikely household objects crafted in this material, note especially a bird cage of c 1700, a *violin (18C), with a musical occasion depicted on it, and an ingenious calendar.

**Room 258**. Sculpture of the 17C, with many terracotta busts and reliefs. *Rombout Verhulst*, Sketch for the tomb of Admiral Tromp; *Bartholomeus Eggers*, G. Munter, burgomaster of Amsterdam (1673); *Artus Quellin*, Bust of the burgomaster Andries de Graef, and reliefs of Cornelis de Graef and his wife. Also sketches for the sculptures now on Amsterdam's Town Hall, now the Royal Palace, on the Dam. Also (attributed to Quellin) Madness, a nude female figure, formerly in the garden of the old lunatic asylum at Amsterdam. **Room 258A**. Delft tapestries (1650). Also a Mantelpiece and portico by *Philips Vingboons* (1639), the great architect of Golden Age Amsterdam and a group portrait of the Regentesses of the Leper House (c 1665) by *Ferdinand Bol*. **Room 259** has gilt leather wall hangings which came into fashion during the 17C, and some handsome furniture; also a case of ivory work (mostly 17C). **Room 260** shows the rather less ornamented furniture of the later 17C. **Room 261**, Chinese screens.

GROUND FLOOR. **Room 162**. Two magnificent dolls' houses, dating from c 1700 and illustrating in miniature typical patrician furnishing. A case of silver, mainly 17C German. **Room 163**, Dutch sculpture. **Rooms 164 and 165**, the latter a large tapestry and carpet hall, exhibit 18C furnishings. Note an elaborate barometer of 1709, and also two paintings (Farmyard, and Parrot, hen and chickens) by *Melchior d' Hondecoeter*. **Room 166**, *Lace work. **Room 167**, an attractively diamond-shaped room, reached through a lobby, with Delft tiles of c 1690 (*Daniel Marot*), contains two large paintings by *Gerard de Lairesse* and *Johannes Glauber*, made as decorations for a room. In **Room 168**, with gilt leather wall hangings of four designs, there are Gobelins tapestries of c 1684 illustrating Ovid's Metamorphoses, and also tapestry (Brussels, 18C) illustrating Diana and her maidens. In **Room 169** are a corner hearth in the style of Daniel Marot, and a rare *Apothecary cabinet. **Rooms 170 and 171** offer a *Collection of Dresden china, while **Room 172** displays Japanese Kakiemon porcelain and derivative European ware.

**Room 173**, Louis XV French furniture and panelling; two portraits by *Louis Tocqué*. **Room 174**, Dutch furniture of the mid 18C, including a large bookcase of 1760. The murals and the fireplace grisaille are by *Jacob de Wit*. **Room 175** displays muffle-fired Delftware (ware fired in a special furnace allowing colours with low heat resistance to be used), and a dolls' house (18C), furnished in Louis XV style. **Room 176**, Louis XV furniture. **Room 177**, Dutch silver (18C). **Room 178** is an attractive oval in plan, the gilded console-tables with mirrors are by *Robert Adam*. **Room 179**, Louis XVI French furniture. Portrait of a boy by *J.-B. Greuze*. **Room 180** displays precious trinkets (18C). **Room 181**. Silver, a case of keys and sculpture. Pallas by *Laurent Delvaux*.

BASEMENT. **Room 24**, Dutch and other glassware, with examples of the 18C stippled technique. **Room 25**, Dutch Louis XVI furniture, c 1775. **Room 26**, a corridor, exhibits Dutch and Belgian silver. **Room 27** is a Dutch Louis XVI room of c 1790, all the furnishings of which came from the same house in Haarlem. **Room 28**, German and Austrian porcelain, with pieces from Höchst, Fulda, Fürstenberg, Berlin, and Vienna. Note the amusing Höchst coiffeur group. **Room 29**, Dutch Louis XVI furnishing. **Room 30** is a gallery in which Dutch and French clothing and accessories are well presented in contemporary settings. **Room 31**, Lace (18 and 19C). **Room 32** Dutch porcelain from Weesp, Loosdrecht, Amstel, and The Hague. **Room 33**, Empire period furniture and silver. **Room 34**, Art Nouveau.

## Dutch History (Ground Floor. Rooms 101–114)

The material derives from the collections of the stadholders, the Admiralty, the offices of the East and West Indies companies, as well as from private individuals—it therefore projects a particular cast onto Dutch history. The collections, arranged generally by subject rather than chronologically, although including some prehistoric material, essentially cover from the Middle Ages to modern times.

**Room 101**. At the entrance, a clock from the tower of the Nicolaaskerk in Utrecht: dating from the 16C the clock strikes the hours and half hours. A case of prehistoric material, mostly ceramic. Altar panels illustrating the disastrous St Elisabeth Flood (near Dordrecht) of 1421 (late 15C copies of lost originals). Contemporary portraits of four lords of Montfoort, three of whom were killed in Count William IV's campaign against the Frisians (1345); these are the oldest known Dutch portraits. Among other portraits are Elizabeth I of England, by an unknown artist; William of Orange by *Adriaen Key*; the Duke of Alva, an old copy of an original by *Willem Key*; Maximilian I (studio of *Joos van Cleve*, c 1510). Other pictures include the Siege of Rhenen (*Master of Rhenen*); the Battle of Gibraltar, when the Dutch under Admiral Heemskerck defeated the Spanish, by *Hendrik Vroom*, c 1625. In the passage between Rooms 101 and 102 can be seen what claims to be the chest in which Hugo Grotius was smuggled out of Loevestein (but see also Delft, Prinsenhof), and also Jan van Oldenbarneveld's walking stick.

**Room 102** (with the gallery 102A) is known as the Seventeenth Century Square. The gallery contains cases with material illustrating 17C everyday life. Not to be missed are examples of Chinese porcelain recently recovered from wrecks. The main floor covers a range of 17C themes, among the many exhibits being a case showing the weapons of a musketeer, a pikeman, and a cuirassier; a model of the siege of 's Hertogenbosch by Prince Frederick Henry (a little dusty at the last viewing, it works best if you crouch down and view from the side); a herald's doublet; *model ships, including a large one of a 17C warship and one of a galleon built for Peter the Great; relics of the expedition of Willem Barentsz. and Jacob van Heemskerck to Nova Zembla (1596–98) in an attempt to discover a north-east passage to the Indies. The many *pictures include several illustrating colonial life (Bengal, Amboina, East Indies, Surinam, with a map of 1737), a picture of the Hoogly river, Bengal, a fascinating if naive glimpse into everyday activities. There is also a series of twelve paintings by *Otto van Veen* (Rubens' teacher, a Hollander living in Antwerp) illustrating the revolt of the Batavian tribe against the Romans; these were well-known images during the 17C, they were engraved as the illustrations to Van Veen's own edition of a history of the Batavian Revolt.

**Room 103**. Sea battles, particularly against England, the main exhibit here being the *Escutcheon of the 'Royal Charles', captured by Admiral de Ruyter. Also a captured Union Jack, the oldest in existence; two large, elaborately carved ships' lanterns; and paintings by the *Van de Veldes*, father and son. **Room 104** contains portraits of admirals and their families, a number by *Bartholomeus van der Helst*. In **Room 105** the main feature is the painted ceiling, originally in the bedroom of William and Mary in their palace at The Hague (before they came to England). **Room 106** is a chapel (normally no adm.). **Room 107**, Colonial history, with particular reference to Ceylon, Japan, and China. Note a Japanese screen with a Dutch ship; a Sinhalese 'Kastane' weapon, an elaborately decorated cannon belonging to the King of Candy, and a portrait by *Govert Flinck*. **Room 108**, pastel portraits of members of the House of Orange by *Johann Tischbein*. **Room 109** covers the formation of the Batavian Republic (1795–1801): political ribbons and badges, silhouettes of the delegates who drew up the constitution; and a delightful family portrait of the Schimmelpennincks by *P. Prud'hon*. In **Room 110** there is a huge painting by *Jan Pieneman* of the Battle of Waterloo, with the Duke of Wellington occupying the central position; a key identifies the many well-known people included. Also by Pieneman, the Prince of Orange at Quatre Bras.

**Rooms 111** and **112** cover the later 19C and the 20C, some of the early photographs being particularly interesting. **Rooms 113** and **114** are used for temporary exhibitions.

## Asiatic Art (Basement. Rooms 11–23)

The main sections are Hindu-Javanese, Japanese, and Chinese. The **Hindu-Javanese Collection** includes stone statuary, fragments of buildings, and bronze and silver figures. In the **Japanese Collection** are sculpture, screens, lacquer, and painting.

The interesting **Chinese Collection** includes prehistoric earthenware (c 2000 BC); a series of six tomb figures, with four horses and two camels (T'ang, 7–10C); a cave temple torso (T'ien-lung-shan, c 7C), showing Indian influence; the bronze head of a warrior (c 1000–1100); Buddha heads of the 7C, one with a gold cap; and, also showing Indian influence, a bronze Siva dancing within a ring of fire.

## Other Departments

The NATIONAL PRINT ROOM (Ground Floor. Rooms 128–133) presents changing exhibitions, the material being either from the museum's permanent collection or on loan for special exhibitions. The permanent collection dates mainly from the 15C on, the 16C and 17C being well represented and including works by Rembrandt and his pupils and by Hercules Seghers. Also represented are works by the German 15C etcher known as the Master of the Amsterdam Print Room; French drawings of the 18C; and Dutch historical prints and portraits, and topographical illustrations. The LIBRARY (entrance 1A Jan Luykenstraat) contains over 45,000 volumes on the history of art, and a large selection of current periodicals, catalogues, etc. (Mon–Sat, 10.00 to 17.00 but closes 12.00 Thurs.) The main STUDY COLLECTIONS (Basement. Rooms 40–47) cover all the main departments of the museum.

# 2   Amsterdam to Den Helder and the Afsluitdijk via Alkmaar (including Texel)

Total distance 99km.—6km *Hembrug*—2km **Zaandam**—16km **Castricum**—10km **Alkmaar**—5km **Bergen**—14km **Petten**—23km **Den Helder**—17km *Hippolytushoef*—6km **Afsluitdijk**.

You can leave Amsterdam (see Rte 1) either by motorway and the Coen-tunnel or, more interestingly, by following a succession of streets NW from the area of the station to meet Nieuwe Hemweg which, beyond the motorway, reaches (*6km*) *Hembrug* where the Noordzee Kanaal is crossed by ferry alongside a great railway swingbridge. The ferry crosses to ZAANSTAD, the name given to the municipality which since 1974 combines the former municipalities of Zaandam, Koog aan de Zaan, Zaandijk, Worm-erveer, Krommenie, Assendelft and Westzaan, an industrialised though not unpleasant belt (often called the Zaanstreek) along the course of the canalised Zaan. Although now amalgamated the individual town names are still widely used, especially for road signs and postal purposes.

*2km* **Zaandam**, the chief place within Zaanstad, is best known for its association with Peter the Great, who came here because of his interest in shipbuilding for which Zaandam was an important centre. A statue of Peter building a boat stands in the town centre (Damplein). Peter the Great (1672–1725) made four visits to Zaandam. In 1697 the Russians sent a mission to the western powers to solicit support against the Turks, Peter attaching himself to this mission as the sailor Peter Mikhailov. As such he came to Zaandam where, on landing, he recognised one Gerrit Kist, who had formerly been in his service, and insisted on staying in Kist's humble wooden home for the few days during which he studied ship designs and did some practical work at Rogge's yard. Kist's house, now the *Czaar Peterhuisje* (Tues–Sat, and second and fourth Sun, 10.00 to 13.00; 14.00 to 17.00), in an alley leading off the Dam, was bought in 1818 by William I of Holland as a gift for the Grand Duchess Anna Paulowna who two years earlier had married the Dutch Crown Prince. She enclosed the house within a brick shelter, and further protection was given in 1865. In 1879 the house was given to Tsar Alexander III who in 1890, amongst other preservation measures, had the house lifted on to stone foundations. Finally, in 1895, Tsar Nicholas II renewed much of the stone building. The house, interesting for itself, contains many souvenirs and pictures and the small box-bed in which Peter slept can be seen. Peter again visited Zaandam in 1698 and twice in 1717.

At **Koog aan de Zaan**, just N of Zaandam, there are several fine old houses, one of which, a merchant's home of 1760 built partly of wood, contains the *Molenmuseum* (Tues–Fri, 10.00 to 12.00, 14.00 to 17.00; Sat, Sun, 14.00 to 17.00), devoted to windmills, of which there were once c 1700, as many as 600 in the Zaanstreek. At **Zaandijk**, just N of Koog and lining the W bank of the Zaan, the *Zaanlandse Oudheidkamer* (Tues–Fri, 10.00 to 12.00, 14.00 to 16.00; Sat, Sun, 14.00 to 16.00) occupying a house of 1706 (No. 80 in the main street) is the regional museum.

**Zaanse Schans**, attractively spread along the river opposite Zaandijk, is a 'village' (established 1960) with windmills and small houses in regional style illustrating local life as it was c 1700. The houses include a grocery, bakery, clock museum, period rooms, clog maker, and print gallery, and there is a centre with a restaurant and exhibitions. The windmills are a mustard mill (where local mustard can be bought), a saw mill, paint mill, and oil mill. Boat excursions can be taken along the river (site always open. Times for individual houses, mills etc. vary, but in principle 10.00 to 17.00. Tues–Sun in March–June and Sept–Oct; daily in July and Aug; Sat and Sun in Nov–Feb).

*Westzaan*, 2km W, has an early 18C church, an orphanage of 1717, and a town hall of 1783; it also preserves the best of the little 17–18C particoloured wooden houses for which the whole Zaanstreek was once known. *Assendelft*, to the W of Westzaan, a village some 6km in length with its S end on the Nordzee Kanaal, was the birthplace of the painter Pieter Saenredam (1596–1665).

To the N and E of Zaanse Schans are the WORMER and PURMER polders, reclaimed by Jan Leeghwater in 1626 and 1622 respectively, today agricultural land broken by a network of small canals but once with several whaling ports. *Jisp*, once such a port, is now a delightful village most of whose small houses are reached by little bridges over canals. The town hall here, with its triple gable, was built by Leeghwater in 1650. *Wormer*, W of Jisp, another former whaling port, has a town hall of 1640. Much of this polder land is a nature reserve with many bird species.

For Purmerend, 5km E of Jisp, and the district of Waterland to its S, see Rte 3.

*16km* **Castricum** (22,700 inhab. VVV, 6 Stationsweg), a mainly modern town, is important for its situation on the E edge of the NOORDHOLLANDS DUINRESERVAAT (ticket, map, etc. from VVV Castricum), an expanse of woodland and dunes of some 5000 ha. stretching along the coast for 14km between Egmond in the N and Wijk in the S. There is another area N of Egmond. The reserve is closed to cars, but there are several parking areas along the E side and along the Zeeweg, the road running to the shore from *Bakkum*, the N extension of Castricum. *De Hoep*, a visitor centre, is on Zeeweg, and *De Duinkant* (July–mid Aug: Sun, 11.00 to 17.00), further S on Geversweg, the road leading into the reserve from Castricum, is a small museum with some archaeological and old domestic material, early maps etc. The reserve has a network of foot and cycle paths, a magnificent beach (frequent bus from Castricum station), picnic areas and two camp sites.

It was at Castricum (and Bergen to the N) in 1799 that a combined British and Russian invasion force, led by the Duke of York and which had landed at Den Helder, was defeated by the French under General Brune. This led to the Convention of Alkmaar, by which the allies withdrew from the country and surrendered all their prisoners.

**Wijk aan Zee** (2500 inhab.), at the S end of the dunes reserve, is a small resort. The mouth of the Nordzee Kanaal is 3km S; on the other side of the canal, crossed by the triple-tube (rail and two roads) Velsertunnel or, more interestingly, by the road across the locks, is *Ijmuiden* (see Rte 5). **Beverwijk** (35,000 inhab.), 4km E of Wijk, is part industrial and part agricultural an centre.

*3km Limmen* is a bulb-growing centre, with a museum, the *Bloembollenmuseum*, at Dusseldorperweg 64 (mid Apri–mid Sept: Mon–Thurs, 09.00 to 12.00, 14.00 to 16.00; Fri, 09.00 to 12.00). *3km Heiloo* is another bulb centre.

*4km* **ALKMAAR** (84,000 inhab.), historically proud of its resistance to the Spanish in 1573 and today famous for its cheese market, lies on the W side of the Noordhollands Kanaal. It is a pleasant place of narrow streets, old façades, and tree-lined canals.

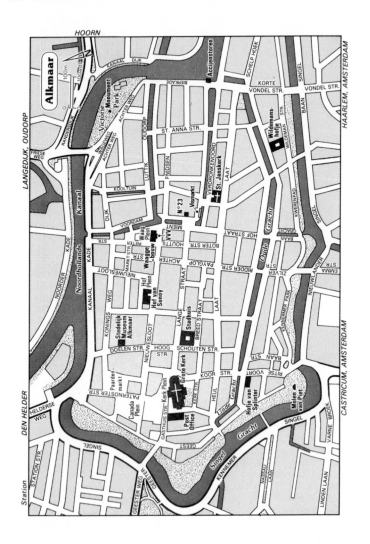

**Centre.** Waagplein; Lange Straat.

**VVV.** Waaggebouw, Waagplein.

**Post Office.** Just W of Grote Kerk.

**Station.** NW of inner town.

**Boats.** Excursions include local canals, the Alkmaardermeer, Zaanse Schans, and Amsterdam.

**History.** In the 10C, when the name first appears, this was a fishing village set among meres and marsh, but before long, perhaps because of its closeness to Egmond, the first territory of the counts of Holland, the place acquired importance and it received a charter in 1254. Alkmaar suffered frequently in the fighting between Holland, Friesland and Gelder, and later, in 1573, it was unsuccessfully besieged by the Spanish under Frederick of Toledo. Alkmaar's commercial importance much increased with the reclamation of the surrounding marshland which started in the later 17C. In 1799 the town gave its name to the Convention of Alkmaar (see Castricum, above). After the Second World War it was 'adopted' by the city of Bath, a gesture commemorated by the Bathbrug, a bridge near the cheese market.

**Natives**. The brother painters *Cesar* and *Allart van Everdingen* (1606–78, 1621–75).

The WAAGPLEIN is the scene of the *****Cheese Market** which is held every Friday (10.00 to 12.00) between about mid April and mid September. The cheeses mainly dealt with are the so-called Edam cheeses which, painted magenta for export, are familiar over much of the world. Dealers and exporters test the cheese by taste, smell, and texture, this last judged by crumbling. The porters, in white costumes and coloured hats, belong to a guild dating back to the early 17C. They form four companies, identified by the colours on their hats and barrows, each company made up of six porters and a collector, and each company foreman being recognised by a badge hanging from a ribbon of the company's colour. Cheese sold is taken by the porters to the Waaggebouw where it is weighed (the weight of each load being marked on one cheese) and then delivered to buyers' warehouses.

The ancient **Waaggebouw** traces its origins to a chapel founded in 1341. In 1582 the chapel was converted to weigh-house, this being the year in which Alkmaar regained its weighing rights, lost earlier because of bad administration (note the inscription 'S.P.Q.A. Restituit Virtus Ablatae Jura Bilancis'). The tower (1599) has a carillon with jousting knights (Fri, 11.00 to 12.00 during market season; also Thurs, 18.30 to 19.30 and Sat, 12.00 to 13.00). The building today houses the *Kaasmuseum* (April–Oct: Mon–Thurs, Sat, 10.00 to 16.00; Fri, 09.00 to 16.00), interesting not only for cheese but also for the interior of this old building. The displays are in two sections—the past and the present—the former in the magnificently timbered upper floor and showing homely vats, presses, churns and suchlike, the latter (with a shop) below.

Nearby, on Houttil, the *Nationaal Biermuseum* (times from VVV) was opened in 1986 in the former De Broom brewery.

A short way SE of the Waagplein, at Appelsteeg 2–5, there is a 16C wooden house in which is embedded a cannon ball from the siege of 1573.

Nieuwesloot, leading NW from the Waagplein, soon passes (N) *Hof van Sonoy*, a late 16C building on the site of the Maria Magdalena Klooster which disappeared c 1500, the buildings coming into the possession of the Van Sonoy family. In the mid 18C the building passed to the Reformed Church. The adjoining *Huis van Achten*, originally part of the Maria Magdalena Klooster, in 1656 became a hospice for eight (hence the name) old men, four of whom had to be Protestant and four Catholic. A short way further NW Doelenstraat leads off north. At No. 3 is the **Stedelijk Museum** (Mon–Thurs, 10.00 to 12.00, 14.00 to 17.00; Fri, 10.00 to 17.00; Sun, Holidays, 14.00 to 17.00) in a building of 1520, once the headquarters of the civic guard. The material here includes plans and pictures of the town, with particular emphasis on the siege of 1573, a collection of antique toys and medieval statuettes from the Grote Kerk. Among the pictures are works by Cesar van Everdingen (portraits of regents. Self-portrait); Maerten van Heemskerk (portraits); Willem van de Velde the Elder (Battle of the Sound, 1658); Pieter de Grebber (Burgomaster Van Teijlingen and his family); Hendrik Vroom (View of Alkmaar in 1638).

Hoogstraat leads S to Lange Straat, Alkmaar's principal street; on the corner is the *Stadhuis*, with a double-stairway entrance. The E wing with the tower dates from the early 16C while the W wing is of 1694. At the W end of Lange Straat stands the **Grote Kerk** (or *Sint Laurenskerk*), a Gothic building of 1470–1520 among the builders of which were the famous Keldermans of Mechelen in Belgium. The nave contains an organ (1643) designed by Jacob van Campen and painted by Cesar van Everdingen, and in the S transept there is a good brass to Pieter Palinck (died 1546) and his wife Josina van Foreest (died 1542) in an advanced Renaissance style (portraits of the pair by Maerten van Heemskerk will be found in the municipal museum). In the apse is the tomb of Count Floris V, who did so much for the benefit of his people and was murdered by the nobles in 1296, and the vault painting here of the Last Judgement (1519) is by Cornelis Buys, the Master of Alkmaar. The stalls and pulpit are of 1655, and the small organ in the N ambulatory, one of the oldest in regular use, dates from 1511.

At its E end Lange Straat meets a small canal; just across the bridge is a house (No. 23) bearing the arms of Alkmaar. The curiosity is that the lions face the wrong way, an insult offered in 1707 to the town authorities with whom the then owner had had a dispute. The *Vismarkt*, just S, was built in 1591 and restored in 1644; note the pump of 1785 and the roof figures. The *Accijenstoren*, at the end of Verdronkenoord running SE from the Vismarkt beside a canal, was put up in 1622 and was the office for excise and tax collection; in 1924 the gate was moved bodily a few metres out of the way of traffic. *St Janskerk*, just S of the Vismarkt, was founded in the 15C and rebuilt after a fire in 1760.

In the S part of the town there are a number of places of interest. Koorstraat runs S from the Grote Kerk to meet the Oude Gracht, the old inner moat, at the SW corner of the bridge being the *Hofje van Splinter* (1646), an almshouse for eight elderly ladies. Beyond, on the main ring canal and standing on the ramparts, there is a corn windmill of 1769 (*Molen van Piet*). Along the S side of the Oude Gracht there are 16–18C façades, beyond (also on the S side and beyond the fourth bridge from the Hofje van Splinter) being *Wildemanshofje* (1714), another hospice for elderly ladies. In *Victoriepark*, at the NE corner of the inner town, a monument, 'Alcmeria Victrix' (1873) commemorates the siege of 1573.

The district to the W of Alkmaar, stretching from roughly Petten in the N to Beverwijk in the S, is called KENNEMERLAND, a name which may derive from the Canninefates, a pre-Roman tribe believed to have lived between here and the Zuider Zee. The three Egmonds here, in a bulb-growing district, are the cradle of the County of Holland and hence of today's state, land here having been given to the Frisian Count Dirk I in 922.

At the inland village of **Egmond aan der Hoef** can be seen the scanty remains of the castle of the counts, destroyed in 1574, while **Egmond Binnen**, also a village and a short way S, is best known for its great abbey, founded in 950 by Dirk II and rebuilt in the 20C (no adm.). The village is also associated with St Adalbert, a Northumbrian companion of St Willibrord, who founded a church here in c 740; this church's successor was destroyed by iconoclasts in 1567, but the main tympanum survives as an exhibit in Amsterdam's Rijksmuseum. Adalbert is remembered by a spring in a field bearing his name (the Adalbertusakker). **Egmond aan Zee** (6000 inhab. VVV, Voorstraat 82A), a popular resort, offers two small museums. The *Museum Oude Scheepsmodellen*, in the Prins Hendrik Stichting, a home for retired seamen at Voorstraat 41, displays ship models, and there is also a museum of local history at Zuiderstraat 7.

At **Langendijk**, 6km NE of Alkmaar, *Broeker Veiling* (May–Sept: Mon–Fri, 10.00 to 17.00) is a curious waterway flower and vegetable auction, claiming to be the oldest in Europe. At the auction room, built on piles, visitors can do their own buying, and there are also a small museum and boat trips.

For **\*Schermerhorn Mill Museum**, 8km E on the Hoorn road, see Rte 3.

The main road follows the Noordhollands Kanaal, but this Route takes small roads to the W of this.

*5km* **Bergen** was where the Duke of York's Russian contingent was defeated in 1799 (see Castricum, above), an event recalled by a monument, while the *Sterkenhuis Museum* (Oude Prinsweg), occupying a house of 1655, contains local material and engravings illustrating the Duke of York's invasion. **Bergen aan Zee**, 4km W, a popular coastal resort, has a marine aquarium. *4km, Schoorl* was the birthplace (1495) of the painter Jan van Scorel. *5km* further on, off *Camperduin*, in October 1797, the Batavian Republic's Admiral J.W. de Winter, a member of the Patriot faction who in 1794 had returned with the invading French from exile, was defeated by the British Admiral Duncan. De Winter was held prisoner for two months, exchanged, then declared by court martial to have properly upheld the honour of the Republic. Northwards from here the chain of dunes ceases and the sea is kept out of the polders by the *Hondsbosse Zeewering*, a massive boulder-dike, the latest development in a series of dikes going back to the 15C. *5km* Petten seems to be at least the fourth village of this name, its predecessors disappearing as the result of the silting up of the tidal Zijpe in c 1365 and a disastrous flood in 1421. The district inland of Petten and stretching northwards beyond Schagen is the Zijpe Polder, drained in 1597.

The road leading N from **Petten** in 6km reaches a road junction. To the W the *Zwanenwater*, a large lake in the dunes, is a nature reserve known for its breeding spoonbills, while *Callantsoog*, on the coast just N of the lake, is popular with dune and woodland walkers. The road leading E from the junction in 2km joins the main Alkmaar-Den Helder road by the hamlet of De Stolpen. **Schagen** (19,000 inhab. VVV, Gedemte Gracht 69), 5km SE, claims ancient origin from a settlement of c 400. Some rights were given in c 1290 by Count Floris V, after which Schagen gradually developed into a commercial centre, receiving more formal charter rights in 1415. Two towers survive of the *Castle* of 1440.

The road northward from De Stolpen runs beside the Noordhollands Kanaal to reach (*23km* from Petten) **Den Helder** (64,000 inhab. VVV, Julianaplein 30), the port and naval base at the N tip of the province of Noord Holland. The car ferry to the island of Texel sails from here.

**History**. In the 17C what had for centuries been no more than a fishing village began gradually to develop into a naval base during the 17C. In 1811 Napoleon fortified Den Helder strongly and built dockyards, and during the reign of William I it became the main base of the Dutch navy. Between 1851 and 1876 the port's commercial importance greatly increased with the opening of the Noordhollands Kanaal.

The sea off Den Helder has been the scene of various military exploits. In August 1673 the admirals De Ruyter and Cornelis Tromp routed the allied French and British off Kijkduin; in January 1794 a detachment of French cavalry rode across the ice and captured a United Provinces' fleet, ice-bound between Den Helder and Texel; and in September 1799 a flotilla landed the Duke of York's 10,000 British and 13,000 Russian troops who were to meet defeat at Castricum and Bergen.

Near the Texel ferry quay, at Hoofdgracht 3, *Helders Marinemuseum* (mid Jan–Oct: Tues–Fri 10.00 to 17.00; Sat, Sun 13.00 to 16.30; June–Aug also Mon 13.00 to 16.30), occupying what was once a store for inflammable materials, covers the history of the Dutch navy generally since 1813, while a more peaceful theme, rescue and lifeboats, is that of the *Reddingmuseum Dorus Rijkers* at Keizerstraat 1A near the town centre (Mon–Sat, 10.00 to 17.00). *Nieuwediep*, the E part of the town, is the port at the mouth of the Noordhollands Kanaal, while *Willemsoord*, to the N, is the naval base (open days in summer).

DIVERSION TO TEXEL. The island of **Texel** (12,200 inhab., but many more in summer), the southernmost of the West Frisian Islands and also the largest (some 25km from N to S and up to 9km broad), is separated from the mainland by the *Marsdiep*, a channel (2km wide) kept free of sand by tidal races. The greater part of the island is polder (reclamation probably started about the 11C), this providing pasturage for some 25,000 Texel sheep, a breed which is farmed worldwide. The west coast, with its beaches, dunes and woods, attracts large numbers of summer visitors. The principal village is Den Burg, in the centre of the southern part of the island, while De Koog on the west coast is the main holiday resort.

Texel is known for its many breeding birds, including gulls, terns, ringed plovers, avocets and spoonbills, and there are a number of nature reserves, the largest being *De Muy* on the west coast between De Koog and De Slufter. Others are *De Geul* (SE), *Waalenburg* (near De Waal), and *De Slufter* (NW). For access, which may be restricted, apply VVV.

VVV. Groenplaats 9, Den Burg.

**Access.** Car ferry from Den Helder. Hourly, or half-hourly, throughout most of the day. Crossing, 20 minutes. No reservations. Motorists must expect delays, especially over weekends in summer. **Accommodation** of all kinds, but reservation essential in summer.

The ferry quay is at the SE of the island, from where a road leads to (6km) **Den Burg** (5000 inhab.), with the VVV and a museum of island history and antiquities. The village of *Oudeschild*, with a small harbour, lies 3km SE, while at *De Waal*, 2km N of Den Burg, there is an agricultural museum (implements, carts, etc.). Northwards from here stretches polder, with, at *Zuideierland*, a small airfield (island viewing flights).

The west coast is one of beaches and dunes, with several roads and paths leading to the sea. The resort of **De Koog**, first developed c 1900, now has accommodation and facilities of all kinds. The woods which run for 7km southward from De Koog, planted after 1900 as a means of stabilising the dunes, have waymarked walks, picnic sites, etc. Here too is a nature recreational centre, which includes a natural history museum (Mon–Sat, 09.00 to 17.00).

This Route now retraces its steps to (5km from Den Helder) *De Kooi* in a bulb-growing district, notably at Breezand, immediately SE. The road runs behind the coast, to the S being the *Anna Paulowna Polder*, named after the Russian consort of King William II, then bears NE along a causeway between the Waddenzee and the small Amstelmeer. After *12km* you reach

*Hippolytushoef*, where in 1918 Crown Prince Wilhelm of Germany took refuge (he returned to Germany in 1923). The town was the chief place of the former island of Wieringen (see Rte 3). *6km* brings you to *Den Oever*, a shrimping port, which stands at the S end of the **Afsluitdijk**, sealing off the IJsselmeer. Part in Noord Holland and part in Friesland, the dike is 30km long and carries a motorway which runs along its foot on the IJsselmeer side and therefore offers few chances of a seaward view as well. The two best stopping places, both combining seaward and IJsselmeer views, are the Monument Tower and Breezanddijk. In addition to the road, there are cycle and pedestrian ways.

Near the Den Oever end a memorial by Mari Andriessen honours Dr Lely, the man behind the Zuider Zee Reclamation Act of 1918 who died in 1929 and thus never saw the completion of his scheme. His 17C predecessor Hendrik Stevin, who drew up the early plans, is remembered by the *Stevinsluizen*, one of the two groups of sluices controlling the water level of the IJsselmeer; alongside there is a navigation lock. Not far beyond, a *Monument Tower* marks the spot where the last gap was closed on 23 May 1932, while nearby an attractive sculpture of a bending man with a stone commemorates the 50th anniversary of the achievement (the sculpture was unveiled by Queen Beatrix in May 1982). Facilities here include multi-lingual explanatory material, coin-binoculars and a café. Beyond, the dike enters the province of Friesland to reach the platform-island of *Breezanddijk*, also with facilities such as a café and a picnic area. Near the northern end of the dike is another group of sluices.

For Den Oever to Medemblik, Enkhuizen, Hoorn and Amsterdam, see Rte 3. For South Friesland, beyond the N end of the Afsluitdijk, see Rte 39.

# 3    Amsterdam to the Afsluitdijk via Hoorn, Enkhuizen and Medemblik

Total distance 93km.—6km *Het Schouw*—3km **Broek-in-Waterland**—3km **Monnickendam** (for **Marken**)—6km **Volendam**—3km **Edam**—17km **Hoorn**—16km **Enkhuizen**—19km **Medemblik**—20km **Afsluitdijk**.

The view to the E, between Amsterdam and Enkhuizen, will gradually change if the Markerwaard is drained and developed.

A pleasant alternative to the main road described below is to leave Amsterdam at its E end by the Zuiderzeeweg which crosses the IJ by swingbridge. At the N end of the bridge you can follow the small lakeside road past meres and waterways through *Uitdam* to Marken and Monnickendam.

By the main road Amsterdam is left by the IJtunnel. After *6km*, at *Het Schouw*, is a road fork which marks the start of the WATERLAND, an attractive region of ditches and meres. This Route bears NE.

ALTERNATIVE ROUTE THROUGH PURMEREND. The road continuing due N beside the Noordhollands Kanaal and across central Waterland in 9km reaches **Purmerend** (52,000 inhab. VVV, Kaasmarkt 20), no more than a fishing village until the reclamation of the local polders in the early 17C (see below) but thereafter a market centre enjoying charter rights it had in fact already received nearly two centuries earlier in 1485. In more recent times the town has combined a commercial role with that of dormitory for Amsterdam. The *Stadhuis* dates from 1591 and a number of façades survive in, for example, William Eggertstraat, a name recalling the benefactor of Amsterdam's Nieuwe Kerk. The town offers two museums. The *Museum Waterland* (Tues–Sun, 12.00 to 17.00; also 19.00 to 21.00 on Fri), at Weerwal 5, mounts several art exhibitions annually, while *Purmerends Museum* (July and Aug: Thurs 11.00 to 13.00), at Kaasmarkt 20, is of more modest and local interest, some emphasis being placed on local Art Nouveau earthenware.

Purmerend lies just E of the motorway which links Zaanstad with Hoorn and generally defines the E boundary of the (S–N) Wormer, Purmer and Beemster polders, all three already diked as early as the 14C but finally reclaimed in 1612–26 by J.A Leeghwater using some 26 windmills. Today this is an inviting district of small roads, canals and meres, mature with trees and rich in attractive small towns and villages. The Wormer and Purmer polders have already been mentioned in Rte 2 under Zaanse Schans. BEEMSTER is one of the Netherlands' most fertile polders, two principal small centres being *Middenbeemster* and *De Rijp*. At the former there is a church of 1623, while the local museum (Betje Wolff. May–Sept: Sat, Sun, 14.00 to 17.00; Tues, Thurs, 10.00 to 12.00, 13.30 to 17.00), at Middenweg 178, is in a former rectory of 1665 in which the writer Betje Wolff lived from 1759–77. De Rijp has a church of 1654 (tower 1661) and a triple-gabled Stadhuis designed by Leeghwater—as distinguished an architect as engineer—in 1630 for the town in which he was born. The local museum (In 't Houten, Jan Boonplein 2. Easter–Oct: weekends, 11.00 to 17.00; in July and Aug, daily except Thurs, 11.00 to 17.00) recalls something of De Rijp's past, prior to reclamation, as a whaling and shipbuilding port. Leeghwater also built the Stadhuis (1613) at *Graft*, a short way W.

Further N, the road to Alkmaar crosses the SCHERMER POLDER, remarkable for the fact that it continued to be drained by windmills, 52 of them, until as recently as 1928. Of these only 11 survive, three being the stepped range near Schermerhorn, brought back into use during the Second World War and today saved largely through the activities of a trust (the Schermermolens Stichting). One of these, immediately S of Schermerhorn beside the Alkmaar road, is the thatched *Museummolen* (May–Sept: Tues–Sun, 10.00 to 17.00. Oct–April: Sun, 11.00 to 16.30), which, with its sails still turning and in just the right setting, is one of the best and most pleasant museum mills in the country. Domestically the visitor sees the cosy small living rooms, with cupboard beds, one of which has transverse shelves for the baby's cot and chamber pot; and, functionally, the sails turn, while glassed-over holes in the floor enable the machinery to be seen and, outside, the great Archimedian screw does its work. Nor is this all in this district. At *Schermerhorn*, for instance, a restored church houses a museum devoted to the curious theme of the Dutch winter, showing sledges, skates, pictures and other material (Museum Hans Brinker, mid June–mid Sept: Tues–Sun, 12.00 to 16.00; Oct–mid June: Sun, 12.00 to 16.00), while at *Ursem*, 3km N, De Prinses combines an old and a modern cheese factory (June–Aug: Mon–Fri, or Sat, tours at 10.00, 11.00, 13.30, 14.30).

3km **Broek-in-Waterland** (2700 inhab.) is a cheese-making town with some wooden houses.

This Route now reaches the triangle around the shallow GOUWZEE formed by Monnickendam, Marken, and Volendam, three places of considerable if rather preserved and artificial charm, with narrow streets, small wooden fishermen's cottages, and costumes, though these are not as much worn as in the past. An over-popular tourist corner, much visited by day excursions (coach and boat) from Amsterdam, the three places in summer tend to become little more than crowded open air museums. Boat services link the three.

*3km* (from Broek-in-Waterland) **Monnickendam** (9500 inhab. VVV, De Zarken 2) has a triple-nave 15C church (restored 1979), with a tall galleried tower, a 15C font, and an oak choir screen dated 1563. The pulpit (1695) was brought from Winschoten. Nearer the port area are the *Speeltoren*, the tower of the old town hall, with clockwork figures, dating from the early 15C and today housing the local museum (mid June–Aug: Mon–Sat, 10.30 to 16.00; Sun, 13.30 to 16.00; also Fri, 19.00 to 21.00); the present *Stadhuis* in a mansion of 1746; and the 17C *Waag*, now a restaurant. Smoked eel is the local speciality.

**Marken**, on the other side of the Gouwzee, can be reached by boat or by road (7km), the last 2km being along the causeway of 1957. Before 1957 Marken was a flat island and, despite tourist boats, enjoyed something of the isolation and attraction of an island. Today the causeway ends at large car and coach parks from which visitors swarm into the village. The costumes, and the painted or tarred wooden houses, many on piles or artificial mounds because of flooding, nevertheless still exert a real charm, the whole, backed by the story of Marken's island past, brought together at the *Marker Museum* (Easter–Oct: Mon–Sat, 10.00 to 16.30; Sun, 12.00 to 16.00). Such isolation as Marken still enjoys will eventually disappear when it becomes incorporated into the Markerwaard.

The main road N out of Monnickendam crosses a waterway, beyond which a minor road bears E to *Katwoude* where a cheese works (De Jacobs Hoeve) can be visited. *6km* from Monnickendam, **Volendam** (17,000 inhab. VVV, Zeestraat 21) is known for its costumes, especially the winged lace caps of the women, and for its small port with little wooden houses, a part of the town long popular with artists though now swamped by tourists, souvenir shops, bars, ice cream stands, etc.

*3km* **Edam** (24,000 inhab. VVV, Damplein 1), an outstandingly picturesque old town with canals, drawbridges, and many old façades, was once a port with several shipyards (De Ruyter's fleet was built here), as such at its most prosperous during the 17C. The town has given its name to a cheese which is famous the world over. The centre is the DAMPLEIN, with the *Raadhuis* (1737), with notable stucco work inside, the post office, and a broad humped pedestrian bridge provided with seats. From the bridge there is a view W to the Speeltoren (see below). The municipal *Museum* (Damplein 8; April–Oct: daily, 10.00 to 16.00), is chiefly notable for its attractive 16C exterior, while Breestraat, alongside, leading N, soon reaches (corner of Eilandsgracht) the 15C *Houtenhuis*, the wooden house, the oldest in Edam. Kerkstraat, parallel to and W of Breestraat, runs N passing (left) the old orphanage (*Weeshuis*) and ending at the *Grote Kerk* (St Nicolaas), a spacious building of the 15C largely reconstructed after a fire in 1602. It is notable for its stained glass (1606–24), mainly heraldic, with trade marks and historical scenes, while a contrasting modern window commemorates the completion of restoration in 1934. The pulpit and screen date from 1649–57. Attached to the S side is the former *Latin School*. You can return to Damplein along Matthijs Tinxgracht, with at the N end, across the water, 16C almshouses. You soon reach the *Kaasmarkt* reached, with its *Waag* of 1592 (cheese can be bought and sent to almost anywhere in the world). Further S rises the pinnacled and leaning *Speeltoren*, a remnant of the 15C Kleine Kerk, with a Mechelen carillon of 1561, one of the oldest in the country.

*17km* **HOORN** (50,500 inhab. VVV, Nieuwstraat 23) is the former principal town of West Friesland. With its waterways and many façades, Hoorn is one of the most attractive towns in Holland.

**History.** First mentioned in a document of 1311, Hoorn received a charter in 1357. Until the end of the 17C, when it was ruined by the silting of the Zuider Zee, it was one of the chief ports in the region, being especially active in herring fishing, the first great net for which was made here as early as 1416. The Spanish occupied the town in 1569, but in 1572 it sided with the northern provinces, soon playing a leading role among the seven towns of the Noorderkwartier (see below).

**Natives** of Hoorn include the navigators Willem Schouten (1580–1625), the first to double the S cape of the Americas which he named Cape Hoorn (now Horn), and Jan Pietersz. Coen (1587–1629), one of the founders of the United Provinces' East Indies empire.

On RODE STEEN (Red Stone, the place of execution), the town centre with a statue of Coen, are the *Waag* (Hendrik de Keyser, 1609; rebuilt 1912) and the *Staten-College* (Council Building), the meeting place of the delegates of the Noorderkwartier, the Seven Towns of Holland N of the IJ (Alkmaar, Hoorn, Enkhuizen, Medemblik, Edam, Monnickendam, and Purmerend). The magnificent façade of 1632 bears the arms of Orange-Nassau, West Friesland, and the Seven Towns, and the wrought iron gates date from 1729. With fine rooms and woodwork the building is as beautiful inside as out.

Today the Staten-College houses the **Westfries Museum** (Mon–Fri, 11.00 to 17.00; Sat, Sun, 14.00 to 17.00). Devoted to the rather specialised story of the relatively obscure district of West Friesland and the Seven Towns, with virtually nothing explained in English, and with a disappointing failure to identify or ascribe many of the pictures and portraits, this may not be a museum of immediate interest to the foreign visitor. Nevertheless it will give pleasure to connoisseurs of sumptuous 17–19C panelled rooms, group paintings and contemporary furniture, glass and china.

The tour starts in the ancient cellars, dating back to the 14C and all that survives of the previous building on this site, occupied first by the Nijenrode family and later by the representative of the Archbishop of Utrecht. Here, in addition to temporary exhibitions, are displayed medieval ceramics; a 14C sarcophagus; 16C façade stones; skeletons from a tumulus at Oostwoud; and material excavated locally during the 1980s, with interesting associated photographs of the excavation work in progress. But to English and Scottish visitors probably the most curious exhibits are two gable stones of 1618 from a local mansion demolished in 1884. One shows Mary, Queen of Scots, and her husband Darnley; the other their son James VI of Scotland (James I of England) and his wife Anne of Denmark. Tradition tells that an early owner of the mansion was a Scottish merchant.

Of the upper rooms special mention may be made of **Room 6** in which there are portraits, several of them of children, by Jan Rotius and W.A. Veen, and of **Room 7** which was the council room of the delegates of the Seven Towns. It is now hung with paintings of the militia by Jan Rotius, the dates ranging from 1649–55. Rotius himself is the left-hand figure by the flag in the group closest to the window. **Room 11** is concerned with the East India Company, noteworthy here being portraits by Jacob Waben of Jan. Pietersz. Coen and of his wife, Eva Ment; a map of Batavia of 1628; a chimney-painting with the governors of the Hoorn section of the company (by Jan de Baen, 1682); views of the port of Hoorn; and several ship models. **Room 12**

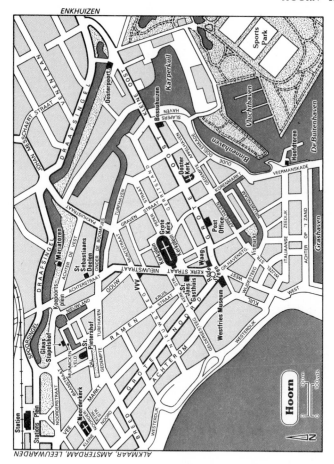

covers crafts and trades; in Room 16 there are a fine fireplace with *carvings of whaling scenes, and also paintings by H. Bogaert, Cornelis van Essen, Floris van Schouten and Jan van Goyen (Landscape with peasant cart). In **Room 18** will be found the oldest picture in the museum, a triptych of 1475–1500, but with the central panel over-painted in 1622 by Jacob Waben.

From Rode Steen two walks are suggested, one generally N and the other generally E and SE.

NORTH. Kerkstraat leads N; on the left you soon reach *St Jans Gasthuis* (1563), also known as *De Boterhal*, where the Westfries Museum holds temporary exhibitions. Opposite stands the large 19C *Grote Kerk*, with its two levels of department stores and roof converted to flats perhaps the most astonishing discovery in Hoorn. Off Kerkplein, on the N side of the church, is the small Admiraliteitspoortje (1607) with, to its N, the former Begijnhof, today of no character though still served by small gateways of 1610 and 1606. Beyond the church Kerkstraat becomes Nieuwstraat in which, by the junction of several roads, stands the pleasing twin-gabled **Stadhuis**, built in 1613, restored in 1903 and now housing VVV; to its left there is a fine gable with a marine theme. The police station, roughly opposite in Muntstraat, occupies the former East Indies House (c 1665). Now follow Achterstraat N; on the E beyond the canal is *Sint Sebastiaans Doelen* (1615), the house of the guild of St Sebastian (note the figures above the door). Achterstraat ends at KOEPOORTSPLEIN, to the E of which, in gardens above the moat, is the *Mariatoren*, a survival of the town defences. From Koepoortsplein this walk bears W into Munnickenveld, a particularly pleasing canal-side corner with 17C houses, with to the N *Glaas Stapelshof* (1682–1932) and to the W *St Pietershof* (1692), a hospital with a pleasant quadrangle. *Noorderkerk* (1441–1519), with good 17C woodwork, is some 300m further west. From Munnickenveld you can return to Rode Steen along Ramen and Kruisstraat.

EAST AND SOUTH-EAST. From Rode Steen, Grote Oost, with several good façades, leads E to the *Oosterkerk*, with a façade of 1606 and a stained glass window of 1620. Further E, near the canal on the corner of the junction with Slapershaven, the *Bossuhuizen* bear sculptured reliefs of the naval battle of 1573 when the Spanish Admiral Bossu was defeated and captured in the Zuider Zee by the United Provinces' fleet under Admiral Diercks. Beyond, across the canal, the *Oosterpoort* (late 16C). Follow Slapershaven S to reach the BINNENHAVEN beside which Oude Doelenkade and Veermanskade, the latter with a row of restored façades, can be followed SW and S to reach the Hoofdtoren, a tower with a belfry of 1651.

The district within the triangle formed by Hoorn, Medemblik and Enkhuizen is known as the DRECHTERLAND, a rich pastoral area with pyramid farms, large farmhouses with all functions contained under a single pyramidal roof, in long rows. A popular summer excursion through this country combines steam train, boat and modern train, the steam train (with buffet) serving Hoorn to Medemblik, the boat plying between Medemblik and Enkhuizen, and a mainline train providing the return to Hoorn (annual timetable from VVV).

*16km* **ENKHUIZEN** (16,000 inhab. VVV Stationsplein 1), though interesting in itself and with many picturesque corners, is most visited for the excellent Zuider Zee Museum. This is in two sections: Indoors (Binnenmuseum) and Outdoors (Buitenmuseum). As explained in more detail below, access to the Buitenmuseum is only by boat; motorists should follow the signs for the main jetty; cyclists and those on foot should make for the Station Jetty (see below).

Enkhuizen is linked by ferries (May—mid Sept) to Medemblik (no cars; twice daily; 1¼ hours); to Staveren (see Rte 39. No cars; three times daily; 1½ hours); and to Urk (see Rte 32A. Compulsory car reservation, Tel: 05277-3407; two or three times daily; 1½ hours).

**History.** Granted its first charter in 1355, Enkhuizen during the 17C had a population of some 40,000 and, later, the largest herring fleet in Holland, but prosperity ended in the late 17C with the silting of the Zuider Zee. In 1572 it was the first town in Noord Holland to throw off the Spanish yoke.

**Natives.** The painters Paulus Potter (1625–54), Jan van Neck (fl. 1587–92), and Dirk Ferreris (1639–93).

The main street is the long, narrow and lively Westerstraat, at the W end of which is the *Westerpoort* (or *Koepoort*) of 1649. After crossing the Oude Gracht canal the steet is pedestrianised. You soon reach on the left the *Westerkerk* (St Gommarus), a 15C building with a detached wooden belfry of 1519 and containing a *choir screen of 1542, with reliefs of Moses, Joshua and the Evangelists, a pulpit of 1568, and a striking modern font of 1958 by H. Verhulst. Just beyond the church, on the S side of the street, the *Weeshuis* (1616 but rebuilt) has a sculptured portal, while near the end of Westerstraat rises the *Zuiderkerk* with a massive tower; dating from 1423–1524, the church contains remains of 15C vault paintings.

A short way N across Westerstraat, at Kaasmarkt 8, the **Waag** of 1559 now houses the local museum (Tues–Sat, 10.00 to 12.00, 14.00 to 17.00; Sun, 14.00 to 17.00) which incorporates the room used by the Guild of Surgeons in the early 17C, whilst just to the SE stands the **Stadhuis** of 1688, a dignified building by Steven Vennecool in which the ceilings and overmantel were painted by the local artists Jan van Neck and Dirk Ferreris. The adjacent *Oude Gevangenis* (1686), long a prison, is now a museum of weapons (VVV for opening times). From here Zwaanstraat crosses the Ooster Haven to reach the indoors section of the Zuider Zee Museum.

The **ZUIDER ZEE MUSEUM** (Rijksmuseum Zuiderzee), its basic theme the way of life of the people around the Zuider Zee and in neighbouring districts prior to the completion of the Afsluitdijk, is effectively two museums, an Outdoors section (the Buitenmuseum) of buildings collected from all around the old Zuider Zee and set up as a 'village', and an Indoors section (Binnenmuseum) concerned largely with Zuider Zee shipping. The two museums are within 300m of one another on the E flank of Enkhuizen between the town and the water, but to avoid local traffic congestion special access arrangements have been made. These are summarised below (see also sketch).

1. The only access to the Buitenmuseum is by ferry, and motorists should follow signs to the car and coach parks, ticket office and embarkation jetty (Main Jetty) which is near the start of the Enkhuizen to Lelystad dike road. Visitors without cars embark at the Station Jetty, from where the ferry takes them to the Main Jetty.
2. Access to the Binnenmuseum is by road.
3. Most visitors will probably wish to see both museums, in which case it is essential to start with the Buitenmuseum. As mentioned above motorists should park at the Main Jetty; others start from the Station Jetty. Boats leave from the Main Jetty every 15 minutes; there are pleasing views of Enkhuizen's waterfront on the way to the Buitenmuseum.

After touring the Buitenmuseum there is a choice between returning by boat to the Main Jetty or walking (5 to 10 minutes) to the Binnenmuseum. The visit to the Binnenmuseum completed, there is another walk (of some 10 minutes, through some attractive corners of the town and passing the squat Drommedaris tower of 1540, once guardian of the harbour) to the Station Jetty and the boat back to the Main Jetty. A long half-day should be allowed for the round of the two museums.

The **Buitenmuseum** (early April–mid Oct: daily, 10.00 to 17.00), opened in 1983 and concerned with the Zuider Zee way of life on land rather than at sea, is an astonishing achievement, comprising as it does some 130 houses and other buildings collected from around the Zuider Zee—and indeed from further afield, for instance Zoutkamp, once on Groningen's Lauwers-

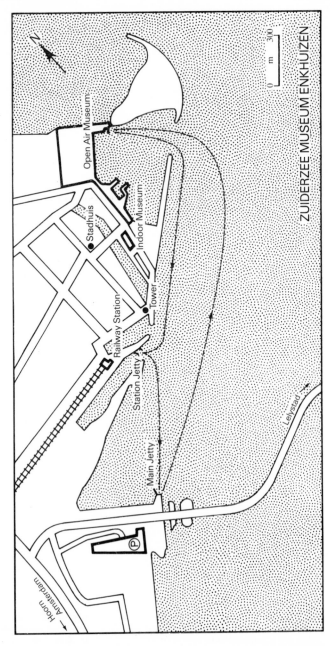

meer—and assembled here as several groups, carefully laid out from the evidence of old records. There is an excellent illustrated English guide and there are also free guided tours lasting about one hour (see also below).

Many visitors will be content simply to wander around, enjoying the frequent picturesque glimpses and poking into the several homely interiors. Others, making use of the plan, may prefer to follow a route which, starting from the ferry jetty and ending at the exit for the Binnenmuseum, takes in the essence of the museum. This route would start with three conspicuous limekilns (from Akersloot), once a commonplace in the local landscape and used for the production of building mortar through the slow burning of shells mixed with peat dust. Passing on the left a row of nine cottages, once lining a street in Monnickendam (the information office is also here and the starting point for guided tours), a right turn leads you through the area of Zoutkamp, a place once so important in the context of fishing from Groningen; the houses here, built of authentic local red clinker bricks, are laid out to a plan shown on an old village map. Beyond, the path curves to pass, on the right, buildings from Enkhuizen and Vollenhove; one of these is the workshop of a brushmaker while another houses an exhibition about three fishermen who drifted for two weeks on an ice-floe. Beyond, the small town of Urk, once an island and now on the reclaimed Noord-Oost Polder, is represented within the loop of the small canal.

The path now returns to the waterfront, there swinging back NW to pass on the left a Hindelopen cottage, now in use as a restaurant, and cross the canal to reach (right) a steam laundry from IJsselmuiden dated from c 1910. The path kinks past houses from Zwartsluis, opposite which a bridge crosses the Gracht. To the left, on the other side, are buildings from Purmerend, Zaandijk and Landsmeer, this last, once a cheese warehouse and today a restaurant, of particular interest for having been brought here in one piece. To the right the path passes another restaurant (once a bakery in Hoorn), a Hoorn pharmacy and a souvenir shop occupying a house from Edam.

You now cross two small bridges to reach (just on the left after the second) a slipway from Wervershoof (1873) with, beyond, a typical West Frisian orchard. Back across the second bridge a row of buildings extends SW within the angle of two small canals, two of these being from the Haarlemmer Houttuinen, today a street near Amsterdam's station but formerly timber yards beside the IJ. One of these now houses an exhibition about the setting-up of the museum. From here a bridge crosses to the Wieringen quarter, with post office and church. Running away from the latter is a line of buildings from Harderwijk, including two farmhouses and a grocer's shop.

Disabled people intending to visit the Binnenmuseum should now leave by the gate opposite the end of the Harderwijk street. Others should make their way generally southward to reach Haven Marken, a replica of the harbour built in 1830 on what was then the island of Marken. Here are a slipway (N side) and, on the S, a group of buildings from Marken, Volendam and Monnickendam, amongst these the former Volendam fish auction office, a gutting and salting shed and curing shelters. Just beyond, this tour ends at a tanning area with two masts between which tanned sails (tanning was usually the job of the sailmaker) were hoisted to dry.

The exit for the Binnenmuseum is a short way further.

The **Binnenmuseum** (early April–mid Oct: Mon–Sat, 10.00 to 17.00; Sun, Holidays, 12.00 to 17.00) fronts on to the Wierdijk of 1567, this name meaning Seaweed Dike and recalling that the medieval dikes were built around a core of seaweed. Opened in 1950, the main part of the museum occupies adjoining old buildings; the Peperhuis, built in 1625 as home and warehouse for a merchant ship-owner, Pieter van Beeresteijn, and a 17C warehouse of the East Indies Company whose ships discharged in the Ooster Haven at the rear. Although devoted essentially to Zuider Zee shipping and associated themes, the museum's scope has broadened in recent years. There is a detailed guide in English.

**Room 1** is the Ship Gallery, a fine hall with four fishing vessels, five pleasure craft, a potato carrier and an ice-boat from Urk. This last is perhaps the most interesting, if only because its function was to keep open communications between the islands of Urk and Schokland and the town of Kampen as well as, not infrequently, to rescue ice-bound ships. **Room 2**, showing much colourful and elaborate work, is concerned with ships' decoration. **Room 3** shows changing exhibitions. **Room 4** illustrates domestic life around the Zuider Zee, including some very ornamentally carved cupboards; painted furniture from Hindelopen and elsewhere; painted sledges and cradles and even a beautifully decorated step-ladder. **Room 5** is for exhibitions, while **Room 6** is the place for crafts and trades such as ship building, sail and rope making and even cheese making, with some fantastically carved and intricate presses. **Room 7** shows carved furniture (unpainted), firebacks and some porcelain and silver.

With **Room 8** there is a return to shipping, the principal theme being fishing, imaginatively illustrated by various nets, the use of which is well shown in diorama form. **Room 9** houses some of the museum's large collection of model ships.

Beyond Rooms 10 and 11, reserved for temporary exhibitions, there comes a series of *Period Rooms with costumed figures. Among the regions represented are Zaan, West Friesland (1890), Hindelopen (early 19C), and Marken, Urk, Spakenburg and Volendam (all c 1930). **Room 16**, the Tile Room, provides a survey of the main types of Dutch tile between 1580 and about 1910.

ENKHUIZEN TO LELYSTAD (32km). This dike road, completed in 1976 as the first step in the reclamation of the Markerwaard, offers an unusual drive, scenically more interesting than the Afsluitdijk because for much of the way the road is along the top of the dike. About half-way a stone monument, unveiled by Prince Claus (14 December 1976), takes the form of a symbolic chain commemorating the linking of West Friesland (a district of the province of Noord Holland) and Flevoland. This road will become of even more interest if the draining and development of the Markerwaard progresses.

Leaving Enkhuizen the road N keeps close to the coast, passing *Andijk* and *Wervershoof* with bulb-fields to the S.

*19km* **Medemblik** (7000 inhab.), today known as a yachting centre, is an ancient town and port granted a charter by Floris V in 1289. By the lively harbour stands the much preserved *Kasteel Radboud* (in origin 13C; exhibitions May–Sept), today a restaurant but once a stronghold of the counts of West Frisia and named after the Frisian pagan king who in 689 was defeated by the Frank Pepin of Herstal at Wijk bij Duurstede and compelled to cede most of West Friesland. The fine Gothic *Sint Bonifaciuskerk*, with some late 17C stained glass, has the tomb of Lord George Murray (1695–1760), the commander of the Jacobite right at Culloden, who died in exile at Medemblik. In summer a steam train runs to Hoorn (see under Hoorn for the triangular Hoorn–Medemblik–Enkhuizen excursion), and at the station of 1869 there is a steam train museum. See Enkhuizen for passenger ferry.

A pleasant diversion can be made into the countryside to the SW of Medemblik. Here *Opperdoes*, 2km SW, is an interesting example of a village built concentrically from a terp mound, while the long village of *Twisk*, almost an extension of Opperdoes, has several 18C and 19C pyramid-roof farmhouses. Further SW, Abbekerk, Hoogwoud, Sijbekarspel, Benningbroek, and Midwoud are all attractive and characteristic rural communities.

The roads N from Medemblik cross the WIERINGERMEER POLDER, much of which was once the island of Wieringen which received a charter as long ago as 1289. In the 1920s a dike was built between Medemblik and Den Oever, the area on the W side then being drained and the island joined to the mainland to form the present polder (prior to this, the coast ran from Medemblik to Kolhorn, now far inland); this was the first stage of the modern Zuider Zee reclamation programme. The polder, much of which is 6m below sea level, became a municipality in 1941. In April 1945 the Germans blew up the dike in two places, completely flooding the polder which, however, was pumped dry by the end of the year; by spring 1946 the land had been resown and the reconstruction of the three villages and 500 farms begun, the task being completed in 1953.

*20km* Den Oever and the Afsluitdijk (see Rte 2).

For Den Oever to Den Helder, Alkmaar, and Amsterdam, see Rte 2; for South Friesland, across the Afsluitdijk, see Rte 39.

# 4   Amsterdam to Hilversum

Total distance 27km.—13km **Muiden**—7km **Naarden**—2km **Bussum**—5km **Hilversum**.

The motorway (A1) leading E out of Amsterdam runs in c *6km* between *Diemen* (N) and *Bijlmermeer* (S), the latter a 'new town' of massive housing blocks planned for some 80,000 people. Beyond, the motorway crosses the Amsterdam-Rijn Kanaal, and is then left for the remainder of this Rte.

*7km* **Muiden** (7000 inhab. VVV, Kazernestraat 10), lying either side of the Vecht river and busy with pleasure and other craft, is best known for its *\*Muiderslot* (Mon–Fri, 10.00 to 17.00; Sun, Holidays 13.00 to 17.00; closes 16.00 in Oct–March. Guided tours only, lasting 1 hr; last tour 15.00.), a red-brick castle attractively set in moated, green surrounds. The castle's builder (1285) was Count Floris V of Holland, who in 1296 was murdered here by noblemen who, it is thought, did not like his policy of granting charters and of generally favouring the common people in preference to themselves. Soon afterwards razed by the Bishop of Utrecht, the castle was rebuilt in 1370–86 on its original foundations. The place knew its best years between 1609 and 1647 when the poet and historian Pieter Hooft was bailiff of Gooiland and castellan of the castle. He attracted many distinguished and regular visitors, including Hugo Grotius the jurist, the poets Joost van den Vondel and Constantijn Huygens, and academics from Amsterdam's Athenaeum Illustre, a group which later became known as the Muiden Circle. After Hooft's death the castle was neglected until restored in

1895–1909, and again in 1948 when it was decided that the interior should be furnished as far as possible in the manner of Hooft's time. The principal room is the Ridderzaal, and the cellars house a restaurant.

*Muiderberg*, 3km E, is a small waterside holiday centre on the Gooimeer. A motorway crosses to Zuidelijk Flevoland (see Rte 29).

**Weesp**, 3km SW up the Vecht, has a town hall of 1776 in which a small museum (mid June–mid Sept: Mon–Fri, 09.00 to 12.00; Sat, 14.00 to 17.00) exhibits Weesp porcelain, made here between 1759 and 1771 by Count van Gronsveldt-Diepenboik, who had been ambassador in Berlin and brought home his interest; generally basically white or clouded brown, the ware tends to be conservative in design and painting, the latter largely the work of French artists, but imaginative spouts, handles, etc. are nevertheless a feature. The *Laurentskerk* dates from 1462 and contains a rood screen of 1525.

For the upper Vecht, see Rte 17A.

The route passes through the district of GOOILAND, stretching SE to Hilversum. With its scenic variety of woodland, moorland, and lakes, the opportunites for boat cruises and water sports, and several pleasing towns and villages, the district is a popular excursion area from Amsterdam. The *Naardermeer*, a reedy lake to the S of the motorway, is a bird sanctuary noted for spoonbills, grebes, and bitterns.

*7km* **Naarden** (16,000 inhab. VVV, Adriaan Dortsmanplein), important as a fortress town, is also known for its Grote Kerk and for its association with the Moravian educationist Komenski, also known as Comenius. The double line of fortifications (generally 1675–85) was first planned after the town was sacked in 1572 by Alva's son, Frederick of Toledo, whose troops gained entry by treachery and then butchered the inhabitants. The town's fortress aspect is the theme of the *Vestingmuseum* at the Turfpoortbastion at the SW edge of the town, with casemates, cannon, dioramas, old prints and much else (Easter–Oct: Mon–Fri, 10.00 to 16.30; Sat, Sun, 12.00 to 17.00). Marktstraat, running NW to SE, cuts the town in half; off the street's southern end is Adriaan Dortsmanplein, named after the architect who was much concerned with the early 17C expansion of Amsterdam and who also designed parts of Naarden's fortifications.

In the town centre, beside Marktstraat, are the Grote Kerk and the Stadhuis. The *Grote Kerk* (May–Sept: daily except Friday, 14.00 to 16.00), originally built between 1380 and 1440, suffered two early fires and was rebuilt in its present form in 1479. The church is known for its early 16C *vault paintings with many panels showing biblical themes, for a wooden choir screen of 1513, and for the annual performance here (week before Easter) of Bach's 'St Matthew Passion'. The tower (45m, 265 steps) affords a wide view over Gooiland and the lower Vecht. The nearby *Stadhuis* (summer, Mon–Fri, 13.30 to 16.30), a Renaissance building of 1601 with a fine interior, is successor to one in Turfpoortstraat (leading off Marktstraat to the S) destroyed in 1572. On the site now stands the *Spaanse Huis* (1615), carrying a stonework depiction of the slaughter of 1572. This Spaanse Huis now houses the *Comeniusmuseum* (March–mid Dec: Tues–Sun, 14.00 to 16.00) with relics of the Moravian (now Czechoslovakia) educationist, philosopher and writer Johann Amos Komenski (1592–1670), exiled from Moravia in 1621. A strong opponent of the contemporary pedantry, he was perhaps the first advocate of what would today be called visual aids. Komenski died in Amsterdam, but is buried here in the *Waalse Kapel* (apply museum) which is on the corner of Jan Massenstraat and Kloosterstraat in the northern section of the town. The chapel was once that of a Franciscan convent, now barracks, and was leased to Czechoslovakia in 1933, Czech artists then converting the interior to a mausoleum. Komenski is also commemorated by a statue, by the Czech sculptor Vincenc Makovsky (1957), near the Utrechtsepoort.

*2km* **Bussum** (33,000 inhab. VVV, Wilhelminaplantsoen 6), adjoining Naarden on the S, is essentially a dormitory town for Amsterdam. From the tourist point of view the main attraction is likely to be the *Rozenwerkerij De Wilde*, on Prinses Irenelaan on the SW edge of the town, claiming to be the largest display of roses in the country.

To the E, beyond woods, are, from N to S, the three towns Huizen, Blaricum and Laren. *Huizen*, on the Gooimeer, is something of a centre for water sports. *Blaricum* and **Laren** (12,000 inhab.) are typical of this region, in which occasional farms are to be found interspersed among modern estates. The latter was for many years the home of Anton Mauve (1838–88), Hague School painter of the Gooiland. The *Singer Museum* (Tues–Sat, 11.00 to 17.00; Sun, 12.00 to 17.00), at Oude Drift 1, is a culture and art centre with a permanent collection of paintings by the founder W.H. Singer (1868–1943) and also works by other 19C and 20C artists, including French and Dutch Impressionists. There is also a *Geological Museum* (Tues–Sun, 13.00 to 16.30) at Zevenend 8A.

*5km* (from Bussum) **Hilversum** (88,000 inhab. VVV, Emmastraat 2) is, with Baarn and Soestdijk-Soest (both in the province of Utrecht, see Rte 16A), one of a group of prosperous residential towns set in park-like country, notable for its gardens and fine trees; the town is perhaps best known as the centre for Dutch broadcasting. The architectural name here is that of W.M. Dudok (1884–1974), local director of public works (1915–28) and from 1928–49 city architect, his principal building being the *Raadhuis* (1931), some 800m W of the station (guide to other buildings from VVV). The *St Vituskerk*, in Emmastraat, 500m S of the station, is a neo-Gothic design by P.J.H. Cuijpers. For those interested in gardens and trees there are the *Blijdenstein Pinetum* (Mon–Fri, 10.00 to 12.30, 13.30 to 16.00) at Van der Lindenlaan 25, with 450 species; the *Costerustuin* botanic garden (daily, sunrise to sunset) at Zonnelaan 2; and the *Corversbos* centre (apply VVV) at Vaartweg 202. Additionally the *De Vaartmuseum* (Mon–Fri, 10.00 to 12.00, 14.00 to 17.00; Sat, Sun, 12.00 to 17.00), at Vaartweg 163, shows local and regional material of many kinds.

The château of *Trompenburg* (no adm.), 2km W immediately S of the village of 's Graveland, was built in the 17C by Admiral Cornelis Tromp.

Hilversum is closely surrounded on the E, S, and W by the province of Utrecht. For nearby places in this province, notably Baarn (6km E), Soestdijk-Soest (7km SE), Amersfoort (16km SE), and the lake area of the Loosdrechtse Plassen (6km SW), see Rtes 16A and 17A. For Utrecht (13km S), see Rte 15.

# 5   Haarlem and Environs

**HAARLEM** (152,000 inhab.), capital of the province of Noord Holland, stands mainly on the W bank of the winding River Spaarne. The inner town, in which are most of the places of interest, is enclosed by this river on the E, the Nieuwe Gracht on the N, the Leidsevaart on the W, and the Raamsingel, Gasthuissingel, and Kampersingel on the S. A small canal, the Bakenesser Gracht, cuts across the NE of the inner town, while, towards the W, a now filled-in canal, Haarlem's oldest moat, is represented by the streets Nassaulaan and Gedempte Oude Gracht. The town has several notable old buildings, especially almshouses (hofjes)—one of which now houses the Frans Hals Museum; access to some is restricted.

**Centre.** Grote Markt.

**VVV.** Stationsplein, N side of Nieuwe Gracht.

**Post Office.** Gedempte Oude Gracht 2.

**Station.** N of Nieuwe Gracht.

**Boats.** Excursions, from Binnen Spaarne (near Gravenstenenbrug), include local waterways; Avifauna (see Alphen, Rte 9); Zaanse Schans (see Rte 2); Kaagerplassen ('Mills and Lakes' tour), a short way N of Leiden.

**History.** Mentioned as early as the 10C, Haarlem started as a settlement on the Spaarne, and it is recorded that the Bakenes, a spit of land into the river, now roughly the NE corner of the inner town, was used by the counts of Holland as a place from which to levy tolls; the early fortification here, the Gravensteen, is recalled by the name of the bridge by the S end of Bakenesser Gracht. In 1245 a charter was granted by Count William II, who also built a hunting lodge and jousting lists on 't Zand, now the Grote Markt. In 1572 Haarlem sided with the insurgent North, soon afterwards being besieged (December 1572 to July 1573) by the Spaniards under Frederick of Toledo, son of the Duke of Alva. The Spaniards eventually took the town, despite the efforts of William the Silent to relieve it and despite also the heroism of the townswomen who formed a company under Kenau Simons Hasselaer, later rewarded for her courage by being appointed Treasurer of the States of Holland and Zeeland. The Spanish success was achieved through the movement of their Zuider Zee fleet, under Admiral Bossu, into the Haarlemmer Meer, thus cutting off the town's only line of supply. Haarlem then offered to surrender on condition that a general amnesty would be granted if 57 of the leading citizens were handed over. Frederick agreed, but three days later started to massacre the garrison, beginning with the Governor, Wigbold van Ripperda; in all he killed some 1800 of the garrison of 4000, all the Calvinist ministers, and several other citizens. In 1576 the town was largely destroyed by fire; in 1577 it was reoccupied without opposition by the army of the States General; and in 1578 (29 May) it saw the plundering and wrecking of many churches and religious houses. From the 17C on Haarlem's story has in the main been one of continuing prosperity.

**Natives and Others.** Haarlem was the birthplace of the architect Lieven de Key (1560–1627) and of the painters Salomon van Ruysdael (c 1600/1603–70) and his nephew Jacob van Ruysdael (?1628/9–82). Also of the painters Bartholomeus van der Helst (?1613–70), Philips Wouwerman (1619–68), the brothers Adriaen and Isaak Ostade (1610–85, 1621–49), Claes Berchem (1620–83), and Jan Wynants (fl. 1643–died 1684). Carel van Mander (1548–1606), Hendrick Goltzius (1558–1617) and Cornelis Cornelisz. (1562–1638), the last a native of the town, laid the foundations of Haarlem's pre-eminence as a centre for art theory, printmaking and painting during the period 1580–1600 and are well represented in the Frans Hals Museum. **Frans Hals**, though probably born in Antwerp, spent most of his life in Haarlem and died here in 1666. In the 15C Haarlem was one of the earliest centres of printing, and Laurens Coster (1370–1440), a native, is claimed to be at least co-inventor with Gutenberg of the art of printing from movable blocks.

In the GROTE MARKT, formerly known as 't Zand and the site of the jousting lists of Count William II, there is a statue by Louis Royer of the medieval printer Laurens Coster. Around the square are the Grote Kerk, the Vleeshal, and the Stadhuis. The large **Grote Kerk** (Mon–Sat, 10.00 to 16.00 or 15.30 in Sept–March) of St Bavo (c 589–654), patron saint of the diocese, was built between c 1400 and 1550, successor to a church of around 1100, probably destroyed by fire in 1328. To the Grote Markt side is attached the former fish market (Vishal), dating from 1768, but successor to a medieval market, while to the Oude Groenmarkt side cling a number of small houses, one of which serves as office and entrance.

The spacious interior has a vaulted cedar ceiling, supported on 28 columns, and there is a small triforium. You enter the south transept, where a tablet on the south-west column of the crossing commemorates the invention of printing (1423) by Laurens Coster, known to be buried somewhere in the church. Moving anticlockwise, the first chapel was that of the Brewers' Guild, the arch keystones depicting St Bavo and St Martin, the guild's patron saint. A curiosity on the central column are records of the heights of a giant called Cajanus and a dwarf called Paap, both of whom lived in Haarlem; their pictures are alongside. By the nave column opposite the chapel are the tombs of F.W. Conrad and Brunings, engineers of the Katwijk sluices (1804–07); also near here are models of 17C warships, the design and gift of a member of the Shipbuilders' Guild. The *choir screen (c 1510) and also the brass lectern are the work of Jan Fyerens, a brass founder from Mechelen who was commissioned by the Shoemakers' Guild. The choir stalls, surmounted by coloured blazonry, are Renaissance work of 1512–75; note the misericords and the armrests. Frans Hals is buried in the choir (slab No. 56). At the NE of the choir ambulatory there are several slabs bearing carved shoes and tools, the tombs of members of the Shoemakers' Guild.

Moving into the north aisle, the chapel under the small organ was the Lady Chapel, with some stone coffins and an old documents chest; this organ (c 1600) was brought here in 1907 from a monastery in Breda. The badly damaged remains of a sculptured group in the N transept were exposed at the time of the Reformation. In the nave north aisle the chapel was that of the Dog Whippers, the top of a column here having a representation of one of these officials whose task it was to keep the church clear of stray dogs.

The great organ was built by Christiaen Müller of Amsterdam in 1735–38 and restored in 1868. For long the largest and finest in existence, and still one of the best organs known, it has 5000 pipes and has been played by Handel and Mozart (at the age of ten). Frequent recitals are given. The group of marble figures below the organ is by J.B. Xaverij (1697–1752); one figure, holding a book, represents poetry, a second with a harp represents music, and the third, to whom the others are paying homage, is the town as patroness. To the left of the organ is a woodcarving, the Seat of the Holy Ghost, recalling the Guild of the Holy Ghost whose task it was to give bread to the poor (see group by *Jan Verspronck* in the Frans Hals Museum).

Moving along the south aisle, the chapel on the right is the Font Chapel, the wrought iron screen of which is interesting for the way it is held to the wall by a small hand. In the left wall beside the chapel is a cannonball which lodged here during the siege of 1572–73. Roughly opposite, the font and pulpit are both of the 17C, though the latter has a 16C sounding board.

The ***Vleeshal**, or meat market, is a highly embellished Renaissance style achievement of Lieven de Key (1602); the columns inside are original

168

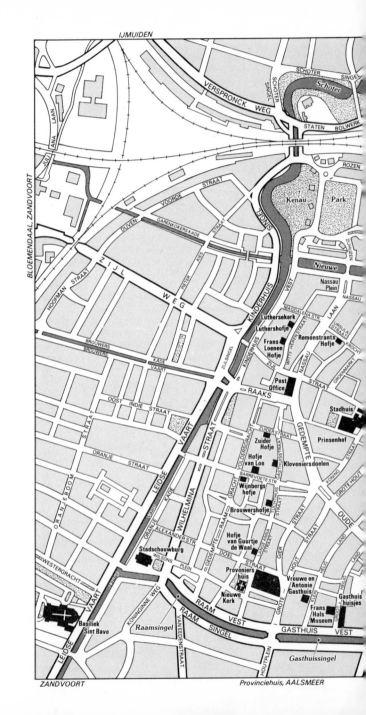

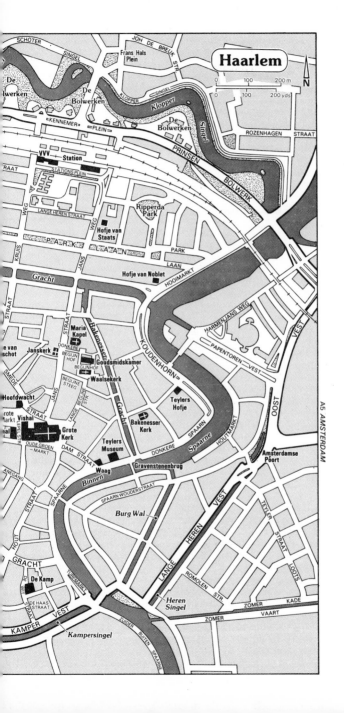

Haarlem

although the remainder of the interior was gutted at the beginning of this century. The building is now used for art exhibitions.

The **Stadhuis**, at the other end of the Grote Markt, originated (1245–50) as the Gravenzaal, the great hall in which the counts of Holland entertained after hunting. It was destroyed in fires of 1347 and 1351, Count William V then giving the site to the town which built a town hall here by the end of the 14C. The centuries that followed saw many alterations, Lieven de Key designing the wing along the Zijlstraat (1620–22) and the date 1630 on the front façade referring to the last major rebuilding. If municipal business allows, visitors are admitted to the great hall (still called the Gravenzaal), where there are some panel-paintings (end 15C) of the counts and countesses of Holland. If you particularly request it, and if there is no meeting in progress for this is a working building still, you may be able to gain admission to the Vroedschapkamer (council chamber) a room decorated c 1630 with a suite of images celebrating Haarlem's history: a tapestry after *C.C. van Wieringen* (c 1580–1633) of the Capture of Damietta (1629), an incident in the Crusades where Haarlem citizens triumphed; *Pieter de Grebber* (c 1600–1652/3), The Emperor augments Haarlem's coat of arms with the sword (1630), and after De Grebber, a tapestry: The Patriarch of Jerusalem augments Haarlem's coat of arms with the Cross (1630). Note also the two fine fireplaces with allegorical and grotesque carvings celebrating reason and civilisation.

At the time of the original Gravenzaal there was a monastery behind, but this also was destroyed in the fires of 1347 and 1351, though the cloister and the library (restored 1963) survive. The name Prinsenhof recalls a residence of the Prince of Orange built in 1590 on the site of the monastery, the church of which was plundered and damaged beyond repair on 29 May 1578.

NORTH OF THE GROTE MARKT. By the corner of the Grote Markt and Smedestraat the *Hoofdwacht* façade dates from c 1650 when the building housed the civic guard. It was in an earlier building on this site that the town's officials met between the granting of the charter in 1245 and the construction of the town hall around the end of the 14C. Jansstraat leads N, with the former *Janskerk* (14–15C) on the left; now housing archives, this was originally the church of a monastery in which the painter Geertgen tot Sint Jans (?1465–?93) lived. Opposite, reached by either Begijnesteeg or Donkere Begijnhof, is the attractive small quarter of the former Begijnhof, with the *Waalsekerk* (from 15C), that of the Begijnhof until passing to the Walloons. Nearby (just N) you can see the exterior of the *Goudsmidskamer* (16C in origin), the guild room of the goldsmiths and silversmiths. Further along Jansstraat, on the right, the *Mariakapel*, next to the neo-classical St Josephkerk, houses a figure of Mercy dating from the Middle Ages and once part of an altar in the Bakenesserkerk.

Jansstraat crosses the Nieuwe Gracht, at the E end of which, on the corner with Hooimarkt, the *Hofje van Noblet* dates from 1761. Jansstraat continues N to cross Parklaan, beyond which on the right is the *Hofje van Staats* of 1730, beyond again being the bus terminal and *Station*. Behind the station and extending E and W the remains of the late 17C fortifications (*De Bolwerken*) have been a public park since the last century.

EAST OF THE GROTE MARKT. Damstraat runs SE and soon reaches the river, on the corner being the *Waag*, dating from 1598 and probably designed by Lieven de Key.

Also near the corner, at 16 Spaarne, is *Teylers Museum (Tues–Sat, 10.00 to 17.00; Sun, 13.00 to 17.00; in Oct–Feb the museum closes at 16.00), founded in 1778 through the bequest of Pieter Teijler van der Hulst, a wealthy merchant, with the aim of encouraging scientific and artistic study. The museum, the oldest established in the Netherlands, is best known for its collections of fossils, scientific instruments, and sketches by Rembrandt, Raphael, Michelangelo, and many others. There are also good paintings (mainly 19C).

**Rooms 1 and 2** show fossils, amber, skulls and several large crystal formations displayed under domes. Among the fossils, Diluvian Man, a primeval bird known today as *Archaeopteryx* and a giant lizard (*Mosasaurus*) are all of some scientific renown. **Room 3**. Physical and astronomical instruments, including Van Marum's electrostatic machine of 1784. **Room 4** is the Oval Room, built in 1780 by Leendert Viervant with a library gallery around the upper part. In this room are a portrait of Pieter Teijler at his desk, more instruments, and also geological specimens, many displayed in unusual and original pyramidal cases. **Room 5**, sometimes used for temporary exhibitions, in principle shows pictures by such artists as Anton Mauve, Jozef Israels and G.H. Breitner.

**Room 6** shows the museum's distinguished *collection of sketches by, amongst others, Rembrandt, Raphael and Michelangelo. These are rotated throughout the year but those by the above are always shown in July and August.

**Room 7**. Paintings, including examples of the Dutch Romantic School. *C. Springer*: Oude Zijds Voorburgwal, Amsterdam (1878); *Andreas Schelfhout*: Winter landscape; *Barend Koekkoek*: Summer landscape, Winter landscape; *A.H. Bakker Korf*: *Tea visit; *N. Pieneman*: Attempt on the life of Prince William in 1582—a very dramatic scene, showing the alarm probably reasonably true to the occasion even though painted some 300 years later; *J.C. Schotel*: sea scenes; *Philip Courbet*: portraits; *H. van Hove*: The Departure; *Wijbrand Hendriks* (once curator of the museum's fine art collection): several works, including a particularly interesting painting of the Oval Room in c 1810 showing the same display cases as are in use today.

To the NE of the museum the Bakenesser Gracht crosses this corner of the town. Beyond are the *Bakenesserkerk* of the late 15C with a mid 16C tower and, a short way further NE, *Teylers Hofje* of 1787. Close to Teylers Museum the Spaarne is crossed by the *Gravenstenenbrug*, this name recalling the ancient fortification from which the early counts levied tolls. Across the bridge Spaarnwouderstraat leads NE to (400m) the **Amsterdamse Poort**, the only remaining town gate; originally built in c 1355, the gate now is mainly of the late 15C.

SOUTH OF THE GROTE MARKT. Grote Houtstraat leads SW, crosses Gedempte Oude Gracht, now a street but formerly the town's oldest moat (see picture by Job Berckheyde in the Mauritshuis in The Hague), and in 500m from the Grote Markt reaches the junction with Gierstraat. Here the *Proveniershuis*, the club house of the St Joris Doelen (the archery order of St George), has a façade dating from 1591. The *Nieuwe Kerk*, a short way W of the Proveniershuis, was built in 1645–49 to a design by Jacob van Campen but has an older tower of 1613 by Lieven de Key. Grote Houtstraat now reaches the Singel waterway, along which Gasthuisvest branches E, the next street being Klein Heiligland, in which No. 64 is the *Vrouwe en Antonie Gasthuis*, an almshouse of the 17C. The next parallel street is Groot Heiligland, a short way up which are (E) the *Gasthuishuisjes*, a series of almshouse homes of c 1610, and, opposite, the **FRANS HALS MUSEUM** (Mon–Sat, 11.00 to 17.00; Sun and Holidays, 13.00 to 17.30; also mid May–early Sept: Sat 19.30 to 23.00).

The museum occupies the former Oudemannenhuis, designed in 1608 by Lieven de Key as a hospice for old men; the building became an orphanage in 1810, remaining such until bought by the city in 1906 when it was restored and enlarged to open as a museum in 1913. In 1981 a new wing was added for modern art. Discounting this new wing, the museum surrounds a courtyard-garden laid out in 17C style, across which the main building represents what were the Governors' Room and the Refectory, this last, structurally still largely intact, today furnished from now demolished Haarlem homes.

Although Frans Hals is still, as he always has been, the essence of this museum, the collections today—some 250 paintings and 450 decorative art exhibits—date from the 16C to the present day and embrace a galaxy of artists and subjects. Additionally there are frequent temporary exhibitions.

For most visitors the highlight of the museum will be the *series of group portraits by Frans Hals, but, as will be seen from the lists below, there is wide and distinguished representation by many other artists. As to the decorative arts, exquisite examples will be found in most of the rooms, these ranging from a dolls' house, faithfully portraying in miniature the rich lifestyle of an 18C merchant, to furniture, lace, tiling, glass and an opulent display of Haarlem silver.

The paintings fall into four groups—Frans Hals; Other Portrait and Group Painters; Landscapes, Still life and Genre; Modern and Contemporary.

The museum entrance from the road is on the E from where an anticlockwise circuit (in principle chronological) is suggested, starting along the north wing, off which is the Modern Art wing, and continuing to the west wing with the best of the Frans Hals groups. The south wing may well be taken over by a temporary exhibition. Following is a selection of the works likely to be found.

FRANS HALS. There are five Civic Guard group portraits—Banquet of the officers of the Civic Guard of St George, painted in 1616 and the earliest of the series; Banquet of the officers of the Civic Guard of St George (1627); Banquet of the officers of the Civic Guard of St Adrian (1627); Officers and sergeants of the Civic Guard of St Adrian (1633), the most appealing of all the groups, remarkable for its vivid life and individual characterisation; Officers and sergeants of the Civic Guard of St George (1639). Other group portraits afford an interesting contrast, showing, as they do, citizens of sober responsibility as compared to the almost swashbuckling members of the Civic Guards—Governors of St Elisabeth's hospital (1641). Governors and Governesses of the Oudemannenhuis (i.e. of this building when a hospice), painted in 1664 when Hals was over 80. Note here that an appropriate landscape painting of the Good Samaritan hangs behind the governesses.

Individual portraits by Frans Hals include Nicoleas van der Meer, Burgomaster of Haarlem (1631); Cornelia Vooght Claesdr., wife of Van der Meer (1631); Archdeacon Zaffius (1611).

OTHER PAINTERS—HISTORY AND PORTRAIT. *Jan van Scorel*: Members of the Brotherhood of the Holy Land after their return from Jerusalem (c 1530); the members are shown in formal procession, and inscriptions record their names and dates of visiting; note how Jan van Scorel literally earmarks himself by folding down the edge of his own inscription. This is the earliest known group portrait in the Netherlands and was one of a series (another is in Utrecht, Centraal Museum) which probably surrounded an octagonal Jerusalem Chapel. Baptism of Christ (c 1530), commissioned when Scorel was living in Haarlem after his return from Italy. *Maerten van Heemskerk*: two wings of a triptych, with the Annunciation on the front, and, on the

*Banquet of the officers of the Civic Guard of St. Adrian by
Frans Hals, 1623, Frans Hals Museum. Perhaps the finest of the
group portraits by Hals in this museum*

back, the Adoration of the Magi and of the Shepherds; St Luke painting
the Madonna and Child (given by the artist in 1532 to the Guild of St Luke)
a strange work the allegory of which is still obscure; Ecce Homo. Crown of
Thorns. *Cornelis Cornelisz.*, an artist whose bravura style influenced the
early work of Frans Hals: Adam and Eve; Baptism of Christ; Judah and
Tamar; The Wedding of Peleus and Thetis (1593). This last was painted for
the town hall; with the Judgement of Paris in the background it is a theme
often associated with peace—Paris' choice, of course, led to his elopement
with Helen and the beginning of the Trojan war. The two Civic Guard
paintings (1584 and 1599), though lesser in scale and immediacy than those
of Hals, were clearly influential on the Hals groups. *Hendrick Goltzius*:
Mercury, Minerva (both 1611) and Tityus bound to the Rock (1613). These
three pictures have recently been reinstated as important works. Goltzius,
an internationally famous printmaker, turned to painting late in his career;
painting, and its status as a liberal art, is clearly the subject of the first two
pictures. *Hendrik Pot*: Apotheosis of William I (the Silent); Parade of the
Arquebusiers. *Jan Verspronck*: Governesses of the Holy Ghost Hospital
(1642); Governesses of St Elisabeth's Hospital; Portraits, including one of
Wilhelmina van Braeckel, wife of Anthonie de Liedekercke, member of a
family also portrayed by *Gerard Terborch*. *Jan de Bray*: Reception of poor
children at the orphanage; Governors of the Orphanage; Governors of the
Leper House; The monumentality and spatial clarity of De Bray's work is
characteristic of the Haarlem Classicists, a group of painters around Pieter
de Grebber who were in direct line from the classicising mannerism of
Cornelis and Goltzius. *Wijbrand Hendriks*: several portraits, including one
of the artist.

LANDSCAPES, STILL LIFE, GENRE. *Hendrik Vroom*: Arrival at Vlissingen in
1613 of Frederick V of the Palatinate with his wife Elizabeth (the 'Winter

Queen', daughter of James I of England). Hendrik Vroom, who specialised in seascapes, was one of the most successful painters of his time, his designs also being employed by tapestry weavers; tapestries after his designs were a royal gift from the States General to James I of England and hung in the old Palace of Westminster until the Great Fire of 1832. *Jacob Matham* (1561–1631) The Brewery 'De Drye Lelyen' at Haarlem and the country house 'Velserende' near Brederode belonging to Jan Claesz. Loo (1627). Matham, stepson of Goltzius, made this unusual *penschilderij* (pen-paint-ing, this is the earliest known) for an ambitious Haarlem brewer—it is unusual in being a *tromp l'oeil* of a print and in combining together with a picture a contemporary indication (in the inscription below) of the recre-ational nature of country house life (see below, Haarlem to IJmuiden, for Brederode Castle). *Jan van Goyen*: Winter Scene (1625); Haarlemmerpoort in Amsterdam. *Pieter de Molijn*: Plundering of a village. *Pieter Saenredam*: Interior of the Nieuwe Kerk, Haarlem (1652). *Adriaen Brouwer*: Tavern interior. *Jan Steen*: Village fair. *Adriaen van Ostade*: Peasant with a pig. *Isaak van Ostade* (brother of Adriaen): Rest at an inn; Barn interior, with a slaughtered pig. *Jacob van Ruisdael*: Landscape with dunes (1650). *Claes Berchem*: Hilly landscape with herdsmen. *Jan Wynants*: Landscape. *Gerrit Berckheyde*: Grote Markt at Haarlem; dated 1676 and showing the Grote Kerk and Vishal. *Wijbrand Hendriks*: several works, including the charm-ingly domestic Interior with a sleeping man and a woman darning. *Isaac Ouwater*: The Amsterdamse Poort, Haarlem, c 1785.

MODERN AND CONTEMPORARY. The Modern and Contemporary Art wing (often with temporary exhibitions) shows paintings, sculpture, graphic art, textiles art and ceramics, the collections embracing not only works by Haarlem artists, but also Dutch Impressionism and Expressionism, Cobra and contemporary trends. Among the many artists are *Jacobus van Looy* (Self-portrait, 1896); *Isaac Israels* (Portrait of the Sultan of Java, 1922); *Jan Sluyters*; *Leo Gestel* (Lady with a large hat; a Cubist work of 1913); *Karel Appel*; *Constant* (Nocturnal Animals; a gouache, abstract fantasy of 1946); and *Sjoerd Buisman* (Leaning Willows; 1981).

Grote Houtstraat is continued southward beyond the canal bridge by the broad streets Houtplein and Dreef. The latter is crossed (500m from the bridge) by Paviljoenslaan, E along which is the *Provinciehuis*, the seat of the administration of Noord Holland, occupying a mansion built in 1788 in which Louis Bonaparte lived for a while, signing his abdication here in 1810. The *Hofje van Heythuizen*, an almshouse of 1651, is off Kleine Houtweg, the next road S off Paviljoenslaan. Dreef continues S to enter the **Haarlemmer Hout**, the large park which is all that survives of the forest which once extended to The Hague. WEST OF THE GROTE MARKT are several almshouses, and are mentioned below in two groups—those N and those S of Raaks.

The *Corrie ten Boomhuis* at Barteljorisstraat 19 remains an active family business, a clock shop founded in 1837; since 1988 it is also a museum dedicated to the everyday heroism of a Dutch family during the German occupation (The Hiding Place Museum: Mon–Sat, 10.00 to 16.30; last tour 16.00; 1 Nov–1 April, 11.00 to 15.30. The Horlogerie/Clockmakers: 9.00 to 18.00; Mon 10.00 to 16.30; closed Sun and holidays). The Ten Boom family were one of the many households who protected '*onderduikers*' (sub-merged—i.e. Jews in hiding); betrayed to the Gestapo in February 1944 the family and about thirty friends were arrested and deported to death camps. The four onderduikers and two Resistance fighters remained hidden behind a false wall on the top floor for two and a half days while the Gestapo lingered, convinced of their presence and hoping to starve them out. Corrie ten Boom survived Ravensbrck and wrote the story. The tiny hiding place with standing room only, and the concealed roof terrace, in exactly the original state are affecting sights.

Barteljorisstraat leads N out of the Grote Markt to reach Kruisstraat, at the start of which (No. 44, W side) is the *Hofje van Oorschot* of 1770. In Ursulastraat, a short way W, is the *Remonstrants Hofje*. Ursulastraat runs into Nassaulaan, the next parallel street to which is Witte Herenstraat with, beside one another, the *Luthersekerk* and *Luthershofje*, the latter having an open air pulpit which can be reached from the church. A short way S, at No. 24, the *Frans Loenen Hofje* was first built in 1607; the attractive small gate is of 1625.

In Zuiderstraat, the road parallel to and to the S of Raaks, there is the *Zuider Hofje*, while in Gasthuisstraat, running S from Zuiderstraat, No. 32 is the *Kloveniersdoelen* (16C), the headquarters of the arquebusiers; the arched gate of 1612 leads to an attractive courtyard. In Barrevoetestraat, the next street to the right, there are two almshouses opposite one another, on the N being the *Hofje van Loo* (No. 7), which, however, lost its courtyard character when the street was widened in 1885, and on the S the *Wijnbergshofje*. Tuchthuisstraat can be followed S from the E end of Barrevoetestraat, with at No. 40 the *Brouwershofje*, while further S, in Lange Annastraat, is the *Hofje van Guurtje de Waal*. For the *Nieuwe Kerk*, further S, see above (South of the Grote Markt).

To the SW, in the angle of Leidsevaart and Raamsingel, stands the *Stadschouwburg*, the municipal theatre of 1918, the anonymous gift of a citizen. You can cross the Leidsevaart here, and 200m S of the bridge is the Roman Catholic **Basiliek Sint Bavo** (J.T. Cuypers, 1906; towers 1930). Built in neo-Gothic style, with almost oriental touches, the basilica, 100m in length, 41.6m broad, and 60 metres high, is one of the largest church buildings in the Netherlands. There is a treasury, and recitals are given on the Adema organ of 1923 (Easter–Sep: Sat, 15.00).

## Environs of Haarlem

HAARLEM TO IJMUIDEN (10km). A choice of roads run N either partly through or just E of the woods and dunes that make up a national park (*De Kennemerduinen*), stretching some 4km to the sea. The local natural history is explained at a centre (in *Overveen*) called Van Vloedlijn tot Binnenduin (summer: daily, 09.00 to 17.00; winter: Sat, Sun, same times), while at *Bloemendaal* there is an open air theatre. *Ruine Brederode* (March–Oct: daily except Sat, 10.00 to 17.00), some 2km further N in wooded surroundings, are the ruins of a castle founded in the 13C, though what is seen today is certainly later. In 1351 the castle was besieged by the Kabbeljauws and surrendered, but it returned to the Hoeks in 1354. Rebuilt in 1464, the place was destroyed by the Spanish during the 1573 siege of Haarlem, thereafter lying in ruins until partial restoration in 1862. The name Brederode first appears in 1244, the beginning of a line of nobles the most famous of whom was Hendrik van Brederode, one of the founders in 1565 of the League of the Nobility, dubbed 'ces gueux' (those beggars) by the counsellors of Margaret of Parma. This castle remained a Brederode possession until the family line died out in 1679.

In *Spaarndam*, 4km E, Frans Hals married his second wife in 1617. At

**Velsen**, 4km N, the Nordzee Kanaal is crossed by the *Velsertunnel*; built in the 1950s the tunnel is 1644m in length (including open sections) and comprises three tubes, one rail and two road. To the S, in Driehuis, *Beeckestijn* is an 18C mansion with period rooms. **IJmuiden** (35,000 inhab.) has developed since the opening in 1876 of the Noordzee Kanaal. This follows the former course of the IJ, and the town lies on the S side of the mouth of the river. The town is both a holiday resort with woods, dunes, beaches, and a breakwater stretching some 1km out to sea, and also an important fishing port with an auction. The *Pieter Vermeulenmuseum* (Mon–Fri, 09.30 to 17.00; also first Sun in month and all Sun during summer, 11.00 to 17.00), at Moerbergplantsoen 22, has natural history exhibits and model ships. The great *sea locks*, however, are perhaps the most interesting feature of the place. The Zuidersluis was completed soon after the opening of the canal, but this quickly proved inadequate and the Middensluis was built in 1896, the depth of the canal at the same time being increased to ten metres. In 1931 the large Noordersluis was opened, 400m long and 50m wide. N of the locks there is now a new sluice, so that the water outlet can be kept clear of the ship locks. A road crosses the locks to the industrial area of **Velser Noord**, from the SW corner of which projects a long breakwater marking the northern entrance to the canal.

For places to the N, see Rte 2.

HAARLEM TO ZANDVOORT (8km). **Zandvoort** (16,400 inhab. VVV, School-plein 1) is, after Scheveningen, the most popular of Holland's coastal resorts (casino, dolphins, etc.). To the N, the *Zandvoort Circuit* is a motor racing track (1948), while to the S, the *Waterleidingduinen* form a dunes park of 3600 ha. These dunes have been a resort of Haarlemmers since time immemorial and the view inland is a familiar sight in landscape paintings.

HAARLEM TO LEIDEN, see Rte 6.


# 6   Haarlem to The Hague via Leiden


## A.   Haarlem to the Hague

Total distance 44km.—10km *Hillegom*—4km **Lisse** (for *Keukenhof*)—4km **Sassenheim**—12km **Leiden**—14km **The Hague**.

Between Haarlem and Leiden this Route runs down the E side of Holland's principal horticultural district (*De Bloembollenstreek*), the main centres being Hillegom, Lisse (Keukenhof gardens) and Sassenheim. As a rough guide the best flowering times are crocus, first half April; tulips, mid April to latter half of May; daffodils and narcissus, April; and hyacinths, second half of April (see Introduction). You can complete the bulb circuit bearing W on the outskirts of Leiden for Katwijk, then head back N through Noordwijk to reach Vogelenzang and Hillegom.

To the E of this Route extends the polder country of the Haarlemmermeer (see Rte 9).

For Haarlem, see Rte 5. *4km. Heemstede* is a garden suburb, on the E edge of which, at Croquiusdijk 27, is the *Croquius Expo* (April–Nov: Mon–Sat,

10.00 to 17.00; Sun, Holidays, 12.00 to 17.00; closes 16.00 in Oct and Nov), one of the three steam pumping stations used in 1849–52 to drain and convert the huge Haarlemmermeer to a polder. This polder was in fact the first to be reclaimed by steam, the three pumping stations doing what previously would have required about 160 windmills. Here today, within the castellated waterside building, is preserved the massive original steam beam engine, built by Harvey and Co., Hayle Foundry, Cornwall. Other exhibits include an ingenious model presentation showing the progressive dates of reclamation in Holland from 1456 onwards and well defining the areas N of Amsterdam drained during the 17C; a good illuminated model illustrating the draining and creation of a polder; some windmill models; and a variety of vintage engines together with vintage maps and drawings.

*2km Linnaeushof* (April–Sept: daily, 10.00 to 18.00) was formerly Harte-camp, a country estate where Linnaeus (or Carl von Linné), the Swedish botanist, then visiting Leiden, lived for a while in 1736–37 as the guest of an English banker, George Clifford. The grounds are now a large recreational park (Europe's largest, it is claimed), with gardens, woodland, picnic areas and over 300 play attractions for children. At *Vogelenzang*, 2km SW, the Frans Rozen nurseries (April–May Tulipshow: daily 08.00 to 18.00; July–Sept Flower Show: daily 09.00 to 17.00) were established in 1789.

A short way S of Linnaeushof you enter the province of Zuid Holland and the main bulb growing strip begins, the first centre being (*4km*) *Hillegom* (19,000 inhab.), site of the National Bulb Centre. *4km* further **Lisse** (20,000 inhab. VVV, Grachtweg 53A) is known for the famous *\*Keukenhof* (end March–end May: daily, 08.00 to 18.30), a park of 28ha. with a magnificent show of bulbs, fine trees, flowering shrubs, a heath garden, ornamental cascades and ponds, and 5000 sq m of glasshouses. Lisse's annual Flower Parade is held at the end of April, and in the town centre, at Heereweg 219, is the *Museum voor de Bloemenbollen Streek* (April and May: daily 10.00 to 17.00; June–March: Tues–Sun 13.00 to 17.00). Although admirable in what it sets out to be, the museum may disappoint the serious bulb fancier for it is concerned with the past rather than the present. The museum is in two parts, the first being a simple and very well presented (text in English) story of this district from remote prehistoric to modern bulb-growing times, while upstairs, showing tools and suchlike, the themes include sorting and storage. Boat trips on the Kagerplassen, a lake system to the S representing a survival from the Haarlemmermeer, are a popular local excursion (departures in summer every half-hour from the Lissebrug. Duration 1½ hours).

Leaving Lisse, immediately on the left of the main road and opposite a garden centre, you will see a mellow, fortified house known as *Huys Dever*; built in 1375 the house, much restored, is now used for exhibitions and concerts. At (*4km*) **Sassenheim** (13,000 inhab.), on the W of the town, are the ruins of the 11–13C *Burcht Teylingen*, the castle in which the unfortunate Jacqueline of Bavaria died in 1436. **Noordwijk aan Zee** (24,000 inhab. VVV, De Grent 8), 8km W across the bulbfields, is a popular coastal resort; the place, too, where the educationalist Dr Maria Montessori (1870–1952) died.

*12km* from Sassenheim is Leiden, see Rte 6B below. In *6km Wassenaar*, seat of the early lords of Leiden, is an elegant residential town with many large houses in parklike grounds. *8km* takes you to The Hague (Den Haag), see Rte 7.

# B.  Leiden

**Leiden** (104,000 inhab.), or in earlier form *Leyden*, a pleasant town with a number of interesting buildings, some attractively situated beside canals, is visited principally for its several excellent museums, notably the Rijksmuseum van Oudheden, the national museum of antiquities. The town is famous for its university, the oldest and most important in the Netherlands and for centuries a seat of international culture.

**Centre.** Stadhuis, Breestraat.

**VVV** Stationsplein, opposite the **Station** at the NW of the town.

**Parking.** Stationsplein and Lammermarkt 250m E (both, and especially the latter, convenient for the Boerhaave, Ethnology, De Valk windmill, and De Lakenhal museums). Hooglandse Kerkgracht and Kaasmarkt (for the Hooglandse Kerk and the Geology and Mineralogy museum). Immediately W of Pieterskerk (for the National Museum of Antiquities).

**Post Office.** Breestraat.

**Boats.** Excursions around local waterways. Also to the Kagerplassen and Brasemmermeer by the Oude Rijn; windmills cruise; Avifauna at Alphen.

**History.** Some authorities associate Leiden with the Roman Lugdunum Batavorum, but it seems more likely that this was in the duneland near The Hague. More probably Leiden started as a settlement at the point where the then important N–S road running between the dunes and the water of the Haarlemmermeer crossed what is now called the Oude Rijn, today insignificant, the main waters of the river having been deflected far upstream into the Waal and the Lek. The place is first mentioned as an appanage of the lords of Wassenaar, and the castle, the mound of which could be of Saxon or even Roman origin, was certainly in existence in the 12C, but the town's prosperity dates from the immigration of the Flemish weavers who settled here after the Black Death (c 1350), Leiden's cloth remaining famous until the 18C. In 1572 Leiden sided with William the Silent, and from October 1573 to October 1574 it was besieged by the Spanish; temporarily relieved in March, it was besieged again in May, the defenders then suffering horribly from hunger and disease. The Burgomaster, Pieter van der Werff, refused to surrender, and at length William relieved the town, but only after cutting the dikes and flooding the whole country between Leiden and Dordrecht; then, aided by a S wind, William's flotilla of boats, under Admiral Boisot and laden with men and provisions, was swept up to the town walls. This was on 3 October, a day still celebrated with fairs and processions. It is said that as a reward for their gallant stand William offered the citizens a choice between the remission of taxes for a period of years or the foundation of a university, and that they chose the latter. In any event William founded the university here in 1575.

  In 1807 the explosion of a barge laden with gunpowder caused the loss of 150 lives and the destruction of many houses.

**Natives and others.** Leiden was the birthplace of many famous artists, including Lucas van Leyden (?1489–1533), Otto van Veen (1558–1629, the master of Rubens), Jan van Goyen (1596–1656), Rembrandt van Rijn (1606–69), Willem van de Velde the Elder and Younger (1611–93, 1633–1707), Gerrit Dou (1613–75), Jan Steen (1625/6–79), Gabriel Metsu (1629–67), Frans van Mieris (1635–81) and his son Willem van Mieris (1662–1747). Other natives were Daniel and Nicolaas Heinsius (1580–1665, 1601–81), the classicists, and Herman Boerhaave (1666–1738), who brought world renown to the university's medical faculty. John of Leyden (Johan Beukelsz, or Buckholdt; ?1508–36) was a leader of the Anabaptist movement which for two years ruled the German town of Münster. The Elzevir family, religious fugitives from Leuven (Louvain), established a press here in 1580 and became important in the story of printing (their house was destroyed in the 1807 explosion). Linnaeus (1707–78), or Carl von Linné after his ennoblement in 1761, the Swedish botanist, took his degree in medicine at Harderwijk in 1735 then came to Leiden where he published his 'Systema Naturae'. For others associated with Leiden, see below under University.

**Summary of Museums and Art Galleries**. Below is a summary, in order of mention in the text, of Leiden's several museums and art galleries. For opening times see under individual entries.

**Pilgrim Fathers Documents Centre**.
**University Museum**: history of the university.
**\*\*Rijksmuseum van Oudheden**: archaeology, Egyptian, Greek and Roman antiquities.
**Rijksmuseum van Geologie en Mineralogie**.
**\*Stedelijk Museum De Lakenhal**: history, art and culture of Leiden; furniture, applied art, 16C and 17C paintings.
**Molenmuseum De Valk**: 18C windmill.
**Museum Boerhaave**: history of science; instruments.
**Rijksmuseum voor Volkenkunde**: Ethnology worldwide.

The town's name, meaning the place on the waterways, is appropriate even today when many of the canals have been filled in. Within an outer ring of canals (the Singels), the inner town is enclosed by the waterways of the Rapenburg running along the W and S, the Oude Vest along the N, and a series of parallel canals on the east. Within these waterways the town is cut from roughly E to W by the Oude Rijn (N) and the Nieuwe Rijn (S), these two combining near the town centre to continue as De Rijn and cross Rapenburg at the NW of the inner town.

## South of De Rijn and Oude Rijn

BREESTRAAT, the main street, runs roughly NW to SE, parallel to and S and W of De Rijn and the Nieuwe Rijn. The **Stadhuis**, about half-way along the length of the street, once one of the most striking works of the Dutch Renaissance, was almost completely destroyed by fire in 1929, but Lieven de Key's façade of 1595 was replaced in 1936. The rings to which horses were tethered can be seen, as also the small town crier's platform, behind which is the standard measure of the 'Rijnlandse roede' (rod). Further NW, on the S side of the street, stands the *Rijnlandshuis* (Lieven de Key, 1596), a well restored building which has housed the local water authority since the date of its construction. Opposite are the *Gehoorzaal*, the 19C municipal concert hall, and the *Waalsekerk*, all that survives of a hospice of St Catharine, founded in 1276.

WEST AND SOUTH OF BREESTRAAT. From roughly opposite the Stadhuis, Pieterskerkchoorsteeg leads SW, a plaque on No. 17A commemorating the Pilgrim Press, run by William Brewster, one of the Pilgrim Fathers (see below). The street ends at the **Pieterskerk**, a large brick church of the 15C, successor to a church consecrated on this site in 1121. The tower, since restored, collapsed in a storm in 1512. The church contains a choir screen with a Renaissance frieze of 1525, and also the monuments of famous savants, notably that of Herman Boerhaave (south transept) by A. de Wapperon. A tomb (of Jan van Kerckhoven, died 1660) in the north transept bears an effigy by Rombout Verhulst. In the choir, one of the many graveslabs is that of Justin of Nassau (died 1631), governor of Breda, and of his wife, and here also were buried John Robinson.

In Kloksteeg, on the S side, is the *Jan Pesijnshofje* (1683, restored 1979), an almshouse with an inscription recording the residence, teaching, and

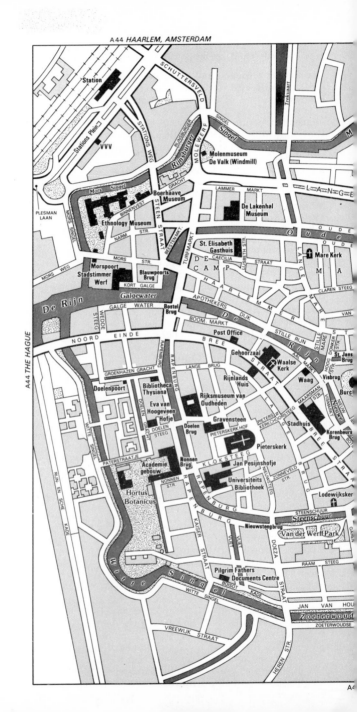

A44 THE HAGUE

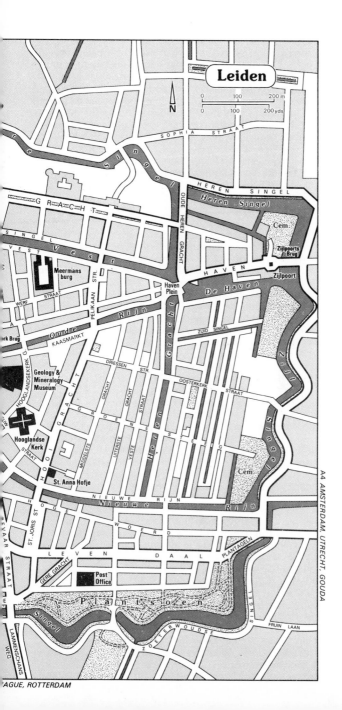

**Leiden**

0     100     200 m

0     100     200 yds

N

SOPHIA STRAAT

Singel

HEREN SINGEL

Heren Singel

OUDE HEREN GRACHT

Cem.

Zijlpoorts Brug

Zijlpoort

HAVEN

De Haven

G R A C H T

SINGEL

V E S T

Vest

Meermans burg

PELIKAAN STR.

Haven Plein

ZUID SINGEL

WERF STRAAT

Rijn

Zijl

Gracht

Oude Rijn

KAASMARKT

Rijn

rk Brug

DRIESSEN STR.

Geology & Mineralogy Museum

GROENE GRACHT

UITERSTE GRACHT

VESTE GRACHT

OOSTERKERK STRAAT

Heren Straat

Singel

HOOGLANDSEKERK G.

Cem.

Hooglandse Kerk

HOOI STRAAT

MIDDELSTE G.

St. Anna Hofje

NIEUWE RIJN

ST. JORIS ST

Nieuwe Rijn

HOOGE

L E V E N D A A L

PLANTAGELN

Post Office

GERE GRACHT

ST. JORIS ST

WOERD

BEVAAR STRAAT

P l a n t s o e n

SINGEL

Singel

LAMMENSCHANS WEG

ZOETERWOUDS

FRUIN LAAN

AGUE, ROTTERDAM

A4 AMSTERDAM, UTRECHT, GOUDA

death here (1609–25) of John Robinson, leader and pastor of the Pilgrim Fathers, who settled in Leiden for some 12 years prior to their departure for America in 1620. Robinson intended to follow, but died before he could do so. The building immediately NW of the church is the *Gravensteen* (13C or 14–17C), the oldest part being the central court. Originally the prison of the counts of Holland, the building later served as a municipal prison and the site of public executions until the 19C; today it houses the university law faculty. Roughly opposite is the *Gymnasium* or *Latin School*, built in 1599 by Lieven de Key and continuing to serve as a grammar school until 1864; Rembrandt was a pupil here.

From the Pieterskerk, Kloksteeg leads W, soon reaching the Rapenburg canal, here crossed by the *Nonnenbrug*, the name recalling the nuns of the convent the buildings of which from 1581 on housed the university (see below). Here a diversion may be made to the S and E.

Immediately to the S, on the E side of Rapenburg, the *Universiteits Bibliotheek*, one of the most important university libraries in the country, occupies the chapel of the former Begijnhof. On No. 68, next door, a plaque commemorates Matthias de Vries (1820–92), lexicographer. Farther E, No. 94 Rapenburg, known as *Het Duyvenhuis* (the pigeon house), was the home during the siege of three brothers who kept pigeons which bore messages between Leiden and William the Silent in Delft. A short way E again, the small Vliet waterway running S was used by Admiral Boisot who relieved the siege, and also in 1620 by the departing Pilgrim Fathers. At No. 2A Boisotkade, at the S end of the Vliet, there is the *Pilgrim Fathers Documents Centre* (Mon–Fri, 09.30 to 16.30), with records and views of Leiden as it then was. Not far beyond the Vliet, Rapenburg may be crossed by the Nieuwsteegbrug to reach VAN DER WERFF PARK, laid out on the site of the houses destroyed when the gunpowder barge blew up in 1807. Here stands a statue (1884) to Van der Werff, the indomitable defender of Leiden during the siege, aspects of which are depicted in reliefs around the base. The *Lodewijkskerk*, N of the park on the other side of the canal (here called the Steenschuur, the town's oldest moat of c 1200), dates from 1538. Built originally as a chapel it was used after the Reformation as a cloth hall. However, when the nearby clandestine Roman Catholic church was destroyed in the explosion, Louis (Lodewijk) Bonaparte offered the cloth hall to the Catholics, their new church thus becoming Leiden's first non-clandestine Roman Catholic church since the time of the Union of Utrecht.

The Nonnenbrug crosses the Rapenburg to the *Academiegebouw*, the former church of the convent of the White Nuns, which since 1581 has housed the core of the **University**. There is a small *Museum* (Rapenburg 73. Wed–Friday, 13.00 to 17.00) devoted to the university's history, and the *Print Room* at 65 Rapenburg includes material on the history of photography (Tues–Fri, 14.00 to 17.00).

From the late 16C to the mid 18C Leiden university occupied a position unrivalled among Europe's seats of learning, numbering among its professors and students such names as Justus Lipsius (Joest Lips, 1547–1606) and Joseph Justus Scaliger (1540–1609), both classicists, the latter succeeding the former as professor; Daniel Heinsius (Daniel Heins, 1580–1655), another classicist, who studied under Scaliger and became professor and university librarian; Hugo Grotius (Huig van Groot, 1583–1645), the jurist and statesman who here took his doctorate in law; Claudius Salmasius

(Claude Saumaise, 1588–1653), the French classical and Arabic scholar who while professor here was in constant dispute with Heinsius; the remonstrant theologian Jacobus Arminius (Jacob Hermanns, 1560–1609) and his opponent Franz Gomarus (1563–1641), two names recalling the politico-religious quarrel which in 1619 led to the execution of Jan van Oldenbarneveld and the imprisonment of Hugo Grotius; Gerhard Vossius (Voss, 1577–1649), German classical scholar and theologian, who here became a close friend of Grotius; the French philosopher René Descartes (1596–1650); and Herman Boerhaave (1666–1738; portrait by Aert de Gelder in the Mauritshuis at The Hague), who made the university's medical faculty world-renowned.

Among the many British associated with the university during the 17C and 18C may be mentioned John Evelyn (1620–1706), the diarist; Oliver Goldsmith (1728–74), poet, playwright, and novelist who though, while at Leiden, dabbled with chemistry and natural science; John Wilkes (1727–97), the agitator, who was here for a short while at the age of 17; and John Robinson (1575–1625), theologian and pastor to the Pilgrim Fathers.

The Leiden Jar, or electrical condenser, takes its name from the experiments here in 1746 of Petrus van Musschenbroek.

Behind the university is the large *Hortus Botanicus*, the botanic garden laid out along the Witte Singel in 1587 and one of the oldest in Europe (entrance Rapenburg 73. Mon–Fri, 09.00 to 17.00; Sun, 10.00 to 17.00. Hothouses, Mon–Fri, 09.00 to 12.30, 13.00 to 16.30; Sun, 10.30 to 12.30, 13.30 to 15.00).

Rapenburg can now be followed N to the next bridge, the Doelenbrug, across which is the **\*\*Rijksmuseum van Oudheden** (see below).

From the W side of Doelenbrug, Doelensteeg leads W with on the right the *Eva van Hoogeveen Hofje*, an almshouse of c 1659, with another entrance gate round the corner in Doelengracht, which you now follow N. The area on the other side of the narrow canal once served as shooting range (doelen = targets) for the Civic Guard and later as barracks. At its N end Doelengracht reaches Groenhazengracht, with, immediately W, the little *Doelenpoort* (1645), bearing a figure of St George anachronistically flanked by cannon and baskets of cannonballs. On Rapenburg, to the E, No. 25 is the *Bibliotheca Thysiana*, built in 1655 by Arent van 's Gravesande, while No. 31 was the house of Herman Boerhaave.

Continuing N along the W side of Rapenburg, the next street W is Noordeinde, off which the second street N is Weddesteeg, in which Rembrandt was born in 1606.

EAST OF BREESTRAAT. Behind the Stadhuis, a little to the N near the confluence of the Oude Rijn and Nieuwe Rijn, stands the *Waag* of 1658, designed by Pieter Post and with sculpture by Rombout Verhulst; this was the last of a series of weigh-houses in this part of the town, the earliest of which is thought to have been put up in 1351. The Visbrug and St Jansbrug opposite are names mentioned as early as c 1200. To the S the Nieuwe Rijn is crossed by the unusual *Korenbeursbrug*, a bridge of 15C origin (roofed in 1825) on which the corn market was held. Within the angle of the rivers, but mostly hidden by buildings, stands the *Burcht*, a 12C and later fortification atop an artificial mound of unknown origin but probably Saxon or even Roman; its gate (1658), at the N end of Nieuwstraat, bears the coats-of-arms of burgomasters (1651–1764).

The nearby **Hooglandse Kerk** is a late Gothic building with a 15C choir, a 16C nave at a lower level than the choir, and the tower of a much older foundation (c 1300) adjoining. Inside the church there is a monument to Burgomaster Van der Werff (died 1604).

A short way N of the church, at No. 17 Hooglandse Kerkgracht, the **Rijksmuseum van Geologie en Mineralogie** (Mon–Fri, 10.00 to 17.00; Sun, 14.00 to 17.00) occupies the former orphanage of the Holy Ghost (founded 1583) for poor orphans and children, an attractive group of 17C and 18C buildings of which the oldest part dates from 1607. Note the sculpture over the entrance of a dove sheltering orphans. The material is excellently displayed on three floors, of which the Ground Floor is used for temporary exhibitions. On the First Floor, to the left, is the Schatkamer, the Treasure Room of precious stones; beyond are rooms devoted to minerals, volcanoes, and petrology. To the right there is a fine minerals display, with a case of tektites and meteorites, and, beyond, a fluorescence room. The Second Floor left side is concerned with geological processes, including erosion of various kinds, rain, chemical effects, plant and animal effect etc. The right side of this floor is devoted to the geology of the Netherlands, with fossils, animal bones, skeletons etc., while the wing beyond displays fossils (plant and animal) from countries other than the Netherlands.

To the E of the Hooglandse Kerk a series of parallel streets (Hooigracht, Middelstegracht, Uiterstegracht, and Vestestraat) run where formerly there were canals or moats. Between Hooigracht and Middelstegracht, at their S end, the *St Anna Hofje* is an almshouse dating from 1507, and, unusual with almshouses, its own chapel.

## North of De Rijn and Oude Rijn

From behind the Stadhuis, Visbrug and St Jansbrug (see above) cross to the elongated island, the districts of DE CAMP (W) and MARE (E), enclosed by De Rijn and Oude Rijn on the S and by the Oude Vest on the north. The streets Stille Mare and Lange Mare run N between the districts to the Oude Vest canal and the street of the same name, near the corner being the domed *Marekerk* (Arent van 's Gravesande, 1638–48), Leiden's first Protestant church. In medieval times the district of De Camp to the W was one with many religious and charitable houses, but, apart from the many evocative street names, the only survival is the *St Elisabethgasthuis* (within Oude Vest, Lijsbeth, and Caecilia streets, 200m W of the Marekerk), a hospice founded in 1428 (but with several additions, notably the chapel of c 1500) which, as a home for the sick and aged, continues to fulfil its original function. Oude Vest followed E from the Marekerk reaches (No. 159) an almshouse, *Meermansburg*, founded in 1683 by Maerten Meerman and Helena Verburg.

HAVENPLEIN, at the E end of the island, stands at the confluence of five waterways. The *Zijlpoort* (250m further E) is a town gate of 1667.

The district to the NW of the island contains four museums. The **\*Stedelijk Museum De Lakenhal** (see below), at 28–32 Oude Singel on the N side of Oude Vest, is the municipal museum in the 17C cloth hall. The **Molenmuseum De Valk** (Tues–Sat, 10.00 to 17.00; Sun, Holidays, 13.00 to 17.00), about 200m N across Noordvest, is a tower windmill of c 1743. The ground floor shows the miller's house with furnishing of about 1900 and a workshop, while, above, models, mill components and suchlike are exhibited. In gardens a short way SW of the windmill are the adjoining Boerhaave and Ethnology museums.

The **Museum Boerhaave** (Tues–Sat, 10.00 to 17.00; Sun, 13.00 to 17.00; may close at 16.00 in Oct–May), also known as the Museum of the History of Science, contains a collection of scientific instruments and other souvenirs of men such as Christiaan Huygens (1629–95), mathematician, astronomer, and physicist; Petrus van Musschenbroek (1692–1761), known for the Leiden Jar electrical condenser; A. van Leeuwenhoek (1632–1723), the microscopist; Gabriel Daniel Fahrenheit (1686–1736), with some of his thermometers; and Herman Boerhaave (1668–1738), the physician. On the ground floor, at the museum N entrance, are a 'sphaera' by Steven Tracy of Rotterdam (late 17C) and a row of globes by Blaeu; beside is a room showing various instruments. At the opposite end of the passage a line of 17C astronomical pendulum clocks demand study for their variety and ingenuity. In the room opposite there is a group of portraits of the Van Musschenbroek family. Upstairs there is some emphasis on anatomy, starting with a huge Simples Chest of 1660, built in the form of a learned book, while further along there is a surgical room displaying some fearsome instruments and equally fearsome old pictures showing some of them in use. In the passage stand cases devoted to the optician and the pharmacist, while adjoining rooms, opposite the surgical room, are largely concerned with microscopy, a portrait of Van Leeuwenhoek hanging above the instruments.

The **Rijksmuseum voor Volkenkunde** (Tues–Sat, 10.00 to 17.00; Sun, Holidays, 13.00 to 17.00), the National Museum of Ethnology. The principal strengths of this broad-ranging collection are, as might be expected, the result of Dutch colonial history. The Hindu-Java section shows bronze, woodwork and some massive stone sculpture, while the display on Religion in Indonesia includes a room filled with temple bells of every design and size. New Guinea, Oceania and Australasia provide a huge geographical sweep, especially noteworthy being some of the models of boats, houses and irrigation equipment; a map showing Oceania population movements, with accompanying models of the craft used; exotic musical instruments and a collection of masks. North America provides glimpses of Indian and Eskimo cultures, while Central America offers a dazzling and colourful Mexican display, in stark contrast to, nearby, sombre grave discoveries (c 800–1200) from Peru and Chile. From Japan and China there are prints, silk screens and lacquer work, together with a whole room devoted to Japanese and Chinese theatre. Tibet, too, has its place here (the museum was visited by the Dalai Lama in 1986) while Buddhism provides another theme, its birth and diffusion illustrated by maps and other material, the latter including a lifesize figure of the Boddhisttva Kuan Yin (China, 13C) and a room in which five large Buddhas from Japan (17–18C) sit in meditation.

To the S, between these museums and De Rijn, here called the Galgewater, are the *Morsport*, a town gate of 1669 at the W end of Morsstraat; and the *Stadstimmerwerf* (municipal carpenters' yard), an attractive building beside the water with an ornamental stepped gable of 1612 by Lieven de Key..

## **RIJKSUSEUM VAN OUDHEDEN** (National Museum of Antiquities).

The museum (Tues–Sat, 10.00 to 17.00; Sun, Holidays, 13.00 to 17.00) was founded in 1818, greatly enlarged in 1826–28, and given extensive rebuilding and rearrangement after the Second World War, new rooms being opened in 1948 and 1951 and the main hall being given over to the Temple of Taffeh in 1979. In 1987 the Koninklijk Penningkabinet (Royal Coin Collection) moved here from The Hague, and a new department of Near East antiquities was opened in 1988. Especially notable are the collections of antique sculptures, the section illustrating the prehistory of the Nether-lands and the Egyptian collection.

The museum occupies three floors, with rooms arranged around the airy main hall which, though now given a false ceiling, rises the height of the building. The material is admirably displayed and explained, the explana-tions for the most part including English text.

GROUND FLOOR. **Classical and Egyptian Sculpture**. The museum en-trance leads straight into the main hall in which stands the *Temple of Taffeh* from Nubia. Built in the 1C AD, the façade was changed for the worship of Isis during the 4C, and during the 8C the building was consecrated as a Christian church. Between 1910 and 1960, because of the construction of the first Asswan dam, the building was for long periods under water, but in 1960, with the building of the new dam, it was dismantled and in 1969 given to the Netherlands in gratitude for her contribution to the rescue of the Nubian monuments.

Beyond the hall a series of rooms extend along its S side, in the first is the *Nehallenia Collection*, Nehallenia was a local Roman goddess, protectress of merchants and sailors. The material, mainly altars or decorative stones from a sanctuary dating from c 200, was first revealed in 1647 when storms moved the dunes near Colijnsplaat in Zeeland, then rediscovered (brought up by fishermen) in 1970. Special exhibits in the *Collection of Greek and Roman Sculpture* beyond, are the votive bust of a woman (Cyprus, c 550 BC) and several heads from Cyprus; a head of Dionysus (2C BC); a marble statue of Trajan from Utica in north Africa (AD 107); nearby, in contrast to imperial Trajan, the homely gravestone of Aurelius Sozomenos, bearing figures not only of his children but also of their nurse; the sarcophagus of Marcellus (AD 350), with scenes from the life of Christ who, unusually, is beardless (this was part of Rubens' collection); terracotta figurines, given by Heinrich Schliemann to Queen Sophia in 1876. Also the *Sarcophagus of a Roman lady, found in 1930 at Simpelveld (Limburg) and dating from the 2C; the reliefs, which are, exceptionally, within the sarcophagus, show the deceased on her couch, and the contents of her living room. Objects found in the tomb, including personal ornaments, are displayed in a nearby case.

The *Egyptian Collection* extends through several rooms and covers from prehistoric to Coptic times. Sarcophagus of Min-Ofer (5 Dynasty, c 2400 BC). *Mastaba, or tomb chamber, of the priest Akhet-Hetep-Her, with a portrait of the occupant on either side of the entrance (5 Dynasty, c 2350 BC); the tomb is notable for its clear and detailed pictorial work. Pedestal for a chapel (13 Dynasty, c 1750 BC). Shrine for a god's statue (26 Dynasty, c 550 BC). Sarcophagus of Iah-mer (27 Dynasty, c 520 BC). *Room of stelae of various periods, many showing fascinating detail and several still pre-serving colouring. Also in this room, wall reliefs from the tomb of Horemheb (18 Dynasty, c 1340 BC). For other Egyptian material see First Floor.

FIRST FLOOR. **Archaeology**. **Classical and Egyptian Antiquities**. On reaching this floor by the main staircase from near the ticket desk, a right turn leads past some elegant Greek jewellery (5–2 BC) from the colonies on the Black Sea, beyond being cases of figurines and small household articles. The north gallery displays the Etruscan material while beyond, in the west gallery, comes first the *Greek and Roman Glass* and then a small *Coptic Collection*.

On the S side the main gallery is given over to the museum's fine collection of *Classical Vases*, perhaps most obviously notable and interesting being three Attic black-figured amphorae given as prizes in the Pan Athenian

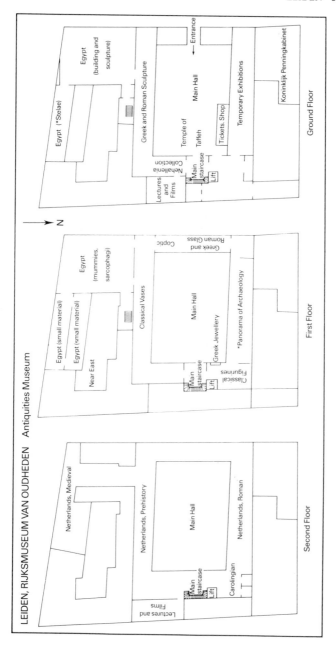

LEIDEN, RIJKSMUSEUM VAN OUDHEDEN Antiquities Museum

N

**Ground Floor**

Egypt (building and sculpture)

Egypt (*Stelae)

Greek and Roman Sculpture

Entrance

Main Hall

Temple of Taffeh

Tickets. Shop

Temporary Exhibitions

Koninklijk Penningkabinet

Nehallenia Collection

Main staircase

Lift

Lectures and Films

**First Floor**

Egypt (mummies, sarcophagi)

Egypt (small material)

Egypt (small material)

Near East

Classical Vases

Main Hall

Coptic

Greek and Roman Glass

Greek Jewellery

*Panorama of Archaeology

Classical Figurines

Main staircase

Lift

**Second Floor**

Netherlands, Medieval

Netherlands, Prehistory

Main Hall

Netherlands, Roman

Carolingian

Main staircase

Lift

Lectures and Films

Games of c 500 BC, and, beyond, a huge Attic funerary amphora, from as long ago as 740 BC yet still bearing an astonishing amount of detail. The rooms behind show more from the *Egyptian Collection*, including several sarcophagi and mummies, some of the latter still covered by coloured beadwork; lengths of papyrus; the Papyrus of Paiser, with scenes from the Book of the Dead (21 Dynasty, 1097–945 BC); several delightful boat models, with occupants (c 2400 BC): a chair from Sakara (18 Dynasty, 1300 BC); and particularly interesting cases showing the working equipment of a scribe, a sculptor and a maker of amulets. Also scarabs, jewellery, bronze temple objects, games and toys, musical instruments, and toilet articles including bronze mirrors. Of particular interest in the *Near East* rooms are a sectioned tell (mound), accompanied by good wall explanations; cylinder seals (3000–600 BC); and a room of jewellery, ornaments and figurines, mostly from Iran.

SECOND FLOOR. **Archaeology of the Netherlands**. The four main sections here are Prehistory, and then the Roman, Carolingian and Medieval periods. The *Prehistory Collection* includes a model of a hunebed (see Rte 30A) with related material alongside; late Neolithic earthenware, with some surprisingly decorated 'striped' beakers; a bronze *Situla (bucket), with also a very bent iron sword, both from a princely tomb of c 500 near Oss (Nijmegen); a late Neolithic wooden bow; and a silver disc bearing animal decoration (1C BC). In the *Roman Period Collection* will be found a case displaying a variety of helmets, swords and a fragment of chain mail, especially noteworthy being a silver-gilt helmet from Deurne (Noord Brabant) belonging to a soldier of the time of Constantine, while the stars of the small *Carolingian Collection* are a magnificent *Jewelled Brooch and an important fresco showing in a room leading off the prehistory gallery.

### *Stedelijk Museum De Lakenhal

This museum (Tues–Sat, 10.00 to 17.00; Sun, Holidays, 13.00 to 17.00), devoted to the history, art, and culture of Leiden and its environs, includes a historical section, furniture, applied art, sculpture, and a small but outstanding collection of 16C and 17C paintings. There are several sumptuous rooms, notably one known as the Grote Pers.

**De Lakenhal** was built in 1640 after a subdued Palladian design by Arent van 's Gravesande, from then until 1800 serving as Cloth Hall, the administrative, exchange, and assay centre for Leiden's important cloth trade. The decoration on the front of the building illustrates aspects of this function, on the main façade are plaques depicting spinning, weaving, dyeing, clothworking, and final inspection; on the cornices there are rams, while along the front a fulling mill is flanked on both sides by bales of cloth and hanks of wool. Little used between 1800–74, other than as a hospital during cholera outbreaks, the building was converted to a museum in 1874. Since then there have been various developments, notably the opening of the Hartevelt Gallery in 1890 and, through the generosity of the Pape brothers, the building of the wing along the Lange Scheistraat in 1918–22; in 1955 the first floor of this wing was arranged to house temporary exhibitions.

The Historical Collection is housed in the original building, in Rooms L (for Lakenhal) 1–16. The Art Gallery occupies Rooms S (for Schilderijen, meaning Paintings) 17–20. Applied Art is for the most part in Rooms P (for Pape) 21–29. The upper rooms, P 30–32, are used for temporary exhibitions, these normally including representative works from the museum's collection of 19C and 20C paintings.

L (LAKENHAL). **Historical Collection**. **Room L1** is the forecourt, the place where the cloth was examined, each bale receiving a seal denoting its type and quality. Architectural fragments have been incorporated into the walls. **Room L2**: armour; examples of weapons carried by the Civic Guard during the 16C and 17C. **Rooms L3** and **L4**: tiles (late 16C–early 19C), including unglazed hearth tiles and also tiled paintings. Furniture of the 17C. Room L5 is a passage out of L2. **Room L6**: archaeological material. **Room L7**, down steps out of L6, is an old Dutch kitchen, the furnishing being largely of the 18C.

Stairs out of L5 lead up to **Room L8**, known as the *Grote Pers (Great Crush) and the finest in the building. The main feature is the Civic Guard groups by *Joris van Schooten*, together with banners from their club house. The stained glass windows, made in 1587 by *Willem Tijbaut* for the Civic Guard house, portray medieval counts and countesses of Holland. The chimney-piece was salved from the town hall fire of 1929, opposite being a case of municipal silver dating from the 17C. **Room L9**, a kind of small anteroom to L10, is the Stempelkamer (Stamp Room), with two presses which were used to stamp the bale seals. **Room L10**, the Staal-meesterskamer, the commonroom of the wool examiners, or syndics, has gilt-leather wall hanging. Pictures include the Board of 1675 by *Jan de Baen*, and De Lakenhal in 1642 by *Susanna van Steenwijck*, an intriguing glimpse of the former business users of this room. **Room L11**, the Gouver-neurskamer, contains a group portrait of the governors (1692) by *Carel de Moor*, and three allegories, painted for this room in 1651 by *Abraham van den Tempel*, ambitious paintings well worth attention, the tendency has been to ignore such attempts at a heroic art which do not fit with traditional ideas of Dutchness. **Room L12**, the Kleermakerskamer, was used by the tailors' guild and L13 by the brewers. This latter intimate small room shows murals illustrating the process of brewing; painted by *Hendrik Meijer* in c 1772 for the now demolished Brewers' Guildhall, these may not be great art, but are nonetheless notable for their charm and detail. **Room L14**, the Chirurgijnskamer (Surgeons' Room), exhibits material from the guildroom of the surgeons, which used to be in the Waag. Note especially the elaborate cupboard of 1679 containing 17C and 18C surgical instruments. **Rooms L15** and **L16**, above the Grote Pers, show miscellaneous material such as pictures, maps, books, weights and measures and some unusual miniature bonework scenes.

S (SCHILDERIJEN). The **Art Gallery**, with pictures of the 16C and 17C, occupies three rooms and a passage, the first room being **S17**, the Hartevelt Gallery, in which the principal work is *Lucas van Leyden*'s *Triptych of the Last Judgement, with Heaven and Hell on the wings, and, on the outside, Saints Peter and Paul. Painted for the Pieterskerk in 1526, this transitional work of the Dutch Renaissance was removed to the Stadhuis a few years later. The whole theme and detail are fantastic, yet at the same time immensely if naively human, from the selection process in the centre to, on one side, the practical fitting of wings prior to the ascent to Heaven, and, on the other, the sinners' fate at the hands of enthusiastic devils. Also in this room, *Lucas van Leyden*: Portrait of an unknown man (1521). *Cornelis Engebrechtsz.*: *Triptych of the Crucifixion, with Abraham's sacrifice and the Brazen Serpent on the wings, Adam's corpse (with donors) in the predella, and Passion scenes outside (c 1512). *Triptych of the Descent from the Cross, with, on the wings, donors and saints (c 1508). Both these works were painted for the abbey of Marienpol, just N of Leiden.

**Room S18** is devoted to landscapes, still life, historical and genre works

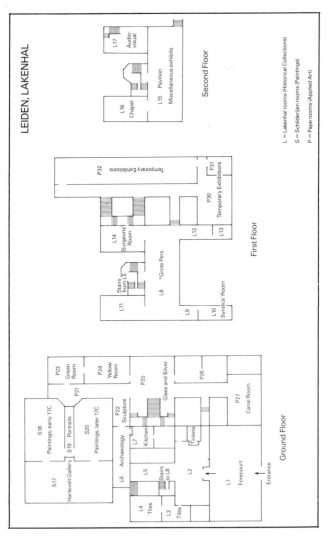

LEIDEN, LAKENHAL

**Second Floor**

L17 · Audio-visual

L16 Chapel · L15 Pavilion Miscellaneous exhibits

L = Lakenhal rooms (Historical Collections)
S = Schilderijen rooms (Paintings)
P = Pape rooms (Applied Art)

**First Floor**

P32 Temporary Exhibitions

P31 · P30 Temporary Exhibitions

L14 Surgeons' Room · L12 · L13

Stairs from L5 · L8 *Grote Pers · L11

L9 · L10 Syndics' Room

**Ground Floor**

P23 Green Room · P24 Yellow Room · P25

P21 · P22 Sculpture · Glass and Silver · P26

S18 Paintings, early 17C · S19 Portraits · S20 Paintings, later 17C

S17 Hartevelt Gallery · Archaeology · L7 Kitchen · Tickets · P27 Canal Room

L6 · L5 · Stairs to L8 · L2 · L1 Forecourt · Entrance

L4 Tiles · L3 Tiles

of the early 17C. *Rembrandt*: Palamedes before Agamemnon (or Clemency
of Titus), an early work of 1626 when the artist was aged 20 showing the
strong influence of the Amsterdam classicist Pieter Lastman, Rembrandt's
most important teacher. *Jan Lievens*: St Jerome, an oil sketch as study for
an etching. *Jan van Goyen*: a series of works (1626–50), the latest being a
*View of Leiden. *Jan Porcellis*: Marine Scenes. *David Bailey*: Vanity. This
is an extraordinary allegory on the transience of human life, playing a game
with layers of reality. **Room S19**, the passage, exhibits 17C portraits, the
artists including *Jan van Ravesteyn, Abraham van den Tempel, Bar-*

*tholomeus van der Helst* and *Frans van Mieris the Younger* (three generations: the artist, his father and his grandfather). Here, too, is an Inn Scene
by *Frans van Mieris the Elder*. In **Room S20** the pictures, among them many
genre scenes, are of the later 17C. *Jan Steen*: Couple reading the Bible.
Laban in search of his household gods. Christ chasing the moneylenders
from the temple, the theme in a 17C setting. *Quirringh Brekelenkam*:
Domestic cares. *A. van Gaasbeek*: *Rest on the flight to Egypt. *Matthijs
Naiveu*: Theatrical presentation. *Jan van Swieten*: Lute player. *Juriaan van
Streeck*: Still life.

P (PAPE). **Applied Art**. **Room P21**, the long ground floor corridor of this
wing, exhibits 18C furniture, notably a clock by *Franciscus le Dieu* of
Leiden and a large cabinet containing Chinese porcelain. **Room P22**, a short
corridor leading off P21, contains 17th and 18C sculpture. Note here a
terracotta group of a Tribunal by *Pieter Xaverij* (1673). **Room P23**, the
Groene Zaal or Green Room (1739), with fine panelling and furniture, was
largely transferred from a house at Arnhem. **Room P24**, the Gele Zaal
(Yellow Room), has panelling and a ceiling from two Leiden houses. The
furniture is of the same Louis XV and Louis XVI period, and paintings here
include works by *J-J. Delin* and *Jan Ekels the Younger*. **Room P25**, originally
intended as the entrance to this Pape extension, contains glass and silver.
Outstanding among the glass exhibits are a large green glass, with scenes
of the relief of Amsterdam and of the Spanish Armada; two covered goblets,
one bearing a view of Leiden; and several pieces of 1648–86 by the local
glass engraver *William van Heemskerk*. The silver includes domestic ware
of the 17C and 18C, guild silver, Communion silver, and some 19C and 20C
silver. **Room P26**, the Biedermeier Room, shows furniture of the Empire
(1800–20) and Biedermeier (1820–50) styles. **Room P27**, the Singel Zaal
(Canal Room), is used for temporary exhibitions and also for changing
exhibitions of the museum's 19C and 20C paintings.

LEIDEN TO KATWIJK AAN ZEE (10km). **Rijnsburg**, beyond the motorway and
known for its flower auction (Mon–Fri, 07.00 to 11.00), was the home of the
philosopher Baruch Spinoza in 1660–63. Around the lower part of the tower
of the *Reformed Church* can be seen the tufa of a tower of the 12C, all that
survives of the abbey church of a house for Benedictine nobles; both abbey
and church were destroyed at the time of the siege of Leiden (1573–74),
and the present church, though with some Romanesque fragments, dates
from 1578 but has undergone many later changes. **Katwijk aan Zee** (39,000
inhab. VVV, Vuurbaakplein 11) is a resort just S of the Oude Rijn. The
lighthouse dates from 1610. The Katwijk sluice, c 2km inland, is a triple
lock built by F.W. Conrad in 1804–07, through which the canalised Oude
Rijn empties into the sea; the several pairs of gates are closed at high tide,
the accumulated water sweeping away the sand which is piled up by the
sea, and which, without this regulation, would dam the stream and return
the Rijnland, the district to the E of Leiden, to the morass which it formerly
was.

# 7 The Hague and Scheveningen

**THE HAGUE**, in Dutch *'s Gravenhaage*, or more generally simply **Den
Haag** (445,000 inhab.), is the administrative capital of the Netherlands, the
home of the court, the diplomatic representation, the government, and of

Parliament. It is also the capital of the province of Zuid Holland. The place differs noticeably from the typical Dutch city, having always been a political and diplomatic rather than a commercial centre and, although there is some modern intrusion, much of the town enjoys an 18C and 19C dignity and elegance with several broad streets and avenues along which are royal and other fine residences. There are excellent shops and a wide choice of museums and art galleries, outstanding being the Mauritshuis and the Gemeentemuseum.

**Centre.** Around the Hof Vijver. Also an extensive pedestrian precinct area just W behind the Buitenhof.

**VVV.** Kon. Julianaplein beside Centraal Station. Mon–Sat, 09.00 to 18.00 or 20.00 in mid April–mid Sept; Sun, 10.00 to 17.00. For postal or telephone enquiries: Groot Hertoginnenlaan 41, 2517 EC, The Hague. Tel: (070) 3546200.

**Post Office.** Bounded by Kerkplein, Nobelstraat and Prinsestraat.

**Station.** Centraal, 1km SE of Hofvijver.

**Public Transport.** Tram and bus folder from VVV, or from HTM (Haagsche Tramweg Maatschappij), Dynamostraat 10. Tel: (070) 3848484.

**Airport.** Schiphol, 44km N. Train, 30 minutes.

**Tours.** The 'Royal Tour' is a bus tour which, though with a royal emphasis, in fact embraces much else including the Ridderzaal (when open) and Scheveningen (bookings and other information from VVV; duration 3 hours). VVV will also provide information on specialised walking and cycling routes, including an Antiques route for antique shops, a Neptune route through old Scheveningen, and even an Art Nouveau route. *Boats.* From The Hague to a Delft pottery works; sea cruises and fishing from Scheveningen.

**History.** Although adjacent to the Roman settlement of Forum Hadriani, today the suburb of Voorburg, The Hague is first mentioned only in 1242 when it appears in a charter as 'Die Haghe' (the hedge). Count William II (died 1256), who appears to have had a hunting lodge here, began in 1250 the construction of a palace more in keeping with his dignity as King of the Romans, a position to which he had been elected in 1247, and his son Count Floris V (died 1296) completed the building. Not until the period of Albert of Bavaria, regent and later Count between 1357 and 1404, did the settlement that had grown up around the palace acquire some importance, in about 1400 becoming known as Haga Comitis (or 's Gravenhaage, the Count's Hedge). In 1586 the Earl of Leicester, the self-appointed Governor General of the northern provinces, summoned the States General to meet at The Hague, and from the time of Prince Maurice of Nassau until the flight of Prince William V in 1795 the town was the residence of the stadholders of the province of Holland and thus, effectively, the political capital of both the province and of the country, a status reflected in the many treaties signed here during this period. In the 17C the town saw the judicial murder of Jan van Oldenbarneveld (1619), the princely splendour of the court of Prince Frederick Henry (1625–47), and the murder by the mob of the brothers Johan and Cornelis de Witt (1672).

Although throughout the 17C and 18C the seat of the government of the United Provinces, The Hague curiously never enjoyed more than the municipal status of village, and it was not until the Napoleonic occupation that this changed with the award of a full civic charter by Louis Bonaparte. During the uneasy period of the United Kingdom of the Netherlands (1814–31), The Hague shared political capital status with Brussels, parliaments meeting alternately in the two cities. King William II (1840–49) did much to beautify the city and make it worthy of a royal residence. In 1899 the first international conference for the suppression of war was held at The Hague, leading to the Permanent Court of Arbitration and the building of the Peace Palace (1913).

**Natives.** Prince William III (1650–1702), Stadholder of Holland and Zeeland and after 1688 King of England, was born here. Also born here were Constantijn Huygens (1596–1687) and his son Christiaan Huygens (1629–95). The former was a poet, scholar, musician, and diplomatist, who studied at Leiden and Oxford and became an admirer and friend of the English poet John Donne, as well as his translator into Dutch. As a diplomatist he headed missions to Venice (1619), England (1621–23) where he was knighted by James I, and France (1666). As a writer, and particularly as a poet, he ranks as one of the most brilliant (and difficult) in Dutch literature; as a statesman he stands out as the most respected patrician figure of his time. It was Constantijn Huygens who proposed the building of the road linking The Hague to the coast at Scheveningen. He also befriended the young Rembrandt and negotiated the commission of paintings from Rembrandt (now in Munich) for the stadholder Frederik Hendrik. Christiaan Huygens, like his father educated at Leiden, was a mathematician, astronomer and physicist. He is best known for his development in 1655 of a new method of grinding and polishing lenses, an early result of which was the discovery of a satellite to Saturn; for his observation (1656) of the Orion nebula; and for his invention (1656) of the pendulum clock. After living in France for many years, he returned to the Netherlands in 1681, devoting the later years of his life to notable research in physical optics.

The painters born in The Hague include Jan van Ravesteyn (c 1570–1657); Daniel Mytens (c 1590–before 1648), 'King's painter' to Charles I of England; Jan Mytens (c 1614–70), nephew of Daniel; and many painters of the Hague School of the 19C, including the brothers Jacob, Matthijs, and Willem Maris, Johannes Bosboom, and Jan Hendrik Weissenbruch.

**Hague Porcelain** was briefly manufactured between c 1776 and 1790, the founder of the firm being Anton Lyncker, a German already active in the trade in Saxony. Not very adventurous in design, the ware reflects contemporary German taste. The firm was primarily concerned with decoration, and for this reason perhaps the painting is good; many Hague pieces, though locally decorated, were fashioned elsewhere.

**Summary of Museums and Art Galleries** The summary below is in order of mention in the text. For opening times see under individual entries.

**Schilderijenzaal Prins Willem V**: royal gallery of the 18C.
**Gevangenpoort**: historic prison.
**Haags Historisch**: story of The Hague.
**\*\*Mauritshuis (Koninklijk Kabinet van Schilderijen)**: one of the world's finest collections of paintings.
**Rijksmuseum Meermanno-Westreenianum**: illuminated manuscripts; applied art; antiquities.
**Museum voor het Poppenspel**: puppets.
**Panorama Mesdag**: H.W. Mesdag's huge panoramic painting of Scheveningen.
**Postmuseum**: many aspects of communications.
**Rijksmuseum H.W. Mesdag**: paintings, mainly by the Hague and Barbizon schools.
**\*Gemeentemuseum**: applied art; 19–20C paintings; musical instruments.
**\*Museon**: the Earth and its people; man and space; worth visiting for its ultra modern presentation techniques.
**Omniversum**: 'Space theatre'.
**Scheveningen Museum**: local history; shipping and fishing.
**Zeebiologisch Museum**: marine life, worldwide.
**Hofwijk**: home of Constantijn Huygens.
**Museum Swaensteijn**: local history, including Roman era.
**Museum Rijswijk**: local history and art.

# A.   Central City

For the purposes of the description below the central city is defined as all
that lies within, on the N, Laan van Meerdervoort and Javastraat; on the E
Prinsessegracht; on the S Zuidwal and Bierkade; and on the W Lijnbaan
and Koningin Emmakade. Within this central area the places of immediate
interest to the visitor are around the Hof Vijver. Additional sections cover
the central districts to the North and East, the West and North, and the
South and South-West of the lake.

## Around the Hof Vijver

The HOF VIJVER (Court Lake), all that survives of the moat which once
surrounded the castle, is an ornamental lake with a small round island.
Along much of the S side of the lake extends the **Binnenhof**, the inner court
of the former castle of the counts of Holland, later the residence of Charles
V and of the Earl of Leicester, and today the home of the Dutch Parliament
and of government offices. Its irregular plan suggests its haphazard growth,
but most of the buildings seen today, though on medieval foundations, have
been either restored or entirely reconstructed. The gateway at the E end,
the *Binnenpoort*, is a 19C reconstruction. The central building, facing the
fountain-statue (1885) of Count William II, who began the first castle here
in 1250, is the *Ridderzaal* (Tourist reception and exhibition on the Dutch
constitution on S side. Conducted tours, including First and Second Chambers when not in use, Mon–Sat, and Sun in July and Aug, 10.00 to 15.55;
closed most Holidays.), or Knights' Hall, a restored late 13C building with
a projecting porch and slender corner turrets. Built by Count Floris V, and
later the meeting place of the Knights of the Order of the Golden Fleece,
the hall is now used for the combined sessions of the First and Second

*The Ridderzaal, or the Knights' Hall, of the Binnenhof,
late 13C (restored)*

Chambers of Parliament, for the ceremonial opening of parliament by the sovereign and for other important occasions. In the same building (but not normally open to the public) are the *Rolzaal* (1511), the place where justice was administered and the scene of the disgraceful trial of Jan van Olden-barneveld in 1619 (he was executed in front of the entrance to the Ridder-zaal), and the *Lairessezaal* of 1688 with allegorical paintings by Gerard de Lairesse.

Within the Binnenhof are various government offices, and also the meeting places of the two chambers of Parliament. The *First Chamber* (N side) was built by Pieter Post in 1660. A staircase and an ante-room, with portraits of stadholders and of famous statesmen and soldiers, precede the chamber itself (formerly the meeting place of the States of Holland) which has a fine ceiling and allegorical chimney-pieces (War and Peace) by Jan Lievens and Adriaen Hanneman. The *Second Chamber* (S side) was built in 1777–90 as a ballroom for Prince William V. Other halls (neither normally open to the public) are the *Statenzaal* (rebuilt 1697) and the *Trêveszaal*, named from the truce (trêve) with Spain which was negotiated here in 1608. The S gate of the Binnenhof, the *Hoofdpoort*, dates from the late 18C; nearby is *'T Goutsmits Keur Huys*, the former home of the Goldsmiths' and Silversmiths' Guild.

The gate at the W end of the Binnenhof, the *Stadhouderspoort*, still showing some 15C work, leads to the BUITENHOF, the old outer court of the castle, today a space in which stands an equestrian statue (1924) of King William II. Behind the Buitenhof good shopping streets (mainly pedestrian) stretch NW and SE, one of the best known of these being the arcaded *Passage* (SE).

The **Schilderijenzaal Prins Willem V** (daily, 11.00 to 14.00), at Buitenhof 35, is the gallery of that prince, restored now as closely as possible to its condition of 1774–95, showing some of the paintings which hung in the original collection. Quite apart from the pictures, it is well worth visiting as a typical gallery of a time when the emphasis was on quantity.

William V was a keen collector of paintings, largely of 17C Dutch works, though after the age of 25 his enthusiasm waned and his interest turned to contemporary paintings. In 1771 he bought this building, formerly an inn, and converted it to serve as his 'cabinet', the 17C and 18C term for what is today normally called a gallery. Such 'cabinets' were standard in mansions and palaces whose owners were unwilling to allow pictures to spoil the effect of their expanses of painted wallpaper, cabinets also allowed the systematic ordering of collections of curiosities which might go far beyond mere picture collections and include coins, natural objects and much else.

The paintings, on the whole reflecting the taste of the time and with some emphasis on genre, are in a single gallery (apart from a small ante-room) and the style of the period required that virtually every inch of wall space be covered. In consequence a good half of the paintings are too high to be enjoyed, and in any case many bear no form of identification. Pictures are from time to time withdrawn for restoration or for temporary exhibition, and there is likely to be some exchange with the Mauritshuis, but names such as Rembrandt, Rubens, Steen, Lairesse, David Teniers the Younger, Willem van Mieris, Schalcken and Wouwerman point to the range of artists whose works may be discovered here.

Nearby stands the **Gevangenpoort**, or prison gate (Mon–Fri, 10.00 to 17.00; Sat and Sun in May–Sept, 13.00 to 17.00), dating from the 14C, an early entrance to the counts' castle, later used as a gaol for political prisoners.

Cornelis de Witt was held and tortured here in 1672, and it was in front of this gate that he and his brother Johan, who had come to help him, were torn to pieces by the mob. Visitors are shown Cornelis de Witt's cell, a cell in which prisoners were starved to death, and a collection of instruments of torture.

Immediately N is the open area of the Plaats, with a statue of Johan de Witt, and further N Kneuterdijk 6 was De Witt's home from 1669; built in 1653, the house was restored in 1960 and is now used for art and other exhibitions.

Lange Vijverberg, with a statue of Jan van Oldenbarneveld, runs along the N side of the Hof Vijver.

In Korte Vijverberg, along the E side of the Hof Vijver, No. 7 today houses the **Haags Historisch Museum** (Tues–Sat, 12.00 to 16.00) sketching the story of The Hague, much use being made of a rich collection of pictures of the city as it once was. Formerly it was the *St Sebastiaansdoelen* (1636). The compact Palladian façade of the **Mauritshuis** (see below) occupies the SE shore of the Hof Vijver. Korte Vijverberg runs into the PLEIN, in which, above an underground car park, stands a statue of William the Silent (Louis Royer, 1848). Around the Plein there are several buildings of interest. That on the N side is the club house of the *Nieuwe of Litteraire Societeit* (known simply as De Witte), one of the leading social clubs in the country. At the NE corner the *Ministerie van Buitenlandse Zaken*, the Foreign Office, occupies a building erected in 1737–41 as the Embassy of Amsterdam to the States General and still bearing the arms of Amsterdam; in 1815 the home of the widow of Prince William V, and after 1853 used for the national archives, the building was taken over by the Foreign Office in 1913. On the S side (the road here being a section of the city's main ancient E–W thoroughfare) is the *Ministerie van Defensie* of 1739–46, while on the W side the large 19C building was once the *Ministerie van Justitie*. Also on this side, but set back, is the *Hoge Raad* (Supreme Court), with in front a row of statues of famous Dutch legal figures, one being Hugo Grotius.

For the * *Mauritshuis**, at the SE corner of the Hof Vijver and housing the Royal Art Gallery, see Section D below. From here you can return to the Binnenhof by the *Grenadierspoort*, a gateway of 1634.

## North and East of the Hof Vijver

Kneuterdijk, with at No. 6 the house of Johan de Witt (see above), leads N out of the Plaats and soon curves east. Within the curve stands an attractive small former palace (18C), while the building on the corner of Parkstraat was in part the house of Jan van Oldenbarneveld. Opposite, on the other corner of Parkstraat, the *Kloosterkerk* (April–Oct or Nov: Mon–Fri, 12.00 to 14.00) is a rebuilding of c 1500 on the site of a Dominican foundation of 1397.

LANGE VOORHOUT, running E, is a broad tree-lined promenade of fine ambassadorial and other mansions, a number of which are of interest. No. 10 (N side) is the *British Embassy*, beyond which the road splits into central and side sections divided by gardens. No. 34 (N side) has since 1819 been the home of the **Koninklijke Bibliotheek**, the Royal Library (reading room entrance at rear at Kazernestraat 39). The building was begun in 1734–36 for Adrienne Huguetan by Daniel Marot and completed in 1761 when the wings were added by Pieter de Swart for her husband Charles van Nassau-Beverweerd; the interior is attractive with period iron and plaster work. The library, with over one million volumes, is concerned with such fields as

social science, history, philology, literature, theology, philosophy, education, etc., and includes some 6000 precious manuscripts (many illuminated);
letters, most written by Dutch savants, artists and statesmen; and a large
collection of printed works spanning the 16C to 18C. Lange Voorhout 44
(N side) was the home in 1624–27 of Constantijn Huygens prior to his move
first to the Plein and later to Voorburg (see below). The *Hotel des Indes*, on
the N side on the corner of Vos in Tuinstraat, was built in 1870 for Baron
Van Brienen, chamberlain to King William III, and became a hotel in 1881;
Paul Kruger, the South African Boer leader, stopped here in 1900, and the
ballerina Anna Pavlova died here in 1931 following a performance at the
city theatre. Facing the point where Lange Voorhout makes a right-angled
turn to the S stands the *Voorhout Paleis*, built in 1760–64 by Pieter de Swart;
formerly the residence of John William Hope (1757–1813), a partner in the
English banking house of Hope and Co. of Amsterdam, the palace is now
mainly used for official receptions.

Lange Voorhout—here nearly 150m wide, broken into several tree-
shaded sections, and on Thursdays in summer the site of an antiques
market—now heads S into the Tournooiveld (former jousting lists), out of
which Korte Voorhout leads E, with, at the start of this road on the S side,
the *Koninklijke Schouwburg*. This, the royal theatre, occupies the wing of
a mansion begun by Pieter de Swart in c 1760 as a palace for Princess
Caroline van Nassau, daughter of Prince William IV, left incomplete in 1795,
and converted to a theatre in 1804, the opening production being Voltaire's
'Semiramis'. The *United States Embassy* is opposite the theatre, while
immediately to the latter's E massive modern government blocks extend to
the Prinsessegracht.

The **Rijksmuseum Meermanno-Westreenianum** (Mon–Sat, 13.00 to
17.00; closed Holidays.) is to the N at Prinsessegracht 30, a building of c
1720 by Jacobus van Dijk, the architect of many other houses along this
canal. Principally devoted to printing and books, both ancient and modern
(the museum is worth visiting for the collection of illuminated manuscripts
alone), the museum also contains antiquities. It is closely associated with
the Royal Library.

Gerard Meerman (1722–71) lived at a house on the corner of Prinsessegracht and Korte Voorhout, destroyed by bombing in 1945. Here he assembled a library and a collection of antiquities that soon became famous
throughout Europe. His son Johan Meerman (1753–1815) continued his
father's work, on his death leaving both house and library to the city, which,
however, refused the bequest on financial grounds, the result being that
the collections were auctioned and scattered in 1824. Baron van Westreenen (1783–1848), a cousin and friend of Johan Meerman and owner of
No. 30 Prinsessegracht, bought as many of the books and antiquities as he
could, these becoming a part of his already extensive private collection. On
his death Baron van Westreenen bequeathed his house and collections to
the state, one condition being that the librarian of the Royal Library should
always be the curator. The state accepted the bequest, the house then being
much altered both inside and out, in this process gaining its present
neo-classical façade. The museum opened in 1852, and in 1960 a museum
of the modern book (Museum van het Boek) was incorporated.

The *antiquities* are mainly Egyptian, Greek, Roman and medieval. They
include an Egyptian papyrus (Book of the Dead); a small wooden figure of
a youth called Mi (c 2000 BC); Greek vases, including an amphora of the
6C BC; Roman material from the Netherlands; icons of the 13C and 14C; a
triptych for a house altar by Niccolo di Tommaso (c 1370); a Bacchante

The Hague
Central

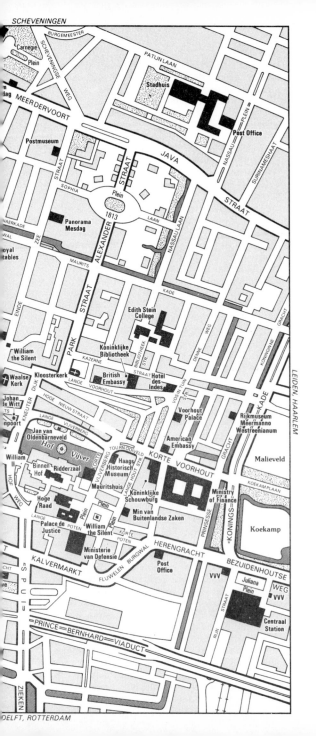

group by Pieter Xaverij (1671); and two Wedgwood busts (18C and 19C) in black basalt of Brutus and Marcus Aurelius. In the *Library* are displayed some of the treasures from the museum's considerable collection of *illuminated manuscripts*. The exhibits are sometimes changed around, but among those likely to be on view are a portion of the Old Testament (6C or 7C); Aristotle's 'Ethics' in French, with grisaille illuminations (1376); a Book of Hours (mid 15C), probably largely illuminated by the Master of Catherine of Cleves; a rhyming Flemish Bible, illuminated by Michiel van der Borch and a Bible, with illumination by Jan van Brugge, made for Charles V of France. The *incunabula*, of which there are over 1200, include early impressions of wooden types, a Blaeu atlas of 1665, and books printed by Gutenberg and Caxton.

The *Museum van het Boek*, a part of the museum since 1960, is concerned with modern books and book production, the emphasis being on Dutch work. The material includes limited editions; standard editions representative of particular trends in paper, design, binding, illustration etc.; experimental typography; greetings and similar cards, and promotional material. Exhibitions on particular themes are mounted regularly.

About 100m NE, across the canal, stands the *Provinciehuis* (1963), seat of the government of the province of Zuid Holland. To the N of this (300m), at Nassau Dillenburgstraat 8, the *Museum voor het Poppenspel* (Sun, 12.00 to 14.00), a department of the Nederlands Theater Instituut in Amsterdam, shows some 1000 puppets of worldwide provenance. For performances (Oct–June) tel: (070) 3280208.

## West and North of the Hof Vijver

The **Oude Stadhuis**, a short way W of the Buitenhof, is a picturesque building dating from 1565 (though with 14C foundations and cellars), enlarged in 1733–39, perhaps by Daniel Marot, and again in 1883. The main façade bears figures of Prudence and Justice by J.B. Xaverij, with Faith, Hope, and Charity above. The interior (not normally open to visitors) is occasionally used for weddings; the Trouwzaal (Marriage Hall) has ceiling paintings of c 1720 by Jacob de Wit.

The **Grote Kerk** or **St Jacobskerk**, just W of the Oude Stadhuis, stands on the site of a 13C church of which a part of the foundations has been found. Today's church (major restoration, 1985–87), though preserving some late 14C work in its transepts, was rebuilt after fires in 1402 and 1539 and is thus mainly of the mid 15C. The tower, which, curiously, is municipal and not church property, dates from 1423 but has a spire of 1959. Inside there are a number of features of interest, notably, on the aisle walls on either side of the W end of the nave, the arms of the Knights of the Order of the Golden Fleece who attended the chapter here in 1456. The pew at the E end of the N aisle, dating from 1647, was reserved for city and visiting dignitaries and originally stood at the W end of the church. In the choir ambulatory there are two windows ascribed to the Gouda artist Dirk Crabeth, these being (N) one representing the Annunciation, and (E) one presented by Charles V and representing the Virgin descending from Heaven and, with her foot on Satan, showing the Child to the sovereign. The lower part of this window was lost, what is seen today being a replacement of 1914. Below this window a stone of 1857 marks the Huygens family vault, in which lie Constantijn and his son Christiaan. In the choir, on the site of the altar, a monument by Bartholomeus Eggers to a design by Cornelis Moninx honours Admiral Jacob van Wassenaer van Opdam, killed in 1665 when his ship was blown up in the battle off Lowestoft; the allegorical figures represent Providence, Courage, Loyalty and Vigilance. The pulpit is a pre-Reformation survival of 1550.

From Groenmarkt, Hoogstraat and its continuation street, Noordeinde, both here pedestrian streets, run NW, in 300 metres reaching (E) the *Waalse Kerk*, built for the Walloon community in 1807 by Louis Bonaparte. The *Old Catholic Church* (Wed, 13.30, 14.30, 15.30; entrance 300m W at Molenstraat 38), dating from 1720–22 and containing good stucco and woodwork, was built in this modest and secluded neighbourhood for fear of intolerance. Further N, Noordeinde crosses an open space in which stands an equestrian statue of William the Silent (Count van Nieuwerkerke, 1845) in front of the *Paleis Noordeinde*. Built in 1553 as a private house, the palace was in 1609 given by the States General to Louise de Coligny, widow of William the Silent; rebuilt in 1640, and enlarged in 1816, it is now used as the Queen's offices. The garden behind, laid out by Prince Frederick Henry, is now a public park, at the N end of which are the *Royal Stables* (1878, restored 1980), still in use as such.

From the Paleis Noordeinde, Noordeinde continues NW to cross Hoge Wal (W) and Mauritskade (E), the canal here being a part of the moat of 1613–19 which encircled The Hague until 1840. The N continuation of Noordeinde is Zeestraat, with, at No. 65B, the **Panorama Mesdag** (Mon–Sat, 10.00 to 17.00; Sun, Holidays, 12.00 to 17.00), not to be confused with the Rijksmuseum H.W. Mesdag, for which see B Northern Quarters), a huge panoramic view (1700 sq m) of Scheveningen, painted in 1881 by H.W. Mesdag with the help of his wife Sientje Mesdag-Van Houten, G.H. Breitner, B.J. Blommers and T.E.A. de Bock. The long passage leading to the panorama contains representative works by Mesdag and his wife, and also a portrait of Mesdag by P. de J. de Jong. At Zeestraat 82 the *Postmuseum* (Mon–Sat, 10.00 to 17.00; Sun, and Holidays, 13.00 to 17.00; closed 25 December, 1 January) covers many aspects of communications, material here including postal, telegraph, telephone and radio equipment, and also a worldwide collection of stamps.

To the E of Zeestraat is the WILLEMSPARK, a compact garden district of elegant houses, embassies and suchlike which has grown up on land sold to the city in 1855 by King William III. At the centre, in the square called Plein 1813, a monument of 1869 commemorates the restoration of independence after the years of French occupation; the statues of King William I and of the leaders of the restoration movement (Karel van Hogendorp, Leopold van Limburg-Stirum and Adam van der Duijn) are by W. Geefs.

Zeestraat ends at Laan van Meerdervoort (W) and Javastraat (E), for all places N of which, including the nearby *Museum H.W. Mesdag* and the *Vredespaleis* (Peace Palace), see B. Northern Quarters.

## South and South-West of the Hof Vijver

Two parallel sequences of main streets run across the southern part of the inner city. The northern sequence, the ancient main E–W thoroughfare, today to a great extent pedestrian precinct, is made up of Bezuidenhout-seweg (immediately S of which is the *Centraal Station*), Herengracht, Korte Poten, the Plein (S side), Lange Poten and then, after crossing the junction of the N–S Hofweg and Spui, Spuistraat and Vlamingstraat. The southern sequence branches S off Herengracht, continuing as Fluwelen Burgwal, Kalvermarkt, Grote Marktstraat, and finally the broad 700m long PRINSE-GRACHT. Places most likely to interest the visitor to this part of the city are along this last street and to its S. The street, once elegant either side of a now drained canal, is today somewhat run-down; nevertheless there are some good 17–18C houses and the district is the object of restoration plans.

No. 6, on the S side, is a late 17C mansion which from 1895 to 1922 was the home of Dr Abraham Bredius (1853–1946), Director of the Mauritshuis from 1889 to 1909, art historian and dedicated collector, notably of 17C paintings. On his death he bequeathed both the house and his collections to the city, but the distinguished Museum Bredius has now sadly closed, though there is talk of showing parts of the collections in other galleries or even in a new one, perhaps combined with another museum.

Roughly opposite the museum, at Grote Markt 8A, the *Groot Boterhuis* was a weigh-house built in 1681 (restored 1983); the building now serves as a café and restaurant offering its customers the unusual experience of being weighed on the original butter scales. A short way down Lange Beestemarkt, off the S of Prinsegracht just W of the Bredius house, the *Hofje van Cornelia van Wouw* is an almshouse of 1565 rebuilt in 1647, while another almshouse, an unusually large one, the *Hofje van Nieuwkoop* of 1658, is at Prinsegracht 79, at the W end of the street.

There are several places of interest to the S of Prinsegracht and Grote Marktstraat—much of the district was the Jewish quarter but which is now more Indonesian and Chinese. Lutherse Burgwal runs S to become Paviljoensgracht, near the S end of which (W) is the *Heilige Geesthofje*, an almshouse of 1616. In the centre of the road here there is a statue (Frédéric Hexamer, 1877) of the Jewish philosopher Baruch Spinoza. In 1670 Spinoza published his 'Tractatus Theologico-Politicus', the theme of which was that freedom of thought was compatible with both religious piety and public good order, but the work aroused such intense partisan interest, and from the Calvinist clergy violent denunciation, that Spinoza moved from Voorburg into The Hague, probably to be near to influential friends. He first lived at Stille Veerkade 32 near here, but spent the last years of his life (1671–77) at what is now the *Domus Spinozana* (Paviljoensgracht 72, adjacent to the statue; no adm.), the house of his Lutheran friends the Van der Spijcks. While here he wrote a protest against the bestial murder of the brothers De Witt, and was only prevented from posting this at the scene of the murder by being locked in the house by his host. Here he was visited in 1676 by Carl Leibniz, and here the following year he died of consumption, possibly exacerbated by inhaling glass dust when he had been a lens grinder.

A short way S, Dunne Bierkade, continued by Bierkade, are pleasant canal-side roads with restored houses. One of these, Dunne Bierkade 18, dates in part to a design of 1640 by Pieter Post, while a building (not visible from the road) behind Nos 18–20 was between 1779 and 1790 The Hague porcelain factory which in 1776 had been established by the German Anton Lyncker in the nearby Bagijnestraat; a good collection of this ware is displayed in the Haags Gemeentemuseum.

Bierkade at its E end reaches Spui which returns N to the city centre. On the W, before reaching Grote Marktstraat, stands the **Nieuwe Kerk**, built in 1649–56 by Pieter Noorwitz and Bartholomeus van Bassen, the first Protestant church in The Hague to be built as such. The hexagonal ground plan with six apses is unusual. The brothers De Witt are buried within; Spinoza's grave is behind.

# B.   Northern Quarters and Scheveningen

From the junction of Laan van Meerdervoort and Javastraat, Schevening-seweg heads N for the coastal suburb of Scheveningen (4km).

This road, a wide avenue, which originated as a project of 1665 by Constantijn Huygens, was a toll road until 1889, although for the inhabitants of Scheveningen it was free. The tollhouse still stands beside the Jewish Cemetery, opposite the Peace Palace.

The **Rijksmuseum H.W. Mesdag** (entrance Laan van Meerdervoort 7F. Tues–Sat, 10.00 to 17.00; Sun, Holidays, 13.00 to 17.00), standing within the angle of Laan van Meerdervoort and Scheveningseweg, houses the collection of 19C paintings, mainly of the Hague School and the French Barbizon School, presented to the country by the banker turned painter H.W. Mesdag (died 1915) and his wife Sientje Mesdag-van Houten (died 1909).

In principle the Hague School pictures, including works by Mesdag, are on the ground floor, staircase, and first floor, while the French pictures are on the second floor (some in later rooms of first floor).

GROUND FLOOR. Hall. A bust of H.W. Mesdag by *Toon Dupuis*. *H.W. Mesdag*: The new mole at Enkhuizen. Room 3. Several works by *H.W. Mesdag*, including Boats by Moonlight, Scheveningen, and Sunset at Scheveningen. *A. Verwee*: Horses on a beach; Sheep on the dunes. Room 4. *Jozef Israels*: Portrait of Sintje Mesdag. *Anton Mauve*: Hut with a straw roof. Room 5. *Anton Mauve*: Going home; The painter at work in a landscape; Peasant woman and cow in a byre. *Willem Maris*: cows. Stairs and Landing, several works by *A. Mancini*, whose bright faces bring a welcome lightness.

FIRST FLOOR. Room 10. *Willem Roelofs*: Windmills. *Jozef Israels*: Old woman. *G. Henkes*: The knitting lesson (a charming study). Room 11. *Jozef Israels*: *Alone in the world; The Harpist. *Jacob Maris*: The Mill. *Matthijs Maris*: The Bride. *Johannes Bosboom*: Church interiors. *B.J. Blommers*: Young girl. Room 12. *J.L. Géricault*: Horses. *B.J. Blommers*: Mother lifting up her child. Here too are a large blue Japanese bowl depicting a ceramics workshop and rich in contemporary detail, and also a case of Japan ware. Room 13. *Paul Gabriel*: Thaw. *Matthijs Maris*: The cook—an amusing portrayal of boredom and reluctance. *H.W. Mesdag*: Winter scene at Scheveningen. *Johannes Bosboom*: Church interior. In this room are also works by *Anton Mauve, Jacob Maris*, and *Willem Roelofs*. Room 14. *Anton Mauve*: Sheep in a copse. *Eugène Delacroix*: Crucifixion. *J.F. Millet*: Peasant and donkey. *Charles Daubigny*: The copse.—Room 15. *J.F. Millet*: Sheep and haystacks. Rest in the vineyard. *B.J. Blommers*: *Small girl paddling. *A. Mancini*: Two lively portraits of ladies.

SECOND FLOOR. Landing. *Charles Daubigny*: several works. Room 18. *C. Troyon*: On the way home; The Cow. *A. Vollon*: Fishing boats in harbour. *T. Rousseau*: Felled trees; Fontainebleau. *N.V. Diaz*: several works. *Charles Daubigny*: Beach scene. Room 19. Several works by *Charles Daubigny, J.F. Millet*, and *C. Troyon*. Room 20. *Charles Daubigny*: Villenville-sur-Mer; Two cows. *A. Monticelli*: Mountain path. *J.F. Millet*: Hagar and Ishmael. *J.B.C. Corot*: two small works. Room 21. *G. Courbet*: Still life; Nude; Self-portrait. *A. Vollon*: Still life. Room 22. *J.B.C. Corot*: several works. *Eugene Delacroix*: Self-portrait. *N.V. Diaz*: Nude.

Scheveningseweg soon crosses Carnegieplein, with the entrance to the garden surrounding the large and conspicuous **Vredespaleis (Peace**

**Palace**), open Mon–Fri, 10.00 to 12.00, 14.00 to 16.00; guided tours 10.00, 11.00, 14.00 15.00; also in May–Sept).

The first international conference for the suppression of war was held in 1899, at the instance of Nicholas II of Russia, at the Huis ten Bosch in the Haagse Bos. As a result the Permanent Court of Arbitration was set up, and to provide this court with a suitable seat and a good library the Scottish-American millionaire Andrew Carnegie placed the sum of one and a half million dollars at the disposal of the Dutch government. After a competition the plans of the architect Louis Cordonnier of Lille were selected from amongst those of more than 200 entrants. The foundation stone was laid by the Russian ambassador, A. Nelidov, president of a second peace conference, in 1907, and the building was declared open in 1913. Since 1922 the palace has housed also the Permanent Court of International Justice, and since 1923 the Academy of International Law has given courses of instruction here.

Built in Flemish Renaissance style, many of the materials and the furnishing for the palace were contributed by various countries from around the world. The woodwork of Javanese teak and Brazilian mahogany and rosewood and the Japanese embroidery are particularly noteworthy, but the whole interior is rich in works of art. The stained glass windows in the Great Hall of International Justice were contributed by Britain.

Roughly opposite the palace Burgemeester Patijnlaan in 400m reaches the modern *Stadhuis* (1953 and later).

Scheveningseweg now runs dead straight between the park areas of the *Scheveningse Bosjes* (E) and *Zorgvliet* (W), parts of both of which have been absorbed by housing estates. The mansion of Zorgvliet was the residence of the poet and Council Pensionary Jacob Cats (1577–1660) who spent his last years here. Beyond the Zorgvliet park a major crossroads is reached, with Professor B.M. Teldersweg branching SE and Johan de Wittlaan SW. Each is now described in turn.

PROFESSOR B.M. TELDERSWEG runs through the Scheveningse Bosjes and in 800m reaches ***Madurodam** (roughly Easter–mid Oct: 09.30 to, according to season, as late as 23.00 or as early as 18.00), a city in miniature (one twenty-fifth scale), imaginary in history and layout but with many well-known buildings of Amsterdam, The Hague, and elsewhere. The 'city' is fully illuminated at night.

The original capital was provided by J.M.L. Maduro and his wife who wished to establish a memorial to their son George Maduro who, as a student and reserve officer, distinguished himself during the German invasion of May 1940 and died in Dachau concentration camp in 1945. A memorial plaque is set in the wall to the left of the entrance. The proposal for the Madurodam project came from Mevrouw B. Boon-van der Starp (died 1959). Additional capital was then raised, the city provided a site, and Madurodam was officially opened by Princess (now Queen) Beatrix (the 'mayoress') in 1952. Profits are applied to general social and cultural charities, especially those concerned with Dutch youth.

Madurodam embraces well over 100 particular features, including churches, schools, theatres, factories, a working railway, canals and a harbour with moving craft, airport, etc. Among the many well-known buildings which can be seen here in miniature are The Hague's Binnenhof, Huis ten Bosch, and Peace Palace; Amsterdam's Dam (with the Royal Palace and the Nieuwe Kerk), Beurs, Westerkerk and the house of Anne Frank,

Jordaan district, and Portuguese synagogue; the Waterpoort at Sneek, the Sassenpoort at Zwolle, the Stadhuis at Gouda, and St. Jans Cathedral at 's Hertogenbosch. Other features are the night illumination, the dwarf trees, and the flowering bulbs in spring. Children will love the house on fire.

For *Westbroekpark* (*Rosarium*), 1km N, see under Scheveningen below.

JOHAN DE WITTLAAN, running SW from Scheveningseweg, passes (N) the large *Congresgebouw* (J.J.P. Oud, 1969) and then reaches the important triple-museum complex contained within Johan de Wittlaan, the E end of President Kennedylaan and Stadhouderslaan. Here, adjacent to one another, are the Haags Gemeentemuseum, the Museon (also sometimes called the Museum voor Onderwijs, or Education), and the Omniversum (also sometimes called the Ruimte, or Space, Theatre). The first two are entered from Stadhouderslaan, the Omniversum from President Kennedylaan. Parking is normally possible either beside the Omniversum or in Stadhouderslaan.

The Haags Gemeentemuseum and the Museon share a common approach path and reception hall, the former museum being to the left, the latter to the right.

The **\*Haags Gemeentemuseum** (Tues–Fri, 10.00 to 17.00; Sat, Sun, Holidays, 12.00 to 17.00), in a building of 1935 by H.P. Berlage, is the city's municipal museum in which are assembled distinguished collections (applied art and 19–20C paintings) from several former museums. Since 1985 the museum has also absorbed the Dutch Costume Museum (Kostuum Museum). Of special note are the collection of musical instruments, spanning the 15–19C and from many parts of the world; the porcelain—oriental, Islamic and Dutch; the Hague silverware; and the 19C and 20C paintings, which include the Hague School and a large collection of the works of Piet Mondriaan.

Throughout much of the year the museum mounts a programme of varied special exhibitions.

The museum, on two floors, is arranged as a system of connecting galleries and rooms around the four sides of a central courtyard-garden. The ground floor contains the applied art collections and the upper floor the paintings and other forms of modern art.

GROUND FLOOR. The approach path, off Stadhouderslaan, enters at the W side of the reception hall. Visitors with specialised tastes or interests will aim for their chosen departments. Others, with a general tour in mind, should move N past, on the left, the museum shop, and then turn right into the S wing to start an anticlockwise round.

The S wing of the ground floor is devoted to ceramics and glass, divided into (left) the Islamic lands and (right) Egypt, Greece and Rome. Beyond the latter, a small area shows material from Asia Minor (15–18C), beyond this again being a series of displays of Chinese ceramics ranging from prehistoric (c 2500 BC) to relatively modern times, the T'ang and Sung dynasty collections being especially noteworthy. A left turn at the end leads through a department (very noisy and full of children) called Spelen met Muziekinstrumenten, or Games with musical instruments.

The greater part of the N wing houses the museum's famous \**Collection of Musical Instruments*, this being in two parts, Non-European and European, the former showing temple bells and many exotic instruments while the latter is a large and varied collection spanning roughly 1450 to the present century. In addition to the instruments themselves, there are some pleasing and interesting paintings (mostly 17C) showing various instruments in use. Beyond the musical instruments, and occupying the NW

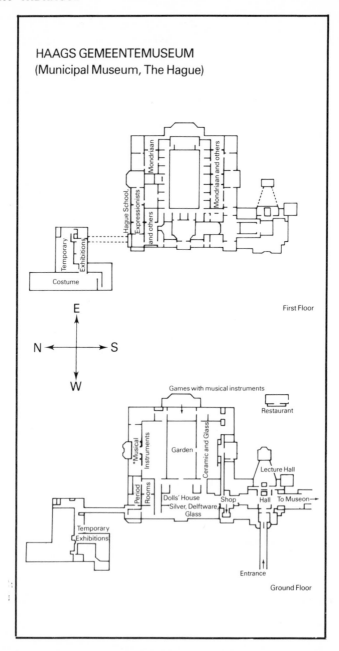

HAAGS GEMEENTEMUSEUM
(Municipal Museum, The Hague)

First Floor

Ground Floor

corner of this floor, there is a series of Period Rooms, some with sumptuous displays of Hague and other silver and porcelain. The west wing—rich in silver, Delftware, Italian ceramic, glass and suchlike—also shows a beautiful, tall, cabinet dolls' house.

The FIRST FLOOR houses the museum's large collection of modern paintings of the 19C to the present day, the emphasis being on *Piet Mondriaan* (most of the S wing; also the E section of the N wing). Among the many other 19C and 20C artists to whom rooms or parts of rooms are devoted may be mentioned the following (it should though be noted that artists are not necessarily confined to the rooms below and that other works may be found elsewhere): room of 19C Landscapes, artists including A. Schelfhout, W.J.J. Nuyen, Barend Koekkoek, Willem Roelofs and J.F. Millet. A room devoted largely to Johan Jongkind, with several local Dutch scenes. A room for, jointly, C.O. Monet, Alfred Sisley, Gustave Courbet and Van Gogh (self-portrait of 1886). Hague School room with works by J.H. Weissenbruch, Jozef Israels and Willem Roelofs. Other rooms show G.H. Breitner and Suze Robertson; Jan Toorop; Anton Mauve and the three brothers Maris; Leo Gestel; J.H. Weissenbruch (several town views and landscapes), A.H. Bakker Korff, Johannes Bosboom and Isaac Israels. Other sections illustrate Cubism (Picasso, Léger), Expressionism (Kirchner), Constructivism (Lissitzky), and works later than 1945.

The KOSTUUM MUSEUM is in an annex off the NW corner of the main building. This is not, as might be thought, a museum of traditional Dutch costume, but, rather, a fairly modest collection of the normal dress worn between the 18C and today. The essence of the museum is a gallery lined by sections which show the development of clothing under various themes, some of these rather odd—Trendsetters; the Poor; Sport; Woman, the Goddess; Romanticism (1895 to Laura Ashley); Status; Restriction of movement; Eroticism; Emancipation of Woman from 1902 to a Chanel suit; Youth; Cultural Confrontation; Emancipation of Men; Anarchy and Punk.

*Museon** (Tues–Fri, 10.00 to 17.00; Sat, Sun, Holidays, 13.00 to 17.00)— ultra modern, bright, colourful and imaginative—must surely represent the last word in the techniques of museum presentation and is worth visiting on this account alone. In principle the basic theme is Education, but the term is misleading because the impact here is educational in the most soaring sense of the word. 'The Earth, our Home', or how people live around the world, is the title of the ground floor permanent presentation; 'Between Man and Nebula' that of the upper level. But these may well change.

But whatever the formal titles, Museon's most notable feature is the way in which the subjects are intermingled, so that at every turn there is something new, contrasting and startling. A desert nomad's tent is pitched alongside modern machinery. Costumed Balinese are neighbours to a spectacular geological display, while a *Tyrannosaurus rex* stands nearby. At one moment the visitor may be attempting to master an electronic explanation of the atmosphere, the next immersed in the tropical rain forest or, perhaps, learning about life in prehistoric Netherlands. A whole room will entrance the photographic enthusiast. Egypt and the pyramids merge with an exhibit entitled The Written Word, tracing the story from ancient pictograms to the word processor and modern pictorial signs. In truth, this museum comes as close as an architectural space can to flicking channels on a television.

The **Omniversum** (Mon–Thurs shows on the hour 11.00 to 16.00; Fri, Sat, Sun, Holidays, on the hour 11.00 to 17.00 and 19.00 to 21.00), officially described as Europe's first space theatre, derives its name from Omnimax, the 70mm projection system, while Universum refers to the space and astronomical aspects of the programmes shown here. In a theatre with a domed screen, the wrap-around projection by Omnimax (Imax Systems Corporation, Toronto), and a six-channel sound system, the audience is totally involved in the spectacular shows such as, perhaps, Earth's creation or a flight through the universe with the help of the Digistar planetarium projector (Evans and Sutherland, Salt Lake City).

**SCHEVENINGEN**, which may be divided into *Scheveningen Bad* (N) and *Scheveningen Haven* (S), is not only The Hague's coastal suburb but also, with its Kurhaus, hotels, fine beach, and many facilities, the most popular resort along Holland's coast.

**History.** Scheveningen originated as an early fishing village which was drowned by the sea in 1570 and rebuilt further inland. The place's development really dates from the construction of the road from The Hague in 1665, though it was not until 1715 that the first resort villa was built. The first formal bathing establishment opened in 1818, and in 1896–1900 the sea wall was constructed. The harbour served as the port of The Hague from the 16–19C, during which time many distinguished people used it as their place of embarkation, including Queen Henrietta Maria of England (1643), after her vain effort to persuade the States General to come to the aid of her husband Charles I; Charles II, in 1650, when he set off to receive the crown of Scotland, and again in 1660, on his restoration, to receive the throne of England, an occasion when Samuel Pepys was much in evidence; and William V (1795), when the stadholderate was finally overthrown by the revolutionary forces acting in concert with the French. The harbour also saw William's son's return in 1813. The town suffered a good deal from German destruction during the Second World War, during which also the ability to pronounce the town's name correctly was treated as a test of whether or not a suspect was genuinely Dutch.

In the early 1970s the decision was taken that Scheveningen should be transformed into a leading European year-round resort, and the year 1978 saw the establishment of the Stichting Scheveningen Bad, a foundation with terms of reference to oversee and co-ordinate all aspects of this venture. The undertaking is well on the way towards completion.

**Boats.** Sea fishing and cruises. Departures from Dr Lelykade, Scheveningen Haven. Tel: (070) 540887.

For the visitor the centre of **Scheveningen Bad** is the *Kurhaus* (1887) which, while retaining its 19C exterior, has been enlarged and modernised as a hotel, with several restaurants, and a *Casino*. The close surrounds include both a residential and an office zone, and an extensive sheltered precinct with shops, restaurants, cafés and recreational facilities. The nearby *Pier* (Oct–March: daily, 09.00 to 17.00; April–Sept: daily, 09.00 to 21.00), replacing one destroyed during the war, extends 400m out to sea as an unusual design with four satellites; among the many attractions are a shell and coral garden, a fishing platform and an aquarium with 60 tanks and a replica of Jules Verne's submarine 'Nautilus'. The *Golfbad*, on the other side of the Kurhaus, is a glassed-in leisure centre the main feature of which is a swimming pool with surf action; other facilities include saunas, solariums, a paddling pool and a sports hall. Alongside, at Strandweg 11, rather different interests are catered for at the *Ambachtelijke Kaarsenmakerij* (Candles Workshop) where the visitor can learn all about the history and manufacture of candles. Visitors can try their skill at dipping, and there is also a shop (Mon–Fri, 08.30 to 17.00; Sat, Sun, 12.00 to 18.00).

Inland, at Neptunusstraat 92, the *Scheveningen Museum* (Tues–Sun, 10.00 to 16.30) is concerned with the story of Scheveningen, with particular emphasis on shipping, while further S, between Nieuwe Parklaan (E) and Haringkade (W), is the *Westbroek Park Rosarium* (daily, 09.00 to one hour before sunset) offering some 20,000 roses of hundreds of varieties; the terrace of the restaurant affords a splendid view.

**Scheveningen Haven**, representing the old fishing village, still maintains a busy fishing industry and something of the earlier character survives in the costume which is still worn by a few of the inhabitants. Dr Lelykade, along the SE side of the harbour, is the departure point for fishing trips and sea cruises, and here too (No. 39) is the *Zeebiologisch Museum* (Mon–Sat, 10.00 to 17.00; Sun, 13.00 to 17.00), showing species of marine life from the oceans of the world. The tower of the church near the sea end of Keizerstraat dates from the 15C and is probably the oldest building in Scheveningen. On Strandweg an obelisk commemorates the landing of Prince William (afterwards King William I) in 1813.

# C.   Outer City and Suburbs

NORTH-EAST. To the NE of the Prinsessegracht, opposite the end of Korte Voorhout, there are two adjoining open areas, the *Malieveld* (N), a former parade ground, now reduced in size by the construction of new roads, and the *Koekamp* (S), with a small lake. These open areas are flanked on the E by a major road, the Utrechtsebaan, beyond which the **Haagse Bos**, a park with lakes, woodland, and some fine avenues, extends E. The *Huis ten Bosch* (no adm.), at the far end of the park and the Queen's official residence, was built in 1645–52 by Pieter Post for Amalia von Solms, widow of Prince Frederick Henry; two wings were added in 1735–37 by Daniel Marot. The heart of the palace is the Oranjezaal, a double-height room entirely decorated with paintings celebrating the life and reign of Frederick Henry by, among others, Jacob Jordaens (Rubens' chief assistant), Cesar van Everdingen, Salomon de Bray, Jan Lievens, Pieter de Grebber and the painter architect Jacob van Campen. Although these are not today the most famous names in the history of Dutch art, many of these artists were at the vanguard of mid 17C classicism which flourished especially in Haarlem and anticipated aspects of that monumental, rational style which can be detected both in later academic traditions and in the limpid clarity of Jan Vermeer. The palace was the meeting place in 1899 of the first international conference for the suppression of war, held at the instance of Nicholas II of Russia. Benoordenhoutseweg (N of the Wood Way) at the end of the wood becomes Leidsestraatweg, off the N of which is *Duindigt Renbaan*, a racecourse for flat and trotting races.

For Waśsenaar, 5km further NE, and also Leiden, see Rte 6.

SOUTH-EAST. A series of suburbs spread along the SE outskirts of The Hague. **Voorburg** is a place of Roman origin (Forum Hadriani). Here the mansion of *Hofwijck* (Westeinde 2: daily except Mon and Fri, 14.00 to 17.00) was built in 1641–43 jointly by Jacob van Campen and Pieter Post for Constantijn Huygens. The house contains portraits, books, correspondence and other material relating to Huygens and his son Christiaan. The *Museum Swaensteijn* (Tues, Thurs, Sun, 14.00 to 17.00; Sat, 12.00 to 16.00), SE of the station at Herenstraat 101, contains Roman remains and local historical material, the emphasis being on engravings and drawings of country mansions. Spinoza lived in Voorburg from 1663–69 or 70. **Rijswijk**

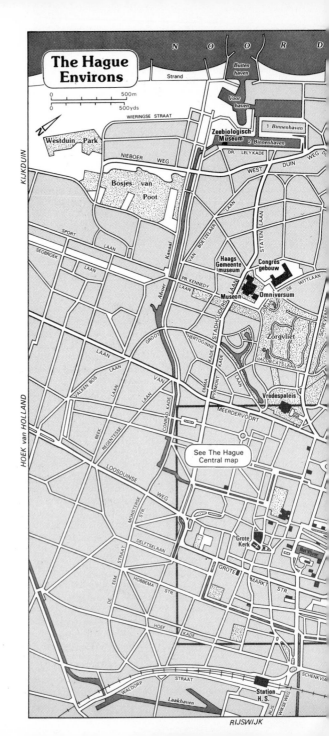

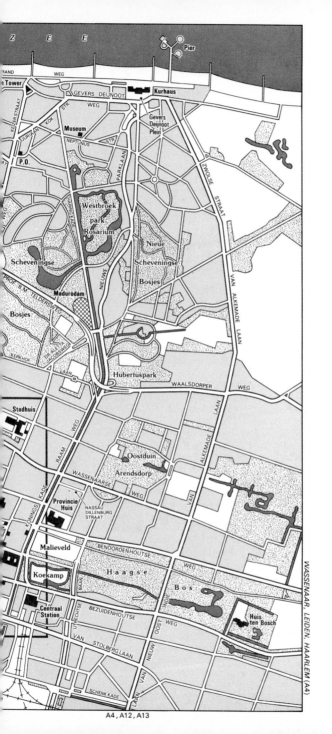

gave its name to the treaty signed in 1697 between France (Louis XIV) on the one side, and the United Provinces, England, Spain, and Germany on the other. Under this treaty Louis XIV recognised Prince William as King William III of England; the treaty also officially transferred the principality of Orange to France. The *Museum Rijswijk* (Tues–Fri, Sun, 14.00 to 17.00; Sat, 10.00 to 17.00), at Herenstraat 67, is a museum of local history and art.

For Delft, 4km SE of Rijswijk, see Rte 8.

NORTH-WEST. **Kijkduin**, on the coast at the NW of The Hague, is a small but developing resort, separated from Scheveningen by the large *West-duinpark*, criss-crossed by many foot and cycle paths and with several outlook points on the dunes. For the WESTLAND horticultural district between Kijkduin and Hoek van Holland, see Rte 11.


# D.  The Mauritshuis—**Royal Picture Gallery

The **MAURITSHUIS** (Tues–Sat, 10.00 to 17.00; Sun, Holidays, 11.00 to 17.00) is a Palladian mansion built in 1633–44 by Pieter Post to designs by Jacob van Campen for John Maurice of Nassau-Siegen, governor of the Brazilian territories of the West Indies Company. It is one of the first buildings in the country to be wholly inspired by Italian models, yet, with its combination of brick and stone, and partly surrounded by water, it remains essentially Dutch. Soon after the death of John Maurice in 1679 the mansion became state property and was used to accommodate distinguished foreigners, one such being Marlborough who resided here in 1704. Soon afterwards the house was gutted by fire. In 1807 the National Library was housed here, but since 1821 the building has been the home of the Royal Picture Gallery. Between 1982 and 1987 the Mauritshuis was closed for major restoration, including the installation of a climate control system, new wall coverings, and the construction under the forecourt of two floors of basement for a study area, storage, offices, etc.

The **Royal Picture Gallery** (*Koninklijk Kabinet van Schilderijen*) is one of the finest collections of paintings in the world. The collection, apart from a few survivals from the collections of Prince Frederick Henry and other Orange princes, was started by Prince William V who assembled some 200 paintings in the Binnenhof, including those of the Slingelandt Collection purchased in 1768. The paintings were carried off to France in 1795 but, thanks largely to the influence of Wellington, most were returned in 1815. King William I increased the collection to 500 pictures, and since 1874 it has progressively been enlarged; by purchase, notably in 1913 when six of the finest works in the Steengracht Collection were acquired, by gift, and by bequest, an important one being that of 1946 from Dr Bredius, director from 1889–1909.

The collection includes some of the famous masterpieces of Rembrandt, Vermeer, Ruisdael, and Jan Steen, as well as of many other masters of the 17C, and the Flemish School is also well represented, with some fine works by Rubens and Van Dyck. Some notable Flemish primitives were given by the Rijksmuseum, Amsterdam, in exchange for a group of Spanish and Italian works. Among the foreign paintings portraits by Holbein are outstanding.

The gallery is on two floors (see plan); this room by room description is based on the layout which followed the major refurbishment of 1982–87. Lack of exhibition space and the accidents of loan policy may mean that any one picture may not be on display at any one time and this is a representative survey. Boards to help you guide yourself around, in all the major languages, are available in slotted boxes in each room.

GROUND FLOOR. **Hal en Trappenhuis** (Hall and Staircase). Fittingly, this great entrance is dominated by portraiture celebrating the Orange family and its royal connections (see also below). *Jan de Baen:* 5. Portrait of John Maurice of Nassau-Siegen for whom the Mauritshuis was built (c 1670). *Adriaen Hanneman:* 429. Portrait of Maria Henrietta, daughter of Charles I of England and wife of Prince William II.

**Van der Weydenzaal** (Van der Weyden Room). A selection of earlier Netherlandish paintings. *Rogier van der Weyden:* 264. Lamentation. *Herri met de Bles:* 957. Paradise—a luminous roundel worth microscopic inspection. *A. Isenbrandt* 958. Virgin and Child. *Master of the Solomon Triptych* 432. Life of Solomon Triptych. *Master of Frankfurt:* 872. St Christopher. *Jan Provost* 853. Virgin and Saints. *Jan Gossaert:* 830. Madonna. 841. Portrait of Count Egmont van Buren-IJsselstein. *Hans Memling:* 595. Portrait of a Man. *Master of the Legend of St Barbara:* 844. Idolatry of Solomon.

**Bosschaertzaal** (Bosschaert Room). Courtly, international and highly refined styles thrived during the Golden Age in the Netherlands—a point often missed by those who emphasise the genre and portrait painting of the 'Dutch tradition'. *Ambrosius Bosschaert:* •679. Vase with flowers in a niche. The Bosschaerts made a good living from painting still lifes; here the landscape view with church, shells, wildlife and choice of flowers comment upon the brevity of life. *Anthonis Mor:* 117. Portrait of Steven van Herwijck. Anthonis Mor was Philip II's principal painter even though the Inquisition was said to have made Spain too uncomfortable for him, driving him home to Utrecht. *Balthazar van der Ast:* 1066. Still life. *Joachim Wttwael:* •223. Venus and Mars surprised by Vulcan. Wttwael, a Utrecht painter, persisted in his Italianate manner until the 1630s; this picture is given an extra preciousness by being painted on a small copper plate—a fashion in Rome and Prague. *Pieter Pourbus:* 881. Portrait of a Man. *Godfried Schalcken:* 158. Portrait of William III of Orange Nassau and of England.

**Troostkabinet** (Troost Gallery). •Pastels by the 18C master *Cornelis Troost*, in a witty and satirical theatrical vein. Note especially the dispute between the astronomers, over the geocentric and heliocentric accounts of the solar system, using plates of food to illustrate their arguments (note too the bemused female servant in the background).

**Goudenzaal** (Golden Room). This grand room overlooks the Hof Vijver and was the principal reception room of the house. The painted decorative scheme of c 1718 (excluding the flower pieces) is by *G.A. Pellegrini*. The furniture by *Daniel Marot*.

**Holbeinkabinet** (Holbein Gallery). This is one of the very best small collections of 16C German painting. *Hans Holbein the Younger:* •276. Portrait of Robert Cheseman, falconer to Henry VIII; 277. Man with a falcon; 278. Portrait of Jane Seymour (contemporary copy). *Lucas Cranach the Elder:* 917. Virgin and Child. *Lucas Cranach the Younger:* 890. Man with a red beard. *Bartholomeus Bruyn:* 889. Portrait of a young woman. *M. Sittow:* 832. Portrait of a man.

**Vlaamingenzaal** (Flemish Room, in fact two adjoining rooms). This room is dominated by Pieter Paul Rubens, an artist much admired at the Orange Court and an artist separated only by political history from the tradition of

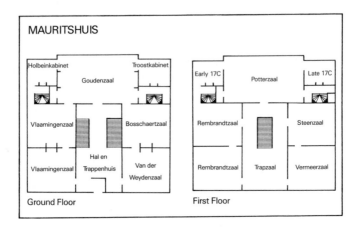

MAURITSHUIS

Holbeinkabinet        Troostkabinet
              Goudenzaal

Vlaamingenzaal                    Bosschaertzaal

                      Hal en
Vlaamingenzaal      Trappenhuis      Van der
                              Weydenzaal

Ground Floor

Early 17C        Potterzaal        Late 17C

Rembrandtzaal                      Steenzaal

Rembrandtzaal      Trapzaal      Vermeerzaal

First Floor

Dutch art. *P.P. Rubens*: 250. Portrait of the artist's first wife, Isabella Brandt. Rubens' first marriage in 1609 to the daughter of an Antwerp burgomaster is the surest testimony of his 'arrival' in Antwerp society; she died in 1627. *P.P. Rubens* and *Jan Breughel*: •253. Adam and Eve in Paradise; collaborative work, in this case between a figure painter and a landscape and animal painter, is typical of artistic practice of the period even outside a particular workshop. *David Teniers the Younger*: 261. The Alchemist. *Adriaen Brouwer*: •919. Quarrel at cards; 847. Inn with drunken peasants. Although a Fleming by birth, Brouwer lived and worked in Haarlem, one of the many emigrants of the War of Rebellion. *Anthony van Dyck*: •239 and 240. Portraits of the painter Pieter Stevens of Antwerp and his wife; 242. Portrait of Quintijn Simons of Antwerp. Although famous in the English-speaking world as a painter of aristocrats, it is in his bourgeois portraits, often of friends, that Van Dyck found the most compelling expression of personality and intimacy. *J. Blommendael*: 361. Bust of Prince William III. *Willem van Haecht*: 266. The Studio of Apelles, an idealised representation of Van der Geest's Kunstkamer in Antwerp. In accordance with contemporary theories of knowledge the gallery is laid out as a kind of three-dimensional encyclopaedia with the reference to the great artist of antiquity lending dignity to the whole. *Jan Brueghel*: 285. Christ delivering souls from Purgatory.

On the **Staircase** (see above) there are more Orange portraits, the most important artist being *Gerrit van Honthorst*: 63. Prince William II; 430. Prince Frederick Henry. Honthorst made his reputation in Italy as 'Gherardo delle Notti' specialising in nocturnal effects in a monumental style derived from Caravaggio. After failing to supplant Van Dyck in London he succeeded Miereveldt as court portraitist at The Hague, producing portraits which are handsome, if bland. *Johan Ziesenis*: 463. Princess Frederica Sophia Wilhelmina; 462. Prince William V; *Hendrick Pacx*: 546. An anachronistic group portrait showing William the Silent, Prince Maurice, Frederick Henry and William Louis of Nassau.

FIRST FLOOR. **Vermeerzaal** (Vermeer Room), on the left at the top of the stairs. A fine and concisely representative selection of 17C Dutch painting. *Jan Vermeer*: *406. Diana and her companions; *670. Girl wearing a turban; *92. View of Delft. The Mauritshuis is worth a visit for these three paintings alone. The Diana picture was discovered to have a signature in 1895, otherwise it would be very hard indeed to relate it to Vermeer's other works. It is one of four early paintings which tackle narrative subjects in a style close to that of the Utrecht Caravaggisti and is the only early work to be seen in the Netherlands. The girl in a turban, despite the lack of an 'everyday' context, is more typical of Vermeer, especially in the puddled handling of paint and command of winsome, haunting expression. Few leave the gallery without buying a postcard of this image. The View of Delft is an hypnotically truthful representation of the town from, it is thought, a window near the St Luke's (Painters') Guild where it originally hung. Several artists specialised in town views during the period, see Jan van der Heyden (no. 868) in the Trapzaal on this floor. The relative scale of objects are rendered so precisely that it seems certain that Vermeer employed a 'camera obscura', a dark box with a lens which projected a scene onto the drawing surface, making this an early example of manual (if not chemical) photography.

*Gerard Terborch*: 744. Mother combing her child's hair. *Pieter Saenredam*: Interior of the Church of St Cunera at Rhenen.

**Steenzaal** (Jan Steen Room). *Jan Steen*: 779. Portrait of an old lady with a lute; 168. The Doctor's Visit; 742. 'What you hear is what you sing'; 170. The Life of Man; 818. Girl eating Oysters. 166. Portrait of a girl. Jan Steen is one of the most various of painters reflecting the amount of travelling he did between towns and the number, therefore, of markets for which he painted his 700 identified pictures. The common theme in his work is the folly of humankind which no doubt accounts for his seeming never to have run out of subject matter.

*Frans Hals*: 459 and 460. Portraits of J.P.Olycan and his wife. *Hendrick Averkamp*: 785. The Pleasures of Winter. *Pieter Claesz*: Still-life with a candle. *Jan de Heem*: 613. Still-life with books. *Jan Porcellis*: 969. Shipwreck. *Jan van Goyen*: 860. View of a Village.

**Potterzall** (Paulus Potter Room). The most striking painting here is by *Paulus Potter*: *136. The Young Bull. Potter died as young as 29, this was painted in 1647 when he was only 22. *Batholomeus van der Helst*: Portrait of Paulus Potter.

Other paintings in the room include Italian influenced landscape subjects. *Cornelis van Poelenburgh*: 1065. Gathering of the gods. *Jan Both*: Italian landscape. *Aelbert Cuyp*: 25. Equestrian portrait of Pieter Roeverer. There are also some examples of genre painting showing a wide range of styles and subjects. *Godfried Schalcken*: 160 and 161. Unheeded Advice, and The Doctor's Visit; two fables for amorous youth. The linking of pictures in such pairs was not unusual. Schalcken was a pupil of Gerrit Dou and continued Dou's 'fijnschilder' (precise painting) style into the early 18C. *Cesar van Everdingen*: *39. Diogenes looking for a man. This is a complicated hybrid of genre, portrait (anachronistic, note the variety of costumes) and history painting; where, asks the philosopher, can I find a real man? *Gabriel Metsu*: 94. Lady at her music.

**Rembrandtzaal** (Rembrandt Room, two rooms). As good a collection of works by Rembrandt as can be found anywhere. *Rembrandt van Rijn*: *148 and 840. Self-portraits at the age of 20 and 60 years. Rembrandt's self-portraits are a unique phenomenon in art history, not because Rembrandt was the only artist to portray himself but because no one else did it so con-

*Two Negroes by Rembrandt, The Mauritshuis, The Hague*

sistently and so prolifically. What the self-portraits were for is a mystery. He did not keep them, they were not a kind of visual diary; they seem to have had different purposes: 148 is a formal exercise in a courtly pose, 840 an appraisal of character with the extra interest of having been painted in the year of Rembrandt's death. 145. Simeon in the temple; 685. Two negroes; 621. David playing the harp for Saul (no longer believed to be by Rembrandt); *584. Homer dictating. Even after his bankruptcy Rembrandt continued to obtain important commissions, this painting was for a Sicilian nobleman who also ordered 'historical portraits' of Aristotle and Alexander. 147. Susanna and the elders.

The room is dominated by *146, The Anatomy Lesson of Dr Tulp. This work established Rembrandt as Amsterdam's leading young portraitist and enabled his move there from Leiden in 1632. The cadaver, Adriaensz 't Kint, was also a Leidener; he was executed for stealing a coat on the previous day. Anatomy lessons, public lectures for doctors as well as the educated elite, involved the illustration of a reading of Vesalius (a 16C Dutch anatomist at Padua University, his book lies open at the bottom right) with an actual body. That this does not represent the event itself is confirmed by the fact that Tulp appears to be discussing the tendons of the arm (he shows the movement of the hand with his own left hand) rather than proceeding first to expose the gut, then the head and lastly the limbs. The drama of the scene is achieved by the variety of response in the sitters, the pyramidal organisation of forms and the chiaroscuro, all features of narrative painting rather than traditional portraiture. Dr Tulp was a very well-connected man and this was a prestigious commission. Interestingly, Rembrandt did not go on to become the portraitist of the highest Amsterdam circles.

*Hendrick Terbrugghen*: 966. The Deliverance of St Peter. *Adriaen van Ostade*: 128 and 129. Two peasant scenes. *Jacob van Ruisdael*: 155. View of Haarlem. Owing to a late-18C passion for collecting romantic views, Ruisdael is better represented in British collections than in his native country. *Philips Wouwerman*: 214 and 215. Leaving and returning to the stables.

**Trapzaal** (at the top of the stairs). *Isaak van Ostade*: 789. Landscape with travellers at an Inn. *Ferdinand Bol*: 585. Portrait of Admiral de Ruyter. *Willem van de Velde the Younger*: 200. Warships on the IJ. 201. Charles II departing from Dordrecht for Delft. *Aert de Gelder*: 40. Judah and Tamar. *Frans Hals*: 1032. Laughing boy. *Jan Weenix*: 206. Dead Swan. *Jacob van Ruisdael*: 728. Evening. 153. A Waterfall. *Salomon van Ruysdael*: 738. River scene. *Pieter Codde*: 392. A Dancing Party. *Frans van Mieris*: 106. A boy blowing bubbles. This motif represents the motif 'Homo Bulla', man is but a bubble, a comment on the transience of human life. *Jan van der Heyden*: 868. View of the Oude Zijds Voorburgwal, Amsterdam. As well as producing some of the most compellingly realistic views in the history of art, Jan van der Heyden invented a pump for the fire brigades and a method of street lighting.

# 8 Delft

**DELFT** (86,000 inhab.) is a compact old town in which the spacious, open Markt, across which a Gothic church and Renaissance town hall face one another, contrasts with the narrow canal-lined streets, often with 17–18C façades, which surround it. The town is known as the place in which William the Silent was murdered, and has given its name to a famous form of pottery.

**Centre.** Markt. All places of principal interest are within a short walking distance.

**VVV.** Markt (SE corner).

**Post Office.** Hippolytusbuurt 12 (near the Oude Kerk).

**Station.** Van Leeuwenhoeksingel (beyond SW of inner town).

**Boats.** Canal cruises from Wijnhaven 6.

**Horse-drawn Carriages** provide a relaxed way of touring the town (Easter–Sept: daily, except Thurs, from the Markt).

**History.** Founded in 1075 by Duke Godfrey III of Lower Lotharingia, Delft passed to the counts of Holland, receiving its first charter from Count William II in 1246. In 1536 the town was almost wholly destroyed by a fire, and it again suffered major damage through a powder magazine explosion in 1654, the painter Karel Fabritius being among the many who lost their lives. In 1584 William the Silent, having been declared an outlaw by Philip II, was assassinated in the Prinsenhof. The first University of Technology in the Netherlands was set up here by the upgrading of the polytechnic (founded 1865) in 1905.

**Natives.** Delft's perhaps most famous native was the scholar, jurist, and statesman **Grotius** (Hugo de Groot; 1583–1645). By the age of 15 he accompanied Jan van Oldenbarneveld on a mission to France; by 17 his writings in Latin were widely acclaimed; and by the age of 20, with a doctorate in law from Leiden, he was occupying important official posts. In the politico-religious dispute that marked the years 1612–18 Grotius pleaded for tolerance and supported Jan van Oldenbarneveld, as a result being sentenced to life imprisonment in the castle of Loevestein. Through the ingenuity of his wife he escaped hidden in a chest (it may be seen here in Delft in the Prinsenhof, though there is a rival claimant in Amsterdam's Rijksmuseum) and took refuge in France. Here he wrote his most important work, 'De Jure belli et pacis' (1625), an analysis of the basic principles of international law. Later he was appointed Swedish ambassador to France. He died at Rostock, after being shipwrecked near Danzig.

Antonie van Leeuwenhoek (1632–1725) made his name in the manufacture of microscopes and in his consequent observations. Amongst other achievements he gave the first accurate description of the red blood corpuscles and was responsible for the first drawing (1683) of bacteria. His work is illustrated in the Museum Boerhaave at Leiden. Another native was Antoon Heinsius (1641–1720), Council Pensionary of the province of Holland (1688) and friend and adviser of Marlborough.

Also born in Delft were the painters Michiel van Miereveld (1567–1641) and Jan Vermeer (1632–75).

**Delftware** traces its origins to Italy, from where potters emigrated to Antwerp early in the 16C, some however soon moving, as Protestant refugees, into the northern provinces where they made Rotterdam and Haarlem their main centres. In the mid 17C the name of Delft began to be known both at home and abroad. Influenced by the Chinese ware being imported by the East Indies Company, early designs were Chinese on blue and white, but other themes, notably Dutch and Italian landscapes, early became popular, these soon being followed by portraits and biblical, genre, and other scenes. The ware, initially tiles, plates and panels, had by the 17C broadened into jars and vases, doorway surrounds, models, etc. By the end of the 18C, partly under pressure of commercial competition, the Delft potteries were in decline, and by the time of the French occupation they had disappeared. The present century has seen a revival (New Delft), dating from 1876 onwards.

Examples of Delftware of all kinds can best be seen at the Huis Lambert van Meerten (see below) or in the showroom of the following factories:

De Porceleyne Fles, Rotterdamseweg 196. This pottery, originally founded in 1653 by David van der Pyet, was refounded in 1876. April–Oct: Mon–Sat, 09.00 to 17.00; Sun, 10.00 to 16.00; Nov–March: Mon–Fri, 09.00 to 17.00; Sat, 10.00 to 16.00.

De Delftse Pauw, Delftweg 133. April–Sept: daily, 09.00 to 16.00; Oct–March: Mon–Friday, 09.00 to 16.00; Sat, Sun, 11.00 to 13.00.

Atelier de Candelaer, Kerkstraat 13 (central). April–Sept: Mon–Fri, 09.00 to 18.00; Sat, 09.00 to 17.00; Sun, 10.00 to 18.00; Oct–March: Mon–Fri, 09.00 to 12.30, 13.30 to 18.00; Sat, 09.00 to 17.00.

Delftware may be bought at these factories, or in many town centre shops.

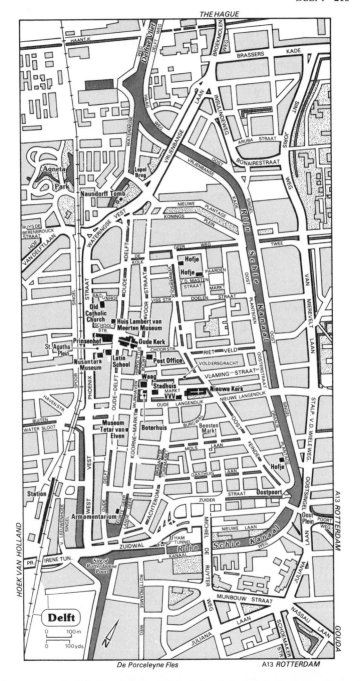

THE HAGUE

HAANTJE

Delftse Vliet

BROEKMOLEN WEG

BRASSERS KADE

INSULINDEWEG

SINT

ARUBA STRAAT

JORIS

BONAIRESTRAAT

WEG

VRIJENBANSE

Agneta
Park

Lepel
Brug

OOST

Naundorff Tomb

VRIJENBANSE

RUYS DE
BERENBROUCK
STRAAT

WATERINGSE VEST

NIEUWE PLANTAGE

KONINGS PLEIN

Rijn Schie Kanaal

SINGEL

TWEE

HOF
VAN DELFTLAAN

DELFT

DE KOLK

GEER WEG

VAN MIEREVELT LAAN

SINGEL

STRAAT

Hofje

Hofje

PAARDEN

V.D. MASTEN
STRAAT

MARKT

BAGIJNHOF

VISS STR

DOELEN STRAAT

Old
Catholic
Church

SCHOOL
STR

VOORSTRAAT

OOST

PLANTSOEN

Huis Lambert van
Meerten Museum

Prinsenhof

Oude Kerk

St. Agatha
Plein

CHOOR STR

RIET VELD

Nusantara
Museum

Latin
School

Post Office

VOLDERSGRACHT

OOSTERSTRAAT

OOST

SPOOR

PHOENIX

Waag

VLAMING STRAAT

HAVEN STR

OUDE-DELFT

Stadhuis

MARKT

Nieuwe Kerk

BUITEN

WIJNHAVEN

VVV

NIEUWE LANGENDIJK

ORANJE

STALP V.D. WIELE WEG

WATER SLOOT

OUDE LANGENDIJK

Museum
Tetar van
Elven

Boterhuis

BURGWAL

OOST

Beesten
Markt

Hofje

KOORNE-MARKT

BRABANTSE
TURFMARKT

MOLS LAAN

EINDE

OOSTSINGEL

A13 ROTTERDAM

Station

VEST

OUDE

LANGE GEER

ACHTEROM

GASTHUIS LAAN

Oostpoort

ZUIDER STRAAT

Oost
Plein

POORT
WEG

Armamentarium

V. LEEUWENHOEK
SINGEL

KORTE GEER

NIEUWE LAAN

JULIANA

PR.
IRENE TUN.

IRENE TUN.

ZUIDWAL

HAM
TUNNEL

Rijn

MICHIEL DE RUYTER

Schie Kanaal

WEG

NASSAU LAAN

HOEK VAN HOLLAND

Site of
Rotterdamse
Poort

KANAAL

ROTTERDAMSE WEG

MIJNBOUW STRAAT

JULIANA LAAN

SCHOEMAKER STR

GOUDA

**Delft**

0        100 m

0        100 yds

N

De Porceleyne Fles

A13 ROTTERDAM

The MARKT is a large, pleasant rectangle with several cafés (open air in summer) and in the centre a statue (1886) of Grotius. The **Nieuwe Kerk** (April–Sept: Mon–Sat, 09.00 to 17.00; Oct–March: Mon–Sat, 10.00 to 12.00, 13.30 to 16.00), at the east end, was founded in 1381 as a wooden church dedicated to Our Lady, but a more permanent building, dedicated to St Ursula, soon started and today's Gothic building grew between 1384 and 1496, the oldest parts being the choir, crossing and east nave. The church suffered severely from the fire of 1536 and explosion of 1654, the main loss being the original stained glass windows (today's glass in the choir and transepts dates from 1927–36). The present spire (P.J.H. Cuijpers) replaces a predecessor destroyed by lightning in 1872. The carillon of 1660, formerly in the tower of the Stadhuis, is by François Hemony.

Inside the most notable feature, in the centre of the apsidal choir, is the *Mausoleum of William I, the Silent* (1614–22), commissioned by the States General, started by Hendrik de Keyser, and probably completed by his son Pieter. The white marble effigy lies on a black sarcophagus; at the prince's feet is his favourite dog, a faithful animal which after his master's death refused food and drink and soon died. The corners of the canopy are supported by allegorical figures of Liberty, Justice, Religion, and Valour, at the head is a seated statue of the prince in full armour, and at the other end, resting on only the toes of the left foot, rises a trumpeting allegory of Fame. Beneath the mausoleum are the *Royal Burial Vaults*; they are not open to the public, but a plan lists those buried and illustrates the arrangement. A number of other memorials merit attention. That to King William I, in the choir, has a marble effigy by W. Geefs (1847); formerly in the Rijksmuseum in Amsterdam, the memorial came to this church in 1905. Above, there is a memorial (1808), with a mourner by Antonio Canova, to Prince William Frederick of Orange, son of Prince William V; he died in 1799 at Padua where he lay below this memorial until his remains and the memorial came to Delft in 1896. On the north side of the choir the *Grotius Memorial* is by H. van Zwoll (1781); a wreath, by E. Marcus of Berlin, was added in 1899 by the delegates of the United States to the international peace conference at The Hague. Grotius is also honoured by a stained glass window in the north transept, a gift of 1931 from the American Bar Association.

Behind the church there is a picturesque corner, with a canal and small bridge sandwiched between the walls of the church and some attractive façades.

The **Stadhuis** (no adm.) stands at the W end of the Markt. Dating from 1618, the building is a Renaissance creation of Hendrik de Keyser who incorporated the 14C tower which was virtually all that survived of the earlier building lost in the fire of 1536. To the left of and behind the Stadhuis are the adjoining *Boterhuis* (1765) and the *Waag* (1770), which has served various purposes, including housing the guild room of the gold and silversmiths, and today is a small theatre.

From this point most visitors will head NW for the Oude Kerk and the Prinsenhof. However, those with a taste for 19C paintings, or with an interest in military matters spanning Roman to modern times, will make their way southwards along the Koornmarkt in which, at No. 67, is the *Museum Tétar van Elven* (May–Oct: Tues–Sat, 11.00 to 17.00), the home of the artist of the same name (1823–96). The house, with stylish furnishing and showing the artist's collection, was presented to the town by his widow. At its S end Koornmarkt becomes Korte Geer in which No. 1 is the square and heavily functional *Armamentarium* (1692 but many times altered), now housing a military museum which includes material formerly in Leiden's now closed Museum General Hoefer (Tues–Sat, 10.00 to 17.00; Sun, 13.00 to 17.00). A short way further S, where three canals meet, was the site of the Rotterdamse Poort. It was from the other side of the water here that Vermeer painted his view of Delft, now in the Mauritshuis in The Hague.

Voldersgracht, the name recalling the fullers who worked here, is a narrow street along a canal running E–W beyond the N side of the Markt. Here there are several 17C façades, including *De Pauw* (the peacock) at No. 6 and, at the street's W end, the *Vleeshal* with its decoration of animal heads; built in c 1650 the Vleeshal was for a period after 1872 used as a corn exchange. The *Vismarkt*, on the corner, still functions as a fish market.

From the Vismarkt a choice of small streets lead the short distance NW to the Gothic **Oude Kerk** (April–Oct: Mon–Sat, 11.00 to 16.00) of St Hippolytus. Started in c 1250 the church was frequently enlarged, the last extension (the NE) dating from the early 16C; the tower has a very pronounced lean.

The interior is known for its monuments, in particular those to the two great admirals, Piet Heyn (1577–1629) and Maarten Tromp (1598–1653). The *Piet Heyn Monument*, at the E end of the church, is by Pieter de Keyser and honours the man best known for his capture in 1628 of the Spanish silver fleet of 20 ships. In the next apse to the north there is the tomb of Elisabeth van Marnix (Nicholas Stone, 1611, the year of her death), daughter of Philips van Marnix van St Aldegonde, secretary to William the Silent, and wife of Karel Morgan, governor of Bergen-op-Zoom.

The *Maarten Tromp Monument* (north choir aisle), believed to be to a design by Jacob van Campen, was executed by Rombout Verhulst (his name appears at the foot of the recumbent figure) and Willem de Keyser, son of Hendrik. Tromp, the admiral who is said to have hoisted a broom at his masthead to proclaim that he had swept the seas clear of the English, defeated Blake off Dungeness in 1652, but was killed in 1653 off Ter Heide near the mouth of the Maas, this last battle being the one depicted here. Samuel Pepys described this monument as 'a sea-fight cut in marble, with the smoke the best expressed that ever I saw'. Two other memorials are in the west part of the church. That on the south-west pillar of the nave commemorates Clara van Sparwoude, a lady who had the curious idea of founding a fund to provide trousseaux for her descendants. Antonie van Leeuwenhoek (1632–1723), the microscopist, has a memorial in the north aisle; erected by his daughter Maria, the memorial was made by G. van der Giessen from a drawing by T. Jelgersma and bears an epitaph by Van Leeuwenhoek's friend the poet Huibert Poot. The daughter Maria (1656–1745) is remembered by an engraving at the lower end of the tomb. The pulpit (1548) merits attention because of its curious perspective carvings, with John the Baptist and the four Evangelists with their symbols. The tomb of Antoon Heinsius (1641–1720) is in the middle of the south aisle.

A short way S of the Oude Kerk stands the modest *St Hippolytus Kerk*, founded as the Chapel of the Holy Spirit and after the Reformation serving various purposes, including that of ammunition magazine. The figures of two girls on the house of 1769 alongside (the Meisjes, or Maidens' House) recall that there was a girls' orphanage here, founded in 1578.

Immediately W of the Oude Kerk, across a canal, an archway off the street called Oude Delft gives access to the **Prinsenhof** (Tues–Sat, 10.00 to 17.00, Sun, Holidays and Mon in June–Aug, 13.00 to 17.00), originally the Convent of St Agatha, founded on this site in c 1400 and enlarged in the early 16C. In 1572 the building, henceforward known by its present name,

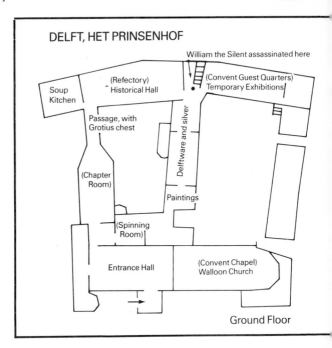

DELFT, HET PRINSENHOF

William the Silent assassinated here

Soup Kitchen

(Refectory) Historical Hall

(Convent Guest Quarters) Temporary Exhibitions

Passage, with Grotius chest

Delftware and silver

(Chapter Room)

Paintings

(Spinning Room)

Entrance Hall

(Convent Chapel) Walloon Church

Ground Floor

became the residence of William the Silent, and it was here that he was assassinated in 1584. After the murder a part of the building was used as a cloth hall, while the remainder housed important guests. In 1799 the place became a barracks, and in 1884 it was decided to make the main hall into a museum, this opening in 1887 as the Historical Hall. The Municipal Museum opened here in 1909; in 1948, after restoration, and aimed at recreating the time of William the Silent, the building opened as the Museum Het Prinsenhof. The Prinsenhof is thus worth visiting both as a former convent and as an elegant mansion closely associated with the House of Orange, as also for the varied contents of the museum.

On entering, the doors to the former convent chapel, now the Walloon Church, are on the right. Note the sloping ceiling, this reflecting the floor of the gallery above, built on a slope so that the nuns could hear Mass without being seen.

The GROUND FLOOR is described roughly clockwise. You pass through a small room into a hall (Chapter Room) with various portraits, and a small altar of c 1500 with wood carving and painted panels. Next comes a short passage in which stands the massive chest in which, it is said, Grotius escaped from Loevestein (but there is a rival claimant in the Rijksmuseum in Amsterdam), beyond being the former refectory, today known as the Historical Hall and housing several particularly fine and well-restored portraits of dignified Delft families. Off the near end of the hall stairs descend to the Soepkeuken (Soup Kitchen) with Delft tile panels; it was from here that soup was supplied to the needy.

Beyond the Historical Hall is the staircase at the foot of which William the

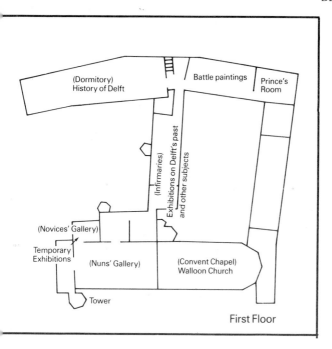

First Floor

Silent, who had just been dining in the hall, was assassinated on 10 July 1584 by a fanatical Catholic, Balthasar Geraerts. The marks of the bullets can be seen, and on the stairs there are pictures of the murder, though, judging from the variety of treatment, these can hardly have been by eye-witnesses. On the other side of the staircase the large hall, once serving as the convent's guest quarters, is now used for exhibitions of contemporary art. The Ground Floor tour continues through a series of rooms showing Delftware, Delft silver and portraits and other paintings, amongst these being views of Delft and pictures of fires and disasters such as the great fire of 1536 and the explosion of the powder magazine in 1654.

The UPPER FLOOR is reached by the stairs below which William was assassinated; at the top, to the left, is a hall showing pictures of battles (Siege of Ostend, Battle of Nieuwpoort). The small room beyond, the Prinsenkamer, houses Orange portraits, including one of Johanna van Stolberg, mother of William the Silent.

The remaining rooms, including the former dormitory to the right after reaching the top of the stairs, are used for exhibitions generally relating to Delft's past. The rooms themselves were once two infirmaries (Nos 18 and 19, the first two leading away from the stairs) and, beyond two small rooms, the gallery of the chapel with the sloping floor.

In the St Agathaplein, immediately SW of the Prinsenhof, the *Nusantara Museum* (Tues–Sat, 10.00 to 17.00; Sun, Holidays, 13.00 to 17.00), housed in the wing of the convent to which the nuns moved when their main building was confiscated in 1572, exhibits mainly Indonesian material, but also mounts temporary exhibitions on wider ethnographic themes.

A short way S of the Prinsenhof are the former *Latin School* (17C) and the *Gemeenlandshuis*, an elaborate blazoned building of c 1520 (restored).

Immediately N of the Prinsenhof along Oude Delft can be seen the gateway of 1658 of the former Saai Greine en Stoffe Hal (the cloth hall into which a part of the building was converted after the assassination), bearing a charming and lively sculptured business scene. In the narrow Schoolstraat adjoining, behind a grille on the wall 75m down on the left, there stands a figure of Charity (1614), ascribed to Nicholas Stone, an English pupil of Hendrik de Keyser and later master mason to James I and Charles I.

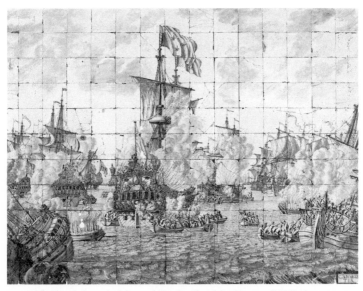

*18C tile picture, in blue, of the Battle of La Hogue (1692), by C. Bouwmeester after R. de Hoogh, Huis Lambert van Meerten Museum*

No. 199 Oude Delft is the **Huis Lambert van Meerten Museum** (Tues–Sat, 10.00 to 17.00; Sun, Holidays, 13.00 to 17.00; also Mon, 13.00 to 17.00 in June–Aug), a 19C patrician mansion visited mainly for its magnificent *collections of Delft tiles and other ware, displayed in a series of beautifully panelled rooms also containing 16–18C furniture. In the room ahead of the entrance, overlooking the garden, there are two portraits (1631) by Paulus Moreelse and a chimney-piece from Hindelopen, while in the room opposite, overlooking Oude Delft, are a portrait by Gerrit van Honthorst and some charming stained glass portrayals of children. On the staircase is a tile picture of the Battle of La Hogue by C. Bouwmeester after R. de Hoogh, and on the landing may be noted the faience pilasters (early 18C) and window columns (1537) from an old Delft house. The upper floor displays several remarkable tile pictures and, in the rooms overlooking the garden, there are cases of 18C and 19C Delftware.

Further N along Oude Delft (W side of the canal) is the old sculptured doorway of the *Begijnhof*, with the *Old Catholic Church* which has a baroque interior. Connoisseurs of minor historical puzzles may continue N some 500m to cross Wateringse Vest and find a small park in which, beside a water tower, is the grave of Karl Wilhelm Naundorff (?1785–1845) who may or may not have been the Dauphin son of Louis XVI and Marie Antoinette, generally supposed to have died in the Temple in Paris in 1795. Perhaps the most plausible of some 40 fellow pretenders, Naundorff claimed to have been smuggled out of the prison in a coffin. He died in Delft, was buried in a tomb inscribed 'Louis XVII' roi de France et Navarre' and, imposter or not, is still protected by a fence bearing the Bourbon lilies.

In other parts of the town you can see three almshouses and also the only survivor of Delft's original seven gates. Two of the almshouses are close to the PAARDENMARKT (Horse Market; parking), which is some 400m NE of the Stadhuis. The *Hofje van Pauw* (entrance Paardenmarkt 52–62) was founded in 1707 for married couples, and the *Hofje van Gratie*, just S in Van den Mastenstraat, was founded in 1575 (rebuilt 1660) for unmarried women. The other almshouse, the *Klaeuwshofje*, founded in 1605, is at the SE of the inner town at Oranje Plantage 58–77. Immediately to its S is the twin-spired **Oostpoort**, dating from the 14C and the only gate to survive the fire of 1536.

# 9   Amsterdam to Rotterdam via Gouda

Total distance 74km. 10km **Schiphol Airport**—6km **Aalsmeer**—10km *Leimuiden*—10km **Alphen**—6km **Boskoop**—8km **Gouda**—12km *Ouderkerk aan der IJssel*—12km **Rotterdam**.

Leave Amsterdam (see Rte 1) by the A4 motorway which crosses the A9 and immediately after a tunnel reaches (*10km* from central Amsterdam) the exit for **Schiphol Airport**. After *3km* you reach the motorway exit for (*3km*) **Aalsmeer** (21,000 inhab.), a sprawling town which is the centre of a flower growing district served by its famous *Flower Auction (Bloemenveiling)* (Mon–Fri, 07.30 to 11.00; arrival before 09.00 is advised), the world's largest and a marvel of colour and efficiency. Visitors can see virtually the whole operation from raised galleries running across the huge hall, windows allowing views into the five auction rooms. The auction is that of the Verenigde Bloemenveilingen Aalsmeer (United Aalsmeer Flower Auction), the co-operative's building covering an area of 42 ha. The process starts with the arrival of the growers, of whom there are approaching 4000 registered, who arrange their flowers on carts which move by powered conveyors; after this the flowers are inspected and given a reference number. Flowers are then called into the appropriate auction hall, each of these having room for over 300 of the 2600 registered buyers, each with a coded disc by which his bids are registered by computer. The auctioneer announces the name of the grower, the flower particulars, and any comments on quality that may have been noted during the earlier inspection, and the auction then starts, buyers bidding by pushing a button to stop one of the two large dials. The dials go backwards from 100 to one, sales thus being effected by reduction (the 'Dutch auction' system which the Dutch call a 'Chinese' auction). Flower carts then move into the main hall where the buyers take over, speed being essential since over 80 per cent of the flowers are exported.

You now follow a small road along the NW shore of the *Westeinder Plas*, a mere some 6km long and 2km wide, a survival of the HAARLEMMERMEER, now a polder, the large lake that lay between Amsterdam and Haarlem and extended SW between what is now the motorway and the coastal dunes. Originally there were four lakes but by the mid 16C flooding and peat cutting had converted these into one, so large that in a storm of 1836 the waters reached the gates of Amsterdam and flooded parts of Leiden. As early as 1643 Jan Leeghwater had proposed reclamation, but it was not until 1840 that work started, the lake, except for peripheral meres, being dry by 1852 (see also Croquius Expo, Rte 6A). After *10km* you enter *Leimuiden*, where the province of Zuid Holland is entered.

Continuing S, with to the W the Braassemermeer, another survival of the Haarlemmermeer, the road crosses the RIJNLAND, a district of canals and polders which was largely waterlogged until the canalisation of the Oude Rijn and the construction of the Katwijk sluices in 1807. The district played an important part in William III's defence against Louis XIV in 1672–74.

*10km* **Alphen aan de Rijn** (55,000 inhab.) was the United Provinces' headquarters during the winter campaign of 1673, and Nicolas Bayard (1644–1707), secretary of the province of New York, was born here. Today the town is known for *Avifauna* (daily, 09.00 to 21.00 or 18.00 in Oct–March), a beautifully laid out bird sanctuary park, with some 275 species from all over the world in surroundings that as closely as possible reflect their natural habitats. Among other attractions are animals such as monkeys and kangaroos, replicas of various well-known buildings, and a choice of boat excursions through the Rijnland polder country.

**Woerden**, 16km E, an ancient place tracing its origins to Roman times, was the French headquarters (Marshal Luxembourg) during the campaign of 1672–74 against William III. A local museum (Mon–Fri, 14.00 to 17.00) now occupies the former *Stadhuis* of 1501 and 1614. Everard Bogardus (1607–47), the first parson in the Dutch colony of New Amsterdam, was born here.

*6km* **Boskoop**, (14,000 inhab.), with nearby Hazerswoude, Reeuwijk, and Waddinxveen, is a centre for tree nurseries, the word 'tree' being used to include, for instance, roses, rhododendrons, and azaleas, ornamental plants and shrubs having been introduced around the end of the 19C. Because of the remoteness of the district the peat here was little dug for fuel, thus allowing the development of a rich soil on which trees were grown at least as early as the 15C. Today there are some 1000 nurseries, many of them small enterprises, and perhaps the most noticeable feature of the area is that these nurseries are within a close network of drainage waterways (total length some 2000km), spanned by countless small bridges.

*8km* **GOUDA** (60,000 inhab.) is a pleasant and compact old town within a typical ring of canals near the confluence of the Gouwe and the Hollandse IJssel. It boasts the largest market square in Holland and is world famous for its local brand of cheese. Syrup waffles (Siroopwafels) are another local speciality. The town is visited principally for the superb stained glass windows in St Janskerk.

**Centre.** Markt, surrounded by pedestrian streets.

**VVV.** Markt.

**Post Office.** Westhaven, 300m S of Markt.

*The Stadhuis, begun 1450; statues of counts and countesses
of Burgundy in the façade*

**Boats**. Day excursions in summer (Biesbos, Willemstad, Rotterdam, Brielle); also for
the Reeuwijkse Plassen.

**History.** Gouda was founded in the 12C and in 1272 received its first charter from
Count Floris V. In the 14C and 15C mainly active in the cloth trade, the town later
turned to a variety of light industries, including the manufacture of clay and other
smoking pipes, pottery, bricks, candles, and of course cheese. The humanist and
theologian Desiderius Erasmus (1469–1536) may have been born here, though Rotterdam seems more likely. He was, though, certainly educated in Gouda, and in 1486 or

1487 he became an Augustinian canon at the nearby monastery of Steyn, where he lived until 1492.

Most places of historical interest are on or close to the MARKT, the spacious irregular triangle at the heart of the town. The **Waag** (July and Aug: cheese weighing, Thursday, 09.30 to 12.00), on the N side, was built in 1668 by Pieter Post and bears a fine and detailed relief by Bartholomeus Eggers depicting the weighing of cheese. The **Stadhuis** (Mon–Fri, 09.00 to 12.00, 14.00 to 16.00), in the centre of the Markt, is especially imposing for being free of other buildings and thus clearly viewed from all sides. Dating from 1450 and possibly the oldest Gothic town hall in the country, the façade carries statues of counts and countesses of Burgundy. The approach stair-case is of 1603, and on the E wall there is a modern carillon, playing every half and full hour with moving figures acting the granting of the charter of 1272 by Count Floris V. Inside there are some good 17C marble groups.

**Markets.** There is a general market on Thursdays (09.00 to 13.00) and Saturdays (09.00 to 18.00), and on Thursdays in summer there are also crafts stalls. But it is the *Cheese Market* (June–Aug, Thurs, 09.00 to 12.00) which is most likely to attract the visitor. The local cheese, made of cows' milk and called Boerenkaas (farm cheese), comes from some 1500 farms in the provinces of Zuid Holland and Utrecht. Each cheese bears an authentica-tion, which also gives the name of the producer and the date of the cheese. Prospective commercial buyers test for moisture, smell and flavour by using a special instrument, and then, if satisfied, negotiate a price with the seller by means of a traditional system of hand clapping. A cheese-making farm (De Driesprong) can be visited at *Bergambacht*, 10km S (daily except Sunday and Holidays).

*\***St Janskerk** (March–Oct: Mon–Sat, 09.00 to 17.00; Nov–Feb: Mon–Sat, 10.00 to 16.00. Carillon concerts Thurs and Sat, 10.00 to 11.00) is due S of the Markt, from which the great length of its nave (123m) can be seen above intervening buildings.

In origin a 13C foundation, a stone church was built in the 14C, but what is seen today is almost entirely 16C rebuilding after destruction by fire caused by lightning in 1552. The church is famous for its magnificent large *\*stained glass windows**. Some (Nos 45–57) date from before the disaster of 1552, but most of the remainder were gifts at the time of the rebuilding from royal and episcopal personages, towns, guilds and others, and it is of interest that they represent both Roman Catholic (1555–71) and Protestant (1572–1603) periods. The 14 best are by the brothers Dirk and Wouter Crabeth, all executed during the Catholic period. These are, in the north nave, Nos 5, 6, 7, 8 and 30; in the south nave, Nos 22, 23, 24 and 31; and around the choir ambulatory, Nos 12, 14, 15, 16 and 18. The remaining windows are largely by the brothers' pupils.

A detailed guide is available in English, but main features are noted below. The description, not always in strict numerical sequence, is clock-wise starting from the west door. No. 1. Freedom of Conscience (1596). Designed by *Joachim Wttewael.* Executed by *Adriaen de Vrije.* Gift of the States of Holland. A chariot, bearing the symbolic figure of Freedom of Conscience and drawn by Fortitude, Loyalty, Concord, Love, and Justice, crushes Tyranny.

Nos 1A, 1B, and 1C are compositions (by *Jan Schouten,* 1931) from old fragments. No. 2. Capture of Damietta by Dutch crusaders in 1219 (1596). By *Willem Thybaut.* Gift of the aldermen of Haarlem. No. 3. Female figure symbolising the city of Dordrecht (1597). By *Gerrit Cuyp*. Gift of the city of Dordrecht. No. 4. Arms of the dike wardens of the Rijnland. (1594). By *Adriaen de Vrije*. Gift of the wardens. No. 5. The Queen of Sheba received by King Solomon (1561). By *Wouter Crabeth*. Gift of the Abbess of Rijnsburg. From here, by looking E and upwards, No. 30 can best be seen. Depicting the story of Jonah, the picture (before 1565) is by *Dirk Crabeth* and was the gift of the Guild of Fishmongers. No. 6. Judith and Holofernes (1571). By *Dirk Crabeth*, the last by this artist (died 1574) and the last during the Catholic period. Gift of Jan van Aremberg, who had been killed in 1568 fighting for the Spanish at Heiligerlee. Jan van Aremberg and his wife are the lowest two figures; the central section depicts the scene immediately after the killing, Holofernes now having been decapitated; the upper section shows Judith and her servant returning to Bethulia, and the head of Holofernes hanging from the town walls. No. 7. Solomon's dedication of the Temple, and, below, the Last Supper (1557). By *Dirk Crabeth*. Gift of Philip II of Spain, who is shown with his wife, Queen Mary Tudor of England. No. 8. Angels chastising Heliodorus, the Temple robber (1566). By *Wouter Crabeth*. Gift of the Duke of Brunswick.

(Nos 32–44, extending from near this part of the church down the central nave, date from 1593–94. Representing the arms of Gouda, these are the first windows of the Protestant period, inserted some 22 years after No. 6. Nos 45–57, around the inner choir and representing Christ and the Apostles, date from before the fire of 1552.) No. 9. Annunciation of the birth of John the Baptist (1561). By *Digman Meynaertsz.* from a cartoon by *Lambert van Noort*. Gift of Dirk van Oudewater, a former burgomaster of Gouda. No. 10. Annunciation (1559). By *Anon* (restored 1655). Gift of the Abbot of Berne, near Heusden. No. 11. Birth of John the Baptist (1562). By *Hans Scrivers* from a cartoon by *Lambert van Noort*. Gift of Herman Lethmaet, Dean of the Mariakerk, Utrecht. No. 12. Birth of Christ (1564). By *Wouter Crabeth*. Gift of the Chapter of the Oude Munster, Utrecht. No. 13. The child Jesus in the Temple (1560). By *Digman Meynaertsz.* from a cartoon by *Lambert van Noort*. Gift of the Abbot of Marienwaard. No. 14. John the Baptist preaching (1557). By *Dirk Crabeth*. Gift of Robert van Bergen, Bishop of Liège.

(Nos 58–64, in a chapel off the NE of the choir, date from 1556–59 and were presented by a variety of donors to the church of the monastery of Steyn (see also History, above) when the monastery, having been damaged by fire, moved into Gouda in 1551. In 1580 this monastery church was demolished, these windows then being brought here and crowded into positions 20 and 21. In 1934 they were moved to this chapel. The artist or artists are unknown. The subjects are the Taking of Christ, the Mocking, Ecce Homo, Calvary, Resurrection, Ascension, and Pentecost.) No. 15. Jesus baptised by John (1555). By *Dirk Crabeth*. Gift of George van Egmond, Bishop of Utrecht, the first window to be presented. Parts of the window were removed by Protestant extremists in c 1622 (God at the top, and what was probably the Trinity before which the donor knelt), but the top portion was replaced in 1932 by *Jan Schouten*, working from a 17C drawing. No. 16. The first preaching by Jesus (1556). By *Dirk Crabeth*. Gift of Cornelis van Mierop of Utrecht. Curiosities worth noting are the 16C clothing and the Dutch vegetation. No. 17. John the Baptist reproving Herod (1556). By *Anon*. Gift by Wouter van Bylaer. No. 18. Mission to Jesus by the followers of John the Baptist (1556). By *Dirk Crabeth*. Gift of the Heye and Ariensz. families. No. 19. Beheading of John the Baptist (1570). By *Willem Thybaut*. Gift of the Commander of the Knights of St John,

Haarlem. Nos 20 and 21 are fragments, composed during restoration in 1933. See also above, Nos 58–64. From here, looking W and upwards, No. 31 can best be seen. Depicting Baalam and his ass (c 1565), the picture is attributed to *Dirk Crabeth* and was the gift of the Guild of Butchers, Gouda. No. 22. Purification of the Temple (1569). By *Dirk Crabeth*. Gift of William the Silent in 1561, who , however, being a rebel by the time the picture was completed, does not appear. No. 23. Offering of Elijah, and, below, Jesus washing the Disciples' feet (1562). By *Wouter Crabeth*. Gift of Margaret of Parma, who is shown kneeling. No. 24. Philip preaching in Samaria (1559). By *Dirk Crabeth*. Gift of Philip de Ligne, lord of Wassenaar. No. 25. The relief of Leiden (1603). Designed by *Isaac van Swanenburgh*, that rare thing, an artist who was also a burgomaster (of Leiden). Executed by *D.J. Verheyden* and, after his death, *D.R. van Douwe*. Gift of the town of Delft, the burgomasters of which are portrayed under the silhouette of Delft half-way up on the left. William the Silent is the left of the two figures in the lower section (left), the other figure probably being Leiden's heroic Burgomaster, Van der Werff. The figure above that of a man carrying a barrel is Admiral Boisot who raised the siege in October 1574. No. 26. Relief of Samaria (1601). By *Cornelis Clock* from a cartoon by *I.N. Swanenburgh*. Gift of the aldermen of Leiden. No. 27. The Pharisee and the publican (1597). Attributed to *Hendrik de Keyser*. Gift of the aldermen of Amsterdam. No. 28. The woman taken in adultery (1601). By *C.J. Wytmans*. Gift of the aldermen of Rotterdam.

The tour ends with three modern windows and one belonging to the 16C series. This last is No. 29, depicting David and the Christian warrior (1596) by *Adriaen de Vrije* and the gift of the northern towns of the United Provinces. No. 28A. Occupation and Liberation, 1940–45 (1947). By *Charles Eyck*. Gift of the citizens of Gouda and others. No. 28B. Arms of contributors (after 1920) to the restoration of the windows (1935). Designed by *D. Boode* and executed by *L.H. Knoll*. No. 28C. Rebuilding of the Temple after the captivity in Babylon (1920). Designed by *H. Veldhuis* and executed by *L.H. Knoll*. Gift of those who before 1920 contributed to the restoration of the windows.

The **Stedelijk Museum** (Mon–Sat, 10.00 to 17.00, Sun, Holidays, 12.00 to 17.00), immediately S of the church, occupies the former Catharina Gasthuis, a building largely of 1665 (the frontage facing Oosthaven may be to a design by Pieter Post) but with some rooms (Nos 2, 3, 4) dating back to 1542 and parts of the cellars to the 14C. Founded in perhaps 1310, the hospice—for transients and local needy—received its name in 1367 and continued to function until 1910. There are entrances from both Oosthaven and Achter der Kerk, the latter being by way of a delightful small gateway of 1609 with an equally delightful sculpted pediment of small figures (the Lazarus Gate, formerly at the entrance to the Leper Hospital).

In addition to the usual regional historical material the museum shows an important collection of 19C and 20C paintings. The description below assumes entry from Achter der Kerk.

Beyond the ticket desk there are some steps, at the top on the left being the hall (2) which was once the main Infirmary (Grote Gasthuiszaal), a function recalled by the inscription above the fireplace. This room, and the small infirmary (3), are today mainly devoted to religious art and show 16C altarpieces, most from Gouda churches or religious houses. Especially notable are a large triptych of 1569 by Dirk Barendsz. (Life of Mary); an Annunciation and an altarpiece by Pieter Pourbus the Elder; and a Flight into Egypt (centre panel of a triptych) by Pieter Pietersz. Vestments and plate are also shown here. Off the main infirmary, at the opposite end to the small infirmary, is the Dispensary (Antieke Apotheek), one of the additions of 1665. Today the room has been arranged as an 18C dispensary with a wealth of pots, bottles and suchlike, and also two 15C paintings by Bartolomeo Vivarini. Beyond the small infirmary come the two Canal Rooms (**4, 5**, Grachtzaal) showing guild material and 16C and 17C paintings, including a powerful Doubting Thomas by Wouter Crabeth.

Four Period Rooms (Stijlkamer, **6, 7, 8, 9**), illustrating 17–19C domestic interiors, continue the tour in a straight sequence, beyond being a fine hall (**10**) known simply as Het Ruim, once the place where beggars, itinerant soldiers and others could find free shelter but today showing guild and Civic Guard material. The room is dominated by Civic Guard groups, notably two painted by Ferdinand Bol (1653) and Cornelis Ketel (1599), but the main treasures here are a *chalice and Eucharist dish of silver-gilt with enamel decoration, presented by Jacqueline of Bavaria to the Civic Guard in 1425. The exquisite detail of the small pictures around the chalice base well rewards close attention. The Kitchen (Gasthuis Keuken) (**11**), off Het Ruim, although as a room dating from 1665 has been furnished and equipped in late 18C style, one particularly homely piece being a baby's high chair complete with foot warmer. Off the other side of Het Ruim is the Chapel (**12**), largely used for temporary exhibitions.

A short stairway ascends out of Het Ruim to reach one room (**14**) showing toys and dolls, and another (**15**) which was granted to the Guild of Surgeons of Gouda (founded 1666) in 1679 by the governors of the hospice. Today it has been restored as closely as possible to its original state.

**Rooms 16** and **17** are the two galleries in which the museum's 19C and 20C paintings are shown, virtually all of these the gift of the painter and collector Paul Arntzenius, born in 1883 and a representative of the later Hague School, which school, together with Barbizon, fired his enthusiasm as a collector. Charles Daubigny, Odilon Redon and T. Rousseau represent Paris and Barbizon; Johannes Bosboom, Paul Gabriel, Anton Mauve, the Maris brothers, Isaac Israels and Jan Toorop are among the artists representing late Dutch painting and the Hague School.

The rooms beyond are used for exhibitions from the museum's collection of contemporary works.

In Spieringstraat, a short way E, the public library is housed in the former *Weeshuis* (orphanage) of 1643. The nearby *Willem Vroesenhuis* (1614) was an almshouse for old men.

Across the canal from the Stedlijk Museum, *De Moriaan* (the Blackamoor), at Westhaven 29, is a merchant's home of 1617 which now houses the Stedelijk Museum's collection of tobacco pipes, tiles, and other ceramics (Mon–Sat, 10.00 to 12.30, 13.30 to 17.00; Sun, Holidays, 12.00 to 17.00).

**Schoonhoven**, 16km SE, an ancient small town at the confluence of the Vlist with the Lek, is known for its manufacture of silver ornaments, especially those worn with peasant costume. The *Nederlands Goud-, Silver-, en Klokkenmuseum* (Tues–Sun, Holidays, 12.00 to 17.00), at Haven 7, is, as its name tells, a museum of gold, silver and clocks. The main town lies pleasantly on either side of the Vlist. The *Stadhuis* dates from 1452, and in the nearby *St Bartolomaeuskerk* there is a fine 16C official pew made from the former rood loft. The *Waag*, further upstream, is of 1617, while towards the Lek stands the *Veerpoort*, a gateway of 1601. A car ferry (frequent) crosses the Lek to **Nieuwpoort**, a particularly attractive small town with tree-lined canals and surrounded by its star-shaped, grass-covered ramparts of 1672. The *Stadhuis* (1697) straddles the main canal.

For Gouda to Oudewater and Utrecht, see Rte 17B.

Motorway A20 offers the fastest route to Rotterdam, but it is pleasanter and more interesting to follow the small road along the E side of the Hollandse Ijssel. *12km Ouderkerk aan der IJssel* was once the estate of Henrik van Nassau-Ouwerkerk (1641–1708), known to the English as Marshal Over-kirk, Marlborough's able lieutenant who did much to ensure victory at Oudenarde and Ramillies. *4km* Krimpen aan der IJssel. From Krimpen aan der Lek, *4km* SE, there is a view across to the Kinderdijk windmills (see Rte 12). *8km* Rotterdam, see Rte 10.

# 10   Rotterdam

**ROTTERDAM** (555,000 inhab.) is a combination of a large, mainly commercial city, the second largest in the Netherlands, and a giant port which ranks as the world's busiest and biggest in terms of commodity capacity. The main city stands on the N shore of the Nieuwe Maas, the waterway which, becoming Het Scheur and then the Nieuwe Waterweg, forms the outlet (some 35km W) of the rivers Rhine and Maas (Meuse). The early town assumed a triangular shape (which it retained until the expansion of the mid 19C), the boundaries of which were (S) Blaak and the Nieuwe Haven, (N) Goudsesingel and Pompenburg, and (W) Coolsingel; it was this tri-angle, and the reclaimed dock area to its S, which was virtually obliterated by the German bombing of May 1940. The combination of port and commercial city, coupled with the destruction of the old city, means that Rotterdam has little of the conventional charm of the typical Dutch town. Instead it is a dynamic place offering a busy and easily viewed port; a fine central area of distinguished buildings; a network of early docks, trans-formed today by imaginative if sometimes startling new housing; excellent shopping precincts; and a choice of museums and art galleries.

**Centre.** Hofplein—Coolsingel—Stadhuisplein—Lijnbaan.

**VVV.** *Main Office*, Coolsingel 67. Tel: (010) 4023260. Mon–Sat, 09.00 to 18.00 or 21.00 on Fri; Sun in April–Sept, 10.00 to 18.00. *Centraal Station*, Tel: (010) 4023268. Mon–Sat, 09.00 to 24.00; Sun, 10.00 to 24.00.

**Post Office.** Coolsingel 32; also Delftsplein 2, just E of the Centraal Station.

**Stations.** *Centraal*, a short way W of Hofplein, for all main lines. Tel: (010) 4-117100. *Noord*, for some through international trains from Hoek van Holland; *Blaak*, for Dordrecht; *Hofplein*, for The Hague and Scheveningen.

**Airports.** *Schiphol*, 56km N; *Zestienhoven*, 6km NW.

**Public Transport.** Metro, tram, bus. Maps etc. from VVV. Or Tel: (010) 4-546890.

**City and Environs Tour.** The main tour is a combined tram and harbour tour, the former lasting one hour, the latter (which can be taken at any time of the day) 75 minutes. April–Sept: daily, from Centraal Station at 13.15. Tel: either VVV office.

**Air Tours.** From Zestienhoven. Luchtvaartmij, De Kroonduif, Zestienhoven, Vliegveldweg 30. Tel: (010) 4-157855. Rotterdam, Delta Project and bulb-fields flights.

**Boats** from Willemskade. Excursions include Harbour (75 minutes); Schiedam—Vlaardingen—Pernis—Botlek (2½ hours); Europoort (5½ hours); Delta Plan (9 hours);

Evening (2¼ hours). For bookings and general information, apply Spido, Willemsplein. Tel: (010) 4-135400.

There are also boat tours of Delfshaven (May–Sept: Wed, 14.00;. Sun, 14.30. Tel: (010) 4-764216). Longer distance tours include the Biesbos, Willemstad, Loevestein, Avifauna, Schoonhoven, Leerdam and Heusden. Rederij Diane, IJsselmonde Hoofd. Tel: (010) 4-826967.

**Diamonds.** Diamond cutting may be seen at the following firms, the first two being central and the third beyond the river close to Zuidplein:

Firma Heetman, Lijnbaan 92 (exhibition Mon–Sat, 10.00 to 17.00; cutting on Friday and Saturday).

Diamonds Manufacturing, Kipstraat 7B (Mon–Sat, 09.30 to 17.00 or 21.00 on Fri).

Sap Juweliers-Diamantairs, Zuidplein laag 100 (Mon– Sat, 09.00 to 17.00).

**Casino.** Hilton Hotel, Weena 10.

**History.** In about 1260 dikes were constructed to regulate the little rivers Schie and Rotte just above their outflow into the Maas and lower down than an older dike beside which the settlement of Overschie had stood since c 1000. On these were founded the towns of Schiedam and Rotterdam, the former, which originally served as the foreport of Delft, receiving a charter in 1275 from Count Floris V. Rotterdam's first charter was granted in 1299, but was soon withdrawn and not replaced until 1328, full privileges being granted in 1340 by Count William IV. In this year a channel was dug to connect the Schie with Rotterdam, this attracting much of the trade of Delft and enabling Rotterdam to outstrip Schiedam, despite the fact that in 1389 Delft dug its own harbour at the mouth of the Schie at Delfshaven. In 1360 Rotterdam, now the triangular shape referred to above, was walled and moated, remaining within this compass for 500 years, the only extensions being reclamation and dock works towards the river.

Rotterdam sided with William the Silent in 1572, long before Amsterdam, and under Jan van Oldenbarneveld as Pensionary it gave hospitality to numerous and useful refugees after the sack of Antwerp in 1585; these were followed 100 years later by Huguenot refugees from France. During this period the port steadily developed; trade relations with England, always important, became even busier with the establishment in 1635 of a 'factory' of the Merchant Adventurers (established by Sebastian Cabot in 1551); and although this moved to Dort (Dordrecht) 20 years later, Rotterdam continued as the most favoured place of residence for English merchants, so that in the 18C there were three English churches and many English names still survive among Rotterdam families.

During the later 18C an already dwindling trade was further weakened first by the silting up of the mouth of the Maas, and then by Napoleon's wars and his deadening 'continental' policy. A canal dug by King William I in 1830 (the Voornsekanaal, now linking the Hartelkanaal with Hellevoetsluis, see Rte 13B) opened up the port to a certain extent, but with the advent of larger ships and the expansion of German industrial production in the Ruhr this was soon found inadequate. Finally an entirely new ship canal, the Nieuwe Waterweg, was begun by Pieter Caland in 1866 and opened in 1872. Prosperity and expansion were now assured, Rotterdam fast developing into Europe's main transit port.

On 14 May 1940 German aircraft destroyed without warning the entire city centre—this after a sordid piece of trickery where the bombing force first flew out as if toward England before doubling back to attack. In 1944 the Germans began a systematic destruction of the port. Immediately the war ended, however, vigorous reconstruction started of both city and port. The former, with a new centre and imaginative innovations such as pedestrian areas, did much to influence Europe's post-war town planning; the port's recovery was such that by 1952 the tonnage of shipping entering Rotterdam equalled the figure of 1938 (25 million tons). See also Port, below.

**Natives and Others.** Desiderius Erasmus (1469–1536), the great Renaissance humanist and theologian, was almost certainly born at Wijde Kerkstraat 3 (house destroyed in 1940), although by some accounts Gouda, where he later studied and became an Augustinian, may have been his birthplace. The son of Roger Gerrit, he seems to have been christened Herasmus, later adopting this as his principal name. Piet Heyn (1577–1629), the admiral who seized the Spanish silver fleet, was born in Delfshaven.

Among the artists born in Rotterdam were Pieter de Hooch (1629–after 1683), Cornelis Saftleven (1607–81), Herman Saftleven (1609–85), Jacob Ochtervelt (1634–1682), Simon de Vlieger (c 1600–53), Hendrik Sorgh (c 1611–70), and Adriaen van der Werff (1659–1722). Grinling Gibbons (1648–1721), the wood carver, is of obscure origin but seems to have been born here, although he was in London by c 1666.

James Scott, Duke of Monmouth (1649–85), son of Charles II and his mistress Lucy Walters, was born in Rotterdam during his father's exile in The Hague. Also born here were Gysbert van Hogendorp (1762–1834), free trader and jurist and founder of his country's present judicial system; J.H. van 't Hoff (1852–1911), founder of stereochemistry; and Mary Louisa Molesworth (1839–1921), novelist and popular writer of books for the young ('Tell me a story', 'The Cuckoo Clock', etc.). Pierre Bayle (1647–1706), the French philosopher and author of the 'Dictionnaire historique et critique', taught philosophy and history in Rotterdam between 1681 and 1693 and died here. H.W. Longfellow, the American poet, visited Rotterdam in 1835, with his first wife Mary Storer Potter, who died here.

**The Port** (see also History, above) can be divided roughly into the older docks near the city centre and the new ones stretching W along the S side of the river. The oldest docks are the Oudehaven and the Leuvehaven, both on the N shore and S of the early triangle, and the small docks at Delfshaven. With the silting of the Maas and the Napoleonic wars trade declined around the turn of the 18–19C, but today's prosperity was assured, if hardly foreseen, when the Nieuwe Waterweg was opened in 1872. Parkhaven, the dock immediately below the Euromast, dates from 1890–1909, and Coolhaven to its W was dug between the wars. On the S shore, opposite the city centre, such docks as the Rijnhaven, the Maashaven and the giant Waalhaven are all of the late 19–20C, the last dating from 1907–30. The post-war years have seen the enormous extension westward along the S shore, reaching through the Europoort as far as the river mouth. Some key starting and completion dates were Botlek (1947–57), Europoort (1957–68), and Maasvlakte (1968–74).

The old docks can be seen as part of the visitor's tour of the city centre. There are two good ways to view the modern docks, one being by Spido boat excursion (see above); the other, for motorists, is to follow the Havenroute, described as a separate section (E) below.

**Routes from Rotterdam.** To Gouda and Amsterdam, see Rte 9; to Hoek van Holland, see Rte 11; to Dordrecht, Gorinchem, and Nijmegen, see Rtes 12 and 25; to Vlissingen (Flushing), see Rte 13. For Delft (14km NW), see Rte 8.

**Summary of Museums and Art Galleries** The summary below is in order of mention in the text. For opening times see under individual entries.

**Boucentrum**: building and architecture.

**Schielandshuis**: history of Rotterdam, in a 17C building.

**\*\*Boymans-Van Beuningen**: fine and applied art, old and new.

**Maritime Museum Prins Hendrik**: maritime; indoor and outdoor, the latter including the *Museumschip Buffel* of 1868.

**Mariniersmuseum**: Dutch Marine Corps.

**Museum voor Land en Volkenkunde**: ethnology, worldwide.

**Belasting (Professor Dr van der Poel)**: taxation, smuggling.

**De Dubbelde Palmboom**: the story of Rotterdam, by themes. Zakkendragershuisje: pewterer's workshop.

**Hendrik Chabot**: paintings by this Rotterdam Expressionist.

**Toy-Toy**: period dolls and mechanical toys.

Rotterdam is described in five sections: A. The Inner City; B. Delfshaven; C. The Outer City; D. The Boymans-Van Beuningen Museum; E. The Havenroute (Port Route).

# A. The Inner City

The HOFPLEIN, at the N end of Coolsingel, is a major road intersection notable for its large central fountain of 1955 by C. van Kralingen. On the NE side is the railway station for The Hague, while Rotterdam's *Casino* is at the Hilton Hotel (Weena 10) at the opposite corner.

The broad Weena leads W out of Hofplein, soon reaching STATIONSPLEIN, with on the N the **Centraal Station** (1957) and on the W the large *Groothandelsgebouw* (1952), Rotterdam's main wholesale business centre. The *Boucentrum* (Mon–Sat, 09.00 to 17.00), at the SW corner of the square, with a relief of 1955 by Henry Moore, is used for exhibitions relating to building and architecture including interior decoration, **Diergaarde Blijdorp** (daily, 09.00 to 17.00 or 18.00 in May–Oct), Rotterdam's zoo, is rather over 1km W of the station. Opposite the entrance a sculpture of a woman athlete (H. Rehm) was inspired by Fanny Blankers-Koen, winner of three gold medals at the London Olympic Games in 1948. Features of the zoo include a large covered complex so that a visit in wet weather can still be worthwhile, a nocturnal house, a children's zoo, and salt and fresh water aquaria. Scientifically the zoo is active in breeding endangered species such as okapi, Père David's deer, and Przewalski horses, while no other zoo in the world breeds as many tigers.

Coolsingel, once a moat but today a wide and important thoroughfare with flowers, trees and cafés, and lined with handsome buildings, runs S from Hofplein. Most of the streets to the W and some of those to the E are pedestrian precincts. The first building of note (E side) is the **Stadhuis**, built by H. Evers in 1914–20. In front stand statues to Jan van Oldenbarneveld (by Charles van Wijk and A.W.M. Odé) and Grotius (by Auke Hettema); the interior is decorated with frescoes by J. Thorn-Prikker. The *Post Office*, immediately S, dates from 1922.

The STADHUISPLEIN is across Coolsingel from the Stadhuis. The war memorial group here (1957) is by Mari Andriessen, and on the building on the SE corner, facing Coolsingel at first floor level, may be seen the *Erasmus Mosaic*, incorporating a figure of the philosopher and symbolising the link between Rotterdam and Basel forged by Rhine navigation. On the pavement below there is a small stone lion, once a feature of the Delft gate which from the 14C until its destruction by German bombing in May 1940 stood behind the Stadhuis near the junction of the Delftsevaart canal and Pompenburg. To the W and S of Stadhuisplein there is an extensive pedestrian precinct shopping district, including the LIJNBAAN, a model of its kind with covered ways, flowers, terraces and cafés. The southern extension of the Lijnbaan is the BINNENWEGPLEIN shopping area, with many of the larger stores. On the SCHOUWBURGPLEIN, immediately W of the Lijnbaan, are, on the S side, the *Schouwburg*, the municipal theatre built in 1947 using rubble from the destroyed city centre, and, on the N side, *De Doelen*, a large building of 1966 with several individual halls used for exhibitions, concerts, congresses and suchlike, while nearby on Korte Lijnbaan there stands a figure, 'Walking Man', by Rodin. Westersingel, the wide road with trees to the W of Schouwburgplein, marks both the boundary of the mid 19C city and roughly also the W limit of the destruction of 1940.

Off Coolsingel the road running E immediately S of the Post Office is Meent, with, opposite the Post Office, the *World Trade Centre*, offering information and a range of facilities to both Dutch and other businessmen.

Meent soon reaches the Delftsevaart canal, from the bridge across which can be seen an interesting housing project along the water, a result of the modern policy of incorporating residential elements in the city centre. The World Trade Centre occupies a part of the **Beurs** (Commercial Exchange), a building of 1938 by J.F. Staal which fills the space along Coolsingel between Meent and BEURSPLEIN, another shopping focus with both department stores and, in the centre, market stalls and boutiques. Hoogstraat, running E from here, was the main street of the old Rotterdam and is still important as a shopping street. Korte Hoogstraat, leading S out of Beursplein, soon reaches the **Schielandshuis** (Tues–Sat, 10.00 to 17.00; Sun, Holidays, 11.00 to 17.00), built in 1665 by Jacob Lois, restored after a fire in 1864 and the only significant older building in this district to have survived May 1940. Originally the house of the Schieland Polder administration, and during the 19C housing the Boymans Museum (which lost many of its collections in the fire of 1864), the building became until 1975 the home of Rotterdam's historical museum, a function which, after over ten years and much restoration, it has in part resumed (see also De Dubbelde Palmboom in Delfshaven), showing art and cultural historical material and, notably, the Atlas van Stolk collection of drawings and prints relating to Dutch history. In the garden there is a statue of Gysbert van Hagendorp (see Natives and Others, above).

**St Laurenskerk (Grote Kerk)** is 200m E of Beursplein beyond the canal. A Gothic edifice of 1409–1525, the church was severely damaged in May 1940, only the walls remaining standing; restoration, started in 1952, was completed by 1968, this work successfully including one of the interior's main features, the series of memorials to distinguished admirals. In front of the church, on Grote Kerkplein, there stands a bronze statue of Erasmus by Hendrik de Keyser (1622).

Coolsingel ends at CHURCHILLPLEIN, some 700m SW of which, and approached by a choice of roads, is the ˙˙**Museum Boymans-Van Beuningen** (see Section D below).

Schiedamsevest, leading S off Westblaak (close to Churchillplein), in 400m reaches the *Scottish Church*, reopened in 1952 replacing a church of 1697.

Immediately SE of Churchillplein stands the conspicuous, white building of the **Maritime Museum Prins Hendrik** (Tues–Sat, 10.00 to 17.00; Sun, Holidays, 11.00 to 17.00). Founded in 1873 under the patronage of Prince Hendrik, brother of King William III, the museum suffered several moves and closures but since 1986 has found its home here. There are indoor and outdoor sections: the former, in the main building, comprises a permanent exhibition outlining many aspects of shipping, surrounded by regularly changing exhibitions. The outdoor section, along the harbour basin (Leuvehaven), will in due course show ships, workshops, a lighthouse, buoys, cranes and suchlike. But the main attraction here is the *Museumschip Buffel*, a Royal Dutch Navy turret-ram of 1868, restored almost entirely to its original condition; the fully equipped upper deck and the contemporary officers' quarters are notable features.

The Maritime Museum is at the head of the LEUVEHAVEN, near the point where it is joined by the small Wijnhaven. Once two of Rotterdam's oldest and busiest docks, this area, together with the Oudehaven just to the E (see below), has been the focus for some imaginative housing development making admirable modern use of this attractive, watery corner. There are also two memorials of interest here, the better known (at the head of

Leuvehaven alongside the museum) being Ossip Zadkine's City Destroyed (1953), expressing the sculptor's outrage on seeing the devastation of the 1940 bombing. The other memorial, overlooking the junction of Wijnhaven and Leuvehaven and likely to be of interest to American visitors, is the colourful Rotterdam Totem, presented in 1982 by the Port of Seattle to commemorate 200 years of official representation between the two cities.

At its foot Leuvehaven is crossed by a bridge, the Nieuwe Leuvebrug, immediately SE of which a pylon (by F. Carasso, 1957) honours the wartime dead of the Dutch merchant navy.

From Nieuwe Leuvebrug you have a choice between NE (followed by crossing the river) or SW towards the Euromast.

NORTH EAST FROM NIEUWE LEUVEBRUG. The riverside road, called Boompjes (Little Trees), represents what was once one of the oldest quays in Rotterdam but is now the western section of the fine promenade which, beyond the bridges changing its name to Maas Boulevard, acts both as a main traffic artery and also as a flood protection dike. The bridges are the railway bridge of 1929 (long-term plans envisage a tunnel) and, just beyond, the Willemsbrug road bridge of 1981, which has taken the place of its predecessor of the same name which crossed just S of the railway bridge. Immediately N of the bridges will be found the **Oudehaven**, as its name suggests Rotterdam's oldest harbour, the place where the Rotte flowed into the Maas and near where the original dike made possible the development of the city. Imaginative planning has now transformed this ancient birthplace of the city into an architecturally exciting corner with, among other designs, some daring cubist housing.

The bridges cross to Noordereiland, an island created in 1876 by the cutting of the Koningshaven channel. Here, at Maaskade 119, is the *Mariniersmuseum* (Tues–Sat, 10.00 to 17.00; Sun, Holidays, 11.00 to 17.00), telling the story of the Dutch Marine Corps from its foundation in 1665.

SOUTH WEST FROM NIEUWE LEUVEBRUG. There is a choice between the main roads—Vasteland, soon becoming Westzeedijk—or the smaller roads closer to and beside the river.

Westzeedijk runs between (N) Museum Park and the *Academisch Ziekenhuis*, the medical faculty of Erasmus University, and (S) Het Park, near the NW corner of which can be seen the *Noorse Kerk*, a characteristic wooden building serving the spiritual needs of Norwegian sailors. Westzeedijk ends at the road roundabout of Drooglever Fortuynplein with access to the Maastunnel and the Euromast (for both see below).

Immediately S of the W end of Nieuwe Leuvebrug is Willemsplein, with, on Willemskade, the embarkation quay for Spido harbour and other cruises. A short way beyond, occupying the corner of Willemskade and Veerkade, stands the **Museum voor Land en Volkenkunde** (Tues–Sat, 10.00 to 17.00; Sun, Holidays, 11.00 to 17.00), Rotterdam's ethnological museum. Behind the dignified façade of 1851 everything was renewed in 1986, being extended and given modern and effective audio-visual and other means of presentation. A large permanent collection is supported by a programme of temporary exhibitions, and there is even a restaurant in which the visitor can choose Third World dishes. Beyond, at Parklaan 14 across the small Veerhaven, there is a museum of a very different kind, the *Belasting Museum Professor Dr van der Poel* (Mon–Fri, 09.00 to 17.00). Here the subject is the history of taxation, the story told through measuring and weighing instruments, paintings, stamps, seals and suchlike, and also by a

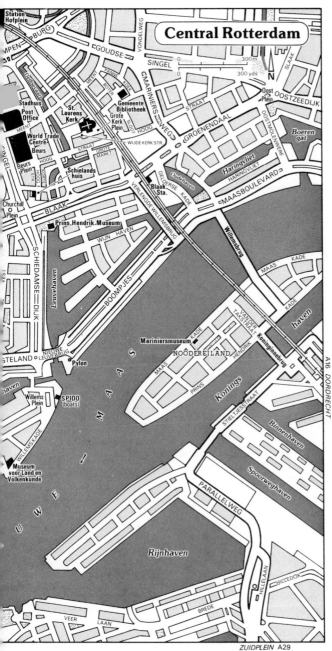

**Central Rotterdam**

section on smuggling. From here Veerhaven, Westerkade and Parkkade run beside the river to reach the Euromast.

The **Euromast**, engineered by H.A. Maaskant and J. van Duin, was erected in 23 days in 1960, but the *Space Tower* is a later addition. Effectively there are two levels, the lower (100m) being the main platform area with two restaurants. Above, the Space Tower soars to reach the Space Cabin (185m), a cabin revolving slowly round the tower (mid March–mid Oct: mast and tower, daily, 09.00 to 22.00; mid Oct–mid March: mast daily, 09.00 to 18.00; tower, daily, 11.00 to 16.00). *Parkhaven*, the dock immediately W of the Euromast, was dug between 1890 and 1909. The adjacent **Maastunnel** (entrance to the N), which crosses the Maas some 12m below the bed of the river, was engineered by J.P. van Bruggen, begun in 1931 and opened in 1942; there are ways for cars, cycles and pedestrians.

# B.  Delfshaven

The district of Delfshaven, rather over 1km W of the Euromast, is served by its own metro station and also by Nos 4, 6, 8 and 9 tram routes. Founded originally as the foreport of Delft with the digging of the Delfshavense Schie canal as early as 1389, but not granted town privileges until 1825, Delfshaven was incorporated into Rotterdam in 1886. The district is worth visiting for its narrow docks which give it something of the quaintness of an old port (architecturally much of Delfshaven is a protected zone), for the two sections of Rotterdam's historical museum to be found here, both in attractive old buildings, and for the place's association with the Pilgrim Fathers. Boat tours in May–Sept: Wed, 14.00; Sun, 14.30.

The part of Delfshaven likely to be of most interest to the visitor will be the narrow peninsula stretching S and bounded by the waters of Voorhaven and Achterhaven (W and E) and Middenkous (S); more precisely you should aim for the E side of Voorhaven. Here (from S to N) the first point of interest, at the S tip, is the *Distilleerketel*, an 18C malt windmill, almost completely destroyed by fire in 1940 but now restored.

Further N, at Voorhaven 12, is the museum of **De Dubbelde Palmboom** (Tues–Sat, 10.00 to 17.00; Sun, Holidays, 11.00 to 17.00), one of the three sections of Rotterdam's historical museum, the other two being the Zakkendragershuisje (see below) and the Schielandshuis in the city centre. However, the presentation here is not so much history in the conventional and chronological sense, but rather by broad themes, the basis being 'living and working in the Maas mouth area from prehistoric to modern times'.

The building was put up as a warehouse in 1825 but has since seen many uses, having served as a cooper's workshop, stables, distillery, furniture factory and coal store. It was much rebuilt in 1861, the façade then acquiring the twin gables which inspired today's name of Double Palm Tree. Much restored prior to opening as a museum in 1975, the interior nevertheless retains its heavy beams, a floor of IJssel bricks and its timbered top floor.

The museum is invitingly arranged in open plan on a ground and four upper levels linked by open staircases. Descriptions are virtually entirely in Dutch, but a two-page summary in English enables the English-speaking visitor to make some sense of the exhibits. Those requiring more in-depth information should contact the information desk about English slide programmes, films and guided tours.

It is probably best to start at the Fourth (top) Floor—with an information desk, café, toilets, etc., and then work downwards. The theme of the Third Floor is 'Water and Land', archaeological finds providing a picture spanning from 6000 BC to medieval times. A reconstructed farmhouse brings the Iron Age to life, the Romans are represented largely by coins and pottery, and the medieval centuries by pictures, models and collections of household objects. The Second Floor concentrates on 'Town and Country' (17C to late 19C), the emphasis being on trades and crafts prior to the industrial era and the exhibits ranging from tile pictures and costume to architecture, with a particularly interesting display on spiral staircase construction. Peat was of course the principal fuel, and exhibits here explain how it was won and also how the resultant meres and bogs were drained by windmills, of which there are several intricate models. Finally, there are the homely workshops of a smith and a carter.

On the First Floor the theme is 'Town and Port', the emphasis being on the latter though there is also material on the growth of Trades Unions, this including some interesting, moralising early 20C posters. 'Industry and Technology' take over the Ground Floor, with industrial archaeology illustrating the growth of industrialisation in the 19C. Here can be seen a paint factory; a jenever (Holland's gin) distillery; cast iron objects providing examples of metal founding; façade ornamentation from industrial buildings; old fire engines, a scissors-grinder's cart and an improbable street-cleaner's bicycle.

Beyond the museum, the *Oude Kerk* faces the water, founded in 1417 as the Chapel of St Anthony, rebuilt in 1716 and restored in 1934–37 and again in 1958–59. A plaque here recalls the Pilgrim Fathers who held a service here before embarking in the 'Speedwell' on 22 July 1620; between Southampton and Plymouth the ship was found to be unseaworthy and the Pilgrims finally made the Atlantic crossing in the 'Mayflower'. Beyond again, at Voorstraat 13, is the *Zakkendragershuisje* (Tues–Sat, 10.00 to 17.00; Sun, Holidays, 11.00 to 17.00), dating from 1653, originally a crane-house for the operation of a sluice and later the guild room of the Guild of the Grain Sack Carriers who were summoned here by the bell in the turret whenever a ship was due, dice then being cast to allot the work. Restored, the house is now a functioning pewterer's workshop, small museum (moulds, tools, stamps) and shop selling pewter.

At the head of Achterhaven a statue (J. Graven, 1870) commemorates Admiral Piet Heyn (1577–1629), born in the adjacent Piet Heynstraat (at No. 6, rebuilt in the 19C); it was he who captured the Spanish silver fleet in 1628. Further E (700m), in Pieter de Hoochweg, the *Anglican Church* of 1930 is successor to one of 1708 which stood at the NE end of Haringvliet in the E of the city. *Coolhaven*, the water along the N of Delfshaven, was the last inner dock to be dug between the wars.

# C.   Outer City

Rotterdam is completely enclosed by motorways, a system known as the Rhomboid with a total length of 41km.

NORTH. The northern motorway (A20), coming from the E, passes N of the district of Kralingen (see below), then S of the twin Bergse lakes, on the E shore of which the *Prinsenmolen* dates from 1648; another mill, 1km E on

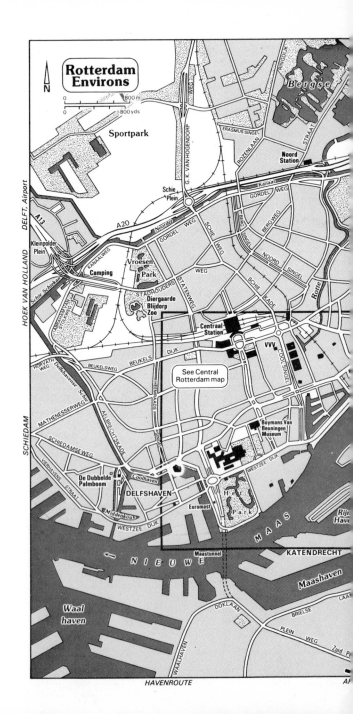

# Rotterdam Environs

N

0 ——— 800 m
0 ——— 800 yds

Sportpark

Bergse

DELFT, Airport

A13

G. K. VAN HOGENDORP WEG

ERASMUS SINGEL

STRAAT

RINGDIJK

Noord Station

ROZENLAAN

Kanaal

Schie Plein

GORDEL WEG

A20

Noorder

GORDEL WEG

SCHIE WEG

BERG SINGEL

BERGWEG

KANAALWEG

Kleinpolder Plein

HOEK VAN HOLLAND

Schie Schiekade

Camping

Vroesen Park

WEG

STADHOUDERS WEG

STATENWEG

NOORD SINGEL

SCHIE KADE

Rotte

Diergaarde Blijdorp Zoo

ABRAHAM VAN STOLKWEG

Centraal Station

VVV

COOLSINGEL

BEUKELS DIJK

HORVATH WEG

Delfshavense Schie

BEUKELSWEG

BEUKELSWEG

HEEMRAADS

See Central Rotterdam map

SCHIEDAM

MATHENESSERWEG

ALBRECHTSKADE

SCHIE

SCHIEDAMSEWEG

Boymans Van Beuningen Museum

VIERHAVENS STRAAT

De Dubbelde Palmboom

Coolhaven

DELFSHAVEN

WESTZEE DIJK

Middenkous

Euromast

Het Park

WESTZEE DIJK

MAAS

Rijn Haven

KATENDRECHT

Waal haven

NIEUWE

Maastunnel

Maashaven

LAA

DOKLAAN

BRIELSE

WAALHAVEN

PLEIN

WEG

Zuid P

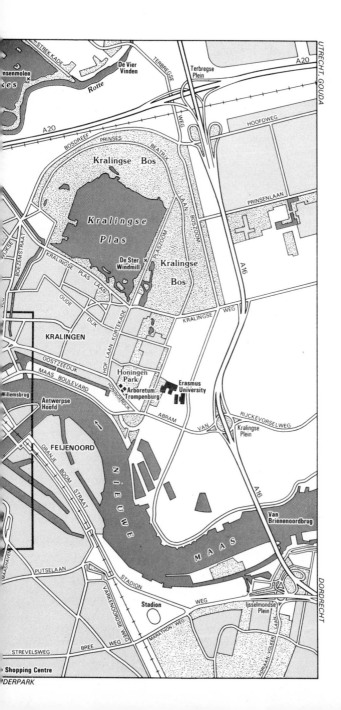

the Rotte and called *De Vier Winden*, is of 1776. Between the lakes, at Berglustlaan 12, the *Museum Hendrik Chabot* (by appointment. Tel: (010) 4-224274) shows the work of this Rotterdam Expressionist artist (born 1894). Due S of the lakes the motorway crosses the little river Rotte, from the early damming of which the city derives its name. Rather over 3km further W the important Kleinpolder intersection is reached, where the A13 heads N for *Zestienhoven Airport* (3km) and *Delft* (see Rte 8), 10km further. Immediately SE of this intersection *Camping Rotterdam* is the municipal site. The A20 continues W for *Schiedam*, *Vlaardingen*, and *Hoek van Holland*, for all of which see Rte 11.

EAST. The E motorway (A16) skirts the E of the district of **Kralingen** (metro) at the NE corner of which, within the loop formed by the motorways, is the large park area of the *Kralingse Bos* (2km by 2km). At the park's centre is the Kralingse Plas, a square lake with on its E bank two windmills, one of which is *De Ster* (1866) where the grinding of snuff and spices is demonstrated (Dec–March: Wed, 09.00 to 16.00; April–Nov: Tues–Wed, 09.00 to 16.00). In the SE part of Kralingen, within the angle of the motorway and Abram van Rijckevorselweg, is the *Erasmus University*, established here in 1970 as successor to the School of Economics, founded on this site in 1913; the medical faculty is in central Rotterdam off Westzeedijk. The *Arboretum Trompenburg* (Mon–Sat, 09.00 to 17.00; tickets from VVV), laid out between 1820 and 1928, is in five parts. The central part (1820) shows oak, copper beech and some blue Atlas cedars; the western part (1870; pinetum 1928) has ash, taxus and a ginkgo; in the E are the herbaceous border, rose garden, heather garden, and cactus hothouse of 1900; the Perenhof (1820) shows species trees and shrubs among original oaks; and Woudesteijn is the home of plane trees and an *Acer cappadocicum* between two *Ulmus glabra*. Not far from the arboretum, 400m N at Groene Wetering 41, will be found the *Toy-Toy Museum* (Sun–Thurs, 11.00 to 16.00; closed July and August) with dolls and mechanical toys of the period 1700 to 1940.

The motorway crosses the Nieuwe Maas by the Van Brienenoordbrug of 1965.

SOUTH. Southern Rotterdam, between the river and the A15 motorway and due S of the main N bank city, is a fast growing residential and commercial district, the post-war result of the opening of the Maas tunnel and of the metro link, although development of this S bank started with the building of the first Willemsbrug in 1874. The centre of the district is the important **Zuidplein**, with the metro station and a huge, fully covered shopping centre, an easily reached and popular objective, especially in wet weather. A short way S, the *Ahoy* is a large sports and exhibition complex standing on the N side of the extensive *Zuiderpark*.

For the districts to the W along the S side of the Nieuwe Maas, see E. Havenroute.

# D.   Boymans-Van Beuningen Museum

The **\*\*Boymans-Van Beuningen Museum** (Tues–Sat, 10.00 to 17.00; Sun, Holidays, 11.00 to 17.00), ranking among the leading art collections in the Netherlands and including paintings, sculpture and applied art, owes its origin to F.J.O. Boymans (died 1847) who bequeathed his collections to the city. In 1849 the museum opened in the Schielandshuis, but in 1864 a fire

*The Prodigal Son by Hieronymus Mosch, c 1510, Boymans-Van Beuningen Museum*

here destroyed some 300 paintings, 13 portfolios of Italian and French drawings and virtually all the museum's prints and ceramics. Through gifts, bequests and purchases the collections were gradually built up again— Bosch's 'Prodigal Son' was acquired in 1931, Kandinsky's 'Lyrical' in 1932, Rubens' 'Achilles' in 1933—and in 1935 the museum moved into its present main building (by A. van der Steur and the then director D. Hannema). Among major acquisitions over the following years were Rembrandt's 'Titus' and a major part of the F. Koenigs Collection of drawings and paintings (Rembrandt, Rubens, Watteau, Bosch) in 1939 and later; the D.G. van Beuningen collection (Brueghel, Titian, Van Eyck) in 1958, thus leading to the addition of this collector's name to the museum's title; and several Kandinsky paintings, acquired in 1964 from the Guggenheim museum.

The year 1972 saw the completion of the new modern art wing, this being followed by the acquisition in 1977–79 of Surrealist works by Dali and Magritte, while 1981 brought enlargement of the applied arts department with a collection of industrial design and historical utensils.

The museum is on two floors. Each wing (old for pre-19C art, new for modern) has its own entrance, but the two are also connected inside. For various reasons—the frequent temporary exhibitions; the need to change pictures around due to lack of space (the museum owns over 250,000 works of art of various kinds); and what seems to be an almost perpetual state of reorganisation—the museum defies any attempt at a reliable room by room description. The following, however, though necessarily mentioning only a small selection, should give an impression of the wealth of the museum's collections. Do not miss the Van Meegeren forgery of a Vermeer (Christ at Emmaus) on your way into the old masters' section.

OLD MASTERS (14–18C). **Dutch and Flemish Paintings, 15—17C.** *Pieter Aertsen (Aertsz)*: Jesus in the house of Mary; Pancakes; Fruit and vegetables. *Bernard van Orley*: Crucifixion, with Margaret of Austria as Charity and Mary of Hungary as Peace; Madonna; *Hieronymus Bosch*: Portrait of an old woman; St Christopher; a curious work, yet in style, with oddities such as a bear being hanged and a fish attached to the saint's staff; *The Prodigal Son (c 1510); *The Marriage at Cana; *Adriaen Brouwer*: Drinking scene; very earthy, with one man passed out, another vomiting, but five survivors hard at it. *Pieter Bruegel the Elder*: **Tower of Babel; a small but theatrical scene in which an uncertain but elaborate structure rises into the clouds. *Gerit Dou*: *The Quack; an amusing and down-to-earth 17C scene of scepticism mixed with hope. *Hubert and Jan van Eyck*: The Three Marys at the Tomb; a brutal contrast between the sorrowing women and the indifference of the sleeping soldiery. *Karel Fabritius*: *Self-portrait. *Jan van Goyen*: *river scenes; Plain, with cattle. *B. van der Helst*: some fine portraits. *Salomon Koninck*: Pontius Pilate; with astonishing lighting of the central figure. *Hans Memling*: Pietà; Two houses in a landscape; Two horses. *Master of the St John Altar*: Birth of John the Baptist; a homely if curious domestic scene with the wan mother being fed broth, while the baby is washed and a servant dries the cloth at the fire.

*Rembrandt*: *Portrait of Titus (1655); a sensitive portrayal of a child within the conventions of the portaiture of learned men; Man in a red cap. *P.P. Rubens*: Hercules and Discordia; Martyrdom of St Lebuinus; England and Scotland crowning the infant Charles; Portrait of a monk; Two Romans; *Landscape at sunset; Portrait of Suzanne Fourment (c 1636–38). *Salomon van Ruysdael*: Seascape; River scene; Portraits. *Pieter Saenredam*: The Mariaplaats with the Mariakerk at Utrecht (1663); Church interiors at Alkmaar and Utrecht. *Jan van Scorel*: *Scholar in a red cap; St Sebastian in a landscape. *Jan Steen*: Extracting the stone; Feast of St Nicholas; Village wedding; Oyster feast. *David Teniers the Younger*: Village scene; Scene at an inn.

**Italian Painting, 14–16C** includes the Florentine Primitives. Also *Tintoretto*: Annunciation; The wise and the foolish virgins; Rape of Proserpine. *Veronese*: Christ at Emmaus; Portrait of a boy; Adoration of the shepherds. *Titian*: Satyr and nymph; Boy with dogs in a landscape.

**Artists of the 18C**. *J.B. Chardin*: The Meal; Still life. *Francesco Guardi*: several works. *Cornelis Troost*: Blind Man's Buff; Interior. *Antoine Watteau*: L'Indifférent (c 1716). **Artists of the 19C** are principally of the French Barbizon and The Hague schools.

OLD APPLIED ART. Roman, Dutch, French and German pewter up to the 17C; the collection includes chalices, tankards, reliquaries and decorated dishes. Candlesticks of the 12–15C. The medieval material includes bronze aquamaniles and censers; French ivories; ornaments spanning prehistoric times, across the Middle Ages and up to the 17C, amongst these some medieval pilgrimage souvenirs; and Netherlands polychrome wood sculpture of the 14–16C. Amongst the Furniture exhibited are examples of Colonial baroque of the 17C, and a large apothecary's chest (Dutch, c 1680) with 72 drawers.

Within the general categories of Renaissance and baroque there are bronze, ceramics, glass and silver collections. The Bronze Collection contains work (15–18C) by Adriaen de Vries, Peter Visscher the Younger, Giovanni da Bologna and Riccio. Ceramic material includes Persian, Turkish and Spanish earthenware, with tiles (10–18C); Dutch, German, French and oriental porcelain and some English earthenware of the late 18C; majolica (15C and 16C) from Italy, France and the Netherlands, the last showing a collection of Delftware up to 1800. The Glass Collection is of many periods and wide provenance, notably Roman, Persian (17C and 18C), Spanish, Venetian, French and Netherlands. The Dutch Silver spans from the 16C to the mid 19C.

MODERN WING. The material here comprises both changing selections from the museum's collections and also temporary exhibitions (some 15 a year) generally designed to illustrate contemporary developments. The divisions between the various modern movements are of course not clear cut, but the museum provides a series of leaflets in English, introduced by an essay on 'Modern Art 1850–1950' covering the several movements.

The following are the principal movements given place in the museum, together with the names of some representative artists. *Impressionism*: Monet, Signac. *Expressionism*: Kokoschka, Kandinsky. The latter is particularly well represented here, as a result of the acquisitions from the Guggenheim museum in 1964. *Surrealism*: Dali, Magritte, Ernst, Paul Delvaux. *Cobra*: Karel Appel. *Pop Art*: Warhol.

Sculptors include Rodin, Degas (his charming 'Young Dancer' of c 1880), Zadkine, Epstein, Moore, Hepworth, Serra, Beuys and Nauman.

The **Print Room** contains prints and drawings (all European schools) spanning the 15–20C. The **Library** is open Tues–Friday, 10.00 to 13.00, 14.00 to 17.00.

# E.   The Havenroute

The HAVENROUTE (Port Route), marked by frequent hexagonal signs, has been arranged by ANWB (the Dutch motorists' club) and the port authority. The route starts from **Europoint** (N of the river), the seat of the port administration (and since 1986 housing the heart of VTMS, the ultra modern Vessel Traffic Management System), runs E towards Delfshaven, crosses the river by the Maastunnel, and then heads W along the S shore to end after some 48km (from the S end of the Maastunnel: excluding diversions) on the N shore of the Maasvlakte at the river mouth opposite Hoek van Holland, a spot as interesting as it can be windy and bleak. ANWB provides an excellent map and accompanying English text, with much commercial and technical detail, and the use of this (obtainable from VVV) is strongly recommended.

The description below, which starts at the S end of the Maastunnel, indicates principal features. Diversions are shown in small print.

DISTANCES. From S end of Maastunnel to NE corner of **Waalhaven**, 2km—
7km **Beneluxplein** (for *Pernis* and *Beneluxtunnel*)—4km **Botlekbrug**
(Oude Maas)—9km **Calandbrug** (for *Rozenburg*, and *Calandkanaal-
Nieuwe Waterweg* diversion)—7km **Dintelhavenbrug** (for
*Europoort*)—3km *Suurhofbrug*—7km **Maasvlakte** (power station)—6km
**Maasmond** (port entrance view)—3km **No. 8 Petroleumhaven**.

The route skirts the E and S sides of **Waalhaven**, dug between 1907 and 1930, the E side being the older part. Piers along the E side are used for timber (No. 1) and multi-purposes (No. 2), the latter also used for the storage of goods for the international terminal markets, such as coffee, tobacco, tea and non-ferrous metals. Between Piers 3 and 4 there are berths for LASH (lighter-aboard ships and their lighters), a type of barge-carrier transporting standard inland barges between the mouths of large rivers (e.g. Rhine and Mississippi). Along the S side of Waalhaven there are berths for inland waterway shipping, including tugs and pushers, and it is also of interest that this area was until the Second World War Rotterdam's airport, a past recalled by streets named after aviation pioneers such as Albert Plesman, first president of KLM, and R.D. Parmentier, captain of the KLM DC2 aircraft which in 1934 won the handicap section in the MacRobertson (England–Australia) Air Race.

You can make a diversion may up the arm dividing Waalhaven from *Eemhaven* with many piers on both sides (containers; rolling cargo; forestry products; daily services to the UK and Scandinavia), a power station, and at Pier 7 the deep-sea container terminal of Multi-Terminals. Here too is the contrasting area of *Heijplaat*, a residential oasis built between 1913 and 1915 as a kind of garden-village for dockyard employees. The 'island' just to the NW between Heysehaven and Werkhaven, once the quarantine station, is now used for a bonded warehouse.

The route, now Reeweg, runs a short way S, passing the head of *Prinses Beatrixhaven* (1965), the place where in May 1966 the first all-container ship between America and Europe docked, and then turns W along Vondelingenweg to the N of which is the busy container area of **Prinses Margriethaven** and **Prins Willem Alexanderhaven**, together forming the world's largest container terminal. Just beyond the latter the road reaches **Beneluxplein**, the large area embraced by the traffic system where motorways A15 (E–W) and A4 (N–S, Beneluxtunnel) cross.

The **Beneluxtunnel** (1967) is just over 1km in length and, at its lowest point, runs 22.5m below the water. Built ahead of the national plan by Rotterdam, Schiedam, Vlaardingen and other authorities, this was a toll tunnel until handed over to the state in 1979.

**Pernis**, lying to the E of the motorway approach to the tunnel, is a large village surrounded by green land. The village dates from the early 14C and its Reformed church (SE quarter of village) has a tower of that date. The village is at Kilometer 1008, this being the distance from the first bridge across the Rhine at Constance. To the W of Pernis is *No. 2 Petroleumhaven*, surrounded by petro-chemical activity (Shell, Mobil) but now too small for the larger tankers.

From Beneluxplein the route continues W along Vondelingenweg, running between the motorway and the huge petro-chemical zone which dominates the N side of the route for virtually the whole of the remainder of its length. Shell, Mobil, and Texaco installations surround both No. 2 Petroleumhaven and No. 1 to its W. Immediately beyond the Shell zone the Oude Maas river is crossed by a bridge and a tunnel. The **Botlekbrug** is a lift-bridge dating from 1955, but with the rapid development both of Botlek, immediately beyond the bridge, and Europoort beyond again, it was soon found inadequate and the **Botlektunnel** was opened in 1980. To the S can be seen the *Spijkenisserbrug* (1978) with its two concrete lifting towers. The *Hartelkanaal*, the exit from which into the Oude Maas is between the Botlekbrug and the Spijkenisserbrug, provides an inland link between Botlek, Europoort, and Maasvlakte. Push-tow units, pushing up to six barges laden with ore, collected from Europoort and delivered via the Rhine to the Ruhr, are a common sight along the canal.

From the W side of Botlekbrug, Oude Maasweg leads N for 2.5km to **Geulhaven**, important as the VTMS Regional Traffic Centre responsible for all shipping on the Oude Maas and Hartelkanaal between Hoek van Holland and the eastern docks and also in the Europoort and Botlek areas. From here too there is a good view across into *No. 3 Petroleumhaven* (W) and across to the *Verolme* shipbuilding and servicing yards (1956–58).

From Botlekbrug the Havenroute continues W past Esso installations to curve N around the head of the *Chemiehaven*, from where, after mechanical unloading, products are taken by conveyor to the nearby **Botlek** basin for transfer to inland shipping. To the SW, between Seinehaven and the Hartelkanaal, the Texaco crude oil tanks receive by pipeline from Europoort and discharge, also by pipeline, to the refineries at Pernis and in Belgium. The route passes the head of Botlek, the road here crossing the dike (1950) of the former Brielse Maas river, now a lake. The unloading of 'agribulk' (grain, oilseeds, animal feeds) is the principal activity here. A good view of Botlek, and across to the *St Laurenshaven* (ore and chemicals), can be had by driving to the end of the short road (Welplaatweg) which runs along the S side of Botlek.

Havenroute heads briefly N, with ore and chemical installations on the E, then bears W to reach the **Calandbrug**, the name honouring Pieter Caland, the engineer who in 1866 started the work on the Nieuwe Waterweg. The bridge, crossing the canal of the same name and conspicuous with its four towers, can be lifted 38 metres in one minute, thus leaving a clearance of 50m for ships.

To the S, the *Brittanniehaven* and *Seinehaven* serve the needs of chemical firms, notably Imperial Chemical Industries. Seaport Terminals, on the N side of Brittanniehaven, handles such cargoes as wood, cellulose and paper. Here too, to the E, is the Quick Despatch Car Terminal (1981), processing, with short-term storage, over 200,000 cars a year.

To the N, protected by dikes on the N and W, is the village of **Rozenburg**, from where a frequent car ferry crosses to Maassluis. A diversion (20km there and back) can be made from Rozenburg along the narrow artificial dike that separates the Calandkanaal from the Nieuwe Waterweg, the former being the approach to Europoort and the latter that for Rotterdam. This diversion offers good views across to the water-side of Europoort (see below), with three petroleum docks (from S to N, Nos 7, 5 and 4) and, finally, Beneluxhaven (see below). The small *Scheurhaven*, near the end of the dike, is used by Europoort harbour tugs, and a drive to the W tip of the dike can offer a rewarding view of the shipping.

Just beyond Calandbrug, *Harmsenbrug* leads S across the Hartelkanaal and the Brielse Meer. For the country beyond, see Rte 13B. After Caland-brug, Havenroute runs between the Hartelkanaal on the S and chemical and oil installations on the N, passing *De Beer*, an international centre for seamen, part of which is a chapel built especially for the crews of Nor-wegian tankers, and in 6km reaching the road fork for **Europoort** (1957–68).

From this point two diversions may be made into **Europoort**, one (just over 3km return) being along Rijnweg to *No. 4 Petroleumhaven*, where tankers unload crude oil for the major companies. The other diversion (6km return) follows Moezelweg and Luxemburgweg to the head of *Beneluxhaven*, departure point for ferry services to England (P. and O. North Sea Ferries to Hull.) This diversion then skirts Dintelhaven, heading N for the grain unloading facilities of Beneluxhaven, handling carriers of upto 200,000 dwt.

The main Havenroute crosses *Dintelhavenbrug* and follows Europaweg to (c 2.5km) the installations of British Petroleum (1967), served by *No. 6 Petroleumhaven* which may be glimpsed through the tanks.

From this point a diversion (8.5km return) northwards leads to *Europoort (Ore)*, or Ertsoverslag, where, on the deep-water Calandkanaal quay, ore is unloaded on to conveyor belts, then either stored or loaded on to the Rhine push-tow units. To the W is the broad *Beerkanaal* (the name meaning 'bear' and not 'beer'), with a station of the municipal pilotage service, which takes over from the state service when vessels leave the open river. To the S is *No. 6 Petroleumhaven* (see above), while across the Beerkanaal is *No. 8 Petroleumhaven* (see below).

Suurhofbrug now crosses the Hartelkanaal, skirts the *Brielse Meer*, with a recreation area on its N shore, passes the *Stenen Baak* (stone beacon), a 17C lighthouse, and continues into open country, with water on both sides. The *Mississippihaven* (N beyond the canal) is used by the very large ore carriers (250,000 dwt), while the Rhine push-tow units are loaded in the adjacent *Hartelhaven*. To the S the *Oostvoornse Meer*, once with the Brielse Meer a part of the Brielse Maas river, is now a lake, formed in 1950 when the river was dammed. The former river mouth is now represented by the Brielse Gat, a sea inlet just beyond the W end of the lake. The road, accompanied by the railway, curves right (there is a short side-road to the shore here) and skirts the Hartelhaven, on the other side of which is the site of the huge Maasvlakte Coal Terminal.

   **Maasvlakte** (Maas Plain), the area through which the road now runs, was reclaimed in 1968–74. Along the W side there are beach parking places and other facilities, and here too starts the 4.5km long Boulder (or Outer) Dike which curves around to the N. The E of the road is dominated by a power station, the largest in the Rotterdam area. Behind the power station the ECT Delta Terminal (1985) stretches along the S shore of *Europahaven*. The terminal has a quay length of 1250m and uses the world's largest container unloading cranes.

   Maasvlakte's conspicuous lighthouse (65m) has superseded that at Hoek van Holland, left too far inland by the progressive extension of the port. At the river mouth (**\*Maasmond**) there is ample parking along the top of the dike, a spot which, though often bleak and windswept, offers a magnificent view across the river entrance (there is even an information board illustrating the shipping that may be seen). To the W are the two towers, each 30m high with lights and helicopter pad, which mark the entrance, incoming vessels then being guided by aligning the central lighthouses before choosing the Nieuwe Waterweg for Rotterdam or the Calandkanaal for Maasvlakte or Europoort. *Hoek van Holland* (see Rte 11) can be seen on the N shore.

The last section of the Havenroute runs E to *No. 8 Petroleumhaven*, with, alongside, its associated oil terminal installations (facility shared by various oil concerns).

The return to Rotterdam may be made through the VOORNE and PUTTEN districts to the S (see Rte 13B).

# 11 Rotterdam to Hoek van Holland

Total distance 27km. 8km **Schiedam**—4km **Vlaardingen**—5km— **Maassluis**—10km Hoek van Holland.

You can leave **Rotterdam**, see Rte 10, by a choice of roads, e.g. Rochussenstraat to Delfshaven, then Schiedamseweg, or by motorway A20. *8km* **Schiedam** (70,000 inhab. VVV, Buitenhavenweg 9) is a compact, ancient town which traces its origin to a dam across the Schie built in c 1260 by Countess Aleida van Henegouwen; 15 years later the place received a charter. Schiedam is known both for its distilleries producing the spirit called 'hollands' or 'jenever' (juniper), and also for shipbuilding.

The town's E flank is defined by Broersvest, a widish main street which forms the southern length of the road which, starting as 's Gravelandseweg, runs S from the motorway to cross the Schie. Here, at the SE corner of the river bridge, stands the pleasing *Proveniershuis* (1756–61), first a leper hospital and then almshouses; there is parking alongside and the neat rectangular court deserves a glance. Just beyond, on the same side of the road, survive the modest ruins of the late 13C castle, while beyond again, across Koemarkt and beside the next water (Buitenhaven), is VVV.

The inner town is immediately W of the Proveniershuis: by car along Boterstraat. The town centre is the small old MARKT, with the *Stadhuis*, an attractive and typical building of 1782, successor to at least two others on this site, one, of wood, destroyed by fire in 1604. The adjacent *St Janskerk* dates from 1425 and has a mainly 17C interior, notably a pulpit of 1600, a font of 1642, and an organ case of 1550. Close by (W), across the water, are the former *Korenbeurs* (Jan Guidici, 1792) and, just N, the *Zakkendragershuisje* (1725), the house at which the grain porters assembled when the bell rang to signal the arrival of a ship. Hoogstraat leads out of the Markt, with at No. 112 the *Stedelijk Museum* (Tues–Sat, 10.00 to 17.00; Sun, Holidays, 12.30 to 17.00), perhaps most interesting as a site and building. Built by Jan Guidici in 1787—with male and female wings separated by a central church—the house not only stands on the site of a hospice founded by Aleida van Henegouwen in 1276 but also continued to function as such until as recently as 1934, thus completing nearly 700 years of service to the needy. The museum shows archaeological and other local material, and embraces the Gedistilleerd Museum with information on local distilling, but there are often temporary exhibitions, these tending to displace the permanent material.

Schiedam is also known for the four windmills which ring the inner town on the W and N. Of these the southernmost two (no adm.) are *De Walvisch* of 1794 and *De Drie Koornbloemen* of 1770. *De Vrijheid* (1785) is at Noordvest 40 and may be visited (Sat, 10.30 to 16.30), as may also the *De Noort* (1794) at Noordvest 38, now serving as a tavern (of Royal Distilleries Erven Lucas Bols Ltd) where both Dutch and foreign distilled drinks can be enjoyed (Mon–Sat; mill operates Sat).

*4km* **Vlaardingen** (76,000 inhab. VVV, Westnieuwland 6) is of interest in the history of the province of Holland as the place where in 1351 the Kabbeljauws supporting Count William V defeated the Hoeks. The *Visserijmuseum* (Mon–Sat, 10.00 to 17.00; Sun, Holidays, 14.00 to 17.00), a mansion of 1740 at Westhavenkade 53, includes an aquarium, models of fishing boats, interesting dioramas explaining fishing techniques, replicas of a typical fishing family's living room and of a fishing company office (both c 1900), and period rooms in Louis XIV and XV style. The *Stadhuis* of 1650 was built to a design by Bartolomeus Drijfhout. At *5km* **Maassluis** (33,000 inhab. VVV, Stadhuis), with a car ferry across to Rozenburg (see Rte 10E), the *Grote Kerk* (1639) has a tower of c 1650 by Arent van 's Gravesande. Maassluis is largely active in the export of the produce of the WESTLAND, a horticultural district (vegetables, fruit and flowers) which, with its many glasshouses, stretches between Maassluis and The Hague. Flowers, of which 75 per cent are exported, are sold through a co-operative (at Honselersdijk) established in 1923 and now with some 2500 members (auction visit, Mon–Fri, 08.00 to 11.00).

*10km* **Hoek van Holland** (8000 inhab.; VVV, Hoekse Brink 23), since 1914 incorporated in the municipality of Rotterdam, is important as the terminus of the boat service from Harwich and of connecting trains from many parts of the continent. The name means not 'Hook of Holland' as is sometimes fancifully believed by English-speakers who see it on the map, but 'Corner of Holland'. It is well worth continuing W beyond the town, at least to the *Semaphore* (coin telescope) from where there is a fine view across the Nieuwe Waterweg to Maasvlakte and Europoort, for both of which see Rte 10E; from here too there is a waterside walk towards the mouth of the Nieuwe Waterweg. There is ample parking in the area and good beaches.

# 12 Rotterdam to Dordrecht and Gorinchem

The direct road is described as Rte 12A. Dordrecht, which lies to the S, is treated separately as Rte 12B.

## A. Rotterdam to Gorinchem

Total distance 41km. 12km motorway junction A16/A15(E) (**Dordrecht**)—5km *Alblasserdam* (for **Molens van Kinderdijk**)—24km **Gorinchem**.

Rotterdam (see Rte 10) may be left by motorway A16, this first reaches the junction with A15(W) and then, some *12km* from the city centre, the junction with A15(E). This Route bears E here, but visitors to Dordrecht should continue S for 7km on A16.

*4km*. You cross the *Noord*, the channel linking the Lek:Nieuwe Maas (N) with the Oude Maas:Beneden Merwede at Dordrecht. *1km Alblasserdam*, immediately N of A15, is at the W end of the ALBLASSERWAARD, a region of polders in the triangle between the Noord, the Lek and the Merwede. It is interesting for the **Molens van Kinderdijk** (3km N of Alblasserdam; entrance at the N near the Lek sluice), a concentration of 19 windmills placed here in c 1740 to drain excess water from the polder into the Lek, a function now performed by powered pumping stations. The mills are put into operation on Saturday afternoons in July and August and are floodlit during the first and second week in September; also one mill is open to visitors from April to September, daily except Sundays. In summer there are boat trips past the mills. The story goes that the name Kinderdijk (child's dike) originates from the stranding here of a cradle with a baby during the St Elisabeth Flood of 1421.

A pleasant, though at first industrialised, minor road follows the S bank of the Lek to (13km) **Groot Ammers**, with a stork colony (*Het Liesveld*) run by the Society for the Protection of Birds, and, 4km further, **Nieuwpoort** (see Rte 9).

*24km* **Gorinchem** (or **Gorcum**. 28,000 inhab.; *VVV*, Zusterhuis 6) is situated on the Linge just below the point where the rivers Maas and Waal unite to form the Merwede. A fortified town as early as the 13C, Gorinchem's present walls date from some three centuries later. *St Janskerk*, in the town centre, has an impressive tower of c 1566 but was otherwise rebuilt in the mid 19C. The local museum (Oud-Gorcum), with an elaborate façade, is at 25 Gasthuisstraat in a house of 1566 curiously named *Dit is in Bethlehem* (Wed–Sun, 14.00 to 17.00). The *Dalempoort* (SE) of c 1600 is the only surviving gate, from the waterfront near here being a distant view across to the castle of Loevestein (see Rte 19). (Ferry, no cars, from Gorinchem to Woudrichem and then to Loevestein.) For the Treaty of Gorinchem (1528) see Province of Gelderland, History.

The district to the NE of Gorinchem between the Linge and the Lek and once sandwiched between the county of Gelder and the bishopric of Utrecht is known as the VIJFHEERENLANDEN (Lands of the Five Lords), because in medieval times it was made up of five small independent lordships. The principal of these was Vianen in the N (see Rte 17C). The others were Hagestein and Everdingen, both to the SE of Vianen, and Arkel and Leerdam in the S on the Linge. From Gorinchem a minor road ascends the Linge to (11km) **Leerdam** (15,000 inhab.), a place known since 1765 for its glass manufacture. The *Nationaal Glasmuseum* (Tues–Fri, 10.00 to 13.00, 14.00 to 17.00; also Sat, Sun, and Holidays in April–Oct, 13.00 to 17.00), at Lingedijk 28, exhibits modern and antique Dutch and other glass. You enter the province of Gelderland just E of Gorinchem. For Gorinchem to *Nijmegen*, see Rte 25.

# B.  Dordrecht

**DORDRECHT** (107,000 inhab.) stands on the S bank of the Oude Maas at the point where this becomes (E) the Beneden Merwede. From here the

Noord channel connects northward to the Lek:Nieuwe Maas, while southward the De Kil channel (toll road tunnel to the Hoekse Waard) provides
the link with the Hollands Diep, both these channels being a section of the
main water communication between Antwerp in Belgium and Rotterdam.
Dordrecht thus lies on what is probably the busiest waterways junction in
the country (that the scene was just as bustling in the 17C is well recalled
by pictures by Jan van Goyen and Abraham Willaerts in the Dordrechts
Museum). Apart from the interest of its active waterfront, Dordrecht offers
many old façades along its generally narrow streets, a magnificent view
from the tower of its Grote Kerk, a good museum (Van Gijn) and a small
but very good art gallery (Dordrechts Museum). The town's name is
sometimes simplified to its early form of 'Dort'.

**Centre.** Bagijnhof-Statenplein.

**VVV.** Stationsweg 1 (opposite the station).

**Post Office.** Johan de Wittstraat (300m S of Statenplein).

**Station.** In the S of the town, c 700m S of Statenplein.

**Boats.** From Groothoofd. To Biesbos, Rotterdam port, Dordrecht port, Heusden,
Alblasserwaard, etc.

**History.** Ancient records suggest that there was a settlement here which was attacked
by the Norsemen in 837, but the real founding of the town was by Count Dirk III in
c 1010 when he built a castle here around which a town grew. Because of its ability to
control passing shipping, this soon became the early power centre of the county of
Holland. Count Dirk IV, fighting the bishop of Utrecht, was killed here in 1049, and
in 1220 the town, now a place of considerable importance, was granted a charter by
Count William I. One of the first towns to declare for the Protestants in 1572, it was the
place chosen that same year for the first meeting of the Estates of the Seven Provinces.
Dordrecht, or Dort as it was then called, was also, in 1618–19, host to the Synod of Dort
at which the Arminians or Remonstrants, the followers of Jacobus Arminius, failed to
gain acceptance for their doctrine that predestination was conditional and not
absolute, the decision going in favour of the rigidly Calvinist followers of Franz
Gomarus, supported by Maurice of Naussau. Overseas trade was stimulated by the
establishment of an English agency here in 1655.

**Natives.** Johan de Witt (1625–75), the Council Pensionary, who was torn to pieces by
the mob at The Hague. Among the artists born here were Ferdinand Bol (1616–80),
Aelbert Cuyp (1620–91), Jacob Cuyp (1594–1651/2), Samuel van Hoogstraten (1627–
78), Nicolaes Maes (1632–93), Godfried Schalken (1643–1706) and Ary Scheffer
(1795–1858). Also, locally active, Abraham van Strij (1853–1926) and Jacob van Strij
(1756–1815).

Places of interest are somewhat scattered, VVV and the station being on
the S; the Grote Kerk and the Van Gijn museum in the NW near the Oude
Maas; and the Dordrechts Museum to the E. The description below suggests two walks, both starting from Statenplein, the first including the
Museum van Gijn and the Grote Kerk, the second the Dordrechts Museum.

STATENPLEIN is a square pedestrian precinct, out of the N corner of which
the small Hofstraat leads to the HOF, a pleasant small square, formerly the
courtyard of an Augustinian house; other entrances are by gateways from
Voorstraat and Steegoversloot. In the E wing the *Statenzaal*, today used for
weddings, concerts and suchlike, was where the Estates of the Seven
Provinces met for the first time in July 1572. To the NW of the Hof,
Steegoversloot meets the long Voorstraat, and near this junction (between
186 and 190 Voorstraat) is the *Muntpoortje*, the entrance to the former mint.
You can now follow Voorstraat, with good façades, N for some 400m to
Boomstraat, which leads W across Boombrug, with a view along the

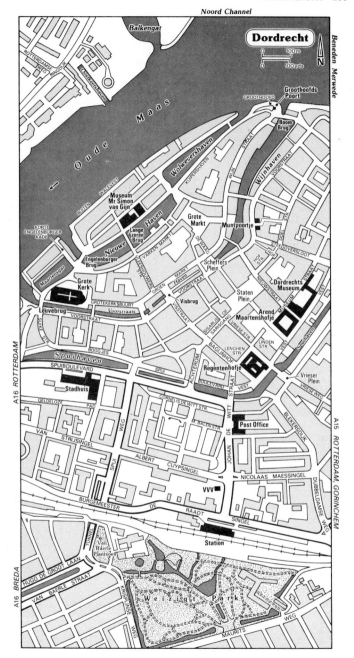

Dordrecht

picturesque Wijnhaven, to the **Groothoofdspoort**, a remnant of the medieval fortifications and once the main entrance to the town. Rebuilt in 1618 and 1692 on the site of an old water-gate, and restored in 1975, this is now a Renaissance gateway decorated with the town arms, symbols, reliefs and a cupola. Boat excursions leave from here (this point, the confluence of the Oude Maas, the Beneden Merwede, and the Noord, claims to be Europe's busiest river junction, passed daily by some 1500 craft).

The return southwards is by Wijnstraat, with more good façades, to SCHEFFERSPLEIN where there is a statue to the painter Ary Scheffer. The small Visbrug, a short distance SW, crosses the main canal of the inner town—Wijnhaven to the N and Voorstraatshaven to the S. Here are a monument to the De Witt brothers by Toon Dupuis and, facing the bridge, *De Vergulde Os*, a fine house of c 1525.

From near the Visbrug, Vleeshouwersstraat runs northwards to the Nieuwe Haven which is crossed by Lange IJzerenbrug, beyond which a turn NE along Nieuwe Haven soon reaches the **Museum Mr Simon van Gijn** (Tues–Sat, 10.00 to 17.00; Sun, Holidays, 13.00 to 17.00; upper floor normally open only Wed, Sat, Sun, Holidays) at No. 29, a house built in 1729 for Johan van Neurenberg (1696–1749), burgomaster of Dordrecht in 1747, and occupied by this family until the early 19C. In 1864 the house was acquired by Simon van Gijn (1836–1922), a banker and art collector, who on his death left the house and his collections to the Old Dordrecht Society. Opened as a museum in 1925, the responsibility was taken over by the municipality in 1949.

On the GROUND FLOOR the Entrance Corridor shows ceremonial weapons, tile pictures and clocks, notably a long-case clock (Albert Vreehuys, 1778) which plays music and shows the date, month and phases of the moon. The Salon, or Tapestry Room (left of the entrance), one of the finest in the museum, is hung with 18C tapestries (probably Brussels) and decorated too with allegorical paintings by Adriaan van den Burgh (1693–1733). Additionally there are two unusual tapestry tables, while showcases display 17C and 18C glass. Across the corridor there are two 19C period rooms with adjacent conservatories. The Dining Room, designed by C. Muysken in 1886 in neo-Renaissance style, has mural and ceiling decoration by Willy Martens (1856–1927), the murals imagining the early inhabitants of the Netherlands. The Music, or Garden, Room will attract the connoisseur of musical instruments, especially notable in the collection here being an organ of 1785, restored in 1970. The 18C and 19C paintings here are mainly by artists of the Dordrecht School; they include a landscape by Jacob van Strij and a portrait of a child by Abraham van Strij.

At the end of the corridor is the Kitchen, with its varied utensils and well-stocked china cupboards arranged as it would have been in c 1800. Note the ingenious syringe for cleaning windows, and how the table and chairs stand on wood so as to be clear of the cold stone floor (nevertheless foot-warmers still seem to have been a requirement).

The Staircase and Gallery are hung with 17C portraits of the De Witt family, and here too is a painting of the Regents of the Orphanage by Adriaan van den Burgh (1732).

On the FIRST FLOOR, along the Corridor, the De Witt portraits continue into the 18C. In the Velouté Room, opposite the top of the stairs and so called because of its velouté wall-hangings of c 1700, the star feature is the chimney-piece with a painting by Dionys van Nijmegen. Also in this room are portraits of Dordrecht magistrates by Jan van Ravesteyn and a rare brass chandelier of the early 17C by Hans Rogier of Amsterdam. The Study, on the left at the end of the corridor, has been left virtually untouched since the days of Simon van Gijn, of whom two portraits hang here. One shows him at the age of 21; in another, by Willy Sluiter, he is in his later years. And a portrait of his wife stands here on an easel. The Renaissance Room, on the right at the end of the corridor, has as its main feature a Renaissance chimney-piece of c 1550 from the Kloveniersdoelen (the House of the Arquebusiers), with a carved wooden frieze (the Wild Men) showing primitive battle scenes, based on a print by the German artist Barthel Beham (1502–40) and said to have been carved in the studio of Jan Terwen, the artist of the choir stalls in the Grote Kerk.

The SECOND FLOOR contains miscellaneous material such as ship models, silver, a case of dolls, a room of toys and models, some particularly good dolls' houses including one of three floors with late 18C interiors, and an interesting maquette of Dordrecht in 1544.

From the museum follow Nieuwe Haven back SW to the Engelenburger-brug. Across this the short Korte Engelenburgerkade ends at a gateway, in origin 1652, beside the Oude Maas.

The **Grote Kerk** (May–Sept: Tues–Sat, 10.00 to 12.00, 14.00 to 16.00; otherwise tours at 10.30 on first and third Saturday of each month), almost immediately S of Engelenburgerbrug, was possibly founded as a chapel in c 1064. What is more certain is that the Lady Chapel was founded before 1285, that the massive tower was begun in 1339, and that most of the present building dates from 1460 to 1502, the period immediately following a disastrous fire of 1457. The builder was Evert Spoorwater of Antwerp, the style being a simplified and spacious development of Brabant Gothic. The Tower (72m; *view), surmounted by four rather inappropriate clocks, is the main feature of the exterior. At the top visitors can see the bells and clock works of 1626; the carillon of 49 bells is usually played on Fridays from 11.00 to noon and on Saturdays from 14.00 to 15.00.

The church is one of the largest in the Netherlands; the nave is 108m long and over 24m high. The choir and nave are surrounded by 23 chapels. The Renaissance *choir stalls are the most important feature of the interior; the work of Jan Terwen between 1539 and 1542, they are the only surviving furnishing from before 1572, the year in which the church became Protestant. The misericords, depicting biblical events, proverbs, everyday scenes, etc., merit particular attention. Above the stalls are battered reliefs, depicting (N) the entry of Charles V into Dordrecht, Roman cavalry, and the story of Mucius Scaevola, the hero of legend who volunteered to kill Lars Porsena who was besieging Rome, but slew his secretary instead; captured and threatened with death, he held his hand in a fire until it was burnt away, an act which so impressed Lars Porsena that he freed Scaevola and withdrew from Rome. Above is a carved children's procession. The panels on the S side depict the Triumph of the Church and the Eucharist. In the N choir aisle there are two 15C frescoes, between these being an interestingly worded English memorial to John Weston, killed in action against the French in 1793. Also worth attention in the church are, at the E end, three windows (by F., A., and J.A. Stoop, 1909) depicting the St Elisabeth Flood of 1421, the fire of 1457 which virtually destroyed the church, and the taking by surprise of Dordrecht in 1480 by Jan van Egmond and 150 English soldiers; the marble pulpit of 1756, with a magnificent wooden canopy by Jan van den Linden; and (W end) the organ built in 1671 by Nicolaas van Hage (mechanism of 1859 by W. Kam).

The second suggested walk, starting from Statenplein, follows Nieuwstraat

SE to Museumstraat, with, a short way left, the ***Dordrechts Museum** (Tues–Sat, 10.00 to 17.00; Sun, Holidays, 13.00 to 17.00), a gallery set in pleasant grounds and with permanent collections of paintings spanning the 17C to the present day. The gallery is also known for its programmes of temporary exhibitions of both older and modern art. Locally born artists are well represented in both the permanent collection and at the temporary exhibitions.

The gallery is on two levels with, in principle, the permanent collection in Rooms 3 to 10, while Rooms 1, 2, 11 and 12 are reserved for the temporaries. The pictures are moved around from time to time but seem unlikely to stray far.

**Room 3**. Several works by *Jacob Cuyp*, including portraits of two worthy and elaborately ruffed ladies. **Room 4** is devoted to the Dordrecht native, *Aelbert Cuyp*, perhaps particularly noteworthy being his Resting riders in a landscape. In **Room 5** the Olympus Ceiling is attributed to *Arnold Houbraken*, while *Jan van Goyen*'s *View of Dordrecht of 1651, providing a lively glimpse of 17C activity on the river, is the best known of the paintings. **Room 6**. *Cornelis Bisschop*: An Interior. *Nicolaes Maes*: Self-portrait; Children in a landscape; Portrait of Jacob de Witt, father of the statesmen brothers; *The Eavesdropper, a well observed and charming scene in an elegant interior.

You should now return to the main staircase (near Room 2), half-way up which stretches a large (7m long) View of Dordrecht by *Abraham Willaerts*, a view looking across the bustling river scene and showing the 17C town stretching from the Groothoofdspoort to the Grote Kerk. Here too on the stairs there are groups by *Samuel van Hoogstraten* who, as well as being a painter and training under Rembrandt (as did the Dortenaars *Nicholas Maes* and *Ferdinand Bol*), was also a writer on art.

In **Room 7** the emphasis is on *Ary Scheffer*, born in Dordrecht but schooled and active in Paris. Works include a portrait of Chopin, a self-portrait, and two portraits of the artist's mother, one of them on her deathbed. In this room, too, are works by *Jozef Israels*, *Abraham van Strij*, and *Jacob van Strij*. Also two interesting pictures by *A.J. Lamme* showing Ary Scheffer at work in Paris, with, in his studio, some of the pictures now hanging in this room. **Room 8**. *Cornelis Springer*: The Church of St Bavo at Haarlem. *A.H. Bakker Korff*: Two charming small works, The Secret and The Festival of 3rd October. **Room 9** shows several typical Hague School works, among the artists being *Anton Mauve*, *Jacob Maris* and *Jozef Israels* (Midday meal at the inn). **Room 10**. *Fantin Latour*: Vase with tea roses. *Isaac Israels*: several works, including *Modiste in a park. *Jan Toorop*: Portraits. *A. Mancini*: some typical portraits of character.

From the Dordrechts Museum you follow Museumstraat SW and soon pass *Arend Maartenshofje*, a hospice with a Renaissance portal of 1625. Lindenstraat and Lenghenstraat, continuing SW, reach Bagijnhof, a main shopping street; and immediately to the SE is the doorway (1775) of the *Regentenhofje*.

A small road SE out of Dordrecht through *Dubbeldam* in 6km reaches a car ferry across the Nieuwe Merwede. To the S of the ferry a signposted nature walk has been laid out along the river bank, a district known locally as the Zuidhollandse Biesbos. For the *Biesbos* proper, across the river, see Rte 19.

For Dordrecht to Breda and Antwerp, see Rte 18A; to Gorinchem and Nijmegen, see Rtes 12A and 25.

# 13 Rotterdam to Middelburg and Vlissingen (Flushing)

This Route, in three sections, crosses the island-peninsulas and wide waters of the unusual and interesting delta region, made up in roughly equal parts of the provinces of Zuid Holland and Zeeland. The first two sections (A and B) describe alternative routes from Rotterdam to Middelburg and Vlissingen. The third (C), starting from Vlissingen, makes a circuit of western Walcheren.

The DELTA PLAN. Despite progressive building of dikes, the flat low-lying delta lands of the Rhine, Maas, and Scheldt have since earliest times suffered disastrous flooding. Among the worst of the floods were the St Elisabeth flood of 1421, which destroyed 72 villages and drowned 10,000 people, and, in modern times, the tragedy of February 1953 when 1850 people lost their lives, 48,000 homes were damaged, many irreparably, and huge areas of the country's most fertile land went under salt water. The islands of Goeree-Overflakkee, Schouwen-Duiveland, Tholen, and St Philipsland were submerged as the result of 67 large and hundreds of small breaches in the dikes, the in-flooding tide depositing sand, salt and mud which killed crops and trees. Urgent work on the major breaches closed one of the worst (at Schelphoek on Schouwen) by August, and by November the last, at Ouwerkerk in the SE of Duiveland, had been repaired. But it was not until around the end of the decade that all the damage had been made good.

Out of this disaster grew the Delta Plan, approved by parliament in 1957, the aim of which was to dam all the delta inlets except for the Nieuwe Waterweg in the N and the Westerschelde (the estuary of the Scheldt) in the S. The order of damming was to be the Veersedam in the S between Walcheren and Noord Beveland, the Haringvlietdam in the N between Voorne and Goeree, the Brouwersdam between Goeree and Schouwen and, finally, widest of all (9km), the Oosterscheldekering between Schouwen and Noord Beveland. During the 1970s, however, important environmental considerations, notably the ecological effects of sealing off the Oosterschelde, including the effect on the important oyster and mussel beds, led to a major change of plan under which this inlet would be closed only in emergency. To achieve this it was decided to construct a costly and elaborate storm-surge barrier rather than the simple, but long, dam previously planned. The completion of this Oosterscheldekering in 1986 also marked the completion of the Delta Plan.

Those interested in the detail of the Delta Plan should visit the **Delta Expo** on the Oosterscheldekering (Rte 13B below).

## A. Via Haringvlietbrug and Zierikzee

Total distance 103km. 24km **Haringvlietbrug**—13km *Oude Tonge*—20km **Zierikzee**—4km **Zeelandbrug**—11km *Zandkreekdam*—5km **Goes**—20km **Middelburg**—6km **Vlissingen (Flushing)**.

Leave Rotterdam (see Rte 10) by the Maastunnel for motorway A29 which (*8km* from the Maastunnel) crosses below the Oude Maas by the *Hei-*

*nenoordtunnel*. A worthwhile short diversion can be made to **Heinenoord**, on the S shore of the Oude Maas just W of the motorway. Here the 18C *Hof van Assendelft* (Tues–Fri, 14.00 to 17.00; Sat, 10.00 to 12.00, 14.00 to 17.00) houses a good regional museum of the Hoekse Waard, a section being an adjacent farmstead (Hofstede Oost Leeuwenstein) with an old schoolroom and shop. The motorway continues S between the districts of BEIJERLAND (W; the word means 'Bavaria' and the district is named after Sabina of Bavaria, wife of Lamoral Count Egmont) and HOEKSE WAARD (E) to reach (*16km*) the **Haringvlietbrug**, opened in 1964 and 1222m in length. The clearance is 14 metres, but the bridge is opened for larger shipping. From the bridge there are fine views to the NW up the broad Haringvliet, and to the E past Willemstad along the Hollands Diep. The S end of the bridge, where there is a road fork, is in a corner of the province of Noord Brabant.

From the road fork the motorway leading SE crosses some of the largest inland-water locks in Europe, just to the E of which is the attractive small town of *Willemstad* (see Rte 18B).

This Route bears W along a dike, immediately re-entering the province of Zuid Holland and reaching the district of OVERFLAKKEE which with GOEREE to the NW (see Rte 13B) is known for its large fields of gladioli. In *13km* you reach *Oude Tonge*.

**Middelharnis** (14,500 inhab.), 7km N, the chief place of Overflakkee, has a *Stadhuis* of 1639 designed by Arent van 's Gravesande, and here too is the *Haringvliet Expo* (April–Oct: daily 10.00 to 17.00) explaining the Haringvliet aspect of the Delta Plan. In the adjoining village of *Sommelsdijk* there is a district museum (May–Oct: Tues–Sat, 14.00 to 17.00; also Wed, 10.00 to 12.00).

Continuing SW this Route crosses the 6km-long **Grevelingendam** (linked since 1986 to St Philipsland, see Rte 18B) and enters the province of Zeeland, the district here being DUIVELAND. Immediately S on the shore, *Bruinisse* is known for the culture of mussels and as a centre for water sports. There are also two modest museums; the Oudheidkamer (Antiquities Room) at Oudestraat 27, and the Visserij en Oorlogsmuseum (Fishing. The Second World War) at Molenstraat 44.

*20km* **Zierikzee** (10,000 inhab. VVV, Havenpark 29) is a very ancient small place with several medieval and other old buildings. Local costume is often worn on market day (Thursday).

**History.** Perhaps founded as long ago as 800, Zierikzee flourished partly through its geographical situation at the crossing of the shipping routes between England and Brabant and Flanders and Holland, and partly because it was able to satisfy the demand for salt, won from the sandy flats around Schouwen. A charter was granted in 1228, and the 13C and 14C saw a steady expansion of the harbour and its surrounds and the first construction of the town's gates.

Many times beseiged, Zierikzee quickly became a strongly fortified place. One main siege was that of 1575 by Requesens and his Spanish troops who waded neck-deep across the Keeten channel under a murderous fire from the United Provinces' fleet. Admiral Boisot, who had relieved Leiden, lost his life in an attempt to raise the siege, and eventually Requesens forced his way in.

The harbour originally reached well into the town, its course now marked by the Oude Haven, still with water, and then the consecutive long rectangular streets Havenpark and Havenplein. Either side of the Oude

Haven entrance there survive two water-gates, the *Noordhavenpoort* with a façade of 1559, and the *Zuidhavenpoort* (15C; restored). Along both Havenpark and Havenplein there are several 17–19C façades.

The N side of Havenpark-Havenplein offers the most rewarding short walk which, starting from VVV, soon reaches the *White Swan* (Havenpark 1, which is where Havenpark and Havenplein meet), a modest but attractive frontage of 1658; the frontage is also interesting for the fact that it collapsed during the 1953 floods, later being rebuilt largely with the original stonework. The *Gasthuiskerk*, just beyond, originally the chapel of St Elisabeth Gasthuis and dating from the second half of the 14C, was enlarged in 1651 and given a gallery, the lower part of which now serves as a part of the market.

A short way further, on the same side and just where Havenplein forks to become Mol, is *'s Gravensteen*, originally built as a jail in the 14C but much altered in the 16C and for a while becoming an official residence. Today, though small, the building is particularly pleasing with its stepped façade, Gothic gable and basket-barred windows. The interior—impressive for its massive beams and other woodwork—now houses the local *Maritime Museum* (May–Sept: Mon–Sat, 10.00 to 17.00), a name which is rather misleading because although the theme is certainly maritime, with, mainly, ship models, many visitors will find the building itself of interest. It was once a jail, and doors with peepholes, scribbled and carved graffiti and suchlike recall the grim old prison in which today's visitor can still see the minute cagelike cells and the battered, primitive loo.

The *Stadhuis*, just W in Meelstraat and with a sumptuous wedding cake spire, dates in part back to service as a meat hall in the 14C but is essentially enlargements and rebuildings of 1550–54 and 1775–79. Today it houses the *Gemeentemuseum* (May–Sept: Mon–Fri, 10.00 to 12.00, 13.30 to 16.30) with local antiquities.

Poststraat, to the S and parallel to Meelstraat, leads W past the post office to the *Grote Kerk*, dedicated to the English missionary Lebuinus (or Liafwin), who was martyred in Friesland in c 776. The church was rebuilt in 1848, but alongside stands the huge unfinished belfry, the *Monstertoren* (69m), begun in 1454 and the work of three generations of the Keldermans family of Mechelen (Malines) in Belgium (Andries, Antoon, and Rombout). According to some records a height of 207m was planned, and it is of interest that a considerable height (167m) was also planned by the Keldermans for the cathedral at Mechelen, although work in fact stopped at 97m. Opposite the church, across Kerkhof, the *Weeshuis* (mid June–Aug: Mon–Fri, 10.00 to 17.00), with a façade of c 1740, has a Regents' Hall with gilt-leather wall-hanging, pictures, ceramics etc. On the N edge of the town the *Nobeltoren* is a gate of the 15C.

For the unusual and attractive ring-villages of Dreischor, Noordgouwe, and Zonnemaire, and the interesting small town of *Brouwershaven*, all to the N of Zierikzee, see Rte 13B.

*4km*. The graceful *Zeelandbrug* (N end), spanning the Oosterschelde and the longest bridge in Europe (5022 metres), stands on 54 piers and rises to a height of 17m above the water. At its S end (*5km*) the bridge reaches the small district of NOORD BEVELAND, formerly an island but now joined to Walcheren; the economy of the district is both agricultural and recreational, the latter because of the increasing development of water sports facilities along the Veersemeer on the S and also at *Colijnsplaat* just W of the S end of the bridge. It was near Colijnsplaat that Roman remains of the Nehallenia cult were found (now in the museums at Leiden and Middelburg). *6km.* The narrow Zandkreek is crossed by the *Zandkreekdam* (1959), beyond being the large district of ZUID BEVELAND, stretching some 45km W to E from Walcheren to the border of the province of Noord Brabant; along the whole of this length run a railway and the motorway A58. The economy is part agricultural, including gardens and orchards, part industrial (SW), and part recreational.

*5km* **Goes** (31,000 inhab.) is the chief town of Zuid Beveland, historically of some interest for being one of the first places to be taken by the Sea Beggars in 1572. In a more recent war it was liberated on 28 November 1944 by 2nd Canadian Division, advancing along the peninsula from the east. Several places of interest are close to the *Grote Kerk*, dating from 1427 but altered and refitted after a fire in 1618; the main feature of the interior is the organ of c 1642 on which concerts are still given. The *Museum van Noord en Zuid Beveland* (Tues–Fri, 10.00 to 16.00, Sat, 11.00 to 16.00) is at Singelstraat 13, immediately S of the church, and just W of the museum can be seen two portals, one of 1655, marking the entrances to an alms-house. To the W of the church, beside a smaller church, the *Slot Oostende* inn stands on the site of a castle of Jacqueline of Bavaria, builder of the town's walls, parts of which still survive. The *Stadhuis* (1775) is at the S end of the large rectangular Grote Markt which has some good façades.

GOES TO WOENSDRECHT. 32km east. There is a choice of road, motorway or railway, all of which run along the narrow isthmus of reclaimed land which links the former island of Zuid Beveland to the mainland and separates the Oosterschelde (N) from the Scheldt estuary proper (S). It was westward along this isthmus that 2nd Canadian Division advanced in November 1944, taking Krabbendijke and Rilland by the 25th, Goes by the 28th, and the next day linking up with the British 52nd Division (see below). **Kapelle**, 5km SE of Goes, is at the centre of a fruit growing district. The Reformed Church (13–14C) is worth visiting for its many medieval •grave-slabs, including especially (east end) the massive slab of Philibert van Tuijll and his wife, and, along the south wall, a row of slabs many of which bear remarkably clear figures meriting study for their features and clothing.

Beyond the *Kanaal door Zuid Beveland*, crossed by bridges and a motor-way tunnel, the land narrows to the isthmus, some 4km in width. To the S is *Kruiningen*, from where a car ferry crosses to Zeeland Flanders.

*Wemeldinge*, at the N end of the canal, and *Yerseke* on the N shore, are water sports and boating centres, the latter also being important for shell-fish culture (mussels and oysters), an industry which can now survive thanks to the decision not to close off the Oosterschelde. A distance of 16km separates the above canal and the more important *Schelde-Rijn Verbind-ing*, the great canal completed in 1975 which links Antwerp in Belgium with the network of waterways to the north. From the road bridge, looking N, you can see the *Kreekrak* locks which incorporate an advanced system for keeping fresh and salt water separated. *Bath*, on the shore to the S, was where a small British force landed as part of the operation of 1809. The canal crosses into Belgium 6km S of the bridge. You reach the border of the province of Noord Brabant 2km beyond the canal; *Woensdrecht* is 5km further on (for this area, see Rte 18B).

ZAK VAN ZUID BEVELAND is the name sometimes given to the remote, quiet district stretching S and SW between Goes and the Westerschelde. At

*Nisse*, in the centre of the area, the church of c 1425 contains old murals and wooden figures of the Apostles, while at *Baarland*, at the SE corner, there are foundations of a 14C castle. (It was between Ellewoudsdijk and Hoedekenskerke that 52nd Division landed—from Terneuzen—on 26 November 1944, then advancing N to meet 2nd Canadian Division coming in along the isthmus from the E, see above.) The roads westward from Goes in c 14km cross into the district (formerly island) of WALCHEREN, divided into two unequal parts by the Kanaal door Walcheren linking Vlissingen (Flushing) and Veere. The SE, with the towns of Vlissingen and Middelburg, is in part industrial, the interior is agricultural, while the coasts, with dunes, woodland, beaches, and since 1959–61 the Veersemeer, are an increasingly popular recreational area. In history Walcheren is perhaps best known for the unsuccessful British expedition of 1809 under Admiral Strachan and Lord Chatham, aimed primarily at Antwerp and designed to encourage the Netherlands to follow the Austrian example and revolt against Napoleon. Vlissingen was taken, and most of Walcheren, at that time fever-laden swamp, was occupied, but with the defeat of the Austrians at Wagram the expedition had to withdraw. In 1944 Antwerp and the opening of the Scheldt were again the Allied objectives, this meaning that the Germans had to be driven out of Walcheren, flooding being the obvious tactic. By the end of October the RAF had made several breaches in the dikes—notably at Westkapelle, Veere, Vlissingen, and Rammekens just E of the last—and most of Walcheren was flooded, remaining so for 13 months. The island was taken by forces landing at Vlissingen and West-kapelle (1 November), these meeting up at Middelburg and Veere on 6 November with those which had advanced from Goes (see above). By the end of 1944 work began on repairing the breaches, the last gap (Rammekens) being closed in February 1946. The damage, though, was immense and it was not until 1954 that the task of replanting and reconstruction was completed.

*20km* (from Goes) **MIDDELBURG** (39,000 inhab.), the capital of the province of Zeeland, is a dignified old town on the W side of the Kanaal door Walcheren and surrounded by a winding moat (the Vest), now pleasantly laid out with gardens and walks and (W and SW) two windmills. German bombing of 17 May 1940 destroyed much of the centre of the town, but many of the buildings have been rebuilt to their former style. Local costume is worn at the Thursday market.

**Centre.** Markt. The main streets, pedestriansised, are Lange Delft and Nieuwe Burg.

**VVV.** Markt.

**Post Office.** Lange Noordstraat 48 (N of Markt).

**Station.** On E side of the Kanaal door Walcheren.

**Boats.** Excursions from opposite the station.

**History.** Although there was an abbey here as early as c 1120, Middelburg, perhaps because of its isolated situation, especially as long as Walcheren was an island, makes little appearance in early history. It was known for its trade in wool and cloth, and in 1574 it was taken by the Sea Beggars under Admiral Boisot. Thus an early adherent to the northern Protestant cause, the town's main focus, its great abbey, was soon dissolved. During the Walcheren expedition of 1809 Middelburg was briefly held by the English. On 17 May 1940 German air attack destroyed a large part of the inner town.

Robert Browne (1550–1633), leader of the Separatist Puritans (or Brownists), precursors of the Congregationalists, after being imprisoned three times emigrated with his followers to Middelburg, where he stayed from 1582–84.

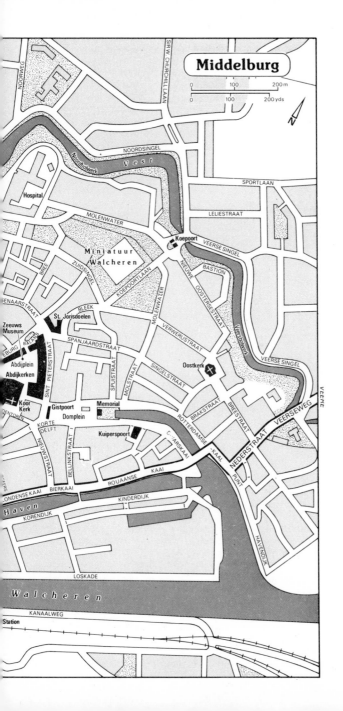

# Middelburg

The inner and oldest part of the town is encircled by a tight ring of streets (diameter 3–400m), the SW section of which is the MARKT, with, on its NW side, the **Stadhuis** (see main entrance notice for tour times), the architectural history of which spans 1452 to the present day. The Gothic façade (in origin 1452–58), facing the Markt and carrying 25 statues of counts and countesses of Holland and Zeeland, was the work of various members of the Keldermans family of Mechelen; the distinctive tower with its pinnacles and the former meat hall, now used for exhibitions, were added between 1506 and 1520; in 1670, and again in 1780–84, additions in a classical style were made along Lange Noordstraat; finally German bombing in 1940 almost completely destroyed the building, restoration following after the war. The interior contains some good tapestries and furniture, and a few interesting paintings.

A turning to the right off Vlasmarkt, the street leading W by the Stadhuis, leads to the *Engelse Kerk* of the late 15C. Originally the church of the Cellite or Alexian Brothers, the building became a tapestry workshop in 1592 (of Jan de Maeght; see also Zeeuws Museum below), an English church from 1629 to 1921, and is now used by the Dutch Reformed Church.

Pottenmarkt, which becomes Lange Viele, runs SW out of the Markt and soon reaches a canal, on the other side of which stands the large *Kloveniers-doelen*, built in Flemish Renaissance style in 1607–11 and until 1787 the house of the Arquebusiers (note the figure at the top). The building was then occupied by the East Indies Company, but became a military hospital from 1795 until 1957. Restored in 1969, it is now used for art exhibitions.

Nieuwe Burg, a pedestrian only shopping street leading NE out of the Markt, soon reaches Groenmarkt with the extensive buildings of the ABDIJ, an abbey founded in c 1120 by Canons Regular and occupied by Premonstratensians from 1128 until its dissolution in 1574, after which it was first used to house the Prince of Orange's staff and then, later, used by the Council of Zeeland. The **Abdijkerken** (14–16C, rebuilt after 1940), three churches in one, have a high octagonal Tower (84m; 230 steps), originally built in the early 14C but repeatedly burnt down, the last occasion being in 1940 when in its flaming crash it wrecked the churches below. Known as 'Lange Jan', the tower carries a large Imperial crown (late March–Sept: Mon–Sat, 10.00 to 17.00). The churches are normally entered at the *Nieuwe Kerk*, the main feature of which is the superb organ case of 1692 by Johannes Duyschot; loaned by the Rijksmuseum, Amsterdam, the case now houses a modern organ. The *Wandel Kerk* contains the magnificent tomb by Rombout Verhulst of the Zeeland brothers Jan and Cornelis Evertsen, admirals killed in the English war of 1666; protected by sandbags this fine monument survived the disaster of 1940. From the Wandel Kerk a huge, high arch (21m) leads to the lower part of the tower. In the *Koor Kerk* there is another famous organ, the so-called Nicolai organ, the case of which was built between 1478 and 1481 and renovated in 1580. Count William II (King of the Romans, died 1256) is buried in this church.

To the E of the churches the *Gistpoort* (or Blauwpoort), dating from 1512 but restored in 1912, stands at the head of the broad Damplein. From here there is access to ABDIJPLEIN, surrounded by post-1940 buildings on the site of the former abbey domestic buildings and now mainly provincial government offices. The cloisters here are of the 15–16C, off which is the reading room of the Provincial Library (no adm. for tourists) occupying the former chapter house.

The **Zeeuws Museum** (Tues–Fri, 10.00 to 17.00, Sat–Mon, 13.30 to 17.00; but seasonal variations), with collections started in 1769, has since 1972 been housed in a series of rooms, thought to have once been abbey dormitories, along the NW side of Abdijplein. Red arrows point the way, starting with the cellar rooms 1 to 3. **Room 1** shows Roman Nehallenia cult altars (the name being that of a local Roman goddess, protectress of merchants and sailors) found near Domburg in 1647 and Colijnsplaat in 1970; **Room 2** prehistoric material, but with also some medieval exhibits; **Room 3** domestic ceramics, decorated bricks, tiles and a medieval sarcophagus discovered serving as a cattle trough.

**Room 4** is called the Curio Room, its principal exhibit being a shell cupboard, one of the museum's oldest possessions (1775) and the achievement of a Zierikzee man called Job Baster whose passion it was to collect shells and stick them on to his dresser. The result may not be to everybody's taste but says much for Baster's industry and skill. A contrast is provided by another early exhibit here, an Egyptian mummy acquired in 1782—an early date for interest in such things. In **Room 5** a mammoth has pride of place, though after 40,000 years there is not a lot of him left. Also shown here are ancient animal skulls and a collection of shells.

A spiral staircase now ascends to **Room 6**, the Tapestry Gallery, with seven tapestries woven locally (some by Jan de Maeght whose workshop was in the Engelse Kerk) between 1594 and 1604 and depicting, with remarkable detail, dramatic sea battles which were fought off Zeeland. While the tapestries are being restored in turn—an undertaking likely to last until well into the 1990s—other loan tapestries are shown. **Rooms 7 and 8** are the 17C and 18C rooms, the former with a powerful portrait of Admiral de Ruyter by Ferdinand Bol (1667), the latter showing porcelain (including Delft) and silver.

Stairs now lead up to **Room 9**, the grandly timbered attic, with two principal themes. One is concerned with the growing and processing of madder, much used for its red dye and once one of Zeeland's most important products. The second and larger theme is regional and local costume, shown either simply as such or incorporated in a scene; a baker's shop (Noord Beveland costume of 1900) or a Walcheren farmhouse interior of 1915. The earliest costume shown is a bridal outfit of c 1800, interesting not only as costume but also for its small size, a reminder of the gap between past and present nutritional standards. **Room 10**, once the abbey granary, is three flights below and generally used for temporary exhibitions.

You can leave Abdijplein on its N side by a doorway of 1679 leading to the small open area called BALANS, on the N side of which is *St Jorisdoelen*, the façade of the guild house of the civic guard company of St George. Originally built in 1582, the house was destroyed in 1940 and rebuilt in 1970; the façade bears the arms of Middelburg, Zeeland, and St George. In Spanijaardstraat, leading away E, there are several good restorations (c 1970). Wagenaarstraat curves W to become Hofplein, on the S side of which are the *Law Courts* (since 1876) in a mansion of 1765. You can return to the Markt by Lange Noordstraat, in which Jacob Cats, the poet and Council Pensionary, lived from 1603–21 at No. 31, and Jacob Roggeveen, the first European discoverer of Easter Island in 1722, at No. 37.

Other places of interest are to the N and E around the inner side of the Vest moat. From the Markt, Lange Delft forms the SE arc of the old inner town. Towards the end of St Jansstraat, leading S off Lange Delft, stands the attractive former *Vismarkt* of 1559. Lange Delft becomes Korte Delft and reaches the broad DAMPLEIN, formed in 1971 by the demolition of

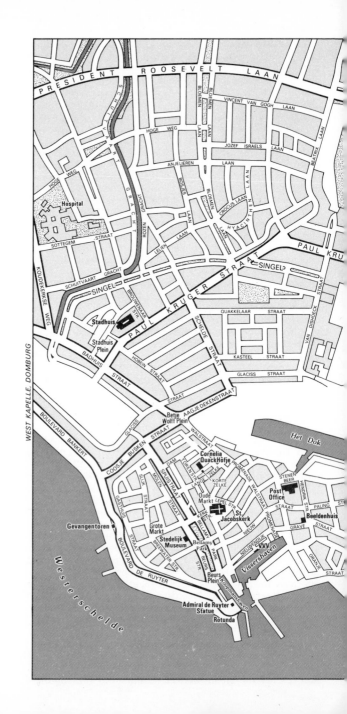

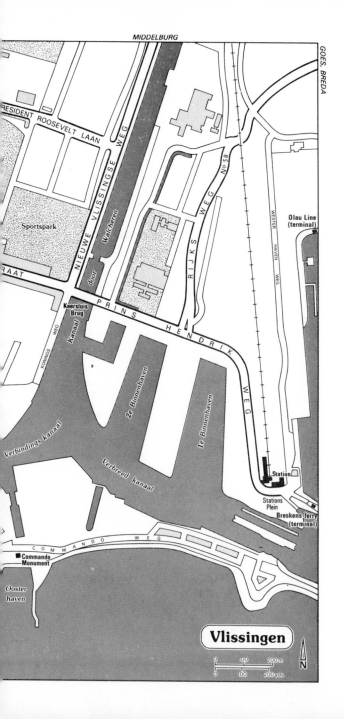

MIDDELBURG

GOES, BREDA

PRESIDENT ROOSEVELT LAAN

NIEUWE VLISSINGSE WEG

Wachtoren

RIJKS WEG

No 58

WESTER HAVEN WEG

Olau Line
(terminal)

Sportspark

door

...RAAT

PRINS HENDRIK WEG

Keersluis
Brug

KONINGS WEG

Kanaal

2e Binnenhaven

1e Binnenhaven

Verbindings kanaal

Verbreed kanaal

Station

Stations
Plein

Breskens ferry
(terminal)

COMMANDO WEG

■ Commando
Monument

Ooster
haven

**Vlissingen**

0    100    200m
0    100    200yds

N

houses which until then divided it into two streets. For the *Gistpoort*, at the W end, see above. At its E end, with a memorial (H.J. Etienne, 1937) to Queen Emma, second wife of King William III and mother of Queen Wilhelmina, the road splits either side of a small harbour inlet, to the S being the *Kuiperspoort* of 1586, a quaint group of warehouses and a gatehouse once occupied by the Guild of the Coopers. To the N of the water, near the Vest, stands the octagonal, domed *Oostkerk*, erected in 1647–67 and the joint achievement of Bartolomeus Drijfhout, Pieter Post, and Arent van 's Gravesande: this is one of the earliest Protestant churches in the Netherlands to have been built as such. You can now follow the Vest northwards to the *Koepoort*, dating from 1735 and the only surviving old town gate. Opposite is the entrance to **Miniatuur Walcheren** (late March–mid Oct: daily, 09.30 to 17.00 or 18.00 in July and Aug), a large model of Walcheren (7000 sq m; scale one-twentieth) showing villages, important buildings, roads, harbours, dikes, dunes and beaches, etc.

You reach *6km* **Vlissingen (Flushing.** 46,000 inhab.; VVV, Nieuwendijk 15) by the road heading due S out of Middelburg along the W bank of the Kanaal door Walcheren. The town has large shipbuilding yards and is an important port, with a car ferry service (Olau Line) to Sheerness in Kent and a busy vehicle ferry service, the main link with Zeeland Flanders, across the mouth of the Westerschelde to Breskens. It is also a popular family holiday resort, with many hotels, a fine promenade, sandy beaches and many points from which the Scheldt shipping can be watched. After war damage the town has been rebuilt to a spacious, open plan, the modern centre being Bellamy Park and the stretch to the N.

**History.** Vlissingen was of little importance until the 15C, but Charles V in 1556 (from West Souburg on the N outskirts) and Philip II in 1559 chose it as their port of embarkation from the Netherlands, the latter leaving with bitter words against his Netherlandish subjects and the alleged faithlessness of his representative, William the Silent. In 1572 Vlissingen was one of the first towns to revolt against Spain, and from 1585–1616 it was, with Brielle, held by England as a 'cautionary town'. The British expedition of 1809 under Lord Chatham succeeded after a destructive bombardment in capturing and briefly holding the town. Modern Vlissingen dates from the arrival of the railway in 1872, and the completion of the docks in 1873. The cross-Channel packet service started in 1875, since running to a series of ports (Sheerness, Queenborough, Folkestone, Harwich).

The harbour installations were badly damaged by German bombing in May 1940. In the Allied operations of October and November 1944 the dikes at Vlissingen and Rammekens were breached by RAF bombing, and on 1 November No. 4 Commando of 52nd Division landed from Breskens and secured a bridgehead, No. 155 Infantry Brigade immediately following to clear the town and capture the German headquarters.

**Natives.** Admiral Michiel de Ruyter (1607–76), the greatest of the admirals of the United Provinces, was born here the son of a ropemaker. Constantin Guys (1802–92), the painter; something of a soldier of fortune, he went to Greece with Byron and acted as war correspondent for the 'Illustrated London News'.

The main town lies behind the adjoining KOOPMANSHAVEN and VISSERSHAVEN. The *Rotunda* by these small docks, with a statue of Admiral De Ruyter (1841), offers a magnificent view across the Westerschelde, with sea traffic to and from Antwerp, pilot boats exchanging the sea and river pilots, and the ferries crossing to Breskens. From here a sequence of coastal boulevards named after admirals (De Ruyter, Bankert, and Evertsen) run NW beside beaches, conspicuous on Boulevard de Ruyter being the *Gevangentoren*, a prison tower of 1699.

In Beursplein, at the head of Koopmanshaven, No. 2 (in origin 1635), now a restaurant, was once the commercial exchange. In BELLAMY PARK beyond, the name commemorating the local poet Jacob Bellamy (1757–86), there are some 16C façades, a statue of Frans Naerebout (1749–1818), a gallant pilot and lifesaver, and a fountain honouring the writers Betje Wolff (1738–1804) and Aagje Deken (1741–1804).

Bellamy, Wolff, and Deken are all names well known in Dutch literature. *Jacob Bellamy* made his reputation as a patriotic poet. *Betje Wolff* and *Aagje Deken* were friends who collaborated in producing novels in letter form; the two ladies were associated with the 'Verlichting' (Enlightenment).

The *Stedelijk Museum* (June–Sept: Mon–Fri, 10.00 to 17.00; Sat, Sun, 13.00 to 17.00. Sept–May: Mon–Fri, 10.00 to 12.30, 13.30 to 17.00; also Sat in May, 14.00 to 17.00), at Bellamy Park 19, shows local material, notably well displayed tiles; several fine pictures, including a particularly interesting large canvas of the town as it was in 1664 from which several surviving features can be identified, including the Bellamy Park, then largely under water; portraits of local worthies; old maps and plans; and ship models. The museum is also proud of its De Ruyter Room, dominated by a copy of Ferdinand Bol's portrait of the admiral. The foregoing is all from the past, but the important present is also stressed by a large model showing the passage of the Westerschelde—its channels, shallows, lights—from Zeebrugge to Antwerp.

To the NE of the park the *St Jacobskerk* (July and August: Mon–Sat, 10.00 to 12.00, 14.00 to 16.30) is a foundation of 1308 rebuilt after a fire of 1911. On Lange Zelke, to the N of the church across the Oude Markt, there is a modern shopping precinct, while on Korte Zelke, just N of Lange Zelke, the *Cornelia Quackhofje* of 1786 is an almshouse for seamen.

Nieuwendijk skirts the Vissershaven, at the end becoming Gravestraat. In Hendrikstraat, running N off Gravestraat, No. 25 is the *Beeldenhuis*, a curious building of 1735 with many statues. Gravestraat, continuing E, becomes Commandoweg, on the S of which (some 500m from Vissershaven) a memorial honours No. 4 Commando, 52nd Division.

For a circuit of western Walcheren, see Rte 13C.

# B.   Via Haringvlietdam, Brouwersdam and Oosterscheldekering

Total distance 153km (via Brouwershaven and Zierikzee) or 106km (crossing the Oosterscheldekering).—13km *Botlekbrug*—17km **Hellevoetsluis**—9km **Haringvlietdam**—7km **Goedereede**—16km **Scharendijke**—14km **Oosterscheldekering (N)**.
    Then either: 17km **Brouwershaven**—7km **Dreischor**—6km **Zierikzee**—40km **Middelburg**—7km **Vlissingen (Flushing)**.
Or: 16km **Veere**—7km **Middelburg**—7km **Vlissingen (Flushing)**.

For the DELTA PLAN see the introductory paragraphs to Rte 13.

For Rotterdam to (*13km* from S end of Maastunnel) the Botlekbrug (or Botlektunnel), see Rte 10E. Rather over 1km beyond the bridge, turn S to cross the *Hartelkanaal* (see as above), beyond which a turn W along Groene Kruisweg (N218) brings you (*9km* from Botlekbrug) to the **Voornsekanaal**, dug in 1830, the first attempt to stimulate Rotterdam's trade, still flagging after the years of French occupation and Napoleon's Continental System. The canal proved inadequate for its purpose and was superseded in 1872 by the Nieuwe Waterweg. This Route now follows the canal, but first a diversion can be made NW into the district of VOORNE.

The principal town (6km beyond the Voornsekanaal) is **Brielle** or **Den Briel** (15,000 inhab.; VVV, Venkelstraat 3), historic on at least three counts—as the first place to be taken from the Spanish (1572) by the Sea Beggars under Willem de la Marck; as a 'cautionary town' held by the English from 1585 to 1616; and as the birthplace in 1597, during the English period, of Admiral Maarten Tromp. Much of the town is an attractive mix of narrow streets, waterways and 16–18C façades, and in Venkelstraat, at No. 3, the former Waag and prison of 1623 are *VVV* and the *Trompmuseum*, the latter, despite its name, concerned more with the local past than with the admiral (Mon, 09.00 to 12.00, 13.00 to 17.00; Tues, 09.00 to 12.30, 13.30 to 17.30; Wed–Sat, 09.00 to 17.00). The small Brielse Maas river flows through the town and, now, immediately out N into the Brielse Meer (see Rte 10E).

At *Oostvoorne* (5km NW), on the Burcht at the SE of this small town, are the remains of the 12C castle of the lords of Voorne.

*8km* **Hellevoetsluis** (30,000 inhab.; VVV, Oostzanddijk 20) was until the development of Den Helder by Napoleon an important and well defended naval base. The port, now increasingly concerned with pleasure craft, briefly became commercially important with the opening of the canal in 1830 as a main approach to Rotterdam, but this ended in 1872 when the Nieuwe Waterweg was brought into use. It was from Hellevoetsluis that William III embarked for England in 1688. Today the town is a very pleasant and lively small port, strung along either side of the canal and surrounded by fortifications, the older bastions of which have in some places been strengthened by late 19C brickwork. The road through the town cuts through the fortifications on both sides, and from the canal mouth there are wide views up the Haringvliet and of its dam to the NW. The town has an unusual museum, the *Brandweermuseum* at Gallasplein 5, showing three centuries of fire-fighting equipment (Tues–Sat, 10.00 to 16.00; closed March–May).

*9km* **\*Haringvlietdam** (N end). This great dam, over 2km in length and with a complex of huge sluices, was completed in September 1970 and has been described as the 'stopcock of the Netherlands', its function being not only flood prevention as part of the Delta Plan but also the control of the always varying volume of water descending the Rhine and Maas. Formerly, when the volume was low, salt water could enter the estuaries, but now, by keeping the sluices closed, the river waters of the Maas, Waal, and Lek are forced along the Nieuwe Waterweg, pushing the salt water back and at the same time keeping this important channel free of silt. The Haringvliet sluices are only fully opened when the river water volume is high.

Ahead you can now see the huge square tower of (*7km*) **Goedereede**, the tower meriting a visit both for the vista from the top and for the small regional museum which it houses. Goedereede, now no more than a village although still the chief place of the district (formerly island) of GOEREE, was a port as early as the 11C, and became of sufficient importance to receive a charter in 1312. The *Tower* (May–mid Sept: Mon–Wed, Fri, 14.00 to 17.00; Thurs and Sat, 11.00 to 17.00) was built between 1467 and 1512, over the centuries serving as shipping beacon, lighthouse, and church tower. A daunting 134 steps climb past the museum to the door of the carillon control, 20 steps above this are the bells, all modern except for one large one made in 1519 from melted down, older bells. A final 65 steps reach the open top of the tower. Alongside the tower there is a church of 1708, standing on the site of the choir of the earlier church, the surviving buttresses of which link the tower and the present church. Adrian Florisz. (1459–1523), later Pope Adrian VI, was priest here. The nearby windmill dates from 1791.

Approaching (*10km*) the N end of the **Brouwersdam**, several roads, all well signed, lead off to beaches with large car parks. The dam, some 6km in length, crosses the border between the provinces of Zuid Holland and Zeeland, here the district of SCHOUWEN, concerned with agriculture and coastal recreational activities and known for its wooded dunes with a great variety of birds. At (*6km*) **Scharendijke**, a holiday place near the S end of Brouwersdam, there is an Aquarium which is half submerged and thus allows an intimate glimpse of the local marine flora and fauna (week before Easter–mid Oct: daily, 10.00 to 18.00; or 22.00 in July and August). From here too in summer local boat excursions can be made.

This Route now bears W along the S shore of the Brouwershavense Gat, then S to (*5km*) *Renesse*, a quiet holiday place with dunes and a fine beach. Slot Moermond (no adm.), 1km E, dating from c 1513 but restored in 1953, was the residence of the lords of Renesse. *5km* on you reach **Haamstede**, between which and the coast extends a dune and woodland area (*De Boswachterij Westerschouwen*), with waymarked paths; here the 57m-high lighthouse was built in 1837.

*4km* **Oosterscheldekering (N)**. At this point you have a choice between bearing E through the attractive and interesting small towns of Brouwershaven and Zierikzee (a distance of 77km to Vlissingen); or crossing the Oosterscheldekering to reach Vlissingen in 30km. If you opt for the former alternative, you may well decide first to drive along the dam as far as the Delta Expo.

VIA ZIERIKZEE. Follow the small shore road E to *9km Serooskerke*. From here the direct road reaches Zierikzee in 10km, but this Route makes a northerly loop to include the interesting small town of Brouwershaven and the unusual ring-villages beyond.

*8km* **Brouwershaven** (3400 inhab.; VVV, Haven Noordzijde 1) is a town of some character, notably for the way in which the small port penetrates the town centre, the spacious Markt; until the mid 19C the port reached as far as today's bandstand. The town is an ancient place, tracing its origin to 1285 when Count Floris V built a dam across a small river which then flowed into the sea here. In 1582, on the instructions of William the Silent, the place was walled, but it lost both commercial and defensive importance in 1682 when flooding not only seriously damaged the town but also covered the surrounds with silt. In 1820 the last surviving gate was pulled down, but in 1838 the Brouwershavense Gat was dredged and buoyed, thus starting a brief period of prosperity, all too soon ended by the opening of the Nieuwe Waterweg.

In the MARKT, where a number of façades have been restored, a statue (1829) honours the poet and Council Pensionary Jacob Cats (1577–1660) who was born here. The *Stadhuis* has a façade of 1559, though the rear of the building is thought to be considerably older. The large *Grote Kerk*, beyond, is generally considered to have been started in 1293 but there was considerable rebuilding during the 14C and 15C.

To the SE of Brouwershaven there are three unusual and attractive ring-villages, villages of terp origin which cluster in a circle around their churches. The villages are *Zonnemaire*, birthplace of Pieter Zeeman (1865–1943), physicist and Nobel prize winner in 1902; *Noordgouwe*, with a church of 1462; and (*7km*) **Dreischor**, the best of the three. Here the church (1340–1475), with a leaning tower having a curious turret built into it, stands at the centre of a ring of green, a small moat, and a small road. The little Raadhuis dates from 1637. A further *6km* brings you to **Zierikzee**, for which and for the continuation to (*40km*) Middelburg and (*6km*) Vlissingen (Flushing) see Rte 13A.

ACROSS THE OOSTERSCHELDEKERING. As already mentioned under Delta Plan in the introductory paragraphs to this Rte 13, the **Oosterscheldekering** (completed 1986) is the massive storm-surge barrier which for ecological reasons superseded the original plan for a conventional dam. The latter would have sealed off the Oosterschelde; the present barrier permits 85 per cent of natural tidal movement and is closed only when there is a threat from storm or dangerously high tide. In brief the complex comprises two artificial islands, with, in the three channels, 66 massive concrete piers between which are suspended the vital steel gates. A *Delta Expo* complex (including a section of the barrier), with multilingual audiovisual and other presentations covering both the Delta Plan generally, and the Oosterscheldekering in particular, has been set up on the artificial island of Neeltje Jans; there is also an associated boat cruise (large water bus) of some 50 minutes (April–Oct: daily, 10.00 to 17.00; Nov–March: Wed–Sun, 10.00 to 17.00; boat cruises roughly April–Sept).

*16km* (from the N of the dam) **Veere**, see Rte 13C. For (*7km*) Middelburg and (*7km*) Vlissingen, see Rte 13A.

# C.   Circuit of Western Walcheren

The circuit described is clockwise starting from Vlissingen. For most of the way around the coast the road runs inland of a strip of woodland, beyond which are dunes and beaches (ample parking). All places mentioned are small holiday resorts. The military expedition of 1809 has of course left no mark; but the Second World War has left some massive bunkers and, at Westkapelle, a natural feature and memorials.

Total distance 46km.—9km *Zoutelande*—4km **Westkapelle**—6km **Domburg**—8km *Vrouwenpolder*—5km **Veere**—7km **Middelburg**—7km **Vlissingen**.

*9km Zoutelande* where the church has a tower of c 1400. In *4km*, **Westkapelle**, perched, in some weathers bleakly, at the northern tip of the mouth of the Scheldt, was the focus of the operations of autumn 1944, the place where the RAF blasted one of the main breaches through the dikes of Walcheren and, with Vlissingen, the site on 1 November of the Allied landings. The dike was repaired by 3 October the following year, but the creek skirted by the road on the approach to the small town remains as a reminder of the flooding. The tall former church tower, built in the 15C and since 1861 serving as a lighthouse, was the first spot secured in 1944 (monument). In the rectangular town centre a pleasing example of modern statuary shows a robust Dutchman repairing a dike, while a stone set into the Gemeentehuis was laid in 1954 by Rear Admiral A.F. Pugsley who ten years earlier had commanded the Naval Assault Group. From the sea dike, first built in 1540, there is a clear view across the Scheldt as far as the area of Zeebrugge, and here today stands the principal memorial—a tank, and a relief of a Commando—to those who lost their lives in 1944.

Beyond Westkapelle the road briefly rides the dike, offering a more open view into the interior than has hitherto been the case, and on the right before Domburg there are concrete defences.

*6km* **Domburg**, the principal small resort on the coast, is the place at which the Roman Nehallenia cult discoveries were made, the material now shown in the Zeeuws Museum in Middelburg. There is a small *Stadhuis* of 1667 (restored 1946) and Domburg was from 1910–20 the home of the painter Jan Toorop. The town forms a single municipality with *Oostkapelle* (4km E), between the two, beside the main road, being the estate of *Westhove*, the castle (no adm.) of which, with two surviving 15C towers, was the summer residence of the abbots of Middelburg. The woodland grounds are open to walkers and the former orangery of the castle now houses the *Zeeuws Museum Natuurhistorie* (Mon, 10.00 to 16.00), a small museum explaining the flora and fauna of Zeeland. After *8km Vrouwenpolder*, a small resort close to the S end of the Veersedam (1961), is well situated both for the sea coast and for the Veersemeer with its recreational facilities. From the NW corner of Noord Beveland, just across the dam, there is a view of the Oosterscheldekering.

The road skirts the Veersemeer to reach (*5km*) the very attractive little town of **Veere** (5000 inhab.; VVV, Ouderstraat 28), a place of considerable importance in the past but today a holiday resort and marina.

**History.** In 1444 Wolfert van Borssele, lord of Veere, married Mary, one of the six daughters of James I of Scotland, a match which led to a monopoly in the Scottish wool trade and special privileges for Scottish merchants which lasted until the French occupation of 1795. After 1795 Veere's importance declined fast, and its role as a port, other than for pleasure craft, finally ended with the completion of the Zandkreekdam and Veersedam in 1959–61.

The late Gothic *Grote Kerk*, with a squat yet imposing tower and dating from the late 15C and early 16C, is the work of Antoon and, later, Rombout Keldermans. It was restored after a fire of 1686, used as a barracks by the British during their Walcheren expedition of 1809, and two years later it served the French as barracks and hospital, five storeys at this time being inserted into the nave. Wolfert van Borssele and his wife, the originators of the town's prosperity, are buried here. The *Stadsfontein*, to the S of the church, was built in 1551, it is said as the result of a promise to the Scottish merchants that they should have good water. The Gothic *Stadhuis* (Evert Spoorwater, 1474–1509), with a Renaissance tower of 1594–99, has a façade adorned with statues of lords of Veere and their wives; the former courtroom now houses the local museum (mid May–mid September: Tues–Fri, 10.00 to 12.00, 14.00 to 16.00; Sat, 10.00 to 12.00). The harbour area is particularly attractive, with the view across the water to the ramparts and, on the quay, the 16C *Schotse Huizen*, the offices and warehouses of the Scottish wool merchants. The adjoining buildings, Het Lammetje (1539) and De Struys (1561), now house a museum, with Zeeland costumes, antique furniture, books and atlases, and a section devoted to fishing; there are also annual art exhibitions (April–Sept: Tues–Sat, 10.00 to 17.00). The *Campveerse-toren*, dating from c 1500 and a relic of the town fortifications, is now a hotel. On the E of the town the Kanaal door Walcheren ends at the Veersemeer.

7*km* Middelburg and 7*km* Vlissingen, for both of which see Rte 13A.

# **14**  Zeeland Flanders (Zeeuws Vlaanderen) (Perkpolder to Sluis)

ZEELAND FLANDERS, all that part of the Netherlands S of the Scheldt estuary (Westerschelde), is completely separated by water from the rest of the country, being accessible by land only through Belgium; this separation arises from the borders drawn after the piecemeal conquest of the lands south of the Great Rivers (from the Spanish) during the stadholderships of Maurice and Frederick Henry. There are, though, excellent vehicle ferry services, in the W between Vlissingen and Breskens and in the E between Kruiningen and Perkpolder. There exists a long-standing plan for a combined bridge, island and tunnel link between Kruiningen and Perkpolder, but so far this has not been financially accepted. The landscape is largely polder, and there are some picturesque small towns in which local costume is sometimes worn on Sundays and market days. During the Allied operations of 1944 the area suffered much damage.

Some of the most historical, beautiful and interesting towns of Belgium (Antwerp, Ghent, Bruges) are only a short distance to the S (see *Blue Guide Belgium and Luxembourg*).

> Total distance 66km.—12km **Hulst**—12km **Axel**—10km **Terneuzen**—10km *Biervliet*—5km *IJzendijke*—9km **Oostburg**—8km **Sluis**.

3*km* (from Perkpolder) *Kloosterzande* owes its name to a refuge (cloister) here of the abbey Ter Duinen at Koksijde on the Belgian coast, today's Reformed Church (1614) standing on the site of the chapel of the refuge. The refuge was destroyed by the Sea Beggars in 1574, a new refuge then being acquired at Hulst, but the parent abbey at Koksijde was wrecked by the Sea Beggars in 1577.

9*km* **Hulst** (19,000 inhab.; VVV, Stadhuis, Grote Markt) is notable for its almost intact ramparts of 1618–21, complete with moats, bulwarks, and three gates, of which the best is the *Gentsepoort* at the town's SW corner. Beside this gate can be seen the amusing Reynard the Fox Monument (1938), put up because Hulst and several nearby places are mentioned in the Flemish version of this earlier story-cycle, written in c 1250 by two men from eastern Flanders called Arnhout and Willem. The *Bagijnepoort* is at the NE of the town, and at the NW the two-way very modernised *Dubbelepoort*, originally built in c 1500 as a land and water-gate. In the GROTE MARKT stands the pleasingly simple *Stadhuis*, the work in 1528–47 of Willem van Sassen, a native of Hulst, on the site of the Schepenhuis which had burnt down in 1485. The interior contains two good paintings, a View of Hulst (1628) by Cornelis de Vos, and Justice (1661) by Jacob Jordaens, while in the entrance lobby a tablet recalls Dutch-Polish military association in 1944–45 (1st Polish Division under General Maczek liberated Hulst on 17 September 1944). Behind the Stadhuis the *Internat Baudeloo* incorporates medieval parts of a refuge of the Abbey of Baudeloo, a Cistercian house in Ghent known to have had a refuge here as early as the 13C.

The large *St Willibrordsbasiliek*, dominating the Grote Markt on the N, was founded in c 1200, but, apart from the four massive central piers and parts of the transepts, what is seen today is a late Gothic church of 1462–c 1533. A number of eminent architects seem to have been concerned in its building, including Evert Spoorwater (choir), Herman de Waghemakere of Antwerp who started the nave in 1481, Mathias and Laurens Keldermans of Mechelen in 1490 and 1528, and the local Willem van Sassen, responsible for the W façade (1533). When Hulst was taken from the Spanish in 1645, the church became Protestant. From 1807 to 1929 it was divided into two, Catholics using the choir and transepts, and Protestants the nave; then, bought by the Catholics in 1929, the church was fully renovated and elevated to a basilica in 1935. The tower, damaged in 1944, was restored in 1958 in singularly inappropriate modern style. Features of the interior are the organ of 1612 (frequently restored and enlarged) by the Flemish master Loys Isore, pictures near the transepts by Jan Maes (fl. 1680–1720) and P.J. Navez (1787–1869), and over 100 graveslabs of the 15–18C.

There are two buildings of note in Steenstraat leading NW out of the Grote Markt. No. 28, with a quaint tower, dates in part back to c 1400 and has been in turn a prison, the home of banker Lombards, a patrician mansion, a refuge of the Abbey Ter Duinen (Koksijde, Belgium) after the destruction by the Sea Beggars in 1574 of the abbey's refuge at Kloosterzande (see above), a residence of the princes of Orange, and now, since restoration in 1978, the *Streekmuseum* (May–August: Mon–Sat, 14.00 to 17.00; Sun in July and Aug, 14.00 to 17.00), the district museum, with archaeological and historical material, costumes, etc. The building opposite is the *Landshuis*, with a façade of c 1725.

For Antwerp, 30km SE, see Rte 18B.

*12km* **Axel** (12,000 inhab.; VVV, Stadhuis) is a small town where costume is worn at the Saturday market. There is a local museum at Noordstraat 11 (April–Sept: Wed–Sat, 13.30 to 17.00; also, in July and August, Fri, 19.00 to 21.00).

At *Overslag* and *Koewacht*, frontier villages respectively 8km S and 8km SE, stone border markers still stand from the time of the Austrian Netherlands (1713–94).

This Route now bears NW for (*10km*) **Terneuzen** (35,000 inhab.; VVV, Burg. Geillstraat 2.), at the N end of the canal of the same name where it meets the Westerschelde and the foreport of Ghent, in Belgium some 30km to the S. The local *Museum* (Tues–Fri, 09.30 to 12.00, 13.00 to 17.00; Sat, 09.30 to 12.00) is at Burg. Geillstraat 2A, and from the waterfront there is a clear view across the Scheldt, over which, from here, were launched the Allied assaults of October to November 1944 against Zuid Beveland and Walcheren. The road W out of the town crosses the series of great locks on the canal.

The first Terneuzen-Ghent canal was dug in 1547. Today's canal was opened to sea-going vessels in 1827, making possible the growth of Ghent's great inland port. A lock of 1968 opened the canal to ships of 60,000 dwt and an even larger facility is planned. The drive along the canal can be an interesting one. The Belgian frontier is just beyond *Sas-van-Gent* (12km from Terneuzen), and from here the road continues S along the W side of the canal, entering an increasingly industrial area, especially on the E bank, and reaching the port of **Ghent**, a city which should certainly be visited—as the seat of the counts of Flanders, whose magnificent feudal fortress 's Gravensteen survives; for its outstandingly attractive medieval quarters; for its museums and art galleries; and for its splendid cathedral, within which is the priceless Van Eyck masterpiece 'The Adoration of the Mystic Lamb'.

*7km*. Continuing W the road passes the head of the *Braakman*. Once a gulf of the sea formed by flooding in 1337 and 1440, it was dammed in 1952 and converted to a large recreational park (boating, swimming, nature reserve, woodland walks).

*Philippine*, 4km S, was built as a fortress by Philip II of Spain. On 20 September 1944 the village was liberated by 4th Canadian Division.

At (*3km*) *Biervliet* a statue in the village centre honours Willem Beukelzoon, who in the 14C invented a method of curing herrings. This invention allowed the Dutch herring fleets to spend months at sea catching and salting the fish and then travelling to ports where the best prices could be found. From this invention came one of the main elements of the country's economic success in early modern times; Beukelzoon also figures in a stained glass window (1661) in the Reformed Church.

*5km IJzendijke* was fortified by Parma in 1587 and taken by Prince Maurice in 1604, the latter then extending the fortifications to plans by Simon Stevinus (1548–1620), the expert in the use of sluices for military purposes; a path now leads around the partially restored ramparts (leaflet available at the museum). The prince also ordered the building of the church (1612–14, extended 1659); the Romanesque arch of the frame of the entrance door may have come from an earlier church. The district museum (West Zeeland Flanders) is at Markt 28 (Mon–Fri, 10.00 to 12.00, 13.30 to 17.00; Sat, Sun, 14.00 to 17.00).

*9km* **Oostburg** (18,000 inhab.), now a lively town and the shopping centre of western Zeeland Flanders, was almost wholly destroyed in 1944. The *Unicorn* in the main street symbolises the rebirth of the town. To the E of the town the creek called *Groote Gat* is a nature reserve.

*5km Draaibrug*, 2km S of which is **Aardenburg** (3900 inhab.), an ancient place known to have been the site of a Stone Age settlement and of a Roman station, and still with parts of its early 17C ramparts, notably the *Kooipoort* at the NW entrance to the town. Further into the town are (left) the early 18C *Weeshuis* (orphanage) and, roughly opposite the Stadhuis, *St Baafskerk*, a foundation of 959, the oldest surviving part of which, the nave, was built in 1225–50. The choir was rebuilt and enlarged in the late 14C, and after war damage the whole church was much restored in 1947–56. The *Gemeentemuseum* (Mon–Fri, 10.30 to 12.15, 13.30 to 17.00), with some Roman and medieval material, is at Marktstraat 18. At *Heile*, 2km SW, there is a small agricultural museum (Mon, Wed–Sat, 10.00 to 12.00, 13.00 to 17.00).

*3km* **Sluis** (3000 inhab.; VVV, St Annastraat 15), an ancient and historic fortified port, is today a lively tourist centre with many day visitors, especially from Belgium.

**History.** Until it silted up towards the end of the 15C a wide and busy estuary (Het Zwin) ran past Sluis, continuing as far as Damme (Belgium) 10km to the SW, and Sluis was already the commercially important foreport of Bruges (Brugge) when it received its charter in 1290. In 1340 the fleet of England's Edward III, commanded by the King in person, sailed up the estuary, he and his Flemish allies then almost totally destroying the French fleet assembled in the Sluis roadstead in preparation for the invasion of England. Some idea of the size of the estuary can be gained from the fact that the

English are reported to have had 250 sail and the French perhaps 200. This battle has been strikingly described by Froissart. Over 200 years later, now with the silting of the Zwin of declining importance as a port, Sluis declared for the Protestant North, but after a siege, which the Earl of Leicester failed to raise, was taken by Parma in 1587; it was retaken by Prince Maurice in 1604, and a Spanish attack of 1606 was defeated. Sluis was badly damaged by bombing in 1944.

The *Stadhuis*, unusual for having a belfry (1375), was all but destroyed in 1944, but restoration was completed by 1960; today it houses both VVV and the small local musuem (June–Sept: Tues–Sun, 10.00 to 12.00, 14.00 to 17.00). On the belfry stands Jantje van Sluis, a wooden figure said to represent an early bellringer but now the symbol of the town; he survived the bombing of 1944 virtually unscathed. The carillon plays every 15 minutes, and in summer there are concerts. A path follows most of the circuit of the ramparts; in the NW section there is a statue of J.H. van Dale (1828–72), a local schoolmaster who compiled the standard Dutch dictionary. The *De Brak* corn mill, the balcony of which offers a good view, can be visited.

*St Anna ter Muiden*, 2km NW, is an architecturally protected village with a green, a 17C pump, and a 17C church with a large 14C tower.

BELGIUM. Sluis is on the Belgian frontier. The popular coastal resort of **Knokke-Heist** is only 9km NW, to its E, overlapping the border, being *Het Zwin* nature reserve and bird sanctuary (see also below). **Damme**, 10km SW, is a delightful and historic old town (founded in the 12C) with a magnificent *Stadhuis. **Bruges**, 7km further, was founded in the 9C, and is, with its beautiful medieval façades, its picturesque canals, magnificent belfry and other historic buildings, and its museums and art galleries, perhaps the most visited town in Belgium.

SLUIS TO CADZAND AND BRESKENS. 21km. The minor road N along the frontier, marking the approximate course of the ancient estuary, in 6km reaches *Retranchement*, built as a fortress in 1622; the present form dates from a realignment of a few years later, with improvements of 1785. The church was built in 1630. To the N is *Het Zwin* nature reserve and bird sanctuary, comprising 150 ha. of dune and marsh, only 25 ha. of which are in the Netherlands. Among the many birds that may be seen are oyster catchers, avocets, storks, greylag geese, golden orioles, and collared doves. **Cadzand**, 3km NE of Retranchement and once on an island, comprises the inland village and *Cadzand Bad*, now a resort with a magnificent beach. The oldest part of the church dates from c 1300, but the small belfry is an addition of 1931. **Breskens** (5000 inhab.), 12km NE, may be reached either by a small coastal road or by the main inland road. The town, best known for its important vehicle ferry to Vlissingen, is also a resort with dunes and beaches. From the car park beyond the harbour there is a particularly good view of the Scheldt shipping.

# PROVINCE OF UTRECHT

**Capital.** Utrecht.

**History.** The province owes its origin to the consecration in c 700 of Willibrord as Bishop of Utrecht. His successors fortified the seat of their see against marauding Frisians and Norsemen, and later against the counts of Holland, the security thus afforded attracting a population to the town which became a power base from which a line of bishops extended their sway to embrace what is now the province of Utrecht, their temporal power extending also by the mid 11C to today's provinces of Overijssel, Drenthe and Groningen. This overlordship lasted until 1527 when Bishop Henry (of Bavaria) sold his temporal powers and possessions to Charles V. Fifty years later, in 1579, the Union of Utrecht was signed and the history of the province becomes a part of that of the United Provinces.

Utrecht is the smallest of the provinces and also the most central. With the historic city of Utrecht roughly at its centre, the province extends from the Eemmeer in the N to the Lek and Neder Rijn in the S, and from the polders of Zuid Holland in the W across to the sandy heaths of the Gelderland border. Besides Utrecht the only large town is Amersfoort, but there are pleasant and interesting small places in the SW (Montfoort and Oudewater, the latter with associations with witches), as also in the SE along the Neder Rijn, notably Wijk bij Duurstede, one of the oldest settlements in the Netherlands, and Rhenen, the inspiration of several artists and with its story of St Cunera, the only survivor of St Ursula's 11,000 virgins. The province offers some of the most pleasant scenery in the Netherlands, including the valley of the Vecht with its many châteaux and the wooded and parklike country between Utrecht and Amersfoort, with the royal palace of Soestdijk.

# 15   Utrecht

**UTRECHT** (230,000 inhab.), the capital of its province, an archbishopric, and the seat of the Netherlands' largest university, combines much that is modern (notably the huge and remarkably ugly Hoog Catharijne shopping precinct) with an old and historic centre, an attractive feature of which is the Oude Gracht canal, an ancient waterway with many bridges and buildings reaching back to medieval times. The Domtoren is the highest church tower in the Netherlands, and there are several museums, outstanding being the Rijksmuseum het Catharijneconvent (ecclesiastical history and art) and the Centraal Museum with its fine collection of paintings (15–20C).

**Centre.** Utrecht has an extended centre embracing the Hoog Catharijne shopping centre to the W and the area around the Domplein (Cathedral) to the E, these twin centres, some 800m apart, being linked by a network of pedestrian precincts. The motor link is the street sequence Vredenburg, Lange Viestraat, and Potterstraat.

**VVV.** There are two VVV in the Hoog Catharijne; the principal one is at the NE corner (Muziek Centrum, Vredenburgkwartier), the other is by the station in the Stationstraverse.

**Post Office.** Neude.

**Rail and Bus Stations.** West side of Hoog Catharijne.

**Boats**. Excursions on city canals, along the river Vecht, and to the Loosdrechtse Plassen.

**History.** To the Romans this place was *Trajectum ad Rhenum* (AD 47), but the 'ford on the Rhine' became disused after the great flood of 839, when the main waters of the Rhine were diverted from the Oude Rijn into the Lek. The name then developed as *Oude Trecht*, or old ford. Long before this flood though, in c 500, the Frankish King Clovis had built a church here. In c 700 St Willibrord was consecrated Bishop of Utrecht, and from now on it became necessary to erect defences against such enemies as the Frisians and Norsemen, the security thus afforded soon attracting population. St Willibrord's successors grew increasingly powerful, becoming secular overlords of what is now the province of Utrecht, and, being under the protection of the German emperors, a thorn in the flesh of the counts of Holland until as late as 1527 (see below). Utrecht was sacked by the Norsemen at the start of the 10C, but the walls were rebuilt and the town began to prosper. In c 1025 Bishop Adelbold built a church (on the site of today's Domkerk), and soon afterwards his successor Bishop Bernold started his plan, still recognisable today, for a Cross of churches with the Domkerk at the centre. The Pieterskerk went up to the E, the Janskerk to the N, and the abbey church of St Paul to the S; the Cross was completed in c 1080 when Bishop Konrad built his Mariakerk to form the foot. From before this time, though, Utrecht had become a frequent residence of the early German emperors who between 1080 and 1250 had a palace near the site of today's Vismarkt. In 1122 the Emperor Henry V (who died here in 1125) granted a charter of privileges, and by the 13C the citizens' council was in local matters often a more powerful authority than the bishops, though conflict between the two continued until 1527 when Bishop Henry (of Bavaria) sold his secular rights to Charles V. The latter then built a castle on the site of today's Vredenburg, but this was demolished in a citizens' revolt against Spanish rule in 1577. Two years later (1579) the city was the scene of the drawing up of the *Union of Utrecht*, the pact by which the seven northern provinces united against Spain. The following year the Roman Catholic see was suppressed. (The see had been raised to the level of archbishopric only in 1559. Although now secularised, the chapter continued to elect archbishops, but in 1724 they were excommunicated for Jansenism, the Jansenist Church of Holland dates from this time, functioning independently of Rome and adopting the name Oud Katholiek. The archbishopric was revived in 1851.) The strong Catholic traditions of the city are reflected in its most famous school of painters, the Utrecht Caravaggisti, who flourished here during the second two decades of the 17C (see Art and Architecture).

In 1585 Utrecht was the residence of the Earl of Leicester, self-styled Governor General of the United Provinces; in 1636 the university was founded; in 1674 a great storm destroyed the nave of the Domkerk and the towers of both Pieterskerk and Janskerk; in 1672 the troops of Louis XIV entered the city, but in 1713, in a later war, he was here forced to assent to the *Treaty of Utrecht*. The city was again occupied by the French between 1797 and 1813.

**Natives and Others.** Utrecht was the birthplace of Adriaen Florisz. (1459–1523), who in 1522 became Pope Adrian VI, the last non-Italian pope until 1978. Painters born here include Anthonis Mor van Dashorst (c 1517/21–76/7), who, working in London (though principally associated with the court of Philip II), became Sir Anthony More; Cornelis van Poelenburgh (?1586–1667); the brothers Gerrit and Willem van Honthorst (1590–1656 and 1594–1666); the brothers Adriaen and Hendrik Bloemaert (c 1609–66 and c 1601–72); Jan de Heem (1606–83/4); and Jan Both (c 1618–52). Godert de Ginkel (1630–1703), Earl of Athlone, William III's general in Ireland, was born and died here. The university was in the 17C and 18C popular with Scottish students who could study Roman Law here, one being James Boswell who in 1763 wrote of Utrecht's 'many beautiful and amiable ladies'.

Utrecht is described in two sections: Central, which includes the Hoog Catharijne and the surrounds of the Domplein; and Southern, which includes the Rijksmuseum het Catharijneconvent, the Spoorweg (railway) Museum and the Centraal Museum.

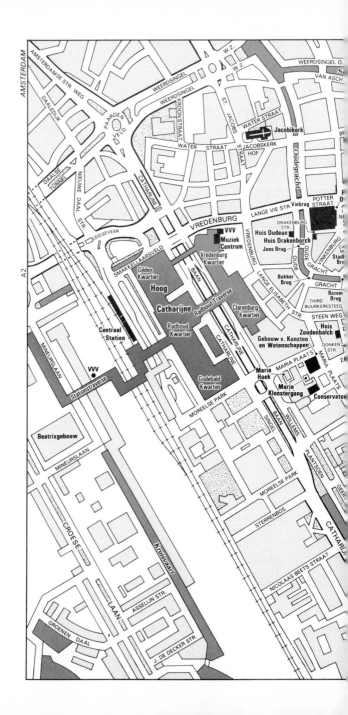

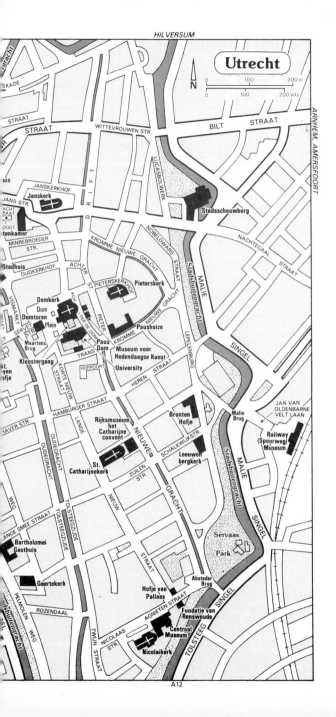

HILVERSUM

## Utrecht

N
0    100    200 m
0    100    200 yds

ARNHEM, AMERSFOORT

SKADE

STRAAT
STRAAT
WITTEVROUWEN STR.
BILT STRAAT

uis
JANSKERKHOF
Janskerk
JANS STR.
ACHT RAAT
OOGT
tenkamer
MINREBROEDER STR.

DRIFT

LUCASBOLWERK

Stadsschouwburg

NACHTEGAAL STRAAT

Stadhuis
OUDKERKHOF
ACHTER ST.
KROMME NIEUWE GRACHT
NOBELDWARS STRAAT
Stadsbuitengracht
MALIE

VISMARKT

Domkerk
Dom
Domtoren
SERVET STR.
Plein

ACHTER DE DOM
ST. PIETERSKERKHOF
Pieterskerk

KROMME NIEUWE GRACHT

LEPELENBURG

SINGEL

Maartens
Brug
Kloostergang
st.
yen
ofje

HOFPOORT

Paus
Dam
TRANS
KORTE NIEUW STRAAT
Paushuize

Museum voor
Hedendaagse Kunst
University

KROMME

HEREN STRAAT

JAN VAN
OLDENBARNE
VELT LAAN

HAMBURGER STRAAT
LANGE
NIEUWE

Brunten
Hofje

Malie
Brug

Railway
(Spoorweg)
Museum

HAVER STR.
OUDEGRACHT

Rijksmuseum
het
Catharijne
convent

ZUILEN STR.
SCHALKWIJKSTR.

St.
Catharijnekerk

Leeuwen
bergkerk

Stadsbuitengracht
MALIE

WEG
TOLSTEEGZIJDE
NIEUW

GRACHT

SINGEL

LANGE SMEE STRAAT
TOLSTEEGZIJDE
STRAAT

Bartholomei
Gasthuis

Servaas
Park

Geertekerk

Absteder
Brug

PELMOLEN WEG
ROZENDAAL

Hofje van
Pallaas

AGNIETEN STRAAT

Fundatie van
Renswoude

SINGEL
TOLSTEEG VAN

sbuitengracht
EL

TWIIN STRAAT
NICOLAAS STRAAT

Centraal
Museum

Nicolaikerk

A12

# A.  Central Utrecht

*HOOG CATHARIJNE is a huge, modern (1973–80), covered and air-condi-
tioned shopping complex to the W of the old city centre. Incorporated with
the railway and bus stations, with several car parks, a hotel, and with some
180 shops, cinemas, restaurants, etc., the complex with some justification
calls itself the shopping heart of Europe. It is divided into seven sections
(Kwartiers). On the W, beyond the station, is the *Jaarbeurskwartier*, adjoining the *Beatrixgebouw* (Jaarbeurs Congreszaal), a large building devoted
to the annual industrial fair. Next comes the *Stationstraverse*, or *Sta-
tionskwartier*, above the railway and town and district bus stations. This
leads into a long wing with, roughly N to S, the *Gildenkwartier*, the
*Radboudkwartier*, and the *Godebaldkwartier*. The Radboudkwartier
crosses by bridge (Radboudtraverse) the Catharijnebaan, a wide street that
was a canal before the building of the complex, to reach another wing, this
one being on two levels. This wing, with the *Clarenburgkwartier* and the
*Vredenburgkwartier*, contains the main VVV and the large department
stores.

Despite good signposting, the complex can be confusing and visitors are
advised to obtain from one of the information offices the guide (*wegwijzer*)
which includes a coloured plan with a numbered key to the shops and other
facilities. At Gildenkwartier 43 there is a *Phonographic Museum* (Tues–Sat,
10.00 to 17.00) with vintage equipment, historical recordings and an 1890s
recording studio.

VREDENBURG, the open space at the NE of the Hoog Catharijne, was the
site of the castle of Charles V.

The *Jacobikerk*, 250m N, a foundation of the early 12C, is a building of the
13–15C with three aisles. The spire of c 1344, flattened in 1812 to make
way for a signal station forming part of the Paris–Amsterdam telegraph link,
was rebuilt in 1953. The church owes its name to the many pilgrims who
visited it on their way to the shrine of St James of Compostela in Spain.

The old centre can be reached either by way of the pedestrian precincts
extending eastward from the Hoog Catharijne, or by following Lange
Viestraat and Potterstraat to the open space called NEUDE, from where the
description below starts. The *Post Office* here, a modern building, stands
on a site occupied in turn by a convent (until 1647), the provincial mint and,
after 1814, the national mint.

A short way into Voorstraat to the N, No. 19 was the *Vleeshuis* (1637), while,
opposite, No. 14 is a curious old house of 1619.

Drakenburgstraat runs along the S side of the Post Office to reach the OUDE
GRACHT, one of the two canals (the other being the Nieuwe Gracht) that
cross the inner town, sections of both of which represent the old course of
the Rhine. The Oude Gracht dates as a canal from the mid 12C, and from
the following century onwards it served as a port along virtually the whole
of its length, many of the cellars seen beside it today originating from the
14C when those of the canal-side houses were extended. In medieval and
later times this section of the canal was a patrician quarter and several of
today's buildings have early origins, notably the *Huis Drakenborch* on the
S corner of the Drakenburgstraat, and, across the canal (No. 99), *Huis
Oudean*, dating from the late 14C; this latter was the residence of the
French Ambassador de Polignac at the time of the Treaty of Utrecht (1713)

and in 1759 it became a hospice for old people. Boat excursions start from this part of the canal (Viebrug), and there is a footpath along the water's edge past the cellars. This path (note the modern small sculpture groups below each lamp post) is followed S and then E, passing first Jansbrug and then Bakkerbrug, near the far side of the latter being a small house of c 1600 but with an 18C gable.

The next bridge is the Bezembrug, by the N end of which stands a rather pretentious building with caryatids (19C) on the site of the medieval hospice of St Barbara. Continuing E, Oude Gracht becomes Stadhuisbrug (14C, when two bridges were joined), while Ganzenmarkt (Goose Market) bears away from the canal. From the centre of Ganzenmarkt a foot tunnel slopes down to the water at the spot which was the site of the municipal crane, represented today by a tree surrounded by a frame marking the base of the crane. At this point the sculpture groups below the lamp posts are again worth noting, especially one (to the left with one's back to the water) of the signing of the Union of Utrecht. The house above, on the corner of Ganzenmarkt and Stadhuisbrug and now known as *Het Keyserrijck* (in origin 1410), was formerly the weigh-house.

The **Stadhuis** is immediately to the E, a building with a Doric façade which in 1824 replaced two medieval houses; it was here that the Union of Utrecht was formally proclaimed, and here too that the Treaty of Utrecht was negotiated and signed. From the Stadhuis, Vismarkt, the site of the fish market as long ago as 1196, runs S beside the Oude Gracht, this section of which marks the western boundary of the Roman station, and soon reaches MAARTENSBRUG. Here, although the Domplein is only a short way NE, a diversion is made SW, the walk returning to Maartensbrug.

The **Buurkerk**, lying two streets back, is Utrecht's oldest parish church. Founded in the 10C, the church, though in part 13C, was largely rebuilt in the 14C and 15C, with a tower in the walls of which Spanish cannon balls fired from the Vredenburg during the citizens' revolt of 1577 can still be seen. Note the carved small figures on the tympanum above the W door. The church was considerably larger than it is today, having a choir which reached almost to the Oude Gracht; demolished in c 1580, this is now recalled by Choorstraat, the street which took its place. A character associated with the church was a lady called Sister Bertken who, because of her shame in being a bastard (by a priest of the Domkerk), occupied a cell in the choir for 57 years until her death in 1514; she became known for her holy writings (see also Maartensbrug below). The church precinct (Buurkerkhof 10) now houses the *Rijksmuseum van Speelklok tot Pierement* (From Musical Box to Street Organ), a unique collection of mechanical musical instruments spanning the 18–20C and as interesting for their mechanical ingenuity as for their flamboyant decoration (Tues.–Sat, 10.00 to 17.00; Sun, 13.00 to 17.00).

Third Buurkerksteeg leads from the W side of the church into Donkerstraat, at the road junction being the *Huis Zoudenbalch* (Donkerstraat 15–19), a rebuilding after a fire in 1903 of the façade of a house of c 1463; Evert Zoudenbalch, the original builder, was treasurer of the Domkerk. Donkerstraat runs S into Zadelstraat, which, followed SW, reaches the MARIAPLAATS, where the pump at the NE of the square is interesting for having until as late as 1863 supplied water which was sold bottled in Amsterdam. Across the square stand the *Conservatorium*, formerly a hospital, and the *Gebouw voor Kunsten en Wetenschappen* (Arts and Sciences), the latter on the site of the Mariakerk of c 1080 which stood at the foot of the Cross planned by Bishop Bernold (see History, above) and which was demolished in two stages in 1813 and 1844. Only the 12C cloisters behind (the *Maria Kloostergang*) survive as a pleasant garden backwater, with, to the NW, a wall plan showing the former layout. Beside the wall plan a passage leads to a small square known as the Mariahoek, out of which another passage between small private gardens passes what was a clandestine Roman Catholic church (17C), unobtrusive and part hidden by houses; after the schism (see History, above) this was a centre of the Old Catholics (with a museum, see the Rijksmuseum het Catharijneconvent). The passage regains Mariaplaats on the S side of the Conservatorium, and from here the return to the Maartensbrug is by Boterstraat, in which, opposite the end of the little Kuipersteeg, can be seen the gateway (1644) of the *St Eloyen Hofje*, a hospice founded in the early 15C by the Guild of Blacksmiths.

At the Maartensbrug a stone picture below a lamp depicts Sister Bertken (see above) being walled into her cell in the Buurkerk. Across the bridge the short Servetstraat passes a doorway of 1634 of the palace of the bishops which has long disappeared. In the small garden (*Bisschops Hof*) tablets on the life of St Martin are from the Domkerk cloisters.

Servetstraat runs into the DOMPLEIN, laid out in 1876. It was in c 700 that St Willibrord founded two churches on this spot, one of these, dedicated to St Martin, being a predecessor of today's Domkerk, and the other, immediately SW, the predecessor of a church of St Salvator, also known as the Oud Munster. This latter was demolished in 1580. Until 1 August 1674 the Domkerk and its tower, the Domtoren, were, except for a short passageway, joined to one another, but on that date a storm destroyed the nave, and tower and church have been separated ever since, though it was not until 1876 that the site was finally cleared to form the Domplein. Tinted stones on the ground show the outlines of both the Oud Munster and of the collapsed nave, while another colour indicates the Chapel of the Holy Cross which once stood between the two churches. A plaque on the wall of the Domkerk shows the site of the Roman station to which Utrecht traces its origin, and a bronze statue (1883) of Count John of Nassau, brother of William the Silent, honours the man under whose presidency the Union of Utrecht was formed. Near the statue a runestone, symbolising the Christianisation of Denmark, considered to have been the direct result of the early Christianisation of Utrecht, was presented by Danes in 1936 on the occasion of the tercentenary of the University of Utrecht.

The **Domtoren** (ascent all year: Sat, Sun, 12.00 to 17.00; also April–mid Oct: Mon–Fri, 10.00 to 17.00; Holidays, 12.00 to 17.00), the highest church tower in the Netherlands (112m), was built in 1321–83 (restored 1901–31), virtually separate from its church, one reason being that the latter was going to take much longer to complete. Inside there are two chapels; that of St Michael, the private chapel of the bishops, and, above, the Egmond chapel used by Bishop George van Egmond and today housing an exhibition. There are 465 steps, bringing climbers to a height of 102m. The **Domkerk** (daily, 10.00 to 17.00 in May–Sept or 11.00 to 16.00 in Oct–April), spanning from c 1254 to 1517, stands on the site of St Willibrord's early church and of its successor built by Bishop Adelbold in c 1025. As noted above, the nave was destroyed in 1674, today's church therefore consisting only of choir and transepts and two chapels of the south nave aisle. In the choir are the tomb, by Rombout Verhulst, of Admiral van Gent, killed in 1672 at the Battle of Solebay, and the cenotaph of Bishop George van Egmond (died

1549); in the second S chapel are the tomb of Bishop Guy d'Avesnes (died 1317) and a 15C wall-painting. In the crypt beneath the choir the hearts of the emperors Conrad II and Henry V, who died at Utrecht (1039 and 1125) but are buried at Speyer in Germany, are preserved. The *Kloostergang*, connecting Domplein with the street Achter de Dom, is the cloister of 1390–1495 (restored 19C and 1963). Over the windows are carved scenes from the life of St Martin, many restored or modern, the originals being in the Bisschops Hof. The mainly late 19C buildings on the S side of the Kloostergang are those of the **University** (*Academiegebouw*), founded in 1636 and first using these buildings in 1893. The buildings incorporate the former chapter house of the canons of the Domkerk, in origin 1495, the place in which the Union of Utrecht was signed in 1579 and now the university auditorium (by appointment. Tel: 030-394252).

The *University Museum* (at Biltstraat 116, about 1.5km NE. Mon–Fri, 10.00 to 17.00; Sun, 13.00 to 17.00) shows material on the history of the university and also an important collection of antique instruments. There is also a large university complex on the E of the city beyond the A27 motorway; here the *Fort Hoofddijk Botanic Garden* is open Mon–Fri, 08.30 to 16.30.

The street ACHTER DE DOM is behind the church. Here, against the wall of the university, there stands a small statue of the French poet François Villon (1431–c 63). The *Museum voor Hedendaagse Kunst* (Tues–Sat, 10.00 to 17.00; Sun, 13.00 to 17.00), at No. 14, offers both a permanent collection and also temporary exhibitions of international contemporary art. Followed S, Achter de Dom reaches PAUSDAM, an open space at the angle of the Nieuwe Gracht and the Kromme Nieuwe Gracht canals, with, at its NE corner, the *Paushuize* (Pope's House), built in 1517 for Adriaen Florisz. (later Pope Adrian VI), a native of Utrecht and tutor to Charles V; being Bishop of Tortosa in Spain at the time, he in fact never saw this house. There are several good façades along the Nieuwe Gracht, a quarter always favoured by the well-to-do, and while here at the Pausdam the visitor should walk a short way along the west bank to the small doorway known as the *Hofpoort* (1620), the gateway of the former law courts. Through this gate, at the end of the lane after it turns, the wall in front has traces of a monastery (of St Paul) built here in c 1050 by Bishop Bernold and forming the south arm of his Cross. Disestablished after 1580, the monastery church became the provincial law courts.

For places further S, see Southern Utrecht.

Achter St Pieter is now followed N out of Pausdam, passing No. 20, the seat of the provincial government, and reaching on the right Pieters Kerkhof with *St Pieterskerk* (Fri, Sat, 09.00 to 12.00, 14.00 to 16.00), built in 1048 by Bishop Bernold (east arm of his Cross) and in part the oldest Romanesque church in the Netherlands; its two west towers fell in the same storm of 1674 that destroyed the nave of the Domkerk, and the church has been much altered and restored (1965). Bishop Bernold's tomb is in the Romanesque crypt.

The large open space of JANSKERKHOF is a short way N. Here stands the *Janskerk* (Mon–Fri, 09.00 to 17.00), also originally built by Bishop Bernold (north arm of his Cross) but with a choir added in 1508–39 and a façade altered in 1682; pavement stonework outlines the original west side towers, one pulled down in medieval times and the other blown down by the storm of 1674. To the S of the church is an equestrian statue of St Willibrord (Albert Termote), and to the W there is a small statue of Anne Frank. Across the road, behind a statue of F.C. Donders, an opthalmic surgeon, stands a building (*Statenkamer*) which is in part a survival of a Franciscan monastery founded in 1247 and between 1581 and 1795 the meeting place of the States of Utrecht; the doorway, with the arms of the province, was built in 1643.

Nobelstraat, running E, in 400m reaches the *Stadsschouwburg*, the municipal theatre built in 1940 by W.M. Dudok, city architect of Hilversum.

Lange Jansstraat leads back to Neude. On the way you can make a turn S into Slachtstraat, off which branches the short Hoogt. Here No. 2 on the corner is a typical citizen's house of the early 17C, while at No. 6 there is a small grocery trade museum (Mon, 14.00 to 16.30; Tues–Sat, 10.00 to 16.30).

# B.   Southern Utrecht

Korte Nieuwstraat leads S out of Domplein, becoming Lange Nieuwstraat which soon passes (E) the *St Catharijnekerk*, a Carmelite foundation of 1468, completed by the Order of St John in 1550, returned to the Roman Catholics in 1815 and now their national cathedral. Today's frontage dates from 1900.

The *Rijksmuseum het Catharijneconvent* (Tues–Fri, 10.00 to 17.00; Sat, Sun, Holidays, 11.00 to 17.00) is behind the church at Nieuwe Gracht 63, a building of 1528–62 which in turn has served as convent, municipal hospital (run by the Order of St John) and barracks. The museum, opened in 1979 and refreshingly modern in its display methods, offers a superb visual survey of the history of Christianity in the Netherlands, combining under one roof the Ecclesiastical Collection formerly a part of the Centraal Museum, the material from the Oud Katholiek Museum, and much from elsewhere. The priceless collections comprise religious statuary (large and small) in stone, wood and plaster, illuminated MSS, books, a wealth of portraits and pictures (many by well known artists, and several curious and interesting), vestments, silver and other ware, etc., as well as, illustrating more modern times, documentation, posters and photographs.

The museum is in two parts, the Kloostergebouw (Convent Building) in rooms surrounding the courtyard of the Convent of St Catharine, and the Grachtenhuis (Canal House), the two joined by an underground passage. The former—with its splendid visual treasures the Netherlands' largest collection of medieval art and likely to be the main objective of most visitors—houses material from the Middle Ages to the 17C. The latter—more for the student of 19C and 20C socio-religious development—continues the story into modern times.

After leaving the ticket desk, you enter the museum proper through a doorway out of the café and are at once confronted with the choice between descending to the underground passage (onderdoorgang) leading to the basement of the Kloostergebouw (where the description below starts) or of ascending to the rooms of the Grachtenhuis.

The official theme of the *KLOOSTERGEBOUW BASEMENT (Kelder) is *Medieval Worship and Piety*, to the layman a hardly compelling and maybe even daunting description. Yet with its wealth of exquisite small exhibits—illuminated MSS, statuettes, breviaries, ivories, etc.—this is perhaps the most absorbing room in the whole museum; an intimate quiet vault walled by a dozen or so cases, each with its individual theme (the Bible, Mass,

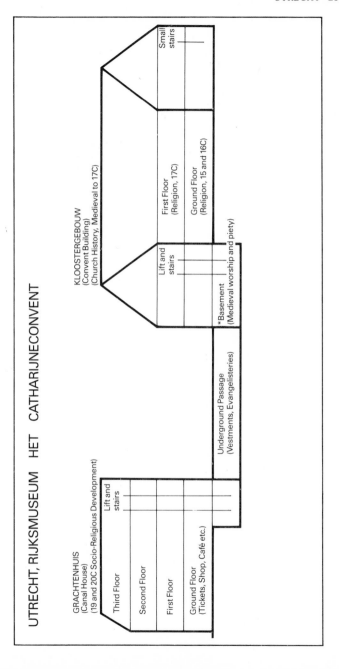

UTRECHT, RIJKSMUSEUM HET CATHARIJNECONVENT

GRACHTENHUIS
(Canal House)
(19 and 20C Socio-Religious Development)

Lift and stairs

Third Floor

Second Floor

First Floor

Ground Floor
(Tickets, Shop, Café etc.)

Underground Passage
(Vestments, Evangelisteries)

KLOOSTERGEBOUW
(Convent Building)
(Church History, Medieval to 17C)

Lift and stairs

First Floor
(Religion, 17C)

Ground Floor
(Religion, 15 and 16C)

*Basement
(Medieval worship and piety)

Small stairs

Devotion, Saints and suchlike), each with its own lighting controlled by the visitor, each a museum in itself. The final theme is Death, this continued, with some dramatic Last Judgements, in the small hall which links the underground passage (for description of which see below) and the basement or kelder.

GROUND FLOOR (Begane Grond). This floor starts with a modest section on *Church Building*, and beyond, going clockwise, *Medieval Church Interiors* with a triptych of c 1540 by Jan van Scorel (with whom the great period of the Utrecht School begins) and others; a Marianum of c 1500 from northern Limburg; a south German Pietà of c 1425; and stone Stations of the Cross, one still showing some colour, dated c 1530, from Westphalia. Under *Religious Representation* are shown smaller figures; triptychs, including one by Cornelis Engebrechtsz; an early 16C painting of Christ, Saviour of the World; and two pictures of the Crucifixion, entertaining in their naivety and detail despite the tragedy of the subject. *Monastic Life* is the theme of the gallery paralleling Medieval Church Interiors. Among the many pictures here are the Abbey and Castle of Egmond by Claes van der Heck (1635); the Abbey of Leeuwenhorst by N. Neth (17C); Portrait of a member of the Order of St John (? Jan van Scorel); and a triptych with several small pictures, possibly by several artists, depicting the life of St Theodosia and the life of Christ (1545). The following sections cover *Veneration of the Saints, Pilgrims* and *Religious Cultural Climate of c 1500*, beyond being the *Reformation* with material on Luther, Calvin, the Council of Trent, etc. Also here is a carved Calvary by Jean Mone, an artist best known for his work in the Church of Our Lady at Halle in Belgium, while pictures include portraits of Luther and Melanchthon by, respectively, Lucas Cranach the Elder and Younger; *Virgin and Child by Cornelis van Cleve; and a delightful ironic Distribution of Holy Grace, the detail of which repays study. The *Freedom Struggle of the Later 16C*, grimly symbolised by a rack, provides the last theme on this floor.

A small stairway now ascends to the KLOOSTERGEBOUW FIRST FLOOR (1ste Verdieping), a long series of rooms carrying the story of religion through the 17C, with themes such as the *Consequences of Revolution, Conflicts within the Catholic Church, the Synod of Dordrecht* (1619), and *Protestants and Catholics*. Here, too, are rooms illustrating the story of this convent building (half-way along this floor) and showing material formerly in the Oud-Katholiek Museum (at the end of this floor). But for many visitors, untutored perhaps in the passions and arguments of 17C Dutch theology, the main attraction along this floor may well prove to be the wealth of pictures, these including, by Rembrandt, *The Baptism of the Eunuch and portraits of Jacobus Arminius and Remonstrants; portraits of Descartes by J.B. Weenix, of N. Stenius by Frans Hals, and of a Praying Begijn by P. de Grebber; and the Holy Family in a Cave (Rest on the flight to Egypt) by Thomas de Keyser.

You should now go down to the UNDERGROUND PASSAGE (Onderdoorgang), in which there is a fine display of vestments, ranging in date from c 1200–1700. Here too are pictures cut from vestments; *Evangelisteries adorned with precious stones; the so-called *Chalice of Lebuinus, an ivory cup of the 9C, with 14C silver mounting (Aachen); and an ancient gavel called the Hammer of St Martin.

In the GRACHTENHUIS the ground floor is administrative, with a café and bookstall. Among the themes illustrated on the floors above—through pictures, portraits, church furnishings, plate, documents, newspapers, photographs and even posters—are *Rationalism and Enlightenment, Church*

*Interiors and Services* (17C and 18C), *Catholic and Protestant Daily Life and Worship* (18C and 19C) and *Developments of the 20C*, these last including Missionary Work, Christian Trades Unions and The Church during the Occupation (1940–45). Among the several pictures are two challenging works by Jan Toorop, The Pilgrim and Girl at Prayer.

The important Centraal Museum is some 400m S along the Nieuwe Gracht, but if you want to visit the Railway (Spoorweg) Museum, you should first make a short diversion E, following Schalkwijkstraat, roughly opposite the Catharijneconvent. This street reaches the gardens flanking the outer canal, with on the street's corner being the *Leeuwenbergkerk*, a church with a mixed history, having been built in 1567 as a hospital for plague victims, then becoming in turn barracks and chemical laboratory until 1930 when taken over for Protestant use. A short way further N the *Bruntenhofje* are almshouses of 1621. Maliebrug crosses the canal, the short Jan van Oldenbarneveldlaan then leading straight to the **Nederlands Spoorwegmuseum** (Tues–Sat, 10.00 to 17.00; Sun, 13.00 to 17.00), housed in the former Maliebaan Station, built in 1874 and a pleasing example of a station of its time.

The indoor exhibition is in the wings either side of the entrance hall, to the right being the historical section, with many technical and specialist aspects but also showing several nostalgic paintings and prints likely to be of more general appeal. The opposite hall is more concerned with modern times. Beyond, there are three long covered platforms and five tracks, all carrying train or tramway rolling stock. On Platform One stands a magnificent row of seven locomotives spanning 1864 (built by Peacock and Co. of Manchester) to the end of steam, with the Longmoor of 1945, built at North British Locomotive Works, Glasgow, for the D Day British Army. And here too stands De Arend (the Eagle), a full-scale copy of a locomotive built in 1869 at Bedlington in Northumberland, drawing three coaches representative of the first Dutch route (Amsterdam to Haarlem, 1839).

The other platforms are reached by a bridge across tracks still in use. On either side of Platform Two there are trams, on one side horse and steam, on the other electric. At Platform Three stands No. 3737 (built 1911 and in service until 1958), the Netherlands' last steam locomotive, with, behind it, beautifully restored carriages of various periods, including examples of 1871 and 1910 and a Wagons-Lits restaurant car, restored in 1976 in, rather surprisingly, Hungary. Opposite there is a more modern train. Finally, any visitor in need of refreshment can repair to a blue Wagons-Lits restaurant car by the front of the museum.

From the Catharijneconvent museum Nieuwe Gracht continues S to the Abstederbrug, where Agnietenstraat bears W. On the N, on the corner of Lange Nieuwstraat, the *Hofje van Pallaas* are almshouses of 1651, while opposite, on the S side of Agnietenstraat, the *Fundatie van Renswoude* (1765) was a school for especially talented poor children.

The *****Centraal Museum** (Tues–Sat, 10.00 to 17.00; Sun, Holidays, 13.00 to 17.00), at Agnietenstraat 1 and founded in 1838, occupies the buildings of the former convent of St Agnes (a foundation of 1420) and also a wing added in 1920. The museum houses the municipal collections of paintings (15–20C); there are also period rooms and sections devoted to archaeology and the story of Utrecht, both city and province. The exhibits are in a basement and on three floors, with also upper and lower mezzanine levels.

In the BASEMENT can be seen the *****Utrecht Ship, an oak sailing vessel of about the 9C AD, dug up in 1930 from the old channel of the Vecht in the NW suburb of the city.

GROUND FLOOR. To the left of the entrance the chapel (1512–16) is frequently used for temporary exhibitions, while straight ahead is the modern art gallery showing works by Dutch artists of the 20C, among the tendencies finding place here being De Stijl, Magic Realism and Fundamental art. To the right of the museum entrance is a series of rooms illustrating dress (mainly 18C and 19C fashion), beyond these being six period rooms, Louis XIV, XV, and XVI to the right and Baroque, Renaissance, and Gothic to the left. Of these the Baroque Room commands the most attention: here hangs Gerrit van Honthorst's wickedly effective *The Procuress, while below there is a sumptuous 17C dolls' house, complete with formal garden. Beyond come the bookstall, café, stairs, and entrance to the garden and Nicolaikerk.

The Nicolaikerk is a 13C building which once served the needs of a village clustered around. The choir is of 1440, and there is a carillon by the Hemony brothers. Stone fragments from various Utrecht churches are exhibited in the interior.

Spiral stairs from the bookstall ascend to the FIRST FLOOR with, on the left, the Acquisitions Hall and Print Room, and to the right an L-shaped series of rooms in which hang some of the museum's best paintings of the 17–19C, the majority of these by Utrecht Old Masters such as Abraham Bloemaert and Gerrit van Honthorst. The pictures are changed around from time to time, but are likely to include some of the following. *Balthasar van der Ast*: Still life. *Dirk van Baburen*: *Entombment (1617); Boy with a Jew's harp (1621); Lute player (1622). *Jan van Bijlert*: portraits. *Daniel de Blieck*: church interiors. *Anthonie van Blocklandt*: Joseph before Pharaoh. *Abraham Bloemaert*: Triumph of Neptune (c 1615); Rest on the flight into Egypt; *Adoration of the Magi (1624); Adoration of the shepherds; Baptism of a Moor; Landscape with dovecot. *Paulus Bor*: Spanish Gipsy (1641); Descent from the Cross. *Ambrosius Bosschaert*: Still life. *Jacob van Campen*: Diogenes. *Joost Droochsloot*: Ice scene. *Gerrit van Honthorst*: David playing the harp (1622). *Granida and Daifolo (1625). Shepherdess with a dove's nest (1625). *Willem van Honthorst*: portraits. *Jan Both, Carel de Hooch, Claude de Jongh, Cornelis van Poelenburgh* and *Jan Weenix*: 'Italian' landscapes. *Paulus Moreelse*: Margaretha van Mansfeldt. *Pieter Saenredam*: church interiors. *Roelant Savery*: Still life (1624), with, beside it, a list of the flowers. *Jan Steen*: The Fortune Teller. *Hendrik Terbrugghen*: Sleeping Mars (1629). The Jolly Toper (c 1622). *Werner van Valckert*: Christ blessing the children. *Joachim Wttewael*: Adoration of the shepherds (1598); *The Artist and his wife (1601); Joseph and his brothers (1605).

Beyond the above series of rooms a passageway leads across above the entrance hall (view down into the chapel) to a room devoted to triptychs and other works by Jan van Scorel who, though not born in Utrecht, lived and worked here for most of his life. Outstanding are the *Lockhorst triptych (1527) and four *portrait groups (first quarter 16C) of members of the Brotherhood of Jerusalem (returned pilgrims), these showing a marvellous variety of expressions (see also Frans Hals Museum, Haarlem).

The MEZZANINE level, off the first floor, shows Applied Art, with a mix of furniture, glass and ceramic spanning five centuries and largely of Dutch provenance.

The SECOND FLOOR has one wing set aside for Educational Projects, and there is also a small room showing Coins and Medals, these including Roman coins found locally and also a virtually complete set of Utrecht coin types. The emphasis on this floor is local-historical and English-speaking

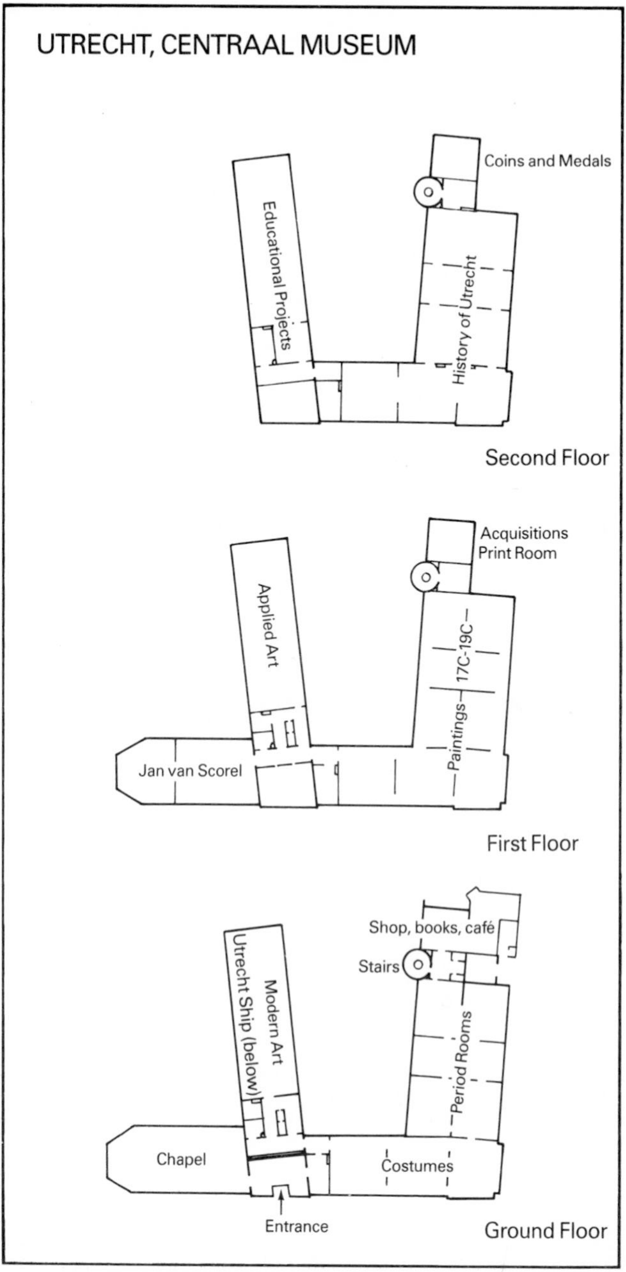

UTRECHT, CENTRAAL MUSEUM

Coins and Medals

Educational Projects

History of Utrecht

Second Floor

Acquisitions
Print Room

Applied Art

17C-19C

Paintings

Jan van Scorel

First Floor

Shop, books, café

Stairs

Modern Art
Utrecht Ship (below)

Period Rooms

Chapel

Costumes

Entrance

Ground Floor

visitors may dismiss it as of limited interest—especially since no language concession is made—but that would be a pity as in fact much of the material is self-explanatory, and much, too, is visually pleasing; as, for instance, a charming, naive triangular hospital scene, well worth studying for its detail, with medical activity in the centre while the sick (sometimes two together) suffer patiently in their regimented cupboard beds. Also noteworthy are two long back-to-back scenes, again delightfully naive, with on one side the Brotherhood of Jerusalem, doubtless confident that their pilgrimage will have ensured for them a successful verdict at the Last Judgement which fills the other side.

To the W of the Centraal Museum the STADSBUITENGRACHT, the outer canal, runs roughly S to N, along this (E bank) being the *Geertekerk* (13C, but much restored), and then the *Bartholomei Gasthuis* (Lange Smeestraat 40), founded in 1407 as a home for the aged and still serving as such. The building was enlarged in the 17C. In the Governors' Room hang large tapestries (1642), known for their perspective effect (by appointment. Tel: 030-310254).

For Utrecht to Amersfoort, Ede, and Arnhem, see Rte 16A; to Doorn, Rhenen, Wageningen, and Arnhem, see Rte 16B; to Amsterdam, see Rte 17A; to Gouda, see Rte 17B; to Vianen, Schoonhoven and Rotterdam, see Rte 17C.

# 16   Utrecht to Arnhem

## A.   Via Amersfoort and Ede

Total distance 62km.—8km **Zeist**—10km **Amersfoort**—26km **Ede**—18km **Arnhem**.

For Utrecht, see Rte 15. *8km* **Zeist** (60,000 inhab.; VVV, Steynlaan 19A), to the S of the road, is an elegant town amid woods and gardens. The château, *Slot van Zeist* (conducted tours, Sat, Sun, 14.30 and 16.30; also Tues–Fri, 14.30 in July and Aug), was built in 1677–86 by Jacob Roman, Daniel Marot working on the interior (period rooms; changing exhibitions). The town and château are associated with the Moravians who established a settlement here in 1764 at a time when, following the persecutions and other difficulties experienced after the building of Herrnhut in 1722–27, land for settlements was provided on their estates by sympathetic noblemen in Germany, the United Provinces, and elsewhere. At (*4km*) **Soesterberg** there is a Royal Netherlands Air Force base, with the service's *Luchtmacht Museum* (April–Nov: Tues–Fri, 10.00 to 16.30; Sun 13.00 to 16.30).

*6km* **AMERSFOORT** (87,000 inhab.), the 'ford on the Amer' (the stream now called the Eem), is a pleasant and lively town of canals, some narrow streets and attractive small squares. There are a number of old buildings, and the two concentric rings of streets mark the circuits of the old ramparts of the (?) 12C and 14–15C.

**Centre.** Hof.

**VVV.** and **Station**. Over 1km SW of Hof, outside the outer ring (Stadsring).

**Post Office.** Stadsring, 400m SW of Hof.

**History.** Although an early settlement, first fortified in the 12C or before, and although receiving a charter in 1259, Amersfoort makes no significant appearance in Dutch history. In 1547 *Jan van Oldenbarneveld* was born here (see National History), and another native was *Jasper van Wittel* (1653–1736), the architect who in Italy was called Vanvitelli.

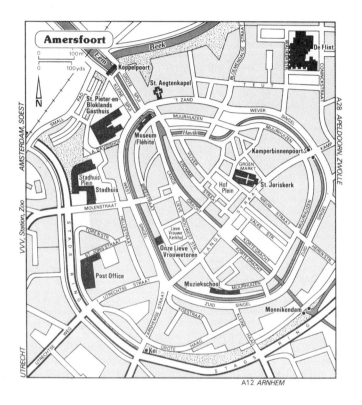

Beside the HOFPLEIN stands **St Joriskerk**, a Gothic building of 1442–1534, restored during the 17C; some of the lower part, notably the base of the tower, is Romanesque work of c 1243. Worth noting also are the S porch of c 1500 and the gallery of the *Botermarkt* (1608) beside it. Inside are a rood screen of the early 16C (restored); the tomb monument of the architect Jacob van Campen (1598–1657); murals of c 1500 (SE chapel) and c 1530 (choir); and a large enclosed pulpit of 1674.

Other places of interest lie close to the ring-canals. NORTH-WEST. The **Museum Fléhite** (Tues–Fri, 10.00 to 17.00; Sat, Sun, 14.00 to 17.00), at Westsingel 50, standing beside the inner canal and facing the Eem, shows prehistoric and historical material relating both to the town and to earlier Utrecht; prehistory (with prehistoric animals) is on the top floor and history on the first and second. Worth looking out for on the first floor are some elaborately carved chests, one bearing a Last Judgement, a Bleau celestial globe of 1603, a View of Amersfoort by Salomon van Ruysdael (loan) and a portrait of Jan van Oldenbarneveld, a native of Amersfoort, by Michiel van Miereveld. In the 19C and 20C rooms two noteworthy exhibits are an ingenious educational alphabet and reading wheel and a telephone exchange used by the Resistance.

Just SE of the museum the short canal called the *Havik*, once the harbour, has several good façades along its sides, while just NE of the museum, on 'T Zand, the *St Aegtenkapel*, a chapel of 1408, is now used for municipal purposes. A short way W, in Achter Davidshof, the *St Pieters-en-Bloklands Gasthuis* (apply Museum Fléhite) was a hospice founded in 1390; the chapel and the men's ward survive from the 14–15C. From near here Grote Spui and Kleine Spui, either side of the Eem, soon reach the *Koppelpoort, a quaint old water-gate of 1400 spanning the river and at one time the home of the Guild of Bargemen; it was restored in 1886 by P.J.H. Cuijpers, but of the road gates on either side only one is complete.

The most notable feature to the SOUTH-WEST is the *Onze Lieve Vrouwetoren*, the beautiful 15C tower with a 17C steeple (100m) of a church destroyed by an explosion in 1787; the carillon is by François Hemony. The adjoining Kerkhof is a very pleasant small square with trees. On the Stadsring, some 300m S, stands the *Kei*, a huge glacial 'erratic' boulder brought into the town by the citizens in 1661. Moving round to the SOUTH-EAST, the *Monnikendam* on the outer ring-canal is a water-gate of c 1430. You can now follow the inner ring-canal northwards, houses along the inner side being known as the *Muurhuizen* (wall houses) because they were built as part of the wall of the inner fortifications. Similar houses will be found at the NORTH-EAST, where also, on the inner canal, is the *Kamperbinnenpoort*, a turreted 13C gate restored in 1932.

Amersfoort's zoo, the *Dierenpark* (mid May–Oct: 09.00 to 18.00; November–mid May: 09.00 to 17.00), is to the SW beyond the station.

At *Oud Leusden*, 3km S of central Amersfoort, are a church tower of c 1300, the oldest in the Netherlands outside Limburg, and also a Commonwealth war cemetery, while to the NW of the village the *Belgenmonument* was put up in 1916 as a mark of gratitude by Belgian refugees.

**Soest** (40,000 inhab.; VVV, Steenhoffstraat 9A), 4km NW of central Amersfoort, and **Baarn** (25,000 inhab.; VVV, Stationsplein 7), 3km further N, are, with Hilversum, to the W in Zuid Holland (see Rte 4), part of a group of prosperous residential towns in park-like surrounds. At *Soestdijk*, between Soest and Baarn, the Royal Palace can be seen from the road; the central building, designed by Maurits Post in 1674 as a hunting lodge for William III, was enlarged after 1816 by Jan de Greef. At Baarn the *Botanische Tuin*, you can visit the botanic garden of the university of Utrecht.

The long, adjoining villages of *Bunschoten* and *Spakenburg*, 10km N of Amersfoort, run down to the Eemmeer, the waterway which separates the province of Utrecht from the reclaimed Zuidelijk Flevoland. The villages are known for their local costume, and in July and August special 'Spakenburg Days' are arranged.

For Amersfoort to Hardewijk (Flevoland) and Zwolle, see Rte 29.

Leave Amersfoort by a southerly road for (*8km*) *Woudenberg* where you make a turn to the E, the road soon crossing into a pocket of the province of Gelderland with the small town of (*4km*) *Scherpenzeel*. You then briefly pass through a corner of the province of Utrecht, the road again entering

Gelderland, and in *14km* (from Scherpenzeel) reach **Ede** (87,000 inhab.; VVV, Achterdoelen 36). Here the *Museum Oud-Ede* (Mon–Fri, 10.00 to 12.00, 14.00 to 17.00; Sat, 14.00 to 16.00), at Museumplein 7, is a district museum housed in a former station of c 1900. The road now runs along the southern part of the Hoge Veluwe national park, for which, as also for (*18km*) Arnhem, see Rte 26.

# B. Via Doorn

Total distance 55km.—8km **Zeist**—10km **Doorn**—9km **Amerongen**—9km **Rhenen**—6km **Wageningen**—4km **Heelsum**—9km **Arnhem**.

For Utrecht to (*8km*) Zeist, see Rte 16A. At *10km* **Doorn** (11,000 inhab.; VVV, Dorpstraat 4), a pleasant small town in wooded surrounds, is known for being the retreat of the deposed German Kaiser William II from 1920–41. He lived at *Huis Doorn* (mid March–Oct: Mon–Sat, 09.30 to 17.00; Sun, 13.00 to 17.00), a manor house which belonged originally to the see of Utrecht, was burnt down in 1332 by Count William III of Holland, was rebuilt, then in the 18C extensively altered, though some of the older parts, notably the round corner tower, were incorporated. When the ex-Kaiser died in 1941, and was buried in a mausoleum in the grounds, Hitler, then occupying the Netherlands, ordered a full military funeral. The interior, furnished in 1920s style, contains 18C French paintings, tapestries, silver, and souvenirs of the Kaiser, including an outstanding collection of snuffboxes of the time of Frederick the Great.

**Wijk bij Duurstede** (8000 inhab.), 8km S, stands at the point where the old, now small stream of the Rhine, the Kromme (winding) Rijn, leaves the main stream, below here known as the Lek—a change which resulted from a great flood in 839. The town has an ancient history, probably starting as the Roman Batavodurum. Later known as Dorestad, it was here in 689 that Pepin of Herstal, the Christian Frankish king who befriended St Willibrord, defeated the pagan Radbod of Frisia, the latter as a result ceding all Frisia between the Scheldt and the Zuider Zee. Between 834 and 846 Dorestad was repeatedly sacked by Norsemen invaders, and in 850 it was granted by the Emperor Lothair to Rorik the Dane as capital and chief port of a short-lived Norse Kingdom of Frisia. In the town the *St Jan Baptistkerk* dates from the 15C, and in a park near the river the ruined *Slot Duurstede* was the castle-palace of the see of Utrecht; a square 13C keep and a late 15C round tower (with a local museum) survive. Throughout the town there are several houses of medieval origin, and a windmill, standing on remains of a rampart tower, recalls Jacob van Ruysdael's famous painting (Rijksmuseum, Amsterdam).

*9km*. It was at **Amerongen** that Kaiser William II first took refuge after his flight from Germany in 1918. The château (April–Oct: Tues–Fri 10.00 to 17.00; Sat, Sun, Holidays 13.00 to 17.00), in origin medieval, was rebuilt by Maurits Post in 1676 after the French wars. In *9km* **Rhenen** (17,000 inhab.; VVV, Frederik van de Paltshof), pleasantly situated on the Rhine, has provided a subject for many artists, including Jan van Goyen, Rembrandt, Pieter Saenredam, and Hercules Seghers. The town is associated with St Cunera, in legend one of the 11,000 virgins who in perhaps the 4C accompanied St Ursula to Rome and who was the only one to escape the subsequent massacre by the pagans at Cologne. The story goes that a Frankish chief took pity on her, bringing her to his estate here at Rhenen where she became much loved because of her care for the poor and suffering. To help her in her good works the chief handed over the keys of his storerooms, an act which so aroused the jealousy of his wife that she strangled Cunera, burying her body in the stables. That evening the horses refused to enter the stables, the body was found, and Cunera was given a ceremonial burial. What happened to the murderess is not recorded. The *Sint Cunerakerk* was built during the 15C, and the many pilgrims to the saint's shrine brought in so much money that a particularly fine tower was added in 1492–1513; church and tower were restored after severe war damage. In medieval times there was a nunnery near the church, but this was pulled down in 1629 to make room for a palace for the exiled King Frederick V of Bohemia (the 'Winter King'); the *Koningstafel*, a hill to the S of the road E of the town, was a favourite spot of his. The *Streekmuseum*, the district museum, is at Molenstraat 25. *Ouwehand*, a short way E of Rhenen on the Arnhem road, is a recreational park, a main feature of which is its zoo (April–Sept: 08.30 to 18.00; Oct–March: 09.00 to 17.00).

The road now enters a district of orchards, crosses into Gelderland, and in *6km* reaches **Wageningen** (32,000 inhab.; VVV, Plantsoen 3), an old town which may have been the Roman Ad Vada and today is known for an important agricultural institution. It was here in the former Hotel De Wereld that the Germans in the Netherlands (under General Blaskowitz) surrendered on 5 April 1945 to General Foulkes, commanding 1st Canadian Corps (memorial). *4km* **Heelsum**, to the N of which was the British parachute dropping and glider landing zone during the Arnhem operation of September 1944 (see Rte 26B). The *Nederlands Jachtmuseum* (hunting and shooting), with weapons and general material on game and game management, is at Kasteel Doorwerth, 3km SE; the castle, 13C in origin, is largely a rebuilding after war damage (April–Oct: Tues–Fri 10.00 to 17.00; Sat, Sun, Holidays 13.00 to 17.00; Nov–March: Sat, Sun, 13.00 to 17.00).

For (*6km*) Oosterbeek (with the Airborne Museum) and (*3km*) Arnhem, see Rte 26.

# 17 Northern and Western Province of Utrecht

## A. Utrecht to Amsterdam

Total distance 36km.—6km **Maarssen**—6km **Breukelen**—4km **Loenen**—20km **Amsterdam**.

As far as Loenen this Route follows the winding course of the river which gives its name to the

VECHT region, from the 16C onwards favoured as a retreat of the well-to-do from both Utrecht and Amsterdam; several of their country mansions are seen. The region was badly damaged by the French in 1672–73.

You leave Utrecht by the road along the E bank of the Amsterdam-Rijn Kanaal. In *5km Slot Zuylen* (mid March–mid Nov: daily, but Sat and Sun in

Oct–Nov, tours at 10.00, 11.00, 14.00, 15.00, 16.00; Sun at 14.00, 15.00 and 16.00) is signed to the right, the approach road crossing the Vecht. This mellow, moated castle in wooded surrounds, built in the late 12C but given a new façade in the 18C, was the home before her marriage of Isabella van Zuylen (1740–1805) who in 1771 married a Swiss and, as Isabelle de Charrière, became known as a novelist. In 1763–64 she was visited here by James Boswell, then a student at Utrecht, the two forming a long-lasting friendship (to Boswell she was Zélide). Opened as a museum in 1952, the castle rooms contain fine furniture, tapestry, porcelain, pictures and documents, including letters written by Alva and William the Silent. Ludger (c 770–809), bishop of the Saxons and first bishop of Münster in Germany, was born in the village. *1km* **Maarssen** (33,000 inhab.) was badly damaged by French troops in 1672, not a single house being untouched. It is now a handsome and prosperous dormitary town for the surrounding cities.

A diversion westward across the canal in 5km reaches the striking castle of *De Haar* (March–mid Aug and mid Oct–Nov: Mon–Fri 11.00 to 16.00; Sun, Holidays, 13.00 to 16.00), surrounded by park and woods beyond the village of Harzuilens. First built in 1165, the castle was enlarged in 1287, destroyed in 1482 by Bishop David of Utrecht, rebuilt in 1505, destroyed by the French in 1672, and finally rebuilt in 1892 by P.J.H. Cuijpers. It was once a home of Franck van Borssele, fourth husband of Jacqueline of Bavaria. The rooms contain tapestries (14C and 15C), Louis XIV–XVI furniture, porcelain, etc.

From Maarssen it is more pleasant to take the small road on the E bank of the Vecht, which in *4km* reaches the mansion of *Oudaen* (14–17C); roughly opposite across the river is the castle of *Nijenrode*, a medieval foundation considerably altered after 1632 and again in 1907 and now used as a business administration centre.

To the E extend the LOOSDRECHTSE PLASSEN, a series of shallow meres, some 6km by 4km, popular for boating and various water sports (boat excursions from *Oud Loosdrecht* at the N). A road along the S side, starting near Oudaen, in 8km reaches Nieuw Loosdrecht, and the château of *Sypesteyn* (May–mid Sept: Tues–Sat, tours at 10.15, 11.15, 14.00, 15.00, 16.00; Sun, Holidays, 14.00, 15.00, 16.00), a reconstruction of 1900 on foundations of a predecessor destroyed in 1580 and now an art gallery and museum. The paintings (16–18C) include works by Paulus Moreelse, Michiel van Miereveld, and Nicolaes Maes, and among the museum exhibits are furniture, weapons, glass, silver, watches and porcelain, including Delft and Loosdrecht ware. This last was made here between c 1771 and 1782 when on the founder's death the factory was moved to Amstel where it functioned until 1820. The ware embraces a wide variety of articles and is known for the high standard of its painting, which often includes attractive landscapes in muted tones. The park has a rose garden.

*2km* **Breukelen** is the village which gave its name to Brooklyn, USA. Largely demolished by the French in 1672, the stones being used to build defence works, the village is nevertheless still attractive with its narrow streets and old bridge over the Vecht. On the E side of the river are the *Stadhuis*, occupying a 17C villa, and also *Gunterstein*, the home of Jan van Oldenbarneveld; first built in the 13–14C and destroyed by the French in 1673, the château was rebuilt in 1681 in classical style.

You can follow either side of the Vecht to (*4km*) **Loenen** (7000 inhab.), and along this stretch from Breukelen are several country houses with gazebos. With its many 18C houses Loenen is perhaps the most picturesque of the Vecht small towns. The design of the church tower was taken from that of the Domtoren in Utrecht; in 1741 a lean of about 117cm was corrected by forcing peat into the foundations, but from some angles the tower still seems to lean. The local castle, *Loenersloot*, with a 13C keep, was restored during the 19C.

*20km* Amsterdam (see Rte 1) is best reached by motorway A2.

# B.   Utrecht to Gouda

Total distance 33km.—15km **Montfoort**—7km **Oudewater**—11km **Gouda**.

*15km* **Montfoort**, which you can reach by a choice of roads leaving Utrecht on the SW, is a small town on the IJssel which grew up around a 12C castle (of which only a gatehouse has survived French demolition in 1672) and settlement and received a charter in 1329. The *Grote Kerk* (or *St Janskerk*) dates from the 15C but has an older tower which is in part 14C, and an association with the Order of St John is remembered by the Order's *Commandery and Cloister* (1544) in Hofstraat. The *Stadhuis* and the *IJsselpoort* are restorations of 16–17C originals. In *7km* you reach **Oudewater** (7000 inhab.), a picturesque old place on the IJssel with many 16–17C façades, is best known for its association with witchcraft, this arising from the reputation for accuracy widely accorded to the town's scales, women coming here to receive a certificate that their weight 'accorded to the natural proportions of the body'. This happened, and for visitors still happens, at the *Heksenwaag* (witches' weigh-house; April–Oct: Tues–Sat, 10.00 to 17.00; Sun, Holidays, 12.00 to 17.00) in the town centre, a building with a façade of 1595 which also served as the commercial weigh-house. The liberal theologian Jacobus Arminius was born in the house next to the Heksenwaag in 1560, and storks nest on the nearby *Stadhuis* of 1588, restored in 1968–72 after a fire. The *St Michielkerk*, in Noorder Kerkstraat, dates in part from the late 12C and is noteworthy for its 13C tower with a saddle-roof. 'Heksenwaagjes', a form of butter biscuit, are a local speciality.

Immediately W of Oudewater, you cross the border into the province of Zuid Holland. For (*11km*) Gouda, see Rte 9.

# C.   Utrecht to Rotterdam via Vreeswijk (Vianen) and Schoonhoven

Total distance 66km.–14km **IJsselstein**.—3km **Vreeswijk (Vianen)**—20km **Schoonhoven**—29km **Rotterdam**.

Follow the motorway A2 S to cross the A12 and in 6km from the crossing you will reach the exit for (*14km* from central Utrecht) **IJsselstein** (17,000 inhab.), a small fortified place which developed from a 13C castle, demolished, except for one early 16C tower, in 1887. Although small, IJsselstein was over a period of centuries in a state of feud with neighbouring Utrecht, as a result being destroyed in 1418 and 1446. The castle's surviving tower (Kronenburgplantsoen 9) can be visited in May–mid Sept: Sat, 14.00 to 16.00; also to be seen here are the Reformed Church (Kronenburgplantsoen 2), in origin of 1310; the Catholic Basilica (Kronenburgplantsoen 46), built in 1887 but with a 12C figure of Our Lady; the *Stadhuis* of 1560 with a small local museum (Wed and Fri, 14.00 to 17.00; Sat, 14.00 to 16.00); and the radio and television tower, at 382m the highest in the country. *3km* (SE) is **Vreeswijk**, a name meaning Land of the Frisians who had a trading centre here in the 9C. On the N bank of the Lek where the river is met by the Merwede canal, Vreeswijk, today with its attractive centre architecturally protected, has long been associated with canals, dams and locks and still preserves the *Oude Sluis*, first built by the city of Utrecht in 1373, it underwent major alteration in 1874. The large *Prinses Beatrix Sluis* in the Lek canal, built in 1938, was until 1950 the biggest lock gate in western Europe.

The small town of **Vianen** (15,000 inhab.) is across the river in the province of Zuid Holland. This was, until 1725 when it was bought by the States of Holland, the principal of the five minute independent lordships (see Vijfheerenlanden, Rte 12) which lay between the rivers Lek and Linge, the lords of Vianen being for some 325 years the great family of Brederode. One of these lords, Reinoud van Brederode (died 1556), and his wife lie in a fine tomb in the *Reformed Church* (14–16C). From the church the straight, broad main street leads past the 15C *Stadhuis* to the turreted 15C *Lekpoort*, and from here a small road to the left passes a pump of 1648, with sculptured decoration, to reach the *Hofpoort* (1353, rebuilt 1658), all that remains of the town's castle.

This Route recrosses the Lek to follow small dike roads westwards through LOPIKWAARD, a quiet district of dikes and pasture with river views, and reaches (*20km* from Vreeswijk) **Schoonhoven** (see Rte 9) in Zuid Holland. *17km* on you reach *Krimpen aan der Lek*, from where there is a view across to the Kinderdijk windmills (Rte 12A). A further *12km* brings you to Rotterdam, see Rte 10.

# PROVINCE OF NOORD BRABANT

**Capital.** 's Hertogenbosch.

**History.** The province has its origins in the duchy of Lower Lorraine which emerged in the 10C during the conflicts which followed the death of Charlemagne. During the following century this duchy splintered into several feudal states (Hainaut, Namur, Limburg and Luxembourg all broke away), leaving a rump which in 1100 joined with the margravate of Antwerp and was ruled, as Duke of Lower Lorraine, by Count Godfrey I of Louvain and Brussels. But until well into the 12C there was territorial and titular dispute between the counts of Louvain and Brussels and those of Limburg, this eventually being resolved in c 1159 in favour of the former. In 1190 Duke Henry I dropped the dignity of Lower Lorraine, instead assuming that of Duke of Brabant, his lands very roughly made up of the present Dutch province of Noord Brabant and the Belgian provinces of Brabant and Antwerp.

The duchy of Brabant survived from 1190 to 1430. Its rulers, normally residing at Louvain (Leuven) in what is now Belgium, included John I (1261–94) who bought the duchy of Limburg in 1283 though his ownership was not established until he defeated and killed the rival claimant, Henry of Luxembourg, in 1288; and John II (1294–1312) and John III (1312–55), two enlightened men who conferred far-reaching privileges. John III was succeeded by his daughter Joanna (1355–1406) who married Duke Wenzel of Luxembourg and whose title was disputed by Count Louis II of Flanders, this leading to a war in which Joanna and Wenzel were supported by the guilds and Louis by the patricians. Wenzel and Louis died in 1383 and 1384 and Joanna ruled until her death over both Brabant and Luxembourg. Duke Anthony (1406–30) died childless, Brabant then passed by inheritance to Duke Philip the Good of Burgundy and its history became merged with the general history of the Netherlands.

It was during the long struggle against Spain that Brabant split into two, the southern portion remaining under Spain and eventually becoming the Belgian provinces of Brabant and Antwerp, while the northern part, conquered by the princes Maurice and Frederick Henry, was eventually ceded to the United Provinces by the Treaty of Münster (1648). Noord Brabant did not, though, rank as an autonomous province but became 'generality land' administered direct by the States General.

The Netherlands' largest province, Noord Brabant extends the length of the Belgian frontier from the Scheldt to Limburg and northwards up to the Maas. Scenically the province is in large part made up of woodland, heath, and some peat fen, much of this having been set aside as recreational land and nature reserve, with public access and usually with walking and cycle tracks. Among such areas may be singled out Beekse Bergen near Tilburg with a safari park, and, in the eastern part of the province, the heath-fen 'peels' (see Rte 20B).

Several of the towns of Noord Brabant—'s Hertogenbosch, Geertruidenberg, Heusden, Grave—are on the sites of Roman stations, though nothing visible survives of this era. Both historically and for what there is to see, the large towns most likely to attract the visitor are Breda and 's Hertogenbosch, while among smaller places Willemstad and Bergen op Zoom, both in the W of the province, repay a visit, as does also Heusden on the Maas for its restored fortifications. Other towns such as Tilburg,

Eindhoven, and Helmond are industrial in character, though the first two have museums of note, textiles at Tilburg and the modern, technological Evoluon at Eindhoven. These last three all have a variety of experimental and modernist architecture, some of it very attractive.

Visitors with young children should not miss the fairy-tale world of De Efteling between Tilburg and Waalwijk (Rte 19); those interested in the story and equipment of the last war should aim for the wooded park of the War and Resistance Museum at Overloon (see Rte 23); while connoisseurs of politico-geographic curiosities will find their way to the village of Baarle-Nassau (Rte 18A).

# 18   Rotterdam to Antwerp

## A.   Via Breda

Total distance 93km.—19km **Dordrecht**—10km *Hollands Diep* (*Moerdijk-bruggen*)—17km **Breda**—15km **Zundert**—6km *Frontier*—4km *Wuustwezel*—22km **Antwerp**. You can leave Rotterdam (see Rte 10) by motorway A16. After *12km* you reach the motorway junction with A15 which bears E (see Rte 12A).

In *7km* the A16 by-passes Dordrecht (see Rte 12B), crossing the Oude Maas by a tunnel of 1977 and continuing southward a short way E of the De Kil channel linking the Oude Maas with the (*10km*) HOLLANDS DIEP, crossed here by the *Moerdijkbruggen* (road and rail bridges). The Hollands Diep, here 1.5km wide and marking the border between the provinces of Zuid Holland and Noord Brabant, was formed in 1421 by the St Elisabeth Flood which also swamped the Biesbos (see Rte 19) a short way east. Before the road bridge was built in 1934–36 traffic was carried on a ferry. The first railway bridge was of 1868–71, but both road and rail bridges have been rebuilt since the last war. *Lage Zwaluwe*, 4km E on the S shore, is one place from which boat excursions can be made into the Biesbos; *Drimmelen*, further E, is another, the duration of the trip from either place being about two hours.

*17km* **BREDA** (118,000 inhab.) is only a few kilometres from the Belgian border and, as a frontier fortress, has suffered much from war. One of the chief towns of the province of Noord Brabant, and with its extensive pedestrian precincts a popular shopping centre, the town's main feature, and its main sightseeing interest for the tourist, is likely to be the Grote Kerk with its many elaborate monuments. Woodland and heath surround much of the town, particularly to the S and E.

**Centre.** Grote Markt.

**VVV.** Willemstraat 17, opposite the **Station** beyond the N edge of the inner town.

**Post Office.** Emmastraat, close to the station.

**History.** Holding Breda as a fief of the German Emperor, the first family to exercise the lordship gave the town a charter in 1252 and then sold the place to the Duke of Brabant in c 1300. A few years later, in 1350, it was bought by Jan I van Polanen, a member of the noble Wassenaer family, and it was he who built the first Polanen castle. In 1394 Johanna van Polanen, an infant, succeeded Jan II, in 1404 marrying Count

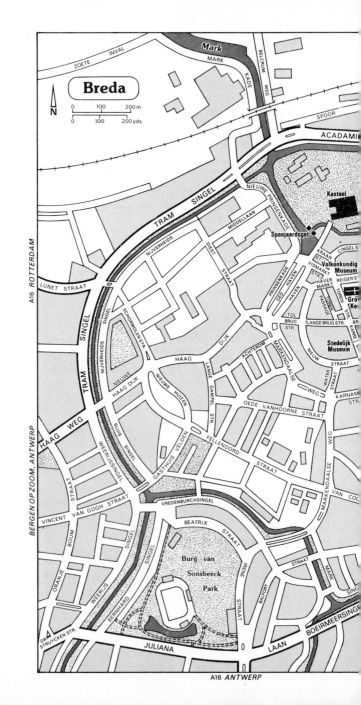

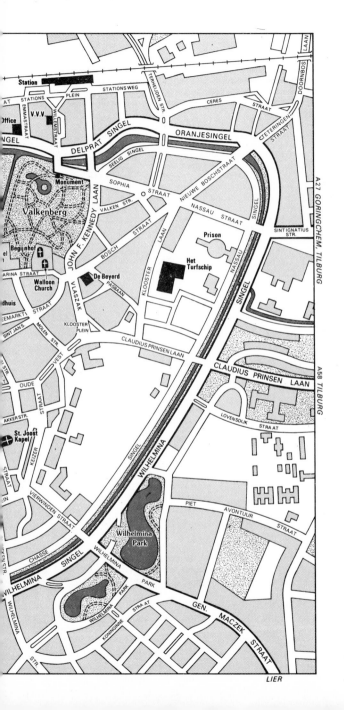

Engelbert I of the house of Nassau and thus starting the line of Breda-Nassau. Of the counts that followed the most notable was the cultured Hendrik III who succeeded in 1504, later rebuilding the castle and extending the town walls out to what is now the Singel. Hendrik's wife was Claudia de Châlons, Princess of Orange, their son Réné de Châlons thus becoming the first Prince of Orange and Count of Nassau. He died childless in 1544, being succeeded (for both Orange and Nassau) by his cousin William van Nassau-Dillingen, better known as William the Silent, who divided his early years between Breda and Brussels.

The Compromise of Breda, a manifesto signed by the Netherlands nobles in 1566 as a protest against the Inquisition, may be regarded as an early move against the Spanish dominion. During the Revolt Spanish troops took Breda in a surprise attack in 1581. In 1590, however, by a clever stratagem, Maurice of Nassau was able to retake the town; Captain De Heraugières and 80 picked men were hidden under a cargo of turves in the peat barge of Adriaen van Bergen who supplied the Spanish garrison with fuel, the barge then being towed into the citadel by the unsuspecting Spanish, who were quickly overcome. But in 1625 Breda, under the command of Justin of Nassau, had to be surrendered to the Spaniards under Spinola, though only after a nine months' siege, an event commemorated in a famous painting by Velazquez ('Las Lanzas' in Madrid's Prado). Prince Frederick Henry retook the town in 1637 and it was finally ceded to the United Provinces in 1648.

Breda was for some time the home of England's Charles II during his exile, and from here he issued the Declaration of Breda (1660), outlining the terms on which he was prepared to accept the throne. The Treaty of Breda of 1667, between England, France, the United Provinces, and Denmark, awarded the colonies of New York (Amsterdam) and New Jersey to the English. In 1696 the Stadholder William III rebuilt the castle.

During the French revolutionary wars, Breda was easily taken by Dumouriez in 1793, evacuated, then retaken by Pichegru in 1795 and held until 1813.

The GROTE MARKT is a rectangle, the S part of which is pedestrian precinct. The *Stadhuis*, with a façade of 1767, stands on the E side, and on the SW the house called *Het Lam* houses the **Stedelijk en Bisschoppelijk Museum** (Wed–Sat, 10.30 to 15.00; Tues, Sun, Holidays, 13.00 to 17.00), covering the story of the town and bishopric; in the 17C a meat hall and also (upper floor, 1617) the guild room of the Guild of Foot Bowmen, the building received a new façade in 1772, became a butter hall in 1861 and was converted to a museum in 1933.

At Nieuwstraat 21, a short way SW, there is a baroque portal. In Ginnekenstraat, some 250m S of the Grote Markt, the *St Joost Kapel* of 1430–40 is the oldest chapel in Breda.

The **Grote Kerk**, at the N end of the Grote Markt, is dedicated to the Blessed Virgin and notable for its many *monuments. Probably started in the 13C, as successor to earlier wooden churches on this site, construction continued with the completion of the chancel in 1410 and of the transepts and nave somewhat later. The fine tower (97m), a rebuilding of one that collapsed in 1457, is of 1461–1509.

The oldest monument of the lords of Breda is that of Jan I van Polanen who bought the lordship in 1350, and of his first two wives. Next is the fine flamboyant canopy sheltering Count Engelbert I (died 1442) of Nassau, his wife Johanna van Polanen who died in 1445, and of their son Jan IV of Nassau (died 1475) and his wife (died 1502); the group kneel at the feet of the Virgin and Child and, above, the arms of Nassau and Polanen remind us that it was the marriage between Engelbert and Johanna that founded the line of Breda-Nassau. Much damaged at the Reformation, this monument was restored in 1860–62 on the orders of King William III. In the side-chapel (Prince's Chapel) opposite is the magnificent *mausoleum of Count Engelbert II (died 1504) and of his wife Cimburga of Baden (died

1501; they in fact lie in the vault below the Engelbert I monument), a striking work (c 1535) of the Italian Renaissance, possibly by Tomaso Vincidor of Bologna. The alabaster effigies of the deceased lie beneath a slab bearing the Count's armour, with four heroes of antiquity (Caesar, Hannibal, Regulus, and Philip of Macedon) as supporters. In the vault below lie Count Hendrik III (died 1538), who commissioned the memorial, and his son Réné de Châlons, the first Prince of Orange-Nassau (died 1544). It is of interest that in 1552 William the Silent had this vault enlarged, probably for himself; however when he was murdered at Delft in 1584 the Spanish held Breda, and Delft thereafter became the Orange-Nassau mausoleum. Nonetheless, the recapture and holding of Breda became a cause close to the heart of the Princes of Orange and their adherents. To the east of the Prince's Chapel is the badly mutilated tomb of Jan II of Polanen (died 1394); opposite, on the wall, is the memorial to the Sieur de Borgnival (died 1536), chief engineer of Charles V; and at the E end can be seen that of Frederik van Renesse (died 1538), counsellor of Charles V, and of his wife (died 1550).

The choir has a good brass screen, presented by Engelbert I in 1412 but with woodwork alterations of the 16C, and also interesting misericords (probably 16C on), many depicting scenes of everyday life, including a motorcycle (1945). Murals of c 1537 adorn the vault of the choir, where also the sculptured bosses have been coloured (both have survived being covered by plaster at the Reformation). In the church's south-west chapel there is a Renaissance bronze font of 1540 by Joos de Backer of Antwerp; the iron crane is by Pieter van Beers of Breda. In the central chapel of the south nave aisle the elaborate brass of Wilhelm van Galen (died 1539), a dean of this church, merits attention. The NW chapel (of St Francis) contains the monument (possibly by Cornel Floris de Vriendt of Antwerp) of Dirk van Assendelft (died 1553) and of his wife Adriana van Nassau (died 1558), with a defaced relief of the Last Judgement and the Brazen Serpent; here too is the tomb of an unknown man, thought to have been one of the architects of the church. In the north transept are a mural (Annunciation, 16C), and a triptych designed by Jan van Scorel and executed by his pupils.

There are many cafés around the small Havermarkt immediately W of the church.

The KASTEELPLEIN, with an equestrian statue of Stadholder William III, to the N of the Grote Kerk, was once a place of execution, and has entered the popular imagination as the scene of the burning of Protestants. The building on the SW corner, known as the *Prins Cardinaal* after the brother of Philip IV of Spain, was formerly an inn at which Oliver Cromwell and Daniel Defoe are said to have stayed, while that at the NW corner houses the *Volkenkundig Museum* (Mon–Sat, 10.00 to 17.00; Sun, 13.00 to 17.00), with ethnographic collections, largely from Indonesia; this building was put up in 1606 for the governor, Justin of Nassau. The *Kasteel*, at the N end of the square, since 1828 a military academy (no adm.), is on the site where a castle has stood since at least 1198. The present building, begun in 1536 by Hendrik III to replace the old stronghold (1350) of the Polanen family, was reconstructed by William III in 1696.

A short walk out of the NW corner of Kasteelplein along Cingelstraat and Kraanstraat reaches the *Spanjaardsgat*, an open sheet of water with a twin-towered gate built in c 1509, popularly but probably incorrectly identified as the spot where the peat barge was moored in 1590; in fact the waterway here was not dug until 1610, and the peat barge probably moored some distance further N.

Catharinastraat, once lined by patrician houses, leads out of the SE corner of Kasteelplein, with almost immediately on left being (No. 9) *Het Huis Wijngaerde*, dating from 1614 and a survivor of the patrician days. Further on, on the left, there is an entrance to the VALKENBERG, a park which until 1912 was the castle garden and which owes its name to a falconry which stood here. At the N of the park, opposite Willemstraat, a monument of 1905 by P.J.H. Cuijpers celebrates the 500th anniversary of the marriage in 1404 between Count Engelbert I and Johanna van Polanen.

The canal beyond marks the N limit of the town between the early 16C when Hendrik III pushed out the walls and 1870–79 when the walls were razed and northward expansion took place. A new station was built in 1975.

The *Begijnhof*, next on the left off Catharinastraat, was founded in 1267 nearer the early castle, then in 1531 built on its present site where it still functions as a religious community. The original chapel later (c 1648) became the Walloon church, and it was here that Pieter Stuyvesant (1592–1672), director of New Amsterdam, later New York, was married. The chapel at the rear dates from 1830. At the E end of Catharinastraat is a fragment of the *Gasthuispoort* (16C), discovered in 1976; the gate was so called because of a hospice which stood outside the walls, this is now the building known as *De Beyard* a short way E at the beginning of Boschstraat, a cultural centre with art exhibitions. The building, with a façade of 1634, has served various purposes, including hospice for poor travellers, hospital for plague victims, lunatic asylum, barracks, and a home for old men. Vlaszak, running S from here, reaches KLOOSTERPLEIN, the name recalling a nunnery which was here until 1645.

**Baarle-Nassau**, 19km SE and reached by a road across some pleasant wooded country, is a geographic and political curiosity where Belgian enclaves (*Baarle-Hertog*) are mixed in with the Dutch village, a state of affairs which originated in 1479 when, for lordship inheritance reasons, the village of Baarle was divided into two parts, these eventually splitting politically between the two Brabants. Some strange situations have thus arisen, e.g. the market place is Dutch, except for one inn, while the old church is Belgian. There are two town halls, police stations, schools, post offices, etc. This unique situation saved Baarle-Hertog from German occupation during the First World War; in October 1915 the Belgians established a radio station here and, in spite of a barbed-wire fence built around the commune by the neutral Dutch, made the village an important focus of Allied espionage.

For Breda to (W) Bergen op Zoom and (E) Tilburg, 's Hertogenbosch and Nijmegen, see Rte 19.

*15km* **Zundert** is the birthplace of the painter Vincent van Gogh (1853–90), the house being on the main street on the E side opposite the Stadhuis. Just N of the house, in the small Vincent van Gogh Plein, a sculpture group, 'Vincent and Theo' by Ossip Zadkine, stands near the small church at which the artist's father was minister. In *6km is the Belgian frontier (see Blue Guide, Belgium and Luxembourg). 4km Wuustwezel* is the centre of a district popular with walkers. The church, in origin 13C, contains a painting of St Sebastian by Guido Reni. *22km* Antwerp (for summary, see end of Rte 18B).

# B.  Via Bergen op Zoom

Total distance 94km.—24km **Haringvlietbrug**—6km **Willemstad**—16km **Steenbergen**—7km **Halsteren**—3km **Bergen op Zoom**—8km *Woensdrecht*—9km *Putte*—21km **Antwerp**.

For Rotterdam, see Rte 10. For Rotterdam to (*24km*) the Haringvlietbrug, see Rte 13A. On the S side of the long bridge the motorway, now in the province of Noord Brabant, bears briefly SE, crossing some of the largest inland locks in western Europe (see below). *6km* (from N end of Haringvlietbrug) **Willemstad** (3000 inhab.), a fortress built by William the Silent in 1565–83 to guard the entrance to the Hollands Diep, is today a most attractive small town interesting mainly for its marina. The star-shaped bastions, of very considerable extent and well preserved, are a main feature. Around the harbour area, with several cafés, are a windmill (1732); the *Stadhuis* of 1587, originally built as a hunting lodge for Prince Maurice; the *Arsenal* of 1793 with a carillon along the front; and a bastion, beyond which is a large car park beside the Hollands Diep and with a good view of the Haringvlietbrug. Boat excursions cruise the Hollands Diep, while the locks, at the S end of the Haringvlietbrug, can be viewed from a special tower.

At *Klundert*, 6km SE, there is a particularly fine free-standing Stadhuis of 1621, a stone near the main entrance showing the height of the flood water in February 1953. The star-shaped bastions around the town have been in part restored.

At (*16km*) **Steenbergen** (13,000 inhab.) the most conspicuous building is the huge *St Gummaruskerk* (1902), with a massive spire, many exterior pinnacles, and a spacious domed interior. At *7km* **Halsteren** (12,000 inhab.) has a handsome *Stadhuis* of 1633 and a church which is in part of the 14C. The Antonius Mill, on the main road S of the town, claims to be one of the best in Noord Brabant.

ST PHILIPSLAND AND THOLEN. Some 7km to the W of Steenbergen and 4km to the W of Halsteren, the *Schelde-Rijn Verbinding* (1975), the canal linking Antwerp in Belgium with the waterways to the N, here the river Eendracht and still often called this, forms the border between the provinces of Noord Brabant and Zeeland. At the village of *Nieuw Vossemeer*, on the E side of the canal, the *Assumburg Windmill* (mid May–early Sept: Sat–Sun, 14.00 to 17.00) houses a windmills museum. Beyond the canal in Zeeland are the polders of (N) St Philipsland and (S) Tholen, both agricultural with fruit orchards and both with coasts increasingly used for marinas and other recreational purposes.

**St Philipsland**, totally submerged during the floods of 1953, is today a prosperous polder linked now by the Philipsdam to the Grevelingendam.

**Tholen** (*VVV*, Markt 13, St Maartensdijk) owes its name to the tolls once levied on shipping using the Eendracht passage. The engineer Cornelius Vermuyden (?1600–83), who in c 1634–37 drained much of the English fens, was born on the island. Thanks to the tolls the little town of *Tholen* at the polder's SE corner enjoyed early prosperity, this being reflected by a graceful Stadhuis of c 1460 and a church dating back to the 13C. The town also retains some sections of its walls.

It was at *St Maartensdijk*, 10km W, that in 1432 Franck van Borssele married the unhappy Jacqueline of Bavaria, and it was from near here in 1572 that the Spanish waded chin-deep across the Oosterschelde in an attempt to relieve Goes, under siege by the Sea Beggars. The Raadhuis has been well restored to its early form of 1628, and the Reformed Church, in part early 15C, has a carillon of 1615. A variety of birds breed by the narrow lake to the S known as the *Pluimpot* (footpath). A Tholen district museum (De Meestoof) is at *St Annaland* in the north (Ascension to mid Sept: Tues–Sat, 15.00 to 17.00).

*3km* **Bergen op Zoom** (46,000 inhab.; VVV, Hoogstraat 2, off the Grote Markt) is an ancient place, historically famed as the strongest fortress in the Netherlands and for the many sieges which it withstood. Of the once all important fortifications little now survives, but the town nevertheless preserves something of its past in the area around the Grote Markt. Situated at the E end of the Oosterschelde, Bergen is surrounded on much of its other sides by a peaceful district of woods, orchards, and lakes. Boat excursions include Zierikzee and Antwerp.

**History.** A settlement here at the confluence of the little Zoom with the Scheldt is known to have been taken by the Norsemen in 880. A castle was built in the 13C, at which time also Bergen was first walled and, lying so conveniently on the Scheldt, it soon became an important trading centre, the annual fair attracting many merchants from England. In 1576 Bergen declared for the United Provinces, and between 1581 and 1622 it was five times besieged unsuccessfully by the Spanish, their commander on the last occasion being Spinola. During the 17C Menno van Coehoorn strengthened the fortifications, and these were extended in 1725, but despite this the French took Bergen in 1747, an event commemorated by the popular French ballad 'La Prise de Berg-op-Zoom', and again, though this time without opposition, in 1795, later successfully holding an English attack in 1814. On 27 October 1944 the town was liberated by the Canadians.
    The story of the lordship of Bergen goes back to around the 10C when it was a fief of the German emperors. In 1533 Charles V raised the lordship to margravate, this being held by a succession of families until finally renounced during the time of the Batavian Republic.

The town centre is the GROTE MARKT, a cheerful place with many cafés, open air in summer. The *Grote Kerk*, dedicated to St Gertrude, is perhaps of most interest for its repeated disasters. Of ancient but shadowy origin, it is known that a replacement church was built during the 14C, of which today only the tower survives, and that during the 15C the structure was much enlarged by Evert Spoorwater and Antoon and Rombout Keldermans. Plundered and wrecked in 1580, the church was totally destroyed when the French took Bergen in 1747. A more modest church was completed in 1752, this, however, being almost completely burnt down during a restoration of 1972. The *Stadhuis* (Mon–Fri, 08.30 to 12.30, 13.30 to 17.30) is something of an architectural hotchpotch. The centre represents a rebuilding after a fire in 1397; the house to the right, formerly the English merchants' centre, was incorporated in 1480; and there is a third old house, this one with an arch, on the left. In 1611 the central and righthand houses were given a new faéade, the message 'Mille periculis supersum' (I overcome a thousand perils) suggesting that its builders had little faith in the Twelve Years' Truce (1609–21) during the long struggle with Spain. Later in the 17C a further building was added at the rear. Inside, in the hall at the foot of the stairs, tablets commemorate that it was people from Bergen op Zoom who in 1660 first settled in what would become New Jersey, USA, and that on 27 October 1944 the town was liberated by the Canadian

Lincoln and Welland Regiment; another tablet expresses the appreciation of the Royal Canadian Legion for the town's promotion of acts of remembrance and for receiving Canadian pilgrims to war cemeteries (there are Canadian and British war cemeteries 2km NE).

Just NW of the Grote Markt, in the Steenbergenstraat, the *Markiezenhof* (mid June–Aug: Tues–Fri, 11.00 to 17.00; Sat, Sun, Holidays, 14.00 to 17.00; other times: Tues–Sun, 14.00 to 17.00), long the palace of the margraves, was rebuilt between 1485 and 1512 by Antoon Keldermans; later, in 1711, the garden wing was redesigned in contemporary French style. With the arrival of the French in 1795 the building served as a military hospital (until 1814), followed by a long period (1814–1957) of use as a barracks. Now thoroughly restored, the Markiezenhof doubles as a cultural centre and museum showing fine art, tapestries, period rooms and a range of decorative art including local ceramic.

Not far to the W of the Markienzenhof stands the massive *Lievevrouwepoort* (or *Gevangenpoort*), built during the first half of the 14C to defend the town's seaward flank. However, with the widening of the fortifications in the following century the gate lost its defensive function and was converted to serve as a prison. The other surviving fortification is the moated *Ravelijn* at the NE of the town, built in the 17C by Menno van Coehoorn.

To the SE the *Wouwse Plantage* is an area of woodland popular with walkers.

For Bergen op Zoom to Goes, see Rte 13A; to Nijmegen, see Rte 19.

*8km Woensdrecht* is at the E end of the isthmus linking Noord Brabant to Zuid Beveland, for the road along which see Rte 13A. From here there is a choice of roads (see also *Blue Guide, Belgium and Luxembourg*), the more westerly crossing the frontier in 5km, then running, with another choice of roads, through Antwerp's busy port to reach the city's centre in c 24km. The main road beyond Woensdrecht in *9km* reaches the frontier at *Putte*, a village in both countries. The grave of the painter Jacob Jordaens (died 1678), who as a Protestant could not be buried in Antwerp, is in the Dutch village. *21km* **Antwerp** is the chief city of Flemish Belgium and one of that country's leading tourist centres, famed for its collections of works by Rubens in the great Gothic cathedral, in the artist's beautiful mansion, and in the Museum voor Schone Kunsten (Fine Arts). Other features of Antwerp are its numerous and diverse superb churches, its historic old quarters, its many museums and art galleries, its lively cafés and restaurants, and a waterfront and port of which most is readily accessible.

# 19 Bergen op Zoom to Nijmegen

Total distance 115km.—12km **Roosendaal**—6km **Oudenbosch**—16km **Breda**—12km **Geertruidenberg**—12km **Waalwijk**—5km **Drunen**—10km **'s Hertogenbosch**—14km **Oss**—16km **Grave**—12km **Nijmegen**.

For **Bergen op Zoom**, see Rte 18B. *7km Wouw*, where the church of St Lambert, built in 1614, badly damaged in 1944 and now restored, retains some of the carvings of the choir stalls of 1690. *5km* **Roosendaal** (56,000 inhab.; VVV, Dr Braberstraat 9), though originating as a peat cutting village in the 13C, is essentially a town of today, an industrial and shopping centre with the latter catered for by a large, partly covered, modern precinct (De Rozelaar). *6km* **Oudenbosch**, where the dominant feature is the huge *Basiliek van de H.H. Agatha en Barbara*, built by P.J.H. Cuijpers and G. van Swaay in 1865–92 as a scaled down copy of St Peter's in Rome, but with a façade derived from St John Lateran. The interior, around which are scattered large statues of saints, contains a canopied fore-altar and a large ornate altar behind, set into the base of the latter being a pleasing small carved Last Supper. A memorial on the space in front of the basilica remembers Dutchmen ('Zouaves') who fought for the Pope and the Papal States during the confused period (c 1860–70) which saw the formation of modern Italy. Roughly opposite the basilica are the buildings of the Monastery of St Louis with a large domed church. *7km* **Etten-Leur**, where the *St Paulushofje* are almshouses of 1681. Here too there is a museum of printing (*Grafisch Historisch Centrum*, Lage Neerstraat 12), with old presses and similar material. *9km* Breda, see Rte 18A.

There is a choice of roads between Breda and 's Hertogenbosch: a southerly one through Tilburg (for those interested in textiles), or a more northerly one (this Route) through Geertruidenberg and Waalwijk (for the Biesbos and those interested in leather and shoes). A direct road (12km) links Waalwijk and Tilburg.

VIA TILBURG. **Tilburg** (154,000 inhab.; VVV, Sportlaan 416A, opposite the station), 19km E of Breda, is an industrial town associated with textiles. For the visitor the town's attraction is likely to be the *Nederlands Textiel Museum* (Tues–Fri, 10.00 to 17.00; Sat, Holidays, 12.00 to 17.00; Sun, 12.00 to 17.00) at Goirkestraat 88 in the northern part of Tilburg. Spread around four levels of a spacious old mill, the museum illustrates aspects such as the treatment of wool, flax, dyeing, weaving (with demonstrations) and design. Tilburg has pleasant wooded surrounds, notably *Beekse Bergen* (daily from 10.00 to 16.00–18.00 according to the time of year; closed about Nov–Easter), a short way S near Hilvarenbeek, a large recreation and safari park. *Oisterwijk*, 7km E of Tilburg and on the edge of woods and lakes, is a summer resort especially popular for walking and cycling and known too for its bird park with, amongst other birds, flamingoes and parakeets (Easter–autumn: daily 09.00 to 18.00).

A27 heading N from Breda in *12km* reaches **Geertruidenberg** (7000 inhab.), an old fortress town (built on the site of a Roman station) beside the motorway bridge across the Bergse Maas just above where it becomes the Amer. From here there are boat excursions (duration 2½ hours) down and across the Amer into the BIESBOS (Reed forest), a large tract of river creeks, meres and reedy marshes, the legacy of the St Elisabeth flood of 1421. Boats also available from Drimmelen and Lage Zwaluwe, respectively 4km and 10km W of Geertruidenberg.

This Rte does not cross the Bergse Maas but turns E for (*12km*) **Waalwijk** (29,000 inhab.; VVV, Grotestraat 245), an industrial town long concerned with shoe making. Here the *Nederlands Leder en Schoenenmuseum* (Tues–Fri, 10.00 to 17.00; Sat, Sun, 12.00 to 16.00), the museum of leather and shoes, is a lot more interesting than might be supposed. The museum will be found in a large hangar-like hall at Elzenweg 25, a road immediately parallel to the Tilburg road in the industrial zone in the SW corner of the town. The comprehensive display, with accompanying illustrations, shows shoes by periods (prehistoric, through Roman and medieval to modern times) and areas, the latter being virtually worldwide. Additionally there is machinery, large and small, while special displays show a factory of 1930, a clog maker's workshop, a tannery of 1870 and a cobbler's living room and workshop. In a more modern context there is a section on specialised footwear, such as military, sport and high fashion. *De Efteling* (roughly Easter–mid October: daily, 10.00 to 18.00), 3km S of Waalwijk, is a recreation park of especial interest to children because of its large and imaginative Fairy Tale Wood; other attractions include a deer enclosure, miniature railway, boating lakes and swimming pool. *5km* **Drunen**, where *Lips Autotron* (April–mid Oct: Mon–Fri, 10.00 to 17.00 or 18.00 in July and Aug; Sat, Sun, 11.00 to 17.00 or 18.00 in July and Aug; Jan–March: Sat, Sun, 11.00 to 17.00), opened in 1972, is a large museum of vintage and veteran cars, motor cycles, and other transport curiosities. The *Loonse* and *Drunense Duinen* to the S have a network of walking and cycle tracks.

DRUNEN TO WOUDRICHEM. 18km **Heusden** (6000 inhab.; VVV, Engstraat 4), on the S bank of the Maas and worth visiting for its restored fortifications, is thought to stand on the site of a Roman post; later, the first church was founded in 717, the town was sacked by Norsemen in 839, and a charter was granted in 1281. The fortifications were the work in 1581 of Jacob Kemp of Gorinchem, and it is to this state that they have now been restored (path; circuit about one hour). At the harbour there are windmills and also the Visbank of 1796.

After crossing the Bergse Maas, you can follow small roads close to the Maas proper, here the border with Gelderland, to (16km from Heusden) **Woudrichem**, at the confluence of the Maas and Waal and another old fortified town. Ferries (no cars) to Gorinchem and across the Maas to the castle of *Loevestein* (April–Oct: Mon–Fri, 10.00 to 17.00; Sat, Sun, 13.00 to 17.00), in Gelderland, built in c 1360 on a commanding site between the rivers. It was here that Hugo Grotius (see also Rte 8) was imprisoned in 1619 as an Arminian, and it was from here that he was rescued by his wife who persuaded him to hide in a chest supposedly carrying unwanted books and linen. The furious castle commandant tried to keep the wife in exchange, but was ordered by the States General to release her. The chest (two claimants) can be seen in the Rijksmuseum at Amsterdam or the Prinsenhof in Delft. The English Admiral Sir George Ayscue, taken prisoner when his ship ran aground in a battle of 1666, was confined here until the following year.

*10km* **'S HERTOGENBOSCH** (89,000 inhab.) is visited principally for its magnificent Gothic cathedral. The capital of the province of Noord Brabant, the town's name is officially abbreviated to *Den Bosch* and it is also known popularly as *'s Bosch*. The triangular inner town is virtually entirely surrounded by water, the Dommel on the W, the double line of the Zuid Willemsvaart and the Aa on the NE, and more water along the line of the Zuidwal on the S.

**Centre.** Markt, from which radiate pedestrian streets.

**VVV.** Markt (*De Moriaan* on the N).

**Post Office.** Kerkstraat, W of St Janskathedraal.

**Station.** W of the Dommel.

**History.** Although the town was probably a Roman station, its name (Duke's Wood) stems from the time of Henry I, Duke of Brabant, who had a hunting lodge here and who conferred a charter on the town in 1185. In the Spanish wars it was vainly assaulted by Maurice of Nassau in 1601 and 1603, but it fell to Frederick Henry in 1629. The

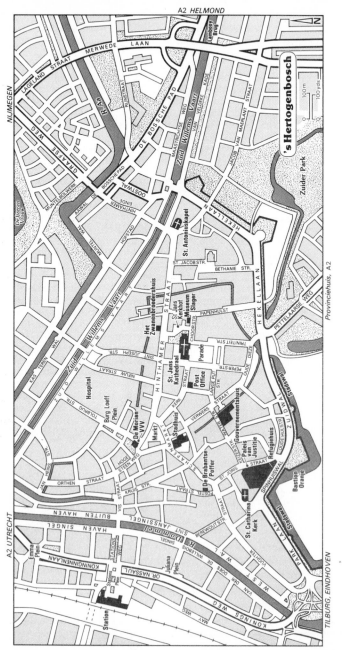

town was taken by the French under Pichegru in 1794. On 24 October 1944 it was liberated by 53rd (Welsh) Division.

**Natives** include the painters Hieronymus Bosch (c 1450–1516) and Theodore van Thulden (1606–69), the friend and pupil of Rubens.

In the MARKT there is a statue of Hieronymus Bosch. *De Moriaan*, on the N and now housing VVV, dates from c 1220 when it was built as successor to Duke Henry I's hunting lodge. Opposite across the Markt the **Stadhuis** (entry normally allowed during working hours), while in origin of the 16C was remodelled in a classical style in 1671. The tower contains a carillon by François Hemony (recitals Wednesdays, 10.00 to 11.00), and the tournament of knights that appears every half hour in the upper part of the façade is by Jacob Roman, responsible also for the fine interior front on the courtyard. In the interior there are frescoes by A. Derkinderen (1895) and paintings by Theodore van Thulden, Jean Brandon (William III and Mary II of England), and others, while in the council chamber a ceiling and chimneypiece are by Roman. The *Raadskeller*, beneath the Stadhuis and dating from 1529, is now a restaurant.

Kerkstraat or Hinthamerstraat both lead E out of the Markt to **··Sint Janskathedraal**, the most outstanding example of Gothic architecture in the Netherlands.

This is the third church to occupy this site, the first being a Romanesque building of c 1200, of which the lower part of today's tower is a survival. This Romanesque church was followed by an early Gothic one, built by Marcelius van Ceulen; the Lady Chapel and the baptistery, either side of the tower, belong to this. The present cathedral dates in all essentials from a rebuilding begun soon after 1336 and continued until c 1550. In 1561 's Hertogenbosch, hitherto a dependency of the bishopric of Liège, was given its own bishop in the person of Franciscus Sonnius, the church then formally becoming a cathedral. On the taking of the town by the Protestants in 1629 the cathedral was largely denuded of its Catholic furnishings, but it was returned to the Catholics in 1810 by Napoleon, and in 1929 the Pope granted the status of basilica.

The *carillon* comprises 48 bells, of which one cast in 1641 by Jacob Noteman is the oldest and heaviest (3500 kg.). There are also two Hemony bells, cast between 1644 and 1663. Most of the other bells were cast by Gillet and Johnstone of Croydon, England. Concerts on Wednesdays, 12.00 to 13.00.

Features of the exterior are the little figures on the buttresses, and the contrast between the very decorated transeptal portals and the plain W end with its red brick tower.

You enter the cathedral by the west gateway, largely a survival of the Romanesque church of c 1200. In the BAPTISTERY, occupying the SW corner of the cathedral and a survival of the second church, the solid copper ·font of 1492 was designed by Alard Duhamel, master mason of the cathedral, and cast by Jan Aerts of Maastricht, but the ingenious wrought iron lever to the three-tiered lid with its many figures is by an unknown smith. The figures supporting the basin represent the cripples at the Pool of Bethesda. The baptistery window (1953) is by Pieter Wiegersma. Adjacent to the baptistery hangs a painting of 1620 by Adriaen Bloemaert depicting Christ as mediator, and nearby, set in the wall, is the small tombstone of Margriet van Auweninge (died 1484), wife of the master mason Alard Duhamel.

The LADY CHAPEL, forming the north-west corner of the cathedral and in part another survival of the second church, contains the venerated 13C wooden figure of Zoete Lieve Vrouw (Sweet Blessed Lady). This figure of Our Lady (dated as c 1250) and that of the Child, probably of about the same date, were discovered during the 14C and united (or perhaps reunited), the group soon becoming known for miracles, 501 of which were recorded between 1383 and 1603. When the Protestants came in 1629 the statue went to the church of Coudenberg in Brussels and did not return to 's Hertogenbosch until 1853.

The NAVE, with double aisles, appears loftier than it really is owing to the absence of capitals in the main arcade. The saints on the piers are men along one side and women along the other, and the pulpit (1567) bears delicate low reliefs of the lives of saints and other themes. The towering organ case (1617) is the work of Frans Symons, a local man, and Gregorius Schysler, a Tyrolean living in Venlo; the original pipes were built by Florens Hoquet (16C), but of these only about a quarter survive. The strange *twisted canopy, at the E end of the nave, is said to be Duhamel's sample work to prove that he had the skill necessary to be appointed master mason.

In the NORTH TRANSEPT there are two grisaille works (originally decorating the panels of doors) by Hieronymus Bosch, and near the S transept (St Anthony's Chapel) stands the cathedral's greatest treasure, the superb *altar of the Passion, an Antwerp retable of c 1500. The carved Crucifixion holds the centre, with, on either side, Christ bearing the Cross and the Lamentation. The painted panels on the left show the Entry into Jerusalem and the Taking of Christ; those on the right the Resurrection and a (rather comic) Ascension; and those on top the Mount of Olives and the Descent from the Cross. Also worth detailed attention are the six delightful carved scenes along the foot of the retable, depicting the birth and youth of Christ, starting with the Annunciation to a clearly startled Mary.

The CHOIR, begun in 1336, contains 15C stalls with lively grotesques, and at their W end two groups, Christ in the Garden and a Crucifixion. Here too in the choir is the tomb of Sir James Ferguson (died 1705) who commanded the Scottish Brigade under Marlborough.

In Hinthamerstraat No. 94 is *Het Zwanenbroedershuis* (Fri, 11.00 to 15.00; closed August), the seat of the Illustre Lieve Vrouwebroederschap (Confraternity of Our Lady), a charitable society founded in 1318 and of which Hieronymus Bosch was later made a member. After 1629 the confraternity became secularised and open to both Protestants and Catholics. Various members of the Royal Family now belong, and in recent times much has been done to promote church music and religious art. The house contains music books of the 15C and 16C and various antiquities, including a remarkable carving of the Vision of the Emperor Augustus, a fragment of an altar made for the confraternity by Adriaen van Wesel in 1475. Roughly opposite the Zwanenbroedershuis, St Janskerkhof leads to the *Museum Slager* (Tues–Fri, and each first Sat and Sun of the month, 11.00 to 17.00) in Choorstraat, with pictures and souvenirs of the 's Hertogenbosch family of artists of that name (late 19C–early 20C).

From near the E end of Hinthamerstraat the 17C ramparts and bastions start. Over a length of nearly 2km these still define the southern edge of the inner town.

There is more of interest in the streets generally to the S and SW of the cathedral. The large square beside the cathedral is called Parade. Lange Put, leading out of the SW corner of the square, soon reaches Verwersstraat roughly opposite (No. 41) the *Gouvernementshuis*, a dignified patrician building of 1769 by Pieter de Swart, bearing the arms of Brabant and once the residence of the provincial commissioner. Today this is the home of *Het Noordbrabants Museum* (Tues–Fri, 10.00 to 17.00; Sat 11.00; Sun, 13.00 to 17.00).

Verwersstraat, followed SE, meets the 17C ramparts at the point where Hekelaan becomes Zuidwal, opposite being Pettelaarseweg which runs SE to (nearly 2km) *Het Provinciehuis* (H. Maaskant, 1971), towering to a height of over 100m. Seat of the provincial government, the building, (open during normal working hours) shows modern art and murals. Zuidwal, followed W, becomes Spinhuiswal, with at this point the *Bastion Oranje* with a huge cannon ('Bose Griet') of 1511. Opposite, on the corner of Spinhuiswal and St Jorisstraat, the *Refugiehuis* (16C), now an arts and crafts centre, was once a monastic refuge; adjoining is the modern *Paleis van Justitie* by Dutour Geerding. St Jorisstraat heads N, to its W being the *Kruiskerk* (or *St Catharinakerk*) with 17–18C paintings by P.J. Verhagen and Theodore van Thulden, and then meets Vughterstraat across which, at Postelstraat 3A, is *De Brabantse Poffer* (16C building), a private museum of Brabant curiosities (Sat, Sun, 13.00 to 17.00; also Tues–Sun in summer).

The *Veemarkt* (cattle on Wed; horses on Thurs) is one of the most important livestock markets in Europe; the halls are on Oude Engelenseweg on the NW edge of the outer town.

In the *Sportpark* (outer town, NE) there is a memorial of 1952 by H. St J. Harrison to the 53rd Welsh Division.

At *Bokhoven*, on the Maas 8km NW of 's Hertogenbosch, the 15C church contains the *tomb, by Artus Quellin, of Engelbert van Immerzeele and his wife Helène de Montmorency (died 1652 and 1649).

For 's Hertogenbosch to Eindhoven, Helmond, and Roermond, see Rte 20.

*14km* **Oss** (50,00 inhab.) is a commercial and market centre. From here it is worth considering a diversion to *Megen* (6km N), an old town still with its street plan of 1645 and preserving also something of its medieval walls. The Gevangentoren (prison tower) here dates from the 14C, and the Franciskanenklooster from the 17C, the latter having a church with a baroque interior.

From Oss the motorway (A50) offers the quickest approach to Nijmegen, but this Route follows the more pleasant road to the S which in *16km* reaches **Grave** (10,000 inhab.), site of a Roman station and later an ancient fortress of the dukes of Brabant, standing at the S end of a bridge over the Maas taken on 17 September 1944 by American 82nd Airborne Division as one of the early objectives of 'Market Garden', the Arnhem operation. The *Hampoort*, a part of the fortifications, dates from 1681.

The Maas marks the border between Noord Brabant and Gelderland. For Wijchen and Hernen, to the W of the road, as also for (*12km*) Nijmegen, see Rte 24.

# 20 's Hertogenbosch to Roermond

There is a choice of two roads, one through Eindhoven, the other through Helmond. The area between the two—before Eindhoven and Helmond are reached, and with names such as Best, Son en Breugel, St Oedenrode, Heeswijk-Dinther and Veghel—was in September 1944 the 'Market Garden' dropping zone for the American 101st Airborne Division whose objectives were the bridges at Best, Son, St Oedenrode and Veghel. There are several memorials (for example, at Son en Breugel and Veghel) and also a museum at Veghel.

# A.  Via Eindhoven

Total distance 79km.—13km *Boxtel*—10km **Best**—10km **Eindhoven**—25km **Weert**—21km **Roermond**.

For 's Hertogenbosch, see Rte 19. In *3km Vught* (23,000 inhab.) is at the junction of the roads to Tilburg (see Rte 19) and Eindhoven. *10km Boxtel* (24,000 inhab.) was the scene of Wellington's first experience of action against the French, as an officer in the Duke of York's unsuccessful expedition of 1795. *10km* **Best**, is commercially known for shoemaking. During 'Market Garden' the bridge here (to the S, over the Wilhelminakanaal) was destroyed by the Germans on 18 September. This led to the isolation of a small party of Americans, one of whom, PFC Joe Mann, was posthumously awarded the Medal of Honour: already badly wounded, he saved the lives of his companions by throwing himself on to a grenade. He is honoured by a memorial (4km E of Best in the woods beside the Son road), in the form of a pelican, with, below, somewhat unreal figures weeping over the fallen soldier. Apart from the pelican symbolism, Mann's story is not told, a matter for regret for this is a popular spot with woodland walkers, few of whom can know what they are looking at.

At *Son en Breugel*, 8km E of Best, the canal bridge was demolished by the Germans on 17 September but taken and rebuilt by American airborne engineers within two days. The Airborne Memorial, in Son in the Europalaan, is a strikingly effective figure of a soldier who, though his parachute is still attached, is already crouched ready to throw his grenade. Breugel was probably the birthplace of Pieter Bruegel the Elder (1525–64), founder of the famous family of Flemish painters.

*Oirschot*, 5km W of Best, has one of the most attractive market squares in the province. The Stadhuis dates in part from 1463, while the Gothic St Pieterskerk, standing on foundations of 1207, was built in 1465–1500.

*10km* **EINDHOVEN** (193,000 inhab.; VVV, Stationsplein) is a mainly industrial town enjoying worldwide renown for its electrical and electronic products. In this context the town is the home of the great firm of Philips and a statue to Dr A.F. Philips, founder of the firm in 1891 as an electric light bulb factory and thus also to a large extent founder of modern Eindhoven, stands on Stationsplein.

The town centre includes Stationsplein and an oval-shaped area running S from here for about 1km. This oval area, bounded by Vestdijk on the E and by Wal on the SW, is largely pedestrianised in its northern part. Outside the above area, but still fairly central, there are two museums. The *Museum Kempenland* (Tues–Sat, 14.00 to 17.00), at St Antoniusstraat 3–5, is a museum of district history, while the **Van Abbemuseum** (Tues–Sun, Holidays, 11.00 to 17.00), at Bilderdijklaan 10, in the S across the Dommel,

A67, VENLO, ROERMOND

offers a permanent collection and temporary exhibitions of the visual arts of the 20C.

But Eindhoven's principal visitor attraction is the *Evoluon (Mon–Fri, 09.30 to 17.30; Sat, Sun, 10.30 to 17.00), situated on the NW edge of the town at the junction of the ring road, the road to Tilburg and Noord Brabantlaan (buses from station). Conceived to celebrate the 75th anniversary of the founding of the firm of Philips, the Evoluon, in the shape of a flying saucer on stilts, is an exhibition devoted to man's skill and ingenuity. The displays are modern, striking and imaginative, an important feature being the extent to which apparatus can be operated by the visitor. Among the themes covered are Daily Life, the Achievements of Science, and the role of Industry in Society. All explanations are in English, and English plans and 'guidophones' are also available.

Visitors with an interest in 'Market Garden' may wish to visit the *Airborne Monument*, to be found in the northern part of the town within the NE angle of John F. Kennedylaan and Airbornelaan. This is the district of Woensel (with a large shopping centre) in the cemetery of which (Europalaan) there is a Commonwealth War Graves plot.

At *Nuenen*, 6km NE, Vincent van Gogh lived and worked in 1883–85 (memorial in Op den Bergh park). The painter's parental home, the vicarage, survives. At *Geldrop*, 6km E of Eindhoven, the castle dates in part from 1403. *Mierlo* Commonwealth and Allied war cemetery is 2km NE of Geldrop.

KEMPENLAND, known for its woods, heath, meadows, and lakes, is the name of the district surrounding Eindhoven, particularly on the S. Here **Valkenswaard** (27,000 inhab.), 9km S of Eindhoven, was as its name suggests once celebrated for its falcons. A road southwards to Hechtel in Belgium passes between two recreation areas, on the E being *Malpie* nature reserve with walking and cycle tracks, and on the W the popular *Het Eurostrand* offering lakes, boating, beaches, heated indoor pool, a campsite, and other attractions. A Commonwealth military cemetery is a short way further S.

Motorway A2 runs SE out of Eindhoven through generally wooded country and in *19km* crosses into the province of Limburg. For *6km* Weert and *6km* Roermond, see Rte 23.

# B.   Via Helmond

Total distance 82km.—18km **Veghel**—17km **Helmond**—26km **Weert**—21km **Roermond**.

As far as Weert the road runs with the Zuid Willemsvaart, the canal cutting across the great loop of the Maas and also connecting to Belgium's Albert Canal. Over its first part the road crosses the MEIERIJ district of woods and many poplar trees.

For places in Noord Brabant to the E of this Route, notably Overloon (War and Resistance Museum) and Boxmeer, see Rte 23.

For 's Hertogenbosch, see Rte 19. At *10km Heeswijk-Dinther*, to the N of the road, there is a castle which is 12C in origin. There is also a district museum, the Meierijsch Museum, concerned mainly with local farming life. *8km* **Veghel** (25,000 inhab.) was a key point in this area of the 'Market Garden' operation. The bridge was seized by the evening of 17 September, but German resistance soon hardened and the SW to NE road, the corridor to Nijmegen which was subjected to repeated counter-attack, quickly became known as Hell's Highway. The *Airborne Memorial* is in the northern part of the town at the junction of Hoogstraat and Kolonel Johnsonstraat (Colonel Johnson lost his life as commanding officer of 501st Parachute Infantry Regiment); the design of Niel Steenbergen, the monument takes the form of a bronze kangaroo, 'kangaroo' having been this local operation's code name. The stone is from the government and people of the

Netherlands, and a tablet on the ground records that it covers an urn containing earth from 50 American states. Behind the monument the large house bearing the date 1870 was an American headquarters; today it carries a screaming eagle, the emblem of 101st Airborne Division. Veghel's museum, *Bevrijdende Vleugels* (June–Sept; Tues–Sun, 12.00 to 17.00), in Asterstraat, shows material on 'Market Garden' and other aspects of the liberation of the Netherlands.

There is a British war cemetery at *Uden*, 8km NE of Veghel. At *St Oeden-rode*, 6km SW of Veghel, Kasteel Henkenshage was the headquarters of General Taylor, commander of 101st Airborne Division. VVV and a small local museum occupy a former hospice, St Paulusgasthuis.

Beyond Veghel the road soon enters PEELLAND, or marsh land, a district which until the beginning of this century was in large part peat bog and in which there is still extensive heath and fen, much of it nature reserve with public access. At *(17km)* **Helmond** (61,000 inhab.; VVV, Markt 211) the *Kasteel* of 1402 today serves as a cultural centre (museum and changing exhibitions), while the *Speelhuis* arts centre forms a part of an architectural curiosity (by Piet Blom) of crazily angled cubes. *Deurne* (8km E of Helmond) was the home of the doctor and painter Hendrik Wiegersma (born 1891). His home here (De Wieger; Mon–Fri, 13.00 to 17.00; Sat, Sun, 14.00 to 17.00) shows works by himself and his contemporaries. *7km* beyond Helmond you cross the A67 motorway, with the *Strabrechtse Heide* to the W, a typical 'peel' nature reserve with foot and cycle paths. **Asten**, 3km SE of the motorway crossing, has a *Museum* (Ostaderstraat 23; Tues–Sun, 10.00 to 17.00) in two parts: one is concerned with carillons, tower clocks, and bells of many kinds; the other part is devoted to nature study with particular reference to the Peelland. *De Groote Peel*, some 8km SE, is a peatland nature reserve with a visitor centre (Mijl op Zeven).

For *(19km)* Weert and *(21km)* Roermond, both in the province of Limburg, see Rte 23.

# PROVINCE OF LIMBURG

**Capital.** Maastricht.

**History.** After some four centuries of Roman rule, during which (late 4C) Limburg became a centre of Christianity with a bishopric first at Tongeren and then at Maastricht, the lands which now very roughly make up today's Dutch and Belgian provinces of Limburg came first under the Frankish kings and then under Charlemagne, on the latter's death becoming for a short period (843–870) a part of Lothair's Middle Kingdom and then in the 10C a part of the duchy of Lower Lorraine. In the 11C Walram of Arlon married the daughter of Frederick of Luxembourg, Duke of Lower Lorraine, by this marriage receiving lands along the Maas, becoming the first Count of Limburg and ruling virtually independently of the parent duchy. Walram's son Henry forced the Emperor Henry IV to recognise him as Duke of Lower Lorraine, thus initiating the long territorial and titular dispute over Lower Lorraine between the counts of Louvain and Brussels and those of Limburg, finally resolved only in c 1159, territorially at any rate in favour of the former; the title of Duke of Lower Lorraine, however, disappeared in 1190, the rivals becoming Duke of Brabant and Duke of Limburg.

In 1280 the then ruler of Limburg, Duchess Irmingardis, died childless and dispute at once arose as her inheritance was claimed by both her husband Count Reinald of Guelders (Gelderland), the man in possession, and by her cousin Count Adolf of Berg. Three years later the latter shrewdly sold his claim to Duke John I of Brabant, and in 1288 Reinald, after a long war which he seemed unlikely to win, in turn disposed of his rights to Count Henry III of Luxembourg. That same year the new rivals met in battle at Woeringen near Cologne where Duke John defeated and killed Count Henry. Now a part of the duchy of Brabant (see Province of Noord Brabant), Limburg enjoyed the privileges conferred by dukes John II and III, but later, on the death childless in 1430 of Duke Anthony, passed with Brabant to Duke Philip the Good of Burgundy, Limburg's history then becoming a part of the general history of the Netherlands.

Under the Treaty of Münster (1648) Spain retained the southern part of Limburg but ceded to the United Provinces the town of Maastricht and all Limburg E of the Maas, this territory now becoming not a province but 'generality land' directly administered by the States General. Not until 1814 were the two parts rejoined as the province of Limburg (of the Dutch-Belgian United Kingdom of the Netherlands), this province including also the southern corner of Gelderland known as the Roermond Quarter (see Province of Gelderland, History). But this unity was shortlived because in 1830 all of Limburg except Maastricht joined the Belgian uprising, the Limburgers then regarding themselves as Belgians until divided again in 1839 by the Treaty of London under which the Netherlands received what, with minor changes, makes up her present province of Limburg (Maastricht, Limburg E of the Maas, and Roermond).

During the First World War the Netherlands remained neutral, although at the war's end she incurred Belgian anger by allowing the retreating German army passage across Dutch Limburg. In the Second World War, when Germany attacked on 10 May 1940, Limburg was at once overrun, and the province suffered severely in the fighting of 1944.

Dutch Limburg now comprises a strip of land some 50km long between the Maas and the German frontier, the rather bleak moorland around Weert and Venray on the W of the Maas in the northern part of the province, the important capital town of Maastricht, and a bulge to the SE. Scenically this SE bulge, at its heart the holiday centre of Valkenburg, is attractively wooded and hilly and very different from anywhere else in the country (it includes the Drielandenpunt, at 321m the highest point in the country). The Roman baths at Heerlen, beautifully incorporated in a special museum, are the most outstanding historical attraction in this part of the province.

Maastricht in the S, and Roermond and Venlo to the N, are Limburg's three large towns, Maastricht, the provincial capital, being the oldest, the most historic and by far the most attractive and interesting. Among smaller places Meerssen has ancient historic associations; Elsloo should be visited for its attractive Schippersbeurs and its church carvings by the Master of Elsloo; and Sittard, Susteren, Venray and, especially, Thorn are all pleasant small towns with churches of note.

The heavy fighting towards the end of the last war is poignantly recalled by the many British war cemeteries as also by the great American and German ones at Margraten and IJsselsteyn.

# 21 Maastricht

MAASTRICHT (113,000 inhab.), the lively capital of the province of Limburg, is known for its picturesque streets and small squares and for its ancient churches and their treasures. The streets and squares contain many pleasing old houses, largely of the 16C and 17C, several of these carefully restored as part of a long-term programme. Remains of the fortifications, dismantled in 1871–78, recall the town's strategic importance and that it withstood as many as 21 sieges.

The Maas flows S to N separating the main town (W) from the district of Wijk, with the station, on the E bank. The river, joined by the small river Jeker at the S of the town, is crossed by five bridges, the two near the town centre, both road bridges, being St Servaasbrug (or the Oude Maasbrug) and, just N, the Wilhelminabrug. Further N there is a railway bridge, beyond this again being the Noorderbrug, while to the S of the town the John F. Kennedybrug carries the main Aachen to Belgium road. Well to the N of the town there is a port on the Juliana Kanaal.

**Centre.** Markt and Vrijthof. Much of the area enclosed by these, the Maas, and the Jeker is pedestrian precinct.

**VVV.** Dinghuis, Kleine Staat.

**Post Office.** Keizer Karelplein, off NW corner of Vrijthof.

**Station.** In Wijk, E bank of the Maas.

**Town tours.** VVV provides leaflets for self-guided town and fortress walks. Additionally, there are official guided walks, duration about 1½ hours (late June–Aug: Mon–Fri, 14.00 from VVV). For those who do not wish to walk, VVV will advise on horse-drawn carriage tours (45 minutes).

**Boats.** Two firms operate cruises. *Rederij Stiphout* (Maas boulevard 27, on the W bank between the St Servaasbrug and the Wilhelminabrug) provide local Maas and Albert Canal cruises (55 minutes). Also cruises to Liège in Belgium, the St Pietersberg caves and a frontier cruise. *Rederij De Bak Balduin* (Maasboulevard, near the Maaspaviljoen) operates to Liège.

**History.** Maastricht started as the Roman settlement of *Mosae Trajectum*, the ford

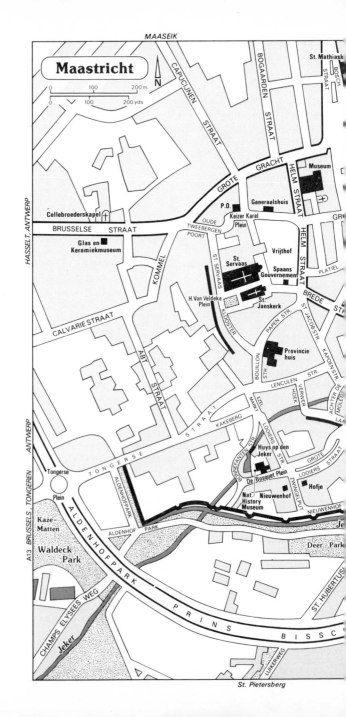

# Maastricht

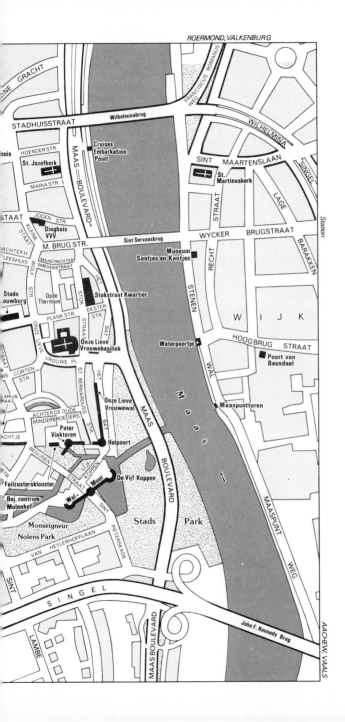

across the Maas on the important road between Cologne and the coast and, in 382 when the Romans were still here, became a Christian centre when St Servatius, first Bishop of Tongeren (13km SW), transferred the seat here, where it remained until removed by St Hubert to Liège in 720, the bishops, however, retaining their local temporal authority. After Roman withdrawal the town passed under the control of the Frankish kings, later surviving the troubled years following the death of Charlemagne until in 1204 it became a joint possession of the dukes of Brabant and the prince-bishops of Liège, a duality recalled today by the street names Grote Staat and Kleine Staat.

In 1576 Maastricht joined in the movement against the Spanish, but in 1579 after a siege of four months it was taken and ruthlessly sacked by Parma. In 1632 it fell to Prince Frederick Henry, and during the 17C and 18C it was three times taken by the French. One of these occasions was 1673 when the Duke of Monmouth was besieging the town on behalf of Louis XIV, England having contributed a contingent of 6000 to help the king against the United Provinces; during this siege Captain John Churchill (later Duke of Marlborough) was cut off and rescued by the 'musketeer' D'Artagnan, who lost his life in this act, and during the same siege Churchill saved Monmouth's life and was later thanked by Louis XIV. In 1830, encouraged by the presence of a Dutch garrison, Maastricht held out for the Dutch against the insurgent Belgians.

**St Servaasbrug**, or **Oude Maasbrug**, originally a 13C wooden bridge of nine arches, was rebuilt in 1684–1716 by François Romain, architect of the Pont Royal in Paris; badly damaged in 1940, it was re-erected on the old lines in 1948. **Wilhelminabrug** (1932), to the N, was also damaged in 1940 and rebuilt. Between the bridges stands the St Jozefkerk Kerk (1661), the former church of the Augustinians, notable for its baroque façade; today the church is used for concerts and exhibitions. Nearby is the embarkation quay for river cruises.

From the W end of Wilhelminabrug, Stadhuisstraat soon reaches the MARKT with, in the middle, the **Stadhuis** (Mon–Fri, 09.00 to 12.00, 14.00 to 17.00), a plain building of 1659–64 by Pieter Post; the tower of 1684 contains a carillon by Hemony. Opening off the domed hall are rooms containing portraits, Gobelins and Brussels tapestries, leather hangings, and some good stucco ceilings, while the Registry Department shows a representative selection from the Glas en Keramiekmuseum (see below). To the N, at the start of Boschstraat, a statue of 1902 incorporating a gas flame honours the Maastricht chemist S.P. Minckelers (1784–1824), the pioneer of the use of coal gas and inventor of gas lighting. Beyond, *St Mathiaskerk* dates from the 13–16C.

From the SW of the Markt, Grote Gracht leads W, Helmstraat soon bearing S off it. Here are the former *Dominicanenkerk* (13C; 14C murals), now used for exhibitions, and, in the adjacent building, the **Limburgs (Bonnefanten) Museum voor Kunst en Oudheden** (Limburg Museum of Art and Antiquities; Tues–Fri, 10.00 to 17.00; Sat, Holidays, 11.00 to 17.00), concerned largely with the history and archaeology of Limburg and Maastricht but also with permanent collections of old and modern pictures, applied art, and documents. The museum takes its name from its former location in the Bonnefanten Klooster (see below). Today, by contrast, the exhibits are scattered around fine, airy, light halls and include a good model of Maastricht (1748–49), at the time when it was being besieged by the French; some huge ceremonial swords; a room of religious statuary, with also a Brabant retable of c 1500; church plate, beautifully displayed below a glass dome; and prehistoric, Roman and applied art sections.

Helmstraat ends at the VRIJTHOF (underground car park), a large and pleasant square with trees and cafés and surrounded by several places of interest. According to one tradition this was a 'free place' or sanctuary, but more probably the name derives from the German for cemetery, two of which are known to have once occupied this site. It was here that William de la Marck, the nobleman turned murderer and robber chief known as the 'Wild Boar of the Ardennes', was executed in 1485; in 1482 he had murdered the Bishop of Liège, but the latter's successor invited him to a feast, seized him and sent him to Maastricht for execution. On the N side of the square the Generaalshuis of 1805 stands on the site of a 7C convent of the White Nuns, while the Post Office is off the NW corner in Keizer Karelplein. A building on the S side of the Vrijthof, the Spaans Gouvernement (1545 but much restored), was the Maastricht residence of the dukes of Brabant and the Spanish kings (arms of Charles V and Philip II). On the ground near the SE corner of the square, there are two round plaques, one commemorating a tree planting of 1973 and the other the liberation of Maastricht in 1944. The Hoofdwacht (1736–73), on the W of Vrijthof, once a guard house, now a military headquarters, stands below St Servaaskerk; this was long the operational headquarters for all the city guard posts.

\*St Servaaskerk (VVV for opening times), the former cathedral and dedicated to St Servatius, first Bishop of Maastricht, is a vast and ancient Romanesque edifice. Successor perhaps to a 6C chapel founded by Bishop Monulphus and sheltering a shrine, the present church was begun in c 950 and although it has been many times altered and enlarged some of this early work can still be found in the nave and crypts. The east apse, originally an extension of the early 13C, is now for the most part restoration and the two square towers are entirely 19C work. The W end is supported by two buttresses thrown across the street, above being two square towers with a neo-Gothic cupola between them. The splendid south portal, the *Bergpoortaal*, rich with foliage and biblical statuary, is of the mid 13C (restored 1883–86).

You enter the church normally either by the south transept, or by the north-west door and along a Gothic porch-gallery, off which is the domed *Keizersaal* (usually no adm.) of the late 12C. The church interior, with round arches on square piers, is lofty and imposing. The aisles and vaults were rebuilt during the 14C and 15C. In front of the narthex there is a statue of Charlemagne (W. Geefs, 1843), against its back being part of a 12C stone screen with a relief of Christ between SS Peter and Servatius. On the north pillar of the crossing stands a (restored) 13C statue of St Servatius, and the brass font, in a chapel off the south aisle, is work of the late 15C.

The *crypts* (fee), though much restored, incorporate a good deal of the original building. In the central crypt, probably the burial place of St Servatius, note the old tiled floor and also the stone chest in which the relics of local saints were gathered after the desecration at the time of the French Revolution. Here too is the tomb of Charles the Simple (died 929), the ruler who in 922 granted the land to the Frisian Count Dirk I out of which developed the county, province, and eventually the nation of the Netherlands; the last of the Carolingian kings, he was reinterred here in 1001. Something of the east crypt can be seen through grilles.

\* *Treasury (Schatkamer)*. The collection includes the copper-gilt chest-reliquary of St Servatius, with 12C reliefs; a bust-reliquary (presented by Parma to replace one destroyed in 1579) with reliefs telling the saint's story; a 15C reredos from Brussels; a 15C head of John the Baptist; St Servatius' drinking beaker (Roman glass); the saint's staff, part of his robe, and his gold pectoral cross adorned with gems and a 10C ivory Christ; a key of electrum (silver and gold alloy), said to have been given to Servatius by Pope Damasus but recast in the 10C; vestments; ivory work.

The Glas en Keramiekmuseum (by appointment. Tel: 043-15088) is at the Municipal Art Academy at Brusselsestraat 77, some 400m to the W. The basis of the collection is Roman, Syrian and 18C and 19C glass and crystal, but a ceramics collection, with the emphasis on local work, is also being built up (see also Stadhuis above). The Cellebroederskapel, roughly opposite, dates to the 16C.

To the S the Protestant St Janskerk (12–15C), with a high 15C tower and some medieval murals, was once the baptistery of the cathedral (VVV for opening times). HENRIC VAN VELDEKEPLEIN here commemorates the poet (c 1140–c 1210), born near Maastricht, whose works, which include the 'Legend of St Servatius', are among the oldest in Dutch literature. On the S side of this small square there is a pleasing 17C mansion.

Out of the NE corner of Vrijthof Grote Staat descends E, at its far end at the junction with Kleine Staat rising the tall *Dinghuis (c 1470; restored 1696 and 1979); a court of justice until the building of the Stadhuis and later used by Napoleon as a prison, the building now houses the VVV. The names Grote and Kleine Staat (rank or status) recall the distinction between the greater and lesser authorities of the dukes and the bishops.

From the Dinghuis Kleine Staat soon reaches the STOKSTRAAT KWARTIER, a quarter of mainly 17C and 18C houses restored between 1957 an 1973. The small square called Op de Thermen, immediately W of Stokstraat and particularly attractive, was the site of the Gallo-Roman baths, and further W in Bredestraat the Stads Schouwburg, the municipal theatre, occupies the former Jesuit church (1604–14).

In ONZE LIEVE VROUWEPLEIN, to the S of Op de Thermen, the gateway of the Wolwaag (1721) survives by No. 27. *Onze Lieve Vrouwebasiliek (closed 12.00 to 15.00) is an ancient foundation much of which dates from c 1000, though there are additions of the 11C and 12C, notably the apse with two squat helm-roofed towers. The extraordinary W front, almost windowless except for the top storey and flanked by circular towers, was evidently built for defence purposes. In the interior the nave, with Gothic vaults, was damaged by alterations during the 18C, but the late Romanesque choir, with its two galleries, and the ambulatory preserve some good capitals. The coupled piers at the east end, with two tiers of capitals illustrating Old Testament history, are especially noteworthy. The late 15C font may be by Jan Aerts. The large crypt (closed, but visible through grilles) is of two periods, the west portion being coeval with the foundations of the church and the aisled E part dating from the 13C. The Treasury (Easter–mid Sept: 11.00 to 17.00) contains the dalmatic of St Lambert, murdered at Liège in 705; a Byzantine cloisonné enamel box (11C); a 13C crystal reliquary; and other similar articles.

From Onze Lieve Vrouweplein, St Bernardusstraat leads S to the sturdy **Helpoort** (1229), the oldest town gate surviving in the Netherlands, with a corner tower of the ramparts beside it; the name was that of a stream which once flowed here. Onze Lieve Vrouwewal, running N from the Helpoort, is also of c 1229. Beyond the Helpoort to the S is an outer bastion (De Vijf Koppen, 1516), while along the ramparts to the W are Pater Vinktoren, a small 14C tower, and the Feilzustersklooster (1647), once a begijnhof. From here it is possible to make your way through the park along the outside of the ramparts, but it is more interesting to return through the Helpoort to St Bernardusstraat and then bear W along Achter de Oude Minderbroeders, which runs along the side of the former Minderbroederskerk (Franciscans), a 13C building, after the banning of the order long used as a barracks and in the 19C restored by Cuijpers to house the provincial archives.

Lang Grachtje, running W from the W end of Minderbroederskerk, is a continuation of the 13C rampart wall. There are some attractive old houses in Tafelstraat and St Hilariusstraat immediately to the N. From the W end of Lang Grachtje, Grote Looiersstraat bears SW, No. 17 here being an almshouse of 1727 and No. 27 (*St Martinshofje*) one of 1715. Opposite the latter there is a charming statue-group of children listening to the local poet Fons Otterdissen. Across the intersection stands the *Natural History Museum* (Mon–Fri, 10.00 to 12.30, 13.30 to 17.00; Sun, 14.00 to 17.00). Among the exhibits are fossils from the St Pietersberg caves. Beside the museum is a huge 6000 kg. quartzite boulder. Zwingelput runs S between St Martinshofje and *Nieuwenhof*, a nunnery, still in use as such, of the 15–17C. At the street's end is a section of second period rampart (early 14C), through which, across the Jeker stream, is the *Deer Park*. The top of the ramparts can be followed W for a short distance, steps then descending into an academic quarter (music conservatoire, built over the Jeker; medical school; sculpture and drama academies, etc.) where modern building has rather marred an otherwise attractive corner. You now take Bonnefanten-straat N, passing the *Huys op den Jeker* (No. 5), an early 17C building straddling the stream, and arriving at the little Ezelmarkt (Donkey Market) with the former *Bonnefanten Klooster* (17–18C), once the convent of the nuns of the Order of the Sepulchre, also known as the 'Bons Enfants', today the library of Limburg university. From beside a statue of a donkey at the start of Looiersgracht a good view is had of the Huys op den Jeker.

From Ezelmarkt, Bouillonstraat and Papenstraat lead back N to the Vrijthof.

The entrance to the **Kazematten (Casemates)**, which originated from min-ing operations of the 16–19C, is in Waldeck Park, near Tongerseplein c 700m SW of the Vrijthof. Some 10km in extent (though only a small part can be visited) the casemates are an elaborate defensive system of bastions, lunettes, and underground rooms and galleries. It was here that D'Artagnan was killed (see History above). VVV for dates of occasional guided tours.

In WIJK, the district on the E bank of the Maas, there are various sites of interest, all close to the river. From N to S the first is the *St Martinuskerk*, the first church built by Cuijpers (1857) and containing a font of 1482 by Jan van Venlo. Further S, in Cörversplein just S of the St Servaasbrug, the *Museum Santjes en Kantjes* (July and Aug: daily, 14.00 to 17.00) shows a rare collection of objects associated with popular piety, including devotional prints, statuettes and prayer books. *Rechtsstraat*, just to the E and running parallel to the river, retains several attractive façades and gables, while the *Waterpoortje*, a short way further S by the junction of Stenenwal and Kaleminkstraat, dates from the 13C as does also the *Maaspunttoren* beyond. From the Waterpoortje, Hoogbrugstraat leads E past the *Beusdaelpoort* (1690) and the *St Gilleshofje* (1759) to reach the station, behind which, in Koningsplein, stands the *Bevrijdings Monument* (by Charles Eyck, of Maastricht), symbolising the breaking of chains with the liberation of 1945.

ST PIETERSBERG CAVES, just beyond the S outskirts of the town, is a hill (110m) formed of marl, a type of sandstone since early times popular for building. As a result the hill has long been used as a quarry and is now honeycombed with caves, described as long ago as AD 50 by Pliny. In the early 18C a fort (now a restaurant) was built on the N slope, its defences being connected to the northern caves; in 1794 this was the scene of subterranean skirmishing between the Dutch and French. During the Second World War the caves were organised as air raid shelters, though in fact little used. They were until recently much used for mushroom cultivation; they are the home of no less than 12 varieties of bat; and they are also noted for the variety of fossils to be found—examples of such are on display in the Natural History Museum. Among the myriad names scrawled here are Parma (1579), Napoleon (1803), and Sir Walter Scott (1840). Two systems may be visited, both on bus routes. The nearer to the town is the *Noord Gangenstelsel* (North Gallery System), for which motorists should follow the St Pietersberg Camping signs from the W end of John F. Kennedybrug. The other system, *Zonneberg* further S, is signed from the W end of John F. Kennedybrug; this system can also be visited in conjunction with a Maas boat excursion (ask VVV about tours of caves and Fort St Pieter).

For South-East Limburg, see Rte 22; for Maastricht to Roermond, Venlo, and Nijmegen, see Rte 23.

**Belgium near Maastricht** (*see also 'Blue Guide, Belgium and Luxembourg'*). **Tongeren** (13km SW). The oldest town in Belgium, originating as a BC Roman camp. Roman remains, including a good length of wall of the 1–2C. Gallo-Roman Museum. Basilica dating from 1240, with a rich *treasury. **Visé** (13km S). Church of St Martin contains the *chasse St Hadelin, a silver and gold coffin reliquary of the 11–12C depicting scenes from the life of the saint. **Liège** (29km S). Palace of the Prince-Bishops. Neolithic traces. Musée d'Ansembourg (Decorative Art). *Musée Curtius in a house of c 1600 (Decorative art; archaeology; glass). Musée d'Armes, with Europe's most complete collection of small-arms. Several historic and interesting churches. Maas (Meuse) cruises.

# 22   South-East Limburg

## A.   Maastricht to Aachen (Aken)

Total distance 29km.—4km **Cadier en Keer**—5km **Margraten**—5km **Gulpen**—11km **Vaals**—4km **Aachen (Aken)**.

For Maastricht see Rte 21. *4km*. **Cadier-en-Keer**, with the *Museum Africa-Centrum* (Mon–Fri, 10.00 to 12.00, 14.00 to 17.00; Sun, 14.00 to 17.00) of the international Society for African Missions. The exhibits, all from West Africa, are arranged by tribes and cover many aspects of tribal life, past and present. Material goes back to as early as the 13C, and includes a curious X-ray picture of a 'magic' killing. *5km* **Margraten** is the site of the impressive *US Netherlands Cemetery*, with the graves of the 8301 members of the American armed forces who in 1944–45 fell in the airborne and ground operations in eastern Netherlands and beyond the Rhine. A feature of the memorial is a stonework pictorial and narrative description of the operations in NW Europe between June 1944 and May 1945. *5km* **Gulpen** is known for the *Gulpenberg* (161m; panorama) immediately S of the small town. *Foreldorada Park*, with a trout hatchery, is 1km W. A magnificent Roman sarcophagus, now in the National Museum of Antiquities at Leiden, was discovered at *Simpelveld*, 6km NE. You reach the German border at (*11km*) **Vaals**, a short way S of which is the *Drielandenpunt* (321m), the highest point in the Netherlands and at the junction of the Dutch, Belgian, and German frontiers. *4km* Aachen.

# B. Maastricht to Valkenburg, Heerlen, and Kerkrade

Total distance 26km.—10km **Valkenburg**—8km **Heerlen**—8km **Kerkrade**.

For Maastricht, see Rte 21. *10km* **Valkenburg** (18,000 inhab., including *Houthem-St-Gerlach* and *Schin op Geul*), an old once fortified town in the pleasant wooded valley of the Geul and known for its caves, is today a lively resort offering a wide variety of attractions, many of them designed for children. These attractions are generally open throughout the season (Easter–Oct: daily, 09.00 or 10.00 to 17.00–19.00 or, in some cases, sunset).

**Centre.** Th. Dorrenplein.

**VVV.** 5 Th. Dorrenplein.

**History.** Although there was a settlement here in Roman times, it was not until the 11C (charter from Emperor Henry IV, 1040) that a town began to develop below the castle built on the hill at about the same time, the result of the granting of these lands to Walram of Arlon. Nominally under the suzerainty of the successive rulers of the Netherlands, Valkenburg held out as a virtually independent lordship from these early days until the arrival of the French in 1795. The early lords were the Walram family, one member of which, Beatrix (died 1277 at Oxford), sister of Count Walram the Red, became the third wife of Richard, Earl of Cornwall, second son of England's King John.

Near the town centre *Kasteel Den Halder*, now housing the provincial VVV, in part dates back to the 14C. The *Casino* is entered from Odapark, just NW of the centre.

Two of the town's 14C gates survive, the *Grendelpoort* (W) and the *Berkelpoort* (E), both below the hills on the S of the town. The former stands on GRENDELPLEIN, a point from which a number of roads fan out to places of interest. The *castle ruins*, the ascent to which starts from here, represent many periods between the 13C and the demolition of 1672. Also near Grendelplein is the *Gemeentegrot* (municipal grotto), believed to be a Roman quarry in origin and in later years, including during the last war, serving as a wartime refuge. Cauberg, leading SW out of Grendelplein, passes the *Lourdesgrot* (1926), a copy of that at Lourdes, and continues past the War Memorial to a sports centre. Daelhemerweg (S out of Grendelplein) soon reaches *Fluwelengrot*, a system of caves which were connected to the castle by secret passages discovered in 1937. Farther S a road climbs to the *Wilhelminatoren* (see below), while further S again is the *Model Steenkolenmijn* (09.00 to 17.00; April–Oct: daily; Nov–March: Sat), a replica coal mine set up by the Dutch State Mines. In ROTSPARK, to the NW of Grendelplein and reached by Plenkertstraat, there are various attractions, including the *Fantoomspelonken* (phantom caves), with 'prehistoric' presentations, and the *Museum Katakomben*, a reproduction expertly set up in 1909–13 of parts of Rome's catacombs.

From the town centre Grotestraat and Berkelstraat lead S and SE to the 14C *Berkelpoort*, beyond which is the start of the cable car up to the *Wilhelminatoren* (160 steps) atop the Heunsberg; other approaches are by foot, or by car off Daelhemerweg below the W of the hill. Near the start of the cable car the *Grottenpanorama*, in one of the district's oldest caves, contains a painted representation (1500 sq m) of the prehistoric world, while further S in the *Spookjesbos* (Fairy Tale Wood) will be found such characters as Snow White, the Seven Dwarfs, and Hansel and Gretel.

*8km* **Heerlen** (93,000 inhab.; VVV, Stationsplein 4) was the Roman *Coriovallum*, a civilian settlement at the crossing of the important roads between Cologne and the Channel coast, and from Xanthen to Aachen and Trier. As Rome weakened during the 3C and the Frankish incursions began the settlement was fortified. Heerlen is visited for its superb *•Museum Thermen* (Tues–Fri, 10.00 to 17.00; Sat, Sun, Holidays, 14.00 to 17.00) in the town centre. Here a bridge leads across the Roman baths, excavated during the 1960s and 1970s, enabling the system to be viewed as a whole. In the adjacent museum proper the exhibits, all well explained in English, include a copy of the interesting Tabula Peutingeriana, a Roman road map of the 4C and a replica of the Simpelveld sarcophagus, the original of which is in Leiden's Rijksmuseum van Oudheden. The *Museum of the Geological Bureau*, with fossils and models illustrating the geology of this southern part of Limburg, is at Voskuilenweg 131 (Mon–Fri, 09.00 to 12.00, 14.00 to 16.00).

HEERLEN TO SITTARD (14km). Children should enjoy the Droomkasteel (Dream Castle: late April–Sept: daily, 10.00 to 18.00) at Heerlerheide, on the N outskirts of Heerlen, with its crowd of figures out of fairy tales and a fantasy castle. Farther N, Kasteel Hoensbroek (daily, 10.00 to 12.00, 13.30 to 17.30; open throughout the day in June–Aug) houses a mixed museum of geological, archaeological and African-Asiatic material; the corner towers of the main building are of the 13C or 14C but everything else is 17C building or rebuilding. The château of Amstenrade, 2km further N, was built in 1781 by B. Digneffe of Liège. At Brunssum, on the German border 3km E of Amstenrade, there is a NATO headquarters. For Sittard, see Rte 23.

*8km* **Kerkrade** (53,000 inhab.) is known for its *Botanic Garden*, laid out in 1939 by the State Mines to demonstrate in particular the flora of Limburg. To the E of the town is the former *•**Abdij van Rolduc**, founded in 1104 by Ailbert, a young priest from Tournai who wished to become a hermit. Three years later Ailbert was joined by a nobleman called Embrico who arrived with his wife and children and proposed that Ailbert's small sanctuary should be developed into a religious house with monastery and convent. Together Ailbert and Embrico then started in 1107 to build a church, this in large part surviving today as one of the most notable Romanesque buildings in the country, famous especially for its clover-leaf crypt (1108; west extension early 13C) with carving on pillars, capitals, and bases, much of it the work of craftsmen from northern Italy. The sarcophagus in the crypt contains the relics of Ailbert (died 1112 at Sechtem on the Rhine), brought here in 1895. The church nave, also with carving, was completed by c 1200. The tomb in the middle of the church is that of Duke Walram III of Limburg (died 1226, but tomb is 17C), lord of Valkenburg and crusader with Richard Coeur de Lion. Of the early monastic buildings virtually nothing survives: today's buildings (youth centre and school) are of the 17–19C. The *Mijn-*

*museum* (Mine Museum), occupying a wing here, was opened in 1974 and tells the story of the Limburg coal mining industry (May–Oct: Tues–Fri, 09.00 to 17.00; Sat, 13.00 to 17.00; also Sun in July, 13.00 to 17.00; Nov–April: first Saturday in month, 13.00 to 17.00).

# 23 Maastricht to Nijmegen

Total distance 131km.—6km **Meerssen**—7km *Beek* (for **Elsloo**)—8km **Sittard**—8km **Susteren**—16km **Roermond**—22km **Venlo**—23km **Venray**—5km **Overloon**—11km **Boxmeer**—7km **Gennep**—18km **Nijmegen**.

For Maastricht, see Rte 21. *6km* **Meerssen** (8500 inhab.), ancient residence of the Frankish kings, was the scene in 845 of a conference between Charlemagne's three sons held to agree plans for repelling the Norsemen, and in 870 of the treaty between Charles the Bald and Louis the German dividing the realm of Lothair II. The 13C *Kloosterkerk*, a striking Gothic building restored by Cuijpers, contains a sculptured *tabernacle (early 16C) and much other interesting carving. The external gallery of the choir and transepts is an unusual feature. *7km* is *Beek*, 2km W of which, beyond the motorway, is **Elsloo** where it is worth driving through the modern village to reach the old one with its narrow cobbled street. Here the attractive *Schippersbeurs* of 1618, once the busy commercial centre for river traders but today a museum of bygones, repays a visit as much for the house as for its contents (Tues, Thurs, 13.00 to 16.00; Sun, 14.00 to 17.00). In the nearby church there are carvings by the Master of Elsloo, notably a lovely St Anna. At *Stein*, 2km N of Elsloo, there are castle ruins close to the Juliana Kanaal. *Steinerbos* is a recreation park with, among many other attractions, dolphin and sealion shows (May–mid Sept: daily, 10.00 to 18.00).

*8km* **Sittard** (44,000 inhab.), with some remains of its walls and in the town centre a number of 16C half-timbered façades, has a pleasant spacious MARKT (parking; pavement cafés) off which are pedestrianised shopping streets. The town has two churches, that of *St Michiel*, on the Markt, dating from 1659–68 and formerly the church of the Dominicans, having a baroque façade and baroque furnishing. In the church of *St Pieter*, three minutes walk away, started in c 1380 and enlarged in the 15C and 16C, the choir stalls, contemporary with the first building of the church, are the oldest in the Netherlands. Sittard war cemetery (Commonwealth and Allied) is on the S edge of the town. At *8km* **Susteren** there is an early 11C Romanesque church; formerly a convent church, it is dedicated to St Amelberga (died after 900) whose tomb is beneath the high altar.

**Maaseik**, 5km NW across the Maas in Belgium, has an attractive market square planted with limes and surrounded by several 17–18C houses. Here a monument of 1864 commemorates the painter brothers Jan and Hubert van Eyck, reputedly born here (Jan in c 1390; Hubert in c 1370). In the early 19C *Stadhuis* on the N side of the square there is a copy of 1926 of the brothers' masterpiece the Mystic Lamb, the original of which is in the cathedral at Ghent. Also on the Markt an 18C pharmacy now serves as the local museum. The parish church of 1840 is noted for its treasury which contains the so-called Eyck Evangelistery of the early 8C, said to have been the property of the two pious ladies who in c 750 founded a convent in

*Aldeneik*, 1.5km E, where a later Romanesque church (11–13C) of their convent still stands.

DIVERSION TO THORN AND WEERT. Thorn can be reached either direct from Maaseik (11km by Belgian N17); or from Susteren by Dutch motorway A2 (15km). Weert, 12km NW of Thorn, can be reached either by minor roads or by A2 and N68.

**Thorn** (3000 inhab.) is a small town with whitewashed 18C houses and a notable abbey church with a baroque interior (Easter–October: daily, 09.00 to 18.00). The church was originally that of an abbey for both sexes founded in c 995 by Ansfrey, a nobleman who later became Bishop of Utrecht, and his wife Hilsondis; thereafter the house was ruled for 750 years by an abbess assisted by a chapter of noblewomen, while canons took care of the liturgical aspect. One prominent later abbess was Clara Elisabeth von Manderscheidt (died 1688) who presented several baroque altars. Around the end of the 13C the church was rebuilt in Gothic style and in the 15C it was enlarged with chapels along the aisles; the only Romanesque survivals today are the west crypt and the base of the tower, the upper level of which is part of a restoration of the whole church by Cuijpers in 1860–80.

You enter the church at the north-west. Along the north aisle there are three chapels: the first is that of St John with a Renaissance altar of 1624 and a Descent from the Cross which is a mirror-image of the same theme by Rubens. In the Chapel of St Michael there is a 17C baroque altar, while in the last chapel, that of the Holy Sacrament, there is a similar altar, this one bearing an Adoration by P.H. Franken, a pupil of Rubens; here too is the monument to Clara Elisabeth von Manderscheidt, the lady wearing canonical dress. In the sanctuary, formerly the choir of the canons, rises the great late baroque *high altar (F.X. Bader, 1769), built in scagliola, while a floor stone (1739) records that Hilsondis, co-founder of the abbey, lies in the church. The SE Chapel of St Lambert (murdered at Liège in 705) contains a 16C triptych and traces of 15C murals.

In the corner steps descend to the Gothic east crypt, with the reliquary of Hilsondis and, in the W wall, niches in which members of the chapter were buried. Two glass coffins here contain the mummified remains of a canon (right) and a canoness (left), the latter perhaps Clara Elisabeth von Manderscheidt. Along the nave's S aisle the chapels are those of the Trinity and the Holy Family, the latter with a baroque altar. At the west end of the nave are a baroque screen and a 15C Marianum ascribed to the Master of Elsloo. Beyond is the Ladies' Choir, the south door of which once led to the domestic buildings, demolished in c 1817. The N door leads through a passage to the Treasury, occupying two rooms of the 14–15C, the first formerly the chapter room and the second, with original tiled paving and vault painting, the records office. The west crypt is 12C Romanesque; it contains a 15C stone font and two windows (Joep Nicolas, 1956) depicting Ansfrey and Hilsondis.

**Weert** (39,000 inhab.; VVV at the Waag, Langpoort, at the S corner of the town's inner ring) was long associated with the counts of Hoorne, one of whom, Philippe de Montmorency (1518–68), was beheaded by the Spanish in Brussels; his grave, marked by a slab of 1841 in front of the altar, is in the 15C *St Martinskerk* off the Markt in the town centre. There is a *Tram Museum* at Kruisstraat 6 about 1km S of VVV (April–Oct: Tues–Sun; also Mon in July, Aug, 14.00 to 18.00). There are British war cemeteries at Nederweert, 3km N, and also as part of the churchyard of Swartbroek, 4km SE of Weert.

*16km* **Roermond** (38,000 inhab.; VVV, Markt 24) stands on the E bank of the Maas at the mouth of the little river Roer. Within the angle of the rivers the inner town is enclosed by boulevards defining the lines of earlier moats—Wilhelminasingel (N), Godsweerdersingel and Willem II Singel (both E), and Minderbroederssingel (W).

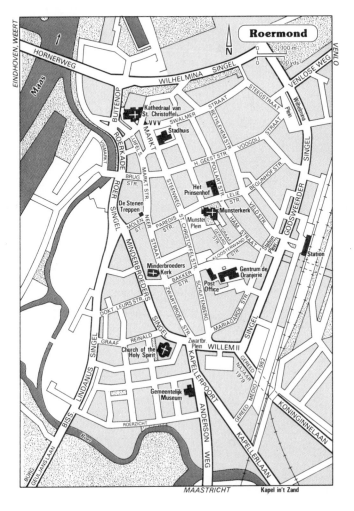

**History.** Roermond, once chief town of one of the 'quarters' of Gelderland, is first mentioned in a document of 1130. The abbey was founded in 1220, and in 1559 the town was made the seat of a bishopric which, with one short interval, it has remained ever since. In the struggle against Alva, Roermond was taken by William the Silent in 1572, the occasion it is said of the first singing of the 'Wilhelmus', now the Dutch national anthem, but six years later it fell without resistance to Parma and in 1579, being almost wholly Catholic, it did not subscribe to the Union of Utrecht. The town remained under Habsburg rule (Spanish or Austrian) until it was incorporated into the modern Dutch province of Limburg in 1814 and 1839.

P.J.H. Cuijpers (1827–1921), the architect of so many Dutch churches as well as the Centraal Station and Rijksmuseum in Amsterdam, was a native of Roermond.

On MUNSTERPLEIN stands the *Munsterkerk* (Fri, Sat, 10.00 to 12.00, 14.00 to 17.00), founded in c 1220 for Cistercian nuns and dedicated to Our Lady, a mainly late Romanesque building with a Gothic west end. Between 1864 and 1891 it was much restored by Cuijpers, a statue of whom (1929) stands in the garden on the S side. The church has a central cupola, four other towers, an elaborately planned apse and a narthex where the Gothic element appears. In front of the high altar is the coloured marble *monument of Count Gerard III of Gelder who died in 1229 (see Province of Gelderland, History), and of his wife Margaret of Brabant who died two years later.

To the N, at the corner of Munsterplein and Pollartstraat, an old people's home occupies *Het Prinsenhof*, built in 1665–1700 as palace of the governors of Upper Gelderland and enlarged during the present century. Farther N, in Swalmerstraat, No. 52 was the former *Karthuizerklooster*, a Carthusian house the monks of which were murdered when Roermond was taken by William the Silent in 1572; the building contains a late Gothic chapel with Rococo plasterwork and an 18C cloister. Followed W Swalmerstraat ends at the MARKT, where the rather plain *Stadhuis* (Mon–Fri, 09.00 to 17.00) in part dates from the early 15C though it was much restored and enlarged around 1700; the cellars include 12–13C fragments, and portraits of rulers of Gelderland hang in the marriage room. To the N the *Kathedraal van Sint Christoffel* (Sat, 14.00 to 17.00) was founded in 1410 and has served as cathedral since 1661; features of the interior are a 16C stone altar and a 13C wooden Crucifixion. Nearby, on the corner of Wilhelminasingel and Buitenop, the *Rattentoren* (no adm.) is the last survival of the medieval town defences.

Neerstraat leads S from the Markt, with at No. 33 *De Stenen Treppen* (Stone Steps), a patrician mansion of 1666. In Minderbroederssingel, to the W of Neerstraat, there are two chuches; the *Minderbroederskerk* (N), once Franciscan and now Dutch Reformed, dates from the 15C, while to the S the circular domed *Church of the Holy Spirit* was built in 1958 by F. Peutz. Further S (200m), at 2–8 Andersonweg, the *Gemeentemuseum* (Tues–Fri, 10.00 to 12.00, 14.00 to 17.00; Sat, Sun, 14.00 to 17.00) contains local antiquities, material on the architect P.J.H. Cuijpers (the museum occupies a part of his house) and work by Roermond artists such as Hendrik Luyten (paintings), Eugene Lücker (etchings) and Louis Raemaekers (caricatures). From near the museum Kapellerlaan leads SE to (1km) the *Kapel in't Zand*, a chapel with a miraculous image of the Virgin (daily, 10.00 to 12.00, 14.00 to 17.00).

At **St Odiliënberg** (5km S) the Romanesque church, formerly that of an abbey, was founded in the 12C but was largely rebuilt in 1880–83; statues from the abbey are in the Rijksmuseum, Amsterdam. At Kerkplein 10 the *Streekmuseum Roerstreek* is the local district museum (Tues–Fri, 10.30 to 16.30; Sat, Sun, 14.00 to 17.00).

For Roermond to Eindhoven, Helmond, and s' Hertogenbosch, see Rte 20, but for Thorn and Weert, see above.

The road NW out of Roermond in *4km* reaches the hamlet of *Asselt* to the

W beside the river, interesting because its little church stands on the site of a Frankish fort; the church itself, a restoration by Cuijpers, is partly of the 11C. Opposite the church there is a small local museum with some prehistoric, Frankish, and Roman material. At (*1km*) **Swalmen** the 17C château of *Hillenraad* was first built in c 1400. After *6km* you reach *Reuver* where a car ferry crosses the Maas to Kessel with mid 12C castle ruins. At (*6km*) **Steyl** the *Missiemuseum* (Mon–Sat, 10.00 to 12.00, 14.00 to 18.00; Sun, 14.00 to 18.00; closes 17.00 in Nov–March) at St Michaelstraat 7 contains ethnographic material (largely from Japan, China, Papua-New Guinea, Indonesia, and Africa), collected by missions and their congregations. *1km* **Tegelen** is, as its name ('tiles') suggests, largely concerned with the manufacture of tiles and ceramics generally, and there is a small ceramics museum in the Gemeentehuis.

*4km* **Venlo** (63,000 inhab.; VVV, Koninginneplein 2), mainly along the E bank of the Maas, was severely damaged in 1944 and has been rebuilt as a leading shopping centre with an extensive spread of pedestrian streets. At the same time a few old corners have survived. The town is also an important centre for the export of market garden produce and is notable for the many glasshouses in its environs.

**History.** A commercial centre since medieval times, Venlo received its first charter in 1345. In 1543 it gave its name to the treaty under which the Emperor Charles V ousted his rival William V of Cleves and formally became Duke of Gelder. During the 16–18C the town changed hands no less than ten times, its loss to the Spanish in 1586 being one of the first fruits of Leicester's military ineptitude. Marlborough took Venlo from the French in 1702; in 1713, under the Treaty of Utrecht, it was ceded to the United Provinces; the ramparts were demolished in 1868; and in the 20C it fell at once to the Germans in May 1940 and was severely damaged in the fighting at the war's end.

**Natives.** Hendrik Goltzius (1558–1617), the engraver and painter, was born near Venlo, as was probably also his uncle, the artist and antiquary Hubert Goltzius (1526–83).

On the MARKT the large *Stadhuis* of 1595 (restored) with its two bulb-capped towers contains a handsome council chamber with paintings by Hendrik Goltzius. From the Markt Lomstraat leads N, off which Kleine Kerkstraat soon bears E to reach *St Martinuskerk*, built in the 15C but with later additions including a tower of 1951 replacing the one destroyed in 1944. Features of the interior include a massive bronze font with a wrought-iron crane (1621), an 18C pulpit and a fine retable. Opposite the church the *Oude Weishoes* (1611), with appropriate wall carving, was once an orphanage, while the nearby *Huize Schreurs* was a patrician mansion of 1588. From the church, St Martinusstraat followed N and then Goltziusstraat followed E reach the *Goltzius Museum* (No. 21) of local history, in part illustrated by period rooms of the 16–18C (Tues–Fri, 10.00 to 16.30; Sat, Sun, 14.00 to 17.00).

To the S of the Markt, Klaasstraat and Parade run generally SE to reach (500m from the Stadhuis) Deken van Oppensingel which flanks the rectangular Julianapark. At No. 8 is the *Museum Bommel-Van Dam* (Tues–Fri, 10.00 to 16.30; Sat, Sun, 14.00 to 17.00), an art gallery with changing exhibitions, mostly of the works of local and contemporary artists.

The road along the E bank of the Maas between Venlo and Gennep (40km) passes 16–17C castles at *Well* and *Heijen*.

This Route now crosses the Maas and heads N for (*13km*) *Horst*. At (*10km*) **Venray** (34,000 inhab.) *St Pieterskerk*, a 15C building restored after severe war damage, is known for its wealth of late Gothic woodcarving, this including a remarkable series of figures of saints and apostles, a Calvary, a Madonna, and a St Peter, all dating from c 1500–25. There is a British war cemetery on the NW of the town, and at *IJsselsteyn*, 9km SW, a German one in which are concentrated the graves (over 31,000) of all the German soldiers who fell in the Netherlands.

The road N out of Venray in *3km* crosses into the province of Noord Brabant and in another *2km* reaches **Overloon**, the scene of particularly fierce fighting in September and October 1944.

Allied artillery bombardment started on 27 September, the occupying Germans as a result evacuating the civilian population. By 29 September the British had been reinforced by the US 7th Armoured Division and there followed a tank battle lasting from 4–8 October, the Germans coming out best. British 8th Army Corps was then given the task of defeating all German forces between Overloon and Roermond. The attack on Overloon was resumed on 11 October with an intense British and American air and ground bombardment, and by 14 October, after a day of house-to-house fighting, the ruined village was in Allied hands. The British war cemetery is to the E of the town.

The **Oorlogs-Verzets (War and Resistance) Museum** (daily, 10.00 to 18.00 or 17.00 in Sept–May) at Overloon comprises a woodland park and museum building in which Allied and German Second World War material is displayed. The collection of photographs and documents is of particular interest. Among the wealth of exhibits are tanks; armoured cars, carriers, and other vehicles; guns and rocket launchers; aircraft, including a V1 flying bomb; a minefield; a Bailey bridge; radar; and one-man submarines. A detailed guide is available in English.

*11km* **Boxmeer** (14,000 inhab.) where the *church*, rebuilt after the destruction of 1944, has an impressive, spacious red-brick interior, including brick confessionals. The monumental tomb (J.B. Xaverij, 1741) of Count Oswald van Bergh (died 1712) and of his wife survived the war damage, and in the crypt, arranged as a simple chapel, the foundations of the earlier church are preserved.

To the N of Boxmeer you cross the Maas to (*7km*) **Gennep** (16,000 inhab.) in the province of Limburg where there is a restored mid 17C *Stadhuis*. In *4km Milsbeek* and *5km Mook*, both with British war cemeteries. On the heath above the latter village was fought the battle of 1574 in which Louis and Henry of Nassau, brothers of William the Silent, were defeated and killed by the Spanish. The road now crosses into the province of Gelderland at a point between the dropping zones on 17 September 1944 of the US 82nd Airborne Division.

*9km* (from Mook) Nijmegen, see Rte 24.

# PROVINCES OF GELDERLAND AND FLEVOLAND

## Province of Gelderland

**Capital.** Arnhem.

**History.** In considering the history of Gelderland (earlier Guelders or Gelder or Gelre) two background facts should be borne in mind. First, that for much of its history the territory embraced a part of what is modern NW Germany, stretching towards the Rhine and including the German town of Geldern from which the province gets its name and which was until the late 14C the principal residence of the counts, later dukes, of Gelder. Second that, again for much of its history, Gelderland was made up of four 'quarters', namely Zutphen, Arnhem, Nijmegen and Roermond, this last including Venlo and the German portion.

By the Treaty of Meerssen (870) the lands which would become Gelderland became a part of the kingdom of East Francia (later the German empire), up to the 11C being ruled by several lords as fiefs of the empire. Of these lords, one Gerard of Wassenburg (died c 1117) emerged as the strongest and can probably be accepted as the first Count of Gelder. Later counts extended their lands, Henry I, grandson of Gerard, in 1131 inheriting the county of Zutphen; Otto I (died 1207) and Gerard III (died 1229; tomb in Roermond's Munsterkerk) taking over the districts of Veluwe and Betuwe; and Otto II (died 1271) receiving the town of Nijmegen as pledge for a loan to the Emperor designate, Count William II of Holland.

Count Reinald II (died 1345), son of Reinald I who had unsuccessfully tried to acquire Limburg, stands out as a leader and organiser, vigorously promoting trade and establishing law and order and so impressing Emperor Louis that he was created Duke and granted lands in East Friesland. But Reinald II's death was followed by some 30 years of dispute, ending in 1374 with the recognition of Duke William of Jülich as ruler, a succession which ended the capital status of the town of Geldern.

The next ruler of importance was Arnold of Egmont (died 1473) who, through a dispute with the Emperor Sigismund, had to fight for his inheritance and in so doing lost Jülich. In return for the support of his subjects he was forced to grant extensive privileges and powers to the States of Gelder, and finally in 1471 he had to sell the reversion of his duchy to Charles the Bold of Burgundy (died 1477) who became Duke of Gelder on Arnold's death in 1473. To this succession, however, there was considerable opposition (Nijmegen fell only after a long siege, and Arnhem too had to be taken by force), but by 1483 the Archduke Maximilian of Austria, who had married Charles the Bold's daughter Mary, seemed firmly established. Nevertheless the Egmont claim survived and the heroic Charles of Egmont, grandson of Arnold, was for several years remarkably successful, between 1492 and 1512 reconquering the duchy, threatening Holland and Brabant, and taking Drenthe and Groningen. Wisely though, he recognised that he could not indefinitely hold out against the power of Austria and in 1528 he signed the Treaty of Gorinchem with the Emperor Charles V, accepting Gelder for life only and as a fief of the empire. Thus when Charles of Egmont died in 1538 the reversion went to Charles V and Gelder was incorporated into the Habsburg dominions (though a rival claimant, William V of Cleves who had been appointed by the States of Gelder, held on to the duchy until ousted under the Treaty of Venlo of 1543).

But Habsburg rule was shortlived. In 1579 the 'quarters' of Zutphen, Arnhem and Nijmegen subscribed to the Union of Utrecht, becoming the province of Gelderland of the United Provinces. The 'quarter' of Roermond, which included Venlo and was almost entirely Catholic, remained Spanish and became known as Spanish Gelderland. Eventually, by the Treaty of Utrecht of 1713, this territory was ceded to Prussia, except for Venlo which went to the United Provinces and the town of Roermond which passed to Austria with the remaining Spanish Netherlands. Under the arrangements following the end of the Napoleonic era Venlo and Roermond were incorporated into the new Dutch province of Limburg.

During the Second World War Gelderland between Grave, Nijmegen and Arnhem was the battleground over which Operation 'Market Garden' (September 1944) and its aftermath were fought, months recalled today by many war cemeteries and memorials as also by much that has been rebuilt.

Gelderland divides into three districts, all of widely different character. At the south-west the BETUWE (Good Land), with rich vegetable and fruit growing acres, extends westward as a long narrow finger between the Neder Rijn and the Waal, the region to the S between the Waal and the Maas being similar. Nijmegen, at the E end, though much rebuilt after widespread war damage, remains Gelderland's largest, oldest, and most historic town, scene of a revolt against the Romans and site of a palace of Charlemagne, while to the W Culemborg and Zaltbommel are both small places of character.

The ACHTERHOEK (Back Corner) makes up the south-east of the province. A pastoral region of meadows, woods, and streams, and containing many large country estates, the district offers relaxed rural touring, scattered villages, and some attractive and interesting small towns such as Doesburg in the W and, in the S on the German border, 's Heerenberg with its moated castle.

The largest and in some ways the most important region of Gelderland is the VELUWE (Bad Land), an expanse of heath, woodland and dunes—some 50km from N to S and not much less in breadth—which fills the whole of the north-west of the province. Although agriculturally speaking the Veluwe deserves its name, it is far from 'bad land' in the context of the modern industry of tourism; with many nature reserves and recreational choices, crossed by networks of walking and bicycle ways, and bordered on the N by the Veluwe Meer with its water sports facilities, the region is the Netherlands' most popular countryside holiday choice yet is at the same time open and large enough to permit escape from the crowd. A part of the SE of the region has been made into the well-arranged yet still wild Hoge Veluwe National Park, within which is the world-famous Kröller-Müller art museum and sculpture garden.

The principal towns around the Veluwe are, at the SE, Arnhem, of tragic wartime notoriety but today with a large variety of recreational possibilities, including both the national park and also the park of the admirable Openlucht (Open Air) Museum; and, further N, Apeldoorn, home of the palace-museum Het Loo and on the edge of the magnificent royal forest. A string of small holiday centres line the NW of the region, amongst these being Nijkerk with early American associations; Harderwijk, an old place which today offers many recreational attractions as well as road access to the interesting Flevoland polders; Nunspeet, near which there is a Veluwe visitor centre; and the uniquely walled old town of Elburg.

**Province of Flevoland**

**Capital.** Lelystad.

The province of Flevoland was created in 1986 out of the polder districts of Oosterlijk Flevoland and Zuiderlijk Flevoland, together with the Noord-Oost Polder, previously a part of the province of Overijssel. For details see Rte 29B which describes the two Flevoland polders, and Rte 32A which crosses the Noord-Oost Polder.

# 24 Nijmegen and Environs

## A. Nijmegen

**NIJMEGEN** (148,000 inhab.), though not the capital of Gelderland (this is Arnhem), is the province's largest town and also, with Maastricht, one of the two oldest in the Netherlands. Rising steeply from the S bank of the Waal the inner town lies within the boulevards which mark the run of the fortifications demolished in 1878; these boulevards, forming a ring of fine fast roads over 2km in circumference, are broken by two large roundabouts, Keizer Karelplein to the SW and Keizer Traianusplein to the E. Severely damaged in the fighting between September 1944 and February 1945, when Nijmegen was in the front line, much of the town has been rebuilt to a new plan.

**Centre.** Plein 1944 and Grote Markt.

**VVV.** Sint Jorisstraat 72 (NW edge of Keizer Traianusplein).

**Post Office.** Van Schevichavenstraat; Station.

**Station.** Beyond W of inner town, 400m W of Keizer Karelplein.

**Boats.** Waal and Maas cruises (Rotterdam, Grave, Venlo, Kleve).

**History.** In 69–70 Claudius Civilis, leader of the Batavian and Frisian German revolt against Rome, occupied the hill (on which the Valkhof was later built) above the river and was besieged by Petilius Cerialis and the Xth Legion who established themselves on the Hunneberg height to the SE (now Keizer Traianusplein), backed by the camp in the area immediately SE of today's Museum Kam. After the defeat of the rebels, Trajan in 105 established Novio Magus (New Market) as a frontier town and fortress protecting the Batavian provinces from Frankish incursions; the town's present name is a corruption from this early one. Afterwards Nijmegen became a residence of Charlemagne and later emperors, and Henry VI (Emperor in 1190–97) was born here in 1165. In 1271 the town passed to Count Otto II of Gelder as a pledge for a loan he had made to Count William II of Holland, the Emperor designate, and in due course it became the chief town of one of the 'quarters' of the duchy of Gelderland, in 1473 refusing to accept Charles the Bold as Duke of Gelderland and submitting only after a long siege. Although subscribing to the Union of Utrecht in 1579 and in 1583 forbidding all Catholic activity, Nijmegen opened its gates to Parma in 1585 and remained under Spanish rule until taken by Maurice of Nassau six years later.

As a frontier fortress Nijmegen was besieged several times; on one occasion, when Turenne took the town in 1672, one of his officers was Captain John Churchill (afterwards Duke of Marlborough), who attracted the general's attention by his bravery. The Peace of Nijmegen (1678–79) between Louis XIV and the Dutch and Spanish brought this war to an end, Louis giving up all claims in the United Provinces.

In *Operation 'Market Garden'*'Market Garden' (17–25 September 1944) the Waal bridges at Nijmegen were a key objective. The Allied forces were the US 82nd Airborne Division which dropped in the area of Groesbeek (5km SE) and, advancing from the S, British 30th Corps. The Americans were successful and the position at Nijmegen was consolidated by the advance of the 30th Corps, a combined assault taking the bridges on the 20th, but the plan to link up with British 1st Airborne Division at Arnhem miscarried and between now and February 1945 Nijmegen was in the front line, over 2000 houses being destroyed and 1800 civilians losing their lives.

On either side of the busy, circular KEIZER KARELPLEIN, with an equestrian statue of Charlemagne, are (NW) the *Schouwburg* (municipal theatre, 1961), and (SE) *De Vereeniging*, a concert and congress hall. From here Bisschop Hamerstraat (commemorating a bishop murdered in China in 1900; statue to the W on Van Schaeck Mathonsingel), prolonged by Molen-straat, leads N towards the town centre. On the right in Molenstraat is the church of *St Pieter Canisius* dedicated to the Jesuit leader of the Counter Reformation who was born in Nijmegen (1521–97). Here a modern nave and façade (Sibbers, Van Dael, and Coumans, 1960) have been well adapted to the Gothic choir of the former Regulierkerk which had been half destroyed by bombing; the spacious interior repays a visit. To the left a short way further PLEIN 1944 is a post-war square in which a monument by Jac Maris honours members of the Dutch armed forces who gave their lives during the Second World War.

KRONENBURGPARK, 200m W of Plein 1944, was laid out around the old moat and ramparts at the end of the 19C by the landscape artist Lieven Rosseels. Fragments of the 15–16C fortifications are preserved, notably the **Kruit-toren** (gunpowder tower, Parkweg 99) in which there are two museums. *Grootmoeders Keukenmuseum* (March–Sept: Mon–Fri, 10.00 to 12.00, 14.00 to 16.00; Sat, Sun, 14.00 to 16.00), or Grandmother's Kitchen, shows kitchen equipment of about the year 1900, while in total contrast there is the *Planetarium en Ruimtevaartcentrum* (VVV for times), with material on the stars and planets and space. Nearby, at Parkweg 65 and yet another contrast, *Het Rondeel*, in another fortress tower, is devoted to mushrooms (Sun, 14.00 to 17.00). The *Station* is 500m to the SW. Immediately W of the *Waalhaven* (beyond the railway and 300m NW of the Kruittoren) was the site of Trajan's Novio Magus.

From the NE corner of PLEIN 1944, the pedestrians only Broerstraat ascends to a main crossroads in the centre pavement of which is the BLAUWE STEEN, a blue slab marking the point which was in medieval times the meeting point of the town's four quarters and thus the town centre.

Grotestraat descends steeply to the Waal. To the W can be seen the railway bridge beside which, in daylight and under heavy fire, American airborne troops crossed the river in rubber boats, taking this bridge and also securing the N approach to the road bridge. To the E are the restored *Brouwershuis* (1621) and the *Besienderhuis* (1525), the latter once the office of the collectors of tolls from incoming ships and now used for exhibitions of modern art. Steps lead up to the *Groene Balkon*, a promenade with a massive supporting wall built as the first stage in the reconstruction of the riverside district. *Velorama*, at Waalkade 107 (E end of the road), is a museum of vintage bicycles (daily 10.00, or 11.00 on Sat and Sun, to 17.00).

In the GROTE MARKT, immediately W of the Blauwe Steen, stands the figure of Mariken van Nieuwmeghen, the misused and seduced heroine of a Dutch medieval folk play, still occasionally revived. The **Waag** (1612) was in turn weigh-house for meat and butter, while the upper floor served as civic militia guardroom. The **Kerkboog**, also in the Markt, is a vaulted passage built by Claes de Waele in 1545 and given its elaborately gabled upper structure in 1606; to its right is the façade of the former *Lakenhal* (Cloth Hall), now a restaurant. Beyond the Kerkboog the **St Stevenskerk** (mid May–mid June and mid Aug–mid Sept: Mon–Fri, 10.00 to 12.30, 13.30 to 17.00; Sat, 10.00 to 13.00; mid June–mid Aug: Mon–Fri, 10.00 to 17.00; Sat, 10.00 to 13.00; Sun, 14.00 to 17.00) dates mainly from the late 14C and early 15C but preserves at the W end portions of a building of c 1254, the year in which the church was founded. The transepts are of c 1552, and the tower (ascent offering fine view) of 1604. Restoration after war damage was completed in 1969. The interior contains the tomb of Catharine of Bourbon (died 1469), wife of Adolf of Gelderland, built in 1512 by William Loemans of Cologne; this Adolf was son of Duke Arnold, and it was partly because of his conspiring against his father that the latter sold the duchy reversion to Charles the Bold of Burgundy. A monument beside the church commemorates the 1800 civilians killed in 1944–45. Facing the S side of the church is the *Latijnse School* (Herman van Herengrave, 1545; now well restored), a school until 1842 and now an architectural office. Note the carving and Latin inscription.

The **Commanderie van St Jan** occupies a commanding position between the Waag and the river. Historically dating back to 1196 and in turn hospital of the Knights of St John (till 1566), a school (1655–78), and Walloon church (1686–1944), the present building, a 1974 reconstruction of the structure of c 1600, now houses the *Stedelijk Museum* (Mon–Sat, 10.00 to 17.00; Sun, 13.00 to 17.00). The ground floor is used for temporary exhibitions, while the upper floor (in part also sometimes used for temporary exhibitions) houses permanent collections covering the history of Nijmegen and its district from Roman times until the 19C. Perhaps most interesting here are the portraits and pictures, including a large pictorial plan of 1669 by Hendrik Geltman; a large canvas by Henri Gascar vividly portraying the signing in 1678 of the Peace of Nijmegen; and a picture by Jan van Goyen of the Valkhof as it was in 1541. Additionally of note are Merovingian and Carolingian coins; a wooden Pietà of c 1520 by Hendrik Douverman; Nijmegen pewter and silver of the 15C and 16C; several immense ceremonial swords; an oak documents chest of 1560; and a neat alabaster relief of the Judgement of Solomon.

The **Stadhuis** (May–Oct: tours Mon–Fri, at 14.00 and 15.30), in Burchtstraat just E of the Blauwe Steen, was built in 1554 by Herman van Herengrave, refaced in 1663 when the statues of imperial benefactors of the town were added, and in 1953 rebuilt in the original style after severe war damage. The interior (reconstructed 1977–80) contains 17C Delft and Gobelins tapestries, paintings and antique furniture. The treaties (1678–79) making up the Peace of Nijmegen were signed here in the Trêvezaal, where there are portraits of the signatories, including those of the English representatives Sir William Temple and his successor Sir Leoline Jenkins.

Opposite the N end of the Stadhuis roads lead to the top of the *Groene Balkon* (see above). Nieuwstraat descends S to the *Marienburgkapel*, once chapel of the sisters of the convent of Mons Mariae.

To the N beyond the end of Burchtstraat is the **Valkhof**, a garden above the river, site of the stand by Claudius Civilis in 69–70 and laid out around the scanty ruins of a palace built on Roman foundations by Charlemagne in 777 and rebuilt in 1155 by Frederick Barbarossa whose son, later Emperor

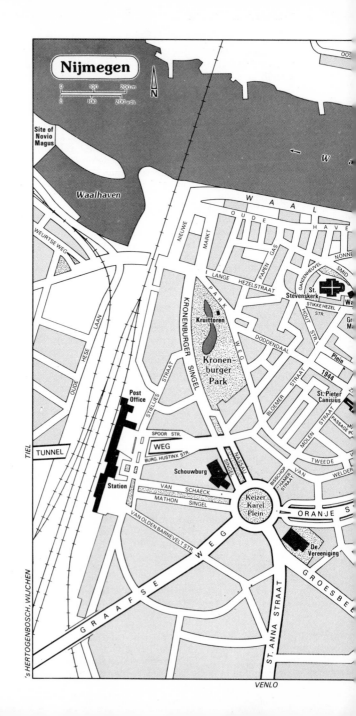

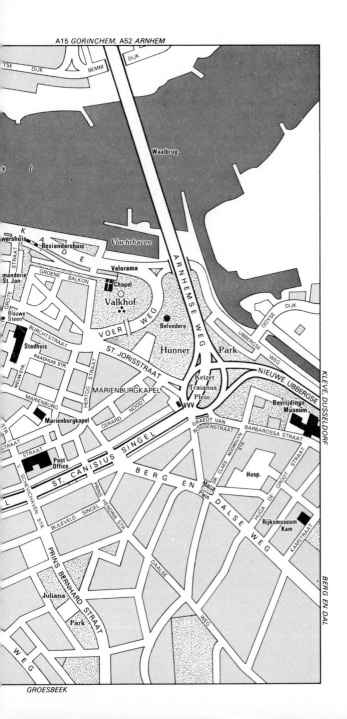

A15 *GORINCHEM*, A52 *ARNHEM*

TSE DIJK
BEMM
DIJK

Waalbrug

KADE

wershuis
**Besiendershuis**
*Vluchthaven*

STRAAT

manderie
St. Jan

GROENE BALKON

**Velorama**

ARNHEMSE WEG

GROTE

Chapel

**Valkhof**

Blauwe
Steen

VOER WEG

**Belvedere**

OOYSE DIJK

BURCHTSTRAAT

**Stadhuis**

RAADHUIS STR.

**Hunner**

**Park**

UBBERGSE

WEG

ST. JORISSTRAAT

HERTOG STRAAT

NIEUWSTR.

MARIENBURG

**MARIENBURGKAPEL**

Keizer
Traianus
Plein

NIEUWE UBBERGSE

KLEVE, DÜSSELDORF

GERARD NOODT

**VVV**

**Bevrijdings
Museum**

**Marienburgkapel**

STR

STRAAT

GRAEDT VAN
ROGGENSTRAAT

BARBAROSSA STRAAT

SINGEL

**Post
Office**

ST. CANISIUS SINGEL

BERG

EN

DR. CLAES NOORDLIJN STR

HUGA DE GROOT STRAAT

Hosp.

L

SCHEVICHAVEN STR

BIJLEVELD SINGEL

PRINS HENDRIK STR

**Maria
Plein**

DALSE

WEG

**Rijksmuseum
Kam**

KAMSTRAAT

PRINS BERNHARD STRAAT

DAALSE

BERG EN DAL

**Juliana**

**Park**

WEG

WEG

GROESBEEK

Henry VI, was born here in 1165. Still habitable in the 18C, the palace was demolished in 1769 by the States of Gelderland and the stonework sold. Today the only recognisable remains are the Romanesque apse of a chapel of Barbarossa's time, and a sixteen-sided chapel built in c 1045 in imitation of Charlemagne's cathedral in Aachen and enlarged in c 1400. A footbridge leads to the *Belvedere*, a ramparts tower rebuilt in 1646 on older foundations and now a restaurant. A public look-out platform offers a fine vista embracing the Waal and the low-lying land stretching N to Arnhem and the Rhine, with the Veluwe hills beyond.

The open HUNNERPARK, immediately to the E and cut by the broad and busy Arnhemseweg, was the scene of fierce fighting in September 1944. Within the park are (W side) some remains of the 15C fortifications; a statue (1927) of St Pieter Canisius and, within a small low brick enclosure, a plaque marking the spot where a capsule was buried on 18 September 1974. The ceremony was attended by Queen Juliana and Allied military leaders, and the capsule, containing official documents relating to Operation 'Market Garden', is not to be opened until the year 2044. On Keizer Traianusplein, at the S end of Hunnerpark and with VVV near its NW corner, are a statue of the Emperor Trajan and also the Verzets (Resistance) monument of 1954. Beside the latter, a tablet honours the Dutch Rover Scout Jan van Hoof, a lad who lost his life by heroically running along the adjacent Waalbrug and, by cutting the wires, prevented the German attempt to blow it up.

Graadt van Roggenstraat, soon becoming Barbarossastraat, leads E out of Keizer Traianusplein. In the latter street, at No. 35, being the **Bevrijdingsmuseum** (Mon–Sat, 10.00 to 17.00; Sun, 12.00 to 17.00), or Liberation Museum, telling the story of September 1944 with a maquette, authentic relics and some dramatic and unique photographs.

The **Rijksmuseum Kam** (Tues–Sat, 10.00 to 17.00; Sun, 13.00 to 17.00), nearby in Museum Kamstraat, is named after G.M. Kam (1836–1922), a distinguished amateur archaeologist who in 1920 presented to the town both this house and his collection of local Roman antiquities. Other collections have since been added.

With its high ground, and with the Rhine defining Rome's frontier, Nijmegen was an obvious Roman strategic key place, their camp occupying the area immediately SE of the museum, bounded by Berg en Dalseweg on the S and Nieuwe Ubbergseweg on the N. After defeating Claudius Civilis, the Xth Legion formed the garrison here and the camp continued in use until about the end of the 2C.

The museum comprises a central hall, surrounded by five ground floor rooms and three upper galleries. The central hall shows pottery and metalwork, notable being Samian ware, probably produced in eastern Gaul; a silver cup, found in the Maas (1C); a bronze portrait, probably Trajan; military equipment such as helmets, shields and harness; and a wealth of minor domestic objects.

Around the central hall Rooms 1 to 5 are arranged clockwise chronologically, Room 1 covering the period 10 BC–AD 70 mainly with finds from burial grounds in the area of the museum. Here, too, are stone blocks bearing reliefs, part of a monumental pillar found in the centre of Nijmegen in 1980 and with one figure possibly representing the emperor Tiberius. Room 2 contains gravestones of the 1C, discovered in the grounds of St Canisius College immediately SE of the museum. Also a small coin display with, alongside each coin, photographic enlargements enabling detail of the original picture to be appreciated. Room 3 is devoted to the Xth Legion which, summoned from Spain, defeated Claudius Civilis in 70 and remained in Nijmegen until transferred to Hungary about 30 years later. Room 5, the next room chronologically, shows discoveries from the Novio Magus, the fortified frontier town which Trajan established in 105 in the area to the W of the railway just beyond today's Waalhaven. Room 4 closes the Roman story with finds (mainly from the area of today's town centre) of the period c 270–400. Additionally there is some material from the immediately following Frankish period.

More general material is displayed around the galleries. North Gallery: kitchen and eating utensils; candleholders and lamps; medical instruments; writing materials; figurines. East Gallery: burial gifts, largely of glass. South Gallery: bronze vessels; jewellery; toilet articles; scales and weights.

# B.  Environs of Nijmegen

The SOUTH-EAST is of interest principally for two unusual open-air museums and, further on around Groesbeek, as one of the 'Market Garden' airborne dropping zones. The approach is by Groesbeekseweg out of Keizer Karelplein, this becoming Nijmegsebaan and in rather over 3km from central Nijmegen reaching the **Heilig Land Stichting**, or Holy Land Foundation, also known as the *Bijbels Openluchtmuseum* or Bible Open-air Museum (Easter–Oct: daily, 09.00 to 17.30). The foundation dates from 1915 and within its extensive grounds reproduces the topography of the Holy Land, with scenes from the life of Jesus. Among individual themes are the nomads with their tents and eastern caravans; shepherds and their flocks; a Palestinian village; a city street of the past, showing Egyptian, Greek, Roman and Jewish houses; and a fishing village.

The *Hotel Sionshof*, at the nearby main crossroads (Nijmegsebaan, Sionsweg, Meerwijkselaan), for four years a German headquarters, was the spot where the American and British forces met on 19 September 1944, the hotel soon becoming an 82nd Airborne Division headquarters (plaque).

The **Africa Museum** (April–Sept: Mon–Fri, 10.00 to 17.00; Sun, Holidays, 11.00 to 17.00; Oct–March: Tues–Fri, 10.00 to 17.00; Sat; Sun, 13.00 to 17.00), on Postweg 1km SW of the Heilig Land Stichting and mainly concerned with West Africa, includes an African village, a small animal park and a modern museum building with collections illustrating African life and art (masks, musical instruments, carved figures). **Berg en Dal**, generally to the N and in, as its name implies, surrounds of hill and valley, is a popular holiday and excursion centre; the *Duivelsberg*, acquired by the Netherlands from Germany under a border agreement of 1963, and *Wylerberg* have waymarked walks and viewpoints.

Nijmegsebaan continues S to reach (11km from Heilig Land Stichting) **Groesbeek**, hub of the American 'Market Garden' drop and an area today with many memorials. The best overall view of the dropping zone is from the *Canadian War Cemetery and Memorial* (N of Groesbeek). The Canadians were much involved in the offensive of 1945 and the memorial bears the names of members of the Commonwealth land forces who died during the campaign in north-west Europe between August 1944 and the war's end and who have no known grave. Many of these died in the *Reichswald*, in Germany just SE of Groesbeek, the scene of bitter fighting during the winter of 1944–45.

SOUTH. Sint Anna Straat, out of Keizer Karelplein, in rather over 1km reaches the large complex of the Katholieke Universiteit, in which, in Thomas van Aquinostraat, is the *Nijmeegs Volkenkundig Museum* which mounts regular temporary ethnological exhibitions (Mon–Fri, 09.15 to 17.00). The *Stadspark de Goffert*, 1km W of the university, is a recreational area with a children's farm, swimming pool and stadium, and, just to the S within the angle of Oude Mollenhutseweg and Weg door Jonkerbos, the Jonkerbos Commonwealth War Cemetery.

Further S, the bridge at *Malden* was a 'Market Garden' objective, blown up, however, by the Germans before the Americans reached it. But the bridge at *Heumen*, farther S again, was successfully secured.

WEST. From Keizer Karelplein, Graafseweg, becoming Wychenseweg, in 9km reaches **Wijchen**, with a 14–15C castle rebuilt during the 16C for the daughter of William of Orange (tours Wed, 13.45 and 15.30). At *Hernen*, 4km NW of Wijchen, there is also a castle, this one of the 15–16C (Easter–Oct: Tues, Thurs, Sat, 10.00 to 12.00, 14.00 to 17.00).

For Nijmegen to Gorinchem and Rotterdam, see Rtes 25 and 12A; to 's Hertogenbosch and Bergen op Zoom, see Rte 19.


# 25 Western Gelderland (Arnhem or Nijmegen to Gorinchem)

This Route describes the long, narrow, westward projection of Gelderland, bordered on the N by the Lek-Neder Rijn and the province of Utrecht and on the S by the Maas and the province of Noord Brabant. The Waal runs through the length of the projection, with the A15 motorway to the river's N and more or less parallel. Much of the Route, and all the eastern part, is through the BETUWE, a vegetable and fruit growing district beautiful with blossom in spring.

> Total distance 86km.—10km (from Arnhem) Motorway Junction A52/A15—32km **Tiel**—11km Buurmalsen—2km Geldermalsen—6km Waardenburg—3km **Zaltbommel**—22km **Gorinchem**.

For Arnhem, see Rte 26. For Nijmegen, see Rte 24.

*10km* (from Arnhem; 7km from Nijmegen) is Motorway Junction A52/A15. It was from the S that the British 30th Corps fought its way in September 1944 in the attempt to link up with the airborne troops dropped near Arnhem. The advance was held up at **Elst** (now within the NW sector of the motorway junction) where the Reformed church was badly damaged; when rebuilding started after the war remains were found of two earlier churches (8–10C), standing on the site of a Gallo-Roman temple.

Follow the A15 motorway W for (*32km*) **Tiel** (30,000 inhab.; VVV, Karenbeursplein 4), on the Waal, the chief town of the Betuwe and the site in early September of an annual festival of fruit and vegetables. Much of the town was rebuilt after war damage. Immediately E, the Amsterdam-Rijn Kanaal meets the Waal through one of Europe's largest inland locks.

This Route now leaves the motorway for (*8km*) the village of *Buren*, where the large former Weeshuis (museum) was founded in 1612 by Maria, daughter of William the Silent (his first wife was Anna van Buren). The crown of the tower of the Reformed church is by Pieter Post (1665). It was from the village of *Buurmalsen, 3km* SW, that Cornelis van Buren, ancestor of President Van Buren of the United States, emigrated.

**Culemborg** (20,000 inhab.; VVV, Herenstraat 29), 8km N on the Lek (car ferry), an old town which received its charter in 1318, was the home of the counts of Culemborch, one of whom was Floris van Pallandt (1532–1613), a leader in the early revolt against Spain. At one end of the straight, broad main street stand the *Binnenpoort*, a gate of 1557, and the mainly 15C *St Barbarakerk*, with good woodwork and patrician monuments. The late Gothic *Stadhuis*, down the street, dates from 1534–39. In the Herenstraat, parallel to the main street, the *Weeshuis* (No. 29), a bequest of 1560 by Elisabeth van Culemborch, houses VVV. Culemborg was the birthplace of Anthonie van Diemen (1593–1645), governor of the East Indies Company and patron of Abel Tasman's voyage of discovery (1642), and also of Jan van Riebeek (1619–77), founder in 1652 of what would be Cape Town; the latter's home, with a well restored double façade, is at Achterstraat 26. The railway bridge across the Lek was built in 1863–68.

*2km Geldermalsen*, beyond which you cross motorway A15 for (*6km*) *Waardenburg* where the castle (no adm.), a 17C and 19C rebuilding and extension of a medieval original, was according to local legend a place where Faust lived with Mephistopheles. Take the motorway (A2) bridge to cross the Waal for (*3km*) **Zaltbommel** (8000 inhab.; VVV, Markt 10), an ancient fortress which successfully resisted the Spaniards in 1599 but fell to Turenne in 1692 and which today has some attractive and interesting old buildings and a number of 16–17C façades. In the rectangular Markt in the N part of the town the *Stadhuis* of 1762 stands in front of some remains of its medieval predecessor, and the *Waag* opposite is of the same date. A short walk N reaches the *Waterpoort* of the 14C with, on the left, remains of a rounded tower. To the E of the Markt rises the 15–16C tower (restored 1958) of the former church of the Hospitallers, with a clock with moving figures and 29 bells of which 20 are ascribed to the Hemony brothers. The road leading S out of the Markt reaches (seven minutes walk) the *Huis van Maarten van Rossem* at Nonnenstraat 5, housing the local museum. Maarten van Rossem (1478–1555) was a general of Duke Charles of Egmont and Gelder; of his house all that survives is the portal of a gatehouse of 1535. A short way E, the mainly 14–15C *St Martinskerk*, founded in 1304, contains 15C murals and late 14C choir stalls, the latter being among the oldest in the Netherlands. Extensive remains of the 14–16C defences enclose the town.

From Zaltbommel there is a choice of roads to Gorinchem. Along the S bank of the Waal a dike road in 14km reaches *Brakel*, with a car ferry to the N bank. For the castle of *Loevestein*, 5km further W on the S bank, see Rte 19. Alternatively you can re-cross the Waal at Zaltbommel and follow any one of a number of roads, including the A15 motorway, W. Approximately *22km* (by any road) is Gorinchem (see Rte 12A) is in Zuid Holland.

For Gorinchem to Rotterdam, see Rte 12A.

# 26   Arnhem and Environs

**ARNHEM** (128,000 inhab.), the capital of the province of Gelderland, became tragically known through the airborne operation of September 1944. Now rebuilt, the town, not without interest in itself, is perhaps most visited for the many features of note in its environs, these including the famous Openlucht (Open Air) and Krüller- Müller museums, the Airborne Museum, the Hoge Veluwe National Park, and a safari park.

The **Battle of Arnhem** (Operation *'Market Garden'*, September 1944). For the general strategic situation prior to the battle, see the article Liberation 1944–45.

The aim of the operation was to prepare the way for an Allied advance which would outflank the German West Wall, thus cutting off the escape route of the Germans still in the western Netherlands, and then swing eastwards to drive deep into Germany. Success might have ended the war in 1944. Combined British and American airborne forces were to drop behind the German lines to capture the bridges over the Maas, Waal and the Neder Rijn, while ground forces were to advance from the Dutch-Belgian frontier to achieve a link-up.

The commander of the 1st Allied Airborne Army was Lt Gen. Brereton. Two American airborne divisions of the 18th US Airborne Corps (Lt Gen. Ridgway), the 101st and 82nd, were to secure bridges in the Son-Veghel area (SE of 's Hertogenbosch) and over the Maas near Grave and the Waal at Nijmegen. Further N, 1st British Airborne Corp's (Lt Gen. Browning) 1st Airborne Division (Maj. Gen. Urquhart) was given the most advanced task, the seizing of the Rhine (Neder Rijn) crossing at Arnhem. The 1st Airborne Division included 1st and 4th Parachute Brigades (Brigadiers Lathbury and Hackett), the 1st Air Landing Brigade (Brig. Hicks), and the 1st Polish Parachute Brigade (Maj. Gen. Sosabowski). The three divisions—two American and one British—were to hold out until 30th Corps (Lt Gen. Horrocks), thrusting N on the ground, could reach them. It was hoped to complete the link-up in two days.

The airborne phase of the operation, which involved almost 5000 fighters, bombers, and transports, and more than 2500 gliders, began in the early afternoon of Sunday 17 September. In the Arnhem area the task of 1st Parachute Brigade was to capture and hold the main road bridge across the river and also a pontoon bridge to the W, today represented by the Roermondspleinbrug; 1st Air Landing Brigade was to protect the dropping and landing zones until the completion of the lift, and then to move to the E of the bridge; 4th Parachute Brigade was to move E to occupy the high ground N of Arnhem, while 1st Polish Parachute Brigade was to land S of the river near Driel and then make for the bridge.

After the first successful landing between 13.00 and 14.00, with drops N and W of Heelsum and Wolfheze some 10km W of Arnhem, 1st Parachute Brigade advanced by three routes towards the town and bridge. The 2nd Battalion (Lt Col Frost) followed the river as planned and, having found the pontoon bridge partially dismantled, captured the N end of the main road bridge at last light (this is the eastern of today's two bridges). They were, though, unable to take the S end. The German reaction was swift and unexpectedly strong and the other British units, trying to advance through and to the N of Oosterbeek, were forced to retire, only some small groups managing to fight through to the bridge. The weather, rapidly deteriorating, hampered further air reinforcement and supply to 1st Airborne Division, while to the S a combination of strong enemy positions and counter-attacks had delayed the advance of 30th Corps, and it was only after a valiant combined British and American attack that the Nijmegen bridges could be taken on the 20th. 1st Airborne Division, although reinforced by landings on the 18th and 19th, came under heavy German pressure led by 9th Panzer Division and amid bitter fighting was forced to fall back on Oosterbeek. 1st Polish Parachute Brigade, which had landed S of the river on the 21st but in smaller numbers and further W than planned, suffered heavy losses in attempting to cross the river to link with the British.

The 600 to 700 men of the 2nd Battalion managed to hold on to the N end of the bridge for three days and four nights—far longer than had ever been planned—but after constant and eventually overwhelming attacks, and with their numbers down to 110, the last resistance came to an end in the early hours of Thursday the 21st. The British held out at Oosterbeek, confined within an ever shrinking perimeter, in the hope that 30th Corps would be able to link up, but although a tenuous link was achieved on the 22nd continued enemy pressure on the whole Allied advance meant that reinforcement in time became impossible. Finally, on the night of the 25th, the position was evacuated, and as dawn broke on the 26th the last of the survivors—2163 out of 10,005—had been withdrawn across the river to Driel. The Allies were not to liberate Arnhem until 13 April the following year with an attack by 49th Canadian Division.

**Routes from Arnhem**. To Utrecht, see Rte 16; to Gorinchem and Rotterdam, see Rtes 25 and 12A; to Zutphen and Winterswijk, see Rte 27A; to Zevenaar, Terborg, and Winterswijk, see Rte 27B; to Apeldoorn and Zwolle, see Rte 28.

# A.  Inner Arnhem

The inner town is enclosed on the W, N, and E by boulevards marking the circuit of ramparts finally levelled in 1853, and on the S by the Neder Rijn (Lower Rhine) a short way below the divergence of the (Gelderland) IJSssel. The Rhine is crossed by two road bridges. The modern bridge to the W, the continuation of the western boulevard called the Nieuwe Plein, carries the main road to Nijmegen; at this bridge's N end is the ROERMONDSPLEIN, a spaghetti-junction around a fountain surrounded by a blue and white stonescape designed to give a water effect. The bridge to the E, carrying the motorway A52, is the John Frost Brug (see below).

**Centre.** Jansplaats-Jansplein, with pedestrian streets to the SE and SW.

**VVV** and **Station.** Immediately NW of inner town, N of Utrechtsestraat.

**Post Office.** Jansplein, just E of Jansplaats. Also Stationsplein.

**Boats.** Excursions along the Rhine and the IJssel; choice of several local and long distance cruises.

**History.** First mentioned in a document of 893 Arnhem may occupy the site of the Roman *Arenacum*. In 1233 the town was both granted a charter and fortified by Duke Otto II of Gelder, and in 1433 it joined the Hanseatic League. A favourite residence of the ducal family, Arnhem was frequently attacked by their rivals the dukes of Burgundy, in 1473 opposing Charles the Bold who had to take the town by force. In 1505 minting rights were granted by Philip the Handsome, and in 1543, after the ducal years of Charles of Egmont and William V of Cleves, Arnhem, as a town of the duchy

352

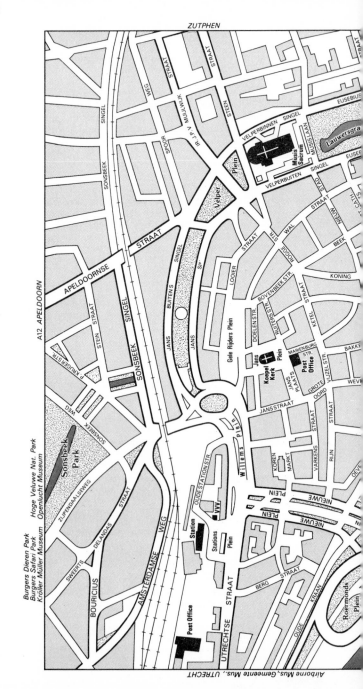

353

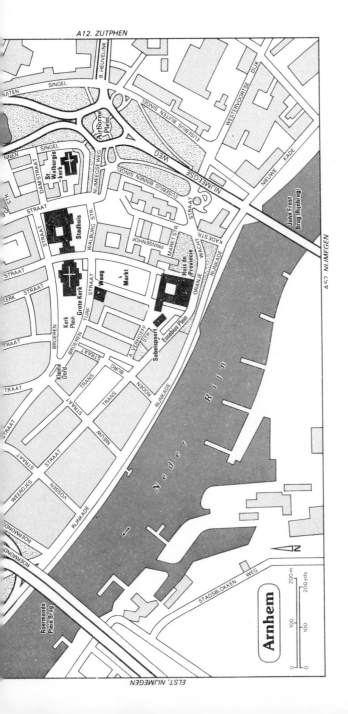

of Gelder, passed to the Emperor Charles V. It was taken from the Spanish in 1585, and it was here the following year that Sir Philip Sidney (see Rte 27A) died of his wounds received at Warnsveld near Zutphen. The ramparts were dismantled after the town had been taken by Louis XIV in 1672, were rebuilt by Coehoorn in the 18C, and finally levelled in 1853.

The WILLEMSPLEIN, an open area of wide road some 300m in length and with a large roundabout at its E end, forms the NW section of the ring boulevards. From the roundabout the road leading N under the railway reaches the N environs of Arnhem (Openlucht Museum, Hoge Veluwe Park, Krüller Müller Museum, etc., for all of which see below). Off the W end of Willemsplein, Nieuwe Plein descends S to the *Roermondspleinbrug* (for Nijmegen), while to the NW of this end of Willemsplein are *VVV* and the *Stations* (railway and bus).

In the INNER TOWN the adjoining Jansplaats and Jansplein are 150m S of the Willemsplein roundabout (through an archway). In the former there is a statue to the Gelderland hero Karel (Charles) of Egmont, Gelre, and Zutphen (1467–1538; see also Grote Kerk below). From Jansplein, Marien-burgstraat leads S to the junction of Vijzelstraat (W) and Ketelstraat (E), this sequence of streets, continued to the W by Rijnstraat and to the E by Roggestraat and the whole length a pedestrian precinct, represent the old main thoroughfare across the town. Rijnstraat 47 was *St Pieters Gasthuis* (1407), at one time the mint.

Bakkerstraat continues S to the large KERKPLEIN, scene of a fleamarket on Friday mornings. The **Grote Kerk** (St Eusebius) was founded by Duke Arnold in 1452, the subsequent building work extending over the following century and the tower being a replacement of that destroyed in the fighting of 1944. Note the curious figures climbing the flying buttresses. Charles of Egmont, whose statue is in Jansplaats, lies in a fine tomb in the choir. The **Stadhuis**, immediately E of the church, was built in the 15C as a palace (it was at one time the home of Maarten van Rossem, Charles of Egmont's general) and was converted to its present use in 1830. The heads on the front represent personages of Van Rossem's time, and the satyr-like figures under the bow-window at the corner have given the building the popular name of Duivelshuis (Devil's House).

To the S extends the MARKT, another large open space, with at the NW corner the *Waag* (1761–68; rebuilt since 1944). The *Huis de Provincie* (Vegter and Brouwer, 1954), seat of the provincial government, stretches across the S side of the Markt, next to it (W) being the *Sabelspoort*, the only surviving fragment of the fortifications built in 1440, with additions of 1642. Walburgstraat, beside the Stadhuis, reaches the Roman Catholic *St Wal-burgiskerk*, a Gothic church of 1422, rebuilt in 1853–54 when the apse was added. Behind the church the E boulevards enclose gardens occupying the site of the moat, a short way S being AIRBORNEPLEIN, a sunken garden within a busy roundabout; in the garden's centre a broken column from the ruins of Arnhem bears the date 17 September 1944. To the S of Airborne-plein the Rhine is crossed by the **John Frost Brug** (also called the *Rijnbrug*), the N end of which was taken and so gallantly held for three days and four nights by the 2nd Battalion of the 1st Parachute Brigade.

# B. Environs of Arnhem

The Environs of Arnhem are described under four directions, North–East, North, West and South. The Hoge Veluwe National Park and the Rijksmuseum Kröller-Müller are described separately as Rte 26C.

## North-East of Arnhem

From Velperplein at the NE corner of the ring boulevards Steenstraat leads NE, beyond the railway becoming Velperweg. *Bronbeek* (daily, 09.00 to 12.00, 12.30 to 17.00), at No. 147, has since 1863 been a home for ex-servicemen, occupying property donated in 1859 by King William III; a museum here shows colonial military material from Indonesia, Surinam and the Antilles. Velperweg crosses the A12 motorway, 600m beyond which Daalhuizerweg heads N for (1½km) *Kasteel Rosendael* (June–mid Sept: Tues–Sat, 10.00 to 17.00; Sun, 13.00 to 17.00), a feudal building with 18C additions which was once a summer residence of the dukes of Gelder. The park offers country walks and the château houses a museum in which pictures and models tell the story of the development of castles, Dutch and elsewhere.

## North of Arnhem

Beyond the railway bridge to the N of the Willemsplein roundabout, the parks of *Sonsbeek* and *Zijpendaal* extend northward for well over 2km as a beautiful area of green slopes, meadows, woods and small lakes. Zijpendaalseweg skirts the W edge of the parks, soon passing *De Witte Molen*, a water mill in origin of the 15C. Still milling flour, today it houses an information centre and exhibition on the natural and cultural development of Arnhem. Beyond, *Kasteel Zijpendael* (Easter–last Sun in Oct: daily, except Sat and Mon, 13.00 to 17.00) shows period rooms.

Zijpendaalseweg becomes Deelenseweg which (3km from Willemsplein) reaches Schelmseweg. Ahead (entrance off the continuation of Deelenseweg) is **Burgers Zoo and Safari Park and Rainforest** (daily, 09.00 to 20.00; last safari train 17.00). Schelmseweg followed E soon reaches the *Nederlands Openlucht Museum** (April–Oct: daily, 09.00 to 17.00; Sat, Sun, 10.00 to 17.00), a large open-air museum founded in 1912 and illustrating the daily life of the ordinary people of the past, the emphasis being on the 19C. The museum offers something like 100 original buildings—mills, farms, workshops, an inn, a school, a church, bridges, etc.—from virtually every part of the Netherlands, all re-erected within a large wooded park and containing contemporary furniture, domestic and trade equipment and suchlike. In addition to the buildings there are specialised attractions such as a Herb Garden, an *Exhibition of Regional Costumes which is the largest and finest in the Netherlands, and craft demonstrations. The museum suggests a choice of three routes, all clearly waymarked: Red (one hour), Green (two hours) and Blue (four hours). Many visitors will be content simply to wander around and enjoy the general setting. Those in search of detail may buy the museum's excellent guide in English (128 pages) with maps, a wealth of background information both domestic and architectural, and every page's text accompanied by illustrations and diagrams.

## West of Arnhem

In these western suburbs and beyond the interest is mainly related to

'Market Garden'. The line Utrechtseweg-Utrechtsestraat represents the axis of the central of the three attempted thrusts from the dropping zones through Oosterbeek and Arnhem to the Rhine bridge. Amsterdamseweg, to the N, would have been the axis of the northern thrust had it not soon been halted in the area N of Oosterbeek.

Leaving Willemsplein, Utrechtsestraat in 500m reaches the large PGEM building (No. 68; parking meters). Opposite, there is a Dutch war memorial, and a plaque on a house (No. 85) a short way back to the E recalls that this was a German SD (security service) headquarters from 1940–44. To the W (100m; N side of the road) another plaque on a house records a gallant stand here by a small group of 1st Airborne Division, this in fact being about the most easterly point reached by the central thrust.

Opposite is the *Gemeentemuseum* (Tues–Sat, 10.00 to 17.00; Sun, Holidays, 11.00 to 17.00). In a garden above the Rhine, the original building, with its cupola, was built by Cornelis Outshoorn in 1873–75, but in 1949–56 reconstruction after war damage included a new section. The museum is largely used for temporary exhibitions, but there are also permanent collections embracing paintings of the 17–19C, modern and contemporary art, archaeology, the history of Gelderland, and a wide range of applied art. Integral features of the museum are the Organ Gallery, the Rhine Room with a view of the river and a 17C painted ceiling.

The hospital, just beyond and on the opposite side to the museum, is *St Elizabeth Gasthuis*, a centre of bitter fighting and effectively the point at which the central thrust was halted before being forced to withdraw to Oosterbeek. The streets Zwarteweg and Alexanderstraat, both immediately W of the hospital, are of some 'Market Garden' interest. On 18 September Maj. Gen. Urquhart (commanding 1st Airborne Division), accompanied by Brig. Lathbury (commanding 1st Parachute Brigade), came forward but were forced to shelter at Alexanderstraat 135. Although pinned down by the ever more vicious fighting, Gen. Urquhart decided that it was vital that he and Lathbury get back to their headquarters, so a breakout was attempted. It achieved little; Brig. Lathbury was wounded and had to remain in the house, while Urquhart and two companions made only the few metres to Zwarteweg 14 where they remained trapped until able to slip away the following day.

The road (now Utrechtseweg) descends to the hairpin junction with Onderlangs. Lt Col John Frost and his batallion managed to slip down this latter road, before the Germans reacted and closed it.

**Oosterbeek** (12,000 inhab.; VVV, Utrechtseweg 216) is today a pleasantly wooded and scattered residential community. But, though the memories may be fading, the memorials, the historical markers, the museum and, above all, the war cemetery provide constant reminders of September 1944. The story is told at the *Airborne Museum* (Mon–Sat, 11.00 to 17.00; Sun, Holidays, 12.00 to 17.00). Opened first in 1947 at Doorwerth, the museum moved in 1978 to this former Hotel Hartenstein where it was opened by Gen. Urquhart whose 'Market Garden' headquarters this had been, at the hub of the ever-shrinking perimeter into which 1st Airborne Division withdrew after failing to break past the area of St Elisabeth Gasthuis and into Arnhem to relieve Lt Col Frost at the Rhine bridge. The house, dating from 1785, was first a private residence, later becoming a hotel and continuing as such until taken over by the museum. Maps, models, commentaries (English and Dutch), contemporary photographs, excellent dioramas, equipment and much else combine here to illustrate the strategy and tactics of 'Market Garden' as also the personal experiences and

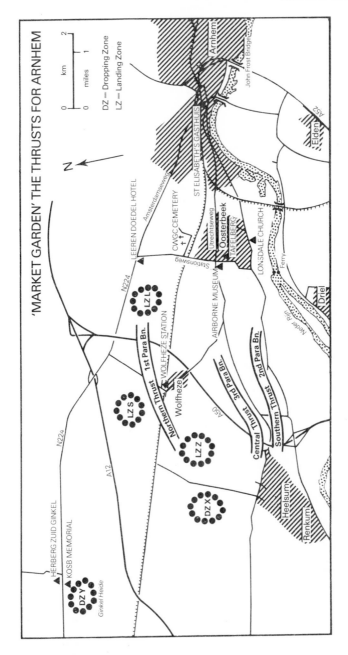

'MARKET GARDEN' THE THRUSTS FOR ARNHEM

DZ = Dropping Zone
LZ = Landing Zone

gallantry of those who fought, whether British, Dutch, Polish, American or German. Opposite the museum stands the *Airborne Monument*. Designed by Jacob Marys, its base was laid as early as September 1945 by Gen. Urquhart and the monument was unveiled by Queen Wilhelmina a year later.

The other focal point in Oosterbeek is the main road crossroads immediately E of the museum. VVV is on the SW corner, opposite (100m down the road to Arnhem at Utrechtseweg 192) being a historical marker, the wording on which, though brief, vividly tells the gallant story of 10th Parachute Battalion. Opposite (NW corner of the crossroads), a low, black geometric design on the lawn of a house is the memorial to 21st Independent Parachute Company.

Pietersbergweg, dropping S from the crossroads, was the axis of the desperate withdrawal during the night hours of 25 September. After passing the *Huize Tafelberg*—the German Field Marshal Model's headquarters, soon in use by the British as a hospital—the road winds down to a T junction at river level, the right arm leading to the recreation area of *Westerbouwing* and the Heveadorp-Driel ferry, the left soon reaching the *Oud Oosterbeek Church* (or, in 'Market Garden' terms, Lonsdale Church, named after the local commander). Founded in the 10C, and a thousand years later the site of a last stand to cover the withdrawal across the river, the church was badly damaged during the fighting and lost its tower. During rebuilding the early Romanesque triple apse was revealed, this now being outlined. Inside are a communion table and silver cup presented by British and Polish units who fought here, and also a carved pulpit presented in 1952 by the people of Boston in Lincolnshire. A short way beyond the church a track branches away on to the polder, and along here are good views of a vital part of the evacuation zone and also eastward along the line followed by Lt Col Frost and his 2nd Parachute Battalion.

From the Oosterbeek crossroads Stationsweg heads N to pass *Oosterbeek Military Cemetery*, where the majority of the British 'Market Garden' casualties lie, and then reach, on the left where the road enters a wood, a historical marker recording that this is where 156th Parachute Battalion (part of the northern of the three thrusts) was halted; unable to make further eastward progress, the survivors fought their way S to Oosterbeek.

Motorists wishing to see something of the Landing and Dropping Zones may continue N to meet (rather over 1km from the cemetery) N224 at the *Leeren Doedel Hotel*, a rebuilding after destruction by RAF attack. It was here that 1st Parachute Battalion, on the N of the northern thrust, was halted by German armour. N224, running W, almost immediately passes (S, by a sports centre) Landing Zone L, the place where the Polish gliders landed on 19 September, only to find themselves in the middle of a battle in which the King's Own Scottish Borderers and 10th Parachute Battalion were desperately engaged. Continuing W, N224 crosses below and above motorways A50 and A12 and in 9km (from Leeren Doedel) reaches the restaurant *Herberg Zuid Ginkel*, with, opposite, a sandy but usually firm enough small road in which to park and visit the *King's Own Scottish Borderers Memorial* bearing a symbolic Dove of Peace. The memorial was erected by the community of Ede and unveiled by Gen. Urquhart in 1960. A nearby boulder bears the words 'Luchlanding 17–18 September 1944', a reminder that this large flat expanse of heathland was Dropping Zone Y, or Ginkel Heide.

You now retrace the N224, and, as soon as you have crossed the A12, make a right turn to flank Landing Zone S (W) and reach *Wolfheze Station*.

Here you can follow the small road westward, running parallel to and alongside the railway which became the axis of the advance by 1st Parachute Battalion. After 2km you should make a turn S, the road cutting between Landing Zone Z (E) and Dropping Zone X (W). Both of these were 17 September objectives, among the first on Landing Zone Z being the gliders of the Reconnaissance Squadron of 1st Parachute Brigade, guided in by flares and some radar set up by 21st Independent Parachute Company (memorial at Oosterbeek crossroads) which shortly before had dropped on Dropping Zone X. On 18 September Landing Zone Z was used by 4th Parachute Brigade.

Beyond, in Renkum, make a left turn for adjacent **Heelsum**. At the town's end, on the right, just before a major intersection with the A50, is the *Heelsum Memorial*, a Pegasus and descending parachutist erected by the local community in 1945 and made of parachute containers, shell cases and a gun.

The eastward road now crosses below the A50, after which you should follow the signs to Oosterbeek. In the woods, a little over half-way between Heelsum and Oosterbeek, a road branches N for Wolfheze; it was at this road junction that the German Gen. Kussin, commandant of Arnhem, who had been conferring with the SS commander at the Hotel Wolfheze, met a platoon of 3rd Parachute Battalion and was killed.

## South of the Rhine

The interest here is almost entirely related to 'Market Garden' and in particular to Maj. Gen. Sosabowski's 1st Polish Parachute Brigade which landed near Driel on 21 September. The assumption was that the Driel-Heveadorp ferry was in British hands, but the Poles all too soon learnt that this was not the case and that, indeed, it was the Germans who manned the northern bank of the river. All attempts, on both sides of the river, to take the ferry failed and, although some Poles and others (elements of 30th Corps from Nijmegen) fought their way across the river, the main Polish force had to dig in around Driel.

Along the dike road (travelling W from Elden) a cycle track signed Oosterbeek indicates the ferry, this also being the heart of the area through which the survivors of 1st Airborne Division, having crossed from near Oud Oosterbeek (or Lonsdale) church in darkness and heavy rain, withdrew towards Nijmegen.

In **Driel**, just beyond, there are two prominent churches, the Polish one (of St Stanislaus), with a clock tower and golden weathervane, being the more easterly of the two. In the entrance porch a memorial honours the fallen Poles and here, too, there is a memorial to a Dutch soldier killed four years earlier. The main Polish memorial is opposite. The gift of the people of Driel (1959), this is made up of a round plinth sheltering an urn of Polish soil and bearing the call 'Surge Polonia'; an angled stone symbolising strength and courage; and a figure representing Youth bearing the jewel of Freedom.

**Heteren**, 3km W, is of American interest. After 'Market Garden', heavy fighting continued, virtually until the end of the war, in the area between Waal and Rhine. In October 1944 American 101st Airborne Division moved in to relieve the British, their memorial being beside the dike road just below and E of the motorway crossing.

# C. De Hoge Veluwe National Park

**DE HOGE VELUWE NATIONAL PARK** lies some 6km N of Arnhem. There are entrances near Schaarsbergen (Rijzenburg), the nearest to Arnhem, at Otterlo (NW), and at Hoenderloo (NE). The park is crossed by over 30km of roads for cars and motor cycles, and also by footpaths, and cycle and horse tracks. The park is open daily, 08.00 to sunset, but see below for the Kröller-Müller Museum, the Sculpture Garden and the Visitor Centre. Entry is expensive but covers all places within the park.

**Bus Service.** In summer (late June–end Aug) there is a special bus service from Arnhem station, crossing the park and making various stops, including the Kröller-Müller Museum and the Visitor Centre; the excursion can be broken at these stops, the same ticket remaining valid for the return to Arnhem.

The park, formerly the private estate of Willem Kröller and his wife Hélène (born Müller), comprises some 5500 ha., of which about half is heath with some patches of drift sand, and half woodland, the latter with roughly equal areas of cultivated trees and of Scotch pine natural seedlings. It is of interest that up to a century ago, when control measures were introduced, drift sand covered about three-quarters of the park. The larger fauna include roe deer, mainly in the S part but also in the N; red deer and moufflons (long-haired sheep from Corsica and Sardinia) across the centre (observation lookout near Hoenderloo entrance); and wild boar, which can be dangerous, in the N woodland. Among the smaller fauna are fox, badger, and polecat. Within the park are the Rijksmuseum Kröller-Müller and a Visitor Centre, entrance to both being included within the park fee.

From the Rijzenburg gate, Kemperbergweg leads N, the first 3km being through woodland, the home of roe deer. After another 1km Reemsterweg (dead end) bears SW across wood and heath, the latter (*Oud Reemster*) being particularly colourful in August and September. Continuing N, Kemperbergweg becomes Wildbaanweg, crossing heath with to the E an area of drift sand (*Deelense Zand*). Woodland is entered again below the hill (E) of *Franse Berg*, best ascended from the N. The foundations at the foot of the hill recall an early attempt by the Krüller-Müllers to build a museum (it was thwarted by the Depression), and here too stands Henry Moore's group 'Three Upright Motifs', placed here in 1965.

The **\*Rijksmuseum Kröller-Müller** (Tues–Sat, 10.00 to 17.00; Sun, Holidays, 11.00 to 17.00, or 13.00 to 17.00 in Nov–March; closed 1 January) is essentially a gallery for connoisseurs of late 19C and 20C art (pictures, sculpture and assemblies), the basis of the museum being the collections of Hélène Kröller-Müller. Presented to the nation in 1934 the collections have been housed since 1938 in this building by Henry van de Velde. The building was extended by W.G. Quist in 1977, and at the rear of the museum lies the large Sculpture Park.

The heart of the Kröller-Müller gift is the famous \*\*Van Gogh Collection (276 works). The museum owns more works of art than it can show at one time, and exhibits are therefore periodically changed around.

The museum is in the form of a letter T, the entrance (the approach to which is flanked by sculpture) being at the lower side of the left arm, which is an administrative wing. The bookstall is at the crossing, and the right arm houses the café, as also sculptures, drawings, etc., mostly dating from after 1950, and temporary exhibitions. The stem of the T, with the Kröller-

Müller collections, is arranged roughly in four sections: Modern, Van Gogh and others, Old Masters and Oriental.

The MODERN section includes rooms devoted to works by J. Lipchitz, B. van der Leck and Charley Toorop (some sensitive self-portraits). In and off the continuing passage are pictures and sculptures by Picasso, Léger (notably perhaps his Soldiers playing cards), Braque, Henry Moore, Barbara Hepworth, Ossip Zadkine (an unobtrusive but effective small Seated Woman) and Piet Mondriaan whose Composition 1917 is in startling contrast to his conventional Beach near Domburg of 1909.

The VAN GOGH COLLECTION includes (to name only a very few works) Head of a peasant with a pipe; *The Potato eaters (much stolen; another version is at the Rijksmuseum Van Gogh, Amsterdam); Head of a woman with a white cap; Sunflowers; *Self-portrait (1887); Peasant seated at a table; View of Saintes- Maries; The Sower; La petite Arlésienne. Among the many other artists represented in this part of the museum are Seurat (a variety of contrasting works); Van Rijsselberghe (notably Family gathering in an orchard); P. Gabriel (Train in a landscape); Fantin-Latour (a severe portrait of Eva Catargi); and Matthijs Maris (Self-portrait).

The small collection of OLD MASTERS includes, by Lucas Cranach the Elder, the eccentric Venus and Amor contrasting with an almost photographic portrayal of the Elector of Saxony; Stag hunt by Lucas Cranach the Younger; Pietà by G. David; *Self-portrait (1564) by S. Pulzone; Tower of Babel by H. van Cleve.

At the end of the museum there are four ORIENTAL rooms showing Chinese ceramics, including Tang horses.

The **Sculpture Park** (April–Oct: Tues–Sat, 10.00 to 16.30; Sun, Holidays, 11.00 to 16.30), at the rear of the museum, a pleasant area of lawns and glades, is the largest in Europe (11 ha.). Among the extensive and varied collection may be mentioned several works by Barbara Hepworth (in an open pavilion); Female figure (1882) by Rodin; Hagar (1971) and The Pair (1929) by Lipchitz; Angel torso (1923) by Epstein; Striding man (1960) by Giacometti; Five balls (1965) by Fontana.

Opposite the museum entrance a bench and enclosure commemorate Martinus Steyn (1857–1916), the last president of the Orange Free State (the Kröller-Müllers were supporters of the Boer cause).

You soon reach a T-junction, the E–W road being Houtkampweg linking the Hoenderloo and Otterlo gates.

At **Otterlo**, 3km W, there is a *Museum of Tiles (it noflik sté)* covering from 1300 to modern times (Tues–Sat, 10.00 to 12.00, 14.00 to 17.00; Sun, 14.00 to 16.00).

Houtkampweg followed E in 1km reaches the *Bezoekers Centrum* (Visitor Centre: April–Oct: daily, 10.00 to 17.00; other months: Sun, 11.00 to 16.00), with material and displays and an Observation Ground explaining all aspects of the park. Here too is a restaurant (*De Koperen Kop*), and a track runs S across Franse Berg. From the Bezoekers Centrum you can make a one-way circuit of the NE corner of the park. Follow Kronkelweg N across the Pheasant Park to reach in 3km a lake and the hunting-lodge of *St Hubertus*; built for the Kröller-Müllers in 1914–20 by H.P. Berlage, the lodge is now used as a meeting place for government ministers (May–October: daily, 10.00 to 12.00, 14.00 to 17.00).

The road W from here (De Wetweg) in 3km reaches the Otterlo gate, at about half-way passing close to (N) a statue (by Mendes da Costa) of the Boer general Christiaan de Wet, another reminder of the Kröller-Müllers' Boer sympathies. Just beyond St Hubertus, Hertjesweg bears SE soon reaching a T-junction where drivers may either turn left for the Hoenderloo gate or right to rejoin Houtkampweg at a car park close to the *Wildkansel*. This is an observation stand in an area where most of the stags herd together, although during the rut (early Sept–mid Oct) they go to the hinds in the S.

# 27 Eastern Gelderland (The Achterhoek)

This Route describes that part of Gelderland which is bounded on the W by the river IJssel, on the N by the province of Overijssel, and on the E and S by the German border. Known as the ACHTERHOEK (Back Corner), this quiet district, offering pleasant rural touring and some interesting small towns, is particularly popular with walkers and cyclists for whom there are networks of tracks (for bicycle hire apply local VVVs). The principal town in the E is Winterswijk, to which two approaches, both starting from Arnhem, are described. The northerly approach is via Zutphen, the southerly via Zevenaar and Terborg.

## A. Arnhem to Winterswijk via Zutphen

Total distance 64km.—12km *Dieren*—12km **Zutphen**—8km *Vorden*—10km *Ruurlo*—12km **Groenlo**—10km **Winterswijk**.

For Arnhem, see Rte 26. As far as Zutphen the road keeps to the W of the IJssel. In *12km* you will reach *Dieren* (16,000 inhab.), where the Apeldoorn canal joins the IJssel; the lock here is notable because of the considerable difference in water levels. In summer a steam train runs between Dieren and Apeldoorn.

The ancient small town of **Doesburg** (10,000 inhab.; VVV, Kerkstraat 6), with several old buildings, is on the E bank of the IJssel 5km SE of Dieren. Although there is no evidence to support a local tradition that the town was founded by the Roman general Drusus (38–9 BC), builder of a military canal linking the Rhine and the IJssel, it is known that there was a settlement here by the year 1000 and that a form of charter was granted in 1237. Between 1701 and 1730 defences designed by Menno van Coehoorn were built, and parts of these survive. The *Martinikerk* (part 15C) claims the curious distinction of being the first in the Netherlands to have been provided with a lightning conductor. The Raadhuis and the Waag are both close to the church, the *Waag* (15C) at the crossroads now being a restaurant. The *Raadhuis*, in origin 14C, was rebuilt in 1665 when the wine-house (left) and the alderman-house (right) were joined. Opposite the Raadhuis is the *Museum Stad en Ambt Doesborgh* of local history. A mustard factory can be visited at Bockholtstraat 2, and boat excursions can be made to Arnhem, Zutphen, and Doetinchem. *Laag-Keppel*, 6km SE of Doesburg, was the home of the Keppel family (see also below under Zutphen-Voorst); the castle is mostly a rebuilding of 1582.

*12km* **ZUTPHEN** (32,000 inhab.; VVV, Wijnhuis, Groenmarkt) is an attractive and interesting old town, which, known in the Middle Ages as *Zutphania Turrita*, still preserves notable remains of its fortifications. The inner, or old town, is enclosed within the IJssel (W), the small river Berkel (W and N), and boulevards and parts of moats on the S and E.

**History.** The line of the independent counts of Zutphen died out when, as the result of his father's marriage to Irmingardis, the heiress to the county, the title passed in 1131 to Count Henry I of Gelder. In the Spanish wars of the 16C Zutphen was taken in 1572 by Frederick of Toledo, and the subsequent massacre of the citizens and sack of the town were factors in strengthening the later resistance of Leiden and Alkmaar. On 22 September 1586, at the battle of Warnsveld a little E of Zutphen, Sir Philip Sidney received his fatal wound (see below). The town was again taken by the Spanish in 1587, but was recovered in 1591. In 1672–74, and again in 1795, it was occupied by the French. Considerable damage was caused during the Second World War.

In the GROENMARKT there are several old houses, one being the **Wijnhuis** (VVV), in origin an inn of the 14C and since 1420 belonging to the town. The present building (1618–27), restored after a fire in 1920 and rebuilt after war damage, contains a carillon by the Hemony brothers. From the Groenmarkt, Lange Hofstraat followed S in about 200m reaches the adjoining Burgerzaal and Stadhuis. The attractive *Burgerzaal* (for entry apply Stadhuis), with a magnificent vaulted interior, dates from 1450 and was restored in 1896 by Cuijpers. Now used for municipal functions, the hall was in turn the place where meat was cooked under official supervision and the sheriff's court. The white-painted *Stadhuis* is in origin 14C but was rebuilt in 1729 and 1956.

Lange Hofstraat ends at the open space called 'S GRAVENHOF, where the course of the foundations of the original castle of the counts (first built in c 1100) is marked out. The **Grote Kerk** (or *Walburgiskerk*), on the E side of 's Gravenhof, dates from the 12C or 13C but was almost completely rebuilt in the latter half of the 15C; the upper stages (1633–37) of the tower were destroyed by fire in 1948. On the north side there is an unusually elaborate portal. The spacious interior is remarkable for its wall-and ceiling-paintings of the 15C and 16C. In the south aisle there are some huge graveslabs and a bronze font (1527) by Gillis van Eynde of Mechelen, resting on couchant lions and bearing figures of the Evangelists; the cover, ornamented with statuettes, is surmounted by a pelican. Just east of the crossing hangs a 15C wrought-iron chandelier with an intriguing frieze of figures. The organ case dates from 1637–43. The former chapter house (1561–64), with curious sculptured and painted capitals, now contains the original *Chained Library, the oldest in Western Europe, with valuable manuscripts and incunabula still fastened to the old reading desks (VVV for opening times).

Between the church and the river stands the *Bourgonjetoren* (1457), with an adjoining section of wall. Here in the mid 14C is said to have stood the world's largest cannon.

About 150m to the E of the church is the **Drogenapstoren** (named after the town trumpeter who lived here in 1555), a fine brick rampart tower of 1444, built as the salt gate giving access to the salt market. From the gate, Zaadmarkt, the former seed market, runs N, at its foot (S) being the public library in a building of 1549, while a short way up on the E side is the *Bornhof*, with a doorway of 1723 bearing lifelike figures. Further up the street No. 88 (W) is the house *De Wildeman* (Tues–Fri, 10.00 to 17.00; Sat,

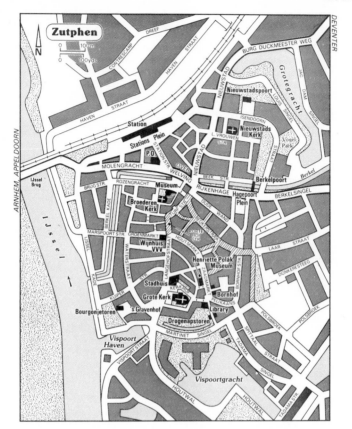

10.00 to 12.30; Sun 14.00 to 17.00), with a hidden Roman Catholic chapel probably dating from 1628. The house now contains the *Museum Henriette Polak*, with the art collection of Henriette A. Polak-Schwarz (1893–1974), known also for her encouragement of young musicians; there are also changing exhibitions of modern art. Prolonging the Zaadmarkt, the Houtmarkt has more old houses: No. 73 has a high 15C gable, No. 75 (1666) stands on the site of the early prison and No. 68 has a gable of 1615.

Houtmarkt leads back to the Groenmarkt. From here Korte Hofstraat is continued NE by Turfstraat which reaches Rijkenhage, a short way along which (E) stands the small ruin of the *Berkelpoort* (14C) and a good section of the old wall. The *Broederenkerk*, just NW of Turfstraat, was begun for the Dominicans in 1293; its cloisters and refectory (N side) now house the municipal *Museum* (Tues–Fri, 10.00 to 17.00; Sat, 10.00 to 12.30; Sun, 14.00 to 17.00). To the N of the Berkel is the Roman Catholic *Nieuwstadskerk* (13–14C), and to the N of this the ruined *Nieuwstadspoort* through which Frederick of Toledo stormed the town in 1572. In Coehoornsingel, to the E beyond the moat (Grote Gracht), there is a statue to Sir Philip Sidney.

**Warnsveld**, a suburb 2km E of Zutphen, is the site of the battle of

22 September 1586 in which Sir Philip Sidney lost his life. Poet, courtier, and militant Protestant, he was fighting for the Dutch against the Spaniards. He was hit in the thigh by a bullet, a wound which proved fatal because in a quixotic gesture he had refused to wear leg-armour because a companion had none. Lying wounded he waved away a cup of water, offering it to a dying soldier and saying 'Thy need is greater than mine'.

*Voorst*, 5km NW on the Apeldoorn road, was the home of Arnold Joost van Keppel (1669–1718) who accompanied William III to England in 1688 and was created Earl of Albemarle in 1697. On William's death he returned to the Netherlands, becoming a general and fighting with Marlborough at Ramillies and Oudenarde.

*Lochem*, 14km E on the Hengelo (Overijssel) road, has a town hall of 1634 and a public library of 1638.

This Route now heads SE, leaving Zutphen by (*2km*) *Warnsveld* (see above) and between here and (*16km*) *Ruurlo* running through a district of châteaux or country mansions of which there are some ten within 4km of either side of the road. *Borculo*, 5km NE of Ruurlo, is known for the damage it suffered in a freak storm of 1925 which blew down the church tower; a small museum (Stormrampmuseum) contains photographs and other material. The lords of Borculo were between 1232 and 1395 the representatives of the bishops of Utrecht in the governing of what is now the province of Drenthe, as such holding the title of burgrave. In *12km* **Groenlo** (7000 inhab.), an old fortified town, was taken from the Spanish in 1597 by Maurice of Nassau, fell to Spinola in 1606, and was taken by Louis XIV in 1627. A Spanish cannon, captured in 1627, stands on the ramparts. The *Grolsmuseum* (Noteboomstraat 15–17; Mon–Fri, 14.00 to 17.00), with local historical and folklore material, occupies a 17C farmhouse, while the *Museum Erve Kots* (daily, 09.00 to 18.00 or dusk; closed Mon in autumn to Easter), a short distance S near Lievelde, is an open air museum illustrating former Achterhoek peasant and farming life. *10km* **Winterswijk** (28,000 inhab.; VVV, Markt 48) lies within 6km of Germany to the N, the E, and the south. At the centre of a quiet countryside of small rivers, meadows, and woods provided with a network of cycle and foot tracks, the town is a popular centre for walkers and cyclists.

# B.   Arnhem to Winterswijk via Zevenaar and Terborg

Total distance 60km.—11km **Zevenaar**—12km *Zeddam*—3km **'s Heerenberg**—3km *Zeddam*—7km **Terborg**—14km *Aalten*—10km **Winterswijk**.

For Arnhem, see Rte 26. *7km Duiven* preserves a 12C church tower. *4km* **Zevenaar** (26,000 inhab.) is an old border town which has many times changed hands. First mentioned in 1049, Zevenaar in the 15C belonged to the counts of Cleves; in 1666 it passed to Prussia, in 1808 to Bonapartist Netherlands, in 1813 back to Prussia and, finally, in 1816 back to the new Kingdom of the Netherlands. The *Pieter Stuyvesant Stichting* (Tel: 08360-24550) shows works by modern artists such as Appel, Corneille, Dubuffet and Giacometti. *Pannerden*, 4km S, is near the present junction of the Rhine and the Waal; further upstream across the Rhine *Schenkenschans*, once a fortress commanding the earlier junction, is where the army of Louis XIV crossed in 1672, one of his principal commanders, Condé, being wounded here. Beyond Zevenaar the main road crosses into Germany, but this Route takes a smaller road skirting the border. After *12km Zeddam* is a pleasant village lying on the E side of wooded hills; here a restored horse-mill (Rosmolen) may be visited, while in the woods to the S rises the hill of *Montferland* on which there is a restaurant occupying in part a late 18C pavilion and standing on a medieval or earlier fortifications mound. In *3km* you reach the old frontier town of **'s Heerenberg** (7000 inhab.) which was the medieval fortress of the counts of Bergh who were staunch Catholics. Count William (1538–86), brother-in-law of William the Silent, at first supported the States General but in 1581 went over to the Spanish side. In 1712 the town was inherited by the princes of Hohenzollern-Sigmaringen. The castle, the church, and the town hall are all close to one another, parts of an estate acquired in 1912 by J.H. van Heek who carefully restored the complex and then presented it to the state. The *castle* (*Huis Bergh*; tour times from VVV) occupies a circular moated enclosure. First built in c 1200, it now has a square keep of c 1400 and domestic buildings restored after fires in 1735 and 1939. The interior contains pictures and antiques, mostly of the 15–17C. The *Reformed church* was originally the castle chapel of 1259 but is now mainly of the 14–15C (restored 1926); nearby are remains of ramparts. The attractive *Stadhuis* was built in c 1500.

*3km Zeddam*, see above. At *7km* **Terborg** (5000 inhab.) the 16–17C château of *Wisch* on the S of the town was rebuilt after war damage of 1945. **Doetinchem** (7km NE 40,000 inhab.; VVV, Walmolen, IJsselkade), chartered in 1237, is the principal town of the Achterhoek. At (*14km* from Terborg) *Aalten* the 15C church has a Romanesque 13C tower, and at *Bredevoort*, 2km further E, there are remains of a moat and rampart. In *10km* you reach Winterswijk, see Rte 27A.

# 28 Arnhem to Apeldoorn and Zwolle

Total distance 58km.—12km *Woestehoeve*—11km **Apeldoorn**—14km *Epe*—15km **Hattem**—6km **Zwolle**.

For Arnhem, see Rte 26. The road N crosses the A12 motorway and enters wooded country which continues until Apeldoorn. After *7km* you pass the *Nationaal Zweefvliegcentrum* (National Gliding Centre), an area extending 5km to the W to the edge of the Hoge Veluwe National Park (see Rte 26C). In *5km Woestehoeve*, where a memorial on the E of the road shortly before the restaurant honours 117 Dutchmen shot by the Germans in 1945 as a reprisal. Roads leading W in 6km reach the Hoenderloo entrance to the national park. After *6km*, *Beekbergen* lies within the municipality of Apeldoorn, with in the 13C church the tomb of Marten Orges, founder in the 17C of the local paper industry.

*5km* **APELDOORN** (144,000 inhab.; VVV, Stationsplein, 800m SE of the central Markt) is a mixture of a modern town and sprawling municipality embracing several surrounding villages. With its parks and gardens, with excellent and convenient shopping, and situated on the edge of the Veluwe, the town is popular as a relaxed holiday centre.

**History**. Although the name Apeldoorn first appears in a document of 793, it was only with the building of the palace of Het Loo in 1685–92 that the place became known. The palace and its grounds attracted many visitors, setting a pattern which continues today. By the end of the 17C Apeldoorn had become a centre of the paper industry, but by the start of the 20C many mills, profiting from the soft local water, had converted to laundries.

The heart of the town is the large MARKT (with convenient underground parking) from which a network of lively pedestrian streets providing everything from excellent shops and cafés to bistros and discos extends SW. The *Oranjepark*, the most central and oldest of the town's parks, is 300 metres NW of the Markt, and Apeldoorn also offers two museums: the *Historisch Museum Marialust* (Tues–Sat, 10.00 to 17.00; Sunday, 13.00 to 17.00), at Verzetstrijderspark 10, caters for local history, while the *Gemeentlijk Van Reekum Museum* (Tues–Sat, 10.00 to 17.00; Sun, 13.00 to 17.00), at Churchillplein 2, shows fine and applied art, both of the past and the present. Among attractions around the town, and all likely to appeal to children, are *Berg en Bos*, an area of natural woodland with gardens which includes the *Apenheul* where monkeys run free and gorillas can be seen on a wooded island (April–June: daily, 09.30 to 17.00; July, Aug: daily, 09.30 to 18.00; Sept–Oct: daily, 10.00 to 17.00; March: Sat, Sun, 10.00 to 16.00); *Malkenschoten*, with a children's farm and zoo, playground, pedalos and other attractions; the *Koningin Julianatoren*, a recreation centre with a fairground; and the *Veluwsche Stoomtrein*, a steam train which in summer links Apeldoorn, Beekbergen, Loenen and Dieren, all to the SE.

But Apeldoorn's outstanding attraction is the **Paleis Het Loo**, on the edge of the town 2km NW of the Markt (*Palace*: Tues–Sun, 10.00 to 17.00. *Stables and Gardens*: April–October: Tues–Sun, 10.00 to 17.00. *Park*: daily, 09.00 to c 18.00).

Built by Prince William III in 1685–92 as a hunting lodge, the palace was a House of Orange residence until 1975, most associated perhaps with Queen Wilhelmina whose home this was from her abdication in 1948 until her death in 1962. She was followed by Princess Margriet, sister of Queen Beatrix, who lived here until 1975. There followed seven years of restoration, aimed at returning the palace exterior and the gardens to something like their 17C appearance, while the interior was partly returned to the 17C and partly left as found so as to record three centuries of House of Orange architectural and decorative taste.

A Rijksmuseum (national museum) since 1984, the palace is not only a record of the House of Orange-Nassau but also houses art collections, both fine and decorative, which in great part belong to the Royal Collection. In the Royal Stables (1906–10) are shown carriages, coaches, sledges, cars of the 1920s and even an anti-gas perambulator, all, except the last, used at one time or another by the royal family or household.

The Gardens divide into four—Lower, Upper, King's and Queen's—while the fine park offers a choice of walks. The adjoining Royal Forest (10,800 ha.) is the country's largest nature reserve (for Game Tours apply VVV, Apeldoorn). *Het Aardhuis*, off the Amersfoort road some 6km W of Het Loo and at the highest point of the Veluwe (107m), was built in 1861 as a hunting chalet for King William III but is now a wildlife and nature information centre (April, May, June, Sept, Oct: daily except Mon, 10.00 to 17.00; July, Aug: daily, 10.00 to 17.00).

The road N out of Apeldoorn passes close to Het Loo. In *14km Epe* has a 14C church, and is a popular small centre for those wishing to enjoy the northern Veluwe. *15km* on, **Hattem** (11,000 inhab.) is a small place with some narrow streets and several attractive buildings, mostly of the 17C.

The turreted *Dijkpoort*, in origin 14C, was restored in 1909, and the *Museum Oud-Hattem*, at Achterstraat 48, is in a restored (?16C) gabled house. The road then crosses the IJssel, with the A28 motorway just to the N, by a bridge which incorporates one of the main girders of London's temporary Waterloo Bridge of 1925–45. *6km* brings you to Zwolle (see Rte 30A) which is in the province of Overijssel.

# 29   North-West Gelderland. Flevoland

This route is in two parts, the first running direct from Amersfoort to Zwolle, the second touring Flevoland.

## A.   Amersfoort to Zwolle

Total distance 67km.—11km *Nijkerk*—18km **Harderwijk**—10km **Nunspeet**—8km **Elburg**—20km **Zwolle**.

For much of the way this road skirts the NW edge of the woodland and dunes of the northern Veluwe, many of the small towns and villages being popular holiday places, especially for walkers and cyclists. Visitor Centre at Nunspeet.

For Amersfoort (in the province of Utrecht), see Rte 16A. You can follow the A28 motorway out of Amersfoort, which soon crosses the Al motorway and 2km beyond enters the province of Gelderland. Leave the motorway at the next exit for (*11km* from Amersfoort) *Nijkerk* (24,000 inhab.), a town founded in 1222. This was the home of Wouter van Twiller (before 1580–1646) who in 1633 was appointed as the second Director General of New Amsterdam (later New York; he ruined the colony's finances and was recalled in 1637), and also of Arend van Curler (1620–67), a successful negotiator with the Indians and founder of Schenectady, New York. In the Reformed church is the tomb of the Van Rensselaer family, but Kiliaen, founder of the colony of Rensselaerwijk (now Albany, Rensselaer, and Columbia counties, New York) is buried in the Oude Kerk in Amsterdam. *9km Putten*, with a 14C church, and *4km Ermelo* are holiday centres. Remains of prehistoric burial cairns may be found on the heathland near the latter.

*5km* **Harderwijk** (33,000 inhab.; VVV, Havendam 58) stands on the south shore of the Veluwe Meer opposite the point at which the Oostelijk and Zuidelijk Flevoland polders meet. A bridge crosses to the polders (see Rte 29B).

**History.** The town is known to have existed as a Hanseatic League port in 1221, and also later as an embarkation port for East Indies sailings. A university, the Gelderse Academie, flourished here between 1648 and 1811, among its distinguished students and teachers being *Herman Boerhaave* (1666–1738) the physician, and the Swedish botanist *Linnaeus* (1707–78); for both of these, see under Leiden, Rte 6. Harderwijk lost its maritime importance with the silting up of the Zuider Zee channels during the 18C, and its outlook on to open water with the creation of the Flevoland polders from 1957 onwards.

Beside Strandboulevard are the *Vispoort*, a relic of the medieval ramparts, and the *Dolphinarium, opened in 1965 and one of the world's largest indoor complexes of its kind, with dolphins, sealions and walrus, all in a variety of shows and settings (March–Oct: daily, 09.00 to 17.00).

The small port is at the N end of Strand Boulevard. At its S end the boulevard curves into Smeepoortstraat, on the left of which is the *Grote Kerk* which lost much of its nave when its tower fell in 1797. A short way beyond, opposite barracks, Donkerstraat (pedestrians only) leads left, with at No. 4 the *Veluws Museum* (May–Sept: Mon–Fri, 09.00 to 17.00; Sat, 13.00 to 16.00; Oct–April: Mon–Fri, 09.00 to 12.00, 14.00 to 17.00) in one of a number of good 18C houses in this part of the town. The museum illustrates the early story of the northern Veluwe and of Harderwijk, particular attention being paid to the prosperous fishing years when the town had a fleet of 171 boats. The first turning right off Donkerstraat leads to the market, and the second (Akademiestraat) to an old tower with a bust of Linnaeus, all that survives of the university. *Veluwe Strand* is a waterside recreation area with fairground, children's boating lake, restaurant etc. Boat excursions lasting about 50 minutes cruise the waters between Harderwijk and Flevoland.

From Harderwijk the road continues N of and roughly parallel to motorway A28, immediately to the S of which the extensive area of woods and dunes includes two nature reserves, the *Leuvenumsche Bosch* and, approaching Nunspeet, the *Hulshorste Zand*, both with walking and bicycle tracks. In *10km* **Nunspeet** (23,000 inhab.; VVV, Stationsplein) is a holiday centre profiting from the countryside to the S and the beaches on the Veluwe Meer. A main attraction (S of the motorway) is the *Zandenbos* visitor centre run by the State Forestry Authority; an exhibition illustrates the flora and fauna of the Veluwe and information is available on all recreational facilities. In the town the *Veluwe Diorama* at Marktstraat 17–19 shows stuffed animals native to the Veluwe.

*8km* **Elburg** (20,000 inhab.; VVV, Jufferenstraat 9), a particularly attractive and compact little walled town, has a rectangular pattern of streets, unusual in the Netherlands, enclosed within virtually complete ramparts.

**History.** The town's name derives from the days when the early marsh dwellers here were forced by flooding to form a settlement on a ridge (elle) on which later, in c 1200, they built a fortification (burcht). Not long afterwards, in 1233, the township received a charter, developing into a port prosperous in both general trade and fishing and joining the Hanseatic League. However, its position was still insecure, and in 1392 the governor, Arent thoe Boecop, moved the people to a safer site a little further inland, laid out the rectangular street pattern and raised defensive walls behind a moat. Over the centuries Elburg has had four town halls.

From the S you enter the walled town by the *Goorpoort* from which Beekstraat runs across the town dividing it into two. In mid-town Beekstraat is crossed by Vispoortstraat (W) and Jufferenstraat (E). If you follow the former, the narrow Royemarijnsteeg soon bears left, along this, by the corner of Krommesteeg (Crooked Alley, the only curving street in the town), is the site of the earliest town hall of c 1200. Vispoortstraat crosses Ellestraat, roughly the site of the first settlement, and reaches the *Vispoort* (1394) in which there is a fishing exhibition, an annexe of the municipal museum (May–Sept: Mon–Fri, 09.30 to 12.00, 14.00 to 17.00).

Near the N end of Beekstraat, Van Kinsbergenstraat branches E, with at No. 5 VVV occupying the *Arent thoe Boekop Huis*, the second town hall; the façade has been restored and the side and rear gables are as in 1396.

Opposite is the 18C *Van Kinsbergen Institute*, formerly a school. Nearby, the *Reformed church*, in part early 15C, contains murals. At Jufferenstraat 6, to the S, is the site of the third town hall (1954), occupying the 15C former St Agnes Abbey; the building now houses the *Gemeente Museum* (Mon– Fri, 09.00 to 12.00, 14.00 to 17.00), the municipal museum in which material on the history of Elburg is exhibited in a Gothic chapel. The street name Ledigestede (Empty Way) just W of the museum recalls that when Boekop built his new town the citizens were slow to move in. The fourth and present town hall is in the modern district of *Oostendorp*, to the E outside the walls.

*12km Wesep* is a part of the municipality of *Hattem*, 4km NE (see Rte 28). For *8km* (by motorway) Zwolle, in the province of Overijssel, see Rte 30A.

# B.  Flevoland

The province of Flevoland, created in 1986 and with its capital at Lelystad, comprises the polders of Oostelijk and Zuidelijk Flevoland, together with, to the N, the Noord-Oost Polder, formerly a part of the province of Overijssel.

For background information on the Zuider Zee and its conversion into today's IJsselmeer with its polders, and also on the development and use of polders generally, see Introduction. For more specific and local information there is the Informatiecentrum Nieuw Land (see under Lelystad below).

Oostelijk and Zuidelijk Flevoland are crossed by motorway A6, linking Amsterdam through Leystad to the Noord-Oost Polder and beyond. There is also a good network of other roads.

**Lelystad** (55,000 inhab.; VVV, Agorahof 2) is named after Dr C. Lely (died 1929), the engineer whose work led to the Zuider Zee Reclamation Act of 1918. In 1966 there was nothing here, by 1981 the population was some 40,000, and by the year 2000 it is planned to have risen to 100,000. Lelystad will not, however, be to everybody's taste, for sadly this new town, with its drab graffiti-daubed central Agora, falls well short of the admirable and imaginative standards achieved elsewhere by Dutch town and architectural planning. The residential surrounds are better, but still send a message of mass construction rather than of character and taste. However, for visitors with an interest in goats there is the *Nationaal Geitencentrum*, with some 500 goats the largest goat business in the Netherlands (in the Gelderse Hout on the E edge of the town).

The *Informatiecentrum Nieuw Land* (April–Oct: daily, 10.00 to 17.00; Nov–March: Mon–Fri, 10.00 to 17.00; Sun, 13.00 to 17.00) is on the W edge of Lelystad close to the start of the dike road across to Enkhuizen (for which see Rte 3). Here advanced exhibition techniques are used to explain the transformation of the Zuiderzee into the IJsselmeer with its polders. Lack of knowledge of Dutch should be no deterrent as there is an audio-visual presentation in English, all main notices are in English and there is also a choice of English books and leaflets.

OOSTELIJK FLEVOLAND. Oostelijk Flevoland, a polder measuring some 25km by 20km, was drained by 1957 and is now well developed, mainly as arable farmland but also for dairy, fruit and mixed farming, while recreational facilities—boating, walking, cycling, nature reserves—abound. A clockwise circuit of some 62km is suggested, leaving Lelystad by the A6 motorway which you leave in *18km* as the motorway approaches the Ketelbrug which crosses to the Noord-Oost Polder. Follow a small road (Ketelmeerdijk) beside the Ketelmeer to (*6km*) **Ketelhaven** with the *Museum voor Scheepsarcheologie* (April–Sept: daily, 10.00 to 17.00; Oct–March: Mon–Fri, 10.00 to 17.00; Sat, Sun, 11.00 to 17.00), a museum of marine construction and ships' inventories based on the astonishing number of wrecks found during reclamation. Old maps and pictures and a variety of artefacts are of interest here, but the star of the museum is a massive merchant ship of c 1650, with, alongside, a series of photographs recording the process of excavation.

At **Dronten** (*6km* S) a memorial by the Stadhuis commemorates the crews, Allied and German, of some 1100 aircraft which during the war crashed into the IJsselmeer; remains of aircraft are still found and there is a special team active in their salvage. From Dronten roads run E to Kampen (12km; see Rte 32A) and SE to Elburg (12km; see Rte 29A).

*8km* **Biddinghuizen** (6000 inhab.) traces its name back to 793, to a distant period, long before the flooding which gradually took shape as the Zuider Zee, when man managed to survive in the peaty marshes here. *Flevohof* (April–Oct: daily, 10.00 to 18.00), 5km SE, is part agricultural and horticultural exhibition and part recreation park. Among the numerous attractions are tropical greenhouses, a miniature train, a children's farm, bowling and a covered and heated swimming pool.

In *9km* SW from Biddinghuizen there is a road junction close to where two canals meet. Futenweg continues SW into Zuidelijk Flevoland (soon passing the junction with N302 which in 5km reaches Hardewijk, see Rte 29A), while Larserweg, beside the canal of the same name, heads N for (*15km*) Lelystad.

ZUIDELIJK FLEVOLAND. Zuidelijk Flevoland, similar in size to Oostelijk Flevoland, was drained in 1968 and is thus less mature than its neighbour. An anticlockwise round of some 73km is suggested, leaving Lelystad by the Oostvaardersdijk which has the open IJsselmeer (Markerwaard) on one side and, on the other, the large watery nature reserve and bird sanctuary of the *Oostvaardersplassen* (no entry). Beyond the reserve the road reaches (*18km*) *De Blocq van Kuffeler*, the Netherlands' largest pumping engine. **Almere** (*5km*), begun in 1975 and with an annual population growth of about 7000, is aiming for a population of 250,000 spread around its scattered sections, the principal of which are Almere-Stad, Almere-Haven and Almere-Buiten. Almere-Stad and Almere-Haven are separated by the A6 motorway, which, 5km SW, crosses the Hollandse Brug and quickly reaches Amsterdam.

A choice of roads lead E to (*25km*) **Zeewolde**, a fast-growing community whose first residents arrived in 1984 and which is already a lively recreational centre with its emphasis on water sports of all kinds. By main road Lelystad is reached in 25km.

NOORD-OOST POLDER. See Rte 32A.

# PROVINCES OF OVERIJSSEL AND DRENTHE

**Province of Overijssel Capital.** Zwolle.

**History.** Little is known about Overijssel prior to the Middle Ages, though among the inhabitants there seems to have been a mixture of Frisians, Saxons, and Franks. By the Middle Ages, however, these lands had become a temporal holding of the See of Utrecht, and as such they passed in 1527 to Charles V when Bishop Henry sold his temporal rights. Fifty years later with the signing of the Union of Utrecht in 1579 Overijssel became one of the seven provinces of the United Provinces.

Overijssel, as its name implies, is the province 'beyond the IJssel', the river (not to be confused with the one of the same name in the S) that, branching from the Rhine near Arnhem, forms the SW border of the province between Deventer, Zwolle (the provincial capital) and Kampen, all old places worth a visit, Kampen being particularly attractively situated on the river.

From the visitor's point of view the province divides roughly into two regions separated by the motorway between Zwolle and Meppel (in Drenthe), close to but well clear of the motorway being the adjoining long rural villages of Rouveen and Staphorst, strung along some 10km and known for their local costumes. The two parts of the province have become loosely known as Western and Eastern Overijssel, the former, with so much that is regarded as typically Dutch, attracting the greater number of visitors. Here is a watery region of broads and canals, in summer busily colourful with pleasure craft cruising between attractive small old towns such as Zwartsluis, Vollenhove, and Blokzijl, as also the curious water-village of Giethoorn.

Eastern Overijssel, though embracing the largely industrial district of Twente and less obviously inviting than the western part of the province, nevertheless offers pleasant pastoral and wooded countryside. The largest town, and also the largest in the province, is Enschede, with some good museums, notably the Rijksmuseum Twenthe with a collection of 16–19C pictures as well as applied art and regional material. Smaller towns, not without historical interest and with some buildings of note, are Almelo, Ootmarsum, and Oldenzaal, the last with an important Romanesque basilica.

## Province of Drenthe

**Capital.** Assen.

**History.** That a part of what is now the province of Drenthe was inhabited in prehistoric times (around 3000 BC) is proved by the great megalithic burial chambers known as Hunebeds, so many of which survive today (see Rte 30A). After this, though, little is known until the 5C and 6C AD, at which time the region was overrun by Saxons from whom eventually emerged various counts holding lands as fiefs from the Frankish and German kings and emperors. Change came in 1024 when the Emperor Henry II gave overall countship (this from 1040 including much of Groningen) to the See of Utrecht, the bishops of which from then on ruled through a burgrave, the title given to an ecclesiastical governor. This post became hereditary, first to the noble house of Coevorden and then (1232) to that of Borculo, this situation continuing until 1395 when Bishop Frederick imposed direct episcopal rule. In 1522 Drenthe fell to Charles of Egmont, but on his death in 1538 it passed to the Emperor Charles V under the terms of the Treaty of Gorinchem (see Province of Gelderland, History), then being incorporated into the Habsburg dominions.

Although taking the Protestant side in the revolt against Spain (Drenthe was overrun by Spain in 1580 but retaken by Maurice of Nassau in 1594), and although a formal appeal was made in 1651, Drenthe, perhaps because of its sparse population, was denied the status of province until 1796 with the declaration of the Batavian Republic. Nevertheless throughout the years of the United Provinces the region preserved its local autonomy, for most of the time having its own stadholders, these from 1722 onwards being the princes of Orange.

The most thinly populated of all the provinces, Drenthe was until the beginning of the 18C little but barren moor and peat bog, the only raised ground being the Hondsrug, the ridge running northwards from Emmen, today because of the many hunebeds along it (see above and Rte 30A) the most interesting and most visited part of the province. Land reclamation has now brought fertility to much of Drenthe, one feature of this being the distinctive Veenkolonien (peat, or fen, colonies) along the NE border with Groningen and also along the German border (see beginning of Rte 36), while Hoogeveen represents a town largely built on filled-in peat canals.

Drenthe's two principal towns are Assen, the not unattractive capital with the provincial museum, and Emmen, visited for its zoo and its hunebeds. Among other places of interest, all around Emmen, are the museum-village of Orvelte, a peat colony museum at Barger Compascuum, and an oilfield around Schoonebeek.

# 30   Deventer to Groningen

## A.   Via Zwolle and Emmen

Total distance 148km.—16km *Wijhe*—13km **Zwolle**—22km **Ommen**—26km **Coevorden**—19km **Emmen**—16km **Borger**—36km **Groningen**.

**DEVENTER** (65,000 inhab.; VVV, Brink 55) is still, as it has been for centuries, a prosperous manufacturing and trading town. Industry, however, is well clear of the inner town which has several picturesque old buildings. The town is known for a honey gingerbread called Deventer Koek.

**History.** A settlement seems to have grown up around a chapel built here in 768, on the hillock still known as the Berg, by the Saxon monk (later saint) Lebuinus or Liafwin, missionary to the Frisians and Westphalians. At this time the IJssel flowed around the foot of the hillock and by the late 9C, despite a Viking attack in 881, the settlement was already being referred to as 'portus', an indication of its commercial importance. By medieval times it was a member of the Hanseatic League.

**Natives and Others.** Deventer was known as a centre of learning. Gerrit Groot (1340–84), founder of the Brotherhood of Common Life, the members of which sought to reproduce the way of life of the early Christians, was born here. Thomas à Kempis (see Zwolle below) was a pupil of Groot's successor, Florentius Radewyn. The Renaissance humanist and theologian Erasmus (?1466–1536) and perhaps also Adriaen Florisz. (Pope Adrian VI) were pupils at the Brotherhood's Latin School, of which today's Gymnasium is the descendant. In 1643 J.F. Gronow or Gronovius (1611–71), the German classicist, became professor of history and rhetoric at the now vanished Athenaeum. Jan Sweelinck (1562–1621), organist of the Oude Kerk in Amsterdam, was born in Deventer, and the painter Gerard Terborch died here in 1681.

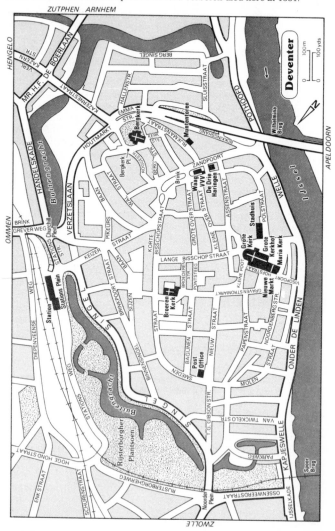

Around the BRINK, the large open space which is the town centre, there are several attractive old houses and restored façades. The *Waag, a Gothic building of 1528 enlarged during the 17C by the addition of a flight of steps, now houses the local museum (Tues–Sat, 10.00 to 12.30, 14.00 to 17.00; Sun, 14.00 to 17.00) while the adjoining building, known as *De Drie Haringen* (1575), an excellent example of the domestic architecture of the period, is now the home of VVV. The *Speelgoed en Blikmuseum* (Tues–Sat, 10.00 to 12.30, 14.00 to 17.00; Sun, 14.00 to 17.00), also on Brink, shows toys (especially mechanical ones), puzzles, books, games, dolls' houses and vintage tinware.

The oldest part of Deventer, the compact BERG KWARTIER, lies generally E of the Brink. With buildings dating from the 13C to the 17C, the quarter has since the 1960s been the object of an important conservation and restoration plan. At the heart of the quarter the *Bergkerk*, the popular name for what is officially the church of St Nicholas, has two early 13C towers. In Roggestraat, with several restored houses, No. 3 is in part a survival of a 14C hospice and Nos 4 and 6 were once breweries, while off Rijkmanstraat will be found the restored Muntentoren complex. Behind this there is a part of the 15C town wall, with some old paving, and another survival of wall can be seen by a small park a little further N.

Keizerstraat leads N out of the Brink for the station. Just off the Brink to the W there are pleasant pedestrian streets, one of which, Korte Bisschopstraat, reaches the *Broerenkerk*, formerly occupied by Friars Minor; a silver chalice here is said to have belonged to St Lebuinus. Lange Bisschopstraat, running roughly S out of Korte Bisschopstraat, ends at the **Grote Kerk**, dedicated to St Lebuinus. The first stone church on this site was built in 937, this being rebuilt in 1040 by Bishop Bernulphus of Utrecht, remnants of whose Romanesque work survive as the primitive *crypt, with an earthen floor and a well, and the four piers of the crossing. After fires in 1235 and 1334 the present Gothic church rose between 1450–1525, the 15C SW tower being added to during the 17C. Restoration work in 1927–40 brought to light 16–17C murals and vault paintings, the finest of which is of the Resurrection and the Day of Judgement. Adjoining the church's W end is the 14C *Mariakerk*, later used as an arsenal and now with small antiques shops built against it.

The **Stadhuis**, across the road from the Grote Kerk, dates from 1662–94 and contains a painting of a council meeting by Gerard Terborch, then burgomaster of the town. The *Landhuis* (from 1632), next door, is now a municipal office.

For Deventer to Almelo, Denekamp, Oldenzaal, and Enschede, see Rte 31.

The Zwolle road, running to the E of the IJssel, in 16km reaches *Wijhe* and then in another *6km Windesheim*, seat of the first house of Canons Regular founded in 1387 according to the precepts of the Brotherhood of Common Life; a fragment of the domestic buildings now serves as the parish church.

*7km* **ZWOLLE** (87,000 inhab.; VVV, Grote Kerkplein 14), the capital of the province of Overijssel and an old place rich in picturesque façades, is of roughly circular shape and completely surrounded by water. This water, the moat of the past, is linked at the NW to the Zwarte Water, along which, in summer, there are boat excursions to the Overijssel lakes.

**History.** Zwolle received its first charter in 1230 from Bishop Willebrand van Oldenburg of Utrecht. Later it is historically most associated with the Augustinian canon and theological scholar and writer Thomas à Kempis (c 1380–1471). Born Thomas Hammerken, son of a peasant from Kempen, between Venlo and Düsseldorf, he passed his life from 1399 onwards at a monastery on the Agnietenberg, a low hill just N of Zwolle, where he wrote his 'Imitatio Christi'. Gerard Terborch (1617–81), the painter who became burgomaster of Deventer, is Zwolle's most distinguished native.

Grote Markt and Grote Kerkplein form the town centre with, running E, the long, pedestrian shopping area along and either side of Diezerstraat.

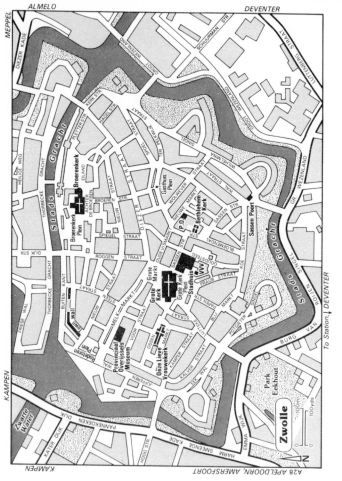

Grote Markt and Grote Kerkplein are separated by the **Grote Kerk** (open on several days in July and August), dedicated to St Michael whose figure, slaying the dragon, is seen above the N door. Built between 1406 and 1446 this Gothic church is successor to a Romanesque one of c 1200, a sculptured tympanum from which, representing Abraham and the three archangels (Michael appropriately being larger than the others) can be seen outside the apse. Noteworthy in the interior are the pulpit (German; 1612–22), the choir screen (1597), and the Schnitger organ of 1721 (concerts in July and August). Attached to the Grote Kerk is the *Hoofdwacht*, the former guard-house of 1614 in front of which stood the scaffold. The words 'Vigilate et Orate' (Watch and Pray) on the façade were presumably an injunction to the officials and other good citizens witnessing executions. The **Stadhuis**, just S of the church, is made up of three buildings; the old town hall, the

vicarage of the church and the new town hall. In the first of these is the
\*Schepenzaal of 1448 (restored 1957), the place from which the city's
administration was conducted over many centuries and still used for
marriages and other civic purposes. Among many fine features are the 15C
woodcarving; the monumental chimneypiece with a painting of 1606 (Last
Judgement) by an unknown artist; the aquamarine and gilt wall lockers of
1449 by Johan van Lübeck, four surviving of an original six; and the 15C
chandeliers, probably by Van der Gheynst of Mechelen, which until c 1580
hung over the magistrates' pew in the Grote Kerk.

To the W of the Grote Markt rises the distinctive pepperpot tower of the
15C *Onze Lieve Vrouwekerk*.

Melkmarkt runs NW out of Grote Markt, with on the left at No. 41 the
**Provinciaal Overijssels Museum** (Tues–Sat, 10.00 to 17.00; Sun, 14.00 to
17.00), housed in the 16C former palace of the stadholders but with an 18C
rococo pediment and main entrance. There are several period rooms,
including a large 17C kitchen and small scullery (the latter with a linen
press and an ingenious window cleaning spray) and a room showing silver
and porcelain, the latter in a magnificent wall cupboard fitted with candle
holders. Other rooms show archaeological material and ceramics of varous
periods (medieval, Renaissance, baroque, Empire and Art Nouveau). The
building known as De Gouden Kroon, across the garden, is mainly used for
temporary exhibitions.

From roughly opposite the museum you can follow Steenstraat N to
Buitenkant where there is a length of renovated town wall. To the E is the
*Broerenkerk*, formerly Dominican, a rebuilding of 1500–12. From here
Broerenstraat returns southward, crossing Diezerstraat, a main shopping
street, to reach Gasthuisplein, out of which Ter Pelkwijkstraat ends at
Wilhelminasingel. This street, followed S past the *Verzetsmonument*
honouring the fighters of the Resistance, reaches the \***Sassenpoort**, a
pinnacled gateway of 1406, the only survivor of the town's original four
gates. Renovated in 1894, the gate now houses provincial archives. You can
return to the Grote Markt by the twisting Sassenstraat, with on the right
the *Bethlehemkerk* and the *Reventer* (refectory), both originally parts of an
Augustinian house founded in 1308, partly destroyed by fire in 1324 and
then rebuilt. Just beyond is the *Karel V Huis*, dating from 1571 and named
from the medallion of Charles V on the façade.

For Zwolle to Meppel and Assen, see Rte 30B; to Lemmer, see Rte 32A; to
Steenwijk, see Rte 32B.

*22km Ommen* (17,000 inhab.; VVV, Markt 1), where a road diverges N for
Hoogeveen and Assen.

Out of Ommen this Route now bears NE, in part along the course of the
Vecht, entering the province of Drenthe just before (*26km*) **Coevorden**
(14,000 inhab.; VVV, 't Kasteel), 2km from the German border, one of the
oldest towns in Drenthe but today primarily an industrial centre. From the
mid 11C until 1232 it was the lords of Coevorden who ruled Drenthe as
burgraves of the bishops of Utrecht; the town received a charter in 1123,
was strongly fortified by Parma in 1580, fell to a scientifically planned
assault by Maurice of Nassau in 1592 and, in 1650, was largely rebuilt to
plans by Menno van Coehoorn, sections of whose fortifications still survive.
The town's street plan, radiating out from the Markt to the sites of the
bastions, still reflects Coevorden's fortress role, while some splendid
façades, notably in Friesestraat and Weeshuisstraat (both out of the Markt)

recall more gracious aspects. The local museum, known as *Drenthe's Veste* (Mon–Fri, 10.00 to 12.30, 13.30 to 17.00; Sat, Sun, 14.00 to 17.00), is just off the Markt in the former armoury (17C) which in 1970 was restored to serve mainly as the public library.

*Schoonebeek*, 9km E, is at the heart of one of western Europe's largest oilfields, with, along and on either side of the German border, over 300 wells. The oil is at a depth of some 800m and, because of low gas pressure, has to be pumped to the surface. A feature of the field is the way in which the pumping installations are to a large extent hidden behind hedges.

Approaching Emmen this Route now enters the region of the prehistoric megalithic HUNEBEDS (giants' graves), many examples of which survive along a corridor running northwards between Emmen and the provincial border of Groningen. These collective burial chambers, built out of erratic boulders probably brought down from Scandinavia by glaciers and the oldest evidence in the Netherlands of man's presence, would have been erected by people of perhaps 3400–2300 BC who settled along this ridge, now known as the Hondsrug, which must have been about the only firm ground above the marshland and lake which made up most of the ancient Netherlands. A typical hunebed consists of a long chamber with a row of uprights and capstones; they were almost certainly originally covered by stone and turf mounds, and from them have been excavated pottery and stone and wood objects, but nothing of metal. Finds are shown in local museums (Emmen, Borger, Assen) and also at the National Museum of Antiquities at Leiden. Many of the sites are signposted.

*19km* **EMMEN** (91,000 inhab.; VVV, Raadhuisplein) lies to the E of the main road; beside the N side of the approach road to the town is a hunebed. The principal town of this corner of Drenthe, Emmen is a scattered municipality, with a separate industrial zone, and is visited principally for its zoo and its hunebeds. VVV, the zoo, and two museums are all close to one another and to a large parking area at the town centre.

The **Hondsrug Museum** (April, May, Sept: Wed–Sat, 10.00 to 12.00, 13.00 to 17.00; Sun, 13.00 to 17.00; June–Aug: Mon–Sat, 10.00 to 12.00, 13.00 to 17.00; Sun, 13.00 to 17.00), at Marktplein 17, shows regional prehistoric and later material, while *Radiotron* (similar opening times), at the same address, is for connoisseurs of vintage telephones, gramophones, cameras, magic lanterns, radio and television sets. The zoo, the **Noorder Dierenpark** (daily from 09.00 to 16.30–18.30 according to season), immediately E of the museums and stretching across to the railway, includes an African savannah in which many animals roam freely, while other features are a collection of South American birds, Europe's largest sealion basin, and the Biochron, a museum of the story of life on Earth.

There are several easily seen hunebeds around the town; one is in woods a short way E of the station (car park and approach from the W); a second has been mentioned above and there are two more on the W edge of the town. One of these is the *Schimmer-Es*, a different kind of monument in the form of a kerbed enclosure (40m long) in which are two burial chambers and a single standing stone (off W side of Odoornerweg between Haagjesweg and Walstraat).

ENVIRONS OF EMMEN. There are several places of outstanding interest within a distance of up to 20km both to the E and to the W of Emmen. Places to the S and N are covered by this Route.

**East of Emmen**. The objective in this direction (11km, near Barger-Compascuum) will be the •*Veenmuseumdorp 't Aole Compas* (mid March–Dec: daily, 09.00 to 17.00, or 18.00). 't Aole Compas means Old Common and this is a large museum-village illustrating the life and work of the former peat colonies (veenkolonien; see introduction to Rte 36), the period being essentially from 1850 to the early years of the present century. The museum is in three principal parts: an Indoor Exhibition, a Peat Moor, and the Peat Colony village. An excellent multilingual guide covers the background of the peat fens and of the people who worked here and also provides a map. And, as a change from walking around, rides can be taken on a peat train and peat barge. Additional interest is provided on certain days by a variety of demonstrations.

The effectively arranged Indoor Exhibition (immediately to the left at the museum entrance; it is best toured clockwise) explains peat digging, stacking and loading on to a barge, and also includes a turf cottage and a remarkable section of the ancient Veenweg, a prehistoric track laid in about 2150 BC and excavated in 1981.

Leaving the main building, the Peat Moor with its nature conservation area is to the left while the Peat Colony Village is ahead. Already size-able—with cottages, baker, inn, grover, smithy and school—the village is expanding and plans include church, post office, more shops and an industrial area.

**West of Emmen**. An interesting circuit of some 37km can be made. Just NW of *Noordsleen*, 7km from Emmen, there are two hunebeds, one of which is immense. *Zweeloo*, 5km further W, is a particularly attractive village with large farms and a church in origin of the 13C. *Orvelte*, 7km NW of Zweeloo and well worth a visit, is a site of an unusual kind; an original local thatched village (largely 17–19C), saved by a trust and now an inhabited village-museum filled with period houses and other buildings and busy with crafts of many kinds. Among the places to be seen are the Tolhuis (where you buy your ticket) with a period living room and informa-tion on bee keeping; a farmhouse of 1729 (Bruntingerhof) showing old agricultural implements; a visitor centre (Drenthehof) providing back-ground on the villages of Drenthe; a shop of 1919; a mill, with, alongside, craft workshops (smith, clogmaker, saw mill and cooper); a hunting and shooting exhibition, and a dairy of 1899. (Only residents' cars are allowed in the village, but there are two large car parks.) The entry ticket, or toll card as it is called here, gives access to the above buildings. Opening times vary, but Orvelte is open for most of the year: Mon–Fri, 09.30 to 17.00; Sat, Sun, 11.00 to 17.00; open till 17.30 in July and Aug.

This circuit now returns E for *Schoonoord* (6km E of Orvelte) where *De Zeven Marken* (Easter–Oct: daily, 09.00 to 17.00) is an open-air museum recalling life in Drenthe as it was around the close of the 19C. Among the buildings are turf huts, an inn, a small lime kiln, a large sheepfold, a farm, a school and a carpenter's workshop of c 1900, while from time to time there are special exhibitions and demonstrations. Emmen is 12km SE of Schoonoord, the road passing a hunebed on the right 3km S of Schoonoord and then running close to those at Noordsleen, mentioned above. Between Emmen in the S and the Groningen provincial border in the N, a distance of some 40km, there is pleasant quiet countryside with many picturesque villages, often built around an open space ('Brink'), and huge, thatched farm buildings. The long, low ridge called the HONDSRUG (Dog's Back), the ridge which was chosen by the builders of the hunebeds, extends along most of this distance. (For the district of the peat colonies along the provincial border to the E, see Rte 36.)

Near (*7km* from Emmen) *Odoorn* there are three hunebeds, one to the N beside the main road and two to the S of the minor road between Klijndijk and Valthe; near the latter two, traces were found during the 19C of a prehistoric pathway. *9km* **Borger** is a typical Hondsrug village. The *hunebed* on its N side is the largest known: 24m long, with 10 capstones and a cross-chamber; while the nearby *'t Flint'nhoes*, in the former work-house, is a museum devoted largely to hunebeds (Easter–Sept: Tues–Sun, 10.00 to 17.00). Between Borger and (*5km*) *Gasselte* there are several hunebeds. In *4km* there is *Gieten*, to the W of which, between the Rolde road and the bypass, there is a large hunebed; and there is another just SW of nearby *Eext*. At (*6km*) *Anlo* the Romanesque church dating from the early 12C is the oldest in Drenthe, and there is a small hunebed beside the minor road leading N out of nearby *Annen*.

*6km* **Zuidlaren** (10,000 inhab.), to the E of the main road, is a pleasingly spacious small town with large green areas and magnificent trees. The *Stadhuis* is in a 17–18C mansion and the *Reformed church* dates from the 13C. Each October (third Tuesday) Zuidlaren is the scene of a large horse market. To the NE of the town the *Zuidlaarder Meer*, part in Drenthe and part in Groningen, is a popular recreational feature. If you take the minor road NW out of Zuidlaren you cross the provincial border in 2km; there is a hunebed just beyond on the west. In *3km* at *Noordlaren*, the 13C church has a saddleback roof to its tower. For (*6km*) Haren and (*6km*) Groningen, see Rte 33.

# B.  Via Zwolle, Meppel, and Assen

Total distance 121km.—29km **Zwolle**—16km *Staphorst*—6km **Meppel**—44km **Assen**—26km **Groningen**.

For prehistoric megalithic hunebeds (giants' graves), a number of which are seen along this Route, see Rte 30A.

For Deventer and (*29km*) Zwolle, see Rte 30A. *12km Rouveen* and *4km Staphorst*, together forming one continuous village strung along some 10km of road, are known for their thatched farms and cottages and for the colourful local costumes, mostly worn on Sundays. These are villages which have in many respects preserved an old-fashioned identity, and visitors are particularly asked not to take photographs without permission. In *6km* **Meppel** (23,000 inhab.; VVV, Kleine Oever 11), just in the province of Drenthe, has a church of 1422 around which and somewhat dwarfed by its large tower there are some nice old houses. Pedestrianised shopping streets will be found behind the church, and there are boat excursions on the NW Overijssel waterways. The *Grafisch Museum* (Mon–Sat, 10.00 to 16.30), at Kleine Oever 11, tells the story of printing, paper making, book binding, etc., with demonstrations on vintage machinery; modern and even future production systems also have a place here.

**Hoogeveen** (45,000 inhab. *VVV*, Raadhuisplein 3), 18km E but quickly reached by motorway, once a peat colony, is now a straggling, largely modern town with broad shopping streets made possible by the filling in of the former peat canals, a process which started with reclamation mea-sures of 1625. The town preserves the medieval custom of summoning worshippers to church by the beating of a drum. The *Museum Venendal*

(Mon–Fri, 10.00 to 12.00, 14.00 to 16.30; Sat, 14.00 to 16.30), at Hoofdstraat 9, is in a patrician mansion in origin of 1653 (though of this period only the cellar survives) but, as seen today, of 1888. The museum shows some prehistoric material, period rooms, decorative art including tiles, costume and pictures of old Hoogeveen.

*9km Havelte*, for Frederiksoord (8km; see Rte 32B). The road now runs with the Drentsche Hoofdvaart, the province's principal canal. *12km Dwingeloo*, to the E of the road, has a small 15C church and in the nearby woods a scientific establishment with a radio-telescope, while at *Diever*, to the W of the road and with a church in part of the 12C, there is De Spiraal, a museum about glass (July and Aug: Mon–Fri, 10.00 to 12.00, 13.30 to 17.30; Sat, 10.00 to 17.00; Sept–June, except Jan: Tues–Fri, 13.30 to 17.30; Sat, 10.00 to 17.00). *9km Hoogersmilde*, where you cross the main road from Leeuwarden to Emmen near a television tower. Signs here direct to the *Herinneringscentrum* (about 10km E near Hooghalen), a memorial and remembrance centre on the site of Westerbork camp, a transit camp through which between 1942 and 1945 the Germans processed a stream of Jewish and other prisoners.

*14km* **Assen** (47,000 inhab.; VVV, Brink 42), with some attractive 19C houses, is the provincial capital of Drenthe. The town centre is the BRINK, prominent on the E side being the former **Provinciehuis**, a complex at one time or other housing the record office of 1885, the abbey church of 1645 and the residence (1650) of the Receiver-General of Drenthe, and now in part the home of the *Drents Museum* (Tues–Fri, 09.30 to 17.00; Sat, Sun, 13.00 to 17.00) devoted to a wide range of local historical themes including archaeology, costume, coins and medals and fine and decorative art. Assen also has an *Automuseum* (April–Sept: daily, 10.00 to 18.00; Oct–March: Sat, Sun, 10.00 to 18.00) at Rode Heklaan 3 (W of the centre) with vintage cars and motor cycles.

At *Rolde*, 5km E, there are three hunebeds, two behind the church and one to the NW at Ballo.

*Veenhuizen*, 12km NW of Assen, was, after Frederiksoord, the second of the free agricultural colonies established (in 1823) by the Society of Charity.

At *(8km) Vries*, the Romanesque tower of the church is the best in the province, while at *Tinaarlo*, 2km E, there is a small hunebed beyond the railway to the E of the village. In *8km Eelde*, with an airfield, forms a single municipality with Paterswolde and Eeldewolde, both to the N. The *Paterswolder Meer*, to the E of the road (or W of the motorway), partly in Drenthe and partly in Groningen, is a recreation area. Beyond the lake the road crosses into the province of Groningen. For *10km* (from Eelde) Groningen, see Rte 33.

# 31   Eastern Overijssel (Deventer to Almelo, Denekamp, Oldenzaal, and Enschede)

Total distance 77km.–17km **Holten**—19km **Almelo**—24km **Denekamp**—8km **Oldenzaal**—9km **Enschede**.

The eastern part of this Route is through the industrial area of TWENTE (Almelo, Hengelo, Enschede). Industry is mainly confined to the towns, between being pleasant countryside of woods and low hills. Twente airport is 5km N of Enschede.

For Deventer, see Rte 30A. In *8km* you reach *Bathmen*, where the church has some 15C murals. At (*9km*) **Holten** (9000 inhab.) there is a Canadian war cemetery. The town is at the S end of a succession of small hills which run N for some 14km to *Nijverdal* and *Hellendoorn* and are known as the SALLANDSE HEUVELRUG, a nature area with the *Noetselerberg*, a forestry authority visitor centre and viewpoint off the Holten to Nijverdal road just S of the latter. It was at Nijverdal in 1833 that Thomas Ainsworth (1795–1841) of Bolton introduced the English power-loom system that revolutionised the textile industry of Twente, and there is a memorial to him in the church at *Goor*, 12km SE of Holten. In *19km* **Almelo** (63,000 inhab.; VVV, De Werf 1), although an industrial town, has at least two buildings of note. One is the *Waag*, just S of Marktplein, the town centre. Although its façade gives the building an older appearance, in fact the Waag was built, as a market hall, only in 1914. Today this is the home of the local museum (Tues–Sat, 13.30 to 17.00). The other building is *Huize Almelo*, in a park to the E of the Marktplein; first mentioned in 1135, today's dignified mansion, once the home of the local counts, dates in its present form from 1662. Almelo is associated with the Regiment of Mortemart, the depot of which was here. Raised by Britain in 1794, the regiment's officers and non-commissioned officers were French refugee royalists and the rank-and-file Germans or French republican deserters; the colours were the fleur-de-lys of royal France, and the regiment was disbanded in Portsmouth in 1802.

The direct road to Enschede now heads SE, but this Route makes a circuit to the NE. In *16km*, **Ootmarsum** (4000 inhab.; VVV, Markt), surrounded by low wooded hills, is known from archaeological discoveries to have been inhabited in Neolithic times. By tradition the town traces its name to a Frankish chieftain called Odemarus, and by written record its founding to a Bishop Radboud, said to have built a chapel here in 917 in which he was buried. Today there are several old façades, a Catholic church dating in part from 1220, and a natural history museum in a 16C building (*Los Hoes*, Smithuisstraat 2B). The *Kuiperberg*, to the S, is the highest point in Twente (orientation table). *8km* on, **Denekamp** (12,000 inhab.; VVV, Kerkplein 2) is another attractive old town in pleasant country. *Huis Singraven*, on Schiphorstdijk, dating in part from the 14C and with a tower of 1661, shows 17C paintings, Gobelin tapestries, furniture and ceramics (VVV for times of conducted tours), while *Natura Docet*, at Oldenzaalsestraat 39, is a museum of natural history and archaeology (Sun–Fri, 10.00 to 17.00). The painter J.B. Jongkind (1819–91) was born at *Lattrop*, 7km N.

*8km* **Oldenzaal** (29,000 inhab.; VVV, St Plechelmusplein), today an industrial town, has ancient origins for it stands on the site of a Frankish fortified farmstead (sala) and is first mentioned, as Aldenzeelen, in a document of c 1000. This ancient past is reflected by the town's circular centre, although modern buildings and gardens now mark the course of the long demolished ramparts. In medieval times Oldenzaal grew in commercial importance, and later it was from here that the Twente textile industry developed and spread. The solid 12C *St Plechelmusbasiliek* is 13C Romanesque with Gothic additions of c 1500. St Plechelm (died 730), whose statue stands outside, was an Irishman, or perhaps Northumbrian, who converted this district. *Het Palthehuis*, a restored mansion, houses the municipal museum (Markstraat 13. Tues–Fri, 10.00 to 12.00, 14.00 to 17.00; Sat, Sun, 14.00 to 17.00).

At **Hengelo** (77,000 inhab.), 9km SW, the most prominent feature is the tower of the modern Stadhuis. Largely rebuilt after devastation at the end of the war, the town is an industrial place (notably electronics and engineering) with a large specialised zone to the S of the station.

*9km* **ENSCHEDE** (145,000 inhab.; VVV, Markt 31), the largest town in Overijssel, is an important industrial centre still largely concerned with textiles but now also much diversified. In 1862 the greater part of the town was destroyed by fire.

In the MARKT stands the **Grote Kerk**, with a Romanesque tower but most of the church a rebuilding of 1865 after the great fire three years earlier (monument beside the church). Worth noting are the stained glass windows by Jan Schouten and, on the exterior wall opposite VVV, a sundial made by a local engineer and astronomer, Coenraad ter Keule, and showing both the time and the month. The *St Jacobuskerk* (RC), also on the Markt, was consecrated in 1933; it has an attractive cloister, Stations of the Cross by Charles Eyck, and a Pietà by Mari Andriessen. From the Markt, Langestraat leads S to reach the impressive **Stadhuis** (G. Friedhoff, 1930–33).

Some 300m E, on the N side of De Klomp, *Elderinkshuis* of 1783 is the only significant survival of the fire. In the VOLKSPARK, rather over 1km W, there is an unusual and moving war memorial (Mari Andriessen, 1953) comprising six statues representing Hostage, Resistance, Soldier of May 1940, Concentration Camp, Jewish Woman and Child, and Bombardment Victim. From the Stadhuis, Raadhuisstraat continues S to the huge HENDRIK JAN VAN HEEKPLEIN, with many shops and on the E side the largely covered market.

Enschede offers three good museums, perhaps the best known being the *Rijksmuseum Twente* (Tues–Sat, 10.00 to 13.00, 14.00 to 17.00; Sun, Holidays, 13.00 to 17.00) at Lasondersingel 129 which is 800m due N of the Markt. The scope here is wide—from prehistory and archaeology, through applied art in many forms, religious architecture and furnishings, folklore, the peasantry and the nobility, to fine art—all this scattered through a sequence of some 14 sections. The fine art collections, showing the works of artists spanning from medieval times to the present day, are outstanding and likely to be the first objective of most visitors, who should turn left at the entrance. Others, with other interests, should turn right.

Section 1, a small room devoted to illuminated manuscripts, is followed by S2 and S3 showing medieval and 16C and 17C paintings including: Lucas Cranach the Elder: portraits of the Elector of Saxony and his wife, the former portly and pompous, the latter demure; portraits by Hans Holbein the Younger, Joos van Cleve and Jacob Elsner; by the Master of Levensbron (c 1510): a gloriously naive Seven Acts of Charity, each a vignette glimpse of contemporary life. Moving into the 16C and 17C, there are two notable works by Pieter Brueghel the Younger, namely a Winter Landscape and a homely Two Men binding Faggots; Joos de Momper contributes River Valley between Hills, Ferdinand Bol one of the seven copies of his portrait of Admiral de Ruyter, Jan van Goyen a View of Nijmegen and Jan Steen his Flute Player.

This point marks the corner of the museum courtyard known as the Beeldentuin II (Sculpture Garden), a clockwise circuit of which leads through S4 and S5, which, together with S7 (for which you should turn right), show works of the 19C and 20C, frequently by means of temporary exhibitions. Here are artists such as Jacob Maris, J.H. Weissenbruch, Anton Mauve, B.C. Koekkoek (a superbly lit *Landscape with oak trees and ruins), Claude Monet (*The cliffs near Pourville) and Isaac Israels (*Two ladies dancing).

Section 6, with 17C Brussels tapestries, marks the start of the museum's applied art collections and continues around Beeldentuin I as a long, narrow gallery showing ceramics (17C and 18C) and tiles (16–19C). S8, parallel to the long S6, is the start of a series of sections or themes (S8 to S14) covering, in turn, Prehistory, with some good models of hunebeds; Religion, with, for instance, a model of the Grote Kerk, medieval fonts and a 15–16C oak chest; the Development of Castles, and also material on the Teutonic Order; the Nobility; the Life and Art of the People; Time and Money, or clocks and coins; and Peasant and Farm, associated with this last being, in the garden of the museum, an 18C farmhouse from eastern Twente.

The **Textiel Industrie Museum** (Tues–Fri, 10.00 to 12.00, 14.00 to 17.00; Sat, Sun, 13.00 to 17.00) is in Industriestraat, off Haaksbergerstraat, 1km SW of the Markt. Housed since 1983 in this large former mill, and devoted to the theme of everyday life in the eastern Netherlands since about the middle of the 19C, the museum has ambitious development plans, but the array of looms of all shapes, sizes and dates is likely to remain as may also the fascinating sequence of living rooms spanning 1700 to 1980.

The **Natuurmuseum en Vivarium** (Tues–Sat, 10.00 to 12.00, 13.30 to 17.00; Sun, 14.00 to 17.00) is at De Ruyterlaan 2, 500m W of the Markt. The museum occupies a basement and ground and first floors, the basement being largely given over to mineralogy with a well displayed if small collection of stones; a vitrine of radioactive stones, with a handwheel enabling these to be revolved past a geiger counter; and a small fluorescent vitrine. On the ground floor there are sections for geology, with small working models of oil rigs, and also shells and corals, while the first floor, largely given over to animals and birds (with some exceptionally well devised dioramas), is perhaps most popular for its vivarium populated by monkeys, hamsters, tortoises, fish, terrapins and even crocodiles.

# 32 Western Overijssel and the Noord-Oost Polder

The western part of Overijssel is a region of marsh, broads and canals, especially popular with pleasure craft. Roads here, often minor, frequently cross canals and delays must be expected while bridges are opened to allow the passage of flotillas of boats. To the W the Noord-Oost Polder, formerly in the province of Overijssel but now a part of Flevoland, stretches across to the IJsselmeer.

Two roads are suggested from Zwolle to the Friesland provincial border; a western approach through the attractive small town of Kampen and then across the polder, and an eastern alternative which meanders through the pleasant canals and broads country.

# A. Zwolle to Lemmer

Total distance 52km.—13km **Kampen**—12km *Ens* (for **Schokland**)—10km **Emmeloord**—17km **Lemmer**.

From Zwolle (see Rte 30A), the road runs to the N of the IJssel.

*13km* **Kampen** (32,000 inhab.; VVV, Oudestraat 85), with towers and spires, façades and gables, is strikingly st rung along the S bank of the river, crossed by a bridge (after 1945) which is last in a succession reaching back to at least 1448. There is a choice of boat excursions, including the IJsselmeer and the Zwartemeer.

The *Stadhuis*, at the town centre, is in two parts. The *Oude Raadhuis* (tour details from VVV) represents a rebuilding in 1543 as a replacement for a medieval predecessor which burnt down. Outside, the statues of Alexander the Great, Charlemagne and the Cardinal Virtues are replacements of 1933–38 by J. Polet, while the interior is distinguished by the fine Schepenzaal. or council chamber, with rich dark oak panelling, a magnificent *chimneypiece of 1545 by Colijn de Nole and a double burgomaster's throne of the same period by Meester Frederik. In the adjoining 18C *Nieuwe Raadhuis* there are portraits of members of the House of Orange spanning from William the Silent to Queen Juliana, while on the outside wall in Vispoort a plaque honours Petra van Staveren, winner of the 100m breaststroke gold medal at the 1984 Olympics. Nearby, on Oude Straat, the graceful *Nieuwe Toren*, on the site of the chapel of the medieval hospital, was built in 1649–64 by Philips Vingboons and has a carillon by François Hemony.

There are also two old houses here in the town centre. The 15C *Gotische Huis* (Oudestraat 158), the residence of wealthy merchants from medieval times until the present century, now houses the local museum (Tues–Sat, 11.00 to 17.00), and the *Vleishuis*, at Oudestraat 119, the former slaughterhouse, though largely 16C dates in part back to 1380.

At the N end of Oude Straat is the *Onze Lieve Vrouwekerk* (or *Buitenkerk*), dating in part (choir) from c 1369 but with nave and transepts of the 15C.

Running SW from the centre, Broederstraat crosses the *Burgel*, the early moat which after expansion of the town in 1462–65 lost its defensive purpose and found itself within the walls. The *Broederkerk* on the corner here dates from 1473–90 and was once part of a Franciscan house. Beyond, taking Broederweg, the continuation of Broederstraat, stands the *Broederpoort*, a gate dating from the 15C expansion but rebuilt in 1615–17 more for decoration than for defence. From here a road (S) skirts the public gardens to reach the *Celle-Broederspoort* (or *Cellespoort*), another gate rebuilt in 1615–17, this also more decorative than defensive.

Cellebroedersweg now returns E across the Burgel, a short way further

E beyond which is the *Bovenkerk* (*St Nicolaas*), a large double-aisled church of 1345–69, by, amongst others, Rotger of Cologne, with a good tower of this period and an apsidal crown of 13 chapels. The interior of light sandstone is particularly pleasing and effective, noteworthy here being the 15C pulpit and font; the choir screen, built with money left in 1550 by a pious widow; the sedilia, rare in the Netherlands; the magnificent organ (1743; Anthony Hinsz) in which are incorporated pipes from the former organ of 1670 by Jan Slegel; the memorial to Hendrik Avercamp (1585–1663), the painter, who worked and died in Kampen; and the memorial to Admiral J.W. de Winter (1750–1812), a native of Kampen and commander of the Batavian Republic's fleet at Camperduin in 1797 (see Rte 2). De Winter died in Paris where he is buried in the Pantheon, but his heart is in the urn here. The *Koornmarktspoort*, close to the church and dating from the 13C and 14C, is the town's only surviving properly defensive gate.

For OOSTELIJK FLEVOLAND, reached by a bridge 4km W, see Rte 29B.

Beyond Kampen the road soon crosses the short waterway linking the Ketelmeer (W) with the Zwartemeer (E) to reach the NOORD-OOST POLDER (province of Flevoland), an area of 48,000 ha. drained in 1942 and after the war developed principally for agriculture. The polder incorporates the former Zuider Zee islands of Schokland and Urk which in Roman times formed a single island. In *12km* (from Kampen) *Ens* is a village first occupied in 1948. **Schokland**, the former island, lies 2km W of Ens. Here the *Museum Schokland* (April–Oct: daily, 10.00 to 17.00; Nov–March: Tues–Fri, 10.00 to 17.00; Sat, Sun, 11.00 to 17.00.), perched on a hillock and including a church of 1834, shows all manner of things found after the draining of the polders. In the garden there are anchors, a section of the local dike (c 1840), graveslabs, and cannon balls. Visitors interested in maritime material found during the draining of the polders should visit the museum at Ketelhaven on Oostelijk Flevoland (see Rte 29B).

**Urk** (9600 inhab.), on the IJsselmeer coast 14km W of Schokland and the other former island, is known for its costumes, most likely to be seen on Sunday. The local museum, *Visserijmuseum*, is at Westhavenkade 44 (Mon–Fri, 10.30 to 17.00; Sat, 11.00 to 13.00). See under Enkhuizen (Rte 3) for car ferry. *Tollebeek*, 6km NE of Urk, is the most recent of the Noord-Oost Polder villages, while *Creil* and *Rutten* on the northward road out of Urk date respectively from 1953 and 1952.

*10km* **Emmeloord** (20,000 inhab.; VVV, Lange Nering Promenade 12), the first settlement after the draining, is the largest place on the polder and stands virtually at its centre. *Marknesse*, 7km E, was settled in 1948; here and to the S around *Kraggenburg* there are orchards. In *7km*, *Bant* was built in 1950. While in *10km*, **Lemmer** (see Rte 39A) is off the polder and in the province of Friesland.

# B. Zwolle to Steenwijk

At Zwartsluis, 16km from Zwolle, there is a choice of roads. That round the W side of the broads (Belter Wijde and Beulaker Wijde) via Vollenhove and Blokzijl is the more picturesque; by this road the distance from Zwartsluis to Steenwijk is 27km. The direct road (17km) passes the curious village of Giethoorn.

For Zwolle, see Rte 30A. In *10km*, **Hasselt**, now a large village on the Zwarte Water, was once a prosperous Hansa town which first received a charter in 1252. The *Stadhuis* dates in part from 1500 (west façade) but has undergone later alterations. The *St Stephanuskerk* was built in 1380 as successor to a church which had been destroyed by fire, but the crown to the tower is a replacement of 1725. In Ridderstraat the *Waterpoortje* is a 14C remnant of the walls. Hasselt was the home of the Lansing family, a name later known in American history through John (1754–1829), a distinguished jurist, and Robert (1864–1928), statesman and chief of the American delegation to the Paris peace conference of 1919. *6km* **Zwartsluis** (4000 inhab.; VVV, Stationsweg 32), on the Zwarte Water where it bends westwards to reach (4km) the Zwartemeer, stands at the junction of several waterways and in the 17C was the site of a strategic fortification, a plan of which can be seen in the *Gemeentehuis*. The *Museum Schoonewelle*, at Museumlaan 2, is a natural history museum devoted to the flora and fauna of this part of Overijssel (Mon–Sat, 09.00 to 12.00, 14.00 to 17.30).

ZWARTSLUIS TO STEENWIJK VIA VOLLENHOVE. Perched on a dike for 4km, the road skirts the Zwartemeer and in *10km* reaches **Vollenhove** (4000 inhab.; VVV, Kerkplein 15), formerly on the IJsselmeer but now facing the E side of the Noord-Oost Polder. The town's name first appeared as long ago as 944; in 1165 it became a fortified seat of the bishops of Utrecht; and in 1354 it received its charter. Around the Kerkplein there are three buildings of interest, namely the arcaded former *Stadhuis* (1621), now a restaurant; the *Onze Lieve Vrouwekerk* of 1434, but with a tower of 1458 which was heightened in 1828; and the former *Latijnse School* (largely 1627), with carved gateposts. To the SE of the town are the ruins of the castle of *Toutenburgh*, in the 16C a seat of the stadholders of Overijssel but largely demolished in the early 19C. In *5km* **Blokzijl** (2000 inhab.; VVV, Kerkstraat 12), first mentioned in 1438, was once a fortress town. Today, the harbour of 1550 is a lively and attractive marina for pleasure craft, around which runs the Bierkade with many well restored 17–18C houses and also a high tide warning gun of 1813.

*12km* **Steenwijk** (21,000 inhab.; VVV, Markt 60) is an old fortified town which has seen much of war. First mentioned in 1141, it was granted a charter in 1225 and was fortified in 1358. A major siege was that of 1523, when the town was taken and sacked by the Gelderland troops of Charles of Egmont. In 1580–81, however, Steenwijk was gallantly and successfully defended against the Spanish by Johan van den Kornput. The Spanish nevertheless took the town the following year, holding it until it was retaken by Van den Kornput in 1592.

The moat and some sections of wall, particularly on the S, still surround the town. From the Markt, the *Kleine Kerk* (1477) is approached by a street in which is the *Waag* with a façade of 1642. The *Grote Kerk* (*St Clemens*), a triple-nave late Gothic building, was begun in c 1400 but, because of repeated war damage, not completed until the end of the 16C. The tower (ascent) was started in 1467 and restored in 1913 when the corner turrets and spire were added.

**Frederiksoord** (8km NE of Steenwijk), until the early 19C barren moorland, was the site of the first of the free agricultural colonies established by an organisation called the Society of Charity. Industries such as rope and mat making and the weaving of jute and cotton were introduced, later followed by tree nurseries, horticulture and general agriculture. Today there are two museums here, one showing shells, the other clocks. The *Zeemuseum*

*Miramar* (Easter–Oct: Mon–Fri, 09.30 to 12.00, 13.00 to 17.30; June–Aug: Mon–Fri, 09.00 to 17.00; Sat, 13.00 to 17.30; Sun, 11.00 to 17.00), at Vledderweg 25, is for shells, corals and fossils. The *Klokkenmuseum* (May–Sept: Mon–Fri, 10.00 to 17.00; Sun, 14.00 to 17.00), at Maj. van Swietenlaan 17, shows Dutch and other clocks spanning 1500 to 1900.

For Steenwijk to Leeuwarden, see Rte 39C.

ZWARTSLUIS TO STEENWIJK VIA GIETHOORN. The road runs NE beside the Meppelerdiep, then forks N to cross the Belter Wijde by a causeway before skirting the E side of Beulaker Wijde. *9km* on, **Giethoorn** (2000 inhab.) is a curious, scattered water-village most of which is inaccessible except on foot or by boat, nearly every house being surrounded by tree-lined canals crossed by footbridges. Giethoorn originated in c 1280 when members of a sect of flagellants were given land here by the lord of Vollenhove. When they started to dig peat they turned up the horns of many wild goats, probably victims of flooding, as a result naming their settlement 'Geyten-horn' (goats' horns). The village's present character grew out of haphazard peat digging, this causing lakes and ponds to form and requiring ditches and canals for transport.

*VVV* is beside the main road and canal, the latter busy with pleasure craft, a short distance N of Beulaker Wijde. From near VVV small roads lead off to car parks, near which 'punters', a local form of punt, await the visitor. The village and its surrounds can be very crowded. Within the village there are such attractions as a museum of stones and crystals (*De Oude Aarde*), an aviary of tropical birds, an exhibition of costumes, a pottery, and a shells exhibition. A large choice of boat excursions is available.

*8km* Steenwijk, see above.

# PROVINCE OF GRONINGEN

**Capital.** Groningen.

**History.** The history of Groningen is closely bound up with that of the Frisians who by the 1C AD inhabited all the coastal zone of what is now the Netherlands, a situation confirmed by Charlemagne whose Lex Frisionum established three districts of Frisia, that of East Frisia being the country between the Lauwersmeer and the river Ems. During the conflicts following the death of Charlemagne Frisia as a whole changed hands several times, but when in 911 it passed to Charles the Simple of West Francia the district of East Frisia asserted its independence, looking to the east for protection and eventually becoming the imperial lands of Groningen.

In 1040 the Emperor Henry III gave the town of Groningen and its immediate surrounds (the Gorecht) to the bishops of Utrecht as an extension of the temporality they had already held in Drenthe since 1024. Ruling through episcopal representatives called burgraves, the bishops at first exercised a measure of authority in the town and the Gorecht—although their authority did not extend to the surrounding Frisian territory known as the Ommelanden (surrounding lands), a complex of local lordships ruled by 'Jonkers' who lived in country manors called 'borgs'—but there was continual struggle between the citizens and the bishops until by the end of the 14C the town, with the Gorecht, had become virtually independent, a state of affairs formally recognised in 1440 when Bishop Dirk II sold to the town the see's rights. The Ommelanden however, although in practice in many respects controlled by the town, remained independent and the whole of what is now the province was not formally united until subjugated by Charles V in 1536.

Although both the town and the Ommelanden subscribed to the Union of Utrecht in 1579, the town withdrew the following year and held out for Spain. However, after being taken by Maurice of Nassau in 1594, it rejoined the Ommelanden in adhering to the union.

Groningen, the province's only town of any size, is a busy administrative, university, and commercial centre with several buildings that are both attractive and of interest and an outstanding coastal and inland shipping museum (Noorderlijk Scheepvaart).

In the surrounding countryside, described as three Routes covering an arc from NW to SE, there are a number of distinctive features. The Lauwersmeer, to the NW, is worth visiting as an example of a large natural bay which has been sealed off for development for agriculture, recreation and military use, all this being well explained at a visitor centre (Expo-Zee). Across the northern part of the province there are many 'circular' villages—usually a central church attractively ringed by grass, a moat and a road. These owe their distant origins to 'terps' (in Groningen sometimes called 'wierden' or 'warften'), man-made mounds thrown up perhaps over 2000 years ago in the constant endeavour to secure living space clear of marsh and flooding; at first mounds for individual homesteads, terps gradually grew in size as villages developed. The mounds as such have now largely disappeared, although traces can still be found. The churches of this district, as also of that extending a short way further SE, are another distinctive feature with their Romanesque or Gothic brick construction, vault paintings and detached towers.

In the SE of the province (Rte 36) there are two very different districts, the Westerwolde with its huge, long farmhouses; and the curious peat-colonies (veenkolonien) along the Drenthe border.

# 33 Groningen

**GRONINGEN** (168,000 inhab.), university town and provincial capital, is the most important town in the northern Netherlands. Its commercial and industrial standing is assured by the Eems Kanaal (1876) which, large enough for sea-going ships, links Groningen with the sea at Delfzijl 25km to the E; the town is also linked by smaller canals to Nieuwe Schans on the German border, to Leeuwarden in Friesland, and to Zwolle and beyond in the S. The inner town is wholly surrounded by waterways, the moats of earlier times. Though damaged during the Second World War, Groningen preserves several fine public buildings and some old houses.

**Centre.** Grote Markt. This is in part a pedestrian precinct, as are also some of the streets off it, notably Vismarkt and Herestraat, running SW and SE.

**VVV** Grote Markt (Naberpassage 3).

**Post Office.** Munnekeholm 1, 500m SW of Grote Markt.

**Station.** S of the southern waterway, 900m S of Grote Markt.

**Boats.** Local and longer distance excursions from opposite the station.

**History.** Under the name '*Villa Cruoninga*', the town and its immediate surrounds (the Gorecht, see history of the province) was in 1040 given by the Emperor Henry III as a fief to the See of Utrecht, the bishops from then on ruling through their prefects, the burgraves. But the authority of the bishops was in practice always limited, and as the town grew in commercial importance, becoming a Hansa member and even providing ships for the Crusades, so also it increasingly asserted its independence, at the same time developing a constitution under which all power, whether commercial, legal or administrative, was concentrated in the hands of the oligarchy of wealthy citizens who formed the Raad, or governing council. The guilds, often so powerful in other Dutch cities, played no significant role in Groningen. Formal recognition of the town's independence came in 1440 when Bishop Dirk II sold to it the See's by now largely theoretical rights.

This formal independence lasted a century, until 1536 when the town and the Ommelanden (see history of the province) were subjugated by Charles V.

With many of its citizens Catholics, it was only reluctantly that Groningen subscribed in 1579 to the Union of Utrecht. The following year it seceded, the consequent siege by Union forces being relieved by the Spanish under whom the town remained until taken by Maurice of Nassau in 1594 and, again reluctantly, rejoining the Protestant Ommelanden to become the capital of the province.

In 1614 the university was founded. In 1672 the troops of Bishop Von Galen of Münster, the ally of Louis XIV, besieged the town, but without success thanks to the provision ships that found their way up the Reitdiep. The fortifications were much strengthened by Menno van Coehoorn in 1698, but were finally demolished in 1874.

**Natives.** The painters Jan Swart (c 1490/1500–after 1553), Jozef Israels (1824–1911) and H.W. Mesdag (1831–1915). Also H. Kamerlingh Onnes (1853–1926), the chemist who first liquefied helium.

GROTE MARKT. The *Stadhuis* in the middle of the square is a classical building of 1802–10 by Jacob Husly. Just to its W, the *Goudkantoor* (Gold Office) was built in 1635 as a tax office but changed its function (to Weights and Measures) and its name during the 19C. At the NE corner of the Grote

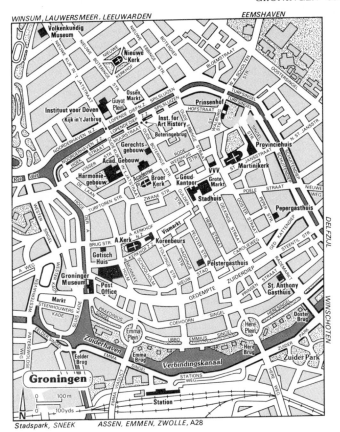

Stadspark, SNEEK    ASSEN, EMMEN, ZWOLLE, A28

Markt rises the graceful, graduated tower of the **Martinikerk**, completed in its present form during the 15C but historically dating back to 1230 to which period belong the east bays of the nave. The tower (nearly 100m), with a Hemony carillon, was started in 1469 but the upper levels were rebuilt in 1627 after a fire 50 years earlier. Inside the church there are 15C and 16C murals and also an organ (restored 1979) dating back to 1480.

NORTH-EAST OF THE GROTE MARKT. At the back of the Martinikerk (Martinikerkhof 12), the older part of the Provinciehuis, formerly a school, has a façade of 1559. The Prinsenhof, to the N, was in the 15C occupied by the Brotherhood of the Common Life (see Deventer, Rte 30A), but it was altered in 1594 to serve as the residence of the Stadholder and given new gateways in 1639 and 1642. Later used as a military hospital, the building today houses radio offices and studios. The garden, laid out in 17C style, is open during the summer.

NORTH-WEST OF THE GROTE MARKT. Oude Ebbingestraat leads roughly N, off which Rode Weeshuisstraat soon branches W. On the left of the latter can be seen the doorway (1627) of the *Weeshuis*, the former orphanage; the doorway bears carved figures and the building preserves something of a 15C nunnery. You can now follow Oude Boteringestraat N, with at Nos 79–81 the Institute for Art History (temporary exhibitions), on the street's W side being the *Gerechtsgebouw* with a double gable of 1612. At the street's end the former inner moat is crossed by Boteringebrug, beyond on the right being the Ossenmarkt with some attractive 17C and 18C buildings. Immediately SW on Guyotplein the *Instituut voor Doven* is an institution for the deaf and dumb founded by Pastor H.D. Guyot (died 1828), a monument to whom stands in the square. Oude Boteringestraat is continued N by Nieuwe Boteringestraat, on the E side of which is the *Nieuwe Kerk* (1664) built to the shape of a Greek cross and containing some good 17C woodwork.

The parallel street to the W of Nieuwe Boteringestraat is Nieuwe Kijk in 't Jatstraat, with at No. 104 the *Volkenkundig Museum* (Tuesday–Friday, 10.00 to 16.00. Saturday, Sunday, 13.00 to 17.00) of ethnology (Gerardus v.d. Leeuw). The street's curious name (Peep into the Creek) is said to be explained by the head of an old man on the house at the SE corner of Kijk in 't Jatbrug; he looks along Noorderhaven to the Reitdiep and recalls the constant lookout kept for the relief boats during the siege of 1672. Oude Kijk in 't Jatstraat returns towards the town centre, on the W being the façade of the *Harmoniegebouw*, formerly home of the music society, with, behind it, university buildings. The university (**Academiegebouw**, 1909) is roughly opposite on Academieplein. Founded in 1614, this academy reached its zenith in the mid 17C when the theologian Franz Gomarus (1563–1641), the adversary of Jacobus Arminius, was teaching here. There is a general *University Museum* (Mon–Fri, 09.00 to 16.00), and the library in nearby Zwanestraat is known for its incunabula and old MSS. The *Broerkerk*, opposite the university, was built by Cuijpers.

SOUTH-WEST OF THE GROTE MARKT. Beyond the Vismarkt, now a flower market, stands the *Korenbeurs*, dating from 1865 and still Western Europe's principal exchange for domestic grain. Around the entrance the statues represent Mercurius, god of commerce, on top, and, on either side, Neptune and Ceres, respectively the deities of the sea and corn. Beyond rises the **Akerk**, more officially *Onze Lieve Vrouwekerk der A*, the A being the name of the small river which near here forms the moat. On a site occupied by a church since the 13C, the present building is a large and much restored 15C structure with a baroque steeple of 1710–12.

Generally to the W of the Akerk there are three museums, two of these, the *Noordelijk Scheepvaart* (Northern Shipping) and *Tabacologisch* (Tobacco) being in the adjoining *****Gotisch Huis** and **Canter Huis** (Brugstraat 24–26), both, though of course restored, in origin of the 13C to 14C. The shipping museum, one of the best of its kind in the country and filled with superb models and striking pictures, covers the story of inland and coastal shipping in the northern provinces; the tobacco museum covers the use of tobacco in Western Europe between about 1500 and 1930.

Quite apart from the interest of the museums, a visit here is rewarding for the buildings themselves, a warren of massive beams and frequent steep stairs, but nevertheless clearly arrowed and explained by a good ground plan (Tues–Sat, 10.00 to 17.00; Sun, 13.00 to 17.00).

The shipping museum occupies Rooms 1 to 8 and 9 to 20, with 18–20 normally used for temporary exhibitions. After Room 8 the visitor is given a complete break by descending steeply through the four tobacco rooms (I to IV). A summary of the room themes is given below.

Room 1. Frisian shipping c 500–1100. Room 2. The Hanseatic period, c 1200–1600. Room 3. The East and West Indies companies in the 17C and

18C; large displays of colonial chinaware; a map by Blaeu of Central America. Room 4. The Frisian Admiralty, 17C and 18C; tile pictures of ships. Room 5. Internal waterways and peat canals after 1650. Room 6. Small shipping, 1750–1900; a period room of a seaman's home of c 1840. Room 7. Small shipping, 1850–1925; seamen's chests; Grocer's shop. Room 8. Ship-building and equipping; small maquette of a shipyard; various workshops, including those of a carpenter, blacksmith, rope maker and sail maker, this last equipped with a massive ancient Singer sewing machine; a display of knots.

You now make a steep descent through the four levels of the Tobacco Museum (Rooms I–IV), with miscellaneous displays of pipes, pouches, cutters, boxes, jars and a period shop.

Rooms 9 and 10 are concerned with loading and ballast, Room 11 with steam. Room 12. Coastal navigation (20C) with a wheelhouse equipped with modern navigation equipment. Room 13. Inland waterway navigation, 19C and early 20C. Room 14. Living conditions along the coast, 18C and 19C; an 18C Ameland interior. Room 15. Fishing, with some complete, if small boats. Room 16. Whaling, including a magnificent action picture of a polar bear at bay; also interesting engravings showing Willem Barendsz. in Nova Zembla, 1596–97. Room 17. Powered inland waterway travel; engines. Rooms 18–20. Paintings, drawings and temporary exhibitions.

To the SW of the Akerk, at Praediniussingel 59, the **Groninger Museum** (Tues–Sat, 10.00 to 17.00; Sun, 13.00 to 17.00) illustrates the past and the culture of the town and the province, offering, too, collections of applied and fine art. Temporary exhibitions, however, often of modern art, are frequent and may well displace the permanent displays. But perhaps the most interesting feature here is the Geldermalsen Porcelain, part of a huge collection which, together with her cargo of tea and silk, went down with the East Indiaman 'Geldermalsen' when, Netherlands bound, she was wrecked in 1752 in the South China Sea. The porcelain (no fewer than 150,000 pieces) was raised by Captain Michael Hatcher in 1985. The collection here, most of it in astonishingly fine condition and of equally astonishing luxury and variety, comprises some 150 pieces donated by Captain Hatcher and also purchases made by the museum.

SOUTH AND SOUTH-EAST OF THE GROTE MARKT. In this part of the town three attractive almshouses can be seen. The *Pelstergasthuis*, or *Heilige Geest Gasthuis*, in Pelsterstraat which drops S out of Vismarkt, is the oldest in Groningen, being founded in c 1267. Much expanded over the centuries, it now comprises three old courtyards and one modern one; the gate on to Nieuwstad is a restoration of 1724. To the E in Rademarkt the *St Anthony Gasthuis* (no adm.) was founded in 1517 and rebuilt in 1696; until 1644 it served as a refuge for plague victims, thereafter until 1844 being a lunatic asylum. The *Pepergasthuis*, also known as the *Geertruidegasthuis*, is in Peperstraat to the north. The gateway dates from 1640, the pediment from 1743 and there are two courtyards, one with 18C façades and a gate of 1651.

OUTSKIRTS AND ENVIRONS OF GRONINGEN. The large and beautiful **Stadspark**, on the SW of the town, includes sports fields, the municipal camping and caravanning site, an ice rink and the *Martinihal* used for exhibitions.

The *Eems Kanaal* leaves from the E side of the town, near its start being the industrial zone and port (*Industrie en Havencomplex*).

At **Noorderhogebrug**, on the town's N outskirts, the octagonal *Wilhelminamolen* (1906) is the largest mill in the province.

At **Haren** (18,000 inhab.), 6km SE, *Hortus de Wolf* (Mon–Sat, 10.00 to

16.45; Sun, 14.00 to 16.45) is the botanic garden of the university; a tropical glasshouse is divided into five climatic sections (monsoon, savannah, desert, sub-tropical, and tropical).

At **Leek**, 14km SW, the estate of *Nienoord* has walking and cycle paths, a children's farm, swimming pool, pottery workshop, etc., and also boat excursions on the Leekstermeer. Here too is the *Nationaal Rijtuigmuseum* (Easter–Sept: daily, 09.00 to 18.00), with coaches, sleds, etc. The church at **Midwolde**, just N of Leek, dates from the 12–13C and contains a monument (1665–69) by Rombout Verhulst with a figure added by Bartholomeus Eggers in 1714.

From Groningen to Zwolle, Emmen, Assen, and Deventer, see Rte 30; to the Lauwersmeer, see Rte 34; to Uithuizen, Delfzijl, and Appingedam, see Rte 35; to Winschoten, Wedde, Ter Apel, and Stadskanaal, see Rte 36.


# 34 Groningen to the Lauwersmeer

An anticlockwise circuit is described starting from and returning to Groningen.

Total distance 78km.—13km *Winsum*—12km **Leens**—15km **Lauwersoog**—10km **Zoutkamp**—12km *Grijpskerk*—10km **Aduard**—6km **Groningen**.

For Groningen, see Rte 33. At (*10km*) Wetsinge, and at Oostum and Feerwerd both to the W of the road, there is mound evidence of early terps. In *3km* you reach *Winsum*. For the district to the E and for the continuation N through Uithuizen, see Rte 35. This Route bears W for (*6km*) **Eenrum** where there is an arboretum with some 500 species of trees and shrubs for sandy soil. *Kloosterburen*, 5km NW, owes its name to a religious house founded here in 1170, believed to have been the earliest foundation in the province. At *6km* **Leens** there is a church of c 1200 in which on Saturday evenings in summer recitals are given on the Hinsz. organ of 1733. *Borg Verhildersum* (Easter–Oct: Tues–Sun, 10.30 to 17.30), just E of Leens and recorded as far back as the 14C, is structurally today of about 1800 and has been arranged in the style of a 19C country mansion. Art exhibitions are mounted in the coach house, and the grounds offer a variety of walks. The nearby (E) *Museum-Boerderij Welgelegen* (April–Oct: Tues–Sat, 13.00 to 16.30; Sun, 10.30 to 17.30), a museum-farm, shows 19C agricultural implements and illustrates various aspects of regional farm life at this period. If, leaving Leens, you take the minor road to the S of the main road, you pass an old pillory which marks the boundary between the municipalities of Leens and Ulrum. Beyond *Ulrum* the road bears N (for the smaller road continuing W see below), reaching the coast and then running W below the dike of 1969 to (*15km* from Leens) the small port of **Lauwersoog** on both the open sea and the Lauwersmeer.

The LAUWERSMEER, a broken and irregular lake of some 8km by 6km, extends across the border between the provinces of Groningen and Friesland, the boundary curving roughly diagonally from NW to SE. Once an expanse of peat, a large bay was formed here by sea flooding during the 10C and 11C, a number of streams thereby acquiring a common estuary. Over the centuries various dikes were built, the first (c 1300) probably near

Oostmahorn on the W side. In 1729 the decision was taken to dam the Dokkumerdiep (SW); the Reitdiep at Zoutkamp was dammed in 1877; and in 1960 the project to seal off the bay from the sea was approved, the work being completed in 1969. One result of this was the isolation of the fishing ports of Dokkumernieuwezijlen and Zoutkamp, and their fishermen now sail from Lauwersoog. The lake receives excess water from both provinces, discharging this into the sea through sluices at Lauwersoog. Long-term plans for the lake surrounds include agricultural land, woodland, recreational facilities (marinas, beaches, camping, chalets), nature reserves, walking and cycle paths and a new road system. There are also some military zones, but these should not significantly affect public access. *Expo-Zee* (signed Lauwersmeer. April–Sept: Tues–Fri, 10.00 to 17.00; Sat, Sun, Holidays, 14.00 to 17.00) at Lauwersoog is an imaginative exhibition covering not only the Lauwersmeer but also Dutch land reclamation generally. The exhibition tells the story from early geological times to the present day, using good dioramas, an illuminated map showing reclamation at various periods, and a film in English.

From Lauwersoog there is a ferry service (crossing 45 minutes) across the 7km of the Waddenzee to the sandy, holiday island of **Schiermonnikoog** (Friesland), some 11km long by 2km broad and with a resident population of around 800. Until the Reformation the island belonged to the monastery of Klaarkamp (see Rte 38). Other than with special permission, cars are not permitted on the island. The ferry runs about four times daily in each direction, and day excursions are popular (bus connections with Groningen and Leeuwarden; large car park at Lauwersoog). There are a few hotels and also camping facilities. (For postal tourist information: VVV Schiermonnikoog, Postbus 13, 9166 ZP Schiermonnikoog; or Tel: 05195-1900. For ferry information: Wagenborg Passagierdiensten, Zeedijk 7, 9976 VM Lauwersoog; or Tel: 05193-9070.)

For places to the W of the remainder of this Route, see Rte 38.

From Lauwersoog the rather desolate but unusual road, along which many species of birds may be seen, can be taken across the reclaimed land to (*10km*) **Zoutkamp** on the mouth of the Reitdiep, a place where tourism is gradually filling the vacuum left by the move of the fishing fleet. From here, small roads S reach the main Groningen to Leeuwarden road between Visvliet and Grijpskerk. At *Burum*, in Friesland just W of Visvliet, an earth-satellite tracking station is a prominent feature, while *Lutjegast*, 3km S of Visvliet, was probably the birthplace of the great navigator Abel Jansz. Tasman (1603–59); there is a plaque on the church wall.

This Route now returns E towards Groningen. At (*12km*) **Aduard** the church occupies what was the refectory of a Cistercian house founded in 1192. When during the troubles of the 16C the abbot and most of the monks retired to Groningen the few remaining monks, now finding their church too big, in 1597 moved into the former refectory, the rest of the abbey soon became a source of building material and consequently disappeared. The church is an outstanding example of early 14C brickwork and its refectory origin gives it an unusual shape and a pleasantly simple and uncluttered vault. The interior merits visiting for its particularly fine early 18C furnishings. Another *6km* brings you back to Groningen.

# 35   North-East Groningen Province (Groningen—Uithuizen—Delfzijl—Groningen)

Total distance 76km.—13km *Winsum*—8km **Warffum**—8km **Uithuizen**—9km *Niekerkje*—12km **Delfzijl**—4km **Appingedam**—22km **Groningen**.

This Route makes a clockwise circuit of the district of FIVELINGO, with large farms (some with parklike gardens suggesting origin as a borg, see below) and many windmills, and known also for its fine brick Romanesque or Gothic churches, often standing on a terp and some also with a detached tower. Few churches are likely to be found open and visitors interested in interiors are advised to consult VVV, Groningen, where an up-to-date list of keyholders is kept. More churches, these also frequently with detached towers, are mentioned in Rte 36.

For Groningen (see Rte 33) to (*13km*) *Winsum*, see Rte 34. At *8km* **Warffum**, *Het Hogeland* (March–Oct: Tues–Sat, 10.00 to 17.00) is an open-air museum showing an inn, a house, shops and local costume. In *4km* you reach *Usquert*. The road S from here leads to Kantens, Toornwerd, and Middelstum, all places whose circular centres indicate terp origins. At Toornwerd a tower of 1487 is all that survives of a church demolished in 1880. In *4km* **Uithuizen**, has a 13C church has a 12C tower. *Menkemaborg* (April–Sept: daily, 10.00 to 12.00, 13.00 to 17.00; Oct–March: Tues–Sun, 09.00 to 12.00, 13.00 to 16.00; closed January), in a park on the E of the town, is a 15C fortified manor house, altered in c 1700. This (with Fraeylemaborg, see Rte 36) is one of the two more or less untouched survivors of the borgs, the homes first of the ruling local lords of the Ommelanden and later of wealthy land owners. Most of the borgs have either been demolished or altered beyond recognition but Menkema survived largely because it was presented to the Groninger Museum. The interior furnishings are generally 17–18C with fine chimney-pieces and other carved work. The Romanesque church at *Oldenzijl*, 2km SE, dates from c 1200.

*4km Uithuizermeeden* has a church which is in part of c 1250 but with an 18C interior. In *5km* you reach *Niekerkje*, to the N of which are an industrial zone and the port of *Eemshaven*. The road now bears SE for (*4km*) **Spijk**, an attractive village in which the inner ring-road and moated church are evidence of a terp. *Godlinze*, 2km SW, with its circular layout, was another terp. The partly 13C church at *Bierum*, 2km SE of Spijk, contains remains of 15C vault paintings.

*8km* **Delfzijl** (25,000 inhab.; VVV, Waterstraat 6), on the mouth of the Eems (Ems) and the foreport of Groningen to which it is linked by the Eems Kanaal, is the largest port on the northern coast of the Netherlands and an industrial town which has much developed with the discovery of salt deposits and natural gas.

From the Zeedijk there is a view across the 10km wide estuary to Germany, the town of Emden being some 25km distant. In the *Noordhoorn Gebouw* (May–Sept: Mon–Fri, 07.00 to 19.00; Sat, 08.00 to 19.00; Sun, 10.00 to 19.00) at Kustweg 7, there are a salt water aquarium and an exhibition of shells.

The circular shape of *Biessum*, immediately W of Delfzijl, shows that there was a terp here, while at *Armsweer* (2km S of Biessum) there are traces of a group of three mounds.

*4km* **Appingedam** (13,000 inhab.; VVV, Blankenstein 2), with an attractive small centre, the Markt, is known for the way in which the houses overhang along the narrow Damsterdiep canal which runs through the town. The arcaded *Stadhuis* in the Markt dates from 1630, and the adjacent church is of the 13–15C but with considerable later additions.

To the N and NW of Appingedam there are several churches of interest, these being from E to W *Marsum* (12C) on a terp; *Leermens*, on a terp, built in the 11C and 13C and having murals and unusual transverse windows in the nave; *'t Zandt*, of the 13C, with vault paintings and a detached tower; *Loppersum* (13C and 15C), with vault paintings of c 1485, 16C screenwork, and a baroque pulpit and stalls; and *Stedum*, a moated 13C church probably on a terp site, with well restored late 15C vault paintings, a curious stone bell-cage pulled up from the ground, and a marble tomb of 1672 by Rombout Verhulst.

*13km Ten Boer* has for a church the chapel of a former Benedictine nunnery, while at (*4km*) *Garmerswolde* the 13C church has 15C vault paintings and a detached tower contemporary with the main building. In *5km* you enter **Groningen** near where the Damsterdiep and Eems Kanaal meet the Van Starkenborgh Kanaal (N) and the Winschoterdiep (S).

# 36 South-East Groningen Province (Groningen—Winschoten—Ter Apel—Stadskanaal—Groningen)

Total distance 117km.—14km **Hoogezand-Sappemeer**—6km *Zuidbroek* (**Veendam**)—7km *Scheemda* 6km **Winschoten—4km** *Blijham* (**Bellingwolde**)—5km *Wedde*—5km *Vlagtwedde* (**Bourtange**)—18km **Ter Apel—16km Stadskanaal**—9km *Nieuwediep*—13km **Hoogezand-Sappemeer**—14km **Groningen**.

For churches, of which there are several of interest along the northern part of this Route, see introductory paragraph to Rte 35.

The return part of this Route, between Ter Apel and Hoogezand-Sappemeer, is through the distinctive landscape of the VEENKOLONIEN (peat colonies) that were planted during the 19C on the peat moors of southern Groningen and eastern Drenthe to cultivate the fertile soil revealed when the top layer of peat had been stripped off. Today the basis of the economy is the potato, from which various by-products such as cardboard have been developed. The region is a dense network of drainage and transportation canals, one result of this being that towns and villages have had to be built to a ribbon-development plan, what is virtually a single street some 35km in length stretching for example from Hoogezand-Sappemeer and Veendam in the N to Ter Apel in the S. There are peat colony museums at Veendam (see below) and Barger Compascuum (•'t Aola Compas, see Rte 30A).

For Groningen, see Rte 33. You can reach *14km* **Hoogezand-Sappemeer** (35,000 inhab.) either by motorway or more interestingly by the road along the N side of the Winschoterdiep. The first of the peat colonies, Hoogezand-Sappemeer is today a long industrial conurbation known for boat building, the boats being launched sideways into the canal.

At *Harkstede*, 6km NW, the church has a 13C tower, the remainder of the building dating from 1695 and being notable for its armorial façade.

The *Zuidlaarder Meer*, with a popular recreation site on its north shore, lies some 5km SW and extends into the province of Drenthe.

A northwards diversion of some 20km, rejoining the main Route at Zuidbroek (6km E of Hoogezand-Sappemeer), is suggested, especially for those interested in churches. *Slochteren* has one of the largest natural gas deposits in Europe, discovered in 1959. The mansion of *Fraeylemaborg* (March–Dec: Tues–Sun, Holidays, 10.00 to 12.00, 13.00 to 16.00 or 17.00), 1km further N, dates from the mid 16C and is, with Menkemaborg (see Rte 35), a rare survival of a large borg. Continuing N, the church at *Schildwolde* dates from 1666 but has an older detached tower, while that at *Siddeburen* has a nave and choir both of c 1200. The road S from Siddeburen passes *Noordbroek*, where the 15C church, with a 14C detached tower, contains 15C vault paintings, and rejoins the main Route at *Zuidbroek*, the 13C church here having a detached tower, unusual because it contains prison cells.

For *6km Zuidbroek*, see above. **Veendam** (28,000 inhab.), 6km S of Zuidbroek, a large peat colony and also once prosperous in boat building, is almost completely surrounded by canals. The town is known for its parks and lakes, and also for the *Veenkoloniaal Museum* (Sun–Fri, 14.00 to 17.00) at Kerkstraat 18. At (*7km* from Zuidbroek) *Scheemda* the Reformed church of 1515 has a detached tower, while there are good contemporary furnishings in the early 18C church at *Midwolda* to the N.

*6km* **Winschoten** (21,000 inhab.; VVV, Stationsweg 21A) is approached through the suburb of *Heiligerlee*, the site of a monastery founded in 1230 from which Winschoten developed, and the site also of the first battle (1568) of the revolt against the Spanish, decisively won by Louis of Nassau; a fine monument beside the road commemorates Adolf of Nassau, killed in the battle (both Louis and Adolf were brothers of William the Silent). An important agricultural centre and market, Winschoten is also known for its three windmills along the road leading in from Heiligerlee. On the Markt, at the S end of the aptly named Langestraat, stands the 13C Romanesque-Gothic church with a detached tower (in which there are former prison cells; also an exhibition on local history), while in the *Stadspark* there is a rosarium with some 250 species.

The 13C church at *Finsterwolde*, 6km N, with a detached tower, is a survival of a former cruciform church.

**Nieuweschans**, 11km E on the German border, has several old houses and a small fortress museum (*Vestingmuseum*). *Oudeschans*, 6km SW of Nieuweschans, originated in 1573 as a star-shaped fortress and something of this design can still be traced.

The district of WESTERWOLDE, bounded on the W by the peat canals and on the E by Germany, extends southwards from Winschoten to Ter Apel. Once woodland and heath, the district is now largely cultivated, a notable feature being huge farmhouses, taking the form of large brick barns to which, attached as a kind of head, are big houses which in many cases are almost of mansion standard. These 'head-farms' may be isolated; or forming a hamlet (e.g. Smeerling); or lining the sides of the long strip of street of a large village or small town as at Bellingwolde (see immediately below), where there is a district museum.

*4km* (from Winschoten) Blijham, 8km E of which is **Bellingwolde** (8700 inhab.), little more than a street (Hoofdweg) some 5km long flanked by 'head-farms' set among magnificent trees. The *Oude Rechthuis* dates from 1643, and *De Oude Wolden* (No. 161) is the district museum for eastern Groningen (Easter–mid Oct: Wed, 15.00 to 17.00; Sat, Sun, 14.00 to 17.00). The 13C church has a detached tower. The road SW out of Bellingwolde continues with farms either side for 5km to *Wedde* (also *5km* direct from Blijham), where the attractive Wedderborg, a restored château reaching in part back to the 14C and standing in a small park, is now used for municipal purposes. In *5km* you reach *Vlagtwedde* where a diversion should be made 6km E to the pleasant and interesting village of **Bourtange**, less than 2km from the German border. The place originated as a star-shaped fortress in c 1593 and the restored fortifications provide an interesting walk, while around the particularly attractive small circular Markt there are restored façades. The local museum, *De Baracquen* (daily, 10.00 to 12.30, 13.00 to 17.00), at Meestraat 3, shows mainly fortress finds. After (*9km* from Vlagtwedde) Sellingen the road runs through marshland.

*9km* **Ter Apel** is a scattered village in beech woods in the SE corner of Groningen, with Drenthe to the W and Germany to the E. Here the late Gothic *monastery church* (1464–1501; Crutched Friars), now serving as a museum (varying exhibitions), is notable for its contemporary rood screen, sedilia, piscina and misericords. Much of the cloister survives, and there is a herbarium (Tues–Sat, 09.00 to 12.00, 13.30 to 17.30; Sun, 13.30 to 17.30).

For the (peat colony) museum at Barger Compascuum, 12km S, see Rte 30A.

This Route now turns N to run for some 35km, mostly in a straight line, through peat colonies and their close network of canals and ditches. The principal place is (*16km*) **Stadskanaal**. *9km* on, **Nieuwediep** is at a crossroads offering a choice. The road northwards returns to Groningen in *27km* via Hoogezand-Sappemeer (see start of this Rte); but it is more interesting, scenically more pleasant, and only some 10km longer, to take the roads to the W through Gieten and Zuidlaren along a part of the hunebed ridge of Drenthe (see Rte 30A).

# PROVINCE OF FRIESLAND

**Capital.** Leeuwarden.

**History.** Today's province of Friesland represents only the central part of the territory which was once the home of the Frisians, the people whom the Romans found settled along a broad strip of coast extending from the Scheldt to the Ems, that is the whole coastal length of what is now the Netherlands. In AD 69–70, although allies (socii) of the Romans (they had been conquered by Domitius Corbulo in AD 47), the Frisians joined the revolt of the Batavians led by Claudius Civilis, and centuries later it seems not improbable that the 'Saxon' invaders of Britain were Frisian adventurers, a suggestion supported by the affinity between the Frisian and English languages. The Frankish northward expansion soon collided with the Frisians who, still heathen despite some conversion in the south by St Amand and St Eloi, in c 630 destroyed the church at Utrecht. But in 689 Pepin of Herstal defeated the Frisian Radbod at Dorestad (today's Wijk bij Duurstede) and forced him to cede all the lands between the Scheldt and the Zuider Zee. With western Frisia now under Frankish control the way was clear for conversion to Christianity, the most notable missionaries being St Willibrord who became Bishop of Utrecht and St Boniface, murdered by the East Frisians in 754.

With Charlemagne all Frisia came under Frankish control, his Lex Frisionum confirming ancient custom and also recognising three distinct districts: West Frisia extending from the Zwin (near Sluis) to the Vlie (near Harlingen), Central Frisia between the Vlie and the Lauwersmeer, and East Frisia between the Lauwersmeer and the Ems. But during the unsettled period following Charlemagne's death the overlordship of Frisia frequently changed hands, finally in 911 falling to Charles the Simple, King of West Francia. At once East Frisia broke away (see Province of Groningen), while in 922 Charles's grant of lands near Egmond to the Frisian nobleman Dirk was the first step in the gradual absorption of West Frisia by the county of Holland, a process completed by the mid 13C.

Central Frisia (today's province of Friesland) remained independent, and when in 1436 Philip the Good on becoming Count of Holland laid claim to it he was restrained by the Emperor Frederick III who declared it to be a direct fief of the empire. This policy of Frederick's was however reversed by his son Maximilian who gave the territory to Albert of Saxony who effectively defeated all resistance. In 1523 Central Frisia was purchased by Charles V, thus becoming merely a part of the vast Habsburg lands.

Central Frisia, becoming the province of Friesland, was a somewhat reluctant signatory of the Union of Utrecht in 1579, asserting its individuality and its independence of the powerful province of Holland by choosing its own stadholders from the line of Count William-Louis of Nassau-Siegen, nephew and son-in-law of William the Silent. This practice continued until 1747 when Jan Willem Friso, having by inheritance become Prince of Orange, was elected as the first Stadholder of all seven provinces.

The **Frisian Language** is spoken by some 350,000 people, enjoys a considerable literature of its own (apart from many translations into Frisian), and is now officially accepted as the Netherlands' second language. Although akin to Dutch and with the same general Germanic ancestry the lineage of the language is different, Dutch having developed through the Frankish dialects while the Frisians spoke a West Germanic tongue. The visitor is unlikely knowingly to encounter Frisian, other than in the form of place names, e.g. *Ljouwert* for Leeuwarden, *Snit* for Sneek.

A feature of Friesland are the huge farmhouses with single roofs covering both the house and the barns; known as 'kop-hals-romp' (head-neck-body) farms, the 'kop' is generally the house, the 'hals' a passage, and the 'romp' the barns and outhouses. Associated with these farms are wide pastures with herds of black-and-white Friesian cattle, the internationally popular breed. Terps are another Friesland feature, especially in the N, originating in the man-made hillocks on which the peoples of some 2000 years ago built homes and settlements clear of marsh and flooding. Few traces of actual mounds survive, but the terp origin of many villages is indicated by their circular shape, frequently with a central church closely ringed by a moat and road. Leeuwarden, though this pattern has here long disappeared, grew out of the amalgamation of three terp settlements.

For the tourist the most attractive and popular part of Friesland is the SW, a country of broads and canals and also of many outstandingly picturesque and historic towns and villages. Leeuwarden, the provincial capital with the excellent provincial museum, is one such town, while others are Franeker with its beautiful Stadhuis and university associations; Harlingen, much of which is architecturally conserved; Bolsward, with another fine Stadhuis; Workum, known for its attractive main square; Sneek, with its early 17C Waterpoort; and Lemmer, threaded by a busy canal. Among many pleasant villages, the two outstanding are Hindelopen, long associated with painted furniture, and the delightful backwater of Sloten.

The holiday resort islands of Vlieland, Terschelling, Ameland and Schiermonnikoog (for this last see Rte 34) all belong to Friesland.

The Frisian winter is more severe than that of the more southerly and less exposed provinces, and skating is often possible. A notable event in exceptionally cold years is the 'Elfstedentocht' (Eleven Towns Tour), a skating race covering some 210km and visiting the eleven chief towns of the province. The decision to race cannot, of course, be taken more than a few days beforehand, but when it is (as in both 1985 and 1986) normal life stops throughout the province and most of the rest of the Netherlands. The winner becomes a national celebrity.

# 37 Leeuwarden

**LEEUWARDEN** (85,000 inhab.), the capital of the province of Friesland, has an inner town not only completely enclosed by waterways but also cut into sections by others, the town centre, with picturesque façades and bridges, extending along one of the inner canals. There are two outstanding museums, the Fries Museum devoted to the province and the municipal and ceramics museum in the Princessehof.

**Centre.** Waagplein.

**VVV.** At the **Station**, to the S beyond the inner town.

**Post Office.** Tweebaksmarkt.

**History.** Leeuwarden traces its distant origins to the amalgamation of three primitive settlements built on terps near where the rivers Ee and Vlie emptied into the marshy Middelmeer, long since drained. First mentioned in documents of the 13C, by which

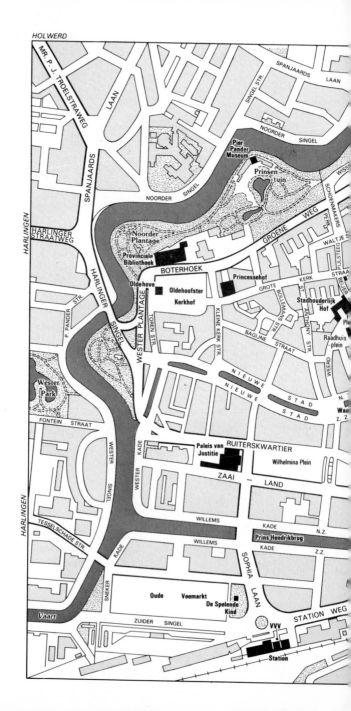

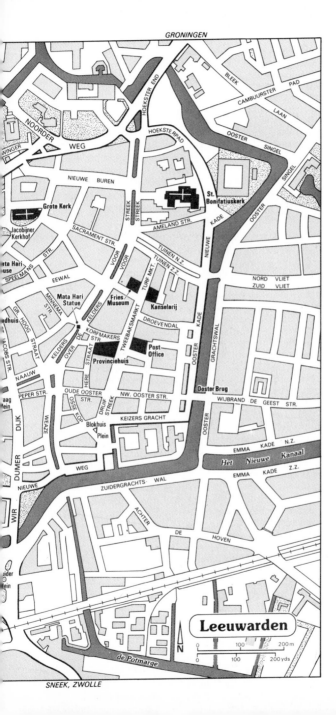

GRONINGEN

BLEEK

CAMBUURSTER PAD

LAAN

NOORDER

WEG

OOSTER SINGEL

SINGEL

HOEKSTER END

HOEKSTERPAD

NIEUWE BUREN

STREEK

STREEK

St. Bonifatiuskerk

OOSTER

KADE

Grote Kerk

SACRAMENT STR.

AMELAND STR.

NIEUWE

Jacobijner Kerkhof

STR.

VOOR

VOOR

TUINEN N.Z.

TUINEN Z.Z.

NORD VLIET

ZUID VLIET

ata Hari use

SPEELMANS

EEWAL

MINNEMA

Mata Hari Statue

KELDERS

Fries Museum

TURF MKT.

Kanselarij

KADE

GR. HOOG STRAAT

KELDERS

OVER DE

KORFMAKERS STR.

TWEEBAKSMARKT

DROEVENDAL

GRACHTSWAL

dhuis

JACOBS STR.

HERE STRAAT

Provinciehuis

Post Office

OOSTER

NAAUW

aag ein

PEPER STR.

OUDE OOSTER STR.

NW. OOSTER STR.

Ooster Brug

WIJBRAND DE GEEST STR.

OSSE KOP

DRUIF STREEK

KEIZERS GRACHT

OOSTER

DIJK

WEAZE

Blokhuis Plein

EMMA KADE N.Z.

Het Nieuwe Kanaal

DUMER

WEG

EMMA KADE Z.Z.

NIEUWE

ZUIDERGRACHTS WAL

WIR

ACHTER

DE HOVEN

uider ein

## Leeuwarden

0    100    200 m

N

0    100    200 yds

de Potmarge

SNEEK, ZWOLLE

time it had already become the centre of an important pastoral district, the town continued to prosper, partly because, being off the main routes of armies, its history was less turbulent than that of most Dutch towns.

**Natives.** Baron Menno van Coehoorn (1641–1704), the fortress engineer. Also Margarethe Geertruide Zelle (1876–1917), better known as Mata Hari, exotic dancer and German spy shot by the French.

The WAAGPLEIN, cut by a canal, is the most attractive and lively quarter of Leeuwarden. The **Waag**, the picturesque weigh-house of 1598 which was later used as a butter and cheese market (until 1884), now houses a bank and a restaurant. Although this is one of the oldest parts of the town, curiously the street leading W, either side of the canal, is called Nieuwestad (new town), the explanation being that the name dates from c 1435 when the town expanded on to the new land resulting from the draining of the Middelmeer; Wirdumer Dijk, a main street S out of Waagplein, was centuries ago a dike holding back the Middelmeer.

To the SW is the large rectangular WILHELMINAPLEIN, with at its W end the neo-classical *Paleis van Justitie* of 1846–52.

Peperstraat, leading E out of Waagplein, soon becomes Oude Oosterstraat, on the corner of which and Ossekop is *De Gladde Gevel*, dating from c 1500 and the oldest house in Leeuwarden. Herestraat, running N from Oude Oosterstraat, ends at Korfmakersstraat, on a canal bridge to the W being a small statue of Mata Hari while to the E Korfmakersstraat leads to Tweebaksmarkt, the old pastry market, with, opposite one another, the *Post Office* and the *Provinciehuis* (part 1784), seat of the provincial government. At its N end Tweebaksmarkt becomes TURFMARKT in which are the Fries Museum and the ornate *•Kanselarij* (1566–71), bearing a statue of Charles V and one of Leeuwarden's finest buildings. It was built for the chancellor George of Saxony, later serving as law court (until 1811) and as the home of the provincial library and archives (until 1976). Today the Kanselarij houses the *Verzets Museum* (Tues–Sat, 10.00 to 17.00; Sun, 13.00 to 17.00) with photographic, documentary and other material about the 1940–45 German occupation and the Resistance.

The *•Fries Museum* (Tues–Sat, 10.00 to 17.00; some Sun, 13.00 to 17.00) has, since 1881, occupied the patrician mansion (1781) of the Van Eysinga family. The most important provincial museum in the Netherlands, it provides a comprehensive survey of Frisian culture from prehistoric times up to the late 19C. There are archaeological and medieval collections, Frisian paintings, notable collections of silver and ceramics, regional handicraft products and costumes.

The museum comprises a Basement, a Ground Floor and two upper floors. On the official ground plan these are identified by the prefixes 0 (basement), 1 (ground) and then 2 and 3, and this same system is used below, with room numbers following the floor level prefixes.

In the *Basement* (0.1 to 0.6) there are an 18C kitchen and also carved stonework from old houses, tablets, murals, stone altars, sarcophagi and statuary.

*Ground Floor.* Rooms 1.1 to 1.5 are generally administrative or used for temporary exhibitions. Room 1.6, called the Grafischmuseum, is devoted to the subject of printing, with several presses and, above the door, an interesting wooden panel showing printers at work. Across the entrance hall (1.1) the corridor (1.7) leads into the mansion proper and shows portraits of its Van Eysinga owners. Room 1.8. A period dining room of the 18C, the

*Portrait by Adriaen van Cronenburg (c 1525–c 1604),*
*Fries Museum*

table set with blue porcelain. Room 1.9 is an ante-room to Room 1.10, a pleasant corner room which was added to the mansion in 1807. Delightful rustic murals, one showing that bridge raising could be woman's work. Rooms 1.11 and 1.12 both show Frisian silver (a drinking horn of 1397 to silver of the 18C), the ceiling of 1.12 showing that this was the music room. Room 1.13, called the Empire Room, shows furniture of the early 19C and has an amusing portrait-group of three children (Disturbed piano lesson, by W.B. van der Kooi) and also a vitrine of miniature silver toys. Room 1.14. Chinese porcelain. Room 1.15, reflecting the 16C, shows several portraits by Adriaen van Cronenburg, the leading Frisian artist of his day. In Room 1.16 hangs the huge sword of the Frisian national hero, Grote Piet. Room 1.17. Church art. Room 1.18. Archaeology, with a chronological survey and some emphasis on the Frisian terps.

*First Floor.* Room 2.1 is a fine staircase beside which hang 23 portraits of the Orange-Friesland Regiment. The corridor 2.2. leads into Room 2.3 in which hang works by W.B. van der Kooi and his pupils. Room 2.5, the

Picture Hall, is best visited next. Here are 17C paintings, including works by artists associated with Friesland such as Wigerus Vitringa, Emanuel Murant and Jan van de Wilde. Also here, a portrait of Saskia by Rembrandt (Saskia was a Frisian), and Child with a bell by Adriaan van der Linde, an attractive child, though, by modern standards, most uncomfortably dressed. Rooms 2.4, 2.6 and 2.7 are all devoted to Hindelopen (famous for its painted furniture), Room 2.6 showing costume and also an interesting painting by Christoffel Bisschop of a man painting what looks like the same cradle which stands beside the costumed lady. Room 2.8. Folk art. Room 2.9 is the island of Ameland room, another place producing painted furniture. Rooms 2.10 to 2.13 are the Christoffel Bisschop rooms. Born in Leeuwarden, Bisschop (1828–1904) worked in Scheveningen where he also assembled an art collection. This he bequeathed to his native province, the collection (tapestries, paintings, furniture, applied art) now shown in the museum in rooms (living room, studio, dining room, bedroom) which as closely as possible represent those in Bisschop's Villa Frisia in Scheveningen. Room 2.14. Italian and early north Netherlands majolica; Delft earthenware; glass of the 17C and 18C. Room 2.15 provides a huge display of porcelain (1600–1800; Dutch and, in particular, Frisian), the bequest in 1892 of the collector A. Looxma Ypey.

*Upper Floor.* Room 3.1. Earthenware (Lemmer, Workum, Harlingen, Makkum). Room 3.2. Makkum earthenware. Room 3.3, called Sport and Play, includes a small dolls' house, behind the windows of which will be found much elegant detail. Room 3.4 returns to Frisian earthenware, largely Harlingen and Makkum, 18C and 19C. Room 3.5 has been arranged as a silversmith's workshop, scattered around being the many tools of his trade, and Rooms 3.6 and 3.7 show a silver shop and a display of Frisian silver. Room 3.8 contains three delightful small shops; a tobacconist of 1800, a grocer of the early 20C, and a 19C chemist. Room 3.9. Frisian costume.

The *St Bonifatiuskerk* (P.J.H. Cuijpers, 1882–84), some 200m N of the Fries Museum, lost a part of its steeple in a storm in January 1976.

Beyond the canal to the NW of the Fries Museum, Sacramentstraat followed NW reaches the **Grote (Jacobijner) Kerk** (June–Aug: Tues–Fri, 10.00 to 11.00, 14.00 to 16.00), rebuilt after the destruction of its predecessor by a fire in 1492 and given major restoration in 1976. The baroque SE entrance known as the Oranjepoortje was added in 1663 at about the same time as the net-vaulted SE chapel. In the choir, which is the mausoleum of the Frisian Nassau family, the tombs were destroyed in 1795 but restored in 1948. On the adjacent Kerkhof are the *Wiesenhuis* (No. 1, 1675), now a music school, and the *Boshuisen Gasthuis* dating from 1652. To the SW of the church, a building on the corner of Grote Kerkstraat and Beijerstraat was the home of Mata Hari; the building now houses the *Fries Letterkundig Museum* with changing exhibitions and material on Frisian writers.

Grote Kerkstraat, with several good façades, continues SW, passing on the right Pijlsteeg in which is the *Fries Natuurhistorisch Museum* (Tues–Sat, 10.00 to 12.00, 14.00 to 17.00; Mon, 14.00 to 17.00) devoted to the flora and fauna of the province. Beyond, along Grote Kerkstraat, also on the right, is the **Museum Het Princessehof** (Mon–Sat, 10.00 to 17.00; Sun, 14.00 to 17.00), the main building of which is a mansion of c 1650 named after Princess Marie-Louise of Hesse-Cassel, widow of the Stadholder Jan Willem Friso, who inhabited it (and altered it) between 1731 and 1765. Room 8 on the ground floor was the princess's dining room and is furnished in the style of her time. The museum specialises in ceramics and, as one of the five ceramics study centres in Europe, provides not only exhibits but also library, studio, and other study facilities. Porcelain from many countries is exhibited, much of the Dutch display being in cases particular to each district and the large collection of Chinese ware, shown in a series of rooms, from prehistoric to modern times. The superbly displayed *Collection of Tiles, the world's largest, includes Dutch, Persian, French and Spanish examples. The museum also shows puppets, weapons, and statuary from Indonesia, and fabrics from various East Indies islands. The annexed *Papingastins* is a 15–16C mansion with unusual towers.

Grote Kerkstraat ends at the large open square called OLDEHOOFSTER KERKHOF, in which stands the 40m high and leaning *Oldenhove* (mid May–Sept: Tues–Sat, 09.30 to 12.30, 13.30 to 16.30), the most conspicuous building in Leeuwarden. Started between 1529 and 1532 by Jacob van Aken and Cornelis van der Goude and intended as part of a cathedral, the project was abandoned because of subsidence. Beside the tower a plan illustrates how the cathedral would have been sited, and its projected ground plan is also laid out on the square. Nearby there is a statue of J.J. Troelstra (1860–1930), Frisian poet and politician. The *Provinciale Biblio-theek*, the provincial library until 1976 housed in the Kanselarij, occupies a long building of 1966 on the N side of the square.

To the W and N of Oldehoofster Kerkhof gardens line the canal, the **Noorder Plantage** being just behind the provincial library while further E is the **Prinsentuin** which from 1648 to 1750 was the private garden of the Frisian Nassau family. Here are the *Verzetsmonument*, the Resistance Memorial by Auke Hettema, and the *Pier Pander Museum* (Tues–Sat, 10.00 to 13.00, 14.00 to 17.00), showing examples of the work of Pier Pander (1864–1919), a noted Frisian sculptor, and also glass and ceramics of the same period.

From Oldehoofster Kerkhof you can return to the town centre by Kleine Kerkstraat and Bagijnestraat, the latter reaching RAADHUISPLEIN and the adjacent HOFPLEIN. The **Stadhuis** here was built in 1715 by Claes Balk and enlarged in 1760 when a fine council chamber was added; the building has a Frémy carillon of 1668 with 39 bells. The *Stadhouderlijk Hof* opposite, now in municipal use as a registry office but formerly the residence of the stadholders, is in origin 16C and 17C but has been much altered. The statue on Hofplein to William-Louis of Nassau-Siegen, the first Frisian Stadholder from 1584 to 1620, is known as 'Us Heit' (Our Father).

In a garden opposite the station stands a pleasing statue by Maria van Everdingen called '*De Spelende Kind*' (Playing Child). To the W is the OUDE VEEMARKT, once the site of great Frisian cattle and agricultural markets, now transferred to the huge *Frieslandhal*, about 1km further W, one of the largest market and exhibition halls in Europe. Just E of the station, in Zuiderplein, a statue by J. Adema called '*Us Mem*' (Our Mother) honours the Frisian cow.

For Leeuwarden to North Friesland, see Rte 38; to Groningen, see parts of Rtes 38 and 34; to Lemmer via Harlingen, see Rte 39A; to Lemmer via Sneek, see Rte 39B; to Steenwijk via Heerenveen, see Rte 39C; to Appels-cha, see Rte 39D.

# 38 North Friesland

A clockwise circuit of some 70km is described.—7km *Stiens*—16km **Holwerd** (for the island of **Ameland**)—8km **Dokkum**—14km *Buitenpost*—24km **Leeuwarden**.

Leave Leeuwarden (see Rte 37) by P.J. Troelstraweg and in *7km* you reach Stiens, 7km W of which is the village of *St Annaparochie* where Rembrandt and Saskia van Ulenborch (1612–42), daughter of a burgomaster of Leeuwarden, were married on 22 June 1634 in the predecessor of the present church, this latter built to an octagonal plan in 1682 as the first Protestant church in Friesland. The village is in the district of HET BILDT, a polder reclaimed in 1508 and settled by people not of Frisian stock. The road continuing N from Stiens passes several windmills. *10km* on, a short way E of Ferwerd, is *Hoogebeintum*, a village standing on the highest terp in Friesland. The church here was built in c 1200. At *6km* **Holwerd** (2000 inhab.) has a 2km-long jetty out to sea from which a car ferry sails to the island of **Ameland**, a crossing of some 12km taking 45 minutes. (About five services a day each way; car reservation compulsory; Tel: 05191-614.)

**Ameland** (3000 inhab.; VVV, Nes) is a long, narrow island of beaches, dunes, and some woodland and marsh, some 24km in length from E to W and with an average width of a little over 2km. In 1895 it was connected with the mainland by a dike (still visible in part today), against which it was hoped that enough mud would silt up to form a permanent causeway. The capital is the village of *Nes*, half-way along the island's length, this also being the ferry quay; the village has several 17–18C houses and also a modest local history museum. For visitors interested in more of Ameland's past there is a small museum of antiquities at Hollum, a village at the W end of the island. Essentially a holiday objective, Ameland offers nature reserves, walking, and horse, pony, and bicycle riding, all of which can be hired; sea fishing; four picturesque villages with narrow streets; tennis, minigolf, etc.; and boat excursions to other islands. There is a wide choice of accommodation ranging from first class hotels through self-catering bungalows to camping sites. The airstrip (round flights; air taxis) is in the western part of the island, and the lighthouse (W end) can be ascended. (For postal tourist information: VVV Ameland, Postbus 14, 9163 ZL Nes; or Tel: 05191-2020. For ferry information: Wagenborg Passagierdiensten, Postbus 70, 9163 ZM, Nes/Ameland; or Tel: 05191-6111.)

From Holwerd this Route bears SE for (*8km*) **Dokkum** (12,000 inhab.; VVV, Grote Breedstraat 1), a pleasant small town, in part walled and moated (1581), with two windmills on the walls and some good façades along the canal. It was here in 754 that the Frisians murdered the English missionary St Boniface (born Wynfryth in Devon). This remarkable man had already preached in Frisia in 716 and 719; later he travelled and converted throughout much of the German empire, being consecrated bishop in 722 and archbishop in 732 and founding many abbeys and bishoprics, including Fulda (where he is buried), Regensburg, Salzburg, Wérzburg, Mainz (of which he was himself bishop), etc. In 754 he gave up his ecclesiastical honours to return to complete his earlier mission in Frisia. The plan of the former abbey church dedicated to him is outlined in the Markt. The *Stadhuis*, on earlier medieval vaults, dates from 1608, the *Waag* from 1752, and there is a small museum of local antiquities in the former building

(1618) of the Frisian Admiralty, transferred to Harlingen during the 17C (April–Sept: Mon–Sat, 10.00 to 17.00; Oct–March: Mon–Sat, 14.00 to 17.00).

For the LAUWERSMEER, 14km NE, see Rte 34.

**Moddergat**, a village on the coast 5km W of the Lauwersmeer, or 10km NE of Dokkum, is an interesting out-of-the-way corner well worth a visit for 't Fiskershûske (March–Oct: Mon–Sat, 10.00 to 17.00), a group of three 18–19C fishermen's cottages now restored as a museum. The cottages, which are at the W end of the long village, stand opposite a memorial commemorating a sea tragedy of 1893 when 83 men and 17 ships were lost. One of the three cottages (De Blaes) provides information about Moddergat's past, including this tragedy, while the next cottage (De Aek), with scale models of fishing craft, illustrates fishing methods and shows all manner of bygones. 't Fiskershûske, of 1794 and the oldest of the three cottages, has as its general theme the portrayal of everyday life here as it was in the 19C.

From Dokkum, the Dokkumerdiep river runs E to Dokkumernieuwezijlen, a former fishing port the fleet of which moved to Lauwersoog when the Lauwersmeer was diked in 1969. The Dokkumerdiep here was dammed in 1729.

At *Janum*, 7km SW of Dokkum, the Romanesque church of c 1200, built on a terp, now serves as a small museum of medieval church art. The church at *Rinsumageest*, 4km E of Janum, has a Romanesque crypt. Nothing survives of the nearby Cistercian house of Klaarkamp, the monks of which once owned the island of Schiermonnikoog.

From Dokkum you can follow a minor road SE beside a canal to (*14km*) *Buitenpost* on the main road between Groningen and Leeuwarden; there is good 17–18C heraldic decoration in the church here. At *Burum*, 5km E on the provincial border, the dish of an earth-satellite station is the most prominent feature.
From Burum to Groningen, see the end of Rte 34.
This Route now returns W following the main road. At (*10km*) *Bergum* there is a typical local 13C church, with a 12C tower and 17C interior woodwork. In *14km* you reach Leeuwarden.

# 39 South Friesland

The most popular part of southern Friesland is the SW, roughly the country to the W of the main road between Leeuwarden, Heerenveen, and Steenwijk. Here there are several most attractive, historic, and often lively towns; a coast of some variety; the great Afsluitdijk dividing the Waddenzee from the IJsselmeer and linking Friesland with Noord Holland; and a beautiful wide swathe of reedy broads and canals, in summer alive and colourful with pleasure craft. This SW district is described below as Rtes 39A and 39B; motorists should be prepared for delays due to the frequent opening of bridges to allow passage to boats. The SE part of the province, much of it peat heath, is described as Rtes 39C and 39D.

# A. Leeuwarden to Lemmer via Harlingen and the Coast

Total distance 83km.—17km **Franeker**—9km **Harlingen**—7km *Zurich* (*Afsluitdijk*)—6km **Makkum**—15km **Hindelopen**—6km *Koudum* (for **Staveren**)—12km **Balk**—11km **Lemmer**.

For Leeuwarden, see Rte 37. In *5km* **Marssum**, a village best known for *Popta Slot* (April–Sept: Mon–Fri, conducted tours 11.00, 14.00, 15.00), the typical and well restored 18C Frisian manor house, furnished in 16–18C style, of Dr Popta, a prosperous lawyer and landowner. The adjoining *Popta Gasthuis* was founded by Popta in 1711, while the church has splendid 17C furnishings including a family pew of 1671. *5km Dronrijp*, with a church tower of 1544, was the birthplace of Laurence Alma-Tadema (1836–1912), the painter, who came to England in 1869 and was knighted on Queen Victoria's 80th birthday. *Winsum*, 5km S of here, is known for the sport of pole-vaulting across water, championship competitions are held in August.

*7km* **Franeker** (13,000 inhab.; VVV, Voorstraat 49) is a particularly pleasant old town which from 1585 until 1810, when it was suppressed by the French, was the seat of an important university which made the town the cultural centre of the northern Netherlands. Pieter Stuyvesant (1592–1672), associated with the early story of New York, studied here.

The town is surrounded by its moat, and a smaller canal encloses the inner town in which the main street is Voorstraat running W–E. At No. 49 the *Museum 't Coopmanshus* (Tues–Sat, 10.00 to 12.00, 13.00 to 17.00; in winter, Sat, 11.00 to 16.00) is housed in twin professors' houses built in 1746 by Dr G. Coopmans who was physician and curator to the university. The museum, opened here in 1946, contains the university senate room with portraits of professors; a period bedroom and kitchen; an interesting model of 17C Franeker; a curious collection of 156 boxes containing data on the nature of trees, presented in 1809 by Louis Bonaparte; paintings and drawings by Frisian artists; collections of silver and porcelain; and a room devoted to Anna Maria van Schurman, resident of Franeker, one of the first women to be admitted to the university of Utrecht and known for her etchings, paper cuttings, embroidered bookcovers, and other handwork. The *Waag*, next door, dates from 1657, and the *Martenahuis*, a little to the E, from 1498 (restored 1946).

At the W end of Voorstraat the open space known as *Sternse Slotland* was the site of the castle.

At the E end of Voorstraat the road forks, Raadhuisplein leading left to the superb *Stadhuis* of 1591, with two gabled façades and an octagonal tower illustrating the transition from Gothic to Renaissance. The sculpture is by Claes Jelles and others, and in the council chamber, hung with stamped leather, there are portraits of Frisian stadholders. Across the small canal is the *Planetarium* (Tues–Sat, 10.00 to 12.30, 13.30 to 17.00; also in May–Aug: Mon, 10.00 to 12.30 and Sun, 13.00 to 17.00), a kind of orrery built in 1744–51 by Eise Eisinga, a self-educated woolcomber. From here, Eise Eisingastraat follows the canal E to a bridge across another canal, on the left across the bridge being the *Korendragershuisje* (Corn Porters' House), a most attractive building of 1634. The right fork from the E end of Voorstraat passes (left) the *Cammingha-stins*, a restored building on the ground floor of which there is a bank and, above, the *Fries Munt en Penningkabinet* (May–Sept: Mon–Fri, 13.00 to 17.00) with a collection of Frisian coins and medals. The *Martinikerk* dates in part from the early 15C. *Botnastins*, across Breedeplaats from the church, the medieval home of the Botnia family, in 1668 became a municipal orphanage; the orphans wore black to distinguish them from those of the *Klaarkamster* orphanage (SE, where Dijkstraat crosses the canal) who wore blue.

*9km* **Harlingen** (16,000 inhab.; VVV, Voorstraat 37), a bustling town and port, is known for its large number of 16–18C houses, virtually the whole of the central part of the town being a conservation zone. The many canals, with shipyards from which boats are launched sideways, are busy with different kinds of craft. Situated opposite the Vliestroom, the main channel through the chain of the Frisian islands, Harlingen enjoys a considerable carrying trade, especially with England. The PORT, already important in the 17C when the Frisian admiralty was transferred here from Dokkum, was greatly extended in 1852 and 1877. A monument called 'De Steenen Man' on the sea wall S of the town honours a Spanish governor, Caspar de Robles, who after a serious flood in 1570 devised an improved method of rebuilding the dike, and a pleasing small statue near the islands ferries quay recalls the tale of Hans Brinker who prevented a flood by holding his fingers in a hole in the dike.

In the town proper Voorstraat is the principal street and the one with most places of specific interest. The neat and attractive *Staduis* (just off Voorstraat) was built in 1730. VVV, at Voorstraat 37, is in a former tobacco factory, with shop and fittings preserved in their original style, while the municipal museum (peak season: Tues–Sat, 10.00 to 17.00; off peak: Tues–Sat, 14.00 to 17.00), at Voorstraat 56, occupies the *Hannemahuis*, an 18C building, enlarged in 1825, which was once the home of the Hannema family who donated it to the town for use as a museum which opened in 1957. On display here is material on the whaling expeditions which sailed from Harlingen from the 16C onwards; shipping exhibits, with a model of the Vliestroom passage; pictures by local artists; Harlingen silver, the work of a guild founded in 1648; and local tiles (16–20C). Harlingen tiles became well known after about 1600, and the industry was revived in 1973 (Aardewerk en Tegelfabriek, Voorstraat 84).

Harlingen is the port for the ferries to the islands of **Vlieland** and **Terschelling**, the operators being B.V. Terschellinger Stoomboot Maatschappij, Willem Barentszkade 21, 8881 BC West Terschelling; Tel: (05620) 6111. There is also an occasional service between the islands.

Vlieland. Two or three services daily each way; no cars. Crossing 25km, c 1½ hours. (VVV, Hafenweg 10, Oost-Vlieland; postal: VVV Vlieland, Postbus 1, 8899 ZN Vlieland; Tel: (05621) 1666.) Stretching SW to NE, the island is 18km long by up to 2km wide and has a resident population of around 1000. The only village is *Oost-Vlieland* at the NE tip, West-Vlieland having been washed away in a storm during the 18C. The 'Lutine', the bullion ship whose bell is rung at Lloyd's of London when news of serious shipping loss is received, was wrecked off Vlieland in 1799. Made up of beaches, dunes and tree plantations, Vlieland is a holiday island with about five hotels, some self-catering bungalows and camping sites. *Het Tromp's Huys* (summer: Mon–Fri, 10.00 to 12.00, 14.00 to 17.00), at No. 99 Dorpsstraat, now the local museum, dates from the 16C and was the office of the Vlie Navigation Commission, the authority controlling local shipping until the establishment of 'admiralties' in c 1600. In 1896 the house was bought by the Norwegian marine artist Betzy Akersloot-Bergen, who as an admirer of Cornelis Van Tromp gave the house his name, and in 1955 it was acquired by the municipality. Among the museum exhibits are Dutch and Scandinavian antique furniture, porcelain, silver and glass; Vlieland bygones; and pictures by Betzy Akersloot-Bergen.

**Terschelling**. Normal and fast services to West-Terschelling. Normal service two or three times daily each way. Crossing 30km, c 1½ hours; reservation essential for cars; Tel: 05620-6111. Fast service (no cars; more expensive), about three times daily each way; crossing 45 minutes. (VVV, Willem Barentszkade 19A, West Terschelling; postal: VVV Terschelling, Postbus 20, 8880 AA West Terschelling; Tel: 05620-3000.)

The ferries arrive at *West-Terschelling*, 4km NE being *Midsland*, the island's main village, while the principal bathing station (*Badpaviljoen*) is 2km N on the N shore. With beaches, dunes, heath and some woodland, Terschelling is essentially a holiday island, having some ten hotels spread between West-Terschelling, Midsland and *Oosterend*, 7km further E. There are also self-catering bungalows and camping sites. The *Brandaris* lighthouse (from 1594) near West-Terschelling can be visited and climbed, and some of the island's old houses have been arranged as small museums. The road ends near Oosterend, beyond which stretch some 12km of empty land and nature reserve (conducted visits). The island's museum, *'t Behouden Huys*, is in West Terschelling (April–Dec: Mon–Fri, 09.00 to 17.00; also Sat in mid May–mid Aug). The *Municipal Centre for Natural History and Landscape*, also in West Terschelling, is open April–Oct: Mon–Fri, 09.00 to 17.00; also Sat and Sun, 14.00 to 17.00 from mid July–mid Sept.

*7km Zurich*, just beyond which the *Afsluitdijk* (see Rte 2) runs SW across the water. This Route continues S for (*6km*) to the village of **Makkum**, a place known for its ceramics work since the 17C and today with a ceramics museum (Easter, May–mid Sept: Mon–Sat, 10.00 to 17.00; Sun, 13.30 to 17.00) in the *Waag* of 1698. The industry is still very active and some firms, with exhibitions, are open for visits (e.g. *Tichelaar* at Turfmarkt 7. Tours, Mon–Fri, 10.00 to 16.00 or 15.00 on Fri).

The ALDFAERS ERF ROUTE (Heritage Route), a round of some 20km within the triangle Makkum, Bolsward and Workum, provides a leisurely alternative to the direct road from Makkum to Workum. The Route, meandering across the south-west Frisian flats and through villages of local character, is officially described as 19C Friesland in a nutshell. The first call might be *Piaam*, just S of Makkum, where *'t Flügelhüs* is a bird museum in which dioramas and slides introduce the rich bird life of this district, but most visitors will head direct to **Allingawier**, 3km SE of Makkum, where *De Izeren Kou* (April–Oct: Mon–Sat, 09.00 to 17.30; Sun, 10.00 to 17.00) is an early 18C farm illustrating farm life as it was before mechanisation. There is also a bakery, at which local specialities can be sampled. **Exmorra**, 3km further E, shows a 19C grocery and the village school as it was in 1885.

**Bolsward** (10,000 inhab.; VVV, Broereplein), 4km E beyond the motorway, is an important dairy farming centre. Claiming to have been known as early as 700, the town was first mentioned in a document of the 10C, received a charter in 1455 and was at the height of its prosperity in the 16C. Opposite VVV in Broereplein, the formerly Franciscan *Broerekerk* has a moulded brick front of 1281. The *Martinikerk*, further N, dates from 1446–66 (but with an older tower) and has some good contemporary choir stalls (some from the Broerekerk), a pulpit of 1662 and vault painting of c 1600.

But the pride of the town is its •*Stadhuis* (to the W of the Martinikerk), a magnificent Renaissance building of 1613–17 (by Jacob Gijsbests) with a bulbous steeple. Further W, the *St Anthonie Gasthuis* (1780) in Nieuwe Markt, and several 17–18C houses in Dijlakker and Groot Zand are worth at least a glance.

The direct road S reaches Workum in 11km, but on the way you could make a short diversion to *Ferwoude* with a carpenter's workshop left exactly as it was on its owner's death around the turn of the century.

*9km* (direct from Makkum) **Workum** (4500 inhab.), a seaport in the 15C, has a most attractive main square in which are the *Stadhuis* (15–18C); the *Waag* of 1650, with grotesque statuary, housing *VVV* and a small museum; and the church of 1515–1615 with a massive detached tower. From the early 18C Workum was active in the export of eels to London, and the Visser family, the people mainly concerned, are remembered by a special room in the Scheepvaart Museum in Sneek (Rte 39B). In *6km*, **Hindelopen** (cars must be parked outside the village), with a tall church tower of 1638, is a very attractive village on a small promontory. The village was once famous for its painted furniture, showing both East Indian and Scandinavian influences, modern copies of which can be found both here and elsewhere in the Netherlands. Original painted furniture, costumes, and other local material can be seen at the *Hidde Nijland Museum* (March–Oct: Mon–Sat, 10.00 to 17.00; Sun, 13.30 to 17.00; see also Fries Museum at Leeuwarden, and Zuider Zee Museum at Enkhuizen). In *6km* you reach Koudum, 2km beyond which the road crosses between broads, the wide main stretch of which extends away to the NE.

**Staveren**, 7km SW of Koudum, once a prosperous port, is now best known as the quay for the passenger ferry link (railway connections) with Enkhuizen in Noord Holland. The service operates only between about May to September; seven services each way in mid season, otherwise three; crossing one hour, 20 minutes. Staveren is supposed to derive its name from Stavo, a deity of the pagan Frisians. Offshore lies the wide grassy sandbank known as the *Vrouwezand*. Legend relates that a rich merchant's wife of Staveren commissioned a ship's captain to bring back from his voyage the most precious cargo he could find. The worthy but unimaginative captain returned with a load of wheat from Danzig, which the lady, furious with disappointment, had tipped into the sea off the harbour mouth. The wheat, germinating, caused the formation of the sandbank that eventually ruined the port. The precise historical context within which to understand this fable is the Baltic Corn Staple of the later 16C and 17C which provided the economic basis of Dutch prosperity, especially for Amsterdam; for several generations the Dutch shipped the enormous surplus of grain from the Baltic area into their home ports and thence across Europe, becoming rich on this trade during a period of famine and war.

*12km* **Balk**, to the S of which the wooded district of GAASTERLAND stretches to the IJsselmeer shore along which there are several bird sanctuaries. There is a small Gaasterland district museum (Klif en Gaast. Easter–Dec: Mon–Fri, 09.30 to 12.00, 13.30 to 17.00) at *Oude Mirdum*, 3km SE of Rijs. The church at *Wijckel*, 3km E of Balk, contains the monumental tomb, by Daniel Marot, of Menno van Coehoorn, the famous fortress engineer whose name survives in that of many town ring-roads. **Sloten**, just NE of Wijckel, is a delightful little moated place with a high-water warning cannon and a small canal through the centre flanked by cobbled roads and old façades.

Only residents' cars are allowed in the village. The local museum, *Stêdhús Sleat*, at Heerenwal 48, is open Easter–autumn: Tues–Fri, 10.00 to 12.00, 14.00 to 17.00; Sat, Sun, 14.00 to 17.00. In *11km* **Lemmer** is a lively small town strung along its canal, and busy with craft moving through the locks between the IJsselmeer and the Friesland broads.

For Lemmer to Zwolle, see Rte 32A; to Leeuwarden via Sneek, see Rte 39B.

# B.   Leeuwarden to Lemmer via Sneek

Total distance 45km.—15km *Deersum*—7km **Sneek**—14km *Spannenburg*—9km **Lemmer**.

Leave Leeuwarden (see Rte 37) by the Zwolle road, and follow this for some 4km then make a right turn on to a smaller road. In *15km* you reach *Deersum*, a hamlet from which a minor road runs NW in 3km reaching *Wieuwerd* where the church crypt, by some peculiar property not fully understood, preserves bodies placed in it. Four such bodies, dating from c 1609, are shown. At *Bozum*, 2km W of Deersum, the late 12C church contains a 13C apse painting of a beardless Christ surrounded by the Symbols of the Evangelists and Saints.

*7km* **Sneek** (29,000 inhab.; VVV, Leeuwenburg 21) is both a lively town and the boat centre for the Frisian broads. The town centre is LEEUWEN-BURG-MARTINIPLEIN. The *Stadhuis*, in Marktstraat to the N of

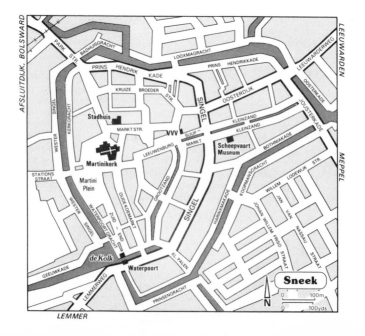

Leeuwenburg, dates from the 15C and has a rococo façade of c 1760 with an elaborate outer stairway; inside there is a collection of weapons. As now seen, the *Martinikerk* is mostly of the early 16C but is successor to others dating back to around 1150. Excavations in 1975 exposed early foundations, and at the W exterior of the church there is an interesting plan of the earlier churches, while the lines of their individual foundations are traced out in stonework. Beside the church stands an old wooden belfry. The *Scheepvaart Museum en Oudheidkamer* (marine and antiquities) is at Kleinzand 14 to the E of Leeuwenburg, a house of which the museum, founded in 1938, moved in 1947 (Mon–Sat, 10.00 to 12.00, 13.30 to 17.00). The marine museum, with several good ship models, illustrates all aspects of Frisian ship activity, both at sea and on inland waterways. Sections include pleasure craft; shipping during the 17–19C, including material on the Frisian admiralty; cargo and fishing boats; and a room devoted to the Visser family who from the early 18C exported eels from Workum to London. In the other part of the museum can be seen archaeological material, Sneek silverware, period rooms, and local craft products. The *Waterpoort* at the S exit from the town is a Renaissance gateway of 1613 with two octagonal towers.

A wide choice of boat excursions is available. Local trips from Oosterkade, Leeuwarderweg or Geeuwkade.

Willem de Sitter (1872–1935), astronomer and mathematician, was a native of Sneek.

*14km Spannenburg* is a hamlet at a crossroads. For Sloten and Wijckel, some 5km SW, see Rte 39A. *Joure* (10,000 inhab.), 9km NE, beyond the motorway, is associated with Frisian clocks; dating from about 1700 these are the hanging type and are known for their decorated cases. *9km* on is Lemmer, see Rte 39A.


# C.   Leeuwarden to Steenwijk via Heerenveen

Total distance 50km.—12km *Grouw*—15km **Heerenveen**—11km **Wolvega**—12km **Steenwijk**.

For Leeuwarden, see Rte 37. In *12km*, *Grouw*, on the Pikmeer, is a water sports centre and has a church with a 12C apse. Beyond (*4km*) Akkrum the road runs across peat bog. In *11km*, **Heerenveen** (37,000 inhab.; VVV, Schans 65A), originating in the mid 16C as a peat settlement, is now a modern shopping centre, but one with a *Stadhuis* which is in a 17C mansion. *4km Oranjewoud* was once the park of an estate owned by the widow of the Stadholder Jan Willem Friso (see also Rte 37, Princessehof). *7km* **Wolvega** (11,200 inhab.) where a statue commemorates Pieter Stuyvesant (1592–1672), born near here and later closely associated with the early days of New York.

For (*12km*) **Steenwijk**, in the province of Overijssel, and from there southward, see Rte 32B.

# D.  Leeuwarden to Appelscha

Total distance 52km.—26km **Drachten**—10km *Duurswoude*—16km
*Appelscha.*

For Leeuwarden, see Rte 37. At (*14km*) the village of *Eernewoude*, 3km S
of the main road, peat carving is shown at the 't Kokelhus Museum
(June–Aug: Mon–Fri, 15.00 to 17.00). The village is on the Prinsenhof lake,
at the NW corner of which the nature reserve of *Oude Venen* is also a water
sports centre. *12km* **Drachten** (42,000 inhab.), where you cross the main
road from Heerenveen to Groningen, started as a simple peat settlement,
though this is hard to believe of today's sprawling industrial and commercial centre.

This Route continues SE through a district of mixed woodland and dunes
to reach (*10km*) Duurswoude, 5km NE of which is the village of Bakkeveen.
Between Bakkeveen and Een (8km E) defence works known as the *Eener*
(or *Zwartendijkster*) *Schans* are said to have been used as a model by Pieter
Stuyvesant when building a fort at New Amsterdam (New York). In *16km*
*Appelscha* is a long peat-colony village surrounded by forest, heath and
sand dunes. The Fachtelooeër Veen (NE), crossed by a footpath, is the
Netherlands' last surviving high fen, and near here is the highest point in
Friesland (26.6m).

For Assen, 14km NE, see Rte 30B.

# INDEX OF ARTISTS

E=Engraver
G=Glassworker, including stained glass
M=Metalworker
P=Painter, including etching, drawing, etc.
S=Sculptor

Place names indicate where most active

# GENERAL INDEX

Topographical names are in CAPITALS.

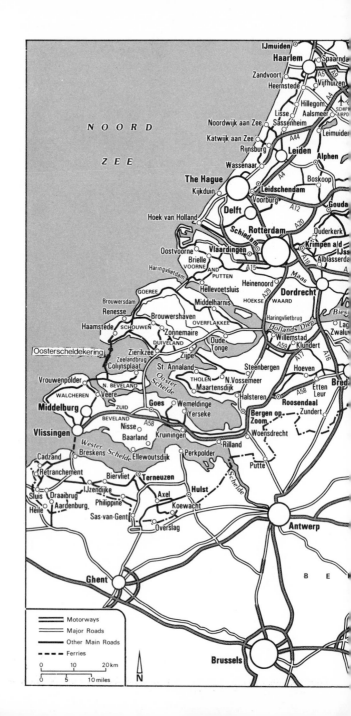

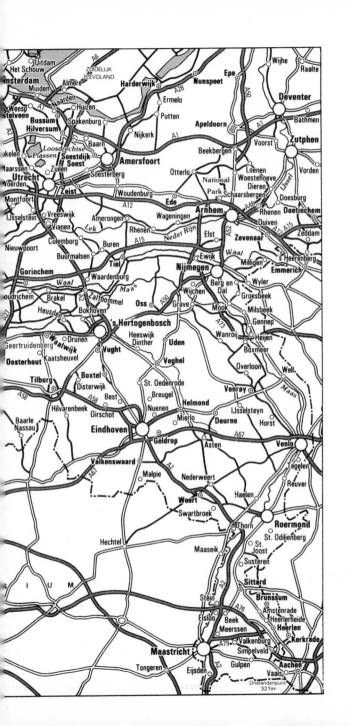

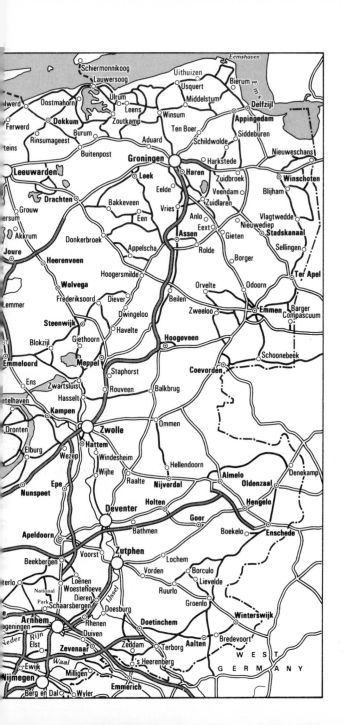

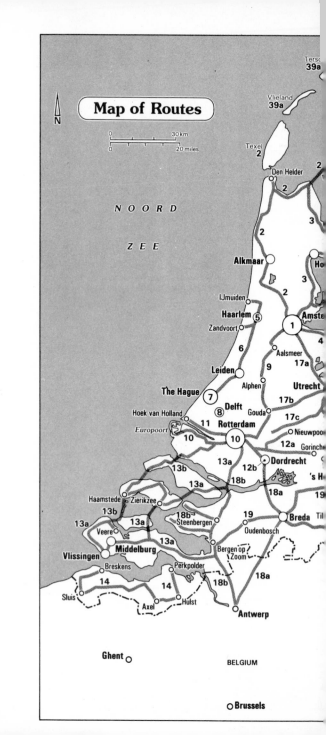

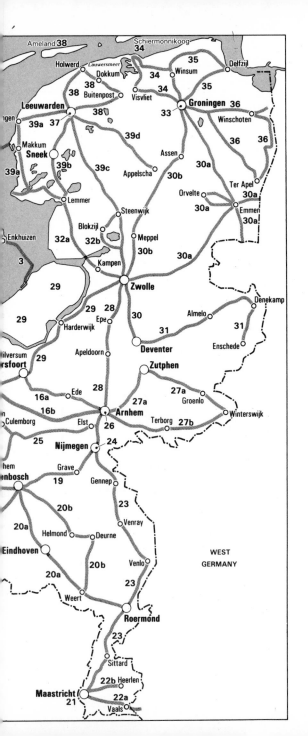

THE PROVINCES OF HOLLAND

0        km        50

0       miles       25

N

GRONINGEN
● Groningen

Leeuwarden

FRIESLAND

Assen ●

DRENTHE

NORTH SEA

IJsselmeer

NOORD HOLLAND

● Lelystad        ● Zwolle

FLEVOLAND        OVERIJSSEL

Haarlem ●

GELDERLAND

Utrecht ●

UTRECHT

Den Haag ●        ● Arnhem

ZUID HOLLAND

GERMANY

ZEELAND

's-Hertogenbosch ●

● Middelburg        NOORD BRABANT

LIMBURG

BELGIUM

● Maastricht